The Complete Wor

The Complete Works of Rosa Luxemburg

VOLUME I, ECONOMIC WRITINGS 1

Edited by Peter Hudis

Translated by David Fernbach,
Joseph Fracchia and George Shriver

VERSO
London • New York

ROSA
LUXEMBURG
STIFTUNG

Verso would like to express its gratitude to Rosa Luxemburg Stiftung for help in publishing this book

ROSA
LUXEMBURG
STIFTUNG

The publisher also gratefully acknowledges the assistance of Dietz Verlag for allowing the publication of translations of "The Industrial Development in Poland," "Introduction to Political Economy" and "Back to Adam Smith" based on Rosa Luxemburg's *Gesammelte Werke*, as well as gratitude, alongside M. Krätke, for providing transcripts of the seven manuscripts from the SPD Party School.

This paperback edition first published by Verso 2014
First published by Verso 2013
© Verso 2013, 2014
English translation of chapters 1 and 4 through 10 and appendix
© George Shriver 2013, 2014
English translation of Chapter 2 © Joseph Fracchia 2013, 2014
English translation of Chapter 3 © David Fernbach 2013, 2014
Introduction © Peter Hudis 2013, 2014

1 3 5 7 9 10 8 6 4 2

Verso
UK: 6 Meard Street, London W1F 0EG
US: 20 Jay Street, Suite 1010, Brooklyn, NY 11201

www.versobooks.com

Verso is the imprint of New Left Books

ISBN-13: 978–1–78168–765–9
eISBN-13: 978-1-78168-331-6 (UK)
eISBN-13: 978-1-84467-975-1 (US)

British Library Cataloguing in Publication Data
A catalogue record for this book is available from the British Library

Library of Congress Cataloging-in-Publication Data
A catalog record for this book is available from the Library of Congress

Typeset in Minion Pro by MJ & N Gavan, Truro, Cornwall
Printed by in the US by Maple Press

Contents

Introduction: The Multidimensionality of Rosa Luxemburg

I.

The depth and breadth of Rosa Luxemburg as theoretician, activist, and original personality was once expressed by her in the following terms:

> I feel, in a word, the need as [Wladyslaw] Heine would say, to "say something great" … I feel that within me there is maturing a completely new and original form which dispenses with the usual formulas and patterns and breaks them down … I feel with utter certainty that something is there, that something will be born.*

This quest for what she called a "land of boundless possibilities" can be regarded as one of her most distinguishing characteristics.

This is most of all evident from Luxemburg's intellectual and political commitments. By the time of her death in 1919 she was renowned as one of the most fiercely independent figures in European radicalism. Refusing to define herself in the terms often adopted by her contemporaries, she issued a searing critique of the inhumanity of capitalism while being no less critical of what she viewed as misguided efforts by radicals to supplant it. Her understanding that capitalism could only be overcome through a thoroughly participatory and democratic process that actively involves the *majority* of the oppressed[†] was a departure from the hierarchical models of electoral politics and revolutionary putschism that defined so many efforts at social change in the twentieth century, just as it anticipates the aspirations of many feminists, ecologists, and Occupy activists struggling in the twenty-first century to avoid the errors of the past.

Luxemburg's quest for a "land of boundless possibilities" is unmistakable to anyone who encounters her numerous political pamphlets, essays, and articles—whether her well-known publications such as *Reform or Revolution, The Mass Strike, the Political Party, and the Trade Unions* or *The Russian Revolution*, or her many lesser-known works that have never been translated in English but which will all appear in the *Complete Works*.[‡] The same is true of

---

* To Leo Jogiches (April 19, 1899), in *Rosa Luxemburg, Gesammelte Briefe*, Band 1 (Berlin: Dietz Verlag, 1989), p. 307. Wladyslaw Heine was a fellow Pole who studied with Rosa Luxemburg at the University of Zurich during the time she was writing her dissertation, *The Industrial Development of Poland*.

† For an especially valuable work that sheds important illumination on Luxemburg's contribution to this conception, see *In the Steps of Rosa Luxemburg: Selected Writings of Paul Levi*, edited and introduced by David Fernbach (Leiden and Boston: Brill, 2011).

‡ One of the difficulties in obtaining access to Luxemburg's entire legacy is that her manuscripts are not found in one place but are in an assortment of archives and libraries, such as the

her voluminous correspondence, which illuminates her original personality and remarkable span of interests—literary, scientific, and political—all grounded in an effort to stay true to what it means to be human.*

What may not have received sufficient attention in some quarters is that Luxemburg's effort to "say something great" is most powerfully exhibited in her four major books—*The Industrial Development of Poland*; *Introduction to Political Economy*; *The Accumulation of Capital*; and *The Accumulation of Capital, or What the Epigones Have Made of Marx's Theory: An Anti-Critique*.† Each is a Marxist analysis of economic phenomena. Taken as a whole, they represent the most comprehensive study of capitalism's inherent tendency towards global expansion ever written. Living as we are at a historical moment in which the logic of capital has now expanded to cover the entire world, the time has surely come to revisit these writings by one of the most important women economists of the twentieth century.

This effort has been hindered, however, by the fact that much of Luxemburg's work (including the bulk of her articles, essays, and letters) has yet to appear in English. This is also true of her economic writings, since until now the Anglophone world has lacked a complete translation of one of her most important books, the *Introduction to Political Economy*. The *Introduction* contains material not found in her other works, critiques of such theorists as Karl Bücher, Werner Sombart and Max Weber; analyses of pre-capitalist societies, such as those in sub-Saharan Africa and pre-Columbian America; and a detailed discussion of the role of wage labor in contemporary capitalism.

The *Introduction* was composed as part of her work as a teacher—a dimension of her work that is little known in the English-speaking world. From 1907 to 1914 she taught history, economics, and social theory at the German Social-Democratic Party's school in Berlin. She devoted considerable time and energy to her teaching and wrote the *Introduction to Political Economy* as a result of her discussions with students at the party school. As part of this work, she composed a number of manuscripts and lecture notes (seven in all survive), which have only recently come to light. Only part of one of these seven manuscripts has

Bonn Archives of the Social-Democratic Party, the SAMPO Federal Archives in Berlin, the Polish State Archives in Warsaw, the International Institute of Social History in Amsterdam, the Russian State Archive for Social and Political History in Moscow, and the Hoover Institution at Stanford University in California.

   * See especially the companion volume to the *Complete Works*, *The Letters of Rosa Luxemburg*, edited by Georg Adler, Peter Hudis, and Annelies Laschitza (London and New York: Verso Books, 2011).

   † Although an impressive number of works on Luxemburg have appeared in the English-speaking world in the past decade, most have focused on her political writings without emphasizing her work as an economic theorist. An important exception is *Rosa Luxemburg and the Critique of Political Economy*, edited by Riccardo Bellofiore (London and New York: Routledge, 2009). See also *Socialist Studies/Études Socialistes*, Vol. 6, No. 2 (2010) for its special issue on Luxemburg.

previously appeared in English;* all are published in full in this volume. They indicate how intently Luxemburg kept up with the latest literature on economic history, sociology, anthropology, and ethnology, and serve as an important supplement to the *Introduction to Political Economy* and *Accumulation of Capital*. Together with a number of her pre-1914 economic writings, such as her dissertation on *The Industrial Development of Poland*, a manuscript of 1897 on the theory of the wages fund, and an essay from 1899 on Marxian value theory, this volume provides a fuller picture of Luxemburg's contribution as an economic theorist than has heretofore been available.

A second volume of her economic writings will contain a new English translation of *The Accumulation of Capital* and *Anti-Critique* as well as the chapter on Volumes 2 and 3 of Marx's *Capital* that she originally wrote for Franz Mehring's biography of Karl Marx. The *Complete Works* will be rounded out with seven volumes of political writings and five volumes of correspondence.

Just as Luxemburg's stature cannot be fully appreciated without taking account of her as a political figure and an inspiring personality, her overall contribution cannot be grasped without engaging with her work as an economic theorist. It is for this reason that we have decided to begin this fourteen-volume *Complete Works* with her economic writings. Surely, separating her oeuvre into economic and political categories is somewhat artificial. As she indicates in her correspondence, her initial approach to economic theory was largely stimulated by a *political* problematic—the expansion of European imperialism into Asia and Africa. She wrote, "Around 1895, a basic change occurred: the Japanese war opened Chinese doors, and European politics, driven by capitalist and state interests, intruded into Asia ... It is clear that the dismembering of Asia and Africa is the final limit beyond which European politics no longer has room to unfold."† Luxemburg's effort to comprehend the phenomena of imperialism and how it points to the dissolution or "the final crisis" of capitalism determined much of the content of her economic work. Meanwhile, many of her "political" writings—such as *Reform or Revolution*—contain brilliant analyses of the economic law of motion of capitalism and its proclivity for cyclical crises. Yet given the amount of time, care, and attention that Luxemburg gave to developing her major economic works, it makes sense to begin the *Complete Works* with the writings that contain her most detailed and analytically specific delineation of Marxian economics. It is here where her brilliance, originality, and independence of intellect—as well as some of her misjudgments and limitations—are most readily visible.

---

* A section of the manuscript on slavery in the ancient world was published in *The Rosa Luxemburg Reader*, edited by Peter Hudis and Kevin B. Anderson (New York: Monthly Review Books, 2004), pp. 111–22.

† To Leo Jogiches, January 9, 1899, in *Gesammelte Briefe*, Band 1, pp. 249–50.

II.

Not long after being forced to flee Poland as a teenager, where she became active in the nascent Polish Marxist movement, Luxemburg moved to Switzerland and enrolled in the University of Zurich. By May 1897 she had earned a Ph.D. in economics—one of the first women in Europe to obtain one. Her dissertation, *The Industrial Development of Poland*, was the first detailed analysis of the development of capitalism in Poland. Based on original research at the Bibliotèque Nationale and Czartoryski Library in Paris, it was a rigorous, empirical study that immediately defined her as a serious theoretician. Unusual for the time, it was published as a book by a major German publisher soon after its completion and was widely (and warmly) reviewed by both radical émigrés and academic economists.*

That *The Industrial Development of Poland* earned Luxemburg a degree and did not explicitly reveal the extent of her commitment to revolutionary politics (Marx is mentioned only once in it) should not be taken to mean she had her eye on an academic career. Instead, the dissertation was central to her effort to come to grips with how the Marxist analysis speaks to her particular homeland. Although Luxemburg did not obtain a major international reputation until the revisionist debate in German Social Democracy in 1898–99, her dissertation already established her as an important *Marxist* thinker.

Central to the dissertation is the theme found throughout her subsequent work: internationalism. She analyzed the economy of Russian-occupied Poland as a part of an increasingly globalized capitalist system by detailing how its industrial development was dependent on goods and skills imported from Western Europe as well as new markets being opened up through Russia's penetration of Asia. Poland's economy, she insisted, was increasingly dependent on global capital; any independent path of national development was foreclosed by economic reality. She wrote, "It is an inherent law of the capitalist method of production that it strives to materially bind together the most distant places, little by little, to make them economically dependent on each other, and eventually transform the entire world into one firmly joined productive mechanism."†

---

*   For the circumstances under which Luxemburg revised her dissertation for publication as a book, see *The Letters of Rosa Luxemburg*, pp. 49, 62, 66, 75, 87–8. Those who praised the work included her dissertation director, Julius Wolf, an important economist in his own right who did not let his objections to the Marxian doctrine get in the way of appreciating his inquisitive and combative student. For Wolf's critique of Marxism, see his *Sozialismus und Kapitalistische Gesellschaftsordung. Kritische Würdigung beider als Grundlegung einer Sozialpolitik* (Socialism and Capitalist Social Organization. An Assessment of Both as a Critical Foundation for Social Policy) (Stuttgart: J.G. Cotta, 1892). Luxemburg's view of Wolf is contained, in part, in the manuscript "Theory of the Wages Fund," written while she attended the University of Zurich, in 1897. It appears here as an Appendix.

†   *The Industrial Development of Poland*, p. 73, below.

This in turn became the basis of her effort to address the question that most bedeviled the Polish Marxist movement from its inception: what position to take on demands for national self-determination. Should the struggle for socialism be inextricably connected to demands for national independence? Or does the former make the latter superfluous? In direct contrast to Marx and Engels, who consistently supported the Polish independence struggles,* Luxemburg opposed all calls for national self-determination for Poland. *The Industrial Development of Poland* represents the economic justification for this political position by arguing that Poland's economy had become so integral to Russia's that any and all calls for national independence had become thoroughly utopian and impractical.

Many of the debates addressed in *The Industrial Development of Poland* were resolved long ago, and not always to Luxemburg's credit. Her contention that the deepening economic links between Finland and Russia signifies "the beginning of the end of Finnish independence in *political* terms"† has hardly stood the test of time; Finland achieved national independence from Russia in December 1917, just as Poland itself did only a few months later. Despite the considerable problems that plagued the Polish economy between the two world wars, her claim that demands for its national independence had become totally impractical have clearly been undermined by the actual historical developments.

At the same time, her dissertation's keen appreciation of the impact of the global economy on efforts to foster capitalistic industrialization means it is not as dated or distant as may appear at first sight. Efforts at industrial modernization that try to seal off a country from the deleterious impact of the world market, she suggests, are inherently counter-productive, since capital accumulation is dependent on a web of influences that extend beyond national borders. Her work counters the claim that development can best be secured by relying solely on a nation's internal resources—a point that many socialists have belatedly begun to discover in recent decades, in light of the painful failures that have accompanied many efforts to pursue a nationalist development strategy in the developing world.

After completing her dissertation, Luxemburg moved to Germany and became a leading figure in the German Social-Democratic Party and Second International. Her reputation secured by her intervention in the revisionism controversy of 1898–99, she became a much sought after public speaker, journalist, political campaigner, and agitator. By 1905–6, when she returned to Poland to participate in the Russian Revolution and penned her famous pamphlet on *The Mass Strike, the Political Parties, and the Trade Unions*, she had become known

---

*   For a recent discussion of Marx's writings on Poland, see Kevin B. Anderson, *Marx at the Margins: On Nationality, Ethnicity, and Non-Western Societies* (Chicago: University of Chicago Press, 2010), pp. 42–79.

†   *The Industrial Development of Poland*, p. 64, below.

as an uncompromising opponent of bureaucracy and political elitism and a firm defender of rank-and-file initiatives and mass spontaneity.

Although some of Luxemburg's biographers have tended to view her work of 1907–14 as less significant than that from 1898 to 1907,[*] the years between the *Mass Strike* pamphlet and the outbreak of World War I actually marked the period in which she produced her most important theoretical work. Much of it was connected to her work as a teacher at the SPD's school in Berlin. Founded in 1906 in response to growing interest in radical ideas following the 1905 Revolution,[†] its aim was to educate party cadres and trade unionists in Marxist theory, history, and sociology.

Luxemburg began teaching at the school in October 1907. Despite lacking any formal experience as a teacher, she plunged into the work with enthusiasm and soon became one of the most popular instructors. Her teaching load was intensive: she lectured five days a week for two hours a day and spent additional time advising and assisting students. She was the only woman on the teaching staff.

Luxemburg's massive theoretical output from 1907 to 1914, much of it devoted to economic theory, was directly impacted by her experience as a teacher. As J.P. Nettl put it, "Undoubtedly the constant polishing of ideas before her students helped Rosa greatly to clarify her own mind on the basic propositions of her political faith."[‡] Luxemburg was in fact deeply invested in critical pedagogy. It reflected her life-long commitment to intellectual and cultural advancement as at the heart of the struggle for a new society. She defined her teaching philosophy thusly:

> We have tried to make clear to them … that they must continue to go on learning, that they will go on learning all their lives … What the masses need is general education, theory which gives them the chance of making a system out of the detail acquired from experience and which helps to forge a deadly weapon against our enemies.[§]

This was part and parcel of her view in the *Mass Strike* pamphlet that "The most precious, because lasting, thing in this rapid ebb and flow of the wave [of

---

[*]   J.P. Nettl referred to the period from 1906–1909 as "the lost years." See Chapter 9 of *Rosa Luxemburg* (London: Oxford University Press, 1966). For a different assessment of this period, see Raya Dunayevskaya, *Rosa Luxemburg, Women's Liberation, and Marx's Philosophy of Revolution* (New Jersey: Humanities Press, 1981), pp. 1–30; and Annelies Laschitza, *Im Lebensrausch, trotz alledem Rosa Luxemburg* (Berlin: Aufbau-Verlag, 1996), pp. 215–429.

[†]   Heinrich Schulz, the SPD's educational expert, explained the impetus for starting the school: "The Russian revolution released a flood of energy and mobility … and the desire for discussing the fundamental questions … [the need for] theoretical education increased accordingly." See Heinrich Schulz, "Zwei Jahre Arbeiterbildung," *Die Neue Zeit*, Band 2, No. 50, September 11, 1908, p. 883.

[‡]   Nettl, *Rosa Luxemburg*, p. 392.

[§]   Quoted in Ibid., p. 394.

class struggle] is its mental sediment: the intellectual, cultural growth of the proletariat."*

Along similar lines, she argued that the ability of the bourgeoisie to throw off the fetters of absolutism, which was so important for the unfolding of capitalism as a global system, could not have occurred without such intellectual revolutions as the Enlightenment that preceded it:

> [P]olitical economy, along with the philosophical, social, and natural-rights theories of the age of Enlightenment, was above all a means for acquiring self-consciousness, a formulation of the class consciousness of the bourgeoisie and as such a precondition and impulse for the revolutionary act.[†]

Ideas, she held, are not merely epiphenomenal—which is one reason why this painstaking Marxian materialist had no problem identifying herself as an *idealist*.[‡]

On the basis of her lectures and discussions at the party school, she decided to work on a full-length book, eventually called *Introduction to Political Economy*. Several of her fellow teachers first suggested the idea of such a book so that her lectures could obtain a wider audience. She began doing research for the book at the end of 1907, and by the summer of 1908 was already looking forward to preparing a manuscript for the printer.[§] As of this period of 1907/08, the content of her planned book closely corresponded to the subjects of her lectures, which were listed as follows: 1) What Is Economics?; 2) Social Labor; 3) Exchange; 4) Wage Labor; 5) The Rule of Capital; 6) Contradictions in the Capitalist Economy.[¶]

As she proceeded to work on the book, she decided to include additional material on pre-capitalist societies that was not part of her initial lectures at the party school. This took her into intense studies of the latest literature on ancient, medieval, and early modern societies. In the summer of 1909 she began preparing the manuscript for publication; in 1910 she completed an initial draft, containing eight chapters. She intended to first publish the work as eight separate brochures or pamphlets and later as a complete book.[**]

---

* *The Mass Strike, the Political Party, and the Trade Unions*, in *The Rosa Luxemburg Reader*, p. 185.

† *Introduction to Political Economy*, p. 140, below.

‡ See *The Letters of Rosa Luxemburg*, p. 118: "As for the statement that it is ridiculous to be an idealist in the German movement, I don't agree with that … Because the *suprema ratio* [supreme principle] with which I have succeeded in all my Polish–German revolutionary practical work is this: always to be myself, without any regard to the surroundings or other people. Indeed, I am an idealist and will remain one, as much in the German movement as in the Polish." (Letter to Jogiches of May 1, 1899.)

§ See her letter to Wilhelm Pieck of August 1, 1908, in *Gesammelte Briefe*, Band 2, p. 365.

¶ This represents one relatively early version of the subjects that she lectured on at the party school. Unfortunately, we have no records of the content of most of her courses from 1907 to 1914.

** The planned table of contents as of 1910 reads as follows: 1) What Is Political Economy?;

In the course of working on the last brochure or chapter in November 1911—dealing with the trajectory of capitalism as a whole—Luxemburg encountered what she called a "puzzling aspect" of a larger subject: namely, *what are the barriers that prevent the continued expansion of capitalism?* She was acutely aware that "What particularly distinguishes the capitalist mode of production from all its predecessors is that it has the inherent impetus to extend automatically across the whole of the earth, and drive out all other earlier social orders."* This drive for global expansion, she held, is the economic basis of colonialism and imperialism. On these grounds, she repeatedly attacked the leading economists of the time, such as Karl Bücher and Wilhelm Roscher, for presuming that capitalism can be understood as a *national* system. Indeed, the study of political economy was termed "national economy" by the German economists of the time—a fact that earned Luxemburg's scorn. However, what establishes the *limits* to capitalist expansion? She wrote,

> Yet the more countries develop a capitalist industry of their own, the greater is the need and possibility for expansion of production, while the smaller in relation to this is the possibility of expansion due to market barriers ... Incessantly, with each step of its own further development, capitalist production is approaching the time when its expansion and development will be increasingly slow and difficult.†

As Luxemburg pondered this issue, she became convinced that Marx failed to explain adequately the limits to capitalist expansion in his formulae of expanded reproduction at the end of Volume 2 of *Capital*, which assumes a closed capitalist society without foreign trade. Luxemburg viewed this as a very serious error, since she took it to imply the possibility of infinite capitalist expansion—something that, if true, would reduce the effort to create a socialist society to being a subjective, utopian wish instead of an objective, historical necessity.

Luxemburg realized that the issue of expanded reproduction was too complex and serious to be briefly dealt with at the conclusion of the *Introduction to Political Economy*. She therefore decided to devote an entire work to the problem. As a result, in January 1912 she broke off work on the *Introduction* in order to begin writing *The Accumulation of Capital*. Published in 1913, it aimed to show that the imperialist destruction of non-capitalist strata is driven by the inability of workers and capitalists to consume or realize the bulk of the surplus value produced through capitalist production. The imposition of capitalist relations upon non-capitalist strata, she argued, is both crucial for further

---

2) Social Labor; 3) Material on Economic History (primitive communism, slave economy, *corvée* economy, guild commerce); 4) Exchange; 5) Wage Labor; 6) The Rule of Capital (rate of profit); 7) Crises; 8) Tendencies of the Capitalist Economy.
   *   *Introduction to Political Economy*, p. 296, below.
   †   Ibid., p. 300, below.

capital accumulation *and* establishes the historical limits to such expanded reproduction.

Neither the problem of expanded reproduction nor her differences with Marx appear in the *Introduction to Political Economy*; indeed, they are not dealt with in her lectures on Volumes 2 and 3 of *Capital* that she gave as part of her work at the SPD school, and which appear here in English for the first time. These issues are reserved for the far more detailed and technical discussion in *The Accumulation of Capital*. But that does not mean Luxemburg gave up on the *Introduction to Political Economy*. She resumed work on it in 1916, when she was imprisoned in the Wronke Fortress for her opposition to World War I, and she continued to work on the manuscript until her release from prison in late 1918.

Her 1916 outline of the *Introduction* included ten chapters, reflecting her much-expanded treatment of pre-capitalist societies.* She appears to have completed much of the manuscript by then and was already envisioning plans for its publication.† However, at the time of her death only five chapters (that is, chapters 1, 3, 6, 7, and the beginning of chapter 10) were found among her papers. It is likely that some of the material was destroyed or lost when the proto-fascist Freikorps ransacked her apartment shortly after her assassination in January 1919.

This volume includes the text of the *Introduction to Political Economy* published after her death by Paul Levi, Luxemburg's colleague and follower, in 1925. The text has to be read with caution, since the version available to us is missing a number of important chapters—such as those on the theory of value, capital and profit, and on the history of crises—and Luxemburg did not get to edit what we do have for final publication. We have every reason to believe, however, that she did compose the missing chapters on value, capital and profit, and crises; the importance she gave to the theory of value, for instance, is evident from much of her work, including an essay from 1899 that is included here, entitled "Back to Adam Smith!" It states,

> But the fundamental difference between Ricardo's and Marx's labor theory of value—a difference not only misunderstood by bourgeois economics, but also mostly misjudged in the popularization of Marx's doctrine—is that Ricardo, corresponding to his universal, natural-rights conception of the bourgeois economy, also

---

*   The planned table of contents as of 1916 reads as follows: 1) What Is Economics?; 2) Social Labor; 3) Economic-Historical Perspectives: Primitive Communist Society; 4) Economic-Historical Perspectives: Feudal Economic System; 5) Economic-Historical Perspectives: The Medieval Town and Craft Guild; 6) Commodity Production; 7) Wage Labor; 8) The Profit of Capital; 9) The Crisis; 10) The Tendencies of Capitalist Development.

†   See her letter to Johann Heinrich Dietz of July 18, 1916, in *Gesammelte Werke*, Band 6, p. 130. As of this point she had completed the first three chapters, while the rest was ready in draft form. She still intended for the respective chapters to appear first as separate brochures or pamphlets, with the complete book published afterwards.

held the creation of value to be a *natural* attribute of human labor, of the individual, concrete labor of individual people. Marx, on the other hand, recognized value as an *abstraction*, an abstraction made by the society under particular conditions, and arrived thereby at a differentiation of the two sides of commodity-producing labor: concrete, individual labor and undifferentiated social labor—a differentiation from which the solution to the *money riddle* springs to the eye as though illuminated by the glow of a bulls-eye lantern.*

Closely connected to the content of the *Introduction to Political Economy* is the series of manuscripts and lecture notes from her work at the party school. Three of the manuscripts—notes on slavery, the history of economic crises, and the history of political economy—were a direct part of her research for the *Introduction*.† In addition, four transcripts of her lectures at the party school have survived that are also connected with the *Introduction*, dealing with Volumes 2 and 3 of Marx's *Capital*, slavery in ancient Greece and Rome, and the Middle Ages.‡ These lectures appear to have been transcribed by Rosi Wolfstein, a student of Luxemburg's at the party school and an important activist in the German socialist movement.§ All appear in this volume in full,¶ for the first time in English.**

The manuscripts and lecture transcripts from the party school are of great importance in illustrating the extent of Luxemburg's historical and empirical knowledge as well as the depth of her critical and analytical intellect. They show how much work she put into keeping up with the latest literature in political economy, anthropology, sociology, and ethnology—all while maintaining a

---

* See "Back to Adam Smith!," pp. 86, below.

† The precise date of composition for these three manuscripts is unknown, but they appear to have been composed between 1909 and 1913.

‡ Rosi Wolfstein made these four transcripts of Luxemburg's lectures in 1912–13.

§ Wolfstein was the wife of Paul Frölich, Luxemburg's biographer. Frölich had access to these manuscripts and typescripts in the 1920s and intended to publish them as part of Luxemburg's Complete Works. That project was cut short, however, by Luxemburg's denunciation by the international communist movement in mid-1920s, and the materials were largely forgotten until six of the seven were rediscovered by Prof. Narihiko Ito in 2001 at the Russian State Archive for Social and Political History in Moscow. The other two manuscripts—Luxemburg's notes on slavery and on the history of political economy—are at the SAMPO Federal Archives in Berlin. See Narihiko Ito, "Erstveröfftenlichung von Rosa Luxemburgs Schrift 'Slavery,'" in *Jahrbuch für Historische Kommunishmus-forschung* (Berlin: Aufbau-Verlag, 2002). I wish to thank Narihiko Ito for making copies of the original manuscripts available to us, and Prof. Michael Krätke for providing us with electronic transcripts of the seven manuscripts.

¶ I wish to thank Éric Sevault for his assistance with some of the footnotes to the *Introduction to Political Economy* and manuscripts from the party school that are found in this volume. See *Rosa Luxemburg, À l'école du socialism, Oeuvres completes*, Tome II (Paris: Agone & Smolny, 2012).

** Luxemburg undoubtedly composed a number of manuscripts in preparation for her lectures and the *Introduction to Political Economy* that have not survived. For instance, there is no manuscript of her research on the Middle Ages, even though we have a lengthy transcript of her lecture on that subject at the party school.

heavy schedule of writing for the socialist press, speaking at rallies and protests, and engaging in the internal debates and polemics of the Second International.*

Her fierce independence is manifest in many of these writings, such as her work on slavery in the ancient world. She took issue with Friedrich Engels, Marx's closest colleague and follower, for claiming that slavery resulted from the creation of private property, arguing, "This explanation cannot, strictly speaking, satisfy us," since slavery arose *earlier*, as a direct result of the dissolution of the primitive agrarian commune. She based much of her research on the same figures that Marx studied in his investigations of non-Western societies at the end of his life, such as the Russian sociologist Maxim Kovalevsky.† Moreover, she showed a pronounced interest in the *positive* contributions of communal social relations in the non-Western world, especially in sub-Saharan Africa—a part of the world that was hardly ever discussed by the European Marxists of her era.

This volume also contains a manuscript on "Theory of the Wages Fund," which sharply attacks the classical theory that the wages of workers is determined by the ratio of the total amount of capital to the population of available workers, by counter-posing that theory to Marx's theory of the surplus army of the unemployed. Luxemburg scholar and biographer Annelies Laschitza has recently discovered that the manuscript was actually composed in 1897, while Luxemburg was at the University of Zurich.‡

III.

What was Luxemburg's specific approach to the study of economic phenomena, especially as shown by *Introduction to Political Economy* and the manuscripts and typescripts that were part of her work at the party school?

It is evident to anyone reading the *Introduction to Political Economy* and the materials composed for her courses at the party school that Luxemburg does not proceed along the lines of Volume 1 of Marx's *Capital*. Unlike Marx, she does not try to delineate the logic of the commodity-form and value production on

---

* The popularity of Luxemburg's lectures was attested to by her secretary and friend Mathilde Jacob: "Even if some of the numerous listeners who came to the Bartsch Assembly rooms in Neukölln [where Luxemburg's lectures were given] on these Sunday mornings did not always agree with her conclusions, everybody followed the masterly dialectical exposition with keen interest." See Mathilde Jacob, *Rosa Luxemburg: An Intimate Portrait*, translated by Hans Fernbach with an Introduction by David Fernbach (London: Lawrence & Wishart, 2000), p. 25.

† Although Luxemburg was asked by Karl Kautsky to help prepare Marx's voluminous manuscripts and unpublished work for publication, she turned down the request. It is therefore unclear if she knew of Marx's "Notebooks on Kovalevsky" or the other materials composed by him at the end of his life on pre-capitalist societies.

‡ Laschitza's tireless research and compilation of Luxemburg's manuscripts, letters and papers, along with the work of Narihiko Ito, Holger Politt, Feliks Tych, and others, has proven of indispensable importance in bringing to light Luxemburg's multifaceted legacy.

a highly abstract level. She instead takes a historical approach by discussing the factors that helped bring the commodity-form and value production into being. However, this does not mean that Luxemburg was writing a straight narrative history. Her aim was not to write a history of capitalism so much as to discuss the central categories of Marx's *Capital* through a historical approach.

Michael R. Krätke has captured the gist of Luxemburg's project in calling it "a problem-oriented representation" that "traces the logic of historical development of the modes of production far beyond the topic of Marx's *Capital*."[*] The latter work is a study of capitalist production and capitalist production alone. It is not mainly concerned with showing how capitalism emerged from pre-capitalist modes of production. Why then does Luxemburg take a more historical approach, and what does this tell us about her theoretical contribution?

It is first of all important to recognize what Luxemburg is *not* doing—trying to popularize the Marxian doctrine. In the period before and after Marx's death in 1883, numerous popularizations of Marx's *Capital* appeared by such figures as Johann Most, Henry Hyndman, Friedrich Engels and Karl Kautsky. Many of these tried to spare readers the trouble of working through the hard, theoretical abstractions found in the opening chapters of *Capital* by treating them as a mere reflection of specific historical phases, such as the transition from simple commodity exchange to generalized commodity production.[†] In some cases, students were even advised to skip Chapter 1 altogether. Luxemburg was not enamored of these efforts to simplify Marx's critique of value production. There is no doubt that she directed her lectures and the *Introduction to Political Economy* to those who might benefit from a primer to Marxian concepts. The issue she faced, however, was how to present the theoretic determinants of *Capital* without falling prey to the superficial summaries so common in the SPD. She sought to make Marx's ideas more accessible, not by rephrasing or abbreviating them in a simplified or vulgarized fashion, but rather by elucidating their complexity by showing how they relate to both the emergence and the dissolution of capitalist society.

In other words, Luxemburg does not bring in history as a way of providing examples of theoretical concepts; instead, the complexity and importance of the concepts are elucidated by analyzing history in their light. The former approach maps the categories directly onto history; the latter enables students to obtain an understanding of the categories on their own terms through a study of history.

Paul Frölich, Luxemburg's colleague and biographer, expressed her approach thusly: "The language is that of the people, but it is not that popularizing style

---

*   Michael Krätke, "Rosa Luxemburgs unveröffentlichte Texte zur Politischen Ökonomie," in *Rosa Luxemburg als politische Ökonomin: Unveröffentlichte ökonomische Schriften* (Berlin: Dietz Verlag, forthcoming).

†   For a critique of this reading of Marx, see C. J. Arthur's *The New Dialectic and Marx's Capital* (Leiden and Boston: Brill, 2002).

which avoids difficulties by flattening out and simplifying the problems, but a straightforward simplicity as is found only in the writings of someone who has a lively view and a complete intellectual mastery of things."* As Luxemburg put it in a letter to Clara Zetkin, her *Introduction to Political Economy* "is not an economic history, as you thought, but a brief analysis of political economy, that is, of the capitalist mode of production."†

No less important, Luxemburg was not simply trying to provide an explanation of capitalism's historical development. She was most of all concerned with tracing out the process of its dissolution. Indeed, the issue of dissolution is central to each specific historical era she explored. In analyzing the "primitive" communist societies of the Incas, Africans, and others, she shows how "private property, class rule, male supremacy, state compulsion, and compulsory marriage" arose out of the internal dissolution of early communal bonds.‡ In analyzing ancient Greece and Rome, she shows how slavery undermined the economic viability of these societies and ultimately led to their demise. In the case of the European Middle Ages, she reveals the damage done by the growth of commodity exchange and private property to the patriarchal solidity of feudal societies. And in analyzing the pre-capitalist societies persisting in her own time, she shows how the impact of European colonialism and imperialism "accomplishes what millennia and the most savage Oriental conquerors could not: the dissolution of the whole social structure from the inside, tearing apart all traditional bonds and transforming the society in a short period of time into a shapeless pile of rubble."§

More than anything else, it is this keen attentiveness to the process of dissolution that characterizes her analysis of capitalism. All of her economic studies—as well as many of her political writings—seek to pinpoint the internal contradictions of value production that lead, of necessity, to the destruction of the existing order. As she wrote in the *Introduction to Political Economy*,

> The capitalist mode of production, for its part, is already, right from the start, viewed in the quite immense perspective of historical progress, not something inalterable that exists forever; it is simply a transitional phase, a rung on the colossal ladder of human cultural development, in the same way as previous social forms. And indeed, the development of capitalism itself, on closer inspection, leads on to its own decline and beyond. If we have up to now investigated the connections that

---

* Paul Frölich, *Rosa Luxemburg* (New York: Modern Reader, 1972), p. 149. See also Krätke, "Rosa Luxemburgs unveröffentlichte Texte zur Politischen Ökonomie": "Popularization does not mean, however, that economic theory is replaced by economic history, it means rather to trace the logic of the historical development of a mode of production, showing their contradictions."

† To Clara Zetkin, late June 1909, in *Gesammelte Werke*, Band 3, p. 39.

‡ See *Introduction to Political Economy*, p. 162, below.

§ Ibid, p. 227, below.

make the capitalist economy *possible*, it is now time to familiarize ourselves with those that make it *impossible*.*

Luxemburg's emphasis on decay also explains why she was so determined to develop a Marxist theory of imperialism. In her view, workers and capitalists cannot supply what is required in terms of demand to "buy back" or realize the bulk of surplus value generated by capitalist production, and consequently imperialism becomes essential if the economy is to continue to expand. But the depletion of non-capitalist strata through imperialist intervention ultimately exhausts the potential for expansion. For that reason, she viewed imperialism as the period of capitalism's "final crisis."[†]

In emphasizing capitalism's tendency towards dissolution, as against developing a theory of capitalism's development, Luxemburg is following the approach of Marx himself, who treated dissolution as the key to any social phenomena. Indeed, that is the essence of Marx's *Capital*. Its primary object of investigation is not the development of capitalism but rather the elements within it that contain the seeds of its destruction. That this was Marx's approach to historical phenomena is also evident from such works as the *Grundrisse* and the *Ethnological Notebooks*.[‡] That Luxemburg took much the same approach—despite the fact that many of Marx's works had not yet been published and were inaccessible to her—indicates that, her differences with Volume 2 of *Capital* not withstanding, she had a far better understanding of Marx's approach than most of his critics and followers.

Luxemburg's emphasis on dissolution is also evident in her attitude toward political economy. The end of the first chapter of the *Introduction to Political Economy* argues that since political economy is the study of the social relations of modern capitalism, the passing of capitalism will spell the end of political economy itself. This indicates that Luxemburg, like Marx, did not see her role as revitalizing political economy so much as undermining its very foundations through a rigorous critique of the capitalist mode of production.[§] This may give the professional economists some discomfort, but Luxemburg's vision was far more expansive than what generally defines that field. Which does not of course

---

*   Ibid., p. 295, below.

†   To Leo Jogiches, January 9, 1899, in *Gesammelte Briefe*, Band 1, pp. 249–50.

‡   For more on the critical importance of the concept of dissolution in Marx's critique of capitalism, see Peter Hudis, *Marx's Concept of the Alternative to Capitalism* (Leiden and Boston: Brill, 2012).

§   See the *Introduction to Political Economy*, p. 144, below: "It is clear then why Marx placed his own economic doctrine outside official political economy, calling it a 'critique of political economy.' The laws of capitalist anarchy and its future downfall that Marx brought to light are certainly a continuation of the political economy that was created by bourgeois scholars, but a continuation whose final results stand in very sharp contrast to the points of departure of this. The Marxian doctrine is a child of political economy, but a child that cost its mother her life."

mean she wasn't intent on mastering the subject as part of an effort to subvert it from within.

IV.

As important as are Luxemburg's contributions to an understanding of the modern world, her limitations are no less instructive. One will search in vain to find in her work a discussion of one of the most important Marxian concepts—the fetishism of commodities. Like virtually all the Marxists of her generation, this dimension of Chapter 1 of *Capital* was largely passed over in silence. It is only with the work of Georg Lukács in the 1920s—who wrote, "[T]he chapter dealing with the fetish character of the commodity contains within itself the whole of historical materialism'"—that it began to obtain the attention it deserved. One will also not find a serious discussion or defense of the Marxian notion of the decline in the rate of profit, which some contemporary economists argue is of crucial importance for understanding the present crisis of global capitalism. Instead, she dismissed the concept on the grounds that "there is still some time to pass before capitalism collapses because of the falling rate of profit, roughly until the sun burns out."†

Most important of all, Luxemburg (like virtually all Marxists of her generation) tended to view the absolute class opposites as anarchy versus organization, by identifying "planlessness" with capitalism and an "organized economy" with socialism. As she writes in *Introduction to Political Economy*, in capitalism there is "the disappearance of any kind of authority in economic life, any organization and planning in labor, any kind of connection between the individual members." She adds, "There is indeed, still today, an over-powerful lord that governs working humanity: *capital*. But its form of government is not despotism but *anarchy*."‡ Although this was the standard view in the Second International, Engels had attacked it many years earlier. The 1891 Erfurt Program, which served as the programmatic and theoretic basis of German Social Democracy, had referred to "The planlessness rooted in the nature of capitalist private production." In his critique of the program, Engels countered: "Capitalist production by *joint-stock companies* is no longer *private* production but production on behalf of many associated people. And when we pass on from joint-stock companies to trusts, which dominate and monopolize whole branches of industry, this puts an end not only to *private production* but also to *planlessness*."§ Of course, that doesn't

---

*   See Georg Lukács, "Reification and the Consciousness of the Proletariat," in *History and Class Consciousness: Studies in Marxist Dialectics* (London: Merlin Press, 1968), p. 170.

†   See Rosa Luxemburg, *The Accumulation of Capital: An Anti-Critique* (New York: Modern Reader, 1972), p. 77.

‡   *Introduction to Political Economy*, p. 134, below.

§   Friedrich Engels, "A Critique of the Draft Programme of 1891," in *Marx-Engels Collected Works*, Vol. 27 (New York: International Publishers, 1990), p. 224.

make society any less capitalistic. Yet despite this, Luxemburg persisted in claiming that "anarchy is the life element of the rule of capital"*—thereby giving short shrift to the despotic plan of capital at the point of production. This is no academic matter, but touches directly on the conception of what constitutes a truly socialist society. For if "market anarchy" is the essence of capitalism, it seems to follow that the abolition of the market and the rule of society by a state-planned economy constitutes "socialism."†

Surely, Luxemburg was correct that one of the historical factors that produced the dissolution of pre-capitalist societies and the rise of capitalism was the increasing role of anarchic relations of commodity exchange. However, she runs up against the following question: does private property emerge as a result of generalized commodity exchange, or is it the other way around? She writes, "We thus come up against a strange contradiction: exchange is only possible with private property and a developed division of labor, but this division of labor can only come about as a result of exchange and on the basis of private property, while private property for its part only arises through exchange."‡ She admits that "we are clearly going round in a circle" and running up against a contradiction. She tries to resolve the matter thusly: "A contradiction may well be something inextricable for individuals in everyday life, but in the life of society as a whole, you find contradictions of this kind everywhere you look … [as] the great philosopher Hegel said: 'Contradiction is the very moving principle of the world.'" The problem, however, is that this way of putting things does not really posit contradiction in a Hegelian sense, in which dialectical duality is resolved through a higher development. She instead poses the contradiction along the lines of a Kantian antimony—that is, of an unresolved and insuperable contradiction.

Marx grappled with a similar contradiction, but he resolved it quite differently. He wrote in his *Economic and Philosophical Manuscripts of 1844*,

> *Private property* thus results by analysis from the concept of *alienated labor*, i.e., of *alienated man*, of estranged labor, of estranged life, of *estranged* man. True, it is as a result of the *movement of private property* that we have obtained the concept of *alienated labor (of alienated life)* in political economy. But analysis of this concept shows that though private property appears to be the reason, the cause of alienated labor, it is rather its consequence, just as the gods are *originally* not the cause but the effect of man's intellectual confusion. Later this relationship becomes reciprocal.§

---

*   *Introduction to Political Economy*, p. 134, below.

†   For more on this, see Peter Hudis, "Rosa Luxemburg's Concept of a Post-Capitalist Society," in *Critique*, Vol. 40, No. 3 (2012), pp. 323–35.

‡   *Introduction to Political Economy*, p. 251, below.

§   *Economic and Philosophical Manuscripts of 1844*, in *Marx-Engels Collected Works*, Vol. 3 (New York: International Publishers, 1975), p.p. 279-80.

Luxemburg did not have access, of course, to Marx's *1844 Manuscripts,* or many of his other writings that contain a far deeper critique of capitalism than the counterpoising of "market anarchy" and "organized plan." That liberatory perspective did not permeate her generation of Marxists—just as it has been outside the purview of many lesser Marxists who came after her.

No one can doubt that Luxemburg had a fiercely independent intellect and personality—to the extent that she was not afraid to take issue with even her closest intellectual mentors. As the entirety of her contribution is made available in the *Complete Works,* we will be in a better position to judge the validity and strength—as well as the possible weaknesses—of her overall contribution to the struggle for human liberation. Reading Luxemburg critically is undoubtedly what she herself would expect of us, as we try to grasp what the revolutionary critique of capital that she devoted herself to means for today.

Peter Hudis

---

* The German edition of the *Complete Works,* published by Dietz Verlag in Berlin, is currently being supplemented by a number of additional volumes containing material that did not appear earlier in the *Gesammelte Werke.* All of these writings will be included in the English-language *Complete Works.*

The Industrial Development of Poland

PREFACE

Although the subject of the following treatise is highly specialized, we are nevertheless convinced that, for a number of reasons, it can be of more than passing interest to Western European readers. Today, in all civilized countries, economic issues stand in the forefront of intellectual life. There is already a widespread recognition that they are the motive forces of all social being and becoming. The political physiognomy and historical destiny of a country are for us like a closed book, sealed with seven seals,* if we do not know that country's economic life and all the resulting social consequences.

It was not so long ago that Poland's name resounded throughout the civilized world; its fortunes stirred the minds of all and brought excitement to every heart. Lately no one any longer hears much about Poland—not since it became an ordinary capitalist country. If one wants to know what has become of the old rebel, and where the destinies of history have steered it, the answer can come only from research into the economic history of Poland in recent decades.

One can view and discuss the so-called Polish question from various standpoints, but for those who see in the material development of society the key to its political development, the solution to the Polish question can be found only on the basis of Poland's economic life and the trends within it. We have attempted in the following treatise to gather together the available material necessary for solving this problem, organizing it as much as possible to provide a clear and overall view. In the process, here and there, we have also taken the liberty of doing some direct finger pointing of a political nature. Thus, the subject that at first glance seemed so dry and specialized may prove to be interesting for political people as well.

This may also be true for other reasons. We live at a time when the mighty Empire of the North is playing an increasingly important role in European politics. All eyes are keeping a close watch on Russia, and people view with concern the alarming advances made by Russian policy in Asia. Soon it may not be a secret to anyone that the most important capitalist countries will, earlier or later, have to be prepared for serious *economic* competition with Russia in Asia. The economic policy of the tsarist empire can therefore no longer be a matter of complete indifference to Western Europeans. Poland constitutes, however, one of the most important and most advanced industrial regions of the Russian empire, one in whose history the economic policies of Russia have perhaps been most clearly and distinctly expressed.

---

* A reference to Book of Revelation in the New Testament, in which John, the author of the fourth gospel, reports that the revelation was secured by seven wax seals.

The material for our study lay scattered in numerous statistical publications, which often contradicted one another, as well as polemical pamphlets, newspaper articles, and both official reports and unofficial ones. No exhaustive work about the history of Polish industry in general, and especially about its present condition, is to be found in the existing literature, neither in the Polish language nor in Russian, nor in German. We believed therefore that we needed to process and digest this ragged, disconnected raw material in order to present it in as finished form as possible, so that the reader could most easily reach significant general conclusions.

I. THE HISTORY AND PRESENT CONDITION OF POLISH INDUSTRY

1. The Period of Manufacture, 1820–50

Toward the beginning of the nineteenth century, political events placed Poland in entirely new circumstances. The partitioning of Poland[*] removed it from the special feudal-anarchic conditions of natural economy that had prevailed under the republic of the gentry—conditions found in Poland for most of the eighteenth century. Poland was brought under a regime of enlightened absolutism, under the centralized, bureaucratic administrative systems of Prussia, Austria, and Russia. The main part of Poland, under Russia, which is of interest to us here, indeed was very soon able, at first as the Duchy of Warsaw[†] and, later, after the Congress of Vienna [as the Kingdom of Poland], to maintain its own constitution based on social estates.[‡] But there was a world of difference between this Congress Poland and the Poland of former times. The entire administrative, financial, military, and judicial apparatus was adapted to that of a modern centralized state. But this apparatus proved to be in glaring contradiction to the economic relations onto which it had been superimposed. As before, Poland's economic life centered on landed property. The development of urban craft production, which had begun in the thirteenth century, had run into the sand by the time of the seventeenth century. At the end of the eighteenth century, attempts

---

[*]   The first partition of Poland between Prussia, Austria–Hungary, and Russia occurred in 1772; the second partition occurred in 1793. The third and final partitioning of Poland occurred in 1795, in which Poland was absorbed in the three surrounding empires.

[†]   The Duchy of Warsaw was established in 1807 by Napoleon. It consisted of Prussian-occupied parts of Poland that were surrendered under the terms of the Treaties of Tilset. It did not function as a truly independent country, serving as a satellite state of France. It was occupied and divided between Prussia and Russia following Napoleon's defeat in Russia in 1814.

[‡]   After the defeat of Napolean, the European heads of state gathered at the Congress of Vienna, from September 18, 1814 to June 9, 1815, to implement a territorial reorganization of Europe. Among other things, the Congress of Vienna established a nominally independent Kingdom of Poland, subordinated to the tsarist regime through a "personal union" with Russia under Tsar Alexander I. This "Kingdom of Poland" is also frequently referred to as "Congress Poland," since the Congress of Vienna founded it.

by the owners of large landed estates (the magnates) to create a manufacturing system likewise fell apart, having gone nowhere. After all, landed property was entirely unsuited to serve as the basis for a modern state organization. Because of its dependence on the world market, which dated from the fifteenth century, the Poland of old had been driven to establish a highly extensive latifundia economy, with the most extreme exactions being imposed on serf labor. These latifundia were managed more and more irrationally, and therefore constantly became less and less productive. The wars of Poland's final epoch, and then Napoleon's economic policies in the Duchy of Poland, especially the Continental System,* and the accompanying drop in grain exports, plus the falling price of grain, followed by the abolition of serfdom in 1807—all these blows of different kinds fell upon landed property, one after the other, over the course of about ten years and brought it to the verge of ruin. But because landed property constituted the main source of revenue in the country, once again the full burden of the relatively large costs of the new administrative system fell on the landed proprietors. The 10 percent income tax on landed property, which Poland had already introduced in olden times, but which was now actually being collected for the first time, was suddenly supposed to be increased to 24 percent. In addition, the burden of quartering troops and supplying the military *in natura*† fell on the nobility.

The result was that landed property soon fell into the clutches of the usurers. While old Poland possessed no urban capitalist class, because of the decay of urban production and trade, such a class surfaced right after the partition of Poland. In part it consisted of immigrating officials and usurers, in part of Polish upstarts who owed their material existence to the country's huge political and economic crisis. This new section of the population now provided the needy gentry with capital. Incidentally, to a large extent the ten-year rule of Prussia (1796–1806) had already laid the foundations for the gentry's indebtedness. During that decade for the first time an organized system of agricultural credit was thrown wide open for the Polish gentry.

For Polish landed property this constituted a veritable revolution. What then took place had been accomplished in Western Europe during the Middle Ages by a slow and gradual process over centuries—the undermining of patrimonial land ownership as the result of usurious interest payments. In Poland this process was brought to completion in less then twenty years. Up until the end of the republic, landed property had been kept free of the usurer. But

---

*   On November 21, 1806, Napoleon prohibited the countries of the European Continent from having any economic dealings with Great Britain. This embargo was meant to isolate England and bring all of Europe under the control of the French Empire. This policy collapsed by 1812 in the face of Britain's economic power, its military control of the seas, and the resistance of several of the European countries to the embargo, especially Russia.

†   That is, with goods in kind.

now, as early as 1821, the landowners had to be saved from destruction by an emergency regulation issued by the government of the Kingdom of Poland—a moratorium.

Under such circumstances, a deficit was a permanent part of the budget of the Kingdom of Poland from the very beginning. The creation of new sources of revenue for the exchequer and of new spheres of economic activity in the country therefore became a condition of existence for the Kingdom from the first moment. Following the example of other countries and driven by immediate needs, the government undertook the establishment of urban industry in Poland.

The decade 1820–30 is the time of origin for Polish industry, or more exactly, for Polish manufacture.

It is indicative that this came about in a way quite similar to that of the earlier origins of Polish craft production, with foreign, mostly German, craftsmen being encouraged to move to Poland. Just as the Polish princes in the thirteenth century tried to attract foreign workers by offering all sorts of privileges, so too did the government of Congress Poland. An entire series of tsarist decrees to this effect were issued in the years 1816–24. The government made houses available free of charge, as well as construction materials, waived rental payments, and established a so-called iron fund for the erection of industrial buildings and housing for industry personnel. In 1816 immigrating craftsmen were assured of freedom from all taxation and other public burdens for six years, their sons were exempted from military service, and they were permitted to bring personal property into the country duty-free. In 1820 the government granted the immigrants free use of building materials from the state forests and established special brickyards to provide them with the cheapest possible bricks.

An 1822 law freed all industrial enterprises, for a period of three to six years, from the obligation to quarter soldiers. In 1820 and 1823 it was decreed that the cities were to hand over locations to these enterprises rent-free for six years. The industrial fund established in 1822 for the encouragement of industrial colonization amounted to 45,000 rubles at the beginning; it was already twice as much in 1823, and from then on, was set at 127,500 rubles annually.[1]

Such manifold attractions did not fail to have an effect. Soon German craftsmen trooped into Poland and settled down. About 10,000 German families immigrated in a few years at this time. In this way, the most important industrial cities of today soon arose: Łódź, Zgierz, Rawa, Pabianice, and others. In addition to craftsmen, the government of Russian Poland called in prominent foreign industrialists to direct its enterprises: [John] Cockerill from Belgium, [Alfons] Fraget, [Philippe de] Girard, and others.* But the government of Congress

---

*   In the original edition the name is given as "Coqueril." John Cockerill was a British-born Belgian entrepeneur whose steel factories in Liège helped spur the industrial revolution in Belgium. After the company that he founded (named after himself) went bankrupt in 1839 due to a banking

Poland did not content itself with the granting of privileges to immigrants and the establishment of German manufacturing towns. Unlike the handicrafts of the Middle Ages, manufacturing could not content itself with a narrow circle of consumption and circulation within one city; to start with, it required a wholesale market and, further, commodity circulation embracing at least the whole country. Together with the foundation of manufacturing colonies, the government had to undertake a whole series of administrative and legislative reforms intended to unify the country economically into a single complex and create the necessary legal forms for internal commodity traffic. The greatest breach in the property relations and especially the landed property relations of old Poland had already been forced by the Napoleonic Code,* introduced in the Duchy of Warsaw in 1808. This had superimposed the legal forms of a modern bourgeois economy in quite finished form onto the economic conditions of a purely feudal natural economy. This code did not have the power to reorganize the mode of production as such, not in the least, but it did undermine the old property relations drastically and thereby hastened their disintegration. With the abolition of perpetual rent, entail, etc., landed property was ripped out of its state of immobility and catapulted into circulation. At the same time, the Napoleonic Code supplied commerce and the commercial courts with legal standards. In 1817, furthermore, chambers of commerce and manufacturing were established and the regulation of trade was brought to a close; in the following year, deed registries were introduced; in 1825, the Agricultural Credit Association was founded.[2] In 1819, the building of highways and the regulation of waterways were begun at government expense; and in 1825, the construction of a canal between the Niemen and the Vistula.[3] Finally, the government also took the lead—as in other countries where manufacture was just beginning—by establishing its own industrial enterprises: model factories, model sheep ranches, and so on. But it gave the strongest foothold to budding manufacturing by establishing the Bank of Poland, which was brought into existence by a tsarist decree of 1828 and organized after the model of the Belgian Societé Generale and the German Seehandlung.† The Bank of Poland was an issuing, investment, deposit,

---

scandal, he traveled to Russia to expand his business and raise funds. He died while staying in Warsaw in 1840. For a study of his company's impact on Russia and Poland, see "John Cockerill in Southern Russia, 1885–1905: A study of Aggressive Foreign Entrepreneurship," *Business History Review*, Vol. 41, No. 3 (Autumn 1967), pp. 243–56. Joseph Fraget (1797–1867) was a French businessman who set up a famous tableware factory in Warsaw, in 1824, with his brother Alfons Fraget
Philippe de Girard was a French entrepreneur who was invited to Russian-occupied Poland in 1825 to help create the country's textile industry. The town in which his biggest factory was located, Zyradów (about twenty-seven miles southwest of Warsaw) is named after him.

    *   The Napoleonic code was established by Napoleon I in 1804 and became subsequently adopted by numerous countries conquered by or allied with France. This comprehensive civil code eliminated many feudal laws by stipulating, among other things, that government jobs be based on qualifications and not birth. It also allowed for freedom of religion.

    †   The German *Seehandlung*, or Prussian Maritime Enterprise, was a trading firm established

mortgage, commission, and industrial bank all in one. Initially endowed with a fund amounting to three million rubles, it also obtained deposits, securities, ecclesiastical funds, fire insurance, pensions, and other capital deposits, which by 1877 came to a total of 282 million rubles. The bank offered credit to industry as well as to agriculture. Over the course of 50 years from its founding it provided credit to commercial and industrial enterprises in the amount of 91 million rubles. The activity of the bank was extremely diverse. It not only established factories itself and engaged in mining and agriculture, but also concerned itself with the transportation system. The first Polish railroad line, from Warsaw to Vienna, completed in 1845, was chiefly the work of the Bank of Poland.

The activity of the government outlined above was the first important factor in the development of industry in Russian Poland. Whatever other circumstances may have affected its subsequent history, it undoubtedly owed its original existence to the initiative and efforts of the government.

We see of course, as has been said, that in other countries, for example, France and Germany, governments have stood beside the cradle of manufacturing and taken its destiny energetically in their hands. But there the governments offered their help only to a natural development of urban production, which moved of itself and by virtue of objective factors such as the accumulation of trading capital, the widening of markets, and the technological development of craft production toward transformation into manufacturing production methods. In Poland, manufacture, like urban handicraft earlier, was a foreign product imported in finished form, which could develop neither a technological nor a social connection to Poland's own economic development. Here, then, the activity of the government was the only positive factor in the rise of manufacture, and this explains to us the predilection, which Polish economists and political journalists have shown, for restating this point over and over; thus, on the whole, its significance is only too often overstated. Above all, they forget that the autonomous Polish government, in the activity that they describe, acted in the most intimate agreement with the Russian tsarist regime, which was guided by intentions that, in national terms, were nothing less than friendly toward Poland.

Moreover, the efforts of the government of Congress Poland encountered highly favorable ground in the form of Poland's tariff relations with other countries. In this respect, the Vienna Congress had made two important decisions affecting Poland: first, it was united with Russia; and second, it was guaranteed free trade with the other parts of the former Polish state, which basically meant the same thing as free trade with Germany and Austria. With regard to unification with Russia, the trade relations between the two countries were regulated by the

---

by Frederick the Great of Prussia in the early 1760s. It served as a predecessor of the Prussian State Bank, established in 1765.

tariffs of 1822 and 1824 in such a way that their products were exchanged almost duty-free.[4] The meaning of this new arrangement for Poland only becomes clear, however, if one focuses on what Russia had been doing since 1810, and especially later under the administration of [Yegor Frantsevich] Kankrin.[*] Russia had pursued an extremely prohibitive tariff policy toward the rest of Europe, often bordering on absurdity, protecting itself on all sides from foreign manufactures with a virtually insurmountable tariff wall. Through the unification with Poland, Russia now became accessible to German goods from that direction, because of the above-mentioned tariffs. The result of this for Poland was that it became the workshop for the processing of half-finished German goods, most of which were imported into Congress Poland duty-free and finished in Poland; they then found their way into Russia as Polish products, again almost duty-free. One particular result was that Poland's large cloth-manufacturing operations came into full bloom in only a few years.[5] Although it was first established in the period 1817–26, Polish cloth manufacturing had already attained, by 1829, a level of production worth 5,752,000 rubles, a substantial amount for that time.[6] That this surprisingly rapid growth resulted almost entirely from Russian consumption is shown by the following table of exports of wool products to Russia, in thousands of rubles:

1823–1,865
1825–5,058
1827–7,218
1829–8,418[7]

If the value of exported products, according to the table above, exceeded the value of those manufactured in Poland, it was because, in addition to the goods finished in Poland, German finished products were smuggled into the country and exported to Russia under Polish labels on a massive scale.

The above-mentioned tariff relationship had yet another important aspect for Congress Poland. It opened a free trade route to China, to which Polish cloth was likewise exported in large quantities. This export specifically amounted to the following, again in thousands of rubles:

1824–331
1826–332
1828–1,024
1830–1,070[8]

---

[*]   Kankrin was Russia's Finance Minister from 1823 to 1844.

Although Poland's entire export trade in the first decade of its industrial development was actually based on only one branch of manufacture, wool production, it nevertheless had great importance for the country, because it had invigorating repercussions on other branches as well, and it acted as a powerful stimulus to immigration by German craftsmen. A historian of the center of the Polish textile industry, the city of Lodz, calls Poland's cloth trade with Russia and China at that time "the main driving force in the development of industry."[9]

In 1831, however, this trade came to an end. There was an uprising in Poland in that year.[*] The uprising brought the development of Polish manufacturing to a standstill for some time, and had the additional lasting effect that the tariff between Poland and Russia was significantly increased.[10] For a long time the competition of Polish cloth in Russia and China had been a thorn in the side for the Russian manufacturers. They repeatedly petitioned the tsarist government for higher tariffs at the Polish border, but had no success until the uprising of 1831, and with it the cessation of Polish cloth exports to Russia. This gave the Russian manufacturers the opportunity to quickly take possession of the abandoned field by expanding their own production and showing the government, with the numbers thus obtained, how much the "Fatherland's" industry had suffered up till then from Polish competition. With the raising of the tariff and, at the same time, the elimination of free transit to China, Polish exports sank rapidly.[11]

In 1834, total exports amounted to 2,887,000 rubles.
Of this, manufactured products accounted for 2,385,000 rubles.
In 1850, total exports amounted to 1,274,000 rubles.
Of this, manufactured products accounted for 755,000 rubles.

This was a heavy blow to Polish wool production. After its value had reached, in 1829—as we saw—the height of 5,752,000 rubles, it sank in 1832 to 1,917,000 and rose only little by little to 2,564,000 rubles in 1850, that is, to half of the earlier amount.[12]

Nevertheless, taken all in all with regard to the further destiny of Polish manufacturing, it was not possible that the closing of the Russian border would have any great significance. In Russia itself there existed neither the prospects of a growing demand for manufactured goods nor the means of transportation capable of shipping in mass quantities. The large cloth export trade [from Poland] can mainly be explained by nothing other than the Russian army's demand for cloth. Moreover, Polish manufacturing had not even had time to provide itself

---

[*]   A military revolt in Warsaw on November 29, 1830, developed into a popular uprising against foreign rule, i.e., the rule of the Russian tsars. Nearly a year later, with the recapture of Warsaw by Russian troops on September 7, 1831, the uprising was suppressed.

with an internal market. So after the closing of the Russian customs border, it slowly undertook to establish a foothold inside the country, promoted by favorable government measures and supported in particular by the Bank of Poland. In the following two decades many branches of production developed well: in the 1830s tanning and the manufacture of soap, and in the 1840s sugar production; also in the 1830s mining, and likewise papermaking.[13] Yet because of the social conditions in Poland fairly narrow limits were imposed on the growth of industry there. The population of Congress Poland amounted to only a small number, four to five million people, and besides, the people lived for the most part in the framework of a subsistence economy. Despite the abolition of serfdom in 1807, forced labor remained the predominant type of work in agriculture, and as a result the landed proprietors, as well as the peasants, were to a large extent cut off from commodity and money exchange. The cities grew only slowly; poor and meagerly populated as they were, they could not provide a strong demand for manufactured goods either. The development of industry was thus a very slow process. Thirty years after Polish manufacture arose, a period in which it oriented mainly toward its own internal market, we see that it was still constrained within totally miniature dimensions. Even in the 1850s the most advanced of all branches of industry, textiles, still operated mainly with manual labor, without steam power, and therefore only with skilled master craftsmen and journeymen and without a trace of female labor. On the whole the fragmentation of production indicates its predominantly craft character, for in the year 1857 we still see 12,542 "factories" in Poland with a total of 56,364 workers and total production worth 21,278,592 rubles: [this means] on the average at each "factory," four to five workers, with production worth 1,700 rubles.[14]

In accordance with the conditions described above, the fact was that urban industry played only a subordinate role in the social life of Poland up until the 1850s and even the 1860s. The same old power of landed property, as ever, set the tone in the economy and the politics of the country. Indeed, the broad mass of landowners with medium-sized properties, those who represented public opinion at that time, viewed up-and-coming urban industry, and the capitalist economy along with it, as a poisonous plant imported from abroad, a "German swindle" that was to blame for the desperate condition of landed property and of the country as a whole.

2. The Transition to Large-Scale Industry, 1850–70

We have made our acquaintance with the first beginnings of industry in Poland and its further development in the limits of the domestic market. We have seen that it owed its origins to the efforts of the government, and that until the 1850s, because of the limited domestic market, it could not get beyond the forms of basic manufacture. But here the first epoch of its history comes to an end, and a new page of that history begins. After the 1850s, a series of new factors made their appearance, and although in and of themselves they were quite varied, in the last analysis all of them definitely contributed to the opening of Russian markets to Polish production and thereby assuring it of a mass market. This gradually brought about a complete revolution in Polish industry and transformed it from manufacture into truly large-scale industry, with mass production. We can therefore designate the second period of its history as the era of large-scale industry. The decades 1850–70 were a time of transition from the first to the second phase.

There were four important factors that revolutionized Polish industry during the above-mentioned transition period.

First, the abolition of the customs barrier between Russia and Poland. In the year 1851 Poland's tariff relations were altered in two ways. On the one hand, the customs barrier, which until then had cut Poland off from Russia, was eliminated; on the other, Poland's independent policy on trade with the outside world was ended and Poland was incorporated into the Russian tariff zone.[15] In this way, ever since that time, Poland has formed a single whole, together with Russia, as far as trade policy is concerned.[16] For Poland the great significance of the tariff reform of 1851 was first of all that it made the totally free export of goods to Russia possible. Thus Polish manufacture had the prospect of producing for a larger mass market, of going beyond the narrow limits of the domestic market and becoming a truly mass-production industry. But a longer period of time was required before these phenomena could fully manifest themselves. At the moment when the tariff barriers between Poland and Russia were eliminated, three important obstacles still stood in the way of truly mass export of Polish manufactured goods to Russia. First, up until then Polish manufacture had been geared mainly to the demands of the domestic market, and thus was not yet capable of the rapid expansion, by leaps and bounds, which to such a great extent characterizes large-scale mass-production industry. Second, no modern means of transportation existed between Poland and Russia. Third, the domestic market in Russia was also of limited dimensions, restricted by the continued existence of serfdom and the natural economy. But soon a complete transformation occurred in all three areas.

Undoubtedly the *Crimean War* [of 1853–56] had a revolutionizing effect on Polish as well as Russian manufacturing. The blockade of Russia's maritime borders stopped the import of most foreign goods; but in part, such goods found a new way through, at the western land borders of Poland, which became the route for a lively transit trade. More important, however, was the mass demand created by the needs of the Russian army, primarily for products of the textile industry. In Russia the growth of the latter in the years 1856–60 amounted to 11.6 percent yearly for cotton spinning, 5.5 percent for cotton weaving, and 9.4 percent for dyeing and finishing.[17] In Poland, an even greater leap may be observed. There the value of production in thousands of rubles was as follows:[18]

	1854	1860	percentage of increase
In the canvas industry	723	1,247	+72
In the wool industry	2,044	4,354	+113
In the cotton industry	2,853	8,091	+183

The era of the Crimean War also caused a deep-going revolution in textile-industry technology, bringing with it the introduction of the mechanical loom and the mechanical spindle in both Russia and Poland. In Lodz in 1854, the Scheibler firm,* which is now a gigantic factory, was founded with 100 looms and 18,000 spindles.[19] The following year, the first mechanical linen-spinning mill was established in Russia, and in 1857, the largest canvas factory in Poland, the Żyrardow [Girards'] factory,† which is still important today, was converted from a hand-operated weaving mill to one run by machinery.‡

The *second* important result was the establishment of a *series of railroad lines* between Poland and the central parts of Russia. In 1862, Poland was connected with St. Petersburg, in 1866 with Volhynia, Belorussia, and Podolia, in 1870 with Moscow, in 1871 with Kiev, in 1877 with southern Russia. Moreover, the feverish building of railroad lines in central Russia opened ever more areas to trade.[20]§ The construction of each new railroad connection to Russia was followed by an increase in demand for Polish products and an expansion of production. To be sure, the Polish uprising [of 1863–64] and the consequent temporary cessation of trade with Russia had a depressive economic effect.¶ But in spite of this,

---

* The Scheibler firm was founded in 1848 by Karol Scheibler, a German industrialist who was a citizen of Belgium. He played an instrumental role in helping to initiate the industrialization of Lodz. By the 1870s his firm was one of the largest textile manufacturers in Europe.

† Zyrardow, a town in central Poland, was founded as a textile factory in 1833. The factory was owned by Philippe de Girard, which the town is named after. Girard was hired by the Kingdom of Poland in 1825 to create a textile industry in the country. He had earlier invented the first flax spinning frame. The factory developed into one of the most important centers of textile production in nineteenth-century Poland.

‡ D. A. Timiriazev (ed.), *Istoriko-statisticheskii obzor promyshlennosti Rossii* (Historico-Statistical Review of the Industry of Russia), Vol. 2, (St. Petersburg, 1883), p. 23.

§ The verst, an old Russian measure of distance, was the equivalent of about two-thirds of a mile, i.e., approximately 3,500 feet to the mile's 5,280 feet.

¶ A wave of peasant revolts in 1860–61 culminated in the popular uprising of January 22, 1863. The rebellion, which occurred in the Kingdom of Poland, and in Lithuania, Belorussia, and parts of Ukraine, was directed against both national and social oppression by the tsarist regime, was bloodily suppressed during 1863 and 1864. Marx, who supported the uprising, considered it one of the most significant revolts of the nineteenth century. See Karl Marx, "Proclamation on Poland by the German Workers' Educational Society in London," in *Marx-Engels Collected Works*, Volume 19 (New York: International Publishers, 1984), p. 296: "The Polish question is the German question.

the decade 1860–70, the period of technological revolution in transport, had the result that while the total value of Poland's industrial production amounted to only 31 million rubles in 1851 (21 million, according to another source), it represented 73 million rubles (according to both sources) in 1872, after 15 years—an increase of 135 percent and 248 percent respectively.[21]

The third factor that contributed to the industrial revolution was *the abolition of serfdom* in Russia in 1861 and in Poland in 1864 and the resulting transformation of agriculture. Now robbed of the unpaid labor power of the serfs, the landowners turned to the employment of wage laborers and the purchase of industrial products, which earlier were made by unpaid labor on the estates. On the other hand, the great mass of peasants now had money to spend, and also became the buyers of factory goods. Connected with this was a tax reform and the beginning of the government's policy of squeezing the Russian peasantry, a policy that violently pushed even the small peasant onto the market with the products of his labor and, as this more and more undermined the natural economy in agriculture, to the same degree it prepared the ground for a money economy and a mass market for manufactured goods. The other result of the reform was the proletarianization of broad layers of the peasantry, thus the "setting free" of a mass of workers who placed themselves at the disposal of industry.

Thus we see in Russia, in connection with the Crimean War, an upheaval in all social relations. The collapse of the old patrimonial form of landed property and of natural economy, the reform of finances and the tax system, and the establishment of a whole network of railways—all this meant the emergence of markets, of new channels and outlets for sales, and of hired hands for Russian industry. But since, in terms of trade policy, Poland formed a single whole with Russia ever since the tariff abolition of 1851, so Polish manufacture was swept into the whirlpool of Russia's economic metamorphosis and was transformed by the rapidly growing market into real mass-production industry.

In addition, in the late 1870s, *a fourth important factor* came onto the scene and helped transform Polish manufacture into the large-scale industry we see in Poland today, and that was the tariff policy of the Russian government.

3. The Period of Large-Scale Industry in Poland

Since the beginning of the century, Russia, as was mentioned, had adhered to a highly protectionist policy. The Crimean War, however, caused a change here, as in all other areas of social life. In the "liberal period" of the 1860s tariffs were significantly reduced. This free-trade turn did not last long, however. Because

---

Without an independent Poland there can be no independent or united Germany, no emancipation of Germany from the Russian domination that began with the first partition of Poland."

of the reforms themselves, especially the costly railroad construction, the government ran enormously into debt to foreign countries, and the gold tariff was introduced in 1877 with the object of getting hold of gold. With this, Russia entered onto a course of ever more stringent protectionist policies.

With the exchange rate of the paper ruble falling, the gold tariff meant an increase in the tariff rate of 30 percent in the first years and of 40 to 50 percent in following years. In 1880 a deficit in the state treasury developed once more as a result of the abolition of the salt tax. To replace that, there followed in 1881 a general tariff increase of 10 percent. In 1882, several individual tariff rates were raised, such as those for linen, wool yarn, chemical products, dyes, etc.; in 1884, a repeated increase in various individual tariff rates occurred, for example that for silk yarn; in 1885, there was a nearly universal increase of tariffs by 20 percent; in 1887, once again a partial rise tariffs on particular items, and the same in 1891.[22]

Obviously the purpose of protectionism, when not fiscal revenue, was above all protection of domestic industry from foreign competition.

The results of such a substantial forcing up of the tariff were twofold. First, the import of foreign manufactured and half-finished goods declined rapidly. The total imports over Russia's European borders in millions of gold rubles annually amounted to:

1851–56	74
1856–61	120
1861–66	121
1866–71	212
1871–76	364
1876–81	326
1881–86	304
1886–91	224
1891	220
1892	219[23]

The import of manufactured and half-finished goods, whose duties much higher than raw materials, shriveled up even more severely than the above table indicates. Thus a place was made in Russian markets for native—Russian and Polish—industry, which was freed to a great extent from foreign competition.

The other natural result was the general climb in commodity prices. It has recently been calculated that the Russian consumer may pay much more for most commodities than, e.g., the German consumer; thus

For tea	304%
For tobacco	687%
For coal	200%
For paper	690%
For linen	225%
For cotton products	357%
For agricultural machinery	159%[24]

As for the metal industry: a pood [36.11 pounds] of wire nails of medium size, for example, costs an American [the equivalent of] 1 to 1.50 rubles, while a Russian pays 3.20 rubles in tariffs alone on this quantity of goods and 4 to 8 rubles for the goods as a whole. In relation to the price of the most important metals, the tariff in 1896 constituted 70 percent for iron ore; 45 percent for finished iron; and 35 percent for steel.[25]

Under such monopoly conditions, Russian and Polish industry began to rake in colossal profits from the domestic market. We can get an approximate notion of these profits from the official statements of the manufacturers themselves. In 1887, for example, the following net profits were declared:

By the Russian Cotton Spinning Mills, St. Petersburg	15.0%
By the Moscow Manufacturing Company	16.0%
By the Balin Manufacturing Company	16.0%
By the Narva Linen Spinning Mill	18.0%
By the Sampson Cotton Spinning Mill	21.3%
By the Yekaterinhof Cotton Spinning Mill	23.0%
By the Rabeneck Cotton Dye Works	25.4%
By the Izmailov Cotton Spinning Mill	26.0%
By the S. Morozov Works	28.0%
By the Neva Cotton Weaving Mill	38.0%
By the Krenholm Works	44.9%
By the Thornton Wool Works	45.0%[26]

From more recent times we have no less astonishing statements of profits in the Russian metal industry. The metallurgical enterprises in southern Russia yield on the average a profit of 50 percent, and the colossal works of the Englishman [John] Hughes as much as 100 percent.* "It is not without interest," writes the

---

* The British entrepreneur John Hughes was actually Welsh, not English. His company, the New Russia Association for Coal, Iron, and Rails Production, contracted with the Russian government in 1869 to build an ironworks and produce rails for Russia's railroads. Hughes brought about seventy British engineers and technicians to southern Russia and founded a town in a coal basin there, the Donets Basin (the so-called, Donbas, now part of Ukraine). The town was given the name "Hughes-ovka"—in Russian, Yúzovka (today Donetsk). Hughes's company built a vast industrial complex, including mines, blast furnaces, rolling mills, metallurgical plants, repair shops, etc.

official organ of Russia's Finance Ministry, "to note how the profits obtained are put to use, giving rise to the impression that the companies, in view of the utter excess of profit, seem unclear, so to speak, about what to do with it all."[27] In other words, they are unsure about the proper category in the official reports to enter their earnings in, so as to veil their shockingly large size.

The influence of monopoly prices on the size of capitalist profits, together with the relationship of the latter to outlays for labor power, is most strikingly shown by the following little juxtaposition. The market price of raw iron in Kiev in July 1897 amounted to 85 kopecks per pood; of that, the costs of production in Russia made up 45 kopecks, including wages at 4 kopecks per pood—with a net profit of 40 kopecks.[28] The relation of profits to cost of production and to wages was thus 10:11 and 10:1 respectively.

The profits of Polish entrepreneurs were in no way inferior to the enormous profits of the Russians, as we will see. At the beginning of the 1890s, dividends from the sugar factories in Poland, for example, amounted to as much as 29 percent.[29] In the textile industry, 40 percent profits were regarded as a normal phenomenon.[30] But these official manufacturers' statements are notoriously 30 to 50 percent smaller than the profits actually obtained.

In this way, after all the main conditions for industrial development—a domestic market, means of transport, an industrial reserve army—were brought into existence in the years 1860–77, the additional tariff policy created a hot-house atmosphere of monopoly prices that placed Russian and Polish industry in an absolute El Dorado of primitive capitalist accumulation. In the year 1877 an era of feverish enterprise and grandiose accumulation of capital began, combined with the bounding growth of production. A picture of Poland's overall industrial development under the impact of the conditions described above may be represented as follows:

| | In millions of rubles | | |
	Total Production	Cotton Industry	Wool Industry	Linen Industry
1860	50.0 (1864)	8.1	4.3	1.2
1870	63.9	10.2	4.0	1.2
1880	171.8	33.0	22.0	5.0
1890	240.0	47.6 (1891)	35.5	6.5[31]

The strongest upswing between 1870 and 1880—for all industry +169 percent, for the cotton industry +223 percent, for the wool industry +450 percent, for the linen industry +317 percent—is chiefly a result of the first three years (1877–80) of the new era in tariff policy. As we will see below, the introduction of the gold tariff brought with it not only the sudden establishment of many new enterprises but also the transfer of a number of German factories from Saxony and Silesia to the western part of Poland. Of the largest factories in Poland, which were inspected in an official inquiry organized in 1886, only 18.1 percent were founded before 1850,

6.8%	in 1850–60
13.6%	in 1860–70
29%	in 1870–80
32.5%	in 1880–86[32]

Thus 61 percent of all large factories were established after 1870. As for the extent of production, it increased by a factor of almost six in the textile industry as a whole, in the period 1870–90. The following table shows quite specifically the influence of the tariff policy. Of the most significant factories:

18.1%	were founded	before 1850,
37.2%		in 1850–77
44.7%		in 1877–86

Thus almost half (today even more) of all the large factories in Poland originated since 1877 as a direct result of the protectionist tariff policy.

This expansion of production went hand in hand with a revolution in the means of production themselves. Everywhere in place of the small, scattered factories appeared modern large-scale industrial enterprises with extensive use of steam power and the latest technology for construction and operation. The concentration of industry in Poland in general is as follows:

	1871	1880	1890
Number of workers	76,616	120,763	ca. 150,000
Value of production (in million rubles)	66.7	171.8	240
For one firm (in rubles)	3,239	8,063	71,248
For one worker (in rubles)	882[33]	1,422	1,600[34]

However here the average figures are, as usual, not suited to giving a true idea of the revolution taking place, since this was of course not accomplished equally in all branches of industry. Most characteristic are the figures for the *textile industry*. Here we find:

	1871	1880	1890
Number of factories	11,227	10,871	635
Number of workers	28,046	45,753	60,288
Production (in million rubles)	18.1	57.6	88.4
Workers per factory	2.5	4.2	95
Production per factory (in rubles)	1,612	5,303	139,298[35]

But within the textile industry the *cotton industry* shows the revolution in the most vivid way:

	1871	1880	1891
Number of factories	10,499	3,881	163
Number of workers	19,894	19,576	26,307
Production (in million rubles)	10.4	30.8	47.6
Workers per factory	1.9	5	162
Production per factory (in rubles)	994	7,950	291,736[36]

The surprising growth of the cotton industry can also be measured in the number of spindles. These amount to:

1836	7,300
1840	27,300
1850	61,300
1863	116,200
1870	289,500
1875	385,500
1879	449,600
1882	467,600
1888	ca. 600,000[37]

According to other sources, the number of spindles grew during a period of ten years (1877–86) from 216,640 to 505,622, i.e., 134 percent. In the same period, the number of spindles in the Russian cotton industry shows an increase of 32 percent (in particular, 45 percent in the Moscow district, 10 percent in the St. Petersburg district); that in the North American industry (1881–91), 30 percent; and in the English, 8 percent. The number of looms grew from 1877 to 1886: in the Russian cotton industry, 46 percent (in particular, 50 percent in the Moscow region, 25 percent in the St. Petersburg region); but in Poland, 139 percent.[38]

The more extensive use of steam power begins only in the 1870s, but since then it has grown quickly.

	1875	1890
Steam horsepower in industry as a whole	14,657	51,800
of that:		
in the textile industry	4,220	26,772
in mining	1,803	10,497[39]

In branches of industry to which excise taxes were not applied, steam horse-power nearly doubled again in the two-year period from 1890 to 1892, growing from 41,303 to 81,346.

In 25 years, the whole outward appearance of the country changed from the ground up. In the midst of this, the little town of Łódź quickly grew into a giant center of the textile industry, into a "Polish Manchester," with the typical appearance of a modern factory city—countless smoking factory chimneys packed tightly one next to the other, a population made up almost exclusively of factory personnel, and a municipal life regulated by factory whistles, revolving exclusively around industry and trade. Here we find a series of gigantic establishments, among which the Scheibler factory, with its yearly production, worth 15 million rubles, and its 7,000 workers, claims first place. In the southwestern corner of the country, on the Prussian border, a whole new industrial area sprang up, as though conjured up out of the ground, where factories suddenly emerged amid forests and rivers, where no cities had even been built, and all else was grouped around the factories from the outset. In the old capital, Warsaw, the collection point for all handicrafts, craft production did increase significantly. But at the same time it frequently fell under the domination of merchant capital. Small and medium-sized independent workshops dissolved themselves into cottage industry, and large warehouses for the products of craftsmen came to the fore as collection points for small production. The trade of the whole country was concentrated from now on in the Stock Exchange and in countless banking and commission firms. Praga, a suburb of Warsaw, became a center of the metal industry with large-scale metallurgical plants. And the gigantic Żyrardów linen factory in Warsaw,* with its 8,000 workers, became a small city unto itself.

---

* The Zyrardow factory was actually 45 kilometers outside of Warsaw.

4. The Main Regions of Polish Industry

We have given a general outline of the development of Polish industry, and it remains for us to illustrate what we have said in greater detail with individual histories of the most important branches of industry, providing a sketch of how factory production is grouped locally, along with its outward appearance.

The industry of the Kingdom of Poland—if one leaves out the insignificant factories scattered about on the east bank of the Vistula and along the Prussian border—is concentrated in three areas, each with its own distinctive physiognomy, each with a character and history different from the others.

The most significant among them is *the Łódź region*. It includes the city of Łódź with its adjoining area, and farther out, the cities of Pabianice, Zgierz, and Tomaszów, as well as some districts of Kalisz province. In 1885, the value of production from this region already amounted to 49 million rubles.[40] Today it is worth at least 120 million.[41] This is the true *textile industry region* of Poland. The history of its main center, *Łódź*, typifies to the greatest extent the history of all Polish industry. It would be difficult to imagine a less favorable place than Łódź for the founding of an industrial city. It is located in a plains area with hardly any forests or water.* Only about ten years ago there were boggy areas here and there on both sides of the main street, so that in some places the town was barely 200 paces wide. The tiny Łódka River is now completely polluted by factory waste, and all necessary water comes to the factories from artesian wells and ponds. In the year 1821 Łódź had only 112 houses with 800 inhabitants. But in 1823 colonization began, Silesian and Saxon cloth makers settled there, and by 1827 the inhabitants of Łódź numbered 2,840, with 322 manufacturing workers among them. In 1837 it had more than 10,000 inhabitants, and in 1840, 18,600, with production worth over 1.1 million rubles annually. As a result of the increased Russian tariff of 1831, however, and the crisis caused by that in cloth manufacturing, the city stopped growing, and the number of inhabitants even declined in 1850 to 15,600.[42] After the 1860s, however, as a result of the causes described above, which all together brought about the opening of the Russian market, there began for Łódź an era of rapid development, followed in the 1870s by growth that was truly tempestuous. For in Łódź we see:

In 1860	32,000 inhabitants	and	production worth 2,600,000 rubles
In 1878	100,000 inhabitants	and	production worth 26,000,000 rubles
In 1885	150,000 inhabitants	and	production worth 36,500,000 rubles
In 1895	315,000 inhabitants	and	production worth 90,000,000 rubles[43]

---

*   However, a small river does run through Łódź.

In the last 25 years in Łódź, there was also a conversion in the kind of cloth produced. Up until the 1870s, cotton goods were made for a limited market, primarily for the well-to-do classes. But when the Russian market was opened to Polish industry and gradually a new class of customers, the working population, began to play the leading role in demand, the textile industry in Łódź had to adjust itself to the new consumers. So the Łódź factories went over to the production of cheaper and simpler cotton goods, such as tricot and other types of cheap cloth, including crude cotton prints, but above all to the production of fustian.* Fabrication of this cloth was first transplanted from Saxony to the city of Pabianice in 1873.[44] Today it is the prevalent kind of cloth produced in the entire region, as the following figures show. Łódź manufactured:[45]

	1881	1886
Lancort[†‡]	29%	27%
Bjas[§]	44%	29%
Fustian	10%	35%
Mitkal[¶]	5.5%	5%
Miscellaneous	11.5%	4%
	100.0%	100%

The drastic change in tariff policy in 1877 also brought into being a new branch of the cotton industry in the Łódź region, namely the fabrication of a so-called mixed yarn of cotton and wool (vigogne).** Before that, this product was massively imported to Russia from Werdau and Crimmitschau,[††] but shortly after the introduction of the gold tariff its entry into Russia was closed. To circumvent this tariff wall, several factories were now transferred directly from Saxony to Łódź by German entrepreneurs, and by 1886 over 39,000 spindles were producing this mixed yarn there.[46]

In this way the current structuring of the large cotton industry in the Łódź region is seen to be a result of the opening of the Russian market and of Russian tariff policy in the 1870s.

---

*   The term "fustian" originally referred to a coarse cloth of cotton and linen, but now means thick cotton cloth with a short nap, such as velveteen or corduroy.

†   Lancort is a cheap kind of cotton cloth originally made in Lancourt, a textile town in Belgium.

‡   Bjas is a fabric woven out of cotton from Bukhara.

§   Bjas is a word that is Arabic in origin. In Russian, the term occurs as *byaz* and sometimes means "coarse calico" but also may refer to a less coarse type of cotton cloth, as used for underwear or sheets.

¶   Mitkal in Russian means calico.

**   The word "vigogne" is derived from a word derived from "vicuña," the very fine wool of the animal (native to the Andean region of South America) that it is named after.

††   Werdau and Crimmitschau were textile towns in the state of Saxony in Germany.

The same factors are no less prevalent in the wool industry of this region. The mighty leap in wool production from a value of four million rubles in 1870 to 22 million in 1880 shows what an effect the Russian market had on this branch of Polish industry. As for the spinning of wool, that industry has an especially great debt to Russia's tariff policy for its present-day level of development. The introduction of the gold tariff in 1877 had as a direct result the relocation of many foreign spinning mills to Łódź; the largest, with 22,000 spindles, was established in 1879 by Allart Rousseau Fils, and today it is still an affiliate of that firm in Roubaix,* from which it also obtains its semi-finished goods.[47] Since the 1870s, Poland has become Russia's source of supply for yarn, and its production of yarn surpasses that in Russia by more than 217 percent; in 1890 in Poland its value amounted to 18,749,000 rubles; in Russia, 5,909,000 rubles. In most recent times, Russian tariff policy has helped two other branches of the textile industry to flourish in Łódź—hosiery mills and knitting mills.[48]

A still more interesting illustration of the effect of Russian tariff policy on Polish industry is offered by the history of *the second region, that of Sosnowiec.*

This encompasses the southwestern part of Piotrków province, lying close to the Prussian border, including the cities of Częstochowa, Będzin, Zawiercie, Sielce, and Sosnowiec. While the Łódź region began its industrial development in the 1820s, the industry of the Sosnowiec region, as has been mentioned, represents a phenomenon of quite recent date.

Up until the 1860s there was nothing to be seen here for miles other than dense pine forests, but within 15 years this forest region was transformed into a busy industrial area whose textile industry was already preparing to give serious competition to that of old Łódź.

Two important circumstances greatly favored the rapid development of industry in the Sosnowiec region. First, the cheapness of fuel. The southern part of Piotrków province contains Poland's coal basin, and having this coal in its vicinity placed youthful Sosnowiec industry in an outstandingly advantageous position in comparison with not only Russia but also the other parts of Poland. The average price of one pood of coal in the regions under discussion is as follows for each location:

Sosnowiec region	2.40 to 9.7 kopecks
Warsaw region	11.22 to 13.0 kopecks
Łódź region	11.50 to 14.9 kopecks[49]

---

* Roubaix was a textile center in France. The firm referred to here, General Company of the Spinning Industry Allart Rousseau Joint Stock Company, operated from 1879 to 1949.

Second, the cheapness of labor. From the outset, this coal industry placed a contingent of "free" female labor and child labor at the disposal of the factories of the region, in the persons of the members of the miners' families. Here too the Sosnowiec region finds itself in a significantly more advantageous position than that of Łódź. Specifically, wages per month in rubles amount to:[50]

	Sosnowiec District			Lodz District		
	Men	Women	Children	Men	Women	Children
Finishing	13.50	10.75	8.50	26.00	18.0	9.75
Wool spinning	29.25	9.0	6.0	28.25	18.25	6.0
Mixed spinning	21.25	10.25	–	22.0	13.0	–
Cotton spinning	15.75	11.0	4.75	21.0	17.75	4.50
Average	20.0	10.25	6.25	24.30	16.6	6.7

The difference in the average [of wages] for the textile industry in Łódź by comparison with that in Sosnowiec comes to + *21.5 percent for men; for women, + 61.9 percent; for children, + 4.7 percent.*

The real reason for the rise of industry in the Sosnowiec region, however, was the new era in Russian tariff policy. Right after 1877 a whole series of Prussian and Saxon factories were simply moved from Germany to Poland. An impressive industry was soon concentrated in one zone three Russian miles wide along the border. Of the 27 most significant factories that could be counted here in the vicinity of the border in 1886, five had been founded before 1877, and 22 in the years 1877–86 (81.5 percent).[51] Production from the factories in Sosnowiec had a value of half a million rubles in 1879, but in 1886 the figure was 13 million, an increase of about 2,500 percent in seven years.[52]

The development of factory production in the Sosnowiec region went hand in hand with surprising growth in the *coal industry*. Supported and, in the 1830s (1833–42), even directly run by the Polish Bank, this industry developed quite slowly up until the 1860s and in 1860 produced a yield of 3.6 million poods[*] of coal. Since that time, three important factors came into play one after the other, providing a powerful impetus to the development of mining: first, the construction of railroads in the 1860s and 1870s; second, the development of factory industry; and third, the prohibitive tariff system. The upturn in coal production can be expressed in the following table, which shows the extraction of coal, in millions of poods:

---

[*]   A pood is eqiuvalent to 16.38 kilograms, or 36.11 pounds.

1860	3.6
1870	13.8
1880	78.4
1890	150.8[53]

Thus, during the twenty-year period 1870–90, coal production increased by 993 percent.

The rail industry is one of the most important buyers of coal. The Polish coal basin and the coal basin in southern Russia [i.e., the Donbas] supply Russia's railroads with fuel. The consumption of the latter amounted to:

	In millions of poods		
	1880	*1885*	*1890*
coal from southern Russia	22.2	34.3	39.8
coal from Poland	10.8	13.8	17.5[54]

But factory industry is a still more important buyer of coal. In 1890 the Łódź region alone used 30.6 million poods of coal, the Warsaw region 26 million, and the Sosnowiec region 40 million poods, in which the iron works played a great role.[55] In 1893, coal consumption in Warsaw came to 35.5 million poods, in Łódź in the same year 36.2 million.[56] And in 1896 coal consumption in Łódź was 41 million poods.[57]

A new epoch in the Polish coal industry begins with the extension of the protective tariff policy to this branch of production in 1884, which imposed a tariff of one-half to two kopecks in gold per pood on the importation of foreign coal, which until then had been duty-free. The immediate result was a great "coal crisis" in Russia, i.e., a great coal shortage as a result of the backward methods of the Russian coal mining industry and its inability to replace the reduced import of English coal with its own coal, proportionate to growing demand.[58]

The Polish coal industry reaped the benefits of this situation; it rapidly expanded its activity and in a few years conquered all the most important markets in Russia: Odessa, Moscow, St. Petersburg, even southern Russia. Although the "coal crisis" was overcome a long time ago, Polish coal has since then driven southern Russian coal from the battlefield, step-by-step, on the Moscow–Kursk railroad line, the Moscow–Brest line, the Kiev–Voronezh line, the Fastov line, the St. Petersburg-Warsaw line, and in part the southwestern lines. In 1894, 5,824,000 poods of coal were delivered to Odessa from Poland, as against 5,300,000 from the southern Russian coal basin [i.e., the Donbas].[59]

It still remains for us to take a look at the [Sosnowiec] region's iron industry. This had behind it a longer history, because even at the time of the Duchy of

Warsaw around 1814, 46 blast furnaces for iron ore could already be counted.[60] However, development proceeded so slowly that up to the 1880s Poland had brought production no higher than 2.5 million poods of pig iron, 1.4 million poods of iron, and 3.9 million poods of steel.[61]

A new page in the history of the Polish iron industry begins with the drastic change in Russia's tariff policy. After the Crimean War the brief period of tree trade lasted somewhat longer for iron than for other commodities, because even with the most stringent protective tariff policy the Russian iron industry could not have satisfied the enormous demand created by the building of the railroads. But here too, from 1881 on, a protective tariff has taken the place of free trade, and after a gradual rise the tariffs were set in 1887 at between 25 and 30 kopecks in gold per pood for pig iron, between 50 kopecks and 1.10 rubles for iron, and 70 kopecks for steel; and the tariff of 1891 brought a further increase in customs duties.[62] We see the direct effect of the upwardly revised tariff in the decline of foreign metal imports to Russia in the following table:[63]

	In millions of poods		
	Pig Iron	Iron	Steel
1881	14.3	6.5	1.4
1890	7.1	5.0	1.0

Metal production in Russia and Poland grew correspondingly. In Poland it was as follows:[64]

	In millions of poods	
	Pig Iron	Iron and Steel
1860	0.7	0.3
1870	1.3 (100%)	0.6 (100%)
1880	2.4	5.5
1890	7.4 (+488%)	7.5 (+1054%)

The *third industrial region, that of Warsaw,* does not have such a distinctive physiognomy as the two already described. Here we find a great diversity of industrial branches, but the most important are *machinery production* and *the sugar industry.* The history of the first is completely told in the following simple comparison. While until 1860 only nine factories producing agricultural machinery existed in Poland, in 1860–85 forty-two new ones were established.[65] Here, as in all earlier cases, we see the same upswing as a result of the radical change in market conditions in the 1860s and 1870s.

Finally, let us take a look at the history of the sugar industry. It had already made its start in the 1820s but until the 1850s was only a subsidiary branch of agriculture, of small dimensions and often run by the landowners themselves. The production of the 31 sugar factories in operation in 1848 did not exceed 177,500 poods, amounting to no more than 5,000 to 6,000 poods per factory. The year 1854 shows the greatest number of sugar factories, when there were 55.[66] After the abolition of serfdom and the revolution in agriculture, sugar production was separated from agriculture and became an independent branch of industry. The number of establishments gradually decreased through the simultaneous concentration of production. In 1870 we still find only 41 sugar factories, but with an annual output of 1.2 million poods. A true revolution, however, was caused in the sugar industry by the tax and customs policy of the Russian government. Namely, in 1867 the singular system of sugar taxation that had applied in Poland until then was annulled and replaced by that of the Russian Empire. The latter was based on taxation not of the finished product actually produced, but on the amount of finished product that was assumed to be produced in every factory, measured by the fixed standard productivity of the press apparatus. In this form the sugar tax naturally became the spur to the improvement of production; it soon moved all sugar factories to introduce the diffusion method, which pushed productivity above the norm taken as the basis for the tax, making the nominal tax of 80 kopecks per pood in reality only 35 or even 20.[67] In 1876, to encourage sugar exports, a rebate of the excise tax on exported sugar was ordered, which in view of the above circumstances acted as the equivalent of a colossal export subsidy. This was yet another spur to a feverish improvement of production methods and to expansion of production. In a few years the sugar industry in Russia and in Poland was transformed into a large-scale, mass-production industry. While Russia had exported only four poods of sugar in 1874, sugar exports in 1877 already amounted to 3,896,902 poods, and the government found itself obliged to "refund" roughly 3 million rubles—half the entire sugar excise tax levied in the Empire.[68] In 1881 the government took steps toward thorough reform of taxation of the sugar industry, but in the meantime the industry had reached very high levels of technological development. In Poland there were:

in 1869–70, 41 factories with an output of 1.2 million poods;
in 1890–91, 40 factories with an output of 4.8 million poods.

From this feverish expansion of production there followed a crisis in 1885, which brought in its wake the establishment of a sugar cartel embracing all of Russia and Poland and thus placed the distinctive stamp of large-scale industry on this branch of production. One peculiar effect of this cartel is that Russian sugar, whose production cost amounts to one and five-sixths pence per pound, is sold outside the Empire for one and two-thirds pence, but in Kiev for four pence per pound.[69] With such monopoly prices, no wonder the sugar factories are able to pay out enormous dividends.

The foregoing picture of industry in Poland would not be complete if it were not at least supplemented with some information about the role of Polish industry in the economy of the Russian Empire in general and, in particular, in comparison with other important industrial regions. The significance of Poland and the two capitals of Russian factory production—St. Petersburg and Moscow—in terms of industrial activity can be generally represented as follows:[70]

1890	Total Production (in millions of rubles)	Per Capita (in rubles)
Russian Empire	1,597	13.5
Moscow region	460	38
St. Petersburg region	242	40
Poland	210	23

As one may see, Polish industry takes *third place* in the Empire, in absolute as well as in relative terms, while Moscow claims first place in absolute terms and St. Petersburg has first place in relative terms. If we single out the two most important branches of production, textiles and mining, we obtain the following comparison:

Of the total production of the Empire (without Finland), which amounted to 82.0 million poods of pig iron, 25.7 million of iron, 34.5 million of steel, and 550 million of coal, the share of the three main regions was as follows (referring only to private businesses):[71]

	Pig Iron	Iron	Steel	Coal
Urals region	36%	56%	7.7%	2.9%
Donets region	40%	6%	42.0%	54.0%
Poland	14%	14%	23.0%	40.0%

Specifically, the most important regions in Russia for metal and coal production are the Donets Basin (in southern Russia) and the Urals region, and Poland is in competition with primarily the former but in part also with the latter for the Russian market. As we see, Poland stands in *second place* in the Empire in mining, right behind the Donbas; only in the production of pig iron does it take third place. Although Poland has only 7.3 percent of the Empire's total population, it has a quarter of the Russian Empire's steel production and two-fifths of its coal production.

Similarly, in the Empire's textile industry Poland plays a very significant role quite out of proportion to the size of its population. The share of the total number of spindles and looms in the Empire's cotton industry, which in 1886 amounted to 3,913,000 and 84,500 respectively, was as follows for the three main regions:[72]

	Spindles	Looms
Moscow region	55%	71.6%
St. Petersburg region	29%	12.8%
Poland	13%	12.5%

Here again Poland stands in *third place*. In the other branches it has a much greater significance, as is seen from the following: Of the total textile industry in the Empire, whose value of production amounted to 580.9 million rubles in 1892, 19.5 percent fell to Poland; its share in individual branches, however, amounted in cotton spinning to 15.6 percent, in cotton weaving to 16 percent, in linen making to 42 percent, in wool weaving and cloth making to 29.6 percent, in wool spinning to 77 percent, and in knitting to 78 percent.[73]

If Poland on the whole is surpassed by the industries of central Russia and the St. Petersburg region, nevertheless in certain important branches of the economy it is ahead of all other parts of the Empire. In particular, Poland's great significance in these branches indicates a far-reaching division of labor between Polish and Russian industry.

5. Poland's Industrial Market

From the foregoing it is clear that Russian markets have been the actual driving forces behind the development of today's large-scale industry in Poland. It would therefore be interesting to hear more precise statements about the extent of the market for Polish commodities in Russia, but this can be determined only with difficulty. As in the statistics of all nations, there exists in those of Russia a great lack of data on internal trade. Here an overview can be obtained only indirectly and approximately. The official investigation carried out in 1886 showed that of the 141 largest factories, which together represent a third of all production,

37 factories with output worth 7,061,984 rubles produce exclusively for Poland,
27 factories with output worth 7,480,645 rubles produce exclusively for Russia,
11 factories with output worth 13,224,589 rubles produce mainly for Poland,

34 factories with output worth 22,824,013 rubles produce mainly for Russia,
32 factories with output worth 19,311,695 rubles produce half for Poland and half
for Russia.[74]

If we assume that the term "mainly" is equivalent to two-thirds, then Polish industry's market can be represented as follows: The 141 factories produce commodities

for Poland to the value of 33,142,228 rubles, equaling 47%;
for Russia to the value of 36,760,698 rubles, equaling 52%.

The general conclusion reached by the investigative commission was that Polish factories sell 50 to 55 percent of their products in Russia.

Some partial data also confirm the above-mentioned conclusion, such as the following figures (in poods) showing where the textile industry of Łódź marketed its goods.[75]

	1884 (crisis)		1885		1886	
	Poland	*Russia*	*Poland*	*Russia*	*Poland*	*Russia*
Cotton and woolen goods	372,390	1,004,286	321,344	1,115,460	443,565	1,507,259
Yarn	45,290	4,524	63,051	99,951	56,583	90,136
Total	417,680	1,008,810	384,395	1,215,411	500,148	1,597,395

Thus the center of the textile industry was already selling three-fourths of its products in Russia by the middle of the 1880s. In the ten years since the above calculations were made, however, the relationship may have shifted to a much greater degree in favor of sales in Russia, since production has grown by roughly half again since then, while it is self-evident that the domestic market could only increase by a small proportion. On the other hand, we have direct evidence that during these ten years the Polish market opened up new areas in Russia, which we will discuss in more detail below. Thus one may assume that the relationship today, at a minimum, is that two-thirds of the products of Polish industry are absorbed by Russia. In fact, this market has spread to include all those branches of industry that constitute the central core of large-scale capitalist production in any country: the textile, metal, and coal industries. Naturally a whole series of smaller industrial branches, such as those producing candy and other confections, or trinkets and gewgaws, etc., are also sending their products to Russia in ever growing quantities.

The advance of the Polish market in Russia offers an interesting picture from a geographical standpoint. As was said, this trade began on a larger scale only in the 1870s. For a long time, however, it was restricted to only the western and southern provinces of the Russian Empire—to Lithuania and Ukraine, thus actually to the old parts of what was formerly Poland. But in the beginning of the 1880s, Poland conquered a new market in the south of Russia, the area called New Russia.[76]* In the middle of the 1880s, Polish trade took another step forward. In 1883 the free transit to Transcaucasia via Batum, agreed to at the Congress of Berlin, was abolished and a tariff border erected.† The Western European countries, above all England, thereby lost a significant market for their products, a market that now passed into the hands of Russian and Polish industrialists. In the year 1885 Polish manufactured goods appeared for the first time in the Caucasus; since then the import of these goods to the three centers of Caucasian trade has grown as follows:[77]

In poods	Batum	Tiflis	Baku
1885–86	39,000	55,000	68,000
1887–88	95,100	200,000	258,000

At the end of the 1880s Polish trade pushed eastward—to the Volga region. Polish deliveries to the center of Volga trade, Tsaritsyn, were: 1887: 55,640 poods; 1888: 73,729 poods; 1889: 106,403 poods.[78]

At the same time Poland began to take part in trade between Europe and Asia; its products appeared at the colossal fairs in *Nizhny Novgorod*, where large Polish warehouses were built beginning in 1889,[79] and also in *Irbit*. Finally, at the end of the 1880s and the beginning of the 1890s, Polish trade stepped onto Asian ground. First, trade relations were entered into with Siberia: in 1888 with *Tomsk* in western Siberia,[80] in 1892 with *Nerchinsk* in southeastern Siberia,[81] and in 1894 Polish commodities appeared in *Omsk* [in central Siberia].[82] During the same time Polish trade in Asia also developed in two other directions, on the one hand to China, on the other to Persia and Asia Minor.

In the course of twenty years, 1870–90, Polish trade found access, step-by-step, to every corner of European Russia. This rapid expansion of the market, as we have seen, turned Polish factory production into large-scale industry in

---

* The term "new Russia" was used by the tsarist government from the mid-1700s onward to refer to Ukraine, Crimea, Bessarabia and parts of southern Russia that it had conquered from the Crimean Khanate, the Ottoman Empire, and other states. The term has been rejected as a description of their homeland by Ukrainians.

† The Congress of Berlin, in which all the major powers of Europe took part, along with the Ottoman Empire, took place June 13–July 13, 1878, and brought an end to the Russo-Turkish war of 1877–78. The decisions of the congress mainly revolved around the partial dismemberment of the Ottoman Empire. Russia obtained several areas in Asia, and Austria-Hungary was given the right to occupy Bosnia-Herzegovina. In addition, several Balkan territories that had previously been under the Turkish rule attained formal independence.

twenty years. Since then, however, it has been preparing itself for a new, important undertaking: *the conquest of Asian markets.* Polish trade has already taken several important steps in this direction. This, however, is doubtless only the beginning of a beginning, and the tremendous prospects that are opening to industry thanks to the Trans-Siberian Railroad* and the major successes of Russian policy in Asia mean a new revolution for Polish industry (among other things), a revolution perhaps even more thoroughgoing than that which it experienced in the 1870s. With great earnestness Polish entrepreneurs are getting ready for this future and steadily directing their attention toward Asia. A museum of products from the Orient has been built in Warsaw, which has the special task of familiarizing Polish producers with the world of Asian commodities and with the tastes, and the needs and requirements, of Asians. The prospectus of the new commercial institution states:

> Sugar and distillery products, machinery and cast-iron pipe, glass, faience, and porcelain, shoes, neckties, and gloves, and fabrics, both cotton and linen, which are made in our country, just a short time ago traveled no farther than to a few neighboring provinces; today they go across the Don and Ural rivers, to the Caucasus, over the Caspian Sea, to China, Persia, and Asia Minor. But in order to carry the process along in this direction as far as possible, our tastes cannot be imposed on those for whom the goods are intended; rather we must pay attention to their tastes, and we must produce what will sell in those markets, but the tastes there are infinitely different from our own ... Out there the type of cloth, the form, the design, the color preferences—all are different from ours ... What we have been producing so far has been intended primarily for the civilized, established layers of the population in those countries. The masses have been beyond the target range of our industry. But if we want to place our industry on a firm foundation and even expand it, we must produce goods that correspond to the habits and tastes of the masses, and therefore we must learn what the needs of those masses are.[83]

Here, then, in a few brief strokes [let us summarize] the history of industry in Russian Poland. Having arisen out of the efforts of the Kingdom of Poland government, it immediately, at the very first moment, made an attempt to take hold of the markets in Russia. When its access to those was impeded, it had to rely more on the domestic sphere of consumption, and so it developed slowly, little by little. The social crisis that Russia went through in the 1860s tore Poland out of its economic immobility and drew it into the whirlpool of capitalist development. With the renewed opening, this time on a definitive basis, of the Russian market regions, Polish industry gained access to a rich and fertile

---

* The Trans-Siberian railroad was inaugurated in 1890. Although it was heralded at the time for opening up eastern Asia to European commerce, it initially had the disadvantage of having only one track, enabling traffic to move in only one direction at a time.

breeding ground, and quickly went through the process of conversion to large-scale industry. Russia's tariff policy gave monopoly advantages to the Russian and Polish capitalists in this enormous sales territory, giving rise to a feverish accumulation of capital. Factory industry now became the dominant factor in the entire life of Polish society, so that a complete and drastic change took place in Polish life during the last twenty-five years.

As we mentioned earlier, up until the 1860s Poland preserved the characteristics of an agricultural country, with the social estate of the landowning nobility dominant in all spheres of public life. The peasant reform* for the most part shattered this preeminence of the landowning nobility.[84] The indebtedness of the landowning nobles was greatly increased by the need to have money capital at their disposal for running their estates [as commercial businesses]. The general crisis of European agriculture that was ushered in, in the 1880s, and the [accompanying] fall of grain prices finished them off.

In this way the whole broad stratum of nobles owning medium-sized land holdings was and is heading toward its ruin more and more every day. Fifteen percent of the estates of the nobility have already passed from those owners into German and Jewish hands, and another 15 percent has been broken up into parcels and sold to peasants. The remaining landed property is burdened with mortgage debt, which amounts on the average to 80 percent of its value, but in two-fifths of the cases the debt amounts to between 100 and 250 percent of the property's value.[85] At the same time, however, industry has grown ever stronger, and soon it will outpace agriculture in all respects. As early as 1880 the value of industrial production was equal to that of grain production.[86] Today it is more than double the value of grain production; the former amounts to at least 23 rubles per capita, the latter only 11 rubles.[87] But even this quantitatively subordinate agriculture has become totally dependent on industry. Whereas Poland was formerly a "breadbasket of Europe," a country that mainly produced grain for the world market, today it barely meets its own needs. Industry has created an internal market that devours the entire output of agriculture. If today Poland still exports substantial quantities of wheat, this happens only because, to make up for that, it imports even larger quantities of inferior types of grain from Russia. Second, agriculture today, in view of the constantly falling price of grain, is forced to emancipate itself more and more from pure wheat production and switch over to the cultivation of so-called industrial crops and to the raising of livestock.[88] It would be superfluous to stress the fact that handicrafts, too, where it has not been destroyed directly by the competition of factories, owes its continued existence to factory industry—in part by working for it directly, in part by profiting from the overall accumulation of capital and the

---

* The tsarist government was forced, as of March 2, 1864, to abolish serfdom in Poland and thereby to guarantee to the Polish peasantry the rights they had won during the fighting and social upheavals of 1863–64.

increased internal consumption that industry has brought with it. Industry has now become the trunk from which all other branches of the country's material existence draw their vital juices. Or to state it more correctly, it is the driving force that revolutionizes all aspects of material existence and subordinates them to itself: agriculture, handicraft, trade, and transport. Poland, a country whose social conditions were previously so unique, has now become a typical capitalist country. The mechanical loom and the steam engine have robbed it of its unconventional physiognomy and placed a levelling international stamp upon it. As early as 1884 Poland was afflicted with an illness specific to capitalism, its first big economic crisis. Already, here and there in the awakening labor movement, the Hippocratic features in Polish capitalism* are coming to light.

PART II. RUSSIA'S ECONOMIC POLICY IN POLAND

The picture we have given in the foregoing of the historical development and present-day condition of industry in Poland is quite different from that presented to us by the history of urban craft production in medieval Poland. Despite the identical nature of their origins—artificial transplantation from Germany carried out by the higher authorities—manufacture in Poland not only did not perish, as urban handicraft did earlier, but developed into large-scale industry, and despite its foreign, German beginnings, it not only sank deep roots in the national life of Poland but also became the dominant factor, actually setting the tone in Polish life.

However, in recent times certain phenomena have appeared that have awakened fears in various quarters about the longer-term future of Polish industry. It is clearly evident that the market in Russia, and in conjunction with it the Asian market that has now been opened, have been the lifeblood of Polish industry. In all these areas, however, it goes without saying that Polish commodities are in competition with Russian ones. A conflict of interest between the Russian and Polish bourgeoisies over these markets appears at first glance to be the natural consequence, a conflict that is bound to become more severe, the more Polish industry grows. On the other hand, it seems to be just as natural that the Russian capitalist class would have the Russian government on its side against the Polish competition, and that the government might use its power to discriminate against Polish industry, and might perhaps reestablish some sort of tariff barrier between Poland and Russia as the simplest and most radical means of doing this. Recently, voices calling for such measures have frequently made themselves heard, and the opinion has been expressed here and there that for Polish industry, after the period of prosperity which it has enjoyed up to now, a new period may begin—one of persecution and punitive measures against Polish industry

---

*   That is, curative elements that can transform it.

by the Russian government—and that as a result, sooner or later, Polish industry is bound to go under.[89]*

Before we conclude our description of Polish industry, then, we still need to go into the question of what the conflict of interest between Polish and Russian factory production is in reality, of how Polish industry is equipping itself for competitive battle with Russian industry, and what the position of the Russian government is with regard to this struggle. In this way, we will be in a position to amplify our account of the history of industry in Poland with a discussion of the prospects for its future.

1. History of the Fight Between Moscow and Łódź

It is, first of all, quite untrue that the competition and conflict between Russia's central industrial region and Polish industry, over which so much of an uproar has been made in the last few years, is a new phenomenon dating only from the 1880s, as is generally assumed. Quite the contrary: this battle is as old as Polish industry itself. As early as the 1820s the government was presented with petitions that, from the Russian side, called for an increase in the Russian-Polish tariffs, and from the Polish side, for the total abolition of the tariff barrier between Poland and Russia. In fact, ever since that time the rivalry has gone on unceasingly. Except for the year 1826, there were 1,831 petitions sent by the Russian entrepreneurs to St. Petersburg[90]—always with complaints about Polish industry and with demands that "the industry of the Fatherland" be supported in its fight against its Polish counterpart. As one may see from [Part One's review of] the history of Polish industry, in the end the government not only did not fulfill the requests of the Russian entrepreneurs, but, on the contrary, abolished the tariff barrier between Poland and Russia in 1851 and so let the contest between the opponent industries take its own course. The battle flared up again intensely in the middle of the 1880s, first because Polish industry at that time, as we have mentioned, took possession of a whole series of new market areas in Russia, in the south as well as the east, and second because, just at that time, the whole textile industry of the Sosnowiec region was seemingly conjured up out of the ground along the Prussian border. But on the other hand, the price of goods, forced up suddenly and severely by the change in tariff policies at the end of the 1870s, had fallen somewhat toward the middle of the 1880s. The Moscow entrepreneurs, upset by this, began "to search for the guilty party."[91] And they found

---

*   In the text of the following endnote by Luxemburg the quotations were in English, and have been reproduced here in the Victorian English in which they were written. As Luxemburg explains at the end of her footnote, she took these quotations, or "excerpts," from the *Blue Book* of the *Royal Commission on Labor, Foreign Reports* (Vol. X, on Russia, 1894). In turn, the *Blue Book* apparently quoted them from Foreign Office *Diplomatic and Consular Reports: On the Trade of Warsaw* of 1888.

it—the Polish competition. Here the battle was led chiefly by the Moscow cotton manufacturers, because of the conquests that Polish cotton goods were making in the Russian markets.

A certain [Sergei Fedorovich] *Sharapov* led the first attack on behalf of the Moscow entrepreneurs in a public speech,* which he gave in 1885, in Moscow and in Ivanovo-Voznesensk,† a speech that later appeared in print. From the start, Sharapov took the loftiest of tones and puffed up the whole campaign [supposedly] waged by Moscow's calico against the accursed fustian from Łódź, portraying it as a historic and heroic combat by the Slavic race against the Germanic. He demonstrated that Polish industry in every way enjoyed more favorable conditions than Russian industry; for example, according to Sharapov, cheaper German credit was at Poland's disposal. It cost only 3.5 to 4 percent, while the entrepreneurs in central Russia had to pay 7 to 8 percent. Second, cheaper raw materials were available to Poland, which also had to pay far lower transportation costs than the Moscow region lying far to the east. Third, Poland enjoyed more favorable rates on the railroads, which it obtained as a result of a private agreement among the railroad companies. Fourth and last, it had to pay significantly lower taxes: in central Russia taxes amounted to 3,600 rubles per 1 million rubles of production; in Łódź, however, the figure was only 1,400 rubles; and in smaller Polish cities, only 109 rubles.[92]

Sharapov called on the government to fight against the "German" industry of Poland and to rescue the Russian *and Polish* elements oppressed by it (!).

The next year, 1886, the Moscow entrepreneurs sent a deputation to St. Petersburg with the "most humble and obedient" request to once again establish a tariff barrier between Poland and Russia.[93]

The government, having been approached in this way, formed a commission in the same year, 1886, consisting of Professors [I.I.] Ianzhul, Ilyin, and [Nikolai Petrovich] Langovoi,‡ which had the task of investigating the conditions of production of the Polish industrial districts and of checking into the claims of the Moscow manufacturers and verifying whether they were correct.[94] The results of this investigation, carried out more seriously and more thoroughly than any other, were as follows:

On the side of Polish industry we see cheaper fuel, smaller fixed capital, lower taxes, a better labor force, and more advantageous spatial concentration of firms in a few locations. On the side of Russian industry, on the other hand, cheaper labor power, smaller transportation costs to the markets (Caucasus, Volga region, Asia), smaller outlays on the workforce (hospitals, schools, etc.),

---

* The reference is to Sergei Fedorovich Sharapov, a conservative Russian politician who argued against the introduction of foreign capital into Russia on the grounds that it undermined domestic industry. He advocated a strong, autarkic national state.

† Ivanovo-Voznesensk was a center of the Russian textile industry.

‡ We have been unable to locate the identity of "Ilyin."

profits from the factory stores, finally a surplus of water to run the cotton weaving and spinning mills.[95] In its conclusions, the commission came out against the introduction of a tariff barrier between Poland and Russia, and likewise against a differential tariff on raw cotton directed against Poland, first because the government "would hardly deem it possible to treat Poland as a foreign country in trade and industrial relations," and second because a higher differential tariff "would appear to the inhabitants of Poland, Russian subjects, as an injustice against them and would doubtless give rise to great dissatisfaction." The commission considered the only just measure to be an increase in the prevailing taxes on Polish industry sufficient to equalize them with Russian taxes.[96]

In 1887 the Moscow entrepreneurs once again presented a petition to the minister of finance at the annual fair in Nizhny Novgorod, in which they requested an increase in the duties on cotton and the introduction of a higher differential tariff at the Polish border.[97] Now the Łódź manufacturers also entered the fray. They answered the above-mentioned document with a counterpetition, in which they sought to prove that they suffered significantly less advantageous conditions of production than their Moscow competitors, that the cotton mills of central Russia yielded profits as high as 8.4 percent, while those in Poland yielded only 7.5 percent.[98] [They also argued] that transport of raw cotton from Liverpool to Moscow cost 35.77 kopecks per pood, but from Liverpool to Łódź, 37.10 kopecks per pood, and that therefore a further worsening of their situation by the introduction of a differential tariff on cotton would make cotton production extremely difficult for them.[99]

In 1888 once again a commission was appointed to investigate the disputed matter, this time under the chairmanship of [an official named] Ber.* Its conclusions this time were very much to Poland's disadvantage, and the commission called for a series of measures to protect the Moscow industrial district against better-situated Polish industry.[100]

On the other hand, also in 1888, the Moscow industrialists again submitted a petition to the minister of finance, in which they complained about how hard-pressed they were by their situation and called on the government to take measures against the "parasitical" industry of Poland.[101]

In 1889 the Łódź industrialists put out a public-relations pamphlet entitled *The Conflict between Moscow and Łódź*, in which they attempted to show through the mouth of "an impartial, nonpartisan observer" that Łódź had to pay more for raw cotton than Moscow did; that the advantage of cheaper fuel, which Łódź had over Moscow, amounted merely to the negligible figure of 0.2 kopecks per arshin of material; that the causes of the more expensive credit in Moscow lay at Moscow's own feet, the result of poor organization; that Łódź suffered

---

* We have been unable to locate the identity of "Ber."

from a shortage of water, paid more for labor, and, finally, made smaller profits than central Russian industry.[102]

In 1890 the system of railroad rates was taken over by the government for [proper] organization. This provided an occasion for forming a new commission and delegating it to investigate, for the nth time, what the competitive conditions of the Polish and central Russian industrial districts actually were, and how, relative to this, the railroad rates on the lines of importance to the competitors should be calculated. This commission, which served under the chairmanship of Lazarev,* a representative of the government's department of railroads, again came to no conclusion. The representatives of the Łódź and Moscow industrialists gave their familiar arguments and counterarguments as best they could. Two arguments from the Polish side were the only new additions, namely, their reference to the use of cheap naphtha residue[†] as fuel in the Moscow industrial district, and the claim that the tax burden was greater in Poland than in central Russia, specifically 5.82 rubles per capita in the Moscow region, but 6.64 rubles in Poland.[103]

The next year, in 1891, once more a well-known economist, this time a man named [V.D.] Belov, was appointed to investigate the conditions of production in Poland and central Russia. This man again came to the conclusion that all the disadvantages were to be found on the Łódź side, while all the advantages were on Moscow's, in particular: cheaper labor power, longer labor time (Moscow 3,429 hours a year, Poland 3,212), cheaper fuel (naphtha residue costs 6 pence per hundredweight, whereas coal for the same amount of heat is significantly more, 10.25 pence per hundredweight), cheaper raw cotton, and, finally, more favorable railroad rates. The same Sharapov who had sounded the first alarm against Łódź in 1885 now asserted, in light of the Belov investigation, that the situation had changed completely since 1885 and that Łódź now absolutely did not deserve to be penalized in any way.[104]

It was necessary [for us] to deal with the various stages of the dispute between Łódź and Moscow as thoroughly as we have in order to demonstrate how difficult it is to arrive at an impartial opinion on this matter, and how cautious one must usually be about accepting any assertions made on this subject, because there is not a single argument which has not been used by both parties, with directly contradictory figures as proof. And it is only too easy to become an unconscious megaphone amplifying the chorus of one or another of these two entrepreneurial groups.

---

*   A possible reference to Semyon Semyonovich Abamelik-Lazareva, a leading Russian mining magnate, industrialist and scholar, who later made important contributions to archeology.

†   Naphtha is a by-product created by the processing of crude oil; it is similar to gasoline. In the period in which Luxemburg was writing, naphtha was often used to heat steam engines (along with kerosene). Naphtha residue is what remains after naphtha has been distilled for obtaining various lighting and heating oils. At the time she was writing, most naphtha residue was produced in Baku, in modern-day Azerbaijan.

After having become acquainted in brief outline with the history of the Moscow-Łódź dispute and the central issues around which it revolves, we want to make our own comparison of the competitive conditions of the two industrial regions in all their main aspects, in order to arrive at an objective assessment of these issues on the basis of quantitative evidence.

2. Conditions of Industrial Production in Poland and Russia

1. *Fuel*. One of the conditions of production that is by far the most important for any factory industry is fuel. For Polish industry this factor is seen by many researchers as the decisive one in its development, and is regarded as the most important in its competitive struggle with Russian industry. So says the report of the above-mentioned commission of 1886: "Fuel is undoubtedly the factor of production that constitutes the most important difference in conditions of production between the *gubernias* [provinces] of central Russia and the Kingdom of Poland."[105] Polish industry possesses large and rich coal-mining districts, while the center of Russian industry, the Moscow region, lies far away from the coal mines of the Donets Basin [Donbas] and is in the main forced to rely on more expensive wood or peat. "The price of wood in Moscow province goes higher every day, and according to the calculations of the engineer Belikov, the cost on the average is between 11.6 and 13.1 kopecks per pood of wood. Peat, whose use in the factories is growing rapidly and which is already being used in Moscow to the extent of 100,000 cords annually, comes to 12 and even 16 kopecks per pood, mainly due to high transportation costs, and its use is in any case only to a factory's advantage if it is in the close vicinity of the peat bog." In Moscow, Russian coal costs 13.3 kopecks [per pood] (from Tula), 17.5 (from Ryazan), and 25 (from the Donbas). English coal also costs 25 kopecks per pood. "How much more relatively expensive the most-used fuels, wood and peat, are—given at the same time the impossibility of replacing them by still more expensive coal—and how vital this question is for Russian industry, can be judged by the following: Average heat production, according to the same engineer Belikov, is 2,430 degrees (F.C.) to 2,700 degrees for wood; for Moscow peat it is 1,920 to 2,800 degrees; the same heat production for coal is 3,280 degrees for that from Tula, but for coal from the Donbas and for English coal it goes far above 5,000 degrees."[106]

Polish industry finds itself in quite a different situation with regard to fuel. The average price of coal in the main centers of industry—Sosnowiec, Łódź, and Warsaw—are, respectively, 2.4–4.95 kopecks, 11.5 kopecks, and 13 kopecks per pood, thus costing less than wood in Moscow, while heat production is of course significantly greater.[107]

Calculated per unit of product, outlays for fuel amount to:[108]

Per pood of cotton yarn		
In Poland	In Moscow	In St. Petersburg
38 kopecks	90 kopecks	53 kopecks

These figures suffice to show the great advantage that Polish industry has in regard to fuel over its Russian competition.

Professor Schulze-Gävernitz nevertheless believes it possible to assert that "natural advantages are of no benefit to Polish industry. Certainly cheaper fuel is pointed to, but according to [D.I.] Mendeleyev's data, compared with the above-mentioned report, this advantage declines to the extent that Moscow goes over to naphtha fuel (for one pood of bituminous coal in Łódź, 12–13 kopecks; for the same heat value in naphtha, 12.75 kopecks)."[109]

With regard to that point, the following should be noted. First, a pood of bituminous coal does not cost 12–13 kopecks in Łódź, as Professor Schulze-Gävernitz says, but 8.75–13.5 (or 8.3–14.7), and a pood of naphtha coal,* i.e., a quantity of naphtha corresponding calorifically to a pood of coal, costs not 12.75 kopecks, but 13–20 kopecks, thus significantly more than coal in Poland.[110] Second, for the present, naphtha accounts for only 20.5 percent of fuel in the Moscow region in general—in particular, it accounts for 29.4 percent in the cotton industry in Moscow and Vladimir provinces[111]—and so naphtha does not affect the conditions of production among the overwhelming majority of the factories in this region.

But third, as far as the future of this fuel method goes, Professor Mendeleyev[†] says in his essay dedicated to the naphtha industry: "The use of this (naphtha residue) as a fuel today, where there is no possibility of utilizing the bulk of the naphtha obtained (as a result of the lack of a pipeline to carry naphtha from Baku to Batum), is a most natural phenomenon, although a unique and temporary one."[112] "For normal fuel needs, particularly for fueling steam engines, where any sort of fuel is suitable, *the use of a fuel as costly as naphtha residue can find wide circulation only temporarily, in those transitional moments of industrial activity in the nation where industry has not had time to 'make its bed' properly*; but today that means, in all countries presumably, that the normal condition is—the use of coal."[113] And still further. "The use today of 130 million poods of naphtha residue in Russia must be regarded as a temporary phenomenon,

---

* Naphtha coal is produced by the distillation of coal tar. Naphtha can also be obtained from shale and crude oil.

† In addition to being a pathbreaking chemist and inventor who first formulated the periodic table of the elements, Mendeleyev helped found the first oil refinery in Russia and wrote extensively on the composition of crude oil. For a study of this dimension of his work, see John Moore, Conrad Staniski, and Peter Jurs, *Chemistry: The Molecular Science*, Vol. I (Belmont, CA: Brooks/Cole, 2008).

which depends, on the one hand, on the lack of demand for naphtha on the world market, and, on the other, on the lack of productivity in the extraction of coal and of its distribution throughout Russia, particularly in the center and the southeast." "The construction of railroad lines from the Donets coal basin to the Volga, and various measures directed toward utilization of naphtha supplies in Baku and toward cheap export of coal from the Donbas, form the current tasks of Russia's industrial development, *and must [necessarily] put an end to today's widespread, irrational use of naphtha residue from Baku for steam boilers.*"[114]

The above quotations, which express the opinion of the best judges on this question, suffice in our opinion to demonstrate that in the comparative valuation of fuels in Poland and in the Moscow region, naphtha fuel in the latter must be disregarded, as a temporary phenomenon. What is now called "naphtha residue" is not some actual by-product of [petroleum] production, but a product of naphtha extraction itself,* which is very insufficiently utilized only as a result of the lack of a market, and to a great extent it is used for fuel rather than for lighting: thus among exports from Baku, in 1891, for example, for every pood of naphtha produced, there corresponds 1.40 poods of naphtha residue, and in 1894 as much as 2.73 poods. Thus the so-called residue actually forms the main product, and naphtha on the other hand the by-product. The abnormality of this phenomenon appears in the quality of the product itself. The "residue" so obtained explodes at 50 degrees, 40 degrees, and even 30 degrees centigrade, while the normal explosion temperature for real naphtha residue cannot be lower than 140–120 degrees. This cheap fuel also has costly results: in the course of the years 1893 and 1894, 20 vessels of the Astrakhan Steamship Company that were fueled with this "residue" were destroyed by outbreaks of fire.[115] Another disadvantage of this type of naphtha fuel is the fact that this residue, because of its chemical composition, is in fact used in much greater quantities to produce a specific effective heat than would be the case with real naphtha residue. The greater consumption of this residue sometimes amounts to 40 percent.[116†] This was confirmed as an established fact by the administration of the St. Petersburg-Moscow railroad line. This makes the most important advantage of naphtha fuel—its cheapness—for the most part completely illusory. Here and there some are already beginning to renounce the use of naphtha residue, as with the Russian Southeastern Railroad, which recently returned to coal. Certainly the consumption of naphtha residue in the central industrial region will in the next few years increase before it will decrease, particularly as a result of overproduction and lower prices. With the Russian government's current vigor in promoting

---

* This is because naphtha residue is what remains after naphtha has been distilled for obtaining various lighting and heating oils.

† Luxemburg's footnote to this sentence was added to her dissertation after it had been approved in May 1897 by Zurich University and while it was being prepared for publication by the Duncker & Humblot book company.

capitalism and pushing aside all obstacles in its way, however, the use of naphtha will soon be reduced to its rational purpose, and factories will be reduced to using wood and coal. In the end, however, Poland's advantage remains in full force, for "in general fuel is half as expensive in Poland as in Moscow."[117]

2. *Labor power.* This aspect of industrial activity is usually cited as proof that Poland has less favorable conditions than Russia because its labor is more expensive than the latter's.[118] Wages are in fact significantly higher in Poland than in Russia, specifically:[119]

	Cotton Spinning	Cotton Weaving	Finishing	Wool Spinning
For men	18.75%	36%	19%	59%
For women	42%	37%	107%	91%
For children	14%	79%	85%	27%
	Wool Weaving	Cloth Making	Half-wool Weaving	Average
For men	31%	13%	60%	32.2%
For women	105%	33%	122%	73.9%
For children	112%	40%	150%	60.0%

Labor time, on the other hand, is significantly longer in Russia than in Poland. "While the 13- to 14-hour-long workday is very widespread in Moscow factories, in Poland it is to be found only in nine factories, and in three of these cases only in separate sections of a factory. While labor time lasting more than 14 hours is absolutely not a rarity in Moscow factories and its outer limit is 16 hours, 14-hour labor time must be described as the outer limit in Poland, and in fact this was found only in two textile factories."[120] In general, 10 to 12 hours were worked in 75 percent of the Polish factories, and so 11 hours can be taken as the average labor time for Poland. In Moscow, the average labor time is more than 12 hours. In Poland, night labor is a rare exception; in Moscow it is widespread. And despite the fact that in Poland the number of workdays in the year is 292, while in Moscow it is only 286, for Poland there are nevertheless only 3,212 labor-hours per year, while the number in Moscow (figured on the basis of only 12 hours a day) is 3,430 hours, thus 218 hours more.[121]

These two factors, lower wages and longer labor time, are usually regarded as important advantages for Moscow industry in its competitive struggle with Polish manufacturing. Yet we believe that this opinion can be shown to be premature and superficial.

First, in comparing wages, usually the wages of male workers in Russia are juxtaposed to those of male workers in Poland, while likewise the wages of female workers in Russia are compared to those of female workers in Poland. This is how the 1886 commission for the investigation of Polish industry, among others, proceeded. This is wrong, as factory inspector Svyatlovsky perceived, insofar as, in Poland, female and child labor is far more extensive than in Russia, so that frequently a female worker in Poland stands counterposed to a male worker in Russia; therefore, the wages of male Russian workers must frequently be compared, not with those of *male* Polish workers, but with those of female Polish workers.[122] In fact, the number of women employed in the Polish textile industry (the industry of most importance with regard to competition) amounts to more than 50 percent of all factory personnel, while in the Moscow region female labor amounts to only 37 percent in the cotton industry and only 28 percent in the wool industry.[123]

If the wages of male workers in Russia are compared with those of female workers in Poland, the picture shifts in many ways to the disadvantage of the Moscow region, or in any case there is an equalization of conditions. The average monthly wages in the textile industry are (in rubles):[124]

	in Poland	in Russia
For men	20.1	15.2
For women	15.3	8.8
For children	8.8	5.5

To obtain true and exact data on relative wage levels in Russia and Poland, it is necessary to consider the composition of the labor force in terms of age and sex in both countries as well as nominal wages. The result thus obtained will in many ways be significantly different from the foregoing. This above all is the corrective that should be applied to the usual conclusions drawn from the comparison of wages.

Second, the fact that the Russian worker frequently receives lodging (and here and there even board) from the factory is often disregarded. This applies not only to single but also to married workers, whose families usually live in the same factory barracks. Here heating fuel [for the workers' housing] is likewise provided by the factory.[125] This should be figured into the wages of Russian workers if one wants to make an exact comparison. Thus the difference even in nominal wages is not so greatly to Poland's disadvantage as would appear from a more superficial comparison.

But there are far more important additional factors showing that factory labor in Poland is significantly more intensive than in Russia.

The Polish worker is first of all more intelligent and better educated, on the average. To the extent that Professor Ianzhul investigated this question, it was shown that in Russia's central region the number of workers who could read and write amounted to 22 to 36 percent of the total; in Poland the number is between 45 and 65 percent.[126]

Furthermore, the Polish worker is better fed than the Russian worker, and this is especially true for women.[127] Third, the workforce in Poland is a stable layer of the population, devoted exclusively to factory labor. In Russia, an observable, although gradually decreasing, portion of the workforce is still made up of peasants who return to the land in the summer, where they perform rough farm labor instead of the more exact kind of work in a factory.[128]

Fourth, the Polish worker is far more individualized in his way of life than the Russian. As was already mentioned, the latter in many cases lives in factory barracks and the worker's board is paid for by the factory. Such a way of life, under certain circumstances, leads to the stunting of individuality. The Russian worker thus remains constantly under the control of his employer and is bound by the factory rules even in his private life. The Moscow factory inspector [Professor Ianzhul] knew of factories where, as he reported, singing—whether in workplace or living quarters—is punished by a fine of five rubles; likewise workers incur a high fine when they pay each other a visit, and so forth.[129] Not infrequently, workers are assigned to an apartment in a damp factory cellar, or in rooms that are built so low that one almost has to go on all fours to get into them.[130] In Poland the situation is different: the worker always runs his own household, and his housing is significantly better overall.

According to the unanimous opinion of all researchers who have made wage labor the subject of their investigation, all the cited factors—education, better housing and food, individual households, in short, everything that raises the living standard of the worker—are of decisive significance for the intensity of his or her activity.[131]

Finally, piece-rate wages predominate in Poland, which, it is generally recognized, raises the intensity of labor to the utmost, while in Russia the time wage predominates.

All the above-mentioned factors make it apparent to us that the labor of Polish factory workers is far more intensive in comparison with that of Russian workers. And this characteristic of the Polish worker so greatly outweighs his higher nominal wages and shorter work time that *in the end he is cheaper for the Polish factory owner than the Russian worker is for his employer.*[132]

Reckoned per pood, wages amount to (in rubles):[133]

	for cotton fabrics	*for cotton yarn*
In Poland	0.77–1.50	0.66–1.20
In Russia	2 and more	0.80–1.50

The difference in the length of the workday in Poland and Russia belongs to the past now, because the workday has recently been reduced by law to 11.5 hours. However, the new measure will primarily be to the advantage of the Polish industrialists in their competitive struggle, perhaps for years to come, even if it will, in time, doubtless become a spur to technical development for the Moscow region. For the Russian worker's productivity, whose lower level depends on so many other factors, will obviously not increase overnight. How justified this conclusion is may be seen from the fact that already in 1892 the Polish factory owners—in part to show a friendly face to the workers, who in May of that year had mounted an impressive strike in Łódź—went to the government with the request that the workday be reduced to 11 hours throughout the Russian empire, a project which foundered primarily because of the resistance of the Moscow industrialists.

3. *Composition of Capital.* This important factor also takes different shapes in Poland and in the Moscow region. In Poland, the total fixed capital of a company is in most cases exceeded by the value of its yearly production. In some cases the latter is even two or three times greater than the former, but on the average the ratio of fixed capital to the value of production is 2:3.2.[134] In Russia, particularly in the central industrial region, this ratio is inverted. Here the value of production (in a particular branch of industry) is often smaller than the fixed capital, or at most the same, and only seldom is it significantly higher. This phenomenon stems from two circumstances. First, far more is spent on buildings for enterprises in Russia than in Poland, because construction materials are quite significantly more expensive.[135] Second, the great majority of factories in Russia include their own factory barracks, which never occurs in Poland.[136]

If, therefore, what Marx calls the "organic composition of capital" (the ratio between constant and variable capital) is "higher" in Russia than in Poland, this has absolutely nothing to do with the higher stage of development of Russian production, but on the contrary with its primitive plant, for the most part. This makes necessary a series of expenditures that have nothing to do with the actual production process. As a result, all other conditions of production and sale being equal, the Polish industrialists are able to realize a greater profit from the sale of their goods on the Russian market, in comparison with the Russian entrepreneurs. In addition, Polish labor, as was shown, is far more intensive.

4. *The turnover time for capital* is much shorter in Poland than in Russia. First, reserves of fuel and raw materials are stocked for long periods in Russia. The high prices and the general shortage of fuel in the interior of Russia mean, for the Russian entrepreneur, the necessity of laying out large sums of money for the purchase of forests or peat bogs. In this way almost every large Moscow factory has put a more or less substantial amount of dead capital into forests and bogs. In addition, wood and especially peat are cheaply and easily delivered only in winter; therefore every Moscow factory lays in reserves of these fuels for a full year, even for two years.[137] In Poland, because of the short distances involved, stocks of coal are laid in for only one to four weeks, at most for three months.

Similarly, in Russia stocks of raw materials, particularly cotton, are laid in for lengthy periods, in Poland only for two to six months.

Second, the Polish industrialist realizes his product much more quickly than does the Russian entrepreneur. The Poles grant their customers only 3 to 6 months' credit, the Russians 12 to 18 months. The Poles, following the English and German model, produce on orders obtained by their traveling agents; the Russians produce according to their own estimates, often stocking for two or three years. This factor also signifies that Polish industrial capital—*ceteris paribus*[*]—is better equipped for the competitive battle.

5. *The concentration of production* is significantly greater in Poland than in Russia. The value of production per factory in those branches of industry not levied with excise duties averaged in rubles:[138]

	1885	1886	1887	1888	1889	1890
In Russia	50,824	52,248	54,601	58,237	58,972	57,578
In Poland	57,875	63,860	71,894	74,051	71,305	71,248

The difference is still greater if particular branches of production are compared. In the coal industry, for example, the situation is as follows. If the number of pits and shafts as well as the quantity of production in Russia are taken to be 100, then one finds in Poland in 1890 6.8 percent pits, 6.2 percent shafts, 70.6 percent production.[139]

Even with the number of mineshafts being 16 times smaller, therefore, coal extraction in Poland equals more than eleven-sixteenths of Russian coal extraction. Five firms account for 85 percent of the entire yearly production of the Dąbrowa region (1893).[140]

In other branches, such as the cotton industry, the gross product per factory is greater in Russia. The smaller concentration of this sort of production in Poland has to do with special circumstances, however, which to go into here would lead us into too much detail and which in any case have nothing to do with the degree of technological development. On the contrary, in Poland, as we will soon see, the yearly value of production per worker is in this as in most branches greater than in Russia.

6. *The technology* of production, lastly, forms the most important difference between Polish and Russian industry. We will compare the most significant branches of production in both countries in terms of technology.

To begin with the textile branch, first the *cotton industry* shows:[141]

---

[*]   All other things being equal.

1890	Factories	Spindles	Looms	Steam Horsepower
Russia	351	2,819,326	91,545	38,750
Poland	94	472,809	11,084	13,714

1890	Production (in thousands of rubles)	Workers	
		Male	Female
Russia	208,581	103,916	83,941
Poland	31,495	10,474	9,535

The technical superiority of the Polish cotton industry is clear from the above comparison. In comparison with the Russian industry, it has: *10 percent of the workers, 15 percent of the production, 35 percent of the steam power.*

For every worker there is 1,110 rubles production yearly in Russia and 1,574 rubles in Poland, that is, 42 percent more. Steam power amounts to 204 for every 1,000 workers in Russia, to 186 for every 1 million rubles of production; it amounts to 685 for every 1,000 workers in Poland, to 439 for every 1 million rubles of production, thus 236 percent and 136 percent more, respectively, in Poland.

Finally, the use of female labor is greater in Poland than in Russia. In the latter, female workers make up 44.7 percent of the personnel, in the former 47.6 percent. According to other accounts, which we noted above and which inspire more confidence because they were ascertained not from summary bureaucratic statistics but by a special commission, the use of female labor in Poland is much higher, and in Russia, on the contrary, much lower.

Roughly the same result is obtained by comparing the *wool industry* in Poland and in Russia. This comparison shows:[142]

1890	Factories	Spindles	Looms	Steam Horsepower
Russia	164	77,474	11,784	2,230
Poland	168	245,892	4,016	6,667

1890	Production (in thousands of rubles)	Workers	
		Male	Female
Russia	21,585	14,471	7,050
Poland	26,199	8,486	6,670

For Poland, in comparison with Russia, this comes out to: *workers 70.4 percent, production 121 percent, steam power 299 percent;* thus for every worker in Russia 1,003 rubles production annually, for every worker in Poland 1,729 rubles, that is, 72 percent more. Steam power amounts to 104 for every 1,000 workers in Russia, to 103 for every 1 million rubles of production; it amounts to 440 for every 1,000 workers in Poland, to 254 for every 1 million rubles of production.

Thus if we take 100 as the number for the steam power per 1,000 workers or 1 million rubles of production in Russia, then we find the same in Poland to be 323 percent and 146 percent more, respectively. In the use of female labor, we see here an even greater difference between Poland and Russia than in the cotton industry, specifically 32.7 percent female workforce in Russia, 44 percent in Poland. The technical superiority of the Polish textile industry is even more evident in the fact that higher grades of spinning yarn and finer sorts of cloth are manufactured in Poland in many branches than in Russia.

Let us turn to the second most important branch of capitalist production, the *coal industry*. We have already mentioned the strong concentration of this branch in Poland. The product extracted annually is as follows:[143]

	Coal in poods	
	from 1 pit	*from 1 shaft*
In the southern Russian region	678,000	240,000
In Poland	7,500,000	2,985,000
	(+1,006%)	(+1,144%)

(Here and below we compare the Polish coalfields with those in southern Russia in particular, because that is where Russia's biggest coal reserves are, and they are the most important for the future.)

A corresponding relationship is discovered when the quantity of production, the number of workers employed, and the steam power used are compared:[144]

1890	*Steam power*	*Workers*	*Production (in millions of poods)*
Russia	6,701	30,077	213.4
Southern Russia region	5,856	25,167	183.2
Poland	10,497	8,692	150.8

Thus, while in Poland (in 1890) one worker extracted 17,348 poods of coal, in Russia the amount was only 7,096 poods per worker and in the southern

Russian region in particular, 7,281 poods, approximately two and half times less than in Poland.

Steam power amounts to:	for every 1,000 workers	for every shaft
Russia	223	8
South Russian district	233 (100%)	—
Poland	1,208 (+419%)	202

From 1890 to 1894, the amount of steam power in Polish mining rose by more than 50 percent: from 10,497 to 15,934.[145]

Of the other important branches of industry we want to single out the *sugar industry*.

Sugar-beet growing itself is carried on in a significantly more rational way in Poland than in the two Russian sugar production regions. For example, the average beet harvest per desyatin[*] in the years 1882–90 was:[146]

Central Russia	73.2–125.3 berkovets[†]
Southwestern Russia	80.1–114.4 berkovets
Poland	88.0–127.6 berkovets

In the year 1895:

Central Russia	51.1–117.4 berkovets
Southwestern Russia	90.0–121.2 berkovets
Poland	94.3–144.5 berkovets

Likewise, the quality of the Polish beet is much higher than the Russian. The sugar content of the juice and its purity are:[147]

1890–91	Sugar content	
	in juice	purity
Southwestern Russia	13.49%	80.85%
Central Russia	13.63%	78.94%
Poland	14.81%	85.20%

---

[*]   A *desyatin* is 2,700 acres.

[†]   A berkovets measures mass and weight in Old Russian. One berkovets is equal to about 163.8 kilograms.

The same superiority of Polish technology is shown by the higher yield of white sugar from the beet juice and the lower yield of molasses.[148]

In 1881–82 to 1890–91 this was on average:

	White sugar	Molasses
Central Russia	7.0–9.47%	3.29–4.24%
Southwestern Russia	7.7–10.48%	3.60–4.31%
Poland	8.2–11.39%	1.53–2.28%

Finally, the utilization of processing by-products is far more intensive and more widespread in the Polish sugar industry than in the Russian. In 1890–91, of 182 factories in the central and southern regions, 10 with 125 osmosis devices conducted the extraction of sugar from molasses by osmosis; of 40 factories in Poland, 24 had 206 osmosis devices.

The above comparative analysis of the most important conditions of production shows that Polish industry is considerably better equipped than Russian and especially central Russian industry. Certainly it is a well-established fact that the Moscow region for its part has an important advantage in the cotton industry, namely the abundance of water, while in this respect the Łódź region suffers from a tremendous shortage, as has been mentioned. On the other hand, Poland lags behind in one of the most important branches of the economy—the iron industry—relative to the natural wealth of Russia, so that it must obtain part of the ore and likewise coke for its ironworks from the southern Russian region. In addition, metal production in the Donbas region is also much more concentrated than in Poland. It is furthermore true that Moscow is located much closer than Poland to the important market outlets for the textile industry, the eastern part of Russia and Asia. However, the advantages that we find in every branch on the Polish side—more capable labor power, cheaper fuel, higher technology in the production process and trade—could in our opinion outweigh numerous advantages of Russian industry. For all the cited factors have an invariant significance, indeed become more decisive in the competitive struggle with every passing day. How very much the significance of industry's distance from markets has already receded into the background, compared with its technical superiority, was recently proved by the amazing spread of the sale of German products in England, and even in the English colonies. Within one and the same customs zone, of course, the outcome of competition in the market depends to a still greater degree on the stage of development of production, i.e., on just those factors that Polish industry has on its side. This is confirmed, among other things, by the fact that the Polish iron industry, for example, despite the relative lack of natural advantages, which has been mentioned, is offering intensely bitter competition to the iron industry in southern Russia and is developing, along with the southern Russian iron industry, more rapidly than in any other region of the empire.[149]

Along with the Polish industrial sector, industry in St. Petersburg is also shaping up into a progressive and technologically rather highly developed Russian industrial region, and it is a particularly favorable circumstance for Poland that in the most important markets it is in competition with the Moscow region—the most anachronistic industrial region in Russia, which is unique in the Empire in its long workday, low wages, truck system, [i.e., paying wages with goods instead of cash] barracks housing for the workforce, and enormous stocks of raw materials—in short, its economic backwardness.

The coexistence of such different levels of production as are represented by Polish and St. Petersburg industry, on the one hand, and Moscow industry, on the other, is only possible because of two circumstances: first, the vastness of the Russian market, in which all competitors are able to find sufficient room for themselves; and second, the hothouse atmosphere created by the [Russian government's] tariff policy, which has made this enormous market the exclusive monopoly of the domestic entrepreneurs—both Russian and Polish.

3. Economic Ties Between Poland and Russia

After the foregoing, it is clear that—if free competition was the only decisive factor in the battle between Polish and Russian industry—the future of the former would be assured, at least to the degree that the capitalist development of the Russian Empire is granted a shorter or longer term by the general fate of the world economy.

However, we have already mentioned the other important factor that is of the greatest significance for the future of Polish capitalism: we mean *the economic policy of the Russian government*. It is all the more necessary to throw some light on precisely this factor, since the question (as is well known) stirred up so much dust a few years ago, and one even comes across the notion that since the middle of the 1880s a real "era of persecution" has dawned for Polish industry.

Actually there are grounds enough to regard all assertions of this sort a priori as baseless. The best and last touchstone for all relevant government economic measures—the growth of industry in Poland up to the present moment, and still at the same impetuous tempo—sufficiently proves (it should seem) that all the uproar about Polish industry's approaching end was wrong. The following tables eloquently display the factual details of this growth:

	1871	1885	1886	1887	1888	1889	1890	1891	1892	1893	1894	1895
Output of total industry (branches not subject to excise tax)	44.4	134.8	137.8	164.5	162.3	168.3	174.2	188.3	228.3	—	—	—
Total output of textile industry*	18.1	66.7	81.4	88.9	89.9	96.6	88.4	100.8	113.4	—	—	—
Pig iron**	1.4	2.5	2.8	3.7	4.8	5.4	7.4	7.5	9.0	9.9	10.7	11.3
Iron**	0.9	4.2	4.6	3.8	3.2	4.0	4.1	4.4	3.7	3.5	3.8	3.6
Steel**	—	2.4	3.1	3.0	3.1	2.4	3.4	3.0	4.0	5.4	6.2	7.9
Coal**	12.6	109.3	120.0	121.1	147.3	151.1	150.8	158.8	176.0	192.1	202.4	221.8

* in millions of rubles
** in millions of poods

As can be seen from the above table, the growth in the seven-year period 1885–92 amounted to: 69 percent in industry as a whole, 70 percent in the textile industry (specifically, 40 percent in cotton spinning and weaving, 77 percent in the wool and cloth industry, 101 percent in all other branches); in mining over the ten-year period 1885–95: 352 percent for pig iron, 229 percent for steel, 103 percent for coal; only in the production of iron do we see a decline, of 14 percent, as in recent times a vigorous development of steel production at the expense of iron production becomes observable in Poland and southern Russia. Still more interesting than the growth during the most recent period (1885–95) is the comparison of this decade with the previous period (1871–85), which is held to be the time of Poland's greatest economic prosperity. The increase, in absolute numbers, amounted to:

Branches not subject to excise tax	Textile Industry	Pig Iron	Iron	Steel	Coal
	(in millions of rubles)		(in millions of poods)		
In the 14-year period 1871–85	90.4	48.6	1.1	5.7	96.7
In the 7-year period 1885–92	93.5	46.7	—	—	—
In the 10-year period 1885–95	—	—	8.8	4.9	112.5

Thus, in view of the above figures, not only does speculation about the incipient decline of Polish industry rest on complete ignorance of the facts, but it is clear, on the contrary, that industry has grown more in the last seven-to ten-year period than in the preceding 14-year period. This becomes most clear when we calculate the growth in both periods *by year*. The average yearly growth in the later period was greater than in the preceding one, specifically: 107 percent in industry as a whole, 90 percent in the textile industry,[150] 20 percent in the production of iron and steel, of coal 63 percent, of pig iron 1,020 percent.

On the other hand, at the end of the first part of our work we also cited Polish industry's recent conquests in Russian and Asian markets into the 1890s. The body of Polish capitalism thus seems to exhibit not one symptom that would justify the claim that it is pining away from some internal malady; on the contrary, the much cried-over invalid grows and blooms "as splendidly as on the first day." But because the question was once raised and for years agitated public opinion in Poland, and also because it is interesting and important enough in itself, it seems appropriate to go into this question more fully and, by a thorough examination of the subject, derive an explanation of what the situation is and can be with regard to the economic policy of the Russian government in general and toward Poland specifically.

With regard to all the statements we have mentioned or quoted about the anti-Polish policy [of the Russian government], it is characteristic that they are based exclusively on particular measures and decrees, sometimes in the sphere of customs policy, sometimes in that of the railway rates system. But it is obvious that no real understanding of government policy can be reached by this road. For first of all, what is being referred to in the case at hand is a most extremely variable quantity: a tariff imposed today, or a railroad rate introduced today, will be lifted tomorrow. This is, in fact, what happened, for example with the differential tariff on raw cotton, which amounted to 15 kopecks in gold more on the Polish border than at the rest of Russia's borders. When it was introduced in 1887, a wail of lamentation went up among the Polish cotton-factory owners, and it was said that Polish industry had received its deathblow. The differential tariff also played the leading role as proof that "the era of persecution" had begun, and it was denounced at every opportunity. But then this tariff difference was once again lifted in the year 1894, on the grounds of the Russian-German trade agreement, making way for a single tariff on cotton at all Russian borders. The same was the case with the differential tariff on coal and coke at the western border, which was frequently represented as a measure aimed directly against the Polish iron industry (see Schulze-Gävernitz, "Der Nationalismus in Russland und seine wirthschaftlichen Träger," p. 347 and after him the English *Blue Book*, Vol. X., p. 9). But in 1894 this tariff was likewise reduced by half. In the same way, railroad rates were changed in part every year, indeed sometimes even more frequently. Thus the actual tariffs and rail rates *by themselves* do not provide a firm foothold from which to gain an insight into Russia's economic policy.

To arrive at a thorough understanding of this policy, it is necessary to disregard particular measures for the present, to look deeper into the economic relations of Poland and Russia on the one hand and their political interests on the other, and to seek to derive from this the economic policy of the latter. Only by following the guidelines thus obtained will it be possible to trace the particular measures of this policy back to their real significance.

First of all, then, what is the nature of the economic ties between Poland and Russia? If one were to form an opinion under the immediate impression of the Łódź-Moscow entrepreneurs' battle, one would be inclined to assume that the Polish and Russian bourgeoisies form two completely separate camps, whose interests run directly counter to one another at every point and who battle against each other using all available means. Such a notion would nonetheless be utterly wrong.

What precludes such a sharp difference in interests from the outset is the thoroughgoing *division of labor* that exists between the industries of these two countries. As we have seen, Poland is for Russia a source of supply for yarn, machines, coal, etc., etc., while Russia furnishes Poland with raw wool, raw iron, coke, and cotton.

Such a relationship already presupposes that the interests of some *Polish* manufacturers coincide with the interests of Russian raw-materials producers, and that the interests of some *Russian* manufacturers coincide with those of Polish producers of half-finished goods. This is confirmed by abundant data. The producers of South Russian wool, the planters of Central Asian cotton, exercise pressure on the system of railroad rates in their own interest to keep transport of their raw product to the Polish manufacturers as cheap as possible. Russian wool weavers likewise seek to encourage the transport of Polish yarn to Russia as much as possible, etc., etc.

Furthermore, from the fact that the battle between the manufacturers and the producers of raw materials and half-finished goods is fought out in the sphere of the *common tariff policy* of the two countries, it follows that the battling parties from Poland would often unite with those from Russia in order to march, hand in hand, with the national enemy against their own brothers. The history of Russian-Polish industry provides examples in quantity. In the year 1850, for example, the Russian government, under the pressure of joint petitions by Polish and Russian wool weavers, reduced the tariff rate on wool yarn. But no sooner had this happened than Polish and Russian spinners, in a touching accord, besieged the government to again push up the tariff rate on yarn, which happened in 1867.[151] Beginning in 1882, the government was solicited by the machine producers to increase the tariff on foreign machinery. "In this connection the initiative was that of the Riga manufacturers, who were followed by the others in *Warsaw*, Kiev, Kharkov, and Odessa with great unanimity."[152] However, when the government had obeyed this wish and increased the tariffs on machinery, a storm of petitions arose from the landed proprietors, again from all over the Empire without differentiation, against the increased price of agricultural machinery.

Just these two examples give us quite a different picture of the relationship between the Polish and Russian bourgeoisies, in their collective endeavors as in their competitive ones. Neither of the two national capitalist classes appears from the inside as a closed phalanx, but on the contrary is fissured, torn by conflicts of interest, split by rivalries. Yet, on the other hand, these different groups, unmindful of the national quarrel, reach out their hands to one another in order to deal their own countrymen an opportune blow to the wallet in the glorious prizefight for profits. Thus it is not national but capitalist parties that are found opposed on the industrial chessboard, not Poles and Russians, but spinners and weavers, machine producers and landowners, and on the flags waving over the combatants one sees not the one-headed and two-headed eagles,* but only the international emblem of capitalism. Finally, the government unexpectedly appears in the strange role of an indulgent mother, who impartially hugs all her profit-making children to her broad bosom, even though they are constantly squabbling with each other, and seeks to appease now the one, now the other, at the expense of the consumers. The above phenomena recur countless times in the history of Polish and Russian industry, and are of such decisive importance for the question under consideration here that it is well worthwhile to give a few more typical cases as examples. It is, for example, most highly instructive to observe how the two main opponents—the entrepreneurs of the Łódź and Moscow districts, whom one would be inclined to accept as representatives of the interests of, respectively, the Polish and Russian bourgeoisies as a whole—try at every opportunity to trip up the other industrial districts of their own countries. Thus the Łódź cotton manufacturers, in their above-mentioned polemic, seek to turn the jealousy of the Moscow manufacturers away from themselves and toward the old Polish wool industry district of Bialystok. They assure their adversaries: "If one can speak of competition, then far more dangerous to Moscow is Bialystok and its district."[153] Meanwhile, these same Łódź entrepreneurs most humbly and obediently denounce their blood brothers of the Sosnowiec district to the Russian government, pointing to the fact that in the latter a full third of the workforce are German subjects, while in the Łódź district—thank God—the figure is only 8 percent. No less brotherly sentiment is displayed by the Moscow capitalists when they come to speak of the affairs of their comrades in the other Russian industrial regions. So we hear them bewail the result of a plan for the regulation of waterways worked out by the Ministry of Transport: "The small expenditures, as with those of many millions, are allotted exclusively to Russia's western and southern zones. The whole central region of Russia has been almost entirely forgotten. This region, this neglected center of Russia, containing key Russian provinces, is relatively poor in waterways," and so forth in the same weepy tone.[154] Here the jealousy of

---

* One-headed and two-headed eagles symbolize Poland and Russia, respectively.

the Moscow capitalists gushes forth with impartiality and true internationalism against all other industrial districts in the Empire without distinction, against Poland and the Volga region, against the Baltic provinces and the Dnieper region.

The following example shows how elastic the notion of national solidarity and the "Fatherland" can be for the Polish capitalists under certain circumstances. In the year 1887 a large Warsaw steel factory was relocated to Yekaterinoslav province in southern Russia, to be nearer to sources of supply of raw iron and coke. Two years later, its owners—Polish capitalists—together with the English, Belgians, Russians, etc., who hold the iron district of southern Russia under their domination—sent a most humble and obedient petition to the government in which they complained about the advantages of the *Polish* iron industry and the competition from that quarter and beg for an increased railroad rate on Polish iron for the protection of the "Fatherland's" industry—this time, the industry in southern Russia.

Last, a classic example of this situation was provided in recent years by the question of the railroad rates for grain. In 1889 new, strongly differential rates were introduced for grain as part of the general regulation of the Empire's rail system, to facilitate exports to other countries from the provinces lying deep in the interior of Russia. However, the result was that masses of grain and flour from the cities of the interior, particularly the Volga region, were sent to the regions lying near the border, thus bringing on a rapid fall in the price of grain in the southern provinces on the Black Sea, in the Baltic provinces, and finally in Poland. Injured in their most virtuous sentiments, the landowners in all these parts of the Empire cried bloody murder, most of all the Polish landowners, who in the beginning tried to take this opportunity to again step forward in the name of all Poland, oppressed by cheap grain. Yet hardly was their national defense crowned by success and the execrated railroad rate partially annulled in the beginning of 1894, when a group of Polish entrepreneurs and merchants entreated the Department of Railroads in St. Petersburg, *by telegram*, to maintain the earlier rate in order, as they put it, not to make bread more costly for the people.[155] Thus the scene shifted from moment to moment, and from a fight between two national parties the question of the railroad rate for grain turned into a dispute between the landed proprietors and the industrialists in Poland. Here the latter marched together with the Russian landowners of the central provinces, while the Polish landowners took the field jointly with the Russian landowners of all the border districts.[156]

This motley grouping of interests was particularly evident in the deliberations on grain tariffs in St. Petersburg in October 1896. On the one side stood the representatives of the Volga district, whose case, as we have seen, was at the same time that of the Polish industrialists; on the other side, the landed proprietors of Livonia, Vitebsk, Odessa, the Polish landowners, and also, what is most interesting, the landowners of the Moscow district. Here Poles and Muscovites appeared on the best of terms, and the Polish landowners and millers declared themselves in full agreement with the program of Prince [A.G.] Shcherbatov, the chairman of the Moscow Agricultural Society.[157]* Almost as if to underline the conflict of interests between industry and agriculture in Poland itself, on the other hand, Chairman Maksimow, of the Polish representation (among others), objected: If Poland were permitted to sell its factory products unhindered in the Russian interior, then it would be highly inconsistent to forbid access to Poland to agricultural products from the interior of Russia.[158]

After the citation of the above examples, which we do not want to pile too high, it ought to be regarded as a proven fact that the interests of the Polish and Russian entrepreneurial groups absolutely do not contradict each other on all points, that, much more often, they tend to mesh together. But also, on the whole, Polish industry is tied up with several important sections of the Russian bourgeoisie by a solidarity of interests, above all with the two most important factors of economic life: the institutions of transport, on the one hand, and those of credit and trade, on the other. It is obvious that the development of Polish industry and, together with this, of the Polish market in Russia is directly in the interests of the Russian credit, commissions, and railroad corporations. To again pull out only two from the abundance of striking examples: the administration of the Russian rail line from Ryazan to the Urals turned to the Warsaw entrepreneurs in the fall of 1894 with the offer to hand over space in all its stations, free of charge, so that the Polish factory owners could have permanent displays of goods there to encourage Poland's market in the Volga region.[159] Thus, while the Moscow factory owners wanted to do battle with their Polish competitors over every market in Russia, the Russian railroad corporations invited this same Polish competition to forge ahead with its goods as deeply as possible into the interior of Russia.

Another characteristic case took place recently as a result of the new tariff on cotton. As long as the above-mentioned difference in customs rates was maintained on the western border, the Łódź factory owners, in order to get around the troublesome tariff, got their cotton via Libau and Odessa, i.e., by means of Russian railroads. When the customs difference was annulled in 1894, cotton transport returned to the old land routes: Bremen-Alexandrovo and Trieste-Granica, thus to German and Austrian railroads. Now the latter used this opportunity to set very low freight rates for cotton and so to monopolize this transport for themselves at the expense of the Odessa-Łódź line. The loss of transport, however, hit the Russian railroads hard, and so the Department

---

* The Moscow Agricultural Society was founded in 1819 as a forum to discuss agricultural policy. Most of its members came from the conservative, landowning nobility. Leading members of the Society, such as Shcherbatov, advocated the elimination of the peasant communes and the establishment of private property and a market economy.

of Railroads in St. Petersburg railway has recently turned to the Łódź factory owners with the question of how much to decrease the freight rates on the Russian lines so that cotton transport would once more go via Odessa. The Łódź factory owners dictated a rate decrease of 30 percent.[160] Likewise the Russian banks, in their own interest, are promoting Polish sales in Russia whenever possible.[161] Once again national borders clash with capitalist interests, and what the national banner might want to tear asunder is nevertheless firmly bound together by capitalist interest.

Finally, there is another area in which the most touching harmony of interests prevails between the whole Polish and the whole Russian bourgeoisie, where they are of one heart and soul: the jealous protection of the profits sought in the domestic market from foreign competition. One can encounter in one section of the Western European press the view that the Polish entrepreneurs are greater believers in free trade than the Russian. Nothing could be more mistaken. In the deep conviction that Russian and Polish workers were created solely to produce surplus value for them, Polish and Russian consumers to assist the realization of surplus value, the Russian government to fend off any invasion of foreign competition into this holy Empire—in this conviction the Polish entrepreneurs are just as firm and unshakable as the Russians. When it comes to taking a stand in defense of these "fundamental rights" of the capitalist constitution vis-à-vis the government, then the Łódź and Moscow factory owners, still bearing the bruises they just inflicted on each other, go shoulder to shoulder into battle. In 1888, one year after the two adversaries, as was mentioned, had sent a petition to the government in which they most sharply fought each other on the question of domestic competition, the Moscow entrepreneurs submitted a series of "most humble and obedient" petitions in regard to tariff policy: on increasing the entry tariffs for products of the textile industry, on reimbursing tariffs paid on raw materials when exported by manufacturers to foreign countries, etc.—all demands that had also frequently been made now as well as previously by the Łódź manufacturers.[162] With reason, then, this organ [Kraj] of the big industrialists of Poland, in discussing this action by the Moscow entrepreneurs, wrote that while much used to be said about the conflict of interests between the two industrial regions, now this petition shows that there is also a community of interests between the two, and indeed on the most important questions.[163]

The same harmony is evident when it comes to defending the monopoly in profits against the "Germans." The Moscow factory owners, as has been shown, saw in the strong representation of German elements in the Polish bourgeoisie a tempting pretext to lend their calico and fustian interests a becomingly patriotic look in the battle against Łódź. When they called on the government for a crusade against the Germans on the Vistula River, they believed they were striking the Polish bourgeoisie right in the heart. When, however, the government issued its well-known decree in 1887,* and when, because of this decree, there was talk on many sides of an era of persecution against the Polish bourgeoisie, then it turned out that the Polish bourgeoisie expressed their dissatisfaction on quite unexpected grounds: namely, for them the Russian government's anti-German measures were not nearly energetic and radical enough. For, as they expressed it, "The government's decree of two years ago concerning language examinations for foreigners brought about an advantageous change, in that it opened up a sphere of action for native forces ... Correspondents from Łódź and inhabitants there have already reported a certain improvement in this situation, *although it is still far from what it could and should be.*"[164]

We have reviewed the many cases of coincidence of interests between the Polish and Russian bourgeoisies. The picture that emerges is absolutely different from that which might be obtained under the immediate impression of the battle cries from Łódź and Moscow. On countless, extremely important questions, the Polish and the Russian bourgeoisies are bound together in a solidarity of interests, in particular groups as much as on the whole. What has created this community of interests is, first, the division of labor in production, which in many ways unified the two into a single productive mechanism; second, still more important, the common tariff borders, which breed solidarity against the outside and merge the entire Polish-Russian bourgeoisie—from the standpoint of the market—into a "national" capitalist class. Finally, there is the common market, which bred an important mutual dependency between Polish production on the one hand and Russian transport on the other. And, as is generally known, this fusion of Russian and Polish economic interests advances every day. This is also, in part, a direct result of the general direction of current Russian tariff policy, which in effect closes the way into Russia not only to foreign manufactured goods but also to foreign raw materials, and creates advantages for domestic raw-materials production, and in pursuit of this task it does not shy away from the greatest sacrifices—out of the pockets of Russian and Polish consumers and taxpayers.

Forced by prohibitive tariffs, Polish industry is changing gradually from the use of German coke and iron ore over to that from the Donets Basin, from American and Indian to Central Asian cotton, from Saxon and Silesian to South Russian wool.[165] To the same extent, the interdependence of Polish and Russian production is growing, and the interests of more and more new circles of the Russian bourgeoisie are becoming tied in with the successes or failures of Polish industry.

Certainly just as much enmity, competition, and rivalry grow out of these same relations between the Polish and Russian bourgeoisies. The same industrial

---

* The decree of March 14, 1887, prohibited foreigners from acquiring real estate in the entire western zone of Russia. In 1892 it was made a condition of employment for all factory official that they have knowledge of Polish or Russian.

division of labor, the common tariff boundaries, and the common markets turn the most varied groups within the bourgeoisie into enemies, and every particular instance of solidarity of interests corresponds to a conflict of interests. As the examples have shown us, landed property opposes industry, production opposes transport, and within each of these groups one region opposes the others and every individual capitalist opposes all the others. But what we glimpse here is a typical picture of capitalist economy, as it puts forth its blossoms in every country. It is the fundamental law of this form of production—*bellum omnium contra omnes**—that is expressed here, and that has nothing to do with national contradictions and borders. Indeed, on the contrary, it ceaselessly wipes away these contradictions and borders within the capitalist class. Certainly if the conflicts of economic interests coincide with national borders within one and the same state, this creates a broad basis, circumstances permitting, for national aspirations. This can only be the case, however, insofar as the enemy nationalities represent different, inherently antagonistic forms of production; if, for example, one country represents small business, the other large industry, one natural economy, the other money economy. In the given case, however, the situation is totally different, since Poland and Russia have gone through a combined development from a natural to a money economy and from small to large industry. Their antagonism, when and where it comes to light, arises not from the dissimilarity but rather the homogeneity of economic structure, and exhibits the characteristics of all capitalist *competitive battles* within one and the same economic mechanism.

The competitive Łódź-Moscow dispute is nothing but a fragment of this general war. Superficially puffed up to supposedly represent Poland's national duel with Russia in the economic battlefield, this dispute in its fundamentals reduces itself to an argument between the Łódź fustian barons and the Moscow calico kings. Following international custom, the two capitalist parties sought first to cover over the trivial cotton object of contention with an ideological national cloak and then to bang the drum as loudly as though their very necks were at stake.

Nonetheless, in reality neither one nor the other party represents the interests of the whole Polish and Russian bourgeoisies. On the contrary, both have countless opponents among their own countrymen. Nor is the fiery competitive battle over domestic markets decisive to or characteristic of the relationship of the disputants. Their rivalry over the domestic markets is contradicted by their solidarity of interests on a whole series of other vital capitalist issues.

In the entire capitalist development of Poland and Russia, which proceeds from an ever stronger bond between the production and exchange of the two countries, the Łódź-Moscow cotton dispute plays an infinitesimally tiny role—if

---

*   A war of all against all.

one is not led astray by the behavior of the squabbling entrepreneurs and keeps the wider perspective of the whole capitalist chessboard in view.[166*]

Only now, from the basis of these material interests, can the economic policy of the Russian government be evaluated and explained. Russia's main concern since the 1870s, as is well enough known, is the promotion of capitalism. To this end the prohibitive tariff policy is followed, the hothouse atmosphere of monopoly prices and profits created in the Empire, the costly means of transport built, subsidies and premiums awarded to "needy" capitalists, etc., etc. From this standpoint, the development of capitalism in Poland (just as in other parts of the Empire) appears as partial realization of the government's own program, its retrogression as a thwarting of this program. But still more important than the Russian government's own economic designs are the objective tendencies of the Russian economy. The bourgeoisie, promoted and protected by the government, already plays a significant role in Russia. The government must now seriously reckon with the bourgeoisie's interests, but also wants to carry through its own. However, the interests of the Russian bourgeoisie, as has been shown, are interwoven with those of the Polish bourgeoisie in the most diverse ways. There is no point at which Polish industry could be dealt a serious and lasting body blow without at the same time grievously wounding the vital interests of one or another group of the Russian bourgeoisie.

The notion that Russia is destroying or could destroy Polish capitalism assumes that Russian economic policy could be made the exclusive tool of the interests of the handful of Moscow calico manufacturers, an assumption based on a misunderstanding of the nature of the bourgeoisie just as much as of the nature of a capitalist government. Given the splits and contradictions of interest within the capitalist class, the government can represent the interests of the latter only *as a whole*; it cannot continually take the standpoint of any particular group of the bourgeoisie without being forced away from this standpoint again by the opposition of the other groups. Even the Russian government—although absolutist—is no exception to this rule. For even in Russia the bourgeoisie is a political tool of the government only to the extent that the government is the tool of the bourgeoisie's economic interests. Were the absolutist Russian government to make itself exclusively the lawyer for the Moscow cotton interests and trample on Polish and therefore Russian capitalist interests for this purpose, it could not help but call forth strong bourgeois opposition to the government in Russia itself. The end result of such a policy could even be efforts by the Russian and Polish bourgeoisies for a reform government that would know how to safeguard their interests as a whole better than the existing regime. It is from this

---

*   The footnote to this sentence is another instance in which Luxemburg added material after the May 1897 approval of her dissertation. This July 1897 addition, for the book version of her doctoral thesis, is apparently from the Russian-language *Newspaper of Trade and Industry* (or more literally, "Commercial-Industrial Gazette").

direction, then, that the question of the future of Polish capitalism is decided: *were it to be injured by the Russian government, the government's efforts would fall to pieces through the violent opposition of the bourgeoisie in Russia and Poland.*

From this standpoint we can also reduce the whole question of the alleged persecution of Polish industry to its true value. All the measures that are usually introduced as proof of Russian anti-Polish economic policy have one common characteristic: namely, that they are all directed to keeping Polish industry from the use of foreign raw materials and to the purchase of Russian raw materials. This was the case with the differential tariffs on cotton, on coal, on raw iron. All these measures were proclaimed not for the advantage of Russian industries competing with Poland and not with the purpose of destroying Polish industry, but to the advantage of Russian raw-materials production, which was also tied to Polish industry, and with the purpose of achieving *a particular configuration* of Polish industry. Precisely the same Russian interests that called forth these measures would form the greatest obstacle to a government policy directed at the destruction of Polish industry.

Yet from the same necessity of satisfying all the so very contradictory interests of the different groups of the bourgeoisie, there arises for the government the necessity of moving in an increasingly zigzag course in its economic policy. All laws of the capitalist method of production are merely "laws of gravity," i.e., laws that do not move in a straight line on the shortest route, but on the contrary proceed with constant deflections in contrary directions. The government's general policy of promoting capitalism, correspondingly, can only be realized as it favors now this capitalist faction, now that. The examples of Russian customs and railroad rate policy given above showed crudely the zigzag course of the Russian government, which at one time protects manufacture at the expense of semi-finished manufacture, at another time takes care of the latter at the expense of the former, at one time patronizes coal mining over iron works, at another time patronizes the iron works at the expense of the "coal interests," favoring sometimes the landowners, sometimes the industrialists. This characteristic of the government's economic policy also means that it can temporarily and on various questions deeply offend one or another *Polish* capitalist group; this is not only not impossible, but follows directly, necessarily, from the nature of the situation. The differential railroad rate for grain, etc., was of this type. However, if all these temporary and one-sided phenomena are torn out of their complicated economic context and puffed up into a doctrine of Russia's anti-Polish economic conspiracy, then what is involved is a complete lack of perspective and overview of the totality of this policy. In the same way, the exaggeration of the skirmish between Łódź fustian and Moscow calico into a deep gulf between the interests of Polish and Russian capitalism reveals the lack of an overview of the totality of the capitalist community of interest. There can be no doubt that the Moscow district, more than any other, has up until now enjoyed particularly loving care from the government, expressed in gifts of every sort. This policy, however, is merely the concrete expression of the encouragement of Russian capitalism in general, since the central district (where nearly a third of the Empire's industry and approximately two-thirds of its textile industry, by value, is concentrated) forms its main branch. The cost of this favoritism toward the Muscovites has not, however, been borne so much by the other industrial regions of the Empire, which in most cases (for example, the customs policy), on the contrary, also benefit, but much more by the other branches of the economy, above all agriculture. In fact, the enmity between the Russian landowners and the Moscow industrialists is much more lasting and bitter than that between Moscow and Łódź. An interesting spotlight on the alleged "national" policy of the Russian government, on the other hand, is thrown by the well-known fact that the southern coal and iron region, which is coddled the most and is absolutely overwhelmed with patronage—at the expense of the Russian metal industry in the Urals as well as the Moscow industrial interests—is a region whose exploitation is mainly in foreign hands: Belgian and English capitalists.

It is as superficial as it is erroneous to ascribe to the Russian government an economic policy of "Great Russian nationalism," in the ethnographic sense. Such a policy exists only in the imagination of the reporter led astray by external appearances. In fact, the tsarist government—just as any other in today's world—maintains not a national but a class policy; it makes a distinction among its subjects, not between *Poles* and *Russians*, but only between those who are "established" [*die "gründen"*] or "have money" [*"besitzen"*] and those who work for a living.[167]

4. Russia's Political Interests in Poland

Above, we have dealt with the economic relations between Russia and Poland, and those unquestionably represent the leading feature in the shape of Russia's economic policy toward Poland. Nevertheless, it would be one-sided to see this policy as determined simply and solely by the interests of the Russian bourgeoisie. For the present, the absolutist government of Russia is more able than that of any other country to carry through its own political interests, its sovereign interests, as well. In this connection, however, the historic state of affairs between the Russian government and Polish industry has formed a unique relationship. It is easy to see that absolutism's interests in terms of Poland are based above all on maintaining and fortifying the annexation. Since the Congress of Vienna, Russia's special attention has been directed to tenaciously suppressing all traces of national opposition in Poland, particularly that of the social class which is the pillar of the opposition, the nobility. In this endeavor, Russian absolutism saw in Poland's industrial bourgeoisie a desirable ally. To bind Poland to Russia through material interests, and to create a counterweight to the nationalist ferment of the nobility in a capitalist class arisen under the very wing of the Russian eagle, a class disposed toward servility not through any tradition of a national past but through an interest in its future—this was the aim of Russian policy, which it followed with its usual iron consistency. It must be admitted that the Russian government did not err in its choice of means, and that it had correctly sensed the nature of the Polish bourgeoisie. Hardly had manufacture sprouted in Poland, hardly had it tasted the honey of the Russian market, when the Polish entrepreneurs felt themselves ready for their historic mission: to serve as the support in Poland for the Russian annexation. Already in 1826 the Polish Finance Minister [Franciszek Ksawery] Drucki-Lubecki* was delegated to St. Petersburg with the most humble entreaty to completely abolish the customs border between Russia and Poland, "so that the two countries would indeed form a single whole and Poland belong to Russia."[168] In this declaration, the entire political program of the Polish bourgeoisie was stated concisely: the complete renunciation of national freedom in exchange for the mess of pottage of the Russian market. Since that time, the Russian government has never ceased supporting the Polish bourgeoisie. We have cited the long list of laws that have been issued since the 1820s to aid industrial colonization of Poland and the development of manufacture, the "iron fund" for the subsidy of industry, the establishment of the Polish Bank, endowed with every conceivable privilege, etc., etc.

This policy was most energetically maintained in the later period; even in the time of Nicholas I we see the Russian government issuing new decrees to the same effect. Nothing was neglected which might transform the noble, rebellious Pole into a capitalist, tame Pole. And the Polish bourgeoisie showed that it possesses a grateful heart, for it has never ceased to thwart and betray national stirrings in Poland with all its might; its disgraceful conduct in the Polish uprisings supplies sufficient evidence of this fact. The most important milestone of this tendency in Russian policy was the abolition of the Russian-Polish customs border in 1851. A historian intimate with the pertinent archives of the Russian government and the best authority on the history of Russian customs tariffs, the Russian author Lodyzhenskii, wrote on this subject:

> The lifting of the customs line between the Empire and the Kingdom was primarily the result of *motives of a political character*. As is well known, an intellectual ferment of a partly *national* and partly socialist character began in Europe in the 1840s. This ferment, in which the population of Russian Poland also participated, disturbed the Russian government up to a certain point and moved it to seek out ways to unite *Poland with Russia as firmly as possible*. One of the main factors that hindered the drawing together of the two countries was their economic separation.[169]

---

* Drucki-Lubecki was Finance Minister from 1821 to 1830. By removing customs barriers between Congress Poland and Russia, he enabled Polish capital to obtain new markets in the East. He also founded the National Bank of Poland, in 1828.

Thus to eliminate this "separation," to fetter Poland to Russia by the material interests of its bourgeoisie, the customs border was abolished. The Russian government still holds to the same standpoint today, and still greets the growing Polish market in Russia as the chain that most tightly shackles the annexed country to Russia. Thus Mendeleyev wrote in his preface to the official report on Russian industry to the Chicago World's Fair in 1893: "The products of this and many other Polish factories find a constantly growing market all over Russia. Through the competition of this industrial region with the Moscow region, the basic goal of Russia's protectionist policy was achieved, on the one hand, and on the other, the assimilation of Poland with Russia, which is appropriate to the peaceable outlook of the Russian people [read: the Russian government— R. L.]."[170] This special role that the Polish bourgeoisie plays toward the Russian government as the bulwark of the annexation also is important in explaining the main point under discussion, i.e., the future of Polish capitalism. It requires, in fact, an enormous dose of naïveté to assume that the Russian government, which has given itself precisely the task of cultivating capitalism in Poland and has for more than half a century used all the means at its disposal to do so, now intends to demolish that same capitalism, force the Polish bourgeoisie over to the opposition, and thus want only destroy its own handiwork. And indeed, solely out of love for the Moscow entrepreneurs, to whose complaints and lamentations the Russian government has turned a deaf ear for half a century! Unfortunately, the Russian government knows better how to protect its ruling interests. What these interests are in regard to Poland we know from the mouths of its representatives: "the peaceable assimilation" of Poland with Russia, i.e., the strengthening of its rule in Poland at any price. This declaration was made in 1893, long after the presumed new course of Russian policy was supposed to have begun.

The best evidence of our interpretation is provided by the recent history of Russia's relations with *Finland*. Here we find on a small scale an exact repetition of Russia's earlier policy in Poland. Finland, at present, remains cut off from the tsarist Empire by a customs border and maintains an independent customs policy toward foreign countries much more liberal than Russia's. Finnish industry is now enjoying all the advantages that have already helped Polish industry to blossom. Likewise Finnish products, particularly those of the metal industry, have found access to Russia thanks to, among other things, lower customs at the Russo-Finnish border than at Russia's other borders, and is now giving Russia's domestic industry fierce competition. The Russian entrepreneurs, to whom this is a thorn in the side, have, of course, not neglected to set in motion a "most humble and obedient" campaign to protect the "Fatherland's" industries against "foreign" rivals—exactly like the campaign against Poland. The government has, under this pressure, likewise twice raised the tariffs against Finland as an economically foreign region, because of its independent customs policy, in 1885 and 1897.

If the Russian government were now to make the interests of this or that group of entrepreneurs the consistent plumb line for its economic policy toward the non-Russian-speaking sections of the Empire, then it would consequently have had to continue along the road to cutting Finland off from Russia with a Chinese wall. But precisely the opposite is in fact the case. The government has already ordered the total lifting of the Russian-Finnish customs border, scheduled for the year 1903, and *the absorption of Finland into the imperial Russian customs zone.* Thus will the "Fatherland's" industries be freed of uninhibited "foreign" competition. And if this has not happened even sooner, it is not consideration for the lamentations of the Russian mill owners that is responsible, but the trade agreement with Germany, through which the tsarist Empire has bound itself for a number of years. It is clear that the impending reform means the beginning of the end of Finnish independence in *political* terms, even if it proceeds first toward demolishing its economic independence.* Here we have before us once more a portion of the general policy of tsarism, which passes over all particular interests in order to spiritually level the various parts of the Empire through the system of Russification, on the one hand, and on the other, to give the unity of the Empire a firm material frame by this economic welding process, and to press the whole thing together in the iron clamps of absolute power—a policy with which we have already become acquainted in Poland.

Of course not everything in the world goes according to the wishes of the rulers. While the Russian government economically incorporates Poland into the Empire and cultivates capitalism as the "antidote" to national opposition, at the same time it raises up a new social class in Poland, the industrial proletariat, a class that is forced by its situation to become the most serious opponent of the absolutist regime. And if the proletariat's opposition cannot have a national character,[†] so it can under the circumstances be even more effective, in that it will logically answer the solidarity of the Polish and Russian bourgeoisie with the political solidarity of the Polish and Russian proletariat.[171‡] But this distant consequence of its policy cannot divert the Russian government from its present course; for the time being, it sees in the capitalist development of Poland only the class of the bourgeoisie. As long as Russia seeks to maintain its rule over Poland in this way, the full blossoming of industry in Poland will remain inscribed in the program of the government. Thus those who await a government policy directed toward the economic separation of Poland take for future phenomena that which belongs to the past, and their insufficient knowledge of history for deeper insight into the future.

---

    *   In actuality, Finland was to become politically independent in December 1917. Poland in turn secured its political independence in November 1918.

    †   This passage indicates the extent to which Luxemburg's economic analysis of industrial development in Poland is integrally connected to her rejection of calls for Polish national self-determination. The latter remains one of the most contentious aspects of her legacy.

    ‡   The first two articles, which are by Luxemburg, can be found in Rosa Luxemburg, *Gesammelte Werke*, Band 1/1 (Berlin: Dietz Verlag, 2007), pp. 37–51 and pp. 94–112 respectively.

5. Russia's Economic Interests in the Orient

Of the highest significance for the question we are dealing with, finally, is the new direction in Russian foreign economic policy that has become evident in the last ten years. Up until that time, Russia's efforts were directed to satisfying its needs for manufactured goods and raw materials through its own production, and emancipating itself from foreign imports. Today its efforts go further; today Russia wants to venture out into the world market and challenge the other capitalist nations on foreign ground. To be sure, this tendency does not stem from the Russian bourgeoisie. Because of the peculiar economic-political development of Russia, politics frequently seizes the initiative in promoting economic development in pursuit of its own interests.

While industry in most capitalist countries, to the extent that the boundaries of the internal market are too narrow, pushes the government to acquire new markets by conquest or treaty, in Russia, on the contrary, tsarist policy sees in industrial exports a means of bringing the countries of Asia, initially chosen as prospective political booty, into economic dependence on Russia. Therefore, while the Russian industrialists for the most part do not lift a finger to win a place in the world market, the government spurs them incessantly in that direction. Everything has been done to impart energy and a thirst for exports: exhortations, invitations, expeditions to investigate new market areas, the construction of colossal railroads such as the Trans-Siberian and the Chinese Eastern, rebates on customs and taxes on exported goods,[172] and finally, direct subsidies to this end. The countries first in consideration here are: China, Persia, Central Asia, and the Balkan states. In 1892 an expedition under the direction of Professor [Alexei M.] Pozdneyev, which was to serve scientific as well as commercial ends, was sent to *Mongolia.*[*] Even earlier the Russians had introduced a postal system there, which was also run by them. In the following year an official of the Finance Ministry, Tomara, was sent to *Persia* to investigate the trade situation there and, particularly important, the reconstruction of the Persian port of Enzeli[†] was begun in order to support Russian trade. In the same year the Russian Finance Ministry worked out a draft regarding the improvement of the routes from the Russian border to Tehran, Tabriz, and Meshed and the establishment of a Russian bank in Persia. In 1896, in order to monopolize the market in eastern Siberia for its own merchants and drive the English from the field, Russia decided to eliminate the free trade zones on the Amur River and at the port of Vladivostok, which had extended to all goods except those on which

---

* For an English translation of the book in which Pozdneyev reported on his 1892 expedition, see Alexei M. Pozdneyev, *Mongolia and the Mongols*, Vol. 1 (Bloomington: Indiana University Press, 1971).

† Enzeli is a port on the Caspian Sea, which was renamed Pahlevi in 1925; after the 1979 Iranian Revolution, the populace of the city restored its original name.

an excise had been levied in Russia. However, the most important measure by which the government hoped to give a boost to Russian trade in Central Asia was the costly construction of the Trans-Caspian Railway.* Russia directed no less—or more exactly, even more—attention toward China. A short time ago China's trade with foreign countries was taken care of by German, French, and English banks.[173]

Therefore, in 1896, the Russian government hurried to found a Russian bank in Shanghai. "One task of the bank," wrote the organ of the Russian Finance Ministry at the time, "is to consolidate Russia's economic influence in China and to thereby create a counterweight to the influence of other European nations. From this standpoint it is particularly important that the bank try to draw as close to the Chinese government as possible, that it collect taxes in China, undertake operations that will bring it into contact with the Chinese treasury, pay interest on the Chinese state debt," and so on.[174] The other Russian measures, for example the construction of the Chinese Eastern Railroad,† are well enough known.

An official inquiry was made recently into the result of these efforts so far, and they turned out to have been an almost total fiasco. In every country where the government wanted to create a market for Russian goods, they would have had to overcome stiff competition from German, French, but above all English industry, and the Russian entrepreneurs had not even remotely risen to this task. Russia was no match for other nations even in its own national territory in eastern Siberia, as long as it had to face them in free competition. Imports in the most important Siberian port, Vladivostok, amounted to:[175]

	In thousands of rubles	
	from Russia	from foreign countries
1887	2,016	3,725
1888	2,121	3,763
1889	2,385	3,325

One consequence of this state of affairs was the above-mentioned decision by Russia to take eastern Siberia into the Empire's tariff zone.

Russian exports to China are likewise hardly worth mention in comparison to those of other nations. Out of total imports of nearly 330 million rubles, Russia participated with only approximately 4.5 million:[176]

---

   *   The Trans-Caspian Railway was built by Russia in 1879 in order to facilitate its expansion into Central Asia. It extended from the Caspian Sea to Tashkent, the capital of Uzbekistan.

   †   Construction on the Chinese Eastern Railroad, which ran through Manchuria and greatly reduced the amount of time it took Russian goods to reach the Pacific, began in 1896, just at the time that Luxemburg was writing the dissertation. Control over the railway later became a contentious issue in Russia's relations with Japan.

	In thousands of rubles
1891	4,896
1892	4,782
1893	4,087
1894	4,488

A similar picture has been provided by the uproar about trade with *Central Asia*. The Trans-Caspian Railway built by Russia, on which such great hopes were set, proved to be a really first-rate trade route—for the English, who now have obtained a way of getting around the high transit duty in Afghanistan. Russian exports to the Trans-Caspian, Khiva, Bukhara, and Turkestan have, after a brief upswing, begun to sink again in the last few years. Of the most important items on record, the exports were as follows:[177]

Year	In thousands of rubles					
	1888	*1889*	*1890*	*1891*	*1892*	*1893*
Total	1,141	1,296	1,685	2,922	2,102	1,854
Products of textile industry	201	245	541	671	397	538
Sugar	422	457	531	1,048	516	510

English imports from India, on the contrary, grew rapidly during the same period thanks to the Russian rail system, as has been officially confirmed from the Russian side. Bukhara, for example, received from the four main stations on this line:[178]

	In thousands of poods						
	1888	*1889*	*1890*	*1891*	*1892*[179]	*1893*	*Total*
Russian products	572	1,176	1,863	923	267	244	5,045
English products	1,160	4,209	8,516	12,761	4,443	16,154	47,243

Russia's exports to *Afghanistan* are in just as bad a way. Imports of products of the Russian textile industry [by that country] amounted to 163,245 poods in 1888–90 (25 months), 10,000 poods in 1893 (12 months), that is, approximately eight times less in the latter year.[180]

Relatively speaking, Russian trade in Persia has had the best success. Russian cotton products make up approximately 30 percent of Persian consumption, and imports of these products amounted to 48,000 poods per year in 1887–90, and 73,000 poods per year in 1891–94.[181]

In the northern provinces of Gilan and Mazanderan, the Russian textile industry has almost supplanted the English, but, in total Persian imports, Russia, according to official evidence, plays a very small role for the meantime. This despite the fact that Russian industry finds itself in the most advantageous situation, since the Persians and Armenians living in the Caucasus, carrying on trade at their own risk, serve Russian industry as the most suitable agents, while the merchants of other nations must have recourse to business on commission, and that only in Persia's larger cities.

The total picture of Russia's exports to its most important Asian markets appears as follows:[182]

1894	In millions of rubles		
	to Persia	to China	to Central Asia
Total	12	4.5	3.8
Food	7.5	0.1	1.7
Manufactured goods	3.5	3.4	0.4
Raw materials and half-finished goods	—	0.7	0.9

We see that the Russian government's program in Asia is still far from being realized, and that, in any case, the result attained corresponds in no way to the amount of effort made in this direction. It would be an error to trace this back to the technological backwardness of Russian industry alone. Certainly Russia is behind other industrial states in this regard, in a whole series of important branches of industry, such as the metal and wool industries, etc., and in order to be able to take up the competitive battle successfully on the world market it would have to unconditionally improve its methods of production. But there is a further and no less important factor involved, which has largely frustrated the government's plans in Asia up until now. For even where Russian industry could have easily won a victory over the English, according to the competent testimony of individual researchers[183] and even the British consuls in Persia—for example, in the production of lower grades of cotton cloth—the Russian industrialists up until now have not been able to go very far. The reason is the entire habitual mode of life [Habitus] of the Russian entrepreneurs, especially those of Moscow, and this was the product of the many years of Russia's protective tariff policy. Pampered by the government with all sorts of gifts and patronage, spoiled by enormous monopoly profits, spoiled further by a colossal domestic market and immunity from outside competition, the Moscow entrepreneurs felt neither the desire nor the need to expose themselves to the rough weather of the world market and contented themselves with normal profits. It is, so to speak, profit-hypertrophy which makes the Muscovites so sluggish and apathetic in the search for possible new markets; they see foreign trade as, at most, a means to either pocket higher export subsidies or to get a huckster's one-time profit by fraudulent goods deliveries and the clumsiest cheating. If neither the one nor the other is in the offing, then the Moscow manufacturer answers the orders that might pour in from outside with stubborn silence.

This method of doing business is clearly shown in connection with Asia. Thus, for example, the Russian calico massively imported to Bukhara and Khiva in 1890 and 1891 was manufactured in such a way that the Moslems could have used it much less for clothing than for dyeing New Year's eggs. In subsequent years the population understandably turned back to English products, and this, more than the cholera epidemic and the bad harvest, brought about the precipitous fall in Russian imports in the years 1892 and 1893.[184] Just as telling is the story of the sugar trade with Asia. So long as the excise tax was rebated on the export of sugar, these exports went rapidly to Persia and Bukhara; when the rebates were suspended, the business once more seemed pointless to the Russians, and exports sank suddenly from 1,047,996 poods in 1891 to 516,021 poods in 1892 and 150,128 in 1893.[185] Another interesting side of the Muscovites' commercial spirit is revealed in their trade with Siberia, where they managed to first send out travelers with samples to win orders, then afterwards declined to fill these orders.[186] Finally, the Muscovites' energy comes to the fore most glaringly in their business with China; approached from there with requests for the establishment of trade relations, they retorted to this importunate demand with silence.[187]

After exhaustive examination of the results of Russia's Asian trade, the organ of Russia's Finance Ministry likewise came to the following conclusion: "The characteristic traits of the non-commercial Slavic (meaning here: Russian) race and the absolute apathy and indolence of the Moscow entrepreneurs are expressed as crudely as they are completely in our trade with Central Asia."[188] The causes of the failure of the Russian market in Asia are formulated in almost the same words by other papers of different viewpoints—Novosti, Novoye Vremya, and the Sankt-Peterburgskie Vedomosti, among others.[189] And recently the organ of the Finance Ministry happened to speak once again on the same theme: "Only Persia," it wrote in January 1897, "can be called a market for the products of our cotton industry; the attempts to conquer the Chinese and Central Asian markets for ourselves can so far not be viewed as successful, and what is partly to blame is our inability to adjust to the demands and customs of the customers, but above all the fact that our entrepreneurs at the moment have it too good at home to want to bother with foreign markets."[190]

Thus it appears that the very essence of the Moscow entrepreneurs, and particularly their efforts to maintain a privileged place by means of a totally artificial Chinese wall, are incompatible with the current tendency of Russian foreign policy and in fact go directly against it. It is clear that the most effective remedy for all Moscow's indolence and its trade practices, as well as for technological backwardness, would be Russia's transition to a liberal tariff policy, which would tear the Moscow district out of the hothouse atmosphere of monopoly and confront it with foreign competition in its own country. To us there is little doubt that the interests of absolutism in Asia, on the one hand, and the expansion of capitalist agriculture and the interests of the landowners, on the other, will sooner or later pull Russia down the road to a more moderate tariff policy. But above all a remedy can be created only in one way, namely by sharpening competition *within* the Russian customs borders, i.e., so that Moscow is ruthlessly abandoned to the unlimited competition of the progressive industrial districts of Poland and St. Petersburg. This viewpoint is also that which the more influential Russian press, such as *Novoye Vremya*, stressed explicitly in connection with the debate over the tsarist Empire's interests in Asia.[191] That the government, for its part, is now in fact preparing to do away with Moscow's economic rut and to force the Muscovites toward modern production and trade methods is best proved by the most recent law on the maximum workday, which indicates the most abrupt break with Moscow's present methods of production, while it also appears as a realization of the *Polish* project of 1892.

To the same degree to which Moscow's economic conservatism is a drag on current Russian policy and becomes more so every day, Polish industry appears once more as tsarism's comrade in arms. We have shown by the comparison between the competitive conditions of Polish and central Russian production how far ahead of Moscow Poland is in terms of technology. For this reason alone, capitalist Poland, as the most progressive industrial district in Russia, which, through competition, unceasingly spurs the others, particularly Moscow, toward technological improvements, realizes the Russian government's current program. But the Polish industrialists are also running ahead of the Russians specifically in the opening up of Asian markets. We have seen how seriously and thoroughly they prepared themselves for this task. Without awaiting the invitation of the government, they themselves seize the initiative and with their own hands forge trade links with foreign countries.

In the only country where Russian trade is relatively flourishing, in Persia, the products of the Polish textile industry make up nearly half of the total textile imports from Russia—approximately 40 percent of the imports via the most important junction, Baku.[192] To Poland also belong the initiatives toward trade relations with Persia, in many respects: as early as 1887, thus before the government had turned its attention to this country, Poland had set about opening up its own trade agency and warehouse in Tehran.[193]

Łódź also immediately made use of the Trans-Caspian Railway to advance into Central Asia with its goods along with St. Petersburg and Moscow.[194] It is the Warsaw district that provides the largely immigrant strata of the populations of Bukhara and Turkestan with glassware, faience, and porcelain, while the inferior Moscow products are bought by the poorer natives.[195] Łódź is, at this point, the only industrial district in the Empire whose textile industry's products have found entry into Constantinople and the Balkan countries.[196] Already in 1887 Poland had taken up trade relations with Romania and Bulgaria.[197] Recently Łódź began to send cotton products directly to Sofia.[198] Indeed, the Polish bourgeoisie, through the use of the Trans-Siberian rail line, may make Warsaw the center of the new, large European-Asian trade routes.[199] "The British manufacturer," wrote the English consul in Warsaw, "may be prepared to find in them (the Polish entrepreneurs) formidable rivals in the markets of the East."[200]

In this way Polish capitalism is working hand in hand with tsarist policy in Asia.

From these so diametrically opposed attitudes of Moscow and Poland toward the aims set by Russian policy, there also follows a totally different current in the public opinion of the two districts. Stronger and stronger grows the party favoring domestic free trade, favoring technological progress, the party that opposes the official guardianship and defense of backward industries, and therefore is sympathetic toward the Polish district; and the Moscow entrepreneurs stand more and more isolated with their ancestral belief in the Trinity: guarantees, bonuses, subsidies. The anti-Moscow temper clearly expressed itself on the occasion of Moscow's petition to the 1893 annual fair in Nizhny Novgorod for the imposition of a tax on Polish traveling agents. Thus we read in *Novosti*:

> During the same fair ... these same representatives of protectionism composed and sent to the Finance Minister a petition regarding a special tax on the traveling salesmen of the Łódź factories, with the unconcealed intention of liberating the Moscow industrial district from Łódź's competition. According to healthy common sense, the Moscow manufacturers should, in the interests of Russian industry and of Russian consumers, merely follow the admirable example of the Łódź manufacturers and employ traveling salesmen, bring the producers closer to the consumers, and so cheapen and make easier the market for its own products. But not nearly so much entrepreneurial spirit lies with the customs and habits of these protection-coddled practical men; they prefer to try various pranks against their competitors.[201]

And, finally, a characteristic excerpt from the official government organ in Warsaw, the *Varshavskii Dnevnik* [Warsaw Journal], on the general tasks of Russia's industrial foreign policy:

> With the opening up of these new markets in Central Asia and Persia, we count on the flourishing of our industries, and we repeat that it is very much to be deplored that the lion's share of the profits go to foreign countries, while only the crumbs remain for our poor workers (!). Our trade with Central Asia and Persia has not yet struck deep roots, and the representatives of Russian trade still have many victories

to win over English competition to conquer those markets for Russia. *In view of the common enemy, the Moscow and Polish entrepreneurs should join forces in order to strive together toward the same goal ... Russia's main goal in the Asian market is at this moment to exclude English goods. It would be a subsidiary question which of the Empire's industrial districts contributes more to the achievement of this goal,* if only the profits of industry on the banks of the Vistula went exclusively to the native population and not, as is the case, to increase the capital for German entrepreneurs, employees, and workers. Were those industries in the hands of Russia or Poland, then we would be far stronger in our battle with England, and our dominance in Central Asia would be secured.[202]

Understandably, the government organ does not neglect to deal a blow in passing at the German industrialists, who are heavily represented in Polish industry; it charges them with ignoring Russian national interests, exclusive, egotistical concern for the "German" interests of their own pockets, etc. But in the main, we find here the actual situation of the moment, pointedly expressed: In view of the present tasks in the world market, the domestic rivalries of the Polish and Russian entrepreneurs stand completely in the background. Insofar as differences exist between them, the blame will be pushed onto the Germans, an element hated just as much by the Polish bourgeoisie, as we have seen. Polish industry in itself, its development, its flourishing, appear here in a new light, as lying directly in the interests of the tsarist government: Once it has served to additionally consolidate the Russian conquest in Poland, tsarism is now assigning Polish capitalism the flattering role of serving in Asia as the harbinger of tsarism's coming appetite for conquest. Indeed, Poland now plays the leading role, as we saw, in the realization of this lofty task, while Moscow's star, i.e., the special Muscovite economic policy, is slowly waning. The new Russian law on the maximum workday signifies that even in the Russian Empire the lovely days of Aranjuez[*]—the days of primitive capitalist accumulation—are almost past.

CONCLUSION

Our task is finished. We believe that we can conclude from the foregoing that all apprehensions about the future of Polish industry—at least insofar as they relate to the danger threatened by the Russian government—are quite groundless and nothing but an uncritical, superficial reflection of the intimate entrepreneurial wrangle between the Łódź and Moscow entrepreneurs. If one looks deeper into the situation, one must arrive at the conclusion that Poland, in economic

---

[*]   Aranjuez, in central Spain, was the site of a palatial residence of the King of Spain in the eighteenth century. In 1808 it was the site of the Mutiny of Aranjuez, a popular uprising against King Charles IV, which was largely a response to an economic crisis that resulted in a sharp drop of industrial production.

terms, not only does not have any separation from Russia in store, but, rather, the tendencies arising from the general internal nature of large-scale capitalist production itself are binding Poland much more strongly to Russia with every passing year. It is an inherent law of the capitalist method of production that it strives to materially bind together the most distant places, little by little, to make them economically dependent on each other, and eventually transform the entire world into one firmly joined productive mechanism. This tendency, of course, works most strongly within one and the same state, within the same political and tariff borders. The capitalist development of Poland and Russia has yielded this result. As long as both countries were predominantly agricultural and indeed natural-economy countries, thus until the 1860s, they remained economically foreign to each other and each represented for itself a closed whole with particular economic interests. Since factory production began here and there on a larger scale, however, since natural economy gave way to money economy, since industry became a determining factor in the social life of both countries, the self-containment of their material existence has more and more disappeared. Exchange and the division of labor have strung thousands of threads between Russia and Poland, and these manifold economic interests are so intertwined that the Polish and Russian economies today increasingly constitute a single complex mechanism.

The process portrayed above is mirrored in many different ways in the consciousness of the different factors in Polish public life. The Russian government sees Poland as a tool for its plans for rule, believes that Poland has unconditionally surrendered to its power and that it has founded a thousand-year empire of despotism. The Polish bourgeoisie sees in this a fundamental of its own class rule in the country and an inexhaustible source of riches; it indulges in the sweetest dreams of the future in its thoughts about Asia and believes itself able to build a thousand-year empire of capital. The various nationalist elements of Polish society perceive the entire social process as a unique, great national misfortune, which mercilessly shattered their hopes for the reconstruction of an independent Polish state. They sense instinctively the power of the economic bonds which capitalism has created between Poland and Russia and, without being able to hold back the fatal process in reality, they can at least put an end to it in their own imagination; they cling in desperation to this illusion and expect the Russian government itself to nullify Poland's hated capitalist development with its own hands and so recreate a basis for nationalism.

We believe that the Russian government, the Polish bourgeoisie, and the Polish nationalists have all equally been struck with blindness, and that the capitalist fusion process between Poland and Russia also has an important dialectical side that they have completely overlooked. This process is bringing to fruition in its own womb the moment when the development of capitalism in Russia will be thrown into contradiction with the absolutist form of government, and then tsarist rule will be brought down by its own works. Sooner or later, the hour will strike when the same Polish and Russian bourgeoisie that is today pampered by the tsarist government will become weary of their political attorney, absolutism, and will checkmate the king. Moreover, this capitalist process is moving with impetuous haste toward the moment when the development of the productive forces in the Russian Empire becomes irreconcilable with the rule of capital and when, in the place of private commodity economy, a new social order based on planned, cooperative production will appear. The Polish and Russian bourgeoisies are hastening this moment with their combined forces; they cannot make one step forward without increasing and pushing forward the Polish and Russian working classes. The capitalist fusing of Poland and Russia is engendering as its end result that which has been overlooked to the same degree by the Russian government, the Polish bourgeoisie, and the Polish nationalists: the union of the Polish and Russian proletariats as the future receiver in the bankruptcy of, first, the rule of Russian tsarism, and then the rule of Polish-Russian capital.

LIST OF WRITINGS USED*

In Polish

F. Rodecki, *Obraz geograficzno-statystyczny Krolestwa Polskego* (Geographical-Statistical Depiction of the Kingdom of Poland), Warsaw[: Drukarni Antoniego Gałęzowskiego i Kompanii,] 1830.

O. Flatt, *Opis miasta Lódzi pod wzgledem historycznym, statystycznym i przemyslowym* (Historical, Statistical and Industrial Description of the City of Łódź), Warsaw[: Drukarnia Gazety,] 1853.

Dr. T. Rutowski, *W sprawie przemyslu krajowego* (On the Question of the Country's Industry), Kraków[: Drukarnia Zwiazkowa], 1883.

W. Zalęski, *Statystyka porównawcza Królewstwa Polskiego* (Comparative Statistics of the Kingdom of Poland), Warsaw, 1876.

J[an] Bloch, *Przemysl fabryczny Królewstwa Polskiego, 1871–1880* (The Factory Industry of the Kingdom of Poland. 1871–80), Warsaw[: Drukarni Cotty], 1884.

Encyklopedia Rolnicza (Agricultural Encyclopedia), Vol. 1, Warsaw[:Drukarnia Artystyczna Saturnina Sikorskiego], 1890; Vol. 2, Warsaw[: Drukarnia Artystyczna Saturnina Sikorskiego,] 1891; Vol. 3, Warsaw[: Drukarnia Artystyczna Saturnina Sikorskiego,] 1894.

---

* Where possible, we have provided the Polish and Russian titles of the works cited. Where we were not able to find the Polish or Russian original, we provide a translation of the title as given in German in the edition of the dissertation found in Luxemburg's *Gesammelte Werke*. The works are listed in the order in which they appear in the original list of writings. With some exceptions (such as Dementyev, Svyatlovsky, Yanzhul) the names of Russian authors have been given according to the US Library of Congress transliteration system. The system for transliterating names from the Russian alphabet into German, which of course was used by Luxemburg, differs substantially from systems for transliterating from Russian to English.

J[an] Bloch, *Landed Property and Its Indebtedness*, Warsaw, 1890.

J[an] Bloch, *O Selskokhozaistvennom Melioratzionnom Kreditye v Rossi i Inostrannykh Gosudarstvakh* (Agricultural Amelioration Credit in Russia and Foreign States), Warsaw, 1892.

J[an] Bloch, *The Peasants' Bank and Parcelization*, Warsaw, 1895.

L. Górski, *Our Mistakes in Agriculture*, Warsaw, 1874.

Dr. J[an] Banzemer, *Obraz przemyslu w kraju naszym* (A Picture of Industry in Our Country), Warsaw[: Drukarni Noskowskiego], 1886.

Magazines

(monthly)

Ateneum, Warsaw.

(weekly)

Przegląd Tygondniowy (Weekly Review), Warsaw.
Kraj (Our Country), St. Petersburg.
Prawda (Truth), Warsaw.

Newspapers

Gazeta Handlowa (Newpaper of Commerce), Warsaw.
Gazeta Polska (Newspaper of Poland), Warsaw.
Kurjer Warszawski (Warsaw Courier), Warsaw.

In Russian

M. Zaveleiskii, *Statistika Tsarstva polskogo* (Statistics of the Kingdom of Poland), St. Petersburg, 1842.

I. Poznanskii, *Proizvoditelnye sily Tsarstva polskogo* (Productive Forces of the Kingdom of Poland), St. Petersburg, 1880.

K. Lodyzhenskii, *Istoriia russkogo tamozhennogo tarifa* (History of the Russian Tariff). St. Petersburg, 1886.

Istoriko-statisticheskii obzor promyshlennosti Rossii (Historico-Statistical Review of the Industry of Russia), D. A. Timiriazev, ed., 2 vols., St. Petersburg, 1883.

Ivan I. Ianzhul, *Istoricheskii ocherk razvitiia fabrichno-zavodskoi promyshlennosti* (Historical Sketch of the Development of Factory Industry), Moscow, 1887.

Fabrichno-zavodskaia promyshlennost i torgovlia Rossii. Vsemirnaia kolumbova vystavka v Chikago 1893 (Factory Industry and Trade of Russia. Report for the Chicago World's Fair 1893), Departament Torgovli I Manufaktur Ministerstvo Finansov (issued by Department of Trade and Manufactures of the Ministry of Finances), St. Petersburg, 1893.

Zemledelie i Lesnaia Promyshlennost' Rossii. Vsemirnaia kolumbbova vystavka v Chikago 1893 (Russia's Agriculture and Forest Industry. Report for the Chicago World's Fair 1893), Rossiia, Departament Gornogo Dela, Ministervo Gosudarstvennykh imushchestv (issued by Russia's Department of Agriculture, Ministry of State Properties), St. Petersburg, 1893.

Gornaia Promyshlennost Roissii. Vsemirnaia kolumbbova vystavka v Chikago 1893 (Russia's Mining Industry. Report for the Chicago World's Fair 1893), Rossiia, Departament Gornog Dela, Ministervo Gosudarstvennykh imushchestv (issued by the Mining Department of Russia's Ministry of State Properties), St. Petersburg, 1893.

G. Simonenko, *Sravnitel'naia statistika Tsarstva Pol'skago I drugikh evropeiskikh stran* (Comparative Statistics of the Kingdom of Poland and of Other European Countries), Warsaw[: Tipografiia Meditsinskoi gazety], 1879.

Petitions by the Imperial Free Economic Society concerning the Revision of Russia's Tariffs, St. Petersburg, 1890.

P. A. Orlov, *A Register of the Factories of European Russia, including the Kingdom of Poland and the Grand Duchy of Finland,* St. Petersburg, 1881.

Materials on Trade and Industrial Statistics of Russia: Data concerning the Factory Industry in Russia for the Years 1885–1887, St. Petersburg: Trade Department of Russia's Ministry of Finance, 1889.

Materials on Trade and Industrial Statistics of Russia: Data concerning the Factory Industry in Russia for the Year 1888, St. Petersburg: Trade Department of Russia's Ministry of Finance, 1891.

Materials on Trade and Industrial Statistics of Russia: Data concerning the Factory Industry in Russia for the Year 1889, St. Petersburg: Trade Department of Russia's Ministry of Finance, 1891.

Materials on Trade and Industrial Statistics of Russia: Data concerning the Factory Industry in Russia for the Year 1890, St. Petersburg: Trade Department of Russia's Ministry of Finance, 1893.

Materials on Trade and Industrial Statistics of Russia: Data concerning the Factory Industry in Russia for the Year 1891, St. Petersburg: Trade Department of Russia's Ministry of Finance, 1894.

Materials on Trade and Industrial Statistics of Russia: Data concerning the Factory Industry in Russia for the Year 1892, St. Petersburg: Trade Department of Russia's Ministry of Finance, 1895.

Reports of the Members of the Commission for Investigation of the Factory Industry in the Kingdom of Poland, St. Petersburg, 1888.

A.S., *Bor'ba mezhdu Moskvoi y Lodzem* ('The Conflict between Moscow and Łódź), St. Petersburg, 1889.

Materialy po statistiki parovykh mashin v rossiiskoi imperii (Materials for Statistics on Steam Engines in the Russian Empire), Rossiia, Tsentral'nyi statisticheskii komitet (issued by the Central Statistical Committee of Russia), St. Petersburg, 1888.

Vladimir Sviatlovskii, *Fabrichnyi rabochii* (The Factory Worker), Warsaw, 1889.

Proizvoditel'nye sily Rossii (The Productive Forces of Russia. For the regional industrial exhibition at Nizhny Novgorod), Rossiia, Ministerstvo Finansov (issued by the Ministry of Finance), St. Petersburg, 1896.

S. Sharapov, *Sobranie sochinenii* (Collected Works), St. Petersburg, 1892.

I. I. Ianzhul, *Report of the Factory Inspector for the Moscow Region*, St. Petersburg, 1884.

I. I. Ianzhul, "The Factory Worker in Central Russia and in the Kingdom of Poland," in the monthly journal *Vestnik Evropy* (European Herald), St. Petersburg), Vol. 1, February issue, 1888.

K. V. Davydov, *Report of the Factory Inspector for the St. Petersburg Region*, St. Petersburg, 1886.

Dr. Peskov, *Report of the Factory Inspector for the Vladimir Region*, St. Petersburg, 1886.

Memorandum of the Warsaw Stock Exchange Commission, on railroad rates for grain. (This work not available from booksellers.*)

N. P. Iasnopol'skii, *Geograficheskoe raspredelenie istochnikov gosudarstvennykh dokhodov v Rossii* (Geographic Distribution of the Sources of State Revenues in Russia), Kiev, 1890.

Sibir' i sibirskaia magistral.' Vsemirnaia kolumbbova vystavka v Chikago 1893 (Siberia and the Great Siberian Railroad. Report for the World's Fair in Chicago), Rossiia, Departament Torgovli, Ministervto Finansov (issued by the the Department of Trade of Russia's Finance Ministry), St. Petersburg, 1893.

R. Mikhailov, "Investigation of Naphtha Residue," *Zapiski russkogo tekhnicheskogo obshchestva* or *Zapiski Imperatorskogo russkogo tekhnicheskogo obshchestva* (Proceedings of the Imperial Russian Technical Society), St. Petersburg, No. 1, January 1898.

Y[evstafy] M[ikhailovich] Dement'ev, *Fabrika: chto ona daet naseleniiu i chto ona u nee beret* (The Factory: What It Gives to the Population and What It Takes Away), Moscow, 1893.

Journals

Trudy Imperatorskogo Svobodnogo Ekonomicheskogo Obshchestva (Proceedings of the Imperial Free Economic Society), published twice a month in St. Peterburg.

Vestnik Finansov, Promyshlennosti i Torgovli (Bulletin of Finance, Industry, and Trade), published weekly in St. Petersburg by the Ministry of Finance.

Newspapers

Novosti (News), St. Petersburg.

Novoe Vremia (New Times), St. Petersburg.

---

*   That is, it was not circulated through the book trade.

Sibir (Siberia), St. Peterburg.

Sankt-Peterburgskie Vedomosti (St. Petersburg News), St. Petersburg.

Torgovo-Promyshlennaya Gazeta (Newspaper of Trade and Industry), St. Petersburg.

In other languages

Blue Book. Royal Commission on Labor, Foreign Reports, Vol. X, Russia, London[: Eyre and Spottiswoode,] 1894.

Th[omas] Brassey, *Work and Wages* [London: Bell and Daldry,] 1872.

Diplomatic and Consular Reports [on Trade and Finance]. [British] Foreign Office. Annual Series:

On the Trade of the Kingdom of Poland, No. 128 [London: Her Majestry's Stationary Office], 1887.

On the Trade of Warsaw, No. 321 [London: Her Majestry's Stationary Office,] 1888.

On the Trade of Poland, No. 1286 [London: Her Majestry's Stationary Office,] 1893.

On the Trade of the District of the Consulate-General at Warsaw, No. 863 [London: Her Majestry's Stationary Office,] 1891.

On the Trade of the District of the Consulate-General at Warsaw, No. 1183 [London: Her Majestry's Stationary Office,] 1893.

On the Trade of the District of the Consulate-General at Warsaw, No. 1449 [London: Her Majestry's Stationary Office,] 1894.

On the Trade of the District of the Consulate-General at Warsaw, No. 1535 [London: Her Majestry's Stationary Office,] 1895.

Foreign Office. Miscellaneous Series Reports:

On the Peasantry and Peasant Holdings in Poland, No. 355 [London: Her Majestry's Stationary Office,] 1985.

On the Position of Landed Proprietors in Poland, No. 347 [London: Her Majestry's Stationary Office,] 1895.

[Gerhart von] Schulze-Gävernitz, "Der Nationalismus in Russland und seine wirtschaftlichen Träger" (Nationalism in Russia and Its Economic Spokesmen), *Preussische Jahrbücher* (Prussian Yearbooks), Vol. 75, Jan.–March, 1894.

S. G., "Die industrielle Politik Russlands in dessen polnischen Provinzen" (The Industrial Policy of Russia in Its Polish Provinces), *Neue Zeit* (Stuttgart), 1893–94, Vol. II, No. 51.

Karl Marx, *Das Kapital: Kritik der politischen Ökonomie*, Vol. 3, Hamburg[:Otto Meissner], 1890.

L[ujo] Brentano, *Über das Verhältnis von Arbeitslohn und Arbeitszeit zur Arbeitsleistung* (On the Relation of Wages and Labor Time to Productivity), Leipzig[: Duncker & Humboldt], 1893.

Back to Adam Smith!*

Previously in this venue Ed[uard] Bernstein reviewed an earlier work by Dr. [Richard] Schüller on "Classical Political Economy and its Antagonists";† now a continuation of these studies has appeared under the title "The Political Economy [*Wirtschaftspolitik*] of the Historical School."‡

The theme in itself is, without a doubt and for several reasons, among the most interesting. Above all, this is because the historical school§ essentially represents the only real national product of the German bourgeoisie in the area of economic theory. In Germany, as elsewhere, the classical liberal period was simply an offshoot of English classicism; but the romantic course of [Karl Ludwig von] Haller and [Adam Heinrich] Müller, however influential it may have been in practice, hardly deserves to be called a school of political economy.¶ [Haller and Müller] made no attempt to advance a positive economic theory and seemingly [their] only literate adherent was, as far as we know, the famous [Karl Ernst] Jarcke who, according to [Ludwig] Börne, was called to the Austrian council from its Prussian counterpart in order to advocate Metternichian policies.** Likewise, [Friedrich] List's "national system" of political economy must be seen rather as a dilettantish attempt than a theoretical doctrine.†† Only the

---

* This essay originally appeared in *Die Neue Zeit*, Year 18, 1899/1900, Volume II, pp. 180–6.

† Richard Schüller was a bourgeois economist associated with the neo-classical Austrian School of economics. See his *Die klassische Nationalökonomie und ihre Gegner. Zur Geschichte der Nationalökonomie und Socialpolitik seit A. Smith* (Classical and Political Economy and its Enemies: On the History of Political Economy and Social Policy Since Adam Smith) (Berlin: C. Heymann, 1895). For Bernstein's review of this work, see "Die klassiche Nationalöknomie und ihrer Gegner," *Die Neue Zeit*, Year 13, 1894/95, Vol. 2, pp. 211–14.

‡ See Richard Schüller, *Die Wirtschaftspolitik der Historischen Schule* (The Political Economy of the Historical School), (Berlin: C. Heymann, 1899).

§ On the historical school of economics see endnote 2 on p. 89 [in *Introduction to Political Economy*].

¶ The "romantic course" in economic theory refers to those who opposed the goals of the French Revolution and industrial capitalism in the name of traditional values. The economic romantics also tended to deny that societies operate according to general economic laws. Haller and Müller were both political reactionaries, resembling in some respects the positions of English theorist Edmund Burke and the French writer and racialist Joseph de Maistre. See Haller's *Restauration der Staatswissenschaft oder Theorie des naturich-geselligen Zustandes* (Restoration of the Science of the State, or the Theory of the State of Nature) (Winterthur: Steiner, 1816–34) and Müller's *Von der Notwendigkeit einer theologischen Grundlage der gesamten Staatswissenschaften* (On the Necessity of a Comprehensive Theological Foundation for Political Science) (Leipzig, 1819).

** Karl Ernst Jarcke, a political and social conservative, originally from Prussia, accepted Metternich's offer to serve in the Austrian government in the 1830s. His main contribution, like that of Haller and Müller, was to extol the virtues of medieval society as superior to the democratizing tendencies of the modern world. See Jarcke's *Handbuch des gemeinen deutschen Strafrechts* (Handbook of German Common Criminal Law) (Berlin: Ferdinand Dümmler, 1830).

†† Marx criticized List as follows: "The whole theoretical part of List's system is nothing but a

historical school offered an entire system of economic doctrine and acquired a numerous following of disciplinary experts and practical men.

It should be added, moreover, that in its internal history the historical school presents an accurate mirror image of the history of the German bourgeoisie. A study of the doctrines, methods, and developmental phases of this school would at the same time deliver a sketch of the development of the German bourgeoisie itself—if, that is, it were treated in relation to the facts of economic and social life.

That Dr. Schüller conceived his task in the manner that we have described cannot at all be confirmed. What he offers is rather a very sketchy series of portraits of significant classical-liberal, reactionary-romantic and historical theoreticians, to which is attached a bundle of general observations, equally simply thrown together, about the different methods of those theoretical tendencies.

Dr. Schüller fully correctly points to the *deductive method* of research as the most salient characteristic of classical-liberal political economy, and also as the basis of the progressive effects of its practice. Equally correct is his assertion that the abandonment of the deductive research method would have as its consequence the lack of any firm principles; and this would result in theoretical infertility and political-economic backwardness. Schüller's whole thing is a warm plea for the method of classical economics and an appeal to today's economists to return to this method. But why the historical school abandoned the research methods of the classicists and how, considering their shallowness and backwardness, to explain their broad and long-lasting influence in German national-economy—to these questions we find no answer from Dr. Schüller. And yet, only through a palpable explication of these questions can something palpable become of Schüller's appeal to contemporary economists in which his entire analysis culminates.

The undivided dominance of the classical economic doctrine at the beginning of our century, even in Germany, is generally known. It is not at all much of an exaggeration, that, as [Alexander von der] Marwitz wrote to Rahel [Varnhagen] in the year 1810, next to Napoleon, Ad[am] Smith is the most powerful monarch in Europe.[*] In Prussia all the statesmen of the Stein–Hardenberg period[†] were students of Ad[am] Smith. Most of official government

---

disguising of the industrial materialism of frank political economy in idealistic phrases. Everywhere he allows the thing to remain in existence but idealizes the expression of it." See "On Friedrich List's Book *Das Nationale System de Politischen Ökonomie,*" in *Marx-Engels Collected Works*, Vol. 4 (New York: International Publishers, 1975), pp. 265–94.

[*]   Alexander von der Marwitz (1787–1814) was a Prussian nobleman; in 1809 he became a friend and lover of Rahel Varnhagen, with whom he carried on an active correspondence. Varnhagen was a prolific writer, critic, and feminist; her *Collected Works* comprise 10 volumes. For more on Varnhagen, see Hannah Arendt, *Rahel Varnhagen: Life Story of a Jewess* (Baltimore: John Hopkins University Press, 2000).

[†]   The Stein–Hardenberg period refers to the reforms of the Prussian state and society

proclamations bear the clear stamp of the classical doctrine. Indeed, even the high ranks of the military—[August Neidhardt von] Gneisenau, [Gerhard von] Scharnhorst, [Job von] Witzleben*—were warm followers of classical liberalism. Smith's theories were the Bible of the entire reform period in Germany that for a short time following the disaster at Jena challenged the hardcore reaction.†

But precisely therein lay the reason why these theories had to lead to opposition. The progressive Stein–Hardenberg reforms arose not from a strong bourgeois movement, not from the society itself. They were rather elicited from the ruling circles by the French attacks and simply imposed by those social circles. Then they soon called forth opposition from two camps: on the one hand, from the side of the feudal Junker class for whom it was a matter of preserving serfdom and, on the other hand, from those elements of the middle class that felt themselves and their interests threatened by the modern reforms, mainly from the artisan class that was still strong at that time but that was severely damaged by the abolition of the guild order and also by the English imports favored by liberal trade policy.

In the first case the opposition expressed itself in Haller's and Müller's reactionary-romantic direction; in the latter, in the older historical school of [Friedrich Julius Heinrich] Soden, [Heinrich] Luden, [Friedrich von] Cölln among others.‡ If in both cases one takes into account the nature of the social

---

promoted by Karl Freiherr vom Stein and Karl August Fürst von Hardenberg following the defeat of Prussia by Napoleon's forces in 1807. The reforms were based on Enlightenment ideals and led to the abolition of serfdom and suppression of guild monopolies. By 1820 this reform movement largely came to an end.

 * Scharnhorst, Gneisenau and Witzleben served as Prussian officers during the Battle of Jena in 1806, when Napoleon's France decisively defeated Prussia. In response, they supported a series of reforms to modernize the Prussian military. Scharnhorst promoted the reorganization of its military from a professional force of noblemen to a national army based on universal service. Gneisenau worked closely with Scharnhorst in promoting these and other reforms, often in the face of opposition from King Friedrich Wilhelm of Prussia. Witzleben allied himself with Scharnhorst's reform efforts with his 1807 book *Ideas on the Reorganization of the Light Infantry*. For more on these efforts to reform the Prussian military, see William McNeill, *The Pursuit of Power: Technology, Armed Force, and Society* (Chicago: University of Chicago Press, 1982), pp. 218–50 especially.

 † In the double battle of Jena and Auerstedt on October 14, 1806, the two main armies of the reactionary Prussian state were defeated by Napoleon's troops. Prussia's defeat prompted a move on the part of a number of its leading intellectuals, politicians and military leaders to implement liberal reforms in Prussia, which was still functioning along feudal lines. This period of reform proved of critical importance in transforming Prussia into a modern state.

 ‡ Friedrich Julius Heinrich, Graf von Soden wrote several works on economics in which he critically discussed the work of Adam Smith. In contrast to Smith's emphasis on the difference between use-value and exchange-value, Soden maintained that the fundamental distinction was between "positive value" and "comparative value"; only the former, he held, is value in the true sense of the word. See his *Nazional-Ökonomie* (National Economics) (Leipzig: J.A. Barth, 1805). Heinrich Luden criticized Smith's work in his *Handbuch der Staatsweisheit oder de Politik* (Manual of Statecraft or Politics) (Jena: Frommann, 1811). Friedrich von Cölln served as an official of the Prussian government during the Napoleonic Wars and was primarily responsible for formulating

foundation from which the two economic directions rebelling against the classical school emerged, then their different theoretical character is easily explained.

The rebellious Junkers, whose protest against the inauguration of bourgeois development found its expression in Haller's romantic school, posited against the reforms that they criticized a very particular, consistent "ideal" medieval feudalism. Just as clear, consistent, and powerful as the Metternichian reaction, as the era of the Holy Alliance,* was the theoretical expression of this politics: the economic theory of the romantic school. It proceeded from certain firm "principles," namely from the principles of the feudal natural economy, that were consistently applied to all questions of political economy.

It was otherwise in the second oppositional camp. If the existence of the middle-class guild-stratum, the master artisans and tradesmen, was threatened by the innovations, it could, on the other hand, not possibly yearn for the times of the undivided rule of feudalism whose iron force left it with bloody wounds. These elements were capable of formulating a specific, positive political-economic programme in the same small degree that they themselves formed a closed social whole. Fluctuating between modern bourgeois development and feudal tradition, fearing the detriments of the one as much as those of the other, they only managed to combat now liberal political economics from a feudal standpoint, then the romantic theories from a liberal standpoint, always reject-ing the consequences of the starting point and getting stuck somewhere in the middle.

The character of the later historical school founded by [Bruno] Hildebrand and [Wilhelm] Roscher is fundamentally different.† If in the earlier case we see the petite bourgeoisie of the guilds protesting against the emerging bourgeois order in the name of the medieval mode of production, now it is the modern bourgeoisie itself that raises an objection to the consequences of its own class rule.

---

taxation policy. After the Battle of Jena he became a firm supporter of the Stein–Hardenberg reforms. See his *Vertrauten Briefe über die inner Verhältnisse am preußischen Hofe siet dem Tode Friedrichs II* (Familiar Letters on the Internal Relations of the Prussian Court Since the Death of Frederick II) (Amsterdam: Peter Hammer, 1807).

* The Holy Alliance was a coalition of Russia, Austria and Prussia, formed in 1815, for the purpose of safeguarding against further European revolutions. It essentially went out of existence in 1825, due to differences between its respective members.

† Wilhelm Roscher is considered the founder of the historical school. The historical school did not share the romantic attachment for the feudal past that Luxemburg criticizes above. Roscher drew more heavily on Smith's ideas than did other members of the older historical school, such as Hildebrand, even though he differed from Smith in numerous respects. He especially held that the classical political economists placed too much emphasis on production and not enough on consumption. Like Hildebrand, Knies, and other members of the older historical school, he opposed Smith's model of perfect competition in favor of emphasizing historical contingency and variability.

With inexorable logic, classical political economy led in the end to an about-face toward self-criticism, toward a critique of the bourgeois order. In England, Ricardo represents the immediate starting point of an entire school of English socialists ([William] Thompson, [John] Gray, [John Francis] Bray, among others); in France [Jean Charles Léonard de] Sismondi follows in the footsteps of [Jean-Baptiste] Say, the first diluter of classical economy; in Germany we find socialist tones already in [Karl Heinrich] Rau, who was followed by [Johann Heinrich von] Thünen und [Johann Karl] Rodbertus;* with Marx the about-face of classical economy into its opposite, the socialist analysis of capitalism, is completed.

One could repudiate the socialist critique, and its consequences, only if one had transcended the starting point, classical economics. The results of the investigation of the bourgeois commodity economy, as the classical doctrine proffered them in a tightly bound system, did not let themselves simply be either corrected or negated. There remained no possibility other than to combat the investigation itself, its method. If the goal of classical economics was knowledge of the foundations and fundamental principles of the bourgeois economy, the historical [school] conversely set as its task the mystification of the internal relations of this economy. For the old historical school, the aversion to the "levelling" or "categorical" [character] of classical liberalism† was merely a protest on behalf of medieval diversification and specialization of the relations that corresponded to the social character of the pre-capitalist mode of production. Here, for Roscher-[Karl] Knies-Hildebrand, the "historical" critique of the classical "absolute theories" is a protest of bourgeois society against the recognition of its own inner laws.‡ Because the purpose, the "historical" calling, the *raison d'être*, of the newer historical school was the veiling of these laws, it thus elevates the *misrecognition* [*Verkennung*] of the laws of social economy to a scientific dogma, to an economic method.

Suum cuique:§ The upsurge of the English bourgeoisie was reflected in the

---

* William Thompson, John Gray and John Francis Bray utilized Smith and Ricardo's labor theory of value to attack the unequal distribution of income that characterizes capitalist society. Karl Heinrich Rau was Wilhelm Roscher's teacher and mentor. A follower of Adam Smith, he placed greater emphasis on the potential role of the state in redressing economic inequality. See his *Lehrbuch der politischen Ökonomie* (Principles of Political Economy) (Leipzig and Heidleberg: C.J. Winter Verlag, 1863). Johann Heinrich von Thünen was not a socialist, though he was critical of the fact that the remuneration of the industrialist is always much greater than that of the workers. See Thünen's *Der isolierte Staat in Beziehung auf Landwirtschaft und Nationaloekonomie* (The Isolated State in Relation to Agriculture and Political Economy), edited by Walter Braueur and Eberhard E.A. Gerhardt (Darmstadt: Wissenschaftliche Buchgesellschaft, 1966 [orig. 1826]).

† The "old" historical school refers to its earliest proponents, which included Wilhelm Roscher, Karl Knies, and Bruno Hildebrand. They opposed the "leveling" or "categorical" character of classical political economy in so far as they rejected the universal validity of economic laws.

‡ Although Knies (like Roscher and Hildebrand) was critical of aspects of bourgeois society, he never considered himself any kind of socialist.

§ Latin for "to each its own."

erection of the grandiose doctrinal edifice of the classical school, in the creation of political economy; the emergence of the German bourgeoisie found its intellectual expression in the self-decomposition and abdication of economics as a science.

Sufficient reason for the historical school's lack of principles, which Dr. Schüller justly chastised although without plausible explanation, is found in the actual historical relations in Germany, in the history of the bourgeoisie, in the increasingly glaring class antagonisms. And likewise, the fact that Roscher's school, despite its pitiful scientific condition and practical sterility, could succeed in attaining such widespread influence is much better explained by the same actual relations than by the circumstance that "the principle directions of the economic and social questions of the present are still in caught up in developmental flux."

Exactly the opposite! Not because the socialist doctrine of political economy (for this is clearly the principle tendency corresponding to the social questions of the present) had not yet emerged, but because it had already attained a high level of development, i.e. it was against this doctrine that the historical school arose in reaction.

Because he does not treat the question in relation to its social foundation, Dr. Schüller commits the double error: for one, of considering the old historical direction in the first decades of the century as one and the same school as that of Roscher whose doctrine was fundamentally different; and furthermore of situating the latter as a result of the absence of a socialist tendency [*Richtung*] rather than conversely as a reaction against the socialist critique.

Dr. Schüller's study wants to be more than a scientific monograph. As we have already mentioned, it fades off into the appeal that the current generation of German economists might return to the methods of classical economy if it wants instead to approach the problems of contemporary social life with the same understanding that the classicists brought to the problems of their time.

This well-meaning appeal, "Back to the Classical Method!"—which clearly represents the guiding thoughts of both of Schüller's economic works—is doubtless very congenial as a desire to bring a fresh draft of air into the stuffy atmosphere of contemporary German political economy. Only, with this advice Dr. Schüller displays once again that, because of his treatment of economic problems apart from their relation to their respective social foundation, the understanding of both the essence of the classical school that he so admired and of contemporary tasks eludes him.

Dr. Schüller traces the greatness of classical economics back to its deductive method, to its treatment of economic problems according to principles. But the deductive method, taken abstractly, is a purely formal scholastic method that says absolutely nothing about the essence of the research method practiced by the Smith's school. If it were just a matter of a "dragging in of universal, preconceived principles into research," then there are still many others who could be seen alongside the classical economists. If, as formulated by Dr. Schüller, the deductive principles of Smith and Ricardo are called economic freedom, labor mobility, and free trade, then the same could be said of Adam Müller's and Haller's patrimonial jurisdiction, serfdom, patriarchal state, etc. As deductions, they are methodologically of equal value. But no one at this time preached such weighty denunciations of the historical school's lack of principles, no one preached with such pathos the necessity of "eternal laws" as the starting point of economic analysis, as did precisely the romantic school.

If therefore the deductive method of classical economics led to the deep understanding of the bourgeois economy, while Haller's and Müller's romantic deductions led only to great esteem for their bearers from the crown prince Friedrich-Wilhelm IV and from Metternich, then that obviously lies in the fact that the classical-liberal deductions corresponded to social development of their time, because they corresponded to the essence of the bourgeois economy.

However, because the general foundations of the bourgeois economy became the absolute "principles" of Ad[am] Smith's and [David] Ricardo's research, for the classicists the modern commodity economy came to represent the absolute, the *normal human* [economy]. And this was the actual basic principle from which they proceeded; this was the real secret of their miracle-working deductive method.

It was precisely this unlimited and fully untroubled belief in what is human normality, in, so to speak, the natural right of the capitalist commodity economy, that allowed the classical political economists that lack of self-examination [*Unbefangenheit*] in research, that lack of consideration of the consequences, that audacious flight to the heights from which they captured with a genial glance the internal relations of the bourgeois mode of production.

The doubts that later arose about the bourgeois order produced on the one hand the vulgar-economic apologists who turned their gaze away from research into the general laws to the rationalization of individual occurrences and, on the other hand, the resignation of the historical school that rejected in advance any research into the foundations of the economy and declared the task of economic science to be the simple description of that which has been and that which is. The bourgeois mode of production forms the foundation and the starting point of all of these economic schools. The belief in the absoluteness and normality of the bourgeois order, however, is peculiar to the classical school, which is precisely what made it *classical*.

This circumstance explains not only the general scientific successes of Smith's school, but also the specific characteristics of its research methods. Cosmopolitanism, the levelling treatment of people, the individualism, the notion of economic self-interest as the sole foundation of all actions, etc., everything that its historical critics attribute to it and chastise as sinful, derives from the same notion of the universal human normality of the capitalist commodity economy, of the commodity producer as the normal human being *par excellence*.

Only, it was this same notion that set certain objective limits to the research of Smith's school—its subjectively unabashed nature, wholly lacking in self-examination. The innermost essence of the bourgeois mode of production, its real secret, can only be deciphered when it is studied in motion, in its historical relativity. And it is precisely this that is excluded *a priori* by the conception of the commodity economy as the normal, absolute form of social production.

Let us take an example. Untroubled by any social consequences, classical economics saw human labor as the single value-producing factor and pursued this theory through to that crystallized clarity that we find in Ricardo's formulation.

But the fundamental difference between Ricardo's and Marx's labor theory of value—a difference not only misunderstood by bourgeois economics, but also mostly misjudged in the popularization of Marx's doctrine—is that Ricardo, corresponding to his universal, natural-rights conception of the bourgeois economy, also held the creation of value to be a *natural* attribute of human labor, of the individual, concrete labor of individual people.[1]

Marx, on the other hand, recognized value as an *abstraction*, an abstraction made by the society under particular conditions, and arrived thereby at a differentiation of the two sides of commodity-producing labor: concrete, individual labor and undifferentiated social labor—a differentiation from which the solution to the *money riddle* springs to the eye as though illuminated by the glow of a bulls-eye lantern.[*]

In order, however, to keep separate the dual character of labor—the laboring people and the value-creating commodity producers— that sat together *statically* in the lap of the bourgeois economy, Marx already had to differentiate *dynamically*, in the sequence of historical time, the commodity producer from the working individual in general, that is, to recognize commodity production as simply a historically particular form of social production. In a word: in order to decipher the hieroglyphics of the capitalist economy, Marx had to approach his research with a deduction *diametrically opposed* to that of the classicists: instead of approaching the matter with the belief in the bourgeois mode of production as the human norm, he approached it with the insight into its historical

---

[*]   Luxemburg is closely following the argument in Chapter 1 of Marx's *Capital* Vol. 1, in which he wrote: "However, the labor that forms the substance of value is equal human labor, the expenditure of identical human labor-power. The total labor-power of society, which is manifested in the values of the world of commodities, counts here as one homogeneous mass of human labor-power ... I was the first to point out and examine critically this twofold nature of the labor contained in commodities. As this point is crucial to an understanding of political economy, it requires further elucidation." See Marx's *Capital* Vol. 1, translated by Ben Fowkes (New York: Penguin Books, 1976), pp. 129, 132.

transitoriness; he had to invert the *metaphysical deduction* of the classicists into its opposite—into the *dialectical.*

The progress of political economy beyond Smith–Ricardo, its further development, was thus brought about precisely by *overcoming* the deductive method of this school, the return to which Schüller preaches still today. This not only because this method, as noted, sets solid limits on knowledge, but also because these limits had already been reached by the classicists. In Ricardo's doctrine the classical economic method had already achieved the most of which it was capable, and it was thrown into the dustbin, not merely as an dangerous instrument that turned against the society being studied, but also as one that was scientifically spent. A return to the method of the classical school would not lead to a new upswing in economics, as Dr. Schüller opines, but would affect a giant retreat. That such a return is *scientifically* impossible is proven precisely by Marx's work that represents a direct continuation of the classical doctrine.

But this return is also *socially* impossible. And this is proven on the other hand by the degeneration of the science of classical economics into both vulgar economics and the historical school. Since the rise of these tendencies, the social relations that have undermined that sanguine classical belief in the absolute character of the capitalist commodity economy have only developed further and in the same direction. Not only are class antagonisms visibly becoming incomparably more glaring, but the self-negation of the capitalist mode of production has also become an obvious fact. It is impossible again to make free trade into the starting point of bourgeois economic policy that it once was while a general return to protective tariffs was taking place; it is just as impossible to begin with the dogma of free competition while production is being increasingly monopolized by cartels. Today, the "principles" of Adam Smith and Ricardo belong, both scientifically and also socially, to the past.

Schüller's exhortation (not sounded for the first time) to return to the method of classical economics is interesting moreover as a fragment of that general "return" that seems to be the watchword of bourgeois social science. Back to Kant in philosophy,† back to Adam Smith in economics! A convulsive

---

*   In *Reform or Revolution*, written in the same period as this article, Luxemburg likewise stated: "The secret of Marx's theory of value, his analysis of money, his theory of capital, his theory of the rate of profit, and consequently of the whole existing economic system is the transitory nature of the capitalist economy, its collapse: thus—and this is only another aspect of the same phenomena—the final goal, socialism. And precisely because, *a priori*, Marx looked at capitalism from the socialist's viewpoint, that is, from the historical viewpoint, he was enabled to decipher the hieroglyphics of capitalist economy." See *Reform or Revolution*, in *The Rosa Luxemburg Reader*, p. 151.

†   The call to go "back to Kant" was raised by a number of German philosophers in the 1860s as part of an effort to combat the legacy of Hegel's dialectical idealism. It led to the German neo-Kantian revival, which dominated central Europe thought until the 1920s. The neo-Kantian movement strongly influenced the thought of Eduard Bernstein and the Austro-Marxists, part of which (as seen in the work of Hermann Cohen, among others) explicitly embraced a moderate

reaching backward toward already superseded positions that is a reliable sign of the hopelessness into which the bourgeoisie has strayed, intellectually as well as socially. But there is no return—just as little in science as in the actual development of society.

But there is only a "forward" along the path of the *dialectical method* that Marx has already taken. All those young political economists, who are, like Dr. Schüller, genuine enough not to find satisfaction in the muddle, in the lack of system or intellect and of the head in contemporary bourgeois economics, and [who are] brave enough to sacrifice class prejudice to scientific knowledge, must become clear about this. Bourgeois theoreticians have for decades been forced to feed upon Marx's doctrine from which every halfway clever thought that appears among them is directly or indirectly derived.[2]

Just as bourgeois society has before it only the alternative of developing into a socialist society or perishing, so too has political economy only the choice of proceeding along the track opened by Marx or declaring its bankruptcy as a science.

---

version of socialism. For more on this, see Timothy Keck, *Kant and Socialism: The Marburg School in Wilhelmian Germany* (Madison: University of Wisconsin Press, 1975); and Michael Friedman's two books, *The Kantian Legacy in Nineteenth Century Science* (Cambridge: MIT Press, 2006) and *A Parting of the Ways: Carnap, Cassirer, and Heidegger* (Chicago: Open Court, 2000).

Introduction to Political Economy[*]

I. WHAT IS POLITICAL ECONOMY?

1

Political economy is a curious science. Difficulties and conflicting opinions arise at the very first step on its terrain, with the most basic question of all: What is the specific object of this science? The simple worker, who has only a rather vague idea of what political economy teaches, will ascribe his lack of understanding to his own inadequate general education. Yet, in some respects, he shares his misfortune here with many learned doctors and professors, who write thick volumes about political economy and deliver lectures to young people studying at the universities. Incredible as it sounds, the fact is that most specialists in political economy themselves have a very confused notion as to what the real object of their specialism is.

Since it is the custom for these learned gentlemen to work with definitions, that is, to reduce the nature of the most complex things to a few well-ordered sentences, we shall seek by way of example to find out from one official representative of political economy what this science is basically about. Let us listen first of all to what the doyen of the German professorial world, the author of countless frightfully thick textbooks on political economy, the founder of the so-called "historical school,"[†] Wilhelm Roscher, has to say on the subject. In his

---

[*] This unfinished manuscript of 1909–10 grew out of Rosa Luxemburg's lecture course at the SPD party school. It was originally designed for publication in eight pamphlets as well as in book form. Luxemburg described its conception as follows: "General title: *Introduction to Political Economy*. Subtitles for the pamphlets: 1) What Is Political Economy?; 2) Social Labor; 3) Material on Economic History (primitive communism, slave economy, *corvée* economy, guild commerce); 4) Exchange; 5) Wage Labor; 6) The Rule of Capital (rate of profit); 7) Crises; 8) Tendencies of the Capitalist Economy" (Róza Luksemburg, *Listy do Leona Jogichesa-Tyski*, 3 vols, Warsaw 1971, p. 98). Her decision to embark on *The Accumulation of Capital* led Luxemburg to break off work on the "Introduction," and she did not take up the project again until her imprisonment at Wronke in 1916. Luxemburg maintained the original basic conception, but now envisaged it as ten pamphlets. This incomplete text was eventually published by Paul Levi in 1925. The six chapters of the manuscript bear the numbers I, III, IV, III, IV and VII, which reflect the changes she made working on the manuscript.

[†] The historical school of economics emerged in Germany in the 1840s as a reaction against the classical political economy of Smith and Ricardo. It dominated much of German academic economic thought for the rest of the century. It is generally divided into three phases: the older historical school, comprising Wilhelm Roscher, Bruno Hildebrand, and Karl Knies; the Younger School, comprising Gustav von Schmoller and Adolph Wagner, and the Youngest School, comprising Werner Sombart and Max Weber. The historical school rejected universal theoretical systems and denied the capitalist economy could be understood in terms of an underlying universal logic or set of laws. They emphasized instead local, cultural, and historical influences on economic behavior. Its thinkers also differed from Smith and Ricardo in placing greater emphasis on the state in fostering economic development. In this qualified sense, some of its proponents considered

first major work, *Grundlagen der Nationalökonomie. Ein Hand- und Lesebuch für Geschäftsmänner und Studierende* [Fundamentals of Political Economy. A Handbook and Textbook for Businessmen and Students], which appeared in 1854 and has since gone through twenty-three editions, we read in Chapter 2, paragraph 16:

> We understand by political economy the theory of national economic life, the theory of the laws of development of the national economy, of the economic life of the nation (philosophy of national economic history according to [Hans Karl Emil] von Mangoldt).* This links up in one direction, like all sciences of national life, with consideration of the individual person; it expands in the other sense to the study of humanity as a whole.†

Does this help "businessmen and students" understand what "national economic theory" is? It is precisely—the theory of national economy.‡ What are horn-rimmed spectacles? Spectacles with a horn-rim. What is a pack-ass? An ass on which burdens are packed. An extremely simple procedure, in fact, for explaining to little children the use of compound words. The only trouble is that anyone who does not already know the meaning of the words in question will be none the wiser, no matter which way round the words are placed.

Let us turn to another German scholar, who currently teaches political economy at the University of Berlin, a luminary of official science famous "far across the land, down to the blue sea," in other words Professor [Gustav von] Schmoller. In the great collective work of German professors edited by Professors [Johannes] Conrad and [Wilhelm] Lexis, *Handwörterbuch der Staatswissenschaften* [Concise Dictionary of the Political Sciences],§ Schmoller

---

themselves to be socialists, although they were hostile to the revolutionary socialist aspirations of Marx and the Marxists.

   * Hans Karl Emil von Mangoldt is primarily known for his theory of prices. See especially his *Grundriss der Volkswirthschaftslehre* (Outlines of Economic Doctrine) (Stuttgart: Engelhorn, 1863).

   † Wilhem Roscher, *Grundlagen der Nationalökonomie, Ein Hand- und Lesebuch für Geschäftsmänner und Studierende* (Foundations of Economics: A Handbook and Guide for Businessmen and Students) (Stuttgart: Cotta, 1900), p. 41. For an English translation, see *Principles of Political Economy* (New York: Arno Press, 1878).

   ‡ The German term for "political economy" (*Nationalökonomie*), literally translated, is "national economy." Hence, as Luxemburg indicates, it is circular to "define" *Nationalökomonie* as the theory of the economy of a given nation.

   § The *Handwörterbuch der Staatswissenschaften* was an important resource in late nineteenth and early twentieth century German economic thought. It was published in four editions. The first edition appeared from 1890 to 1895, the second from 1895 to 1901, the third edition between 1909 and 1911, and the fourth and final edition from 1923 to 1929. The first three editions were edited by Johannes Conrad, Wilhelm Lexis, L. Elster, and Edgar Loening, who were part of the Verein für Sozialpolitik (The Association for Social Politics). For more on this influential publication, see Vitantonio Gioia, "Arthur Spiethoff: From Economic Crisis to Business Cycle Theory," in *Crises and Cycles in Economic Dictionaries and Encyclopedias*, edited by Daniele Besomi (London and New York: Routledge, 2012), pp. 361–2.

gives the following answer to the question what this science might be, in an essay on economic theory:

> I would say that it is the science that seeks to describe, define, and explain in causal terms national economic phenomena as a coherent whole, which naturally presupposes that national economy has already been correctly defined. At the center of this science stand those phenomena of division and organization of labor, of commerce and the distribution of income, of social economic institutions, supported by particular forms of private and public law, that are typically found among present-day civilized peoples, and that, controlled by the same or similar mental forces, produce similar or identical arrangements or forces, presenting in their total description a statics of the present economic civilized world, a kind of average constellation. Starting from this point, the science has gone on to investigate the differences between particular national economies, the various forms of organization here and there, and thus to inquire as to the combination and series in which these different forms emerge, and has in this way come to the notion of a causal development of forms and a historical succession of economic conditions; it has thus added to the static treatment a dynamic one. And as, from its first appearance, it already came by way of ethical-historical value judgments to the positing of ideals, it has continued to maintain this practical function to a certain degree. Alongside theory, it has posited practical lessons for life.[1]

Phew! Let's pause for breath. What was all that? Social economic arrangements—private and public law—mental forces—similar and the same—the same and similar—statistics—statics—dynamics—average constellation—causal development—ethical-historical value judgments ... For ordinary mortals, this has the same numbing effect as a millwheel turning in the brain. In his insistent drive for knowledge, and his blind confidence in the spring of professorial wisdom, he makes the painful effort of going through the whole nonsense twice and three times, trying to extract some conceivable meaning. Unfortunately this is all needless trouble. What we're offered is precisely nothing but echoing phrases, hollow words screwed together. An unmistakable sign of this is that anyone who thinks clearly, and has a genuine mastery of his subject matter, also expresses himself clearly and understandably. Someone who expresses himself in obscure and high-flown terms, if he is not a pure philosophical idea-constructor or a fantasist of religious mysticism, only shows that he is himself unclear about the matter, or has reason to avoid clarity. We shall go on to show that the obscure and confusing language of bourgeois scholars as to the nature of political economy is not accidental, but actually expresses two things: both the unclearness of these gentlemen themselves, and their tendentious, stubborn rejection of a real explanation of the question.

That the clear definition of the nature of political economy is indeed a contentious question is suggested by a certain external circumstance. This is the fact that the most contradictory views are expressed as to the *age* of this science. For example, the late Adolphe Blanqui—a well-known historian and professor of political economy at the University of Paris, and brother of the famous socialist leader and Commune fighter Auguste Blanqui*— started the first chapter of his *History of Political Economy,*† published in 1837, with the following epigraph: "Political economy is older than people think. The Greeks and the Romans already had their own." Other writers on the history of political economy, however, for instance the former *Dozent* at the University of Berlin, Eugen Dühring, consider it important to stress that political economy is much younger than people generally believe: according to them, this science only properly arose in the second half of the eighteenth century.[2]

To cite socialist judgments on this question, Lassalle in the preface to his classic polemical text of 1864 against Schulze-Delitzsch, *Kapital und Arbeit* [Capital and Labor], made the following assertion: "Political economy is a science that is only at its beginnings and still to be constructed."‡ Karl Marx, for his part, gave the first volume of his economic masterwork *Capital* that appeared three years later, representing the fulfillment of the expectation expressed by Lassalle, the subtitle "Critique of Political Economy." In this way, Marx placed his own work outside the previous political economy, considering this as something confined and superseded, and setting out to criticize it. It is clear that a science that one lot of people maintain is almost as old as the written history of humanity, a second lot that it is scarcely a century and a half old, a third lot that it is still in diapers, and others again that it has already run its course and the time has come for its critical burial—it is clear that such a science presents a rather peculiar and tangled problem.

We would receive equally poor advice if we were to ask one of the official representatives of this science to explain the remarkable fact that political economy, as currently prevailing opinion holds, only arose so late, scarcely a hundred and fifty years ago. Professor Dühring, for example, in a great flood of words, argues that the ancient Greeks and Romans had scarcely any scientific

---

*   Auguste Blanqui actually did not directly participate in the Paris Commune of 1871, since he was arrested shortly before the uprising and was in prison during most of it. His followers, however, played an important role in the Commune.

†   Adolphe Blanqui, *Histoire de l'économie politique en Europe, depuis les anciens jusque à nos jours* (Paris: Guilloumin, 1837). See *History of Political Economy in Europe*, translated by Emily J. Leonard (New York: G.P. Putnam's Sons, 1880).

‡   Ferdinand Lassalle, *Herr Bastiat—Schulze von Delitzsch, der ökonomische Julian, oder Kapital und Arbeit. In Ferdinand Lassalle's Reden und Schrifte.* Neue Gesammtausgabe. Mit einer biographischen Einleitung hrsg. von Eduard Bernstein, Volume 3 (Mr. Bastiat-Schulze Delitzsch, the Economic Julian, or Capital and Labor) (Berlin: Verlag der Expedition des Vorwärts, 1893), p. 18. For Marx's critique of this work of Lassalle, see the "Preface to the First Edition" of *Capital* Vol. 1, pp. 89–90.

notion of political-economic matters, only "unsound," "superficial," "most commonplace" ideas taken from everyday experience, while the whole of the Middle Ages was extremely "unscientific."[3] Which learned explanation does not take us a single step forward, not to mention the fact that it is also quite misleading, particularly in its generalization about the Middle Ages.

A different original explanation is offered by Professor Schmoller. In the same essay that we cited above from the *Handwörterbuch der Staatswissenschaften*, he tells us:

> For several centuries, individual private and social economic facts were observed and described, individual truths of national economy recognized, and economic questions discussed in systems of ethics and law. These relevant individual parts could only be united when questions of national economy acquired previously unsuspected importance for the ruling and administration of states, from the seventeenth through to the nineteenth century, when numerous writers concerned themselves with them and instruction of students in them became necessary, while at the same time the rise of scientific thinking in general led to the accumulated propositions and truths of national economy being combined, by way of certain fundamental ideas—such as money and exchange, state economic policy, labor and the division of labor—into connected systems, as was attempted by major writers of the eighteenth century. Since this time, national economic theory or political economy has existed as an independent science.[4]

If we briefly summarize this long speech, we obtain the lesson: individual political-economic observations, which existed as separate facts for a long while, came together in a particular science when this was required for the "ruling and administration of states"—i.e. governments—and it became necessary for this purpose to teach political economy in universities. What a wonderful and classic explanation from a German professor! First a chair is founded, when this is "required" by the praiseworthy government, to be occupied by an assiduous professor; then of course the corresponding science has also to be created, otherwise what could the professor teach? Doesn't this remind us of the master of court ceremonies who maintained that there would always have to be monarchies, otherwise what would be the function of a master of ceremonies? For the basic contention here is indeed that political economy came into being because the governments of modern states needed this science. The command of the powers that be is the genuine birth certificate of political economy. It is completely in character with the way of thinking of a present-day professor who, as scientific valet of the Reich government of the day, agitates "scientifically" as need arises for certain naval, customs or tax proposals, or as a battlefield hyena preaches chauvinist national hatred and intellectual cannibalism during a war— it is completely in character to imagine that the financial needs of princes, the interests of "royal treasuries," a word of command from governments, is all that is needed to conjure a new science out of the ground. For the rest of humanity, however, those not paid out of the exchequer, such a notion has its difficulties. Above all, this explanation only raises a new puzzle. For we then have to ask: what happened so that around the seventeenth century, as Professor Schmoller maintains, the governments of modern states suddenly felt a need to dupe their dear subjects according to scientific principles, whereas for countless centuries they had managed quite successfully in the old-fashioned way, without such principles? Should we not turn all this upside down and see the new-fangled needs of "royal treasuries" as simply a modest consequence of that great historical transformation out of which the new science of political economy arose around the middle of the nineteenth century?

In brief, after failing to learn from this learned guild what political economy actually deals with, we do not even know when and why it arose.

2

One thing, at any rate, is established: in all the definitions of bourgeois specialists we have cited above, it is always a question of "national economy." And "political economy" is only a foreign word for the theory of national economy. The concept of national economy stands at the center of discussion for all official representatives of this science. What then actually is this national economy? Professor Bücher, whose work *Die Entstehung der Volkswirtschaft* [The Rise of the National Economy] enjoys a high reputation both in Germany and abroad, offers the following information:

> The national economy is formed by the totality of arrangements, dispositions and procedures that the satisfaction of the needs of an entire nation demands. This national economy, again, breaks down into numerous particular economies, which are connected with one another by trade, and dependent on one another in a variety of ways as a result of the fact that each undertakes particular tasks for all the others and has the others undertake such tasks for it.[5]

Let us try to translate this learned "definition" into the language of ordinary mortals.

If the first thing we hear is the "*totality* of dispositions and procedures" that are designed to satisfy the needs of an entire nation, we are forced to consider everything possible: factories and workshops, agriculture and stock-raising, railways and warehouses, but also church preaching and police surveillance, ballet performances, civil servants and observatories, parliamentary elections, national guards and military associations, chess clubs, dog shows and duels—for all these and an endless chain of other "dispositions and procedures" serve today to "satisfy the needs of an entire nation." The national economy would then be everything that takes place under the sun, and political economy a universal science "of all things and more," as the Latin tag goes.

The generous definition of the Leipzig professor evidently has to be restricted somewhat. Very likely he only wants to refer to "arrangements and procedures" that serve to satisfy the *material* needs of a nation, or more precisely, the satisfaction of such needs by material things. And even then the "totality" would be far too widely conceived, and easily float off again into the mist. Yet we shall try to find our way here as best we can.

People all need, in order to live, food and drink, a protecting roof, clothing in cold regions, as well as all kind of articles of daily use in the home. These things may be simpler or more refined, be supplied sparingly or abundantly, but they are indispensable for the existence of any human society and must consequently be constantly produced by people—we are not in the land of Cockaigne.* In every kind of culture, as well, there are all kinds of objects that serve to improve life and satisfy intellectual and social needs, such as weapons for defense against enemies: among the so-called savages, dance masks, bows and arrows and idols; for us, luxury goods, churches, machine-guns and submarines. The production of all these articles requires, in turn, various natural materials, as well as the various tools with which they are produced. These materials, too, such as stones, wood, metal, plants etc., are obtained from the earth by human labor, and the tools that are used in this connection are likewise the product of human labor.

If this rough-hewn notion is temporarily satisfactory, we could conceive the national economy as follows: each nation constantly creates by its own labor a mass of things that are necessary for life—food, clothing, buildings, household articles, jewelry, weapons, religious objects, etc.—using the materials and tools that are indispensable for their production. The way in which a nation performs all this labor, how it distributes the goods produced among its individual members, how it consumes them and produces them afresh in an endless cycle—all this together forms the economy of the people in question, a "national economy." This would then be more or less the meaning of the first sentence in Professor Bücher's definition. But we have to go into rather more detail.

"This national economy, again, breaks down into numerous particular economies, which are connected with one another by trade, and dependent on one another in a variety of ways as a result of the fact that each undertakes particular tasks for all and has others undertake such tasks for it." Here we come up against a new question: What are these "particular economies" that the "national economy," which we have taken pains to conceive properly, breaks down into?

---

* Cockaigne is a medieval mythical land of plenty, with abundant luxury and pleasure and ease of living.

The first thing that suggests itself would be individual households, family economies. Indeed, each nation in the so-called civilized countries does consist of a number of families, and each family as a rule also conducts its "economy." This private economy consists in the family obtaining certain monetary incomes, whether from the employment of its adult members or from other sources, with which it in turn meets its needs for food, clothing, housing, etc.; and in this connection, if we think of a family economy, it is usually the housewife, the kitchen, the wash-tub and the nursery that form the center of this notion. Are these then the "individual economies" into which the "national economy" breaks down? We get into a certain confusion here. The national economy, as we have just understood it, involves first and foremost the production of all those goods that are used as food, clothing, housing, furniture, tools and materials for life and labor. At the center of the national economy stands *production*. In family economies, on the other hand, we see only the *consumption* of the objects that the family obtains ready-made out of its income. We know that most families in modern states today buy almost all their foodstuffs, clothing, furniture, etc. ready-made from shops or markets. In the domestic economy meals are prepared only with bought foodstuffs, and clothes generally made from bought material. Only in very backward rural districts are there still peasant families who provide for most of their needs by their own household work. Of course there are on the other hand, even in modern states, many families who do produce various industrial products at home, such as domestic weavers and garment workers; there are even, as we know, whole villages where toys and similar things are produced on a mass scale domestically. But here the product manufactured by these families belongs exclusively to the entrepreneur who ordered it and paid for it; not the slightest part of it goes into their own consumption, into the economy of the home-working family. For their own household economy, these domestic workers buy everything ready-made out of their meager wages, in the same way as other families. Bücher's statement that the national economy breaks down into many individual economies would thus lead to something like the following result: the *production* of the means of existence of a whole nation "breaks down" simply into the *consumption* of means of subsistence by individual families—a statement that looks much like utter nonsense.

An additional doubt also arises. According to Professor Bücher, these "individual economies" are "connected with one another by exchange" and completely dependent on one another because "each undertakes particular tasks for all others." What kind of exchange and dependence does this mean? Is it for example exchange between friends and neighbors, of the kind that takes place between various private families? But what does such exchange actually have to do with the national economy, with the economy as a whole? Any capable housewife, indeed, will maintain that it is better for the household and for domestic peace that as little exchange as possible takes place between neighbors in different houses. And as to precisely what this "dependence" involves, it is impossible to see what "tasks" the household economy of pensioner Meyer is supposed to undertake for the household economy of headmaster Schulze and "all others." We have clearly taken a completely wrong turn here, and have to tackle the question from a different direction.

It evidently cannot be individual family households into which Professor Bücher's "national economy" breaks down. Shouldn't it rather be such things as factories, workshops, and agricultural holdings? One fact seems to confirm that this leads us onto the correct path. All these businesses are where various things really are produced and manufactured that serve the maintenance of the whole nation, while on the other hand there is real exchange and mutual dependence among them. A factory making trouser buttons, for example, is completely reliant on the tailoring workshops where it finds outlets for its goods, while the tailors in turn can't produce proper trousers without buttons. On the other hand, the tailoring workshops need materials, and this makes them reliant on the weavers of cotton and wool, who in turn depend on sheep-rearing and the cotton trade, etc., etc. Here we really can see a ramified connection of production. It is of course rather pompous to speak of "tasks" that each of these businesses "undertakes for all others," when what we have is the most ordinary sale of trouser buttons to tailors, of wool to spinning plants, and the like. But we have to accept such flowery language as unavoidable professorial jargon, as they love to wrap the profitable little deals of the business world in a bit of poetry and "ethical value judgments," as Professor Schmoller so nicely puts it. It is just that still more serious doubts arise at this point. The individual factories, agricultural holdings, coalmines and iron works are said to be so many "individual economies" into which the national economy "breaks down." But this concept of an "economy," at least as we have now conceived the national economy, must evidently include within a certain orbit both the manufacture of means of subsistence and their use, both production and consumption. In these factories, workshops, mines and plants, however, only production takes place, and indeed only for others. What are consumed here are only the materials and tools that are needed for labor. The finished product, for its part, in no way enters into consumption within the same business. Not a single trouser button is consumed by the manufacturer and his family, let alone by the factory workers, nor are iron tubes consumed by the iron-works proprietor's family. Besides, if we try to define the "economy" more closely, we must always understand by it something whole, to a certain extent entire unto itself, more or less the production and consumption of the most important means of subsistence required for human existence. Today's individual industrial and agricultural businesses, however, as every child knows, only produce a single product, or at most a few products, which would be far from sufficient for human maintenance, most of these moreover being not at all consumable, just one part of a food product, or a raw material or tool needed for this. Present-day production facilities are precisely just fragments of an economy, having no meaning and purpose of their own in economic terms, so that they immediately strike even the untutored eye as not forming any "economy" by themselves, but only a shapeless little splinter of an economy. So if we say that the national economy, i.e. the totality of arrangements and procedures that serve to satisfy the needs of a people, breaks down again into individual economies, which are factories, workshops, mines, etc., we could equally well say that the totality of biological arrangements that serve to perform the functions of the human organism is the human being itself, which breaks down again into several individual organisms that are the nose, ears, legs, arms, etc. The present-day factory, in fact, is no more an "individual economy" than the nose is an individual organism.

This route too thus leads to an absurdity—proof that the artful definitions of bourgeois scholars, constructed simply on the basis of external characteristics and word-splitting, have an evident reason in this case to circumvent the true heart of the matter.

Let us now attempt to subject the concept of national economy to a closer examination.

3

We are told about the needs of a nation, about the satisfaction of these needs in an interconnected economy, and in this way about the economy of a nation. Political economy would then be the science that explains to us the nature of this national economy, i.e. the laws according to which a nation creates and increases its wealth by labor, distributes this among individuals, consumes it and creates it afresh. The object of the investigation should thus be the economic life of a whole nation, in contrast with a private or individual economy, whatever the latter might mean. It appears to confirm this notion that the epoch-making book published in 1776 by Adam Smith, who is seen as the father of political economy, bore the title *The Wealth of Nations.**

The first thing we must ask, however, is whether there really is such a thing as the economy of a nation. Do nations each conduct a separate household, a closed economic life? Since the expression "national economy" is especially popular in Germany, let us turn our attention to this country.

The hands of German workers, male and female, produce each year tremendous quantities of all kinds of useful products. But is all this produced just for the use of the population living in the German Empire? We know that an enormous proportion of German products, growing every year, is dispatched

---

*   Adam Smith, *An Inquiry into the Nature and Causes of the Wealth of Nations*, two volumes (London: W. Strahan and T. Cadell, 1776).

to other countries and parts of the world, for the use of other nations. German iron products go to various neighboring European countries, and further afield to South America and Australia; leather and leather goods go from Germany to all European states; glass products, sugar and gloves find their way to England; animal hides to France, England and Austria-Hungary; the dye-stuff alizarin* to England, the United States and India; phosphates for artificial fertilizer to the Netherlands and Austria-Hungary; coke to France; coal to Austria, Belgium, the Netherlands and Switzerland; electrical cable to England, Sweden and Belgium; toys to the United States; German beer, indigo, aniline and other coal-tar dyes, German pharmaceuticals, cellulose, gold articles, stockings, cotton and woolen materials and clothes, and German locomotive rails are dispatched to almost all trading countries across the world.

Conversely, however, the German people are reliant at every turn in their labor, as well as in daily consumption, on products of other countries and nations. We eat bread from Russian wheat and meat from Hungarian, Danish and Russian cattle; the rice that we consume comes from the East Indies and North America, tobacco from the Dutch East Indies and Brazil; we receive cocoa beans from West Africa, pepper from India; lard from the United States; tea from China; vegetables from Italy, Spain and the United States; coffee from Brazil, Central America and the Dutch East Indies; meat extract from Uruguay; eggs from Russia, Hungary and Bulgaria; cigars from the island of Cuba; pocket watches from Switzerland; sparkling wine from France; cattle hides from Argentina; feathers for beds from China; silk from Italy and France: flax and hemp from Russia; cotton from the United States, India and Egypt; fine wool from England; jute from India; malt from Austria-Hungary; linseed from Argentina; certain kinds of coal from England; lignite from Austria; nitre† from Chile; quebracho for tanning from Argentina; construction timber from Russia; cork from Portugal; copper from the United States; tin from the Dutch East Indies; zinc from Australia; aluminum from Austria-Hungary and Canada; asbestos from Canada; asphalt and marble from Italy; cobblestones from Sweden; lead from Belgium, the United States and Australia; graphite from Ceylon, phosphoric lime from America and Algeria; iodine from Chile ...

From the simplest foodstuff eaten every day to the most sought-after luxury goods and the materials and tools needed for them, the greater part come directly or indirectly from foreign countries, entirely or in one or other component, and are the product of other people's labor. To make our life and work possible in Germany, we have almost all other countries, peoples and parts of the world work for us, and we work in turn for all these countries.

---

*   Alizarin is a red dye used in textile production. Originally obtained from the roots of plants of the madder genus, it was first chemically synthesized by German scientists in the 1860s.

†   Nitre is the mineral form of potassium nitrate; it is also known as saltpeter.

In order to get an idea of the enormous scope of this exchange, let us cast a glance at the official statistics for imports and exports. According to the *Statistisches Jahrbuch für das Deutsche Reich* [Statistical Yearbook of the German Empire], 1914 edition,* Germany's total trade (net of goods arriving in Germany for re-export) was as follows.

Germany imported in 1913:

Raw materials	to the value of	5,262 million marks
Semi-finished products		1,246 million marks
Finished products		1,776 million marks
Foodstuffs and consumer goods		3,063 million marks
Live animals		289 million marks

In total, 11,638[†] million marks, or close to 12 thousand million. In the same year, Germany exported:

Raw materials	1,720 million marks
Semi-finished products	1,159 million marks
Finished products	6,642 million marks
Foodstuffs and consumer goods	1,362 million marks
Live animals	7 million marks

In total, 10,891 million marks or nearly 11 billion marks. Germany's annual foreign trade thus amounts to more than 22 billion marks.

The situation is the same, to a greater or lesser extent, in other modern states, precisely those with which political economy has been exclusively concerned. All these countries produce for one another, partly even for the most far-flung parts of the world, while likewise consuming all along the line products from all other parts of the world.

In the light of such a tremendously developed reciprocal exchange, how are we to draw the borders between the "economy" of one nation and that of another? Should we speak of so many "national economies" as if these could be treated as separate territories in economic terms?

Of course, the increasing international exchange of goods is no new discovery, unknown to bourgeois scholars. Official statistical surveys and their annually published reports have long since made the facts reported the common property of all educated people; businessmen and industrial workers, moreover,

---

* See *Statistisches Jahrbuch für das Deutsche Reich*, edited by the Imperial Statistical Office (Berlin: Puttkammer & Mühlbrecht, 1914). The *Statistisches Jahrbuch* was published yearly, beginning in 1880.

† The small differences in this and the following addition result from Luxemburg ignoring the thousands in the component categories.

know them from their daily life. The fact of rapidly increasing world trade is so universally known and recognized today that it can no longer be challenged or doubted. But how is this question conceived by the academic specialists in political economy? As a purely external chance connection, as the export of a so-called "surplus" in the products of one country over and above its own needs and the import of what is "lacking" in its own economy—a connection that in no way prevents them from continuing to speak as before of the "national economy" and "national-economic theory."

Professor Bücher, for example, proclaims, after he has lectured us at length about the present-day "national economy" as the highest and final stage of development in the series of historical economic forms:

> It would be a mistake to conclude from the successful easing of international trade in the liberal age that the era of national economy is on the decline and making way for an era of world economy ... We certainly see today in Europe a series of states that renounce national autonomy in their provision of goods to the extent that they are forced to obtain considerable quantities of their food and consumer goods from abroad, while their industrial production capacity has grown far beyond the national need and supplies regular surpluses that have to seek their utilization in foreign lands. But the existence alongside one another of such industrial and raw-material producing countries that are mutually reliant, this "international division of labor," should not be taken as a sign that humanity is on the brink of reaching a new stage of development, and be opposed to earlier stages under the name of a *world economy*. For, on the one hand, no economic stage has guaranteed complete ability to satisfy its own needs in the long term; each leaves certain gaps, which have had to be filled in one way or another. On the other hand, at least up to this time, no signs of this so-called world economy have yet appeared that depart from those of the national economy in their essential characteristics, and it is very doubtful whether such will appear in the foreseeable future.[6]

Still bolder is Professor Bücher's younger colleague [Werner] Sombart, who declares point-blank that we are not moving into a world economy, but on the contrary increasingly departing from this:

> The civilized peoples, I would rather maintain, are today (as far as their overall economy goes) not fundamentally more, but rather less linked with one another by trading relations. The individual national economy today is not more but actually less involved in the world market than a hundred or fifty years ago. At least ... it would be wrong to assume that international trade relations are acquiring a relatively growing importance for the modern national economy. The opposite is the case.

Professor Sombart is convinced that "individual national economies are becoming ever more complete microcosms [i.e. small closed worlds—R.L.] and that the internal market increasingly overshadows the world market in importance for all lines of trade."[7]

This blatant foolishness, which recklessly flies in the face of all daily perceptions of economic life, most happily underlines the stubborn reluctance of the gentlemen of the scholarly guild to recognize the world economy as a new phase of development of human society—a reluctance that it is well worthwhile to note, and whose hidden roots we shall go on to examine.

So, because at "earlier economic stages," for example at the time of King Nebuchadnezzar, "certain gaps" in people's economic life were filled by exchange, *present-day* world trade has nothing to teach us, and we still have a "national economy." That is Professor Bücher's opinion.

How indicative this is about the crude historical conception of a scholar whose fame is based precisely on supposedly acute and deep insights into economic history! With the help of a fatuous schema, he brings the international trade of the most varied stages of economy and civilization, separated by millennia, under a single category. Of course there never has been any social form without exchange, and there is not today. The oldest prehistoric discoveries, the most primitive caves used as dwellings by "antediluvian" human beings, the most primitive graves from early times, all give evidence of a certain exchange of products already between distant regions. Exchange is as old as human culture itself, it has ever been a constant accompaniment of this and its most powerful promoter. In this general knowledge, quite vague in its generality, our scholar now drowns all particularities of different eras, levels of civilization and economic forms. Just as all cats are grey in the dark, so in the obscurity of this professorial theory all forms of exchange, no matter how diverse, are one and the same. The primitive exchange of an Amerindian tribe in Brazil, who every now and then happen to exchange their uniquely woven dance masks for the artfully made bows and arrows of another tribe; the gleaming warehouses of Babylon, where the splendors of Oriental court life were accumulated; the ancient market of Corinth, where at the new moon Oriental cloth, Greek pottery, paper from Tyre, Syrian and Anatolian slaves were offered for sale to rich slave-owners; the medieval maritime trade of Venice, supplying luxury goods to European feudal courts and patrician houses—and the present-day capitalist world trade, which has brought East and West, North and South, all the oceans and corners of the world into its net, and year in, year out moves tremendous quantities of goods hither and thither—from the beggar's daily bread and firewood through to the artworks most sought after by rich connoisseurs, from the simplest fruit of the soil through to the most complicated tool, from human labor-power, the source of all wealth, through to the deadly instruments of war—all this is one and the same for our professor of political economy: simply the "filling" of "certain gaps" in the independent economic organism! ...

Fifty years ago, Schulze von Delitsch taught the German workers that each person nowadays first of all produced for himself, but "those products he does not need himself ... he exchanges for the products of others."[8] Lassalle's response to him remains unforgettable:

Herr Patrimonialrichter* Schulze! Have you no idea at all about the real pattern of social labor today? Didn't you come from Bitterfeld and Delitzsch? In what century of the Middle Ages are you still living with these ideas? ... Have you no inkling that social labor today is precisely characterized by the fact that each person produces precisely what he cannot use himself? Have you no inkling that this has to be so, ever since the rise of modern industry, that the form and essence of present-day labor lies in this, and that without the sharpest emphasis on this point it is impossible to understand a single page of our present-day economic conditions, not a single one of our present-day economic phenomena?

According to you, then, Herr Leonor Reichenheim in Wüste-Giersdorf produces first of all the cotton yarn that he needs for himself. The surplus, which his daughters cannot work up into more stockings and nightshirts for him, he exchanges.

Herr Borsig first of all produces machines for his family's needs. He then sells the surplus machines.

The workshops making mourning clothes provide first of all for deaths in their own families. But if there are too few of these, and some mourning clothes are left over, they exchange them.

Herr Wolff, proprietor of the local telegraph office, first has messages come in for his own instruction and pleasure. And when he's had his fill, if there are any left over, he exchanges them with the stock-exchange sharks and newspaper editorial offices against their surplus newspaper reports and shares! ...

In conclusion, it is precisely the distinctive character of labor in *earlier* periods of society, to be sharply emphasized, that at this time people produced first of all for their own needs and parted with the surplus, i.e. they principally pursued a natural economy.

And it is again the distinctive character, the specific determination of labor in *modern* society, that each produces only what he in no way does need, i.e. that everyone produces exchange-values, whereas previously they produced use-values.

And do you not understand, Herr Schulze, that this is the necessary "form and manner of performing labor," ever more prevailing, in a society in which the division of labor has developed to such a degree as it has in modern society?[9]

---

* As *Patrimonialrichter*, Schulze-Delitsch was a magistrate in charge of adjudicating matters of inheritance.

What Lassalle tried here to explain to Schulze about capitalist private enterprise applies more each day now to the economic pattern of highly developed capitalist countries such as England, Germany, Belgium or the United States, in whose footsteps the others are following one after the other. And the attempt by the progressive patrician from Bitterfeld to mislead the workers was only more naïve, but no cruder, than the tendentious arguments of a Bücher or Sombart against the concept of a world economy today.

Punctilious civil servant that he is, the German professor loves proper order. For the sake of order, he also likes to arrange the world nicely into the pigeon-holes of a scientific schema. And in the same way as he places his books on the shelves, so he has also divided the different countries onto two shelves: on the one hand, countries that produce industrial goods and have "a surplus" of these; on the other, countries that pursue agriculture and stock-raising and whose products meet a shortage in other lands. This is how international trade arises, and what it is based on.

Germany is the one of the most industrialized countries in the world. According to this schema, its most vigorous trade should be with a large agricultural country such as Russia. How is it then that Germany's most important trading partners are the two other most industrialized countries: the United States and Britain? Germany's trade with the United States in 1913 amounted to 2,400 million marks, and with Britain to 2,300 million; Russia only came in third place. And especially as regards exports, the leading industrial state in the world is precisely the greatest customer for German industry: with 1,400 million marks' worth of annual imports from Germany, England stands in first position, leaving all other countries far behind. The British Empire, including its colonies, takes a good fifth of German exports. What does the professorial schema say about this remarkable phenomenon?

Here industrial countries, there agricultural ones—that is the rigid skeleton of world economic relations with which Professor Bücher and most of his colleagues operate. Back in the 1860s, however, Germany was an agricultural country; it had a surplus of agricultural products and had to obtain the most necessary industrial goods from England. Since then, it has also been transformed into an industrial country, and the most powerful rival to England. The United States is doing the same as Germany did in the 1870s and 80s, in a yet briefer interval; it is already well along this path. America is still one of the largest grain-producing countries in the world, along with Russia, Canada, Australia and Romania, and according to its last census (which dates from 1900) as many as 36 percent of its total population is still employed in agriculture. At the same time, however, the country's industry is striding forward at an unmatched speed, so that it presents a dangerous contender to England and Germany. We could set up a prize competition for our great faculties of political economy to define whether the United States, in Professor Bücher's schema, should be classified as an agricultural state or an industrial one. Russia is slowly following on the same path, and as soon as it casts off the fetters of an obsolete form of state it will catch up, thanks to its tremendous population and inexhaustible natural wealth, and appear in our own lifetimes alongside Germany, England and the United States as a powerful industrial country, if it does not indeed overshadow them. The world is precisely not a rigid skeleton, unlike the wisdom of a professor; it is living, moving and changing. The polar opposition between industry and agriculture, from which international exchange is supposed to emerge, is thus itself something fleeting; it will steadily shift ever more from the center of the modern civilized world to its periphery. What is happening meanwhile with trade within this ambit of civilization? According to Bücher's theory it should steadily dwindle. But instead—a miracle!—trade is growing ever greater between the industrial countries themselves.

Nothing is more instructive than the picture that the development of our modern economic region offers in the last quarter of a century. Despite the fact that there have been real orgies of tariff raising in all the industrial countries and major states of Europe, as also in America, i.e. mutual artificial barriers to "national economies," world trade has not stopped developing in this period—it has pursued a furious course. And that increasing industrialization and world trade go hand in hand, even a blind person can see from the example of the three leading countries: England, Germany and the United States.

Coal and iron form the core of modern industry. Coal production from 1885 to 1910 rose as follows:

in England	from 162 to 269 million tons
in Germany	from 74 to 222 million tons
in the United States	from 101 to 455 million tons

Pig iron production rose in the same period

in England	from 7.5 to 10.2 million tons
in Germany	from 3.7 to 14.8 million tons
in the United States	from 4.1 to 27.7 million tons

At the same time, annual foreign trade (imports and exports) rose from 1882 to 1912

in England	from 13,000 to 27,400 million marks
in Germany	from 6,200 to 21,300 million marks
in the United States	from 5,500 to 16,200 million marks

If however we take the total foreign trade (imports and exports) of *all* the more important countries on earth in recent years, this rose from 105,000 million marks in 1904 to 165,000 million in 1912. That means a growth of 57 percent in eight years! There is not even a close parallel to this breath-taking pace of economic development in the whole of previous world history—"the dead ride swiftly."[10] The capitalist "national economy" seems in a hurry to exhaust the limits of its capacity, to shorten the remission period in which it can justify its existence. And what does the schema of "certain gaps" and the clumsy dance between industrial and agricultural countries have to say about this?

Yet there is no longer such a puzzle in modern economic life.

Let us take a closer look at the tables for German imports and exports, instead of resting content with total sums of goods exchanged or their major economic categories; let us examine as an experiment the most important kinds of German trade.

Two facts immediately strike the most superficial observer. The first is that in several cases one and the same type of commodity figures in *both* columns, even if in different quantities. Germany sends enormous quantities of machinery abroad, but it also imports machinery from abroad to the considerable annual sum of 80 million marks. Likewise, coal is exported from Germany while at the same time foreign coal is imported into Germany. The same holds for cotton goods, woolen yarn and finished goods, also for hides and skins, and many other goods that are not included in this table. From the standpoint of a crude opposition between industry and agriculture, which our professor of political economics uses like Aladdin's lamp to illuminate all the secrets of modern world trade, this remarkable duplication is quite incomprehensible; it even appears completely absurd. What is happening here? Has Germany a "surplus over and above its own needs," or on the contrary "certain gaps"? Both in coal and in cotton goods? And in cattle hides? And a hundred more! Or is a "national economy" supposed always to show some kind of "surplus" and "certain gaps"? Aladdin's lamp is flickering insecurely. Clearly the observed facts can only be explained if we assume that there exist more complicated and far-reaching economic connections between Germany and other countries, a ramified and detailed division of labor that allows for certain kinds of the same products to be produced in Germany for other countries, other kinds abroad for Germany, creating a continuous to and fro in which individual countries appear only as organic parts of a greater whole.

Besides, anyone must be struck at first glance in the table above by the fact that imports and exports do not appear here as two separate phenomena in

In 1913

Germany imported	million marks	Germany exported	million marks
Cotton, raw	607	Machines of all kinds	680
Wheat	417	Iron products	652
Wool, raw	413	Coal	516
Barley	390	Cotton goods	446
Copper ore	335	Woolen goods	271
Cattle hides	322	Paper and paper products	263
Iron ore	227	Skins for fur	225
Coal	204	Iron ingots	205
Eggs	194	Silk goods	202
Skins for fur	188	Coke	147
Chilean nitre	172	Aniline and other dyestuffs	142
Raw silk	158	Clothing	132
Rubber	147	Copper goods	130
Pine planks	135	Leather uppers	114
Cotton yarn	116	Leather goods	114
Woolen yarn	108	Toys	103
Pine, raw	97	Sheet iron	102
Calf skins	95	Woolen yarn	91
Jute	94	Iron tubing	84
Machines of all kinds	80	Cattle skins	81
Lamb, sheep and goat skins	73	Iron wire	76
Cotton goods	72	Rails, etc.	73
Lignite	69	Pig iron	65
Wool, combed	61	Cotton yarn	61
Woolen goods	43	Rubber goods	57

need of explanation, on the one hand by "gaps" in a country's own economy, on the other by its "surpluses," but that they are instead linked causally together. Germany's tremendous cotton import is quite evidently not the result of its population's own needs, but is rather designed from the start to make possible the great export of cotton goods and clothing from Germany. Likewise, the connection between the import of wool and the export of woolen goods, and between the tremendous import of iron from abroad and the tremendous export of iron goods of every shape and form, and so on. Thus Germany imports in order to be able to export. It does not artificially create "certain gaps" so as to subsequently transform these gaps into as many "surpluses." The German "microcosm" thus appears from the start, in all its dimensions, as a fragment of a greater whole, as a single workshop in the world.

But let us examine this "microcosm" rather more closely, in its "ever more perfect" self-satisfaction. Let us imagine that by some kind of social and political catastrophe the German "national economy" were actually cut off from the rest of the world and left to its own devices. What picture would this then present?

Let us start with the daily bread. German agriculture has twice as high a yield as that of the United States; in terms of quality it holds first place among the world's agricultural countries, and it is only outdone by the still more intensive cultivation of Belgium, Ireland and the Netherlands. Fifty years ago, Germany with an agriculture that was then far more backward was one of the granaries of Europe; it fed other countries with the surplus of its own bread. Today, despite the higher yield, German agriculture is not nearly sufficient to feed its own people and its own cattle: a sixth of the foodstuffs needed have to be obtained from abroad. In other words, if the German "national economy" were to be cut off from the world, a sixth of the population, some 11 million Germans, would be deprived of their sustenance.

The German people spend 220 million marks each year on coffee, 67 million on cocoa, 8 million on tea, 61 million on rice; they spend at least another 10 million marks on various spices, and 134 million on imported tobacco. All these products, which even the poorest people today cannot dispense with, which are part of everyday habit and subsistence, are not produced in Germany at all (or, as in the case of tobacco, only in small quantities), since the German climate is unsuited to them. If Germany were to be permanently closed off from the world economy, the subsistence of the German people, which corresponds to its present level of civilization, would collapse.

Let us turn from food to clothing. Both the underwear and the outer clothing of the broad mass of people are today made entirely from cotton, the underwear of the richer bourgeoisie from linen and their outer garments from fine wool and silk. Neither cotton nor silk are produced in Germany at all, and no more is the highly important textile jute or the finest wool, Britain having a world monopoly on these; Germany also has a great shortfall in hemp and flax. If Germany were permanently cut off from the world, both raw materials from abroad and outlets for exports would disappear, and all classes of the German people would be deprived of their most essential clothing; the Germany textile industry, which together with the clothing industry today provides a livelihood for 1,400,000 adult and juvenile workers of both sexes, would be ruined.

We can go on. The backbone of today's large-scale industry is what is known as heavy industry, i.e. machine production and metallurgy; and the backbone of these is metal ore. In 1913, Germany consumed some 17 million tons of pig iron. Its own production of pig iron also amounts to 17 million tons. At first glance, it might look as if the German "national economy" could cover its own needs in terms of iron. But the production of pig iron requires iron ore, and we find that Germany's own demand for iron ore alone amounts to some 27 million tons, a value of more than 110 million marks, while 12 million tons of higher-quality iron ore costing more than 200 million marks, ore without which the German

industry and trade from the rest of the world is just as much a legend as is the adequate supply of the German population by domestic agriculture, and that the supposed self-sufficiency of the German "microcosm" during the World War was based on a couple of fairy-tales.

Finally, we come to the outlet for German industry, which we showed was provided to such a high degree by all other parts of the world. For the duration of the war this was replaced by the state's own military needs. In other words, the most important branches of industry: metallurgy, textiles, leather and chemicals, underwent remodeling and were transformed exclusively into industries supplying the armed forces. Since the costs of the war were borne by German tax-payers, this transformation of industry into war industry meant that the German "national economy," instead of sending a large part of its products for exchange abroad, surrendered them to continuing destruction in the war, burdening the future products of the economy for decades to come with the loss arising, by way of the public credit system.*

If we take all this into account, it is clear that the miraculous success of this "microcosm" during the war represented in every respect an experiment in which the only question was how long it could be extended without the artificial construction collapsing like a house of cards.

One further glance at a remarkable phenomenon: If we consider Germany's foreign trade in its total amounts, it is striking that its imports are significantly greater than its exports: the former amounted in 1913 to 11,600 million marks, the latter to 10,900 million. And this relationship was in no way an exception for the year in question, but can be noted for an extended number of years. The same holds for Great Britain, which in 1913 showed imports to a total of 13,000 million marks and exports to 10,000 million. How is such a phenomenon possible? Perhaps Professor Bücher can explain it for us with his theory of the "surplus" over a country's own needs and of "certain gaps."

If the economic relations between the different "national economies" amount to no more than the fact that, as the professor teaches us, these "national economies," just as at the time of Nebuchadnezzar, cast off certain "surpluses," i.e. if simple commodity exchange is the only bridge over the void dividing one of these "microcosms" from another, it is clear that a country can import exactly as much in goods from abroad as it exports of its own. But in simple commodity exchange money is only an intermediary, and the foreign products are paid at the end of the day in one's own commodities. How then can a "national economy" manage the artifice of permanently importing more from abroad than it exports from its own "surplus"? Perhaps the professor will jest with us that the solution is the simplest thing in the world, the importing country only needs to settle the

---

*   This suggests that Luxemburg did not consider a "war economy" as any sort of panacea for the problem of capital accumulation. As she notes, the debts incurred through incessant militarization can become an important impediment to further economic growth.

excess of its imports over its exports in cash. "Only," indeed! The luxury, year in year out, of filling the bottomless pit of its foreign trade with a considerable sum of money that will never be seen again is something that at most a country with rich gold and silver mines of its own could afford, which is not the case with either Germany or France, Belgium or the Netherlands. Besides, there is a further amazing surprise: not only does Germany steadily import more goods that it imports, it also imports more money! In 1913, German imports of gold and silver came to 441.3 million marks, its exports to 102.8 million, a relationship that has been approximately the same for years. What does Professor Bücher with his "surpluses" and "gaps" have to say about this puzzle? The magic lamp is flickering gloomily. Indeed, we begin to suspect that behind the puzzling character of world trade there must in fact be quite other kinds of economic relations between individual "national economies" than simple commodity exchange; to regularly obtain from other countries more than you give them is evidently only possible for a country that has some kind of economic claim over others that is completely different from exchange between equals. And such claims and relations of dependence between countries exist in fact at every turn, although these professorial theories know nothing of them. One such dependence relationship, in the simplest form, is that between a so-called mother country and its colony. Great Britain draws from its largest colony, India, an annual tribute of more than 1,000 million marks. And we accordingly see that India's exports of goods are some 1,200 million marks greater than its imports. This "surplus" is nothing more than the economic expression of the colonial exploitation of India by British capitalism—whether these goods are directly bound for Great Britain, or whether India has to sell to other states each year goods to a value of 1,200 million marks specifically for the purpose of paying this tribute to its British exploiters.[11] But there are also other relationships of economic dependence that are not based on political rule. Russia annually exports around 1,000 million marks' worth more of goods than it imports. Is it the great "surplus" of agricultural products over the needs of its own "national economy" that drains this immense flow of goods each year out of the Russian Empire? But the Russian peasant, whose corn is taken out of the country in this way, is well known to suffer from scurvy due to undernourishment, and often has to eat bread mixed with tree bark! The massive export of his grain, through the mechanism of a financial and taxation system designed for this purpose, is a matter of life or death for the Russian state, in order to meet its obligations to foreign creditors. Since its notorious defeat in the Crimean war,* and its modernization by the reforms of Alexander II,† the

---

    * A major war fought between Britain, France, and the Ottoman Empire from 1853 to 1856 against Russia over control of the Balkans and the Dardanelles, which resulted in Russia's defeat. With its use of such new technologies as the railway and the telegraph, it is widely considered the first truly "modern" war.

    † This refers primarily to Russian Tsar Alexander II's freeing of the Russian peasants from

Russian state apparatus has been financed to a high degree by capital borrowed from Western Europe, principally from France. In order to pay interest on the French loans, Russia has to sell each year large quantities of wheat, timber, flax, hemp, cattle and poultry to Britain, Germany and the Netherlands. The immense surplus of Russian exports thus represents the tribute of a debtor to his creditors, a relationship matched on the French side by a large surplus of imports, which represents nothing other than the interest on its loan capital. But in Russia itself, the chain of economic connections runs further. The borrowed French capital has served principally in the last few decades for two purposes: railway building with state guarantees, and armaments. To this end, Russia has developed since the 1870s a strong heavy industry—under the protection of a system of high customs tariffs. The borrowed capital from the old capitalist country France has fueled a young capitalism in Russia, but this in turn requires for its support and expansion a considerable import of machinery and other means of production from Britain and Germany as the most technologically advanced industrial countries. A tie of economic connections is thus woven between Russia, France, Germany and Britain, in which commodity exchange is only a small part.

Yet this does not exhaust the manifold nature of these connections. A country like Turkey or China presents a new puzzle for our professor. It has, contrary to Russia but similarly to Germany or France, a large surplus of imports, amounting in many years to almost double the quantity of exports. How can Turkey or China afford the luxury of such a copious filling of the "gaps" in their "national economies," given that these economies are not nearly in a position to export corresponding "surpluses"? Do the Western powers offer the crescent and the realm of the pigtail each year a present of several hundred million marks, in the form of all kinds of useful goods, out of Christian charity? Every child know that both Turkey and China are actually up to their necks in the jaws of European usurers, and have to pay the British, German and French banks an enormous tribute in interest. Following the Russian example, both Turkey and China should on the contrary show a surplus of exports of their own agricultural products in order to be able to pay this interest to their West European well wishers. But in both these two countries the so-called "national economy" is fundamentally different from the Russian. Certainly, the foreign loans are likewise used principally for railway building, port construction and armaments. But Turkey has virtually no industry of its own, and cannot conjure this out of the ground of its medieval peasant subsistence agriculture with its primitive cultivation and tithes. The same is true in a slightly different way for China. And so not only the whole of the population's need for industrial goods, but also everything necessary for transport

---

serfdom, with his decree of March 3, 1861. Other reforms implemented in the early years of his reign included ending corporal punishment in the military, reorganizing the judiciary, and allowing for limited self-government in rural districts and large towns through the *zemstvo* system.

construction and the equipment of army and navy, has to be imported ready-made from Western Europe and constructed on site by European entrepreneurs, technicians and engineers. The loans are indeed frequently tied in advance to supplies of this kind. China, for example, obtains a loan from German and Austrian banking capital only on condition that it immediately orders a certain quantity of armaments from the Skoda works[*] and Krupp;[†] other loans are tied in advance to concessions for the construction of railways. In this way, most European capital migrates to Turkey and China already in the form of goods (armaments) or industrial capital in kind, in the form of machinery, iron, etc. These latter goods are not sent for exchange, but for the production of profit. Interest on this capital, along with further profit, is squeezed from the Turkish or Chinese peasants by the European capitalists with the help of a corresponding taxation system under European financial control. The bare figures of a preponderance of imports for Turkey or China, and corresponding European exports, thus conceal the particular relationship that obtains between the rich big-capitalist West and the poor and backward East that it bleeds dry with the help of the most modern and developed communications facilities and military installations—and with it the galloping ruin of the old peasant "national economy."

A still different case is presented by the United States. Here we again see, as in Russia, an export figure well above that of imports—the former came to 10,200 million marks in 1913, the latter to 7,400 million—but the reasons for this are fundamentally different from the Russian case. Right from the beginning of the nineteenth century, the London stock exchange has absorbed vast quantities of American loans and shares; speculation in American company formation and stocks, until the 1860s, regularly announced like a fever patient's thermometer an impending major crisis for British industry and trade. Since then, the outflow of English capital to the United States has not ceased. This capital partly took the form of loan capital to cities and private companies, but mostly that of industrial capital, whether American railway and industrial stocks were sold on the London stock exchange, or English industrial cartels founded branches in the US in order to circumvent the high tariff barrier, or else to take over companies there by purchasing their shares, in order to get rid of their competition on the world market. The United States possesses today a highly developed heavy industry that is advancing every more swiftly, and that,

---

* The Skoda works, taken over by Emil Skoda in 1869, was the largest industrial conglomerate in the Austro-Hungarian Empire, and during the twentieth century became one of Europe's most important steel works and munitions manufacturer.

† Friedrich Krupp AG Hoesch-Krupp, launched by Friedrich Krupp (1787–1826) and led for many years by industrialist and inventor Alfred Krupp (1812–87), was the largest company in Europe at the beginning of the twentieth century, specializing in metal production and armaments. The company later became central to the rearmament of Germany under the Nazis. Gustav Krupp (1870–1950), who headed the company from 1909–43, was the only person to be indicted for war crimes in both World War I and World War II.

while it continues to attract money capital from Europe, itself exports industrial capital on an increasing scale—machinery, coal—to Canada, Mexico and other Central and South American countries. In this way the United States combines an enormous export of raw materials—cotton, copper, wheat, timber and petroleum—to the old capitalist countries with a growing industrial export to the young countries embarking on industrialization. The United States' great surplus of exports thus reflects the particular transitional stage from a capital-receiving agricultural country to a capital-exporting industrial one, the role of an intermediate link between the old capitalist Europe and the new and backward American continent.

An overview of this great migration of capital from the old industrial countries to the young ones, and the corresponding reverse migration of the incomes drawn from this capital and paid as annual tribute by the young countries to the old, shows three powerful streams. England, according to estimates from 1906, had already invested 54,000 million marks by this time in its colonies and elsewhere, from which it drew an annual income of 2,800 million marks. France's foreign capital at this time amounted to 32,000 million marks, with an annual income of at least 1,300 million. Germany, finally, had invested 26,000 million, which yielded 1,240 million annually. These great main streams, however, ultimately break down into smaller tributaries. Just as the United States is spreading capitalism further on the American continent, so even Russia—itself still fueled completely by French capital, and English and German industry—is already transferring loan capital and industrial products to its Asian hinterland, to China, Persia and Central Asia; it is involved in railway construction in China, etc.

We thus discover behind the dry hieroglyphs of international trade a whole network of economic entanglements, which have nothing to do with simple commodity exchange, which is all that the professorial wisdom can notice.

We discover that the distinction Herr Bücher makes between countries of industrial production and countries of raw-material production, the flimsy scaffolding on which he hangs the whole of international exchange, is itself only a crude product of professorial schematism. Perfume, cotton goods and machines are all manufactured goods. But the export of perfume from France only shows that France is the country of luxury production for the thin stratum of the rich bourgeoisie across the world; the export of cotton goods from Japan shows that Japan, competing with Western Europe, is undermining the traditional peasant and handicraft production throughout East Asia, driving it out by commodity trade; while the export of machinery from England, Germany and the United States shows that these three countries are themselves propagating heavy industry to all regions of the world.

We thus discover that one "commodity" is exported and imported today that was unknown in the time of King Nebuchadnezzar as well as in the whole of the antique and medieval periods: *capital*. And this commodity does not serve to fill "certain gaps" in other countries' "national economies," but quite the reverse—opening up gaps, rifts and splits in the edifice of traditional "national economies," and acting like gunpowder to transform these "national economies" sooner or later into heaps of rubble. In this way, the "commodity" capital spreads still more remarkable "commodities" on an ever more massive scale from various old countries to the whole world: modern means of transport and the destruction of whole indigenous populations, money economy and an indebted peasantry, riches and poverty, proletariat and exploitation, insecurity of existence and crises, anarchy and revolutions. The European "national economies" extend their polyp-like tentacles to all countries and people of the earth, strangling them in a great net of capitalist exploitation.

4

Cannot Professor Bücher believe in a world economy, despite all this? No. For the scholar explains, after he has carefully surveyed all regions of the world and discovered nothing: I cannot help myself, I see nothing in the way of "special phenomena" that "deviate in essential characteristics" from a national economy, "and it is much to be doubted whether such things will appear in the foreseeable future."[12]

Let us now leave trade and trade statistics completely aside, and turn directly to life, to the history of modern economic relations. Just a single small passage from the great colorful picture.

In 1768, [Richard] Arkwright built the first mechanically driven cotton spinning plant in Nottingham, and in 1785 [Edmund] Cartwright invented the mechanical loom. The immediate result in England was the destruction of handloom weaving and the rapid spread of mechanical manufacture. At the start of the nineteenth century there were, according to one estimate, around a million handloom weavers; they were now fated to die out, and by 1860 no more than a few thousand remained in the whole kingdom, out of more than half a million factory workers in the cotton sector. In 1863, Prime Minister [William] Gladstone spoke in Parliament of the "intoxicating augmentation of wealth and power"[*] that the English bourgeoisie had obtained, without the working class winning any share of this.

The English cotton industry draws its raw material from North America. The growth of factories in Lancashire conjured up immense cotton plantations in the southern United States. Blacks were imported from Africa for the deadly work on these plantations, as well as those of sugar, rice and tobacco. The African slave

---

[*]   Marx cited this April 16, 1863 speech by Gladstone in *Capital* Vol. 1, p. 806. He earlier quoted directly from Gladstone's speech in his "Inaugural Address of the Working Men's International Association." See *Marx-Engels Collected Works*, Vol. 20 (New York: International Publishers, 1985), p. 7.

trade expanded tremendously, whole tribes were hunted down in the "dark continent," sold off by their chiefs, transported across immense stretches over land and sea, to be auctioned in America. A literal black *"Völkerwanderung"** took place. At the end of the eighteenth century, in 1790, there were by one estimate only 697,000 blacks; by 1861 there were over four million.

The colossal extension of the slave trade and slave labor in the South of the United States triggered a crusade by the Northern states against this un-Christian atrocity. The massive import of English capital in the years 1825–60 made possible a vigorous railway construction in the Northern states, the beginnings of their own industry and with it a bourgeoisie enthusiastic for more modern forms of exploitation, for capitalist wage-slavery. The fabulous business of the Southern planters, who could drive their slaves to death within seven years, was all the more intolerable to the pious Puritans of the North because their own climate prevented them from establishing a similar paradise in their own states. At the instigation of the Northern states, slavery in every form was abolished for the whole of the Union in 1861.† The Southern planters, whose deepest feelings were injured, answered this blow with open revolt. The Southern states declared their secession from the Union, and the great Civil War broke out.

The immediate effect of the war was the devastation and economic ruin of the Southern states. Production and trade collapsed, the supply of cotton was interrupted. This deprived English industry of its raw material, and in 1863 a tremendous crisis broke out in England, the so-called "cotton famine." In Lancashire, 250,000 workers lost their jobs completely, 166,000 were only employed part-time, and just 120,000 workers were still fully employed. The population of this district was racked by poverty, and 50,000 workers asked Parliament in a petition to vote funds to enable their families to emigrate. The Australian states, which lacked the labor-power required to begin their capitalist development—after the indigenous population had been almost completely exterminated by the European settlers—declared that they were prepared to accept unemployed proletarians from England. But the English manufacturers protested vigorously against the emigration of their "living machinery," which they would need again themselves as soon as the anticipated revival of industry took place. The workers were refused the funds for emigration, and had to bear the full weight of the crisis and its terrors.

Denied American supply, English industry sought to obtain its raw material elsewhere, and turned its attention to the East Indies. Cotton plantations

---

*   This term, literally "migration of peoples," particularly connotes the Germanic and Slavic migrations into Europe of the first millennium AD.

†   Luxemburg is mistaken here. It was not until January 1, 1863 that the Emancipation Proclamation granted freedom to all slaves in the Confederate states, though this could only be applied when and where these states were occupied by Union forces. Slavery in all US states and territories was finally banned by the Thirteenth Amendment in 1865.

were feverishly started here, and rice cultivation, which had provided the daily food of the population for millennia and formed the basis of their existence, had to give way in large areas to the profitable projects of speculators. In the wake of this suppression of rice cultivation, the next few years saw an extraordinary price rise and a famine that carried off over a million people in Orissa alone, a district north of Bengal.

A second experiment took place in Egypt. To take advantage of the opportunity provided by the American Civil War, the Egyptian khedive, Ismail Pasha, began cotton plantations as rapidly as possible. A real revolution took place in the country's property relations and rural economy. Large area of peasant land were stolen, being declared royal property and transformed into very large-scale plantations. Thousands of workers were driven to forced labor on the plantations at the end of the whip, to build dams and canals for the khedive, or to pull ploughs. But borrowing the money needed to obtain the most modern steamploughs and hulling machines led to the khedive sinking ever deeper in debt to English and French bankers. This large-scale speculation ended with bankruptcy after only a year, when the end of the American Civil War brought the price of cotton down by three-quarters in the space of a few days. The result of this cotton period for Egypt was the rapid ruin of its peasant agriculture, the rapid collapse of its finances, and finally the swift occupation of the country by the English army.*

Meanwhile the cotton industry made new conquests. The Crimean War of 1855 [interrupted] the supply of hemp and flax from Russia, leading to a major crisis of linen production in Western Europe. The collapse of the old system in Russia, with the Crimean War, was followed right away by a political transformation, the abolition of serfdom, liberal reforms, free trade and the rapid building of railways. A new and stronger market for industrial products was thus opened up within this great empire, and the English cotton industry was the first to penetrate the Russian market. At the same time, in the 1860s, a series of bloody wars opened up China to English trade.† England dominated the world market, and the cotton industry made up half its exports. The period of the 1860s and 70s was the time of most brilliant business deals for the English capitalists, as well as the time when they were most inclined to guarantee their "hands" and secure

---

* On July 11, 1882 Great Britain began a military offensive against Egypt. The war concluded with a siege of Cairo on September 14, 1882. Egypt became a British protectorate, although it remained nominally part of the Ottoman Empire.

† This refers to the Opium Wars of 1839–42 and 1856–60, in which Britain insisted on its "right" to import opium into China in defiance of Chinese law and authority. The first Opium War of 1839–42 forced China to grant Britain trade and territorial concessions, including control of Hong Kong; the second Opium War of 1856–60, codified in the Treaty of Tientsin, to which France, Russia, and the US were also signatories, opened numerous foreign ports to Europeans and legalized the import of opium. It signalled the decline of the Qing Dynasty and the era of European colonial domination of China.

"industrial peace" by small concessions to the workers. It was in this period that the English trade unions, with the cotton spinners and weavers in the lead, achieved their most striking successes, as well as the time when the revolutionary traditions of the Chartist movement* and the Owenite ideas† finally died out among the English proletariat, ossifying into conservative trade unionism.

But the page soon turned. Everywhere on the continent that England exported its cotton products there gradually developed a local cotton industry. Already in 1844, the hunger revolts of the handloom weavers in Silesia and Bohemia‡ had been the first heralds of the March revolution [of 1848].§ In the English colonies, too, an indigenous industry arose. The cotton factories of Bombay soon competed with the English, and in the 1880s helped to break England's monopoly on the world market.

In Russia, finally, the rise of cotton manufacture in the 1870s inaugurated the age of large-scale industry and protective tariffs. In order to circumvent the high tariff barrier, whole factories along with their staff were taken from Saxony and the Vogtland⁋ to Russian Poland,** where the new manufacturing centers of

---

*   Chartism was a working-class movement for radical political and economic reform in Britain between 1838 and 1848. Named after the "People's Charter" of 1838, which called for universal male suffrage, a secret ballot, an end to property qualifications for voting, pay for members of Parliament, constituencies of equal size, and annual elections for Parliament, the movement also led to massive work stoppages, strikes, and demands for improved working conditions. Chartism is considered to be the world's first mass working-class labor movement. For a recent study of the movement, see David Black and Chris Ford, *1839: The Chartist Insurrection* (London: Unkant, 2012).

†   This refer to the followers of Robert Owen (1771–1858), utopian socialist and pioneering figure of the cooperative movement. The Owenites argued for the creation of cooperatively organized, self-sustaining townships that combined industry and agriculture without class distinction or private property. In the early 1830s the Owenites also embraced the formation of an equitable labor exchange system in which members of cooperatives would be remunerated by means of labor notes instead of money. The movement died out by the mid-1840s, although Owen (who was highly regarded by Marx) had an enduring impact on later socialist movements.

‡   The spontaneous revolt of weavers in Silesia and Bohemia between June and August 1844 were the first large-scale working class movement in Central Europe. In response to a severe economic depression that pushed living conditions for many below subsistence, weavers attacked the homes and warehouses of merchants and destroyed machines as well as the property deeds to them. The young Karl Marx was deeply impacted by the revolt, viewing the weavers' attack on the instruments of their oppression as a sign of a profound level of class consciousness. See "Critical Marginal Notes on the Article 'The King of Prussia and Social Reform. By a Prussian,'" *Marx-Engels Collected Works*, Vol. 3 (New York: International Publishers, 1975), pp. 189–206.

§   The "March Revolution" refers to the series of revolutions that broke out in numerous German states at the beginning of 1848. Initially dominated by middle-class revolutionaries demanding political freedom, an end to censorship, and governance based on democratic constitutions, the revolutions included a working-class dimension that also called for a transformation of economic relations and living conditions. In response to increased working-class militancy, the middle-class forces wavered in forcefully taking on the conservative forces centered in Prussia and Austria, which eventually defeated the revolutions.

⁋   Vogtland is in southeastern Germany, comprising parts of the state of Bavaria, Saxony, and Thuringia, bordering the Czech Republic.

**   The Congress of Vienna in 1815 had designated Russian-occupied Poland as the "Kingdom of Poland," placing it under complete Russian control. This re-confirmed the third partition of

Lodz and Zgierz* grew into big cities at a Californian pace. In the early 1880s, unrest in the Moscow-Vladimir cotton district forced the first labor protection laws in the tsarist empire. In 1896, 60,000 workers from the St Petersburg cotton plants carried out the first mass strike in Russia.† And nine years later, in June 1905, 100,000 workers in Lodz, the third center of the cotton industry, with German workers among their leaders, erected the first barricades of the great Russian revolution ...

Here we have, in a few lines, 140 years in the history of a modern branch of industry, a history that winds its way through all five continents, hurls millions of human lives hither and thither, erupting in one place as economic crisis, in another as famine, flaming up here as war, there as revolution, leaving in its wake on all sides mountains of gold and abysses of poverty—a wide and blood-stained stream of sweat from human labor.

These are convulsions of life, actions at a distance, that reach right into the innards of nations, while the dry figures of international trade statistics give only a pale reflection of them. In the century and a half since modern industry was first established in England, the capitalist world economy has taken shape at the price of the pains and convulsions of the whole of humanity. It has seized one branch of production after another, taken hold of one country after another. With steam and electricity, fire and sword, it has obtained entry into the most remote corners of the earth, has torn down all Chinese walls, and through an era of world crises, periodic common catastrophes, it has initiated the economic interconnection of present-day humanity.‡ The Italian proletarian, expelled from his misery at home by Italian capital, who migrates to Argentina or Canada, finds there a ready-made new yoke of capital imported from the United States or England. And the German proletarian who remains at home and tries to make an honest living, is dependent for his weal and woe at every turn on the course of production and trade throughout the world. Whether he finds work

---

Poland of 1795, which divided the country between Russia, Prussia, and the Austro-Hungarian Empire.

*   Zgierz is a town in central Poland, just north of Lodz. At the time Zgierz was a center of light industry, based on textile production.

†   The 1896 St. Petersburg strike was in response to the refusal of the owners of the textile factories to pay wages for the week of May 15–17, when the enterprises were closed because of the coronation of Tsar Nicolas II. As the strike expanded, the workers raised demands for a reduction of the working day from thirteen hours to ten and a half. On June 4 a general strike was declared, involving 30,000 workers in eighteen factories. It was the most significant revolt of the Russian working class to that point.

‡   Luxemburg's words here closely follow Marx and Engels's discussion in the *Communist Manifesto*: "The bourgeoisie, by the rapid improvement of all instruments of production, by the immensely facilitated means of communication, draws all, even the most barbarian, nations into civilization. The cheap prices of its commodities are the heavy artillery with which it batters down all Chinese walls, with which it forces the barbarians intensely obstinate hatred of foreigners to capitulate." See *Marx-Engels Collected Works*, Vol. 6 (New York: International Publishers, 1976), p. 488.

or not, whether his wage is sufficient to feed his wife and children, whether he is condemned to spend several days of the week in enforced idleness, or to work day and night in infernal overtime—all this constantly varies depending on the cotton harvest in the United States, the wheat harvest in Russia, the discoveries of new gold or diamond mines in Africa, the outbreak of revolution in Brazil,* tariff battles, diplomatic turmoil and war across five continents. Nothing is so striking today, nothing has such decisive importance for the whole shape of today's social and political life, as the yawning contradiction between an economic foundation that grows tighter and firmer every day, binding all nations and countries into a great whole, and the political superstructure of states, which seeks to split nations artificially, by way of border posts, tariff barriers and militarism, into so many foreign and hostile divisions.

But none of this exists for Bücher, Sombart and their colleagues! For them, all that exists is the "ever more complete microcosm"! They see far and wide no "special phenomena" that would "depart in essential characteristics" from a national economy. Is this not puzzling? Would a similar blindness on the part of the official representatives of science be conceivable for phenomena that leap to the eye of any observer in their plenitude and their dazzling, lightning-like intensity, in any area of science other than that of political economy? Certainly in natural science, a professional scholar who tried to express the view publicly that the earth did not revolve round the sun, but the sun and all other stars revolved round the earth as their center, who maintained that he "did not know any phenomena" that would contradict this view "in essential characteristics"—such a scholar could be sure of being met by the Homeric laughter of the entire educated world, and would end up having his mental health examined at the instigation of troubled relatives. Of course, 400 years ago not only did the spread of such views go unpunished, but anyone who undertook to refute them publicly would himself run the risk of ending on the scaffold. In those days, preservation of the mistaken view that the earth was the center of the universe and the heavenly bodies was a pressing interest of the Catholic church, and any attack on the imagined majesty of the earth in the universe was at the same time an assault on the spiritual rule of the church and its tithes on the earth. In those days, accordingly, natural science was the ticklish nerve center of the prevailing social system, and mystification in this realm was an indispensable instrument of subjugation. Today, under the rule of capital, the ticklish point of the social system is no longer faith in the mission of the earth in the blue heaven, but rather faith in the mission of the bourgeois state on earth. And because thick fog is already rising and gathering over the powerful waves of the world economy, because storms are in preparation here that will brush

---

* A possible reference to the Federalist Riograndense Revolution of 1893–95 in southern Brazil, launched by monarchists against the declaration of the Brazilian Republic in 1889. The revolutionaries, called Maragotos, were defeated at the Battle of the Pulador.

away the "microcosm" of the bourgeois state like a henhouse in an earthquake, the scientific "Swiss guards" of the rule of capital stand before the gate of their stronghold, the "national state," ready to defend it to the last gasp. The first word of present-day political economy, its basic concept, is a scientific mystification in the interest of the bourgeoisie.

5

Political economy is frequently defined for us in the simple formula that it is "the science of people's economic relations." Those who offer this kind of formulation believe they have navigated the reefs of the "national economy" and the world economy by universalizing the problem into something indefinite and speaking of "people's" economic relations in general. Tossing the problem up into thin air, however, does not make it any more clear, but may well just confuse it even more, as the question then arises as to why and wherefore this special science of "people's" economic relations—i.e. of *all* people at all times and in all circumstances—should be necessary.

Let us take any example we like of people's economic relations, as simple and transparent as possible. Let us place ourselves in the time when the present world economy did not yet exist, when commodity trade flourished only in the towns while in the countryside a natural economy still prevailed, i.e. production for one's own need, with the large landed proprietors as well as on the small peasant holdings. Let us take, for example, the relations described by Dugald Stewart in the Scottish highlands in the 1850s:

> In some parts of the Highlands of Scotland ... every peasant, according to the Statistical Account, made his own shoes of leather tanned by himself. Many a shepherd and cottar too, with his wife and children, appeared at Church in clothes which had been touched by no hands but their own, since they were shorn from the sheep and sown in the flax-field. In the preparation of these, it is added, scarcely a single article had been purchased, except the awl, needle, thimble, and a very few parts of the ironwork employed in the weaving. The dyes, too, were chiefly extracted by the women from trees, shrubs, and herbs.*

Alternatively, we can take an example from Russia, where only a relatively short time ago, in the late 1860s, the peasant economy could be commonly described as follows:

---

* Karl Marx, *Capital* Vol. 1, p. 616, note 27. Marx is quoting from Stewart's *Collected Works*, Vol. 8, edited by William Hamilton (Edinburgh: Thomas Constable and Sons, 1855), pp. 327–8.

The land that he [the farmer of the Viasma district in the province of Smolensk—R.L.] cultivates provides him with food and clothing, almost everything that is necessary for his existence: bread, potatoes, milk, meat, linen, cloth, sheep pelts and wool for warm clothing ... All that he buys with money are boots and a few personal items such as belt, cap and gloves, as well as some necessary household equipment: iron and wooden dishes, poker, kettle and the like.[13]

Today there are still peasant economies of this kind in Bosnia and Herzegovina, in Serbia and Dalmatia. If we were to put to one of these self-sufficient peasants in the Scottish Highlands or Russia, Bosnia or Serbia the usual professorial questions of political economy about "economic purpose," "creation and distribution of wealth" and the like, he would stare at us in amazement. As to the reason why he and his family work, or to put it in scholarly terms, the "motivating force" that drives their "economic activity," he would exclaim: Well, we have to live, and food doesn't just drop from the sky. If we didn't work, we'd die of starvation. So we work to get by, to eat our fill, to put clothes on our back and have a roof over our head. As to *what* we produce, "what orientation" we give our labor, that's another foolish question! We produce what we need, what any peasant family needs to live. We grow wheat and rye, oats and barley, we plant potatoes, we keep a few cows and sheep, chickens and ducks. In winter we do the spinning, which is women's work, while men are busy with axes, saws and hammers making whatever the house needs. You can call this a "rural economy" or a "business," whatever you like, but at all events we have to do a bit of everything, as all kinds of things are needed in the home and the fields. How do we "divide" these tasks? Another strange question! The men naturally do what needs male strength, the women take care of the house, the cows and the henhouse, the children help with this and that. Or are you saying that I should send my wife to chop wood while I milk the cows myself? (The good man is unaware—we can add here—that there are many primitive peoples, for example the Brazilian Amerindians, where it is precisely the woman who gathers wood in the forest, digs up roots and goes to pick fruit, while among the herding peoples of Africa and Asia men not only look after the cattle but also milk them. In Dalmatia today, you can still see a woman carrying a heavy load on her back with a strong man complacently riding his donkey alongside, puffing away at his pipe. This "division of labor" seems just as natural to them as it appears obvious to our own peasants that the man should chop wood and his wife milk the cows.) And besides, this question about my "wealth"! That again, every child in the village understands. A wealthy peasant is one who has a full barn, a well-stocked stable, a respectable flock of sheep and a large henhouse; a peasant is poor if he runs short of flour already by Easter, and water drips through his roof when it rains. What does an "increase in wealth" depend on? No question about it. If I had a larger plot of land, I would naturally be richer, and if in summer, Heaven forbid, we had a heavy hailstorm, everyone in the village would be impoverished in the space of twenty-four hours.

Here we have let the peasant patiently answer the learned questions of political economy, but we are certain that, before the professor who arrived with his notebook and fountain pen to make a scientific study of such a peasant household in the Scottish Highlands or Bosnia had asked even half of his questions, he would already have been shown out of the door. In fact, all relationships in this kind of peasant economy are so simple and self-evident that their dissection with the scalpel of political economy seems an idle game.

The objection can of course be made that we perhaps chose an unfortunate example, by focusing on a tiny self-sufficient peasant household whose extreme simplicity is determined by its scanty resources and dimensions. So let us take another example. Leaving the small peasant household to continue its modest existence in a remote corner of the world, we turn our attention to the highest summit of a powerful empire, the household of Charlemagne. This sovereign, who made the Germanic Empire the most powerful in Europe at the start of the ninth century, undertaking no fewer than fifty-three crusades for the expansion and strengthening of his realm,* and uniting under his scepter not just present-day Germany but also France, Italy, Switzerland, the northern part of Spain, Holland and Belgium, was also very concerned with economic conditions on his lands and estates. He drafted personally a special legislative decree on the economic principles of his estates, consisting of seventy paragraphs, the celebrated "*Capitulare de villis*,"† i.e. law about landed estates, a priceless gem of historical survival which has happily come down to us through the dust and mildew of the archives. This claims very special attention for two reasons. Firstly, most of Charlemagne's estates subsequently developed into powerful imperial cities: Aachen, Cologne, Munich, Basel and Strasbourg, for example, along with several other towns, were at this time agricultural estates of the emperor. Secondly, Charlemagne's economic institutions became a model for all major spiritual and temporal landed estates of the early Middle Ages; these adopted the survivals of ancient Rome and the refined way of life of its noble villas, transplanting them into the coarser milieu of the young Germanic warrior nobility,

---

*   At the end of the eleventh and beginning of the twelfth century, as the Catholic Church sought to inspire the faithful to take part in the Crusades against the Muslims, a legend was propagated that Charlemagne's wars of conquest had paved the way for them. In fact, these "crusades" of Charlemagne were military expeditions aimed at conquest and were not primarily motivated by religious considerations.

†   Capitularium were a series of administrative acts issued by the Frankish Merovingian and Carolingian dynasties. The Capitulare de Villis Imperialis was issued by Charlemagne around 800, and (among other things) delineated the plants (89 in all, some but not all of medicinal value) that should be included in gardens throughout his empire. The list was probably compiled by Abbot Benedict of Aniane.

and his prescriptions for the cultivation of vineyards and gardens, fruit and vegetables, fowl, etc. were an act in the history of civilization.

Let us take a closer look at this decree. The great emperor demanded here, above all else, to be served honestly and have his properties looked after so that his subjects living on them were protected against poverty; they should not be overburdened with labor; if they worked at night, they were to be compensated for this. But the subjects for their part were to take diligent care of the vineyards and put the pressed wine into bottles to avoid damage. If they evaded their duties they were chastised "on the back or elsewhere." The emperor also lay down that bees and geese were to be kept on his domains; the birds were to be kept well and increased. The stocks of cows and brood mares were also to be expanded, and the greatest care taken of sheep.

We desire, the emperor continued, that our woods are managed properly, that they are not uprooted and that sparrowhawks and falcons are kept there. Fat geese and chickens should be always available for us; eggs that are not consumed in the household should be sold on the market. Each of our estates should keep a store of good featherbeds, mattresses, covers, tableware of copper, lead, iron and wood, chains, kettle-hooks, axes and drills, so that nothing needs to be borrowed from other people. The emperor further prescribed that an exact account be kept of the harvests from his estates, and he lists: vegetables, butter, cheese, honey, oil, vinegar, turnips "and other trifles," as it says in the text of the famous decree. He continues that on each of his estates there should be various artisans, a sufficient number fluent in every craft, and he again lists the precise kinds in detail. He also made Christmas Day the date on which he required accounts of his wealth, and the smallest peasant did not count each head of stock and each egg on his holding more carefully than the great Charlemagne. Paragraph 62 of the decree states: "It is important that we know what and how much we have of all these things." And he again lists: oxen, mills, wood, ships, wine stocks, vegetables, wool, linen, flax, fruit, bees, fish, hides, wax and honey, old and new wine, and whatever else was supplied to him. He adds, as generous consolation for the dear subjects who were to supply all this: "We hope that all this does not appear too hard to you, for you can demand the same for your part, since everyone is lord of his property." Further, we find exact prescriptions as to the way in which wines should be packed and transported, these apparently being a particular concern in the great emperor's governance: "Wine should be carried in barrels with firm iron hoops and never in skins. As for flour, this is to be carried in doubled crates and covered with leather, so that it can be brought across rivers without damage being done. I also want exact account to be made of the horns of my goats, male and female, as well of the skins of the wolves that are shot each year. In the month of May, merciless war against the young wolf cubs should not be neglected." Finally, in the last paragraph, Charlemagne lists all the flowers, trees and plants that he wants to have tended in his garden: roses, lilies, rosemary, gherkins, onions, radishes, caraway, etc. The famous decree more or less comes to an end with a list of varieties of apple.

This is a picture of the imperial economy in the ninth century, and although we have here one of the most powerful and richest princes of the Middle Ages, anyone must admit that his economy, along with the principles on which it was managed, are surprisingly reminiscent of the dwarf-size peasant holding that we considered above. Here too, the imperial landlord, if we were to put to him the familiar basic questions of political economy about the nature of wealth, the purpose of production, the division of labor, etc., etc., would refer with a royal wave of the hand to the mountains of grain, wool and flax, the barrels of wine, oil and vinegar, the stables full of cows, oxen and sheep. And we would be equally at a loss to know what "laws" of political-economic science were to be investigated and deciphered in this economy, since all the connections, cause and effect, labor and its result, are as clear as day.

The reader might draw our attention here, once again, to the fact that we have taken a misleading example. It is clear after all from Charlemagne's decree that this was not dealing with the public economic relationships of the Germanic Empire, but rather with the private economy on the emperor's estates. But it would certainly be a historical error for anyone to try to oppose these two concepts in the context of the Middle Ages. The capitulary does indeed refer to the economy on the estates and properties of Charlemagne, but he managed this economy as ruler, not as a private person. Or more accurately: the emperor was a lord on his domains, but likewise any noble lord in the Middle Ages, i.e. in the time *after* Charlemagne, was more or less such an emperor on a small scale, i.e. he was by virtue of his free noble domain a legislator, tax collector and judge for the population on his estates. The very form of Charlemagne's economic dispositions, as we have mentioned them, shows that these were indeed acts of government: they make up one of his sixty-five laws or capitularies which, drafted by the emperor, were made known at the annual imperial assemblies of his magnates. And the regulations about radishes and iron-clad wine barrels derive from the same fullness of power and are drafted in the same style as, for example, the admonitions to the bishops in his "*Capitula episcoporum*," in which Charles gives the bishops a box on the ears and warns them energetically not to curse, not to get drunk, not to visit places of ill-fame, not to keep women or charge too high a price for the holy sacraments. We may go where we please in the Middle Ages, but nowhere in the countryside do we find an economic enterprise for which Charlemagne's does not offer a model and a type, whether it is the estates of noble lords or the simple peasant holding, whether we have an

---

*   The Capitula Episcoporum was a series of written instructions sent to bishops and their clergy, beginning shortly before 800, which aimed to raise the rural priesthood to a level of chastity and literacy in the face of the widespread corruption that dominated the priesthood at the time.

individual peasant family operating for itself or a communally operating mark*
community.

What is most striking in both examples is that here the needs of human life
directly govern and determine labor, and the result thus corresponds so exactly
to intention and need that the relationships maintain, whether on a greater or
smaller scale, this surprising simplicity and transparency. Both the small peasant
on his holding and the great monarch in his court know quite exactly what they
want to achieve by their production. And no magic is required to know this: both
want to satisfy the natural human needs for eating and drinking, clothing and the
conveniences of life. The only difference is that the peasant sleeps on a straw sack
and the great lord on a soft featherbed, one drinks beer and mead, or just plain
water, while the other has fine wine on his table. But the basis of the economy and
its task of directly satisfying human needs remains the same. The result corresponds in the same self-evident way to the labor that proceeds from this natural
task. Here too, again, there are differences in the labor process: the peasant works
along with his family members, and the fruits of his labor correspond to the
extent of his holding and his share in the common land; more precisely—since
we are speaking here of medieval serf labor—he what is left over after providing dues and labor services for the lords and the church. The emperor or any
other noble lord does not work himself, but has his subjects and subordinates
work for him. But whether a peasant and his family work for themselves, or all
together under the management of a village headman, or under the lord's bailiff,
the result of this labor is still nothing other than a particular sum of means of
subsistence in the wider sense, i.e. precisely what is required, and more or less in
the amount required. No matter which way you look at an economy of this kind,
there is no puzzle to be found in it that could only be solved by profound investigation and a special science. The slowest-witted peasant in the Middle Ages knew
precisely what his "wealth"—or rather, his poverty—depended on, leaving aside
the natural phenomena that visited both lord's and peasant's lands from time
to time. He knew quite precisely that his distress as a peasant had a very simple
and direct cause: first of all the boundless extraction of labor services and dues
on the part of the lords, and secondly the theft by these same lords of common
lands—woods, meadows and waters. And what the peasant knew he cried aloud
to the world in the peasant wars, and showed by setting fire to the houses of his
bloodsuckers. What remains for scientific investigation here is only the historical
origin and development of those relationships, the question as to how it could
happen that throughout Europe the formerly free peasant landholdings were
transformed into noble estates extracting dues and tolls, the formerly free peasantry into a mass of subjects liable to serf labor and later also to monetary dues.

---

* The *Mark* was an ancient Germanic communal form of village organization that survived
in modified form into modern times. Luxemburg subsequently uses the term more universally,
applying to what she saw as similar forms in various societies around the world.

The situation looks completely different as soon as we turn to any phenomenon of *present-day* economic life. Let us take for example one of the most remarkable and outstanding phenomena: the *trade crisis*. We have all experienced already several major crises of trade and industry, and are familiar from our own observation with the process classically described by Frederick Engels in the following terms:

> Commerce is at a standstill, the markets are glutted, products accumulate, as multitudinous as they are unsalable, hard cash disappears, credit vanishes, factories are closed, the mass of the workers are in want of the means of subsistence; bankruptcy follows upon bankruptcy, execution upon execution. The stagnation lasts for years; productive force and products are wasted and destroyed wholesale, until the accumulated mass of commodities finally filter off, more or less depreciated in value, until production and exchange gradually begin to move again. Little by little the pace quickens. It becomes a trot. The industrial trot breaks into a canter, the canter in return grows into the headlong gallop of a perfect steeplechase of industry, commercial credit, and speculation, which finally, after breakneck leaps, ends where it began—in the ditch of a crisis.*

We all know that a commercial crisis of this kind is the terror of every modern country, and the way in which such a crisis is heralded is already very instructive. After a spell of some years of prosperity and good business, a vague rumor begins in the press here and there, with reports of some disturbing news about bankruptcies on the stock exchanges; then the spots in the press become larger, the stock exchange ever more turbulent, the central bank raises the discount rate, making the supply of credit more difficult and limited, until news about bankruptcies and unsalable stocks falls like a cloudburst. The crisis is then in full swing, and the struggle now is about who bears responsibility. The business people blame the brusque refusal of credit by the banks, the banks blame the speculative craze of the stockbrokers, they in turn blame the industrialists, the industrialists blame the lack of money in the country, and so on. And when business finally begins to get under way again, it is once more the stock exchange and the newspapers that note the first signs of improvement, until hope, calm and security again appear for a while. What is remarkable about all this, however, is the fact that the crisis is seen and treated by all those involved, by the whole society, as something that stands outside the realm of human will and human calculation, like a blow of fate inflicted on us by an invisible power, a test from heaven of the same order as a severe storm, an earthquake or a flood. Even the language in which the newspapers like to report a crisis is fond of such

---

* Frederick Engels, *Anti-Dühring. Herr Eugen Dühring's Revolution in Science*, *Marx-Engels Collected Works*, Vol. 25 (New York: International Publishers, 1987), p. 263.

expressions as "gloomy clouds are gathering over the formerly bright skies of the business world," or, if a sharp increase in the discount rate is announced, they inevitably use the headline "Storm Signal," just as we later read about the thunder passing and the horizon brightening. This way of writing expresses rather more than mere fatuousness on the part of the ink coolies of the business world, it is precisely typical of the strange effect of the crisis, its apparently law-like character. Modern society notes its approach with terror, it bends its neck and trembles at the hail-like blows, it awaits the end of the test and then raises its head again, at first timid and unbelieving, then finally relieved.

This is precisely the way that, in the Middle Ages, people awaited the outbreak of a great famine or plague, the way that country folk today suffer a heavy thunderstorm and hail: the same helplessness and impotence in the face of a severe trial. And yet famine and plague, even if ultimately social phenomena, are initially and immediately the results of natural phenomena: a harvest failure, the spread of disease-inducing germs and the like. Thunder is a basic event of physical nature, and no one, at least at the present stage of science and technology, is able to bring about a thunderstorm or to avert one. But what is this modern crisis? It consists, as we know, in too many commodities being produced without finding an outlet, with the result that trade and industry come to a halt. The production and sale of commodities, trade and industry—all these are purely human relations. It is people themselves who produce commodities, and people themselves who buy them; trade is conducted between one person and another, and in the circumstance that make up the modern crisis we do not find a single element that lies outside of human action. It is therefore nothing other than human society itself that periodically provokes the crisis. And yet we also know that the crisis is a real trial for modern society, that it is expected with dread and suffered with desperation, that it is not wanted or wished for by anyone. Apart from a few stock-exchange sharks who try to enrich themselves quickly during a crisis at the expense of others, but frequently fail in the process, the crisis is for everyone at the very least a danger or a disturbance. No one wants the crisis, and yet it comes. People create it with their own hands, yet they do not intend it for anything in the world. The medieval peasant on his little plot produced partly what his lord required, partly what he himself needed: grain and meat, provisions for himself and his family. The great medieval lord had others produce for him what he wanted and needed: grain and meat, fine wines and fine clothes, means of subsistence and luxury goods for himself and his household. Present-day society however produces what it neither wants nor can use: crises. It periodically produces means of subsistence that it cannot consume; it suffers periodic hunger alongside tremendous stocks of unsold products. Need and satisfaction, the purpose and the result of labor, no longer match; between them stands something unclear and puzzling.

Let us take another example, all too well known to workers of all countries:

unemployment. Unemployment is no longer, like crises, a cataclysm that visits society from time to time. It has become today, to a greater or lesser degree, a constant and everyday accompaniment to economic life. The most well-organized and well-paid categories of workers, who keep lists of their unemployed, show an uninterrupted series of figures for each year, even each month and week; these figures fluctuate substantially, but they never completely peter out. How powerless present-day society is in the face of unemployment, this dreadful scourge of the working class, is shown each time that the scale of this evil becomes so great that it forces legislative bodies to concern themselves with it. The regular course of such discussions, after a lengthy to-ing and fro-ing, culminates in the decision to conduct an inquiry, an investigation, into the present number of unemployed. The main thing here is to measure the present state of the evil, as the level of water is measured with a depth gauge in times of flood, and in the best case weak palliative measures are taken in the form of support for the unemployed—generally at the cost of those in work—with a view to dampening the effects of the evil, without the slightest attempt being made to do away with the evil itself.

In the early years of the nineteenth century, Reverend [Thomas] Malthus, the great prophet of the English bourgeoisie, proclaimed with the heart-chilling brutality that was characteristic of him:

> A man born into a world already occupied, whose family has no means of supporting him or of whose labor society has no need, has not any right to demand any portion whatever of food. He is really one too many on the land. No cover is laid for him at the great banquet of Nature. Nature tells him to go away, and does not delay herself to put the order into execution.*

Official society today, with its characteristic "social-reforming" hypocrisy, scorns such crass expressions. In practice, however, it finally tells the unemployed proletarian, "whose labor it does not need," to "go away" in one way or another, quickly or slowly, to leave this world—the increasing figures of disease, infant mortality and crimes against property during every great crisis speak for themselves.

The comparison we have made between unemployment and flood even shows the striking fact that we are less *impotent* in the face of elemental events of a physical kind than we are towards our own, purely social, purely human affairs! The periodic spring floods that do such damage in the east of Germany are ultimately only the result of the current neglected state of water management.

---

* Thomas Malthus, *An Essay on the Principle of Population, as It Affects the Future Improvement of Society, with Remarks on the Speculations of Mr Godwin, M. Condorcet, and other Writers* (London: J. Johnson, 1803), pp. 531–2. This celebrated passage appeared only in the earlier editions of Malthus's book, and was subsequently omitted.

The present level of technology already affords sufficient means for protecting agriculture from the power of water, even for making good use of this power; it is just that these methods can only be applied at the highest level of a large-scale, interconnected, rational water management, which would have to refigure the whole area affected, appropriately disposing arable zones and meadows, building dams and sluices, and regulating rivers. A great reform of this kind can certainly not be undertaken, partly because neither private capitalists nor the state are willing to provide the resources for such an project, partly because on the large scale that would be needed, the barriers of a whole range of private landowning rights would be infringed. But society today does have the resources for tackling the water danger and harnessing the raging element, even if it is not in a position to use them at this time. On the other hand, this society has not discovered a method for combating unemployment. And yet this not an element, a natural phenomenon of physics, but a purely human product of economic relations. And once again here we come up against an economic puzzle, a phenomenon that no one intended, no one consciously strove for, but which all the same appears with the regularity of a natural phenomenon, over people's heads as it were.

But we need in no way take the case of these striking phenomena of present-day life, crises or unemployment, calamities and cases of an extraordinary nature, which in popular imagination form an exception to the usual course of things. Let us take one of the most familiar examples from everyday life, repeated a thousand times in all countries: *the fluctuating prices of commodities*. Every child knows that the prices of goods are in no case fixed and unchangeable, but on the contrary, go up and down almost daily—sometimes, indeed, every hour. If we pick up a newspaper, and turn to the report on the commodities market, we can read the price movements of the previous day: wheat rather weak in the morning, somewhat livelier in the afternoon, rising towards the close of business, or else falling. The same goes for copper and iron, sugar and vegetable oil. And likewise with shares in different industrial firms, government and private bonds, on the stock market. Price fluctuations are a constant, daily, quite "normal" phenomenon of contemporary economic life. These price movements, moreover, cause a daily and hourly change in the wealth of those who possess all these products and papers. If the cotton price rises, then the wealth of all dealers and manufacturers who have stocks of cotton in their warehouses also rises temporarily; if prices fall, their wealth dwindles similarly. If copper prices rise, then the owners of shares in the copper mines grow richer, and if these fall, they grow poorer. In this way, people can become millionaires or beggars in a few hours as a result of simple fluctuations in price, as reported in a stock-market telegram, and this is the essential basis of the whole giddiness of stock-market speculation. The medieval lord could grow richer or poorer as a result of a good or a bad harvest, or enrich himself as a robber baron making a good catch by waylaying a passing merchant, or—and this was the most well-tested and favored method—increase his wealth by pressing more out of his peasant serfs than he managed previously, by increasing the services and dues he demanded. Today, a man can suddenly become rich or poor without doing the slightest thing himself, without lifting a finger, without any kind of natural event, even without anyone having given him something or violently robbing him. Price fluctuations are likewise a secretive movement, guided behind people's backs by an invisible power, and causing a continuous shift and fluctuation in the distribution of social wealth. The movement is noted in the same way as temperature is indicated on a thermometer, air pressure on a barometer. And yet commodity prices and their movements are obviously a purely human affair, with no magic involved. It is no one but people themselves who produce commodities with their own hands and determine their prices, simply that here again their action gives rise to something that no one intended or had in mind; here again, the need, end and result of people's economic action come into blatant imbalance.

What is the reason for this, and what are the obscure laws that make people's own economic life today bring about such strange events behind their backs? This can only be revealed by scientific investigation. It has become necessary to solve all these puzzles by way of strenuous investigation, deep reflection, analysis and comparison, in other words to make explicit the hidden connections that bring it about that the results of people's economic action no longer coincide with their intentions and their will—in sum, their consciousness. The lack of consciousness within the social economy thus becomes a task for scientific research; and here we have arrived directly at the root of political economy.

In recounting his journey around the world, Darwin says of the inhabitants of Tierra del Fuego:

> They often suffer from famine: I heard Mr. Low, a sealing-master intimately acquainted with the natives of this country, give a curious account of the state of a party of one hundred and fifty natives on the west coast, who were very thin and in great distress. A succession of gales prevented the women from getting shellfish on the rocks, and they could not go out in their canoes to catch seal. A small party of these men one morning set out, and the other Indians explained to him, that they were going a four days' journey for food: on their return, Low went to meet them, and he found them excessively tired, each man carrying a great square piece of putrid whale's-blubber with a hole in the middle, through which they put their heads, like the Gauchos do through their ponchos or cloaks. As soon as the blubber was brought into a wigwam, an old man cut off thin slices, and muttering over them, broiled them for a minute, and distributed them to the famished party, who during this time preserved a profound silence.[14]

So much for the life of one of the most backward peoples on earth. The limits within which their will and deliberate ordering of their economy can operate are here still extremely narrow. People here are still completely tied to the apron strings of external nature, and depend on its favor and disfavor. But within these narrow limits, the organization of the whole small society of some hundred and fifty individuals prevails. Concern for the future is only expressed in the wretched form of a stock of putrid whale's blubber. But this putrid stock is divided between everyone with due ceremony, and everyone similarly participates in the work of seeking food, under planned leadership.

Let us turn to a Greek *oikos*, the household economy of antiquity with slaves, which by and large also formed a "microcosm," a little world unto itself. Here extreme social inequality already prevails. Primitive need has been transformed into a comfortable surplus of the fruits of human labor. Physical labor has become the curse of some, idleness the privilege of others, with those who work even becoming the property of the non-workers. Yet here again, this relationship of domination involves the strictest planning and organization of the economy, the labor process and distribution. The determining will of the master is its foundation, the whip of the slave overseer its sanction.

On the feudal manor of the Middle Ages, the despotic organization of labor receives early on the visage of a detailed code elaborated in advance, in which the plan and division of labor, the duties of each as well as their claims, are clearly and firmly defined. On the threshold of this period of history stands that fine document that we have already cited: Charlemagne's *"Capitulare de villis,"* which still revels joyously and brightly in the wealth of physical enjoyments to which the economy is completely directed. At its end we have the baneful code of services and dues which, dictated by the unrestrained financial greed of the feudal lords, led to the German peasant war* of the sixteenth century,† and made the French peasant still 200 years later into that miserable and semi-bestialized creature who was only shaken to struggle for his human and civil rights by the shrill alarm clock of the great Revolution. But, until the broom of revolution swept away the feudal manor, this peasant was still in the misery of the relationship of direct mastery that firmly and clearly defined the relations of the feudal economy as an unavoidable fate.

Today we have neither masters nor slaves, neither feudal barons nor serfs. Freedom and equality before the law have in formal terms done away with all despotic relationships, at least in the old bourgeois states; in the colonies, as is

---

* The German Peasants' War was a massive popular revolt that swept Central Europe from 1524 to 1526. It involved almost half a million peasants (as well as many artisans and town dwellers), and represented both an economic and religious revolt against oppressive living conditions (especially concerning the destruction of the commons and debt peonage) and social hierarchy (especially among the clergy). It was put down with great bloodshed; as many as 100,000 peasants were massacred.

† The manuscript wrongly says "fifteenth century."

well known, these same states have frequently themselves introduced slavery and serfdom. Everywhere that the bourgeoisie is at home, *free competition* rules economic relations as their one and only law. This means the disappearance from the economy of any kind of plan or organization. Of course, if we look at an individual private firm, a modern factory or a large complex of factories and plants such as Krupp's, alternatively a great agricultural enterprise such as those of North America, we find here the strictest organization, the most far-reaching division of labor, the most refined planning based on scientific knowledge. Here everything works beautifully, directed by a *single* will and consciousness. But we scarcely leave the factory or farm gate than we are met already with chaos. Whereas the countless individual components—and a private firm today, even the most gigantic, is only a fragment of the great economic network that extends across the whole earth—whereas the fragments are most strictly organized, the whole of the so-called "national economy," i.e. the capitalist world economy, is completely unorganized. In the whole, which stretches across oceans and continents, no plan, no consciousness, no regulation prevails; only the blind reign of unknown, uncontrolled forces plays its capricious game with people's economic fate. There is indeed, still today, an over-powerful lord that governs working humanity: *capital*. But its form of government is not despotism but *anarchy*.

And it creates this anarchy by having the social economy bring about results that are unexpected and puzzling even to the people involved; it turns the social economy into a phenomenon that is foreign to us and alienated, whose laws we have to discover in the same way as we investigate the phenomena of external nature, which govern the life of the vegetable and animal realms, changes in the earth's crust and the movements of heavenly bodies. Scientific knowledge must subsequently discover the meaning and rule of the social economy, which no conscious plan has dictated in advance.

It is now clear why bourgeois political economists find it impossible to clearly pinpoint the nature of their science, to put their finger into the wound of their social order, to denounce it in its inherent criminality. To discover and confess that anarchy is the life element of the rule of capital means in the same breath to pronounce a death sentence, it means saying that its existence is only granted a temporary reprieve. It is clear now why the official scientific advocates of the rule of capital seek to conceal the matter with every kind of word-spinning, to direct attention away from the core to the outer shell, from the global economy to the "national economy." At the very first step across the threshold of political-economic knowledge, with the first fundamental question as to what political economy actually is and what is its basic problem, the paths of bourgeois and proletarian knowledge already diverge. With this first question, however abstract and immaterial for present social struggles it may appear at first sight, a special tie is already drawn between political economy as a science and the modern proletariat as a revolutionary class.

6

Once we adopt the perspective we have now reached, many things that first appeared uncertain now become clear.

To start with, the question of how old political economy is. A science whose task is to disclose the laws of the anarchic capitalist mode of production could naturally not arise earlier than this mode of production itself, not before the historical conditions for the class rule of the modern bourgeoisie had gradually been assembled by political and economic changes over the centuries.

According to Professor Bücher, of course, the origin of the present-day social order was something extremely simple, having little to do with preceding economic development. It was in fact the result of the superior will and elevated wisdom of absolutist princes.

"The construction of the *national economy*," Bücher explains—and we already know that for a bourgeois professor the concept "national economy" is only a mystifying description of capitalist production—

> is essentially a result of the political centralization that began with the rise of the territorial state model towards the end of the Middle Ages, and is reaching its culmination today with the creation of the unitary national state. The concentration of economic powers goes hand in hand with the bending of political special interests to the higher purposes of the whole. In Germany, it was the larger territorial princes who sought to bring the modern state idea to expression, in struggle with the landed aristocracy and the cities.[15]

But princely power also wrought the same great deeds in the rest of Europe—in Spain, Portugal, England, France, and the Netherlands.

> In all these countries, if to a varying degree, the struggle with the separate powers of the Middle Ages took place: the great nobles, the cities, provinces, spiritual and temporal corporations. Initially, it was a question of abolishing the independent circles that stood as an obstacle in the way of political concentration. But at the underlying foundation of the movement that led to the development of princely absolutism, there still slumbered the world-historical idea that the new and greater tasks of human civilization required a united organization of whole peoples, a great living community of interest, and this could only arise on the basis of a common economy.[16]

We have here the finest flowering of that serviceability in matters of thought that we have already noted among German professors of political economy. According to Professor Schmoller, the science of political economy arose at the command of enlightened absolutism. According to Professor Bücher, the whole capitalist mode of production is simply the fruit of sovereign will and the heaven-storming plans of absolutist princes. It would of course be very unfair to the great Spanish and French despots, not to mention their petty German counterparts, to raise the suspicion that in their boisterous games with the arrogant feudal lords at the end of the Middle Ages, or their bloody crusades against the cities of the Netherlands, they troubled themselves with any kind of "world-historical ideas" or "tasks of human civilization." This would mean turning historical events upside down.

Certainly, the establishment of large centralized bureaucratic states was an indispensable precondition for the capitalist mode of production, yet it was just as much itself only a *consequence* of the new economic requirements, so that it would be far more justifiable to turn Bücher's proposition around and declare that the construction of political centralization was "essentially" a fruit of the maturing "national economy," i.e. of capitalist production.

But if absolutism had an incontestable share in this process of historical preparation, it played this part with the same stupid lack of thought of a blind instrument of historical developmental tendencies, and could likewise contradict these same tendencies whenever the occasion arose. Thus the medieval despots by the grace of God considered the cities allied with them against the feudal lords simply as objects for blackmail, which they betrayed again to the feudal lords at the first opportunity. Thus they viewed the newly discovered regions of the world, with all their population and culture, immediately and exclusively as a suitable field for the most brutal, pernicious and crude plunder, to fill the "princely treasuries" with gold nuggets as quickly as possible, for a "higher cultural purpose." In the same way, later, we had the stubborn resistance to interposing between the "grace of God" rulers and their "loyal peoples" that sheet of paper, called a bourgeois parliamentary constitution, which is just as indispensable for the unhindered development of the rule of capital as is political unity and the large centralized states themselves.

It was in fact quite other powers at work, great shifts in the economic life of the European nations as they emerged from the Middle Ages, that pioneered the move to the new form of economy.

Once the discovery of America and the circumnavigation of Africa, i.e. the discovery of the sea route to India, had led to an unforeseen upswing and a shift in trade, the dissolution of feudalism and the guild regime was a powerful tendency in the towns. The violent conquests, land acquisitions and plundering expeditions in the newly discovered lands, the great spice trade with India, the extension of the slave trade supplying black Africans to the American plantations, very soon created in Western Europe new wealth and new needs. The small workshop of the guild artisan with all its fetters proved an impediment on the necessary expansion of production and its rapid progress. The great merchants created a way out by gathering artisans together in large factories outside the city precincts, so as to have them produce more speedily and better, untroubled by the narrow-minded guild regulations.

In England, the new mode of production was introduced by a revolution in the agricultural economy. The blossoming of wool manufacture in Flanders, with its great demand for wool, gave English feudal nobles the impulse to transform large expanses of agricultural land into sheep-walks, which meant the larger part of the English peasantry being driven out of house and home. This meant the creation of a massive number of property-less workers, proletarians, at the disposal of the emerging capitalist manufacture. The Reformation worked in the same direction, with the confiscation of church properties, some of which were handed to the court nobility and speculators, others squandered, with the greater part of their peasant population likewise driven from the soil. The manufacturers and capitalist farmers thus found a massive poor and proletarianized population, outside both feudal and guild restrictions, who, after a long martyrdom of vagabond existence, and bloody persecution by law and police, found a safe haven in wage slavery for the new class of exploiters. There immediately followed also the great technological transformations in manufacturing, which made it possible increasingly to use greater numbers of unskilled wage proletarians in place of skilled artisans or alongside them.

All this pressure and striving towards new relationships came up against feudal barriers and the misery of decomposing conditions. The natural economy that was determined by feudalism and in its very nature, as well as the impoverishment of the popular masses by the limitless pressure of serfdom, naturally restricted the domestic market for manufactured goods, while at the same time the guilds continued to fetter the most important condition of production, labor-power, in the towns. The state apparatus with its endless political fragmentation, its lack of public security, its jumble of tariff and trade-policy confusion, inhibited and burdened the new trade and production at every turn.

It was clear that the rising bourgeoisie in Western Europe, as representative of free world trade and manufacture, had in some way or another to clear all these obstacles out of the way, if it did not want to completely renounce its world historical mission. Before it broke feudalism to pieces in the great French Revolution, it first struggled with it critically, and the new science of political economy thus arose as one of the most important ideological weapons of the bourgeoisie in its struggle against the medieval feudal state and for the modern state of the capitalist class. The new economic order that was breaking through appeared right away in the form of new and rapidly arising riches, which poured over West European society and stemmed from quite different, more profitable and apparently inexhaustible sources than the patriarchal methods of feudal peasant slavery, which in any case had already reached the end of their natural life. The most striking source of the new enrichment was at first not the emerging new mode of production, but rather its pacemaker, the powerful upswing of world trade on the emergence from the Middle Ages—in the rich Italian commercial republics on the Mediterranean and in Spain, where the first questions of political economy arose, as well as the first attempts to answer them.

What is wealth? How do states become wealthy, and how are they made poor? This was the new problem, once the old notions of feudal society had lost their traditional validity in the whirlpool of new relations. Wealth is gold, for which anything can be bought. Trade therefore creates wealth. So those states become rich that are in a position to bring much gold into the country and not let any out. World trade, therefore, along with colonial conquests in the newly discovered lands and manufactures that produce goods for export, must be promoted by the state, while the import of products from abroad, which would draw gold out of the country, is forbidden. This was the first doctrine of political economy, which appeared in Italy already at the end of the sixteenth century, and came to prevail generally in the seventeenth century in England and France. And no matter how crude this doctrine was, it did offer the first sharp break with the mental universe of feudal natural economy, the first bold criticism of it, the first idealization of trade, of commodity production, and in this form—of capital: in sum the first program of a state policy after the hearts of the young bourgeoisie struggling to advance.

The focus soon switched from the merchant to the commodity-producing capitalist, but still only cautiously, under the mask of humble servant in the anteroom of the feudal lord. Wealth is by no means gold, which is simply the mediator in commodity trade, so the French *lumières** proclaimed in the eighteenth century. What a childish confusion to see gleaming metal as the firm basis of fortune! Can I eat metal if I'm hungry, or can it protect me from the winter cold? Didn't the Persian king Darius, with all his gold treasure, suffer from dreadful pangs of thirst on the battlefield, and would have willingly given it all away for a sip of water?† No, wealth means the gifts of nature in foodstuffs and materials, with which all of us, king and beggar alike, satisfy our needs. The more lavishly a population satisfies its needs, the wealthier a state is, as it can draw all the more in tax. But who is it that coaxes nature to make corn into bread, to make the thread from which we spin our clothes, the wood and ore from which we build houses and machinery? Agriculture! It is agriculture, not trade, that forms the true fount of wealth. The mass of the agricultural population, accordingly, the peasant masses whose hands create the wealth

---

* The French *lumières* were the members of the French Enlightenment, which included such individuals as Rousseau, Voltaire, Diderot, D'Holbach, and others.

† A reference to Darius III, the last king of the Archaemenid Empire of Persia. After suffering major defeats in several battles with Alexander the Great, he retreated eastward (towards present-day Afghanistan). With Macedonian and Greek forces in hot pursuit, two of his generals stabbed him with a lance and left him to die. When the Macedonian troops arrived, they found him crying out for water—a result of his serious wounds. He died soon thereafter.

of everyone, must be rescued from their boundless misery, protected from feudal exploitation, raised up to well-being! (And in this way I shall also find a market for my goods, the manufacturing capitalist quietly adds.) The great lords of the land, therefore, the feudal barons, into whose hands the whole wealth of agriculture flows, should be the only ones who pay taxes and maintain the state! (Which means, the capitalist again murmurs into his beard with a smile, that I also need pay no taxes.) Agriculture, accordingly, work in the bosom of nature, need only be freed from all the chains of feudalism, for the springs of wealth to flow in their natural abundance for people and state, and the supreme happiness of all people to stand automatically in a necessary harmony with the whole.*

If in these Enlightenment doctrines could be clearly heard already the approaching rumble of the storming of the Bastille [in 1789], the capitalist bourgeoisie soon felt strong enough to throw off the mask of obsequiousness, place itself sturdily in the foreground and demand without beating about the bush the restructuring of the whole state to suit them. Agriculture was in no way the only source of wealth, Adam Smith declared in England in the late eighteenth century. All wage labor that was harnessed to commodity production created wealth, whether on the farm or in manufacture! (Any kind of *labor*, said Adam Smith; but for him and his followers—who were already no more than a mouthpiece for the emerging bourgeoisie—people who labored were by nature capitalist wage-laborers!) For all wage-labor created, besides the most necessary wage for the worker's own subsistence, also rent to maintain the lord of the land and a profit as the wealth of the owner of capital, the entrepreneur. And this wealth was all the greater, the larger the number of workers in a workshop who were harnessed to labor under the command of a single capital, and the more detailed and meticulous the division of labor among them. This then was the true natural harmony, the true wealth of nations: from any kind of work, a wage for the laborers, a wage that kept them alive and forced them to further wage-labor; a rent sufficient for the careless life of the lords; and a profit attractive enough to make it worthwhile for the entrepreneur to pursue his business. *Everyone* is provided for without the clumsy old methods of feudalism. Promoting the "wealth of nations," therefore, meant promoting the wealth of the capitalist entrepreneur, who keeps the whole system in motion and with it the golden vein of wealth—the bleeding of wage-labor. Away then with all chains and obstacles of the good old days, as well as the more recent paternal methods of the state. Free competition, the free blossoming of private capital, the whole apparatus of taxation and state in the service of the capitalist entrepreneur—and everything will be for the best in this best of all worlds!

---

*   The position summarized here by Luxemburg corresponds to the views of the French Physiocrats, a school of economics (whose most important proponent was Francois Quesnay) that held that agricultural labor is the source of all value.

This was the economic gospel of the bourgeoisie, with all the wrappings peeled away, and with it political economy finally acquired its fundamental and true form. Of course, the practical reform proposals and advice of the bourgeoisie to the feudal state came to grief as hopelessly as all historic attempts to pour new wine into old bottles. In twenty-four hours the hammer of revolution succeeded in doing what half a century of reforming patchwork had failed to do. It was in fact the conquest of political power that provided the bourgeoisie with the conditions of their supremacy. But political economy, along with the philosophical, social and natural-rights theories of the age of Enlightenment, was above all a means for acquiring self-consciousness, a formulation of the class consciousness of the bourgeoisie and as such a precondition and impulse for the revolutionary act. Even in its palest offshoots, the work of bourgeois world-renovation in Europe was fed by the ideas of classical political economy. The bourgeoisie in England, in its stormy period of struggle for free trade, with which it inaugurated its supremacy on the world market, drew its weapons from the arsenal of Smith and Ricardo. And even the reformers of the Stein-Hardenberg-Scharnhorst era, who wanted to give Prussia's feudal plunder a more modern touch after the blows received at the battle of Jena,* if only to enhance its capacity for survival, developed their ideas from the doctrines of the English classics, so that the "young German"† political economist [Alexander von der] Marwitz could write in 1810 that along with Napoleon, Adam Smith was the most powerful ruler in Europe.‡

If we understand then why political economy first arose some hundred and fifty years ago, its later destiny becomes clear from the same point of view. If political economy appears as a science of the particular laws of the capitalist mode of production, its existence and function are evidently linked to the existence of this, and lose their foundation once this mode of production ceases to exist. In other words: political economy as a science has played out its role as soon as the anarchic economy of capitalism makes way for a planned economic order, consciously organized and managed by the whole of working society. The victory of the modern working class and the realization of socialism accordingly mean the end of political economy as a science. This is where a

---

*   This refers to the reforms inaugurated in Prussia by Karl Freiherr vom Stein, Karl August Fürst von Hardenberg, and Gerhard Johann David von Scharnhorst following the defeat of Prussian forces by Napoleon at the battle of Jena-Auerstedt in 1806. Prussia's defeat (it lost half its territory to the French) led an effort to reorganize its government along "rational" and "enlightenment" principles. The reforms included the abolition of serfdom and suppression of the guilds.

†   "Young Germany" (*Junges Deutschland*) was a movement of progressive writers from 1830 to 1850 that advocated democracy, socialism, equal rights, and the emancipation of women. Its foremost representatives were Heinrich Heine, Ludwig Börne and George Herwegh. Luxemburg was a great admirer of the movement.

‡   Alexander von der Marwitz, a Prussian nobleman, stated in a letter to Rahel Varnhagen in 1810, "Next to Napoleon, [Adam Smith] is now the mightiest monarch in Europe." For more on their relationship, see Hannah Arendt, *Rahel Varnhagen: Life Story of a Jewess*.

particular connection arises between political economy and the class struggle of the modern proletariat.

If it is the task and object of political economy to explain the laws of the origin, development and spread of the capitalist mode of production, it is an unavoidable consequence that it must as a further consequence also discover the laws of the decline of capitalism, which just like previous economic forms is not of eternal duration, but is simply a transitional phase of history, a rung on the endless ladder of social development. The doctrine of the emergence of capitalism thus logically turns into the doctrine of the decline of capitalism, the science of the mode of production of capital into the scientific foundation of socialism, the theoretical means of the bourgeoisie's domination into a weapon of the revolutionary class struggle for the liberation of the proletariat.

This second part of the general problem of political economy has of course not been solved by either French or English scholars from the bourgeois class, still less their German counterparts. One man drew the final consequences of the theory of the capitalist mode of production, a man who stood from the start on the class position of the revolutionary proletariat: Karl Marx. With this, socialism and the modern workers' movement was placed for the first time on an unshakeable foundation of scientific knowledge.

Socialism goes back for thousands of years, as the ideal of a social order based on equality and the brotherhood of man, the ideal of a communistic society. With the first apostles of Christianity, various religious sects of the Middle Ages, and in the German peasants' war, the socialist idea always glistened as the most radical expression of rage against the existing society. But in this ideal form, which could commend itself to any social milieu at any time, socialism remained no more than a golden fantasy, as unachievable as the appearance of the rainbow against the background of clouds.

It was in the late eighteenth and early nineteenth century that the socialist idea first appeared with vigor and force, freed from religious enthusiasm, but rather as an opposition to the terror and devastation that emerging capitalism wreaked on society. Yet this socialism too was basically nothing but a dream, the invention of individual bold minds. If we listen to the first forerunner of the revolutionary uprisings of the proletariat, Gracchus Babeuf, who carried out an attempted coup during the great French Revolution for the forcible introduction of social equality,* the only fact on which he was able to base his communist strivings was the gaping inequality of the existing social order. He did not tire, in his passionate articles and pamphlets, likewise in his speech in his own defense before the tribunal that sentenced him to death, of painting this in the most

---

* This refers to Babeuf's "Conspiracy of the Equals," in which he sought (along with Philippe Buonarroti, Sylvain Maréchal and Germain Charles Augustin-Alexandre Darthé) to overthrow the Directory in the waning days of the French Revolution, in 1796, and forcefully impose a regime based on equality and shared property. The Conspiracy proved a failure.

dismal colors. His gospel of socialism was a monotonous repetition of charges against the inequality of the existing order, against the sufferings and pains, the misery and humiliation, of the working masses, at whose expense a handful of idle people grow rich and rule. It was enough for Babeuf that the existing social order deserved to collapse, and it could in fact have been overthrown a hundred years earlier if there had been a group of determined men to seize state power and introduce a regime of equality, as the Jacobins* of 1795 sought to seize political power and introduce the republic.

The socialist ideas represented by the three great thinkers: [Claude Henri] Saint-Simon and [Charles] Fourier in France, [Robert] Owen in England, in the 1820s and 30s, with far greater genius and brilliance, relied on quite different methods, but essentially rested on the same foundation. Certainly, none of these three had in mind a revolutionary seizure of power for the realization of social-ism; on the contrary, they were, like the whole generation that followed the great Revolution [of 1789], disappointed by all social overthrow and all politics, and avowed supporters of purely peaceful propaganda methods. Yet the basis of the socialist idea was the same for all three: in essence, this was simply the project and invention of a mind of genius, who recommended its realization to tortured humanity, in order to redeem them from the hell of the bourgeois social order.

These socialist theories thus remained, despite the force of their criticisms and the spell of their future ideals, without significant influence on the real move-ments and struggles of contemporary history. Babeuf and his handful of friends sank like a frail bark in the powerful counter-revolutionary wash, without at first leaving any trace but a short illuminating line on the pages of revolutionary history. Saint-Simon and Fourier only founded sects of enthusiastic and talented supporters, who after a while scattered or took new directions, after they had spread rich and fertile stimulus in terms of social ideas, criticisms and initia-tives. It was Owen who had most effect on the mass of the proletariat, yet even his influence, after inspiring an elite troop of English workers in the 1830s and 40s, subsequently disappeared without trace.

A new generation of socialist leaders emerged in the 1840s: [Wilhelm] Weitling in Germany, [Pierre Joseph] Proudhon, Louis Blanc and Blanqui in France. The working class, for its part, had already embarked on struggle against the rule of capital, it had given the signal for class struggle in the elemental insurrections of the Lyons silk weavers in France,† and in the Chartist movement

---

* The Jacobin Club was a revolutionary circle of middle-class democrats who led the French Revolution of 1789 during its most radical phase, in 1793–94.

† The revolts of the silk weavers in Lyon in 1831 and 1834 were the first independent politi-cal actions of the French working class. The uprising of 1831 was in response to the refusal of the manufacturers to accept the higher wages for weavers that had been negotiated earlier. The workers routed government troops, who were forced to abandon the city before crushing the revolt, a week later. Another revolt broke out in 1834 over the arrest and firing of workers who had taken part in an earlier strike.

in England. But there was no direct connection between these spontaneous stirrings of exploited masses and the various socialist theories. The revolutionary proletarian masses did not have a definite socialist goal in mind, nor did the socialist theorists seek to base their ideas on a political struggle of the working class. Their socialism was to be realized by cleverly thought-out arrangements, such as Proudhon's "people's bank" for fair exchange of goods, or Louis Blanc's producer associations.* The only socialist who counted on political struggle as a means to carry out the social revolution was Blanqui, who was in this way the only genuine representative of the proletariat and its revolutionary class interest in this period. But his socialism was basically a project that was achievable at any time, as the fruit of the determined will of a revolutionary minority and a sudden overthrow that this would achieve.

The year 1848 was to see both the culmination and the crisis of this earlier socialism in all its varieties. The Paris proletariat, influenced by traditions of earlier revolutionary struggle and roused by various socialist systems, passionately clung to the vague ideas of a just social order. As soon as the bourgeois monarchy of Louis-Philippe was toppled,† the Paris workers used their position of power to demand from the terrified bourgeoisie the realization now of the "social republic" and a new "organization of labor." For the achievement of this program, the proletariat afforded the provisional government the celebrated timeframe of three months, during which time the workers starved and waited, while the bourgeoisie and petty-bourgeoisie quietly armed and prepared the subjection of the workers. The period ended with the memorable butchery of June, in which the ideal of a "social republic" achievable at any time was drowned in the streaming blood of the Paris proletariat.‡ The revolution of 1848 did not introduce the realm of social equality, but rather the political rule of the bourgeoisie and an unprecedented upswing of capitalist exploitation under the Second Empire.

At the same time, however, that socialism of the old schools seemed buried forever beneath the demolished barricades of the June insurrection, the socialist idea was placed on a completely new footing by Marx and Engels. These two sought the basis for socialism not in moral repugnance towards the existing

---

*   Proudhon advocated the "abolition" of money while retaining commodity exchange, by substituting money with notes or "chits" denoting the hours of labor performed by the worker. Marx sharply criticized Proudhon's approach in *The Poverty of Philosophy*, the *Grundrisse*, *Capital*, and other writings. Louis Blanc, a leader of the 1848 Revolution in France, advocated the creation through existing government institutions of "national workshops" to eliminate unemployment and poverty. Although an opponent of Bonapartism, he did not support the Paris Commune and remained largely aloof from the events of 1871.

†   Louis-Philippe was overthrown in February 1848, during the French Revolution of that year. He had come to power in 1830, and was the last king to rule France.

‡   On June 23, 1848, the populace of Paris rose up in a major insurrection, becoming known as the June days. It was brutally crushed by the forces of reaction. The June massacres paved the way for Louis Napoleon to assume power on December 2, 1848.

social order nor in cooking up all kinds of possible attractive and seductive projects, designed to smuggle in social equality within the present state. They turned to the investigation of the *economic* relationships of present-day society. Here, in the laws of capitalist anarchy itself, Marx discovered the real starting-point for socialist efforts. If the French and English classics of political economy had discovered the laws by which the capitalist economy lived and developed, Marx took up their work half a century later precisely at the point where they had broken this off. He discovered for his part how these same laws of the present-day social order acted towards their own downfall, by increasingly threatening the existence of society with the spread of anarchy and forming a chain of devastating economic and political catastrophes. It was thus, as Marx showed, the developmental tendencies of the rule of capital itself that at a certain stage of their maturity made necessary the transition to a planned mode of production, consciously organized by the whole working society, if the whole of society and human culture were not to collapse in the convulsions of unleashed anarchy. And the rule of capital hastened this fateful hour ever more energetically by bringing together its future gravediggers, the proletarians, in ever greater masses, by spreading itself over all corners of the earth, producing an anarchic world economy and in this way creating the basis for the proletariat of all countries to combine in a revolutionary world power for the abolition of capitalist class rule. In this way socialism ceased to be a project, a beautiful fantasy or even an experiment of particular groups of workers in separate countries. As the common program of political action of the international proletariat, socialism is *a historical necessity*, since it is a fruit of the economic developmental tendencies of capitalism.

It is clear then why Marx placed his own economic doctrine outside official political economy, calling it a "critique of political economy." The laws of capitalist anarchy and its future downfall that Marx brought to light are certainly a continuation of the political economy that was created by bourgeois scholars, but a continuation whose final results stand in very sharp contrast to the points of departure of this. The Marxian doctrine is a child of political economy, but a child that cost its mother her life. Political economy found its completion in Marx's theory, but also its conclusion as a science. What is still to follow—apart from the detailed development of Marx's doctrine—is simply the transformation of this doctrine into action, i.e. the struggle of the international proletariat for the realization of the socialist economic order. The end of political economy as a science thus amounts to a world historical act: its transformation into the practice of a world economy organized according to a plan. The final chapter of political-economic doctrine is the social revolution of the world proletariat.

The particular connection between political economy and the modern working class thereby proves to be a reciprocal relationship. If political economy, as this was extended by Marx, is on the one hand more than any other science the indispensable basis for proletarian enlightenment, on the other hand the class-conscious proletariat of today forms the only comprehending and receptive audience for the doctrine of political economy. At an earlier time, it was only with the decaying ruins of the old feudal society before their eyes that [François] Quesnay and [Pierre] Boisguilbert in France, Adam Smith and [David] Ricardo in England, full of pride and enthusiasm for the young bourgeois society and with a firm belief in the impending thousand-year rule of the bourgeoisie and its "natural" social harmony, fearlessly directed their penetrating gaze into the depths of the laws of capitalism.

Since then, the proletarian class struggle that has risen ever more powerfully, and especially the June insurrection of the Paris proletariat, has long since destroyed the faith of bourgeois society in its divine mandate. Since it has eaten from the tree of knowledge of modern class antagonisms, it shuns the classical nakedness in which it showed itself to the creators of its own political economy. It is clear today however that it was these scientific discoveries from which the spokesmen for the modern proletariat drew their most deadly weapons.

For several decades now, therefore, it is not just socialist political economy, but bourgeois political economy as well, in so far as this is genuinely scientific, that finds a deaf ear among the possessing classes. Unable to understand the teachings of their own great ancestors, and still less to accept the Marxian teaching that emerged from these and tolls the death knell of bourgeois society, today's bourgeois scholars produce under the name of political economy an inchoate brew of garbage from all kinds of scientific ideas and self-interested confusions, no longer pursuing the goal of investigating the real tendencies of capitalism, but only striving for the opposite aim of concealing these tendencies in order to defend capitalism as the best, eternal, and only possible economic order.

Forgotten and betrayed by bourgeois society, scientific political economy now seeks its audience only among the class-conscious proletarians, finding with them not just theoretical understanding but also vigorous fulfillment. It is political economy more than anything else to which Lassalle's well-known words apply: "If science and the workers, these two opposite poles of society, embrace one another, they will overwhelm in their arms all obstacles of civilization."[17]

III. MATERIAL ON ECONOMIC HISTORY (I)

1

Our knowledge of the earliest and most primitive economic forms is very recent. In 1847, Marx and Engels wrote in the first classic proclamation of scientific socialism, the *Communist Manifesto*, that "the history of all hitherto existing society is the history of class struggles."* But around the very same time that the creators of scientific socialism announced this notion, it began to be shaken by new discoveries on all sides. Almost every year brought formerly unknown insights into the ancient economic conditions of human society, leading to the conclusion that there must have been enormous stretches of time in past history in which there were not yet class struggles, since there was no division into different social classes, no distinction between rich and poor, and no private property.†

In the years 1851 to 1853, the first of Georg Ludwig von Maurer's epoch-making works was published in Erlangen, the *Einleitung zur Geschichte der Mark-, Hof-, Dorf- und Stadt-Verfassung und der öffentlichen Gewalt* [Introduction to the History of the Mark, Court, Village and Town Constitution],‡ casting a new light on the Germanic past and the social and economic structure of the Middle Ages. Several decades before, in some particular places—Germany, the Nordic countries and Iceland—people had already stumbled upon remarkable survivals of age-old agricultural arrangements that indicated the former existence of common ownership of land in those places, the existence of an agrarian communism. At first, however, no one knew what to make of these survivals. According to an earlier point of view, widespread since the writings of [Justus] Möser and [Nikolaus] Kindlinger, the cultivation of the soil in Europe was undertaken by individual households, each of whom was allocated a separate holding that was the household's private property. Only in the later Middle Ages, it was believed, were the formerly scattered dwellings brought together into villages for the sake of greater security, and the formerly separated household plots bundled together as village ones. Improbable on closer consideration as this notion appears, the

---

* See Marx and Engels, *Manifesto of the Communist Party, Marx-Engels Collected Works*, Vol. 6 (New York: International Publishers, 1976), p. 482.

† Engels sought to address this after Marx's death, by qualifying the statement "The history of all hitherto existing society is the history of class struggles" with a footnote to the 1888 edition of the *Manifesto* that read, "That is, all written history." Marx, however, who had studied the work of Morgan, Haxthausen and Kovalevsky prior to and independent of Engels, did not choose to qualify the sentence when he co-authored the Preface to the second Russian edition of the *Manifesto* in 1882.

‡ Georg Ludwig von Maurer, *Einleitung zur Geschichte der Mark-, Hof-, Dorf- und Stadt-Verfassung und der öffentlichen Gewalt* (Introduction to the History of the Mark, Manor, Village and Town Constitution) (Munich: C. Kaiser, 1854).

most unbelievable thing is what has to be assumed about its origin, i.e. that dwellings often quite far removed from one another were torn down simply to rebuild them in a different place, and further, that each person voluntarily gave up the convenient situation of his private fields around his house, which he was free to cultivate how he liked, in order to receive land that was divided into narrow strips scattered across open fields, whose cultivation was completely dependent on his fellow-villagers—unlikely as this theory was, it continued all the same to prevail until the mid nineteenth century. Maurer was the first to combine these various particular discoveries into a bold and wide-ranging theory, and he demonstrated conclusively, on the basis of immense factual material and the profoundest research in old archives, proclamations and legal institutions, that common property in land did not arise for the first time in the late Middle Ages, but was rather the typical and general age-old form of the Germanic settlements in Europe from the very beginning. Two thousand years ago and still earlier, in that first misty age of the Germanic people, who did not yet have any written history, the prevailing conditions were fundamentally different from those of today. There was then among the Germans no state with written obligatory laws, no divide between rich and poor, rulers and workers. They formed free *tribes* and *clans*, which wandered across Europe for a long time until they settled first temporarily and eventually permanently. The first cultivation of land in Germany, as Maurer showed, was undertaken not by individuals, but by whole clans and tribes, as it was in Iceland by larger societies known as *frändalid* and *skulldalid*—i.e. friendships and retinues.[*] The oldest information about the ancient Germans, which we have from the Romans, authenticates this notion, as does the examination of institutions that have survived. The first peoples who populated Germany were migrating pastoralists. Like other nomads, stock raising and the possession of rich meadows for this was their main concern. In the long run, however, they could not exist without agriculture as well, as was also the case with other migrant peoples old and new. And it was precisely in this condition of nomadic economy mixed with agriculture, yet with stock-raising still apparently their main activity and cultivation something subordinate, that Julius Caesar found the Germanic populations of the Suevi or Swabians.[†] Similar conditions, customs and institutions were also noted among the Franks, Allemanni, Vandals[‡] and other Germanic tribes. All these

---

[*] In many ancient northern Scandanavian societies, the land was originally cultivated by groups based on intimate kinship ties. These were called frändalid and skulldalid, which means an association of friends. Such lands could not be alienated.

[†] The Suevi, or Swabians, were a Germanic people originally from east of the Elbe. In the first century BC they unsuccessfully tried to enter Gaul and settled between the Rhine and the Danube, in southwestern Germany.

[‡] The Allemanni were originally an alliance of several German tribes, located in the Upper Rhine, in southwestern Germany and northern Switzerland. By 800 AD they were absorbed by the Franks. The Vandals were an eastern German tribe that may have originally come from Sweden.

Germanic populations settled as coherent tribes and clans, rapidly cultivating the land and gathering together whenever more powerful tribes pressed one way or another, or their pasture was no longer sufficient. Only when the migrating tribes had become peaceful and none of the others any longer pressed them, did they remain for a longer time in these settlements and thus gradually acquired fixed territories. This settling down, however, whether at an earlier or a later date, whether on virgin land or on former Roman or Slavic possessions, took place by whole tribes and clans. In this process, each tribe, and each clan within a tribe, took over a particular area, which then belonged in common to everyone involved. The ancient Germans did not know any *meum* and *tuum*[*] in connection with land. Each clan rather formed as it settled a so-called mark community, which cultivated, partitioned and worked in common the land that it held. Each individual received by lot a share of the fields, which he was only given to use for a definite time, the strictest equality being observed in this sharing of the land. All economic, legal and general affairs of these mark communities, which generally also formed a "hundred" of arms-bearing men, were handled by the assembly of mark members itself, and this also chose the mark leader and other public officials.

It was only in mountain, forest or marshy districts, where lack of space or cultivable land made denser settlement impossible, as for example in the Odenwald,[†] Westphalia and the Alps, that the Germans settled as individual households. Yet these too formed into communities, with meadows, woods and pastures rather than fields being the common property of the whole village, the so-called "common land" (*Allmende*), and all public affairs being dealt with by the mark community.

The tribe, as the ensemble of many such mark communities, generally around a hundred, most often came into play only as the highest judicial and military unit. This mark-community organization, as Maurer showed in the twelve volumes of his great work, formed the foundation as well as the smallest cell of the whole social network, from the very start of the Middle Ages through to quite recent modern times, with feudal manors, villages and towns, in different modifications, all emerging out of it, and its ruins can be seen right to the present day in certain districts of Central and Northern Europe.

When the first discoveries of age-old common property in land in Germany and the Nordic countries became known, the theory was put forward that this was a particular and specifically Germanic institution, which could only be

---

In the fifth century they invaded northern Africa, Sicily, Corsica, and Sardinia, and sacked Rome in 455 AD. Their kingdom was destroyed in the sixth century by the Eastern Roman Emperor Justinian I.

    *   Latin for "mine and yours."

    †   The Odenwald is a mountain range in southwestern Germany, in the northern part of Baden-Würtemberg.

explained in terms of the particularities of the Germanic national character. Although Maurer himself was quite free from this national view of Germanic agricultural communism, and pointed out similar examples among other peoples, it generally remained a fixed assertion in Germany that the old rural mark community was a peculiarity of Germanic public and legal relations, an emanation of the "Germanic spirit." Yet almost at the same time as Maurer's first publications on the ancient village communism of the Germans, new discoveries came to light in a quite different part of the European continent. Between 1847 and 1852, the Westphalian Baron von Haxthausen, who had traveled in Russia in the early 1840s at the invitation of Tsar Nicholas I, published in Berlin his *Studien über die inneren Zustände, das Volksleben und insbesondere die ländlichen Einrichtungen Russlands* [Studies on the Internal Conditions of Russia, the Life of its People and Especially its Rural Institutions].* From this work the world learned to its astonishment that in the east of Europe fully analogous institutions still persisted. The age-old village communism, whose ruins in Germany had to be unveiled with difficulty from the overlays of later centuries and millennia, was suddenly found alive and kicking in the enormous empire to the east. In both the book mentioned above, and in his later work published in 1866 in Leipzig on *Die ländliche Verfassung Russlands* [The Rural Constitution of Russia],† Haxthausen demonstrated that the Russian peasants knew nothing of private property in fields, meadows and woods, the village as a whole being the real owner of these, while individual peasant families obtained only temporary use of parcels of land—by drawing lots just as with the ancient Germans.‡ In Russia, at the time when von Haxthausen traveled and investigated, serfdom was still in full force, and at first glance it was thus all the more striking that under the rigid surface of a harsh serfdom and a despotic state apparatus the Russian village presented a little closed-off world unto itself, with rural communism and the communal handling of all public affairs by the village assembly, the *mir*.§ The German discoverer of these peculiarities explained the Russian

---

* August Freiherr von Haxthausen, *Studien über die inneren Zustände, das Volksleben und insbesondere die ländlichen Einrichtungen Russlands* (Studies on the Internal Conditions of Russia, the Life of its People and Especially its Rural Institutions) (Hanover: Hahn, 1847–52).

† See August Freuherr von Haxthausen, *Die ländliche Verfgassung Russlands* (The Rural Constitution of Russia) (Leipzig: Brockhaus, 1866).

‡ Several recent studies have cast doubt on some of Haxthausen's findings on the grounds that he made generalizations about Russia as a whole on the basis of conditions that prevailed only in certain areas. See especially T. K. Dennison and A.W. Carus, "The Invention of the Russian Rural Commune: Haxthausen and the Evidence," *The Historical Journal* (2003), Vol. 46, pp. 561–82.

§ The *mir* refers to the communal possession of the land as well as the association of representatives that govern the working of the land. For Marx's analysis of the *mir*, see *The Late Marx and the Russian Road: Marx and "the Peripheries of Capitalism*," edited by Teodor Shanin (New York: Monthly Review Press 1983), pp. 95–133. A comparison of Marx and Luxemburg's studies of the *mir* can be found in "Accumulation, Imperialism, and Pre-Capitalist Formations: Luxemburg and Marx on the non-Western World," by Peter Hudis, *Socialist Studies/Études socialistes*, Vol. 6, No. 2 (Fall 2010), pp. 75–91.

rural commune as a product of the ancient Slavic family community, as this is still found among the southern Slavs of the Balkan countries and as it fully existed in the Russian law books of the twelfth century and later. Haxthausen's discovery was seized on with jubilation by a whole intellectual and political tendency in Russia, by *Slavophilism.** This tendency, bent on a glorification of the Slavic world and its particularities, its "unspent force" as against the "lazy West" with its Germanic culture, found in the communist institutions of the Russian peasant community its strongest point of support over the next two or three decades.† Depending on the respective reactionary or revolutionary branch that Slavophilism divided into, the rural community was seen either as one of the three authentic basic Slavic institutions of Russiandom: Greek Orthodox belief, tsarist absolutism, and peasant-patriarchal village communism, or conversely as a suitable point of support for introducing a socialist revolution in Russia in the immediate future, and thus making much earlier than in Western Europe the leap directly into the promised land of socialism.‡ The opposing poles of Slavophilism both completely agreed, however, that the Russian rural community was a specifically Slavic phenomenon, explicable in terms of the particular national character of the Slavic tribes.

In the meantime, another moment in the history of the European nations had appeared, bringing them into contact with new regions of the world and making them very perceptibly aware of particular public institutions and age-old cultural forms that belonged neither to the Germanic nor to the Slavic orbit. This time it was not a matter of scientific investigations and learned discoveries, but rather the heavy-handed interests of the European capitalist states and their experiences in practical *colonial policy*. In the nineteenth century, in the age of capitalism, European colonial policy struck out on new paths. It was no longer, as in the sixteenth century with the first attack on the New World, a matter of the speediest plunder of the treasures and natural wealth of the newly discovered tropical lands in terms of precious metals, spices, valuable adornments

---

*   Slavophilism was an intellectual movement in nineteenth century Russia that opposed Western European influences and promoted Russian nationalism. It had adherents on the Right as well as the Left. Among its early proponents were Aleksei Khomyakov, Ivan Kireyevsky, and the brothers Ivan and Konstantin Aksakov.

†   See Marx's letter to the editorial board of the Russian-language publication *Otechestvennye Zapiski* of 1877, in speaking of Alexander Herzen: "My reproach against this writer had been that he discovered the Russian commune not in Russia but in the book by Haxthausen, a Prussian government councilor; and that, in his hands, the Russian commune merely served as an argument to show that old, rotten Europe must be regenerated through the victory of pan-Slavism." *Late Marx and the Russian Road*, p. 134.

‡   Luxemburg did not know of Marx's draft letters to Vera Zasulich of 1881, in which he discussed the possibility that Russia could achieve a socialist transformation ahead of the industrially developed West. The draft letters were not published until 1924. However, what was available to her was the Preface to the second Russian edition of the *Communist Manifesto* of 1882, in which Marx and Engels state that "Russia's peasant communal land-ownership may serve as the point of departure for a communist development." See *Late Marx and the Russian Road*, p. 139.

and slaves, in which the Spanish and Portuguese had achieved so much. Nor was it a matter of important opportunities for trade, with various raw materials from overseas countries being imported for the European market, and valueless trash and plunder being pressed on the indigenous peoples of these countries, in which the Dutch of the seventeenth century were the pioneers and served as a model for the English. Now, as well as these earlier methods of colonization, which are still in full bloom here and there today and have never gone out of style, we had a new method of more persistent and systematic exploitation of the population of the colonies for the enrichment of the "home country." This was designed to serve two purposes: first, the actual seizure of land as the most important material source of wealth in each country, and second, the continuous taxation of the broad mass of the population. In this double effort, the European colonial powers necessarily came up against a remarkable rock-hard obstacle in all these exotic lands, i.e. the particular property institutions of the indigenous peoples, which opposed a most stubborn resistance to plundering by the Europeans. In order to seize land from the hands of its former proprietors, it was first necessary to establish who these proprietors were. In order not just to decree taxes, but also to be able to collect them, it had to be established who was liable for such taxes. Here the Europeans in their colonies came upon relationships quite foreign to them, which directly overturned all their notions of the sanctity of private property. The English in South Asia had the same experience of this as the French did in North Africa.

The conquest of India by the English, begun in the early seventeenth century with the gradual seizure of the entire coastline and Bengal, only ended in the nineteenth century with the subjection of the highly important Punjab in the north. After political subjection, however, came the difficult work of the systematic exploitation of India. Everywhere they went, the English experienced the greatest surprise: they found the most varied peasant communities, large and small, which had occupied the land for millennia, cultivating rice and living in quiet, orderly conditions, but—oh horror!—no private owner of the land was to be found anywhere in these tranquil villages. No matter whom you asked, no one could call the land or the parcel he worked *his own*, i.e. no one was allowed to sell, lease, mortgage it or pawn it for arrears of taxation. All the members of these communities, which sometimes embraced whole large clans, sometimes only a few families who had branched off from the clan, stuck doggedly together, and ties of blood were everything to them, while individual ownership was nothing. Indeed, the English to their amazement were forced to discover on the banks of the Indus and the Ganges similar models of rural communism against which even the communist customs of the ancient Germanic mark or Slavic village community seemed almost like the fall into private property.

As the English tax authorities reported from India in 1845, "We can see no permanent shares. Each possesses the share that he cultivates only as long as the agricultural work continues. If a share is left untilled, it falls back into common land and can be taken over by anyone else, on condition that he cultivates it."[18]

At the same time, a government report on the administration of Punjab from 1849 to 1851 stated:

> It is highly interesting to observe how strong the sentiment of blood kinship is in this community, and the consciousness of stemming from a common ancestor. Public opinion so strictly insists on the maintenance of this system that we not uncommonly see how persons are allowed into it even if their ancestors had not participated in this common ownership for one or even two generations.[19]

"With this form of possession of land," wrote the report of the English state council on the Indian clan community, "no member of the clan can prove that he owns this or that part of the common land, but only that he possesses it for temporary use. The products of the common economy are placed in a common bank, from which all needs are met."[20] Here, therefore, we have no distribution of the fields at all, even for the agricultural season; the peasants of the community possess and work their fields undividedly and in common, they bring the harvest into a common village store, which the capitalist eye of the English had to see as a "bank," and fraternally meet their modest needs from the fruits of their common labor. In the northwestern corner of the Punjab, close to the border with Afghanistan, other very remarkable customs were encountered, which scorned any notion of private property. Here, while the fields were indeed divided and even periodically changed around, it was not—what a miracle!— individual families that exchanged their plots with one another, instead whole villages rotated their land every five years, with the whole community migrating. As the English tax commissioner James wrote from India in 1852 to his superiors: "I cannot fail to mention a most peculiar custom that has persisted in some districts until today: I mean the periodic exchange of lands between individual villages and their subsections. In some districts only fields are exchanged, in others even dwelling houses."[21]

Once again, therefore, we have the particular characteristics of a certain family of peoples, this time an "Indian" peculiarity. The communist institutions of the Indian village community, however, indicate their traditional age-old character both by their geographical location and particularly by the strength of blood ties and kinship relations. It was precisely the earliest forms of communism preserved in the oldest inhabited parts of India, the north-west, that clearly indicated the conclusion that communal property along with strong ties of kinship was attributable to thousand-year-old customs, linked with the first settlements of the immigrant Indians in their new home, present-day India. Sir Henry Maine, professor of comparative law at Oxford and former member of the government of India, took the Indian rural community as the

subject of his lectures as early as 1871,[*] placing it alongside the mark communities that Maurer had demonstrated in Germany and [Erwin] von Nasse in
England,[†] as age-old institutions of the same character as the Germanic rural
communities.

The venerable age of these communist institutions also struck the amazed
English in a further way, i.e. by the stubbornness with which they resisted the
tax and administration skills of the colonizers. It took a struggle of decades,
with every kind of coup de main, enormity, and unscrupulous attack on the
people's old laws and prevailing notions of right, before they could bring about
an incurable confusion of all property relations, general insecurity and the ruin
of the great mass of peasants. The old ties were broken, the quiet seclusion of
village communism torn asunder and replaced by discord, disharmony, inequality and exploitation. The result was enormous *latifundia* on the one hand, and an
immense mass of millions of dispossessed peasant tenants on the other. Private
property celebrated its entry in India, and with it typhus and scurvy due to
hunger became a constant presence in the marshes of the Ganges.

But even if, in the wake of the discoveries of the English colonizers in India,
this ancient rural communism, already now found among three such major
branches of the great Indo-Germanic family of peoples—Germanic, Slavic and
Indian—was seen as an ancient peculiarity of the Indo-Germanic group of
peoples, uncertain as this ethnographic concept may be, the concurrent discoveries of the French in Africa already went far beyond this orbit. What we had
here were discoveries that showed among the Arabs and Berbers of North Africa
exactly the same institutions as had been found at the heart of Europe and on
the Asian continent.

Among the Arabic nomadic herdsmen, land was the property of the clan.
This clan property, so the French scholar [Rodolpho] Dareste wrote in 1852,[‡]
was handed down from generation to generation, and no individual Arab could
point to a piece of land and say: This is mine.

Among some branches of the Kabyles,[§] who had been completely Arabized,

---

[*] Luxemburg was probably not aware that Marx had taken extensive notes on Maine's work
at the end of his life. See "Marx's Excerpts from Henry Sumner Maine, *Lectures on the Early History
of Institutions*," in *The Ethnological Notebooks of Karl Marx*, transcribed and edited by Lawrence
Krader (Assen: Van Gorcum, 1972), pp. 285–336.

[†] See Erwin von Nasse, *Über die mittelalterliche Feldgemeinschaft in England* (On the
Community Field System in Medieval England) (Bonn, A. Marcus: 1869).

[‡] This is a reference to Dareste's *De la Propriété en Algérie, commentaire de la loi du 17
juin 1851* (Paris: A. Durand, 1852). The work was cited by Kovalevsky. Unknown to Luxemburg,
Marx also called attention to Dareste's work in his "Notebooks on Kovalevsky." See *Karl Marx über
Formen vorkapitalischer Produktion: Vergleichende Studien zur Geschichte des Grundeigentums*,
edited by Hans-Peter Harstick (Frankfurt: Campus Verlag, 1977), p. 94.

[§] The Kabyles are a Berber people living in North Africa. They comprise a large percentage
of the non-Arab population of Algeria and Tunisia. Many have retained their distinct language and
culture.

the clan associations had already very much decayed, yet the power of the clans still remained strong: they took common responsibility for taxes; they bought livestock together for division among the different branches of a family as food; in all disputes over possession of land the clan council was the highest authority; settlement among the Kabyles always required the agreement of the clans; and the clan council likewise disposed of uncultivated lands. The prevailing rule, however, was the undivided property of a family, which did not just include in the present-day European sense an individual couple, but was rather a typically patriarchal family, like that of the ancient Israelites as described in the Bible—a large circle of kinship, consisting of father, mother, sons and their wives, children and grandchildren, uncles, aunts, nephews and cousins. In this circle, said another French researcher, [Aristide] Letourneux, in 1873,* it was the custom for the oldest family member to dispose of the undivided property, though he was in fact *chosen* for this office by the family, while in all more important cases, in particular where the sale and purchase of land was involved, the whole family council had to be consulted.

This was the situation with the population of Algeria at the time that the French colonized it. France had the same experience in North Africa as the English had in India. Everywhere, the European colonial policy met with stubborn resistance on the part of age-old social associations and their communistic institutions, which protected individuals from the exploitative grip of European capital and European financial policy.

At the same time as these new discoveries, a half-forgotten memory from the first days of European colonialism and its quest for booty in the New World now appeared in a new light. The yellowed chronicles of the Spanish state archives and monasteries preserved the curious tale from centuries ago of the miraculous South American country where already in the age of the great discoveries the Spanish conquistadores had found the most remarkable institutions. The hazy reports of this South American land of marvels found their way into European literature already in the seventeenth and eighteenth centuries, reports of the empire of the Incas, which the Spanish had discovered in what is now Peru and where the people lived with complete common property under the paternal theocratic government of generous despots. The fantastic ideas of this legendary communist realm in Peru persisted so stubbornly that in 1875 a German writer could refer to the Inca kingdom as "almost unique in human history" in being a social monarchy on a theocratic foundation, in which "the greater part of what the Social Democrats strive for today as their conceived ideal, but at no time have achieved," was carried out in practice.[22] In the meantime, however, more exact material on this remarkable land and its customs had appeared.

---

*   See Aristide Letourneux, *La Kabylie et les coutumes kabyles* (Paris: Imprimerie nationale, 1872–73); reissued by Éditions Bouchène (Paris) in 2003.

In 1840, an important original report by Alonzo de Zurita, one-time auditor to the royal council in Mexico, on administration and agrarian relations in the former Spanish colonies, was published in French translation.* And in the mid-nineteenth century, even the Spanish government was stirred to rescue old information about the conquest and administration of Spain's American possessions from the archives and bring it to light. This made a new and important documentary contribution to the material on social conditions of ancient pre-capitalist stages of culture in overseas lands.

Already on the basis of Zurita's reports, the Russian scholar Maksim Kovalevsky concluded in the 1870s that the legendary realm of the Incas in Peru had been simply a country in which the same age-old agrarian communist relations prevailed that Maurer had already found in many places among the ancient Germans, and that were the predominant form not just in Peru but also in Mexico and throughout the new regions of the world conquered by the Spanish. Later publications made possible an exact investigation of the old Peruvian agrarian relations, and revealed a new picture of primitive rural communism—again in a new part of the world, among a different race, at a quite different cultural stage and in a quite different era, than had been the case with previous discoveries.

Here we had an age-old agrarian communist constitution, which—prevailing from time immemorial among the Peruvian tribes—was still fully alive and well at the time of the Spanish invasion. Here too, a kinship association, the clan, was the only proprietor of the land in each village, or in a few villages together, and here too, the arable land was divided into lots and distributed annually by lot to the members of the village; here too public affairs were settled by the village community, which also elected the village head. Indeed, on the distant continent of South America, among the Amerindians, living traces were found of a communism so far-reaching as seemed quite unknown in Europe: there were immense common buildings, where whole clans lived in common quarters with a common burial place. It was said of one such quarter that it was occupied by more than 4,000 men and women. The capital of the so-called Inca emperor, the town of Cuzco, consisted of several such common quarters, each of which bore the particular name of a clan.†

---

   *   See Alonzo de Zurita, *Rapport sur les différentes classes de chefs dans la Nouvelle-Espagne, sur les lois, les mœurs des habitants, sur les impôts établis avant et depuis la conquête, etc., etc.* (Report on the Different Classes of the Leaders of New Spain, the Laws, Customs of the Inhabitants, the Taxes Assessed Before and After the Conquest, etc.), translated by M. Henri Ternaux-Compans (Paris: A. Bertrand, 1840). First published in Spanish in the sixteenth century, the book is considered an important source for the early history of Mexico.

   †   Cuzco served as the Incan capital from the thirteenth century until its conquest by the Spanish in 1532. The city was divided into four parts (or *suyos*), corresponding to the major parts of the Incan Empire. Leaders of these four parts of the Empire were required to live in Cuzco part of the year.

From the mid-nineteenth century, therefore, through to the 1870s, a wealth of material came to light that eroded and soon tore to shreds the old idea of the eternal character of private property and its existence from the beginning of the world. After agrarian communism had been discovered as a peculiarity of the Germanic people, then as something Slavic, Indian, Arab-Kabyle, or ancient Mexican, as the marvel state of the Peruvian Inca and in many more "specific" races of people in all parts of the world, the conclusion was unavoidable that this village communism was not at all a "peculiarity" of a particular race of people or part of the world, but rather the general and typical form of human society at a certain level of cultural development. The first reaction of official bourgeois science, i.e. political economy, was obstinately to resist this knowledge. The English school of Smith and Ricardo, which prevailed throughout Europe in the first half of the nineteenth century, simply denied the possibility of common property in land. Just as earlier on the crude ignorance and narrow-mindedness of the first Spanish, Portuguese, French and Dutch conquerors in newly dis-covered America completely failed to understand the agrarian relations of the indigenous population, and in the absence of private owners simply declared the whole land "property of the emperor," available to the exchequer, so in the age of bourgeois "enlightenment," the great luminaries of political-economic learning proceeded in the same way. In the seventeenth century, for example, the French missionary [Jean-Antoine] Dubois wrote about the Indians: "The Indians possess no property in land. The fields that they work are the property of the Mongol government."* And a medical doctor of the Montpellier faculty, François Bernier, who traveled the lands of the great Mogul in Asia and pub-lished in Amsterdam in 1699 a very well-known description of these countries, exclaimed in amazement: "These three states, Turkey, Persia, and India, have denied the concept of *meum* and *tuum* in relation to the ownership of land, a concept that is the foundation of everything fine and good in the world."† Exactly this same crass ignorance and lack of understanding of everything that appeared different from capitalist culture was shown by the scholar James Mill, father of the celebrated John Stuart Mill, when he wrote in his history of British India: "On the basis of all the facts we have considered, we can only reach one conclu-sion, that landownership in India fell to the conqueror, for if we were to assume that he was not the landowner, we would not be in a position to say who the owner was."‡

---

* Cited in Maksim Kovalevsky, *Obshchinnoe Zemlevadenie. Priciny, khod i posledstviia ego razlozeniia*, p. 158. See Jean-Antoine Dubois, *Description of the Character, Manners and Customs of the People of India, and of their Institutions, Religious and Civil* (London: Longman, Hurst, Rees, Orme and Brown, 1816).

† Cited in Kovalevsky, *Obshchinnoe Zemlevadenie*, p. 158. Bernier's book was first published in 1670, not 1699. See François Bernier, *Voyages, contenant la description des États du Grand Mogul* (Travels, with a Description of the States of the Grand Mogul) (Amsterdam: Paul Marret, 1670).

‡ Kovalevsky, *Obshchinnoe Zemlevadenie*, p. 159. Taking François Bernier as his main

The idea that ownership of land simply belonged to the Indian peasant communities who had worked it for millennia, that there could be a country, a great social culture, in which land was not a means for exploiting the labor of others, but simply the foundation of the existence of working people themselves, was something that the brain of a great scholar of the English bourgeoisie was unable to accept. This almost touching limitation of the intellectual horizon to the four walls of the capitalist economy only shows that the official science of the bourgeois enlightenment has an infinitely narrower horizon and cultural-historical understanding than the Romans had two thousand years ago, with their generals like Caesar, and historians like Tacitus, handing down to us extremely valuable insights and descriptions on the economic and social relations of the Germanic barbarians that they saw as strange and savage.

Just as today, so previously too, bourgeois political economy as the intellectual defense forces of the prevailing form of exploitation had less understanding than any other science of different forms of culture and economy, and it was reserved for branches of science that were somewhat more removed from the direct conflict of interest and struggle between capital and labor, to recognize in the communist institutions of earlier times a generally prevailing form of economic and cultural development at a certain stage. It was jurists such as Maurer and Kovalevsky, and the English law professor and state councilor for India, Sir Henry Maine, who first came to understand agrarian communism as an international primitive form of development that appeared among all races and in all parts of the world. And it was a legally trained sociologist, the American Lewis Henry Morgan, who discovered the necessary social structure of primitive society as the basis for this economic form.*

The great role of kinship ties among the ancient communist village communities struck scholars, both in India and in Algeria, as well as among the Slavs. In the wake of Maurer's studies, it was established in the case of the Germans that it was always in the form of clans, i.e. kinship groups, that they pursued their settlement in Europe. The history of the antique Greeks and Romans showed

---

source, Mill argued that the sovereign was the sole possessor of the land in India. This served as the basis of the theory of "Oriental Despotism." In his "Notebooks on Kovalevsky," Marx rejected Mill's claim (later repeated by his son John Stuart Mill) that the monarch exerted "despotic" control over village communal life. As Lawrence Krader notes, "J.S. Mill never pierced through to the practical meaning of the doctrine of the sovereign as landowner and landlord, as Marx was able to do." See *The Asiatic Mode of Production, Sources, Development and Critique in the Writings of Karl Marx.*

    * Marx was much more cautious about making such generalizations about "primitive communism" in his studies of Morgan, Maine, and Kovalevsky. Unlike Engels, he did not treat "primitive communism" as a single, undifferentiated stage of human history. As he put it in one of his draft letters to Vera Zasulich (1881), "The history of the decline of the primitive communities still has to be written (it would be wrong to put them all on the same plane; in historical as in geological formations, there is a whole series of primary, secondary tertiary and other types). So far, only very rough sketches have been made." See *Late Marx and the Russian Road*, p. 107, as well as *The Ethnological Notebooks of Karl Marx.*

all along the line that the clan had always played the greatest role for them, as a social group, an economic unit, a legal institution and a closed circle of religious practice. Finally, almost all reports of travelers in so-called savage countries agreed remarkably on the fact that, the more primitive a people was, the greater the role of kinship ties in the life of that people, and the more that these governed their economic, social and religious relations and ideas.*

Scientific research was thus presented with a new and highly important problem. What actually were these kinship ties that were so important in ancient times, how had they come to be formed, what was their connection with economic communism and economic development in general? On all these questions, it was Morgan who first offered an insight in his epoch-making book *Ancient Society*. Morgan, who had spent a large part of his life among an Indian tribe of Iroquois in the state of New York, and had made a most thorough study of the conditions of this primitive hunting people, came by comparing his own results with facts known about other primitive peoples to a new and wide-ranging theory about the forms of development of human society over the immense expanses of time that preceded any historical information. Morgan's pioneering ideas, which retain their full validity today despite the wealth of new material that has since appeared and corrected several details of his presentation, can be summarized as follows.

1. Morgan was the first to bring scientific order into prehistoric cultural history, both by defining its particular stages and also by revealing the underlying driving force of this development. Until then, the immense temporal extents of social life that preceded any written history, as well as the social relations of the primitive peoples still living today, with all their motley wealth of forms and stages, formed an uncharted chaos, from which only individual chapters and fragments had been brought to light by scientific research here and there. In particular, the descriptions "savagery" and "barbarism," which were customarily used as a summary description of these conditions, had only a meaning as *negative* concepts, descriptions of the lack of everything that was considered characteristic of "civilization," i.e. of well-mannered human life as seen through contemporary eyes. From this point of view, properly mannered social life, appropriate to human dignity, began only with those conditions described in written history. Everything that belonged to "savagery" and "barbarism" indifferently formed only an inferior and embarrassing stage prior to civilization, a half-animal existence which present-day civilized humanity could only regard with condescending disparagement. Just as the official representatives of the Christian church regard all primitive and pre-Christian religions as simply a long series of errors in the quest of humanity for the only true religion, so for

---

*   Some modern anthropologists no longer accept Morgan's claim that all forms of "primitive" society are based on kinship instead of political relations, though others still agree with his premise.

the political economists all primitive forms of economy were merely unsuccessful attempts that preceded the discovery of the one true form of economy: that of private property and exploitation with which written history and civilization begins. Morgan dealt this conception a decisive blow by portraying the whole of primitive cultural history as an equally valid—indeed an infinitely more important—part in the uninterrupted developmental sequence of humanity, infinitely more important both on account of its infinitely longer duration in comparison with the tiny section of written history, and also on account of the decisive acquisitions of culture that were made precisely in that long dawn of human social existence. By filling the descriptions "savagery," "barbarism" and "civilization" for the first time with a positive content, Morgan made them into precise scientific concepts and applied them as tools of scientific research. For Morgan, savagery, barbarism and civilization are three sections of cultural development, separated from each other by quite particular material characteristics, and themselves each breaking down into a lower, middle and upper stage, which again are distinguished by particular concrete achievements and advances. Pedantic know-alls today may rail that the middle stage of savagery could not simply begin, as Morgan believed, with fishing, the upper stage with the invention of the bow and arrow, and so on, since in several cases the sequence was the other way round, and in other cases was dependent on natural conditions—objections that can indeed be made against any historical classification, if this is conceived as a rigid schema of absolute validity, an iron fetter on knowledge instead of a living and flexible guideline. Morgan's epoch-making service remains exactly the same, that he originated the investigation of prehistory with this first scientific classification of preconditions, just as it is Linnaeus's service to have supplied the first scientific classification of plants. Yet there is one great difference. [Carl] Linnaeus, as we well know, took as the basis of his systematization of plants a very usable but purely external characteristic—the sexual organs of plants—and this first makeshift had later, as Linnaeus himself well recognized, to make way for a deeper natural classification from the standpoint of the developmental history of the plant world. Morgan, on the contrary, made his most fruitful contribution to research precisely by the choice of the basic principle on which he built his system: he made the starting point of his classification the proposition that it is the kind of social labor, *production*, that in each historical epoch from the first beginnings of culture plays the main role in determining human social relations, and that its decisive advances are likewise so many milestones in this development.

2. Morgan's second great achievement bears on the family relations of primitive society. Here too, on the basis of comprehensive material that he obtained by an international survey, he laid down the first scientifically founded sequence of developmental forms of the family, from the earliest forms of quite primitive society through to today's prevailing monogamy—i.e. legally established

permanent marriage of a single couple, with the dominant position of the man. Of course, here too material has emerged to require several corrections of detail to Morgan's developmental schema of the family. The basic lines of his system, however, as the first ladder of human family forms derived strictly from the idea of development, from the grey of prehistory through to the present, remain a lasting contribution to the treasury of social science. This area, too, Morgan enriched not simply by his systematic conception, but also by a fundamental idea of genius about the relationship between the family relations of a society and its prevailing kinship system. Morgan was the first to draw attention to the striking fact that among many primitive peoples the actual relations of sexuality and descent, i.e. the actual family, do not coincide with the kinship categories that people ascribe one another, or with the reciprocal duties that derive from these ascriptions. He was the first to find an explanation for this puzzling phenomenon purely in materialist and dialectical terms. "The family," he says, "represents an active principle. It is never stationary, but advances from a lower to a higher form as society advances from a lower to a higher condition. ... Systems of consanguinity, on the contrary, are passive; recording the progress made by the family at long intervals apart, and only changing radically when the family has radically changed."[*]

We find, then, that among primitive peoples, systems of consanguinity remain valid that correspond to an earlier and already superseded form of family, just as people's ideas and notions generally remain tied for a long while to conditions that have been superseded by the actual material development of society.

3. On the basis of the developmental history of family relations, Morgan offered the first exhaustive investigation of the ancient clan associations that are found at the beginning of historical tradition among all civilized peoples—among the Greeks and Romans, the Celts and Germans, the ancient Israelites—and that still exist among most primitive peoples that survive today. He showed that these associations resting on blood relationship and common descent are on the one hand only a high stage in the development of the family, while on the other hand they are the basis of the whole social life of peoples—in those long stretches of time when there was not yet a state in the modern sense, i.e. no organization of political compulsion on a fixed territorial basis. Each tribe, which itself consisted of a certain number of clan associations, or, as the Romans called them, *gentes*, had its own territory, which belonged to it as a whole, and in each tribe the clan

---

[*] Lewis Henry Morgan, *Ancient Society, or Researches in the Line of Human Progress from Savagery through Barbarism to Civilization* [1877] (New Brunswick NJ: Transaction Publishers, 2000), p. 435. Luxemburg made use of the German edition, *Die Urgesellshaft oder Untersuchung über den Fortschritt der Menschheit aus der Wildheit durch die Babarei zur Zivilisation* (Berlin: J.H.W. Dietz Verlag, 1891). This idea of Morgan's has long been rejected by some Marxist and non-Marxist anthropologists.

association was the unit in which a common household was run communistically, in which there were no rich and poor, no idlers and workers, no masters and slaves, and where all public affairs were dealt with by the free vote and decision of all. As a living example of these relations that all peoples of present-day civilization went through, Morgan described in detail the *gens'* organization of the American Indians, which was in full bloom at the time of the conquest of America by the Europeans:

> All the members of an Iroquois gens were personally free, and they were bound to defend each other's freedom; they were equal in privileges and in personal rights, the sachem and chiefs claiming no superiority; and they were a brotherhood bound together by the ties of kin. Liberty, equality, and fraternity, though never formulated, were cardinal principles of the gens. These facts are material, because the gens was the unit of a social and governmental system, the foundation upon which Indian society was organized. A structure composed of such units would of necessity bear the impress of their character, for as the unit so the compound. It serves to explain that sense of independence and personal dignity universally an attribute of Indian character.[†]

4. The gentile organization led social development to the threshold of civilization, which Morgan characterizes as that brief recent epoch of cultural history in which private property arose on the ruins of communism and with it a public organization of compulsion: the state and the exclusive dominance of man over woman in the state, in property right and in the family. In this relatively brief historical period fall the greatest and most rapid advances in production, science and art, but also the deepest fissure of society by class antagonism, the greatest misery for the mass of the people and their greatest enslavement. Here is Morgan's own judgment on our present-day civilization, with which he concludes the results of his classical investigation:

> Since the advent of civilization, the outgrowth of property has been so immense, its forms so diversified, its uses so expanding and its management so intelligent in the interests of its owners, that it has become, on the part of the people, an unmanageable power. The human mind stands bewildered in the presence of its own creation. The time will come, nevertheless, when human intelligence will rise to the mastery over property, and define the relations of the state to the property it protects, as well as the obligations and the limits of the rights of its owners. The interests of society are paramount to individual interests, and the two must be brought into just and harmonious relations. A mere property career is not the final destiny of mankind, if

---

*   The *gens* (plural, *gentes*) was a clan or family group in ancient Rome that shared a common name, traceable to a common ancestor. Descent was through the male heir.

†   Morgan, *Ancient Society*, pp. 85–6.

progress is to be the law of the future as it has been of the past. The time which has passed away since civilization began is but a fragment of the past duration of man's existence; and but a fragment of the ages yet to come. The dissolution of society bids fair to become the termination of a career of which property is the end and aim; because such a career contains the elements of self-destruction. Democracy in government, brotherhood in society, equality in rights and privileges, and universal education, foreshadow the next higher plane of society to which experience, intelligence and knowledge are steadily tending. It will be a revival, in a higher form, of the liberty, equality and fraternity of the ancient gentes.*

Morgan's achievement had wide-ranging significance for the knowledge of economic history. He placed the ancient communistic economy, which up till then had only been discovered in isolated individual cases and not explained, on the broad footing of a consistent and general cultural development, and particularly of the gens constitution. Primitive communism, with the democracy and social equality that went together with it, were thereby shown to be the cradle of social development. By this expansion of the horizon of the prehistoric past, he showed the whole present-day civilization, with private property, class rule, male supremacy, state compulsion and compulsory marriage, as simply a brief transition phase that, just as it arose itself from the dissolution of age-old communist society, is bound to make way in turn in the future for higher social forms. In this way, however, Morgan gave powerful new support to scientific socialism. While Marx and Engels showed by way of the economic analysis of capitalism the unavoidable historical transition of society to the communist world economy in the very near future, thus giving socialist efforts a firm scientific basis, Morgan in a certain sense supplied the work of Marx and Engels[†] with a full and powerful underpinning, by demonstrating that a communist and democratic society, even if in different and more primitive forms, embraced the whole long past of human cultural history prior to present-day civilization. In this way, the noble survivals of the dim past offered a hand to the revolutionary efforts of the future, the circle of knowledge was harmoniously closed, and from this perspective the present-day world of class rule and exploitation, which presented itself as the one and only world of civilization, the highest aim of world history, appeared as a tiny transitional stage on the great forward march of human culture.[‡]

---

*   Ibid., pp. 561–2.

†   Although it was widely known at the time that Marx studied Morgan's work shortly after *Ancient Society* was published, there are considerable differences between Marx and Engels's appraisal of Morgan's work. Marx tended to be more critical of Morgan's formulations and conclusions, although he also expressed appreciation for his work. Since Marx's *Ethnological Notebooks* were not published until the 1970s, Luxemburg was most likely unaware of these differences.

‡   Marx himself disclaimed efforts to identify his "materialist theory of history" with a unilinear evolutionism positing a single course of human development. As he wrote in response to a Russian critic who attributed such a unilinear perspective to him, "He absolutely insists on

2

Morgan's "ancient society" formed as it were a subsequent introduction to the *Communist Manifesto* of Marx and Engels. It was only natural that it should provoke a reaction in bourgeois science. Within two or three decades from the mid-nineteenth century, the concept of primitive communism made its entry into science on all sides. As long as it was a question of honorable "Germanic antiquity," "Slavic tribal peculiarities', or the historical excavation of the Peruvian Inca state and the like, these discoveries did not overstep the realm of scientific curiosities, without contemporary significance or any direct connection to the interests and struggles of today's bourgeois society. So much so that staunch conservative or moderately liberal statesmen such as Ludwig von Maurer or Sir Henry Maine could claim the greatest merit for these discoveries. Soon, however, such a connection was established, in two different directions. Colonial policy, as we have seen, involved a collision of palpable material interests between the bourgeois world and primitive communist conditions. The more that the capitalist regime began to establish itself as all-powerful in Western Europe after the mid-nineteenth century, in the wake of the storms of the February revolution of 1848, the sharper this collision grew. At the same time, and precisely after the February revolution, a new enemy within the camp of bourgeois society, the revolutionary workers' movement, played an ever-greater role. After the June days of 1848 in Paris, the "red specter" never again vanished from the public stage, and in 1871 it reappeared in the dazzling light of the struggle of the Commune, to the fury of the French and international bourgeoisie. In the light of these brutal class struggles, primitive communism as the latest discovery of scientific research showed a dangerous face. The bourgeoisie, clearly affected in their class interests, scented an obscure connection between the ancient communist survivals that put up stubborn resistance in the colonial countries to the forward march of the profit-hungry "Europeanization" of the indigenous peoples, and the new gospel of revolutionary impetuousness of the proletarian mass in the old capitalist countries. When the French National Assembly was deciding the fate of the unfortunate Arabs of Algeria in 1873, with a law on the compulsory introduction of private property,* it was repeatedly said, in

transforming my historical sketch of the genesis of capitalism in Western Europe into a historico-philosophical theory of the general course fatally imposed on all peoples, whatever the historical circumstances in which they find themselves placed ... But I beg his pardon. This is to do me both too much honor and too much discredit." See *Late Marx and the Russian Road*, p. 136.

    * The National Assembly met in Bordeaux on February 13, 1871, at which it fostered French control of Muslim land in Algeria through the expropriation of indigenous communal holdings by French capitalists and speculators. The Warnier Law was named after August Warnier, a French politician who was elected to the National Assembly in July 1871. The Warnier Law greatly facilitated land purchases from the indigenous peoples of Algeria, accelerating the break-up of their traditional communal relations of working the land in favor of private land ownership.

a gathering where the cowardice and bloodlust of the conquerors of the Paris Commune still trembled, that the ancient common property of the Arabs must at any cost be destroyed, "as a form that supports communist tendencies in people's minds."* In Germany, meanwhile, the glories of the new German Empire, the "founders' time"† and the first capitalist crash of the 1870s,‡ with Bismarck's "blood and iron" regime and the anti-Socialist law,§ greatly inflamed class struggles and made even scientific research uncomfortable. The unmatched growth of German Social Democracy,¶ as the theories of Marx and Engels become flesh, sharpened to an extraordinary degree the class instinct of bourgeois science in Germany, and a reaction against the theories of primitive communism now set in most forcefully. Cultural historians such as [Julius] Lippert and [Heinrich] Schurtz, political economists such as [Karl] Bücher, sociologists such as [Carl Nicolai] Starcke, [Edward] Westermarck and [Ernst] Grosse, now united in a keen combat against the doctrine of primitive communism, and particularly Morgan's theory of the development of the family and the previously universal prevalence of a kinship constitution with equality between the sexes and general democracy. This Herr Starcke, for example, in his *Primitive Familie* of 1888,[23] called Morgan's hypotheses about kinship systems a "crazy dream … not to say a feverish delusion."[24] But more serious scholars, too, such as Lippert, author of the best cultural history that we have, took the field against Morgan. Basing themselves on obsolete and superficial reports of eighteenth-century missionaries who were completely untrained in economics or ethnology, and themselves quite ignorant of Morgan's wide-ranging studies, Lippert described the economic conditions of the North American Indians, the very same people whose life with its finely developed social organization Morgan had penetrated more thoroughly than anyone else, as evidence that among hunting peoples in general there is no common regulation of production and no "provision" for the totality and for the future, rather nothing but a lack of regulation and consciousness. The foolish distortion by narrow-minded European missionaries of the communist institutions that actually existed among the Indians of North America

---

* Probably unbeknownst to Luxemburg, Marx quoted from the same sentence of Kovalevsky in his notebooks on his work. See "Excerpts from M.M. Kovalevsky," in *The Asiatic Mode of Production*, p. 405.

† This refers to the period of German history lasting from 1815 to the formation of the German Empire in 1871.

‡ In May 1873 three major Viennese banks went bankrupt, producing a financial crisis that soon spread to Germany.

§ The Anti-Socialist Laws (officially termed the "Law Against the Public Danger of Social Democratic Endeavors") was introduced by Bismarck in 1878 and lasted until 1890. Although it did not explicitly ban the Social-Democratic Party, it banned newspapers, public events, and trade unions that the government considered "subversive."

¶ The German Social-Democratic Party grew rapidly following the expiration of the Anti-Socialist Laws in 1890. By 1912, the SPD obtained the most votes of any party in Germany. It had over a million members and hundreds of publications.

was taken over by Lippert quite uncritically, as shown for example by the following quotation he offers from the history of the mission of the Evangelical Brothers among the Indians of North America by [Georg Heinrich] Loskiel in 1789. "Many among them" (the American Indians), says our excellently oriented missionary,

> are so lethargic that they do not plant for themselves, but rather rely completely on others' not refusing to share their stores with them. Since in this way the more diligent do not benefit from their work any more than the idlers, as time goes on ever less is planted. If a hard winter comes, so that deep snow prevents them from going hunting, it is easy for a general famine to arise, which often leads to many people dying. Hunger then leads them to eat the roots of grass and the inner bark of trees, particularly of young oaks.*

"By a natural connection, therefore," Lippert adds to the words of his source, "the relapse into earlier carelessness leads to a relapse to an earlier way of life." And in this Indian society, in which no one "may refuse" to share his store of provisions with others, and in which an "Evangelical Brother" constructs in a quite evidently arbitrary fashion the inevitable division between the "diligent" and the "idlers" along European lines, Lippert finds the best proof *against* primitive communism:

> Still less at such a stage does the older generation care to equip the younger generation for life. The Indian is already far removed from primitive man. As soon as someone has a tool, he has the concept of ownership, but only limited to this. This concept the Indian already has at the lower stage; *but in this primitive ownership any communist trait is lacking; the development begins with the opposite.*[25] [Emphasis R.L.]

Professor Bücher opposed to the primitive communist economy his "theory of individual search for food" on the part of primitive peoples, and the "immeasurable stretches of time" in which "people existed without working."[26] For the cultural historian Schurtz, however, Professor Bücher with his "insight of genius" is the prophet that he follows blindly.[27] The most typical and energetic representative of reaction, however, against the dangerous doctrines of primitive communism and the gentile constitution, and against Morgan as the "church father of German socialism,"[28] is Herr Ernst Grosse. At first sight, Grosse is

---

* Quoted in Julius Lippert, *Kulturgeschichte der Menschheit in ihrem organischen Aufbau* (The Cultural History of Humanity in its Organic Structure) (Stuttgart: F. Enke, 1886) Vol. 2, Part 1, p. 40. See Loskiel's *Geschichte der Mission der evangelischen Brüder unter den Indianern in Nordamerika* (History of the Mission of the Evangelical Brothers among the Indians of North America) (Barby an der Elbe: Brüdergemeinen, 1789).

himself a supporter of the materialist conception of history, i.e. he attributes various legal, kinship and intellectual forms of social life to the prevailing relations of production as their determining factors. "Only a few cultural historians," he says in his *Anfänge der Kunst* [The Beginnings of the Arts] published in 1894,

> seem to have grasped the full significance of production. It is however far more easy to underestimate this than to overestimate it. Economic activity is likewise the center of life of every cultural form; it influences all the other factors of culture in the deepest and most irresistible way, while being itself determined not so much by cultural factors as by natural ones—geographical and meteorological. It would be correct in a certain sense to call the form of production the primary cultural phenomenon, besides which all other branches of culture appear only as derivative and secondary; not of course in the sense that these other branches have arisen from the stem of production, but rather because, despite their independent origins, they have always been formed and developed under the overwhelming pressure of the prevailing economic factor.[29]

It would seem at first sight that Grosse himself had learned his main ideas from the "church fathers of German Social Democracy," Marx and Engels, even if he understandably takes care not to betray with a single word from which scientific corner he has taken over ready-made his superiority over "most cultural historians." Indeed, he is even "more Catholic than the pope" in relation to the materialist conception of history. Whereas Engels—along with Marx the joint creator of the materialist conception of history—assumed for the development of family relations in primitive times through to the formation of today's legally accredited compulsory marriage a progress of forms independent of economic relations, founded on the interest of preserving and multiplying the human species, Grosse goes a great deal further. He puts forward the theory that at all times the form of family is simply the direct product of the economic relations prevailing at the time. "Nowhere," he says, "does the cultural significance of production appear with such clarity as in the history of the family. The strange forms of human families, which have inspired sociologists to still stranger hypotheses, appear surprisingly understandable as soon as they are considered in connection with the forms of production."[30]

Grosse's book published in 1896, *Die Formen der Familie und die Formen der Wirthschaft* [The Forms of Family and the Forms of Economy], is devoted completely to proving this idea. At the same time, however, Grosse is a determined opponent of the doctrine of primitive communism. He too seeks to demonstrate that human social development began not with common property but with private property; he too strives, like Lippert and Bücher, to show from his standpoint that the further we go back in ancient history, the more exclusively and all-powerfully the "individual" and his "individual ownership" prevails.

Of course, the discoveries of primitive village communities in all parts of the world, and clan associations—or kinship groups as Grosse calls them—in connection with these, cannot be simply denied. It is just that Grosse has the clan organization*—and this is his own particular theory—emerge as the framework of a communist economy only at a particular stage of development, i.e. with the lower agricultural stage, to dissolve again at the stage of higher agriculture and make way once more for "individual ownership." In this way, Grosse triumphantly turns the historical perspective established by Morgan and Marx directly on its head. According to this, communism was the cradle of human cultural development, the form of economic relations that accompanied this development for measureless extents of time, only to decline and dissolve with civilization and make way for private property, this epoch of civilization facing in turn a rapid process of dissolution and a return to communism in the higher form of a socialist social order. According to Grosse, it was private property that accompanied the rise and development of culture, making way temporarily for communism only at a particular stage, that of lower agriculture. According to Marx and Engels, and likewise Morgan, the beginning and end point of cultural history is common property and social solidarity; according to Grosse and his colleagues of bourgeois science, it is the "individual" and his private property. But this is not enough. Grosse is not only an express opponent of Morgan and primitive communism, but of the whole developmental theory in the realm of social life, and pours scorn on those childish minds who seek to bring all phenomena of social life into a developmental series and conceive this as a unitary process, an advance of humanity from lower to higher forms of life. This fundamental idea, which serves as a basis for the whole of modern social science in general, and particularly for the conception of history and doctrine of scientific socialism, Herr Grosse combats as a typical bourgeois scholar, with all the power at his command. *"Humanity,"* he proclaims and emphasizes, *"in no way moves along a single line in a single direction; rather, its paths and goals are just as varied as are the conditions of life of different peoples."*[31] In the person of Grosse, therefore, bourgeois social science, in its reaction against the revolutionary consequences of its own discoveries, has reached the same point that bourgeois vulgar economics reached in its reaction to classical economics: the denial of the very lawfulness of social development.[32] Let us examine this strange historical "materialism" of the latest champion to defeat Marx, Engels and Morgan.

Grosse has a good deal to say about "production," he is always referring to the "character of production" as the determining factor that influences the whole of culture. But what does he understand by production and its character?

---

* A clan organization here refers to a group whose members share a common ancestor, land rights, and rules of marriage.

The economic form that prevails or dominates in a social group, the way in which the members of this group gain their subsistence, is a fact whose main features can be directly observed with sufficient assurance everywhere. We may remain much in doubt as to the religious and social notions of the Australians, but not the slightest doubt is possible as to the character of their production: the Australians are hunters and gatherers of plants. It is perhaps impossible to penetrate the mental cultural of the ancient Peruvians, but the fact that the citizens of the Inca empire were an agricultural people is open for anyone to see.[33]

By "production" and its "character," therefore, Grosse simply means the particular main source of a people's sustenance. Hunting, fishing, pastoralism, agricul-ture—these are the "relations of production" that have a determining effect on all other cultural relations of a people. The first thing to note here is that, if no more than this meager discovery is involved, Herr Grosse's exaggeration about "most cultures" is certainly quite unfounded. The knowledge that the particular main source that a given people draw on for their sustenance is extraordinarily important for their cultural development, is in no way Herr Grosse's spanking new discovery, but rather an age-old and honorable element in all doctrines of cultural history. This knowledge led in particular to the conventional division of peoples into hunters, pastoralists and agriculturalists, which is found in all cultural histories and which Herr Grosse finally adopts himself after a great deal of to-ing and fro-ing. But this knowledge is not only quite old, it is also quite false—at least in the bland version of it that Grosse offers. If all we know is that a people lives from hunting, pastoralism or agriculture, we do not yet know any-thing about its relations of production or the rest of its culture. The Hottentots in Southwest Africa today, whose herds, which formed their previous source of livelihood, have been taken away by the Germans and who have been supplied with modern shotguns, have been forcibly made into hunters.* The relations of production of this "hunting people," however, have nothing at all in common with those of the Indian hunters of California, who still live in their primitive seclusion from the world, and are themselves very different from the hunting companies of Canada, which supply American and European capitalists with tradable animal pelts for the fur trade. The pastoralists of Peru, who before the Spanish invasion kept their llamas communistically in the cordilleras under Inca rule, the Arab nomads with their patriarchal herds in Africa or the Arabian pen-insula, the present-day peasants in the Swiss, Bavarian and Tyrolean alps, who pursue their long-established "*Alpenbücher*" in the midst of the capitalist world,

---

* The "Hottentots" was the derogatory name given by the South African Afrikaners to the Khoikhoi peoples of what is now Namibia and southwestern South Africa. From 1904 to 1907, Khoikhoi peoples living in Namibia joined forces with the Nama and Herero peoples to combat German imperialism. Many of them perished as a result of genocidal reprisals by the German colonial authorities.

the half-wild Roman slaves who kept the enormous herds of their masters in the wastes of Apulia, the farmers in today's Argentina who fatten up immense herds for the Ohio slaughterhouses and processed-meat factories—these are all examples of "pastoralism," each presenting a totally different type of production and culture. As for "agriculture," this embraces such a broad scale of the most varying kinds of economy and levels of culture—from the ancient Indian clan community to the modern latifundium, from the tiny peasant holding to the knightly estates east of the Elbe, from the English tenant system to Romanian *"jobbaggio,"* from Chinese peasant horticulture to Brazilian slave plantations, from the women's hoe-tillage of Haiti to the giant North American farms with steam and electric machinery—so that Herr Grosse's showy revelations about the significance of production only display a glaring lack of understanding of what "production" really means. It was precisely against this kind of crude and coarse "materialism," which takes into consideration only the external natural conditions of production and culture, and which found its best and most exhaustive expression in the English sociologist [Henry Thomas] Buckle, that Marx and Engels directed themselves. What is decisive for the economic and cultural conditions of people is not the external natural source of their sustenance, but rather the connections that people form between one another in their labor. The *social* connections of production determine the question: what form of production prevails among a given people? Only when *this* aspect of production has been thoroughly grasped is it possible to understand the determining influences of a people's production on its family relations, its concepts of right, its religious ideas and the development of its arts. Most European observers, however, find it extraordinarily difficult to penetrate the social relations of production of so-called primitive peoples. In contrast to Herr Grosse, who believes he already knows a world when he knows nothing more than that the Peruvian Incas were an agricultural people, Sir Henry Maine says: "The characteristic error of the direct observer of unfamiliar social or juridical phenomena is to compare them too hastily with familiar phenomena apparently of the same kind."[34]

The connection between forms of family and "forms of production" understood in this way is expressed in the following terms by Herr Grosse:

> At the lowest stage, people feed themselves by means of hunting—in the broadest sense of the term—and by the gathering of plants. This most primitive form of production is also associated with the most primitive form of division of labor—the physiologically based division between the two sexes. While the provision of animal food falls to the man, the foraging of roots and fruits is the task of the woman. Under these conditions, the economic center of gravity lies almost always on the male side,

---

* The *jobbaggio* was a form of *corvée* labor in which peasants were required to perform unpaid service to the feudal lords during emergencies. Over time, the requirements became more and more onerous. For Marx's discussion of the *jobbaggio*, see *Capital* Vol. 1, pp. 347–8.

and as a consequence the primitive form of family everywhere bears an unmistakably patriarchal character. Whatever the ideas about blood relationships may be, primitive man stands in fact as lord and master among his wives and children, even if he does not recognize his progeny as blood relations. From this lowest stage, production can continue in two directions, according to whether the female or the male branch of the economy undergoes a further development. But which of these two branches becomes the stem depends above all on the natural conditions in which the primitive group lives. If the flora and climate of the land immediately suggest and reward the conservation and subsequent care of food plants, then the female branch of plant gathering gradually develops into plant cultivation. In fact, with primitive agricultural peoples this occupation is always found in women's hands. The economic center of gravity accordingly shifts to the female side, and as a result we find among all primitive societies that support themselves predominantly by agriculture a matriarchal family form or at least the traces of this. The woman stands now at the center of the family as the main provider and landowner. The construction of a matriarchy in the strict sense, however, the actual rule of women, occurs only in very infrequent cases—in particular where the social group is not exposed to attacks by external enemies. In all other cases, the man regains as protector the supremacy he lost as provider. In this way, the family forms develop that prevail among most agricultural peoples, presenting a compromise between the matriarchal and the patriarchal direction. A large part of humanity, however, has undergone a completely different development. Those hunting peoples living in regions that place difficulties in the way of agriculture, while they offer animals that are suitable and profitable for domestication, have advanced not like the former to plant cultivation, but instead to that of animals. Livestock breeding, however, which gradually developed out of hunting, appears exactly like its predecessor as a privilege of the man.[*] In this way, the economic superiority of the male side that is already present is strengthened, and this relationship finds consistent expression in the fact that all peoples who feed themselves principally from livestock stand under the rule of the patriarchal family form. Besides, the commanding position of the man in stock-raising societies is further increased by another circumstance that is similarly connected directly with the form of their production. Stock-raising peoples are always inclined to warlike entanglements and consequently to the development of a centralized organization for warfare. The unavoidable result is an extreme form of patriarchy in which woman becomes a slave without rights under a husband endowed with despotic power.

But those peaceful agricultural peoples among whom women rules as the breadwinner in the family, or at least enjoys to some extent a freer position, are generally subjugated by the warlike stock-raisers and take over from them,

---

[*] Modern anthropologists tend to dispute this. For instance, in the highlands of New Guinea pig farming (a central aspect of social life) is the responsibility of women.

along with other customs, the despotic rule of the man in the family. "And so we find all civilized nations today under the sign of a more or less sharply marked patriarchal family form."[35]

The remarkable historical destinies of the human family depicted here, in their dependence on forms of production, thus follow the schema: hunting period—individual family with male supremacy; stock-raising period = individual family with still worse male supremacy; period of lower agriculture = individual family with sporadic female supremacy, but later subjection of agriculturalists by stock-raisers, i.e. here individual family with male supremacy; and as the apex of the edifice, period of higher agriculture = individual family with male supremacy. Herr Grosse, we can see, is very serious in his rejection of modern developmental theory. For him there is no development of family forms at all. History begins and ends with the individual family and male supremacy. What Grosse does not notice is that after he has showily promised to explain the origin of family forms from forms of production, he actually presupposes the family form as something always already given, i.e. as the individual family, as a modern household, and assumes this unchanged under *all* forms of production. What he actually pursues as different "family forms" with the change of epochs is simply the question of the relationship of one sex to the other. Male supremacy or female supremacy—this is the "family form" according to Grosse, which in a completely harmonious manner he reduces as crudely to an external characteristic as he simplifies the "form of production" to the question of hunting, stock-raising or agriculture. That "male supremacy" or "female supremacy" can embrace dozens of different family forms, that there can be different kinship systems within the same cultural stage of "hunters"—none of this exists for Herr Grosse, as little as does the question of the social relations within a form of production. The reciprocal relationship of family forms and production forms here comes down to the following ingenious "materialism": the two sexes are seen from the start as business competitors. Whoever feeds the family also rules in the family, so the philistine believes, and so also does the civil code. The bad luck of the female sex, however, is that only exceptionally in history—at the low stage of tillage agriculture—were they the leading provider of food, and even then they generally had to give way to the warlike male sex. And so the history of the family form is basically no more than a history of women's slavery, in all "forms of production" and despite all forms of production. The only connection between family forms and economic forms is thus in the end simply the slight difference between somewhat milder and somewhat severer forms of male supremacy. In conclusion, the first message of redemption for enslaved woman in the history of human culture appears as the Christian church, which at least knows no distinction between the two sexes in the blue ether of heaven, even if it still does so on earth. "By this doctrine, Christianity endowed women with an elevated position before which the arbitrary will of the male must bow,"[36]

Herr Grosse concludes, finally, after wandering far and wide on the waters of economic history, dropping anchor in the harbor of the Christian church. How "surprisingly understandable," then, those forms of family appear that have inspired sociologists to "strange hypotheses," when they are viewed "in connection with the forms of production"!

The most striking thing, however, about this history of the "family form" is the treatment of the clan association or kin group, as Grosse calls it. We have seen the tremendous role that clan associations played in social life at earlier levels of culture. We have seen—particularly in the wake of Morgan's epoch-making investigations—that they were the actual social form of people before the development of the territorial state, and continued for a long while after to be both the economic unit and the religious community. How do these facts stand in the light of the remarkable history of Grosse's "family forms"? Grosse evidently cannot simply deny the existence of a kinship constitution among all primitive peoples. But since this contradicts his scheme of individual families and the dominance of private property, he seeks to reduce their significance as close to zero as he can, except for the period of lower agriculture: "The power of kinship arose with lower agriculture, and it decays with it as well. Among all higher agricultural peoples, the kinship order has already either disappeared or in the process of doing so."[37] Grosse thus lets the "kinship power" and its communist economy burst into the midst of economic and family history like a pistol shot, simply to have it fall back and dissolve right away. How the origin and existence of the kinship order and its functions are to be explained in the millennia of cultural development before lower agriculture, since for Grosse they had at this time neither an economic function nor a social significance vis-à-vis the individual family, and what these kinships were that led their shadowy existence among hunters and stock-raisers against the background of separate families with private housekeeping, remains a private secret for Herr Grosse. Just as little is he concerned that his story stands in blatant contradiction with certain generally recognized facts. Kin groups are seen as acquiring importance only with lower agriculture; they are then generally linked with the institution of blood revenge, with religious observance and very frequently with animal names. All these things however are far older than agriculture, and must therefore according to Grosse's own theory derive from relations of production of far more primitive cultural periods. Grosse explains the kinship order of higher agriculturalists, such as the ancient Germans, Celts and Indians, as a legacy from the period of lower agriculture, when they had their roots in the female rural economy. But the higher agriculture of cultured peoples did not arise from female tilling, but rather from stock raising, which was already pursued by men, and where consequently, according to Grosse, the kin groups were without significance in relation to the patriarchal family economy. According to Grosse, the kinship order is meaningless with these nomadic pastoralists, and only comes to prevail for a while with settlement and agriculture. According to the most respected scholars, however, the agrarian constitution followed a quite opposite direction: as long as pastoralists followed a nomadic way of life, kinship associations were the most powerful in every respect, whereas with settlement and agriculture the kinship constitution begins to loosen and decline in relation to the local association of agriculturalists, whose community of interest is stronger than the traditional blood ties, and the kinship community is transformed into the so-called neighborhood community. This was the view of Ludwig von Maurer, Kovalevsky, Henry Maine and [Emile] Laveleye,* and the same phenomenon has more recently been noted by [Konstantin] Kaufman among the Kyrgyz and Yakuts of Central Asia.

We should finally mention that Grosse is understandably unable, from his point of view, to offer the slightest explanation of the most important phenomena in the field of primitive family relations, such as matriarchy (mother-right), and confines himself to shrugging his shoulders and declaring matriarchy "the rarest curiosity in sociology"; that he makes the incredible assertion that among the Australians ideas of blood relationship had no influence on their family systems, and the still more incredible assertion that among the ancient Peruvians there was no trace of kinship groups; that he bases his ideas about the agrarian constitution of the Germanic people on Laveleye's obsolete and unreliable material; and that finally he echoes the same Laveleye's fabulous assertion that "still today" the Russian village community that prevails among a population of 35 million forms a kinship community with blood relationship, a "family community," which is about as true as it would be to claim that all the inhabitants of Berlin formed "still today" a great family community. All this specially enables Grosse to treat the "church father of German Social Democracy," Morgan, as a dead dog.

The above examination of Grosse's treatment of family forms and kinship gives an idea of how he treats the "forms of economy." The entire proof that he directs against the assumption of primitive communism rests on "yes, but," with unchallengeable facts being admitted, but others contrasted to them in such a way that what is unwanted is diminished, what is wanted is exaggerated, and the result correspondingly dressed up to look good.

Grosse himself reports of the lower hunters:

Individual possession, which among all lower societies consists principally if not exclusively in movable goods, is here almost completely insignificant; the most valuable piece of property, however, the hunting ground, belongs to all the men of a tribe in common. It follows that the proceeds of hunting have to be divided from time to time among all members of a horde. This is reported for example among the

---

* See especially Émile Louis Victor de Laveleye, *De la Propriété et de ses formes primitives* (Property and its Primitive Forms) (Paris: Baillière, 1877).

Botocudos* (Ehrenreich, "Über die Botocudos," in *Zeitschrift für Ethnologie*, XIX, 31†). In some parts of Australia, similar customs exist. Thus all members of a primitive group are and remain more or less equally poor. Since there are no essential differences of wealth, a main source for the origin of tribal differences is lacking. In general, all adult men have equal rights within the tribe.[38]

In the same way, "membership of a kin group has in some (!) connections a fundamental influence on the life of the lower hunter. It ascribes him the right to use a particular hunting ground, and it gives him the right and duty of protection and revenge" (p. 64). Similarly, Grosse concedes the possibility of a kinship communism among the lower hunters of central California.

But for all that, the kinship group here is loose and weak, there is no economic community. "The mode of production of the Arctic hunters however is so completely individualist that the kinship connection is scarcely able to resist centrifugal tendencies."[39] Likewise, among the Australians, the use of the common hunting land "in hunting and gathering is generally pursued not at all in common, but each individual family conducts a separate economy." And in general, "the lack of food does not permit lasting unification of large groups, but forces them to disperse" (p. 63).

Let us turn then to the higher hunters.

It is true that "land among the higher hunters is indeed as a rule the common property of the tribe or kinship group" (p. 69), true that we directly find at this stage large buildings as common quarters for such groups (p. 84), while we also learn: "The extensive dams and defenses that [Alexander] Mackenzie saw in the rivers of the Haidah‡ and that in his estimation must have required the work of the whole tribe, were supervised by the local chief, without whose permission no one was allowed to fish. They were thus very likely seen as the property of the whole village community, to which the fishing waters and hunting grounds undividedly belonged" (p. 87).

But "movable property here has acquired such an extension and importance that despite the equal possession of land a great inequality of wealth can develop" (p. 69), and "as a rule, food, so far as we can see, is no more seen as common property than are other movable goods. Thus the domestic kinship groups can only to a very limited sense be described as economic communities" (p. 88).

We move then to the next higher cultural stage, that of nomadic stock-raising (pastoralism). Here again Grosse tells us:

---

* The Botocudos is the name European explorers and colonizers gave to the Aimorés or Krenak peoples of eastern Brazil. Devastated by European colonization, they were forced from their homelands to Minas Gerais, where small numbers of their descendants still survive.

† The full article is "Über die Botocudos," by P. M. A. Ehrenreich, in *Zeitschrift für Ethnologie* 19 (1887), pp. 49–82.

‡ The Haidah are the Native American inhabitants of Queen Charlotte's Island and other islands off the western coast of Canada.

It is true that "even the most restless nomads do not roam in unbounded spaces, they all rather move within a quite firmly limited region, which is seen as the property of their tribe and which is frequently divided again among the individual separate families and kin groups" (p. 91). Furthermore: "The land in almost the whole region of stock-raising is the common property of the tribe or kin group" (p. 96). "The land is naturally the common property of all kin group members and as such is divided by the kin group or its chief between the different families for their use" (p. 128).

But "the land is not the most valuable possession of the nomad. His greatest wealth is his herd, and livestock is always (!) the separate property of the individual families. The stock-raising kin group has never (!) developed into a community of economy and possession."

Finally we have the lower agriculturalists. Here, *it is true* for the first time that the kinship group is admitted to be a completely communist economic community.

But—and here this "but" follows hard on the heels—here too "industry undermines social equality" (when Grosse talks of industry he naturally means commodity production, being unable to differentiate the one from the other), "creating a movable individual property, which prevails over the common property in land and destroys this.'" And despite the community of land, "the separation between rich and poor already exists here."[40] Communism is thus reduced to a brief interval of economic history, which moreover begins with private property and ends with private property. *Quod erat demonstrandum.**

3

In order to assess the value of Grosse's schema, we shall turn directly to the facts. Let us examine the economic form of the most backward peoples—if only with a fleeting glance. Who are these?

Grosse calls them the "lower hunters," and says of them:

The lower hunting peoples today form only a small fragment of humanity. Their imperfect and unfruitful form of production condemns them to numerical weakness and cultural poverty, and they are everywhere on the retreat in the face of larger and stronger peoples, now continuing their existence in inaccessible primal forests and inhospitable deserts. A large part of these wretched tribes belong to pygmy races.† It is precisely the weakest peoples who are forced by the stronger in the

---

*   Latin for "That was to be demonstrated."

†   Pygmies are not a race, but a term used for a variety of cultures and ethnic groups around the world in which individuals are of diminutive stature. The term derives from the ancient Greek term for "dwarf" and has no morphological or cultural significance. Most "pygmies" prefer to be referred to according to their respective ethnic group (Aka, Mbuti, Twa, etc.).

struggle for existence into the regions most hostile to culture, and thereby condemned also to cultural stagnation. Yet representatives of the oldest economic form
are still found today on all continents with the exception of Europe. Africa houses
many such hunting peoples who have grown small; unfortunately, however, we so
far have information only on one of these, the Bushmen of the Kalahari desert*
[in German South-West Africa—R.L.]; the lives of the other pygmy tribes are still
hidden in the darkness of the central African forests. If we turn from Africa to
the East, we find first of all in central Ceylon [off the southern tip of the Indian
peninsula—R.L.] the dwarf hunting people of the Vedda,[†] then on the Andaman
islands the Mincopie,[‡] in inland Sumatra the Kubu[§] and in the mountain wilder-
nesses of the Philippines the Aeta[¶]—three tribes who again belong to the small races.
The whole of the Australian continent was peopled with lower hunting peoples
before the European settlement; and if in the last half of this century the indigenous peoples have been driven out of the greater part of the coastal regions by the
colonists, they still persist in the deserts of the hinterland. In America, finally, from
the extreme south to the far north, we find a whole series of groups of an extreme
cultural poverty. In the rain-and storm-lashed mountain wastes around Cape Horn
[the southern tip of South America—R.L.] dwell the inhabitants of Tierra del Fuego,
whom more than one observer has declared to be the poorest and crudest of all
humans. Besides the Botocudos with their evil reputation, many other hunting tribes
still wander through the forests of Brazil, including the Bororó who are somewhat
familiar to us thanks to the studies of [Karl] von den Steinen.[**] Central California [on
the west coast of North America—R.L.] has a number of tribes at a level only little
above the most wretched peoples of Australia.[41††]

---

   *   "Bushmen" is a generalized term for a wide variety of African indigenous peoples, such
as San, Sho, Barwa, and Kung. They form part of the Khoisan group. Those in the Kalahari have
traditionally been hunters and gatherers.
   †   The Vedda are indigenous hunter-gatherers of Sri Lanka who also practiced a form of slash
and burn agriculture.
   ‡   The Mincopie is a term applied to indigenous hunter-gatherers off the coast of India, who
subsist largely from fishing and eating shellfish.
   §   The Kubu are nomadic peoples of the forests of southern Sumatra who live by hunting and
the cultivation of tubers.
   ¶   The Aeta are indigenous inhabitants of Luzon, in the northern Philippines, who were pos-
sibly the first inhabitants of the archipelago.
   **   The Bororó are an Amazonian people living in southern Matto Grosso. Claude Lévi-
Strauss discusses them at length in his famous work, *Tristes Tropiques*. Karl von den Steinen, a
German ethnologist, studied them during several trips to central Brazil in the 1880s.
   ††   Since Australia was the only continent exclusively populated by hunter-gatherers at the
time it was discovered by Europeans, many early colonial settlers and commentators assumed that
its populace was the most "backward" of any on earth. Marx himself did not share this view, as seen
from his discussion of the Australian aborigines in his critical notes on the work of John Lubbock.
See Marx's *Ethnological Notebooks*, pp. 339–51.

Without continuing any further with Grosse, who strangely also counts the Eskimos* among the lowest peoples, we shall now dwell on some of the tribes mentioned above in search of traces of a socially planned organization of labor.

Let us turn first of all to the Australian cannibals,† who according to several scholars exist at the lowest level of culture that the human race displays on this earth. Among these aborigines we particularly find the already mentioned primitive division of labor between men and women; the latter principally see to vegetable food as well as wood and water, while the men are responsible for hunting and providing animal food.

We also find here a picture of social labor that is the direct opposite of the "individual search for food" and offers an example right away of how the most primitive societies see to it that all labor-power needed is diligently applied, for example:

> All the males in the Chepara tribe‡ are expected to provide food, if not sick. If a man is lazy and stays in the camp, he is jeered at and insulted by the others. Men, women, and children leave the camp early in the morning for the purpose of hunting for food where they think that game will be plentiful. The men and women carry the various catches to the nearest water hole, where fires are made and game is cooked. The men, women, and children all eat together amicably, the food being distributed among them by the old men equally to all the men, women, and children. After the meal, the women carry what is left of the cooked food to the camp, men hunting by the way.[42]

Now some further information on how production is planned among the Australian aborigines. This is in fact extremely complicated, and worked out in the utmost detail. Each Australian tribe is divided into a number of groups, each one being named after an animal or a plant that it honors, and possessing a demarcated part of the tribe's total territory. One particular territory thus belongs for example to the kangaroo-men, another to the emu-men (the emu is a large bird similar to an ostrich), a third to the snake-men (the Australians even eat snakes), etc. According to the findings of the most recent scientific research, these "totems," as we have already mentioned in another connection, are almost always animals and plants that the aborigines make use of as food. Each of these groups has its chief, who takes the lead in the hunt. The animal or plant name and the cult corresponding to it are not an empty form: each particular group of

---

    * This is the name French explorers gave to the Inuit peoples of Siberia, Greenland, and Arctic North America.

    † Although many European travelers to Australia brought back tales of "cannibalism" on the part of the aboriginal peoples, there is little documented evidence that it widely prevailed.

    ‡ The Chepara is an indigenous group living in the Australian state of Queensland.

aborigines is in fact obliged to provide the animal or plant food of its name, and to take responsibility for the supply and continuation of this source of food. And each of these groups does this not for itself, but above all for the *other* groups in the tribe. The kangaroo-men, for example, are obliged to provide kangaroo meat for the rest of the tribe, the snake-men to provide snakes, the caterpillar-men a certain caterpillar that is seen as a delicacy, and so on. All this is bound up with strict religious observances and great ceremonies. It is almost a universal rule, for example, that the people of a particular group may not eat their own animal or plant totem, or only in great moderation, although they must provide this for others. A man in the snake-group, for example, if he kills a snake—even in times of great hunger—must refrain from eating it himself, but rather bring it back to the camp for the others. In the same way, an emu-man will only consume emu meat with extreme moderation, and never take the eggs and fat of the bird— which are used as a remedy—for himself, but hand them over to his fellow tribes people. On the other hand, other groups may not hunt or gather and consume the animal or plant without the permission of the corresponding totem men. Each year, a festive ceremony is held by each group, with the object of secur- ing the multiplication of the totemic animal or plant (by way of singing, wind instruments and various religious ceremonies), with only the other groups being allowed to eat it. The time for such ceremonies to take place is decided for each group by its chief, who is also in charge of the ceremony. And this time is directly bound up with the conditions of production. In central Australia, animals and plants suffer from a long dry season, while the short wet season leads to an increase in animal life and a vigorous plant growth. Most of the ceremonies of the totem groups are then held as the good season approaches. According to [Friedrich] Ratzel, it is a "comic misunderstanding" to say that the aborigines call themselves after their most important foodstuffs.[43] In the system of totem groups briefly indicated above, however, anyone can already recognize at first glance an elaborate organization of social production. The individual totem groups are evidently just limbs in an extensive system of division of labor. All the groups together form an ordered and planned whole, and each group also conducts itself in a quite ordered and planned way under a unitary leadership. And the fact that this system of production assumes a religious form, the form of various food taboos, ceremonies, etc., merely shows that this production form is of *age-old date*, that this organization has existed among the aborigines for many centuries or even millennia, so that it has had time to ossify into rigid formulas, and what originally were mere expediencies for the purpose of producing and providing food have become articles of a belief in secret connections. These con- nections, discovered by the Englishmen [Walter Baldwin] Spencer and [Francis James] Gillen, are also confirmed by another scholar, [James George] Frazer, who expressly says, for example:

We have to bear in mind that the various totemic groups in totemic society do not live in isolation from one another; they intermingle and practice their magic powers for the common good. In the original system, if we are not mistaken, the kangaroo-men hunted and killed kangaroo for the benefit of all other totemic groups as well as their own, and it would have been the same with the caterpillar totem, the hawk totem and the rest. Under the new system [i.e. in the religious form—R.L.], in which a totemic group was forbidden to kill and eat its own totem, the kangaroo-men continued to provide kangaroos, but no longer for their own consumption; the emu-men continued to see to the multiplication of emus, although they were no longer allowed to enjoy emu meat; the caterpillar-men continued their magic arts for the procreation of caterpillars, even if these delicacies were now destined for other stomachs.*

In sum, what appears to us today as a religious system was in age-old times a simple system of organized social production with a far-reaching division of labor.

If we now turn to the distribution of products among the Australian aborigines, we find an even more detailed and complex system. Each part of a wild animal killed, each bird egg found and each handful of fruit gathered, is carefully allocated according to quite firm rules to particular members of the society for their consumption. For example, what the women gather in the way of plant food belongs to them and their children. The proceeds of the men's hunting is divided according to rules that differ from tribe to tribe, but which in all tribes are extremely detailed. The English scholar [Alfred William] Howitt, for example, who studied the populations in southeastern Australia, chiefly in the state of Victoria, found the following kind of distribution:

> It is assumed that a man kills a kangaroo at a distance from the camp. Two other men are with him but are too late to assist in killing it. The distance from the camp being considerable, the kangaroo is cooked before being carried home. While the first man lights a fire, the others cut up the game. The three cook the entrails and eat them. The following distribution is made. Men 2 and 3 receive one leg and the tail, and one leg and part of the haunch, because they were present, and had helped to cut the game up. Man number 1 received the remainder that he carried to the camp. The head and back are taken by his wife to her parents, the remainder goes to his parents. If he is short of meat, he keeps a little, but if, for instance, he has an opossum, he gives it all away. His mother, if she has caught some fish, may give him some, or his wife's parents may *give him some of their share*; and they also would in such a case give her some next morning. *Children in all cases well cared for by their grandparents.*[44]

---

* Cited in Felix Somló, *Der Güterverkehr in der Urgesellschaft*, pp. 61–2, which gives the source as I. G. Frazer, "Observations on Central Australian Totemism," *Journal of the Anthropological Institute*, 1899, p. 284.

The following rules prevail in one tribe. With a kangaroo, for example, the hunter takes a piece near the loin, the father receives the backbone, ribs, shoulder and head; the mother the right leg and the younger brother the left foreleg. The father gives the tail and another piece of the back to his parents, the mother gives a part of the thigh and the shin to her parents. With a koala, the hunter keeps the left ribs for himself, the father receives the right hind-leg and mother the left, the elder brother receives the right foreleg and the younger brother the left. The elder sister receives a piece along the backbone, the younger one the liver. The right rib portion belongs to the father's brother, a side piece to the maternal uncle, and the head goes to the young men's camp.

In another tribe, however, the food obtained is always divided equally among those present. If a wallaby (a smaller species of kangaroo) is killed, and there are ten or twelve people, each of them receives a part of the animal. None of them touches the animal or any part of it until they have been given their portion by the hunter. If the person who killed the animal happens not to be present while it is being cooked, no one touches it until he returns. The women receive equal portions to the men, and children are carefully seen to by both parents.[45]

These various modes of distribution, which differ from one tribe to another, also reveal their age-old character by the way that they appear in ritual forms and are summed up in sayings.[46] This expresses a tradition that may go back several millennia, and is seen by each generation as an unbreakable and strictly maintained rule that has been handed down. But two particular features of this system stand out very clearly. Above all, among the Australian aborigines—perhaps those humans who have remained most backward—it is not only production but also consumption that is planned and organized as a common social affair; and secondly, this plan evidently aims at the provisioning and security of all members of society, according both to their needs in terms of food and to their productive power. Under all conditions, special care is taken of old people, who in turn care look after the small children along with the mothers. The entire economic life of the Australian aborigines—production, division of labor, distribution of foodstuffs—has thus been planned and organized in the strictest way from earliest times by way of firm rules.

From Australia we turn to North America. Here in the West, the sparse remnants of Indians living on the Isla del Tiburón in the Gulf of California* and a narrow strip of the adjacent mainland present a particular interest, thanks to their complete isolation and their hostility to outsiders, which is how they have preserved their age-old customs in a very pure state. In 1895, United States scientists undertook an expedition to study this tribe, and the results of this were

---

* The Isla del Tiburón is the largest island in the Gulf of California and the largest island in Mexico. "Tiburón" is Spanish for "shark." It is the traditional homeland of the Seri Indians. In 1975 the Mexican government granted the Seri title of communal property with regard to the island.

described by the American [William John] McGee.* According to his report, the Seri Indian tribe—the name of this now very sparse people—is divided into four groups, each of these being named after an animal. The two largest are the pelican group and the turtle group. The customs, practices and rules of these groups in relation to their totemic animals are kept strictly secret, and were very hard to ascertain. But if we learn right away that the diet of these Indians consists principally of the meat of pelicans, turtles, fish and other sea creatures, and bear in mind the previously described system of totemic groups among the Australian aborigines, we may assume with a high degree of certainty that also among these Indians off the Californian coast the secret cult of totemic animals and the division of the tribe into corresponding groups expresses nothing other than the survivals of an age-old, strictly organized system of production with a division of labor, that has ossified into religious symbols. This view is reinforced, for example, by the fact that the supreme protective spirit of the Seri Indians is the pelican, but it is also this bird that forms the basis of that tribe's economic existence. Pelican meat is the main food, pelican skins are used as clothing and bedding, as shields, and as the most important articles of exchange with outsiders. The Seri's most important form of labor, hunting, is still practiced according to strict rules. Hunting pelicans, for example, is a well-organized common undertaking "with at least a semi-ceremonial character." Pelican hunts may take place only at particular times, in such a way that the birds are protected during their breeding season, so as to secure their progeny. "The butchery [the massive slaughter of these top-heavy birds presents no difficulties—R.L.] is followed by a gluttonous feast, in which the half-famished families gorge the tenderer parts in the darkness, and noisily carouse in the carnage until overcome by slumber. Next day the matrons select the carcasses of least injured plumage and carefully remove the skins."⁴⁷ The feast lasts for several days, with various ceremonies being associated with it. This "gluttonous feast," therefore, and the noisy "gorging in darkness," which Professor Bücher would certainly note as a sign of purely animal behavior, is actually very well organized—its ceremonial character is sufficient proof of this. The planned character of the hunt is combined with strict regulation of distribution and consumption. The common eating and drinking proceeds in a definite sequence: first comes the chief (who is also leader of the hunt), then the other warriors in order of age, then the oldest woman followed by her daughters in order of age, and finally the children also by order of age, with the girls, particularly those approaching marriageable age, enjoying certain preference by the connivance of the women:

---

*   In 1895, United States scientists undertook an expedition to study the Seri tribe. The results were described by William John McGee in *The Seri Indians* (Washington, DC: Smithsonian Institution, 1898).

[E]very member of the family or clan is entitled to necessary food and raiment, and it is the duty of every other person to see that the need is supplied. The stress of this duty is graded partly by proximity (so that, other things equal, it begins with the nearest person), but chiefly by standing and responsibility in the group (which again are reckoned as equivalents of age), whereby it becomes the business of the first at the feast to see that enough is left over to supply all below him; and this duty passes down the line in such wise as to protect the interests of the helpless infant...*

From South America, we have the testimony of Professor [Karl] von den Steinen about the wild Indian tribe of the Bororó in Brazil. Here again we have above all the typical division of labor. The women obtain plant food, look for roots with a pointed stick, climb with great agility up palm trees, collecting nuts and cutting the palm kernels, seeking fruits and the like. The women also prepare plant food, and manufacture the cooking pots. When the women return home, they give the men fruit, etc. and receive whatever meat is left over. Distribution and consumption are strictly regulated. According to von den Steinen:

> If Bororó etiquette in no way prevents them from sharing their meals, they have other strange customs for this, which clearly show that tribes where the proceeds of hunting are scarce have to search somehow for ways to forestall quarrels and disputes. One rule here is particularly striking: *no one cooks the game that he has shot himself, but gives it to someone else to cook!* The same prudent foresight is practiced for valuable hides and teeth. If a jaguar is killed, a great feast is held and the meat is eaten. But *it is not the hunter* who receives the hide and the teeth, but rather... the closest relative of the tribesman or woman who most recently died. The hunter is honored, and is presented by everyone with macaw feathers [the Bororós' most prized ornament—R.L.] and bows decorated by oassú ribbons. The most important measure to preserve peace, however, is bound up with the office of *medicine man*,[48]

or, as European like to say in such cases, the magician or priest. This person must be in attendance at the killing of any animal, but it is particularly important that every animal killed, as well as plant food, is only distributed and consumed by way of particular ceremonies. Hunting takes place on the initiative and under the leadership of the chief. The young and unmarried men live together in the "men's house," where they work together, produce weapons, tools and ornaments, spin, hold wrestling matches and also eat together, in strict discipline and order, as we have already mentioned above. "A family one of whose members dies," says von den Steinen, "suffers a great loss

---

* McGee, cited in Somló, p. 128 (W. G. McGee, *The Seri Indians*, p. 273).

For everything that the dead person used is burned, thrown into the river or placed in the bone-basket, so that he will have no occasion to return. The hut is then completely evacuated. But the bereaved are given presents, bows and arrows are made for them, and there is also the custom that, if a jaguar is killed, the hide is given *"to the brother of the last woman who died or to the uncle of the last man who died."*[49]

A fully worked-out plan and social organization thus prevails in both production and distribution.

If we pass through the American mainland down to the most southerly point, we find here a primitive people at the lowest level of culture, the Fuegians, who inhabit the inhospitable archipelago at the tip of South America, the first information on them being brought back to Europe in the seventeenth century. In 1698, the French government sent an expedition to the southern ocean, in response to French pirates who had been plying their trade there for many years.* One of the engineers on board kept a diary that has survived, and contains the following summary information about the Fuegians:

> Each family, that is, father and mother, along with those children not yet married, has its pirogue (a canoe made of tree bark), in which they carry everything they need. They sleep at night wherever they find themselves. If there is no ready-made hut, then they build one ... They make a small fire in the middle, around which they lie together on grass. When they feel hungry, they cook shellfish, which the eldest man among them distributes in equal portions. The main occupation of the men, indeed their duty, consists in building huts, hunting and fishing; looking after the canoes and gathering shellfish falls to the women ... They hunt for whales in the following manner: Five or six canoes put out to sea together, and when they find a whale they pursue it and harpoon it with large arrows whose points made of bone or stone are very skillfully cut ... When they kill an animal or a bird, or catch the fish and shellfish that are their regular food, they divide these among all the families, since they are ahead of us in possessing almost all their combined means of subsistence in common.[50]

From America we turn to Asia. Here we are told the following about the pygmy tribes of the Mincopie on the Andaman archipelago (in the Gulf of Bengal) by the English researcher E[dward] H[orace] Man, who spent twelve years among them and obtained a more exact knowledge of them than any other European.†

---

* The French pirates, based in what is now Haiti, spent seven years plundering the coast of South America in the late 1600s. In response, on December 18, 1698, the French government sent an expedition to the southern seas, funded by the twenty richest financiers in France.

† See Edward Horace Man, *On the Aboriginal Inhabitants of the Andaman Islands* (London: Tübner, n.d.). Reprinted as *On the Aboriginal Inhabitants of the Andaman Islands* (New Delhi: Mittal, 2001).

The Mincopie are divided into nine tribes, each consisting of a considerable number of small groups of between thirty and fifty individuals, though sometimes as many as 300. Each of these groups has its leader, and the whole tribe has a chief who stands above those of the individual communities. Yet his authority is very limited; it consists principally in holding assemblies of all the communities that belong to his tribe. He is the leader in hunting and fishing and on migrations, and he also settles disputes. Work within each community is done in common, with a division of labor between men and women. Hunting, fishing, obtaining honey, constructing canoes, bows and arrows and other tools falls to the men, while the women bring in wood and water as well as planting food, producing ornaments and cooking. It is the duty of all men and women who stay at home to care for children, the sick and the aged, and to keep the fires going in the various huts; each person capable of work is obliged to work for themselves and the community, and it is also the custom to make sure that there is always a reserve of food to provide for any strangers who may arrive. Small children, the weak and the aged are the special object of general attention, and they have an even better deal in terms of the satisfaction of their daily needs than do the other members of the society.

The consumption of food is governed by definite rules. A married man may only eat together with other married men or bachelors, never with other women or with his own household, unless he is already of a prescribed age. Unmarried people take their meals separately—male youths in one place, girls in another.

The preparation of meals is the customary duty of the women, who see to this while the men are away. But if they are particularly occupied with obtaining wood and water, as on feast days or after a particularly successful hunt, then one of the men does the cooking, and when this is half finished, divides it among those present and leaves the further preparation to them, which they do on their own hearths. If the chief is present, he receives the first and indeed the lion's share, then come the men and after them the women and children in succession; what remains belongs to the distributor.

In the manufacture of weapons, tools and other articles, the Mincopie generally spend a remarkable time and great diligence, being able to spend hours on end laboriously working a piece of iron with a stone hammer in order to form a spear or arrowhead, to improve the shape of a bow, etc. They devote themselves to these tasks even when no immediate or foreseeable necessity drives them to such efforts. They cannot be accused of greed—it is said of them—as they often present (a misunderstood European expression for "distribute") the best that they possess, and preserve for their own use objects that are in no way better worked, still less making better ones for themselves.[51]

We conclude this series of examples with a sample from the life of the primitive peoples of Africa. Here, the pygmy Bushmen of the Kalahari desert are frequently taken as an example of extreme backwardness and the lowest stage of human culture. German, English and French researchers agree in saying that the Bushmen live in groups (hordes), conducting their economic life in common. Their small bands are marked by complete equality, in respect of means of subsistence, weapons, etc. The foodstuffs that they find on their travels are collected in sacks that are emptied out in the camp. As the German scholar [Siegfried] Passarge reports: "The day's harvest then makes its appearance: roots, tubers, fruits, grubs, rhinoceros birds, bullfrogs, turtles, grasshoppers, even snakes and iguanas."[52] The booty is then divided among all.

> The systematic gathering of vegetables, for example fruits, roots, tubers, etc., as well as smaller animals, is the business of women. They have to supply the horde with supplies of this kind, and the children help with this. Men will occasionally also bring back something that they accidentally happen upon, though for them gathering is only a secondary matter. The main task of men is hunting.[53]

The proceeds of the hunt are consumed by the horde in common. Space and food are provided around the common fire for traveling Bushmen from allied hordes. Passarge, as a good European with the intellectual spectacles of bourgeois society, immediately remarks on the "exaggerated virtue" with which the Bushmen share the last morsel with others—this being a token of their cultural incapability![54]

It is apparent, then, that the most primitive peoples, and particularly those far removed from settled existence and agriculture, who stand in a sense at the starting point of the chain of economic development as far as this is known to us from direct observation, offer a quite different picture of relations than we see in Herr Grosse's schema. What we have on all sides is not "dispersed" and "separate" household economies, but rather strictly regulated economic communities with typical features of communist organization. This is a question of the "lower hunters." As for the "higher hunters," the picture of the kinship economy of the Iroquois, as described for us in detail by Morgan, is quite sufficient. But stock-raisers, too, provide sufficient material to give the lie to Grosse's bold contentions.[55]

The agricultural mark community, accordingly, is not the only primitive communist organization that we find in economic history, but rather the most developed one, not the first but the last. It is not a product of agriculture, but rather of the immeasurably long earlier traditions of communism which, born in the womb of the gens organization, was finally applied to agriculture, where it precisely reached an apogee that heralded its own decline. In no way therefore do the facts confirm Grosse's schema. If we then ask for an explanation of the remarkable phenomenon of a communism that emerges in the midst of economic history only to immediately disappear again, Herr Grosse offers us, with one of his clever "materialist" explanations:

We have seen in fact that among the lower agriculturalists, the kin group has particularly acquired so much more force and power than among the peoples of other cultural forms, because it appears here initially as a community of dwelling, possession and economy. But the fact that it has taken such a form here is explained in turn by the nature of the lower agricultural economy, which unites people, whereas hunting and stock-raising disperse them.[56]

Spatial "uniting" or "dispersal" of people in work thus decides whether communism or private property are to prevail. It is a pity that Herr Grosse has forgotten to enlighten us why woods and meadows, in which people are most likely to live "dispersed," precisely remain common property for longest—in some places down to the present day—whereas the agricultural land on which people "unite" was the earliest to transfer to private ownership. And further, why the form of production that "unites" people more than any other in the whole of economic history, i.e. modern large-scale industry, far from generating any kind of common property, has produced the strictest form of private property, i.e. capitalist property.

We see then that Grosse's "materialism" is one more proof that it is not enough to talk about "production" and its importance for the whole of social life in order to conceive history from a materialist perspective, and that separated from its other aspect, from its revolutionary idea of development, historical materialism becomes a crude and ungainly wooden crutch, instead of, as with Marx, a stroke of genius of the scientific spirit.

But what this shows above all else is that Herr Grosse, who talks so much about production and its forms, is unclear about the most fundamental concepts of relations of production. We have already seen how what he understands right away by forms of production is such purely external categories as hunting, stock raising and agriculture. But in terms of answering the question as to the form of property within each of these "forms of production"—that is, the question whether there is common property, family ownership or private ownership, and to whom such property belongs—Grosse merely distinguishes between categories such as "landownership" on the one hand and "moveable possessions" on the other. If he finds that these belong to different owners, he then asks which is "more important": the "moveable" possessions on the one hand, or immoveable landed property on the other. And whichever appears "more important" to Herr Grosse, he takes as decisive for the form of property in this particular society. He decides, for example, that among higher hunters, "moveable possessions have already acquired such an importance" that they are more weighty than landed property; and since moveable possessions such as foodstuffs are private property, Grosse does not recognize any communistic economy here, despite the self-evidence of common property in land.

But distinctions of this kind made according to purely external

characteristics—such as those of moveable versus immoveable possessions—
do not have the slightest significance for production, and are more or less on
the same level as Grosse's other distinctions—in family forms between male
supremacy and female supremacy, or in forms of production between dispersed and uniting activities. "Moveable possessions," for example, may consist
of foodstuffs or raw materials, ornaments and cult objects, or tools. They may
be produced for a society's own use or for exchange. Depending on this, they
will have a very different significance for relations of production. In general,
Grosse judges the production and property relations of different peoples—and
he is here a typical representative of present-day bourgeois society—according
to foodstuffs and other objects of consumption in the broadest sense. If he finds
that such objects of consumption are possessed and used by individuals, this
demonstrates for him the rule of "individual property" among the people in
question. This is the typical manner in which primitive communism is "scientifically" refuted today.[57] According to this profound point of view, a community
of beggars which collects and consumes its scanty takings in common, such as
is very common in the East, or a band of thieves who enjoy their stolen goods
together, are pure examples of a "communistic economic society." A mark community, on the other hand, which possesses its land in common and works it
together, but in which the fruits are consumed on a family basis—each family
from its piece of land—is called "an economic community only in a very limited
sense." In short, what is decisive for the character of production from this point
of view is the right of ownership over means of consumption and not over means
of production, i.e. the conditions of distribution and not those of production.
We have reached here a key point in conceptions of political economy, which is
fundamentally important for the understanding of all economic history. But we
shall now leave Herr Grosse to his fate, and turn our attention to this question
in a more general fashion.

4

Anyone who embarks on the study of economic history, and wants to discover
the various forms that the economic relations of society have presented in their
historical development, must first of all be clear as to what feature of economic
relations is to be taken as the touchstone and measure of this development.
In order to find one's way among the wealth of phenomena on any particular
terrain, and particularly their historical succession, complete clarity is required
as to what element it is that is as it were the inner axis around which the phenomena revolve. The particular element that Morgan, for example, took as the
measure of cultural history and touchstone of its present level, was the development of productive technology. In this way he did indeed grasp and reveal
the root of the whole cultural existence of humanity. For our purposes here,

however, those of economic history, Morgan's measure is not sufficient. The technology of human labor precisely shows the stage that humans have reached in the mastery of external nature. Each new step in the perfection of productive technology is at the same time a step in the subjugation of physical nature by the human mind, and thereby a step in the development of human culture in general. But if we particularly want to investigate the forms of production in society, the relationship of people to nature is not enough; what we are interested in here is first and foremost a different aspect of human labor, i.e. the relations in which people stand *to one another* in work; what interests us is not the technology of production but its social organization. For the cultural level of a primitive people it is very important to know that they are familiar with the potter's wheel and practice pottery. Morgan takes this important advance in technology as the marker of an entire cultural period, which he describes as the transition from savagery to barbarism. But on the basis of this fact we can still judge very little about the form of production of this people. For this we would first have to discover a whole series of conditions, for example who practices pottery in this society, whether all members of the society or only some of them, for example that it is women who supply the community with pots, whether the products of pottery are destined only for the community's—perhaps a village's—own use, or rather serve for exchange with others, whether the products of each person who practices pottery are used only by themselves, or whether everything manufactured serves all members of the community in common. We see that there are ramified social connections in a position to determine the character of the form of production in a society: the division of labor, the distribution of products among consumers, exchange. But all these aspects of economic life are themselves determined by one decisive factor, production. The fact that the distribution of products and exchange can only be consequent phenomena is apparent at first glance. So that products can be distributed among consumers, or exchanged, they must first of all be manufactured. Production itself is therefore the first and most important element in a society's economic life. In the process of production, however, what is decisive is the relations in which those who work stand to their means of production. All work requires particular raw materials, a particular workplace, and then—particular tools. We already know what a high importance the tools of labor and their manufacture assume in the life of human society. Human labor-power intervenes to perform work with these tools and other dead means of production, and to produce the means of consumption, in the broadest sense, that are needed for social life. The relation of those who work to their means of production is the first question of production and its decisive factor. And by this we do not mean the *technical* relation, not the greater or lesser perfection of the means of production with which people work, nor the way in which they proceed with their work. We mean rather the *social* relation between human labor-power and the dead means of production, i.e. the question as *to whom the means of production belong.* In the course of time, this relationship has changed many times. Each time, however, the whole character of production has changed along with this—the pattern of the division of labor, the distribution of products, the direction and scale of exchange, and finally the whole material and intellectual life of society. According to whether those who work possess their means of production in common, or individuals each work for themselves, or do not possess anything but are rather along with the means of production themselves the property of non-workers as means of production, or are chained unfree to the means of production, or as free people who possess no means of production are forced to sell their labor-power as a means of production—we accordingly have either a communist form of production, or a small peasant and handicraft one, or a slave economy, or a feudal economy based on serfdom, or finally a capitalist economy with the wage system. And each of these economic forms has its particular type of division of labor, distribution of products and exchange, as well as its own social, political and intellectual life. It is enough in human economic history for the relationship between those who work and the means of production to radically change, for all other aspects of social, political and intellectual life to change radically as well, so that a whole new society emerges. Of course, there is a continuing inter-action between all these aspects of a society's economic life. Not only does the relationship of labor-power to the means of production influence the division of labor, the distribution of products and exchange, but all of these react in turn on the relation of production. But this kind of action is different. The prevail-ing kind of division of labor, distribution of wealth and particularly exchange at a given economic stage may gradually undermine the relation between labor-power and the means of production from which they themselves arose. Their form however is only altered if the relation between labor-power and means of production has become obsolete and a radical transformation takes place, a literal revolution. Thus the respective transformations that occur in the relation between labor-power and means of production form the visible great mile-stones on the road of economic history, they mark out the natural epochs in the economic development of human society.

How important it is for the understanding of economic history to be clear about what is essential in this history is shown by examining the partition of economic history that is most current and most celebrated in German politi-cal economy today. We refer to that of Professor Bücher. In his *Entstehung der Volkswirtschaft* [The Rise of the National Economy], Bücher explains how important a correct partition of economic history into epochs is for its under-standing. In pursuit of this task, however, he does not just tackle the question and show us the result of his rational investigations, but rather prepares us first for a proper evaluation of his own work, by holding forth with great compla-cency on the inadequacy of all his predecessors.

"The first question," he says,

> that the political economist has to raise, if he wants to understand the economy of a people in a remote epoch, will be "Is this economy a *national* economy? Are its phenomena of the same nature as those of our present-day exchange economy, or are the two different in nature?" Yet this question can only be answered if we do not shy away from investigating the economic phenomena of the past with the same means of conceptual articulation and psychologically isolating deduction that have produced such brilliant results for the economy of the present in the hands of the masters of traditional "abstract" political economy.
>
> We cannot spare the more recent "historical" school the reproach that, instead of penetrating into the nature of earlier economic epochs by the above kind of investigation, it has, almost unnoticed, transferred the customary categories abstracted from the phenomena of the modern national economy to the past, and has spent so long kneading the concepts of exchange economy until they seem applicable to all economic epochs, for better or worse … Nowhere can this be more clearly seen than in the way that the distinctive features of the present economic mode of the civilized peoples are characterized in contrast to the economy of past epochs of peoples of low culture. This is done by proposing so-called *stages of development*, in indicating which the basic features of the course of development of economic history are summarized in a nutshell … All earlier attempts of this kind suffer from the failing that they do not lead into the essence of things, but stick to the surface.[58]

What partitioning of economic history then does Professor Bücher propose? Let us hear.

> If we are to grasp this whole development from a *single* perspective, this can only be a perspective that leads us right into the essential phenomena of political economy, and at the same time also embraces the organizational aspect of earlier economic periods. This is nothing other than the relation in which the production of goods stands to their consumption, recognizable from the length of the path that goods cover from the producer to the consumer. From this perspective, we can divide the whole of economic development into three stages, at least for the peoples of Central and Western Europe, where it can be historically traced with sufficient exactitude:
>
> 1. The stage of self-contained domestic economy (pure subsistence production, exchange-less economy), at which goods are consumed in the same economic unit as that in which they are produced;
>
> 2. The stage of urban economy (production for clients or stage of direct exchange), at which goods move directly from the producing economic unit to the consuming one;

3. The stage of national economy (commodity production, stage of circulation of goods), at which goods must as a general rule pass through a series of economic units before they are consumed.[59]

This schema of economic history is interesting first of all for what it does *not* contain. For Professor Bücher, economic history begins with the mark community of European civilized peoples, thus already with higher agriculture. The whole millennial period of primitive relations of production that preceded higher agriculture, relations in which countless populations still find themselves today, Bücher characterizes, as we know, as "non-economy," the period of his famous "individual search for food," and "non-labor." For Bücher, economic history starts with the final form of primitive communism, in which, with fixed settlement and higher agriculture, the beginnings of the unavoidable break-up and transition to inequality, exploitation and class society are already present. If Grosse contests communism for the whole developmental period prior to the agricultural mark community, Bücher simply strikes this period out of economic history.

The second stage of "self-contained urban economy" is another epoch-making discovery that we owe to the "insight of genius" of the Leipzig professor, as Schurze* would say. If the "self-contained domestic economy," for example that of a mark community, was characterized by the fact that it embraced a circle of individuals who satisfied all their economic needs within this domestic economy, then in the medieval town of Western and Central Europe—as it is only this that Bücher understands by his "urban economy"—the very opposite was the case. In the medieval town there was no common "economy" of any kind, but rather—to adopt Professor Bücher's jargon—as many "economies" as there were workshops and households of guild artisans, each of whom produced, sold and consumed for himself—even if under general guild and town rules. But even taken as a whole, the medieval guild town of Germany or France was no "self-contained" economic zone, as its existence was precisely based on reciprocal exchange with the countryside around, from which it drew foodstuffs and raw materials, and for which it manufactured handicraft products. Bücher constructs around each town a self-contained orbit of countryside that he encloses in his "urban economy," by conveniently reducing exchange between town and country simply to exchange with *peasants* in the immediate surroundings. And yet the manors of rich feudal lords, who were the best customers for urban trade and who had their seats partly scattered across the countryside far from town, partly within the town—particularly in the imperial and episcopal cities—here, however, forming a distinct economic zone, Bücher leaves entirely

---

*   We have been unable to locate the identity of "Schurze." The reference may actually be to Hermann Schulze-Delitzsch.

out of account, just as he completely ignores foreign trade, which was extremely important for medieval economic relations and particularly for the long-term destiny of cities. As for what was really characteristic of the medieval cities, however, that they were centers of *commodity production*, which became here for the first time the prevailing form of production, even if on a limited territory, Professor Bücher ignores it. Conversely, for him, commodity production only begins with the "national economy"—as we well know, bourgeois political economy likes to describe the present-day capitalist economic system with this fiction, i.e. as a "stage" in economic life, whereas what is characteristic is precisely that it is not just commodity production, but *capitalist* production. Grosse calls commodity production simply "industry," in order to show the superiority of a professor of economics over a mere sociologist.

But let us turn from these side issues to the main question. Professor Bücher presents the "self-contained domestic economy" as the first "stage" of his economic history. What does he understand by this expression? We have already mentioned that this stage begins with the agricultural village community. But besides the primitive mark community, Professor Bücher also counts other historical forms as belonging to the stage of "self-contained domestic economy," in particular the antique slave economy of the Greeks and Romans, and the medieval feudal manor. The entire economic history of civilized humanity, from its grey dawn through classical antiquity and the whole of the Middle Ages down to the threshold of modern times, is brought together as a single "stage" of production, to which is opposed the medieval European guild town as the second stage, and the present-day capitalist economy as the third stage. Professor Bücher thus classes the communist village community leading its calm existence somewhere in the mountain valleys of the Punjab, the household of Pericles in the heyday of Athenian civilization, and the feudal court of the bishop of Bamberg in the Middle Ages,* as one and the same "economic stage." But any child with even a superficial knowledge of history from school textbooks will understand that relations that are basically different are being squeezed here into a single category. On the one hand we have in the communistic agricultural communities a general equality of the mass of peasants in possession and law, no class differences or at most very embryonic, while on the other hand, in ancient Greece or Rome as well as in feudal medieval Europe, we have the most glaring development of social classes—freemen and slaves, lords and serfs, the privileged and those with no rights, wealth and poverty or misery. On the one hand the general duty to work, on the other a clear opposition between the enslaved mass of working people and the ruling minority of non-workers. And again, between the ancient slave economy of the Greeks or Romans, and the medieval

---

* The Bishopric of Bamberg (in Bavaria) was established in 1007 to encourage the spread of Christianity in Germany. In the twelfth century the Bishopric rose to great power and prominence.

feudal economy, there is the powerful distinction that ancient slavery eventually led to the downfall of Greco-Roman civilization, whereas medieval feudalism threw up urban guild handicrafts and urban trade, and in this way eventually generated modern capitalism within its womb. Anyone, therefore, who brings under one schema all these economic and social forms, these historical epochs, that are in fact poles apart, must be applying a highly original measure to economic epochs. The measure that Professor Bücher applies, in order to create the night of his "self-contained domestic economy" in which all cats are grey, he himself explains to us, by assisting our understanding with a helpfully bracketed parenthesis. "Exchange-less economy" means that first "stage" stretching from the beginning of written history to the modern age, which is followed by the medieval town as the "stage of direct exchange" and then by the present economic system as the "stage of circulation of goods." We thus have non-exchange, simple exchange or and complicated exchange—or to put it in more usual terms: absence of trade, simple trade, developed world trade; this is the measure that Professor Bücher applies to economic epochs. The main and basic problem of economic history for him is whether the merchant has already made his appearance or not, whether he is one and the same person as the producer, or a separate person. The professor is very welcome to his "exchange-less economy," which is nothing more than a professorial fantasy, still not discovered anywhere on earth, and amounting to a historical invention of staggering boldness in being applied to ancient Greece and Rome, or to the feudal Middle Ages from the tenth century on. But to take as measure of the development of production not relations of production but relations of exchange, to take the merchant as the fulcrum of the economic system and the measure of all things, even when he does not yet exist—what a brilliant result of "conceptual articulation, psychological-isolating deduction," and above all, what "penetration into the essence of the matter," which scorns "sticking to the surface"! Isn't the old undemanding schema of the "historical school," the partition of economic history into three epochs of "natural economy, money economy and credit economy," much better and closer to reality than the pretentious personal fabrication of Professor Bücher, who not only turns up his nose at all "previous attempts of this kind," but takes as his own basic idea the same rejected "sticking to the surface" of exchange, distorting it by his pedantic word spinning into a completely inappropriate schema?

"Sticking to the surface" of economic history is indeed no accident with bourgeois science. Some bourgeois scholars, such as Friedrich List, partition economic history according to the outward nature of the most important sources of food, proposing epochs of hunting, stock raising, agriculture and industry— partitions that are not even adequate for an external history of civilization. Others, such as Professor [Bruno] Hildebrand, partition economic history according to the outward form of exchange, into natural economy, money economy and credit economy, or else, like Bücher, into an exchange-less economy, an economy with direct exchange and one with commodity exchange.* Still others, like Grosse, take as their starting-point for judging economic forms the distribution of goods. In a word, the scholars of the bourgeoisie push to the forefront of historical consideration exchange, distribution, consumption—everything except the social form of *production*, which is precisely what is decisive in every historical epoch, and from which exchange and its various forms, distribution and consumption with their particular features, always follow as logical consequences. Why is that? For the same reason that moves them to present the "national economy" i.e. the capitalist mode of production, as the highest and final stage of human history, and to dispute its further world-economic development and associated revolutionary tendencies. The social pattern of production, that is, the question of the relationship of those who work to the means of production, is the core point of each economic epoch, but it is the sore point of every class society. The alienation of means of production from the hands of those who work, in one or another form, is the common foundation of all class society, since it is the basic condition of all exploitation and class rule. To divert attention from this sore point, and focus on everything external and secondary, is not so much a deliberate effort on the part of bourgeois scholars as rather the instinctive refusal of the class whose intellectual representatives they are to eat the dangerous fruit of the tree of knowledge. And a thoroughly modern and celebrated professor such as Bücher shows this class instinct with his "insight of genius," when with a wave of the hand he forces such major epochs as primitive communism, slavery and serfdom, with their fundamentally different types of relation of labor-power to the means of production, into one little box of his schema, while permitting himself elaborate hair-splitting in relation to the history of trade, distinguishing with pedantic self-importance, and holding up to the light, "domestic work (in brackets: domestic tasks)," "wage work," "handicraft," "work on the customer's premises," and similar fatuous rubbish. The ideologists of the exploited masses, the first communists, the earliest representatives of socialism, also wandered in darkness and remained in limbo with their preaching of equality among men, so long as they directed their accusations and struggle principally against unjust distribution, or—like some socialists in the nineteenth century—against modern forms of exchange. Only after the best leaders of the working class realized that the forms of distribution and exchange themselves depend on the organization of production, for which the relationship of working people to the means of production is decisive, only then were socialist strivings placed on a firm scientific footing. And on the basis of this unitary conception, the scientific position of the proletariat is distinguished from that of the bourgeoisie in its approach to economic history, just as it is in relation to political economy. If it lies in the

---

* See Friedrich Bruno Hildebrand, *Die Nationalökonomie der Gegenwart und Zukunft* (Frankfurt am Main: J. Rütten 1848).

class interest of the bourgeoisie to conceal the crux of economic history—the pattern of the relationship of labor-power to the means of production—and its changing historical character, the interest of the proletariat is conversely to bring this relationship to the fore and make it the measure of a society's economic structure. And for this it is not merely indispensable for workers to bear in mind the great milestones of history that divide the ancient communistic society from subsequent class society, but equally too the distinctions between the various historical forms of class society themselves. Only by being clear about the specific economic peculiarities of primitive communist society, and the no less particular features of the ancient slave economy and medieval serfdom, is it possible to grasp with due thoroughness why today's capitalist class society offers for the first time a historical leverage for the realization of socialism, and what the fundamental distinction is between the world socialist economy of the future and the primitive communist groups of primitive times.

IV. MATERIAL ON ECONOMIC HISTORY (II)

1

Let us take a look at one of the mark communities that has been researched most thoroughly in terms of its internal structures—the German.

As we know, the Germans settled by tribes and clans. In each clan, the male head of the household was allocated a building site along with a plot of land in order to set up house and farm there. A portion of the land was then used for agriculture, and each family would obtain a lot on it. It is true that according to Caesar,* around the beginning of the Christian era, one tribe of Germans (the Suevi or Swabians) cultivated their farmland collectively without first partitioning it among the families; yet yearly repartitioning of the lots was already a common practice when the Roman historian Tacitus wrote, in the second century CE.† In isolated regions, such as around Frickhofen in Nassau,‡ yearly repartitioning still survived in the seventeenth and eighteenth centuries. In the nineteenth century, it was still the custom in a few regions of the Bavarian Palatinate§ and on the Rhine to draw lots for farmland, although they took place at longer intervals: every three, four, nine, twelve, fourteen or eighteen years. This land, in other words, was definitively turned into private property only around the middle of the last century. In a few regions of Scotland as well, there was repartitioning of farmland up until recently. All of the lots were originally

---

* See Julius Caesar, *The Conquest of Gaul*, translated by S.A. Handford (New York: Penguin Books, 1982), pp. 94–7 and pp. 137–8.

† See Tacitus's *Germania*, translated by J.B. Rives (Clarendon: Oxford University Press, 1999). Tacitus wrote the book around 98 BC, but it was not discovered until the early 1500s.

‡ Frickhofen is a town in northwestern Germany, in the modern state of Hessen.

§ The Bavarian Palatinate, or Rhenish Bavaria, was a kingdom of the German Confederation.

the same size, matching the average needs of a family as well as the potential yield of the soil and the labor available. Depending on the quality of soil in the various regions, they amounted to fifteen, thirty, forty or more *Morgen* of land.*
In most parts of Europe, the lots were passed down by inheritance through individual families, as the repartitioning of land became rare and eventually fell out of practice in the fifth and sixth centuries. Still, this only applied to the farms. All of the land that was left over—woodland, meadows, bodies of water and unused parts—remained the unpartitioned, collective property of the mark. From the yield of the woodland, for example, the needs of the community were negotiated and what remained was distributed.

The pastures were used in common. This unpartitioned mark or common land survived for a very long time; it still exists today in the Bavarian Alps, Switzerland and the Tyrol, as well as in France (in the Vendée†), in Norway and Sweden.

In order to ensure complete equality in the partitioning of farmland, the land was first divided by quality and situation into a few fields,‡ and each field was cut into several narrow strips corresponding to the number of mark members. If a member of the mark had doubts about whether he had received an equal share, he was allowed at any time to call for a new measurement of the total land. Anyone who resisted him was punished.

But even after periodic repartitioning and allocation by lot fell into disuse, the *work* of all members of the mark community, including farm work, remained totally communal and subject to strict regulation by the collectivity. This meant above all the general obligation of everyone possessing a share of the mark to work. Residency alone was not enough to be an actual member of the mark. For this, each person not only had to live in the mark, but also had to cultivate his holding himself. Anyone who failed to cultivate his portion of land for a number of years lost it for good, and the mark could hand it over to someone else to cultivate. Work itself was also under the direction of the mark. In the early period after the Germans established settlements, the centerpiece of their economic life was stock raising, conducted on communal fields and meadows under communal village herdsmen. They used fallow land as pasture for livestock, as well as farmland after the harvest. This followed already from the fact that the times for seeding and harvest, the alternation between tilling and fallow years for

---

* Luxemburg gives these areas in *Morgen*, a traditional German measure. The *Morgen* varied considerably from one part of Germany to another, but in many areas it was equivalent to between one-half to two-and-a-half acres. It roughly corresponded to the amount of land that a farmer could plough in a given morning.

† The Vendée is a mainly rural and agricultural department in the Pays-de-la-Loire region of west central France, on the Atlantic ocean. It was the center of a famous peasants' revolt against the revolutionary government of 1793.

‡ Luxemburg uses here the old-fashioned term *Flur*, adding that these *Fluren* were also known as *Oesche* or *Gewanne*.

each field, and the sequence of sowings, were collectively decided and everyone had to comply with the general arrangement. Each field was surrounded by a fence with gates, and was closed from seedtime until harvest; the opening and closing dates of the field were decided by the entire village. Each field had an overseer, or field guardian, who had to uphold the prescribed arrangement as a public official of the mark. The so-called field processions of whole villages were organized as festivals; children were also brought to these, and given a box on the ear to make them remember the boundaries and be able to attest to them later on.

Stock raising was conducted in common, and the members of the mark were not allowed to keep individual herds. All the village's animals were divided into common herds according to the kind of animal, each with its own village herdsman and an animal to lead the herd. It was also decided that the herds should have bells. In each mark, the right to hunt and fish anywhere on its territory was also common. No snares could be laid, nor any pits dug, without first notifying the rest of the community. Mineral ore and the like that was dug out of the subsoil of the mark from deeper than a ploughshare belonged to the community and not to the individual finder. The craftsmen needed to reside in each mark. Each farming family, indeed, made most of the items they needed for everyday life themselves. They baked, brewed, spun and wove at home. Yet certain crafts became specialized early on, especially those having to do with the manufacture of farm implements. Thus, in the woodland community of Wölpe in Lower Saxony,* the members of the mark were to "have a man of each craft in the forest to make useful things from wood."[60] Everywhere, it was decided what amount and kind of wood the craftsmen were to use, in order to protect the forest and use only what was necessary for the members of the mark. The craftsmen received their necessities from the mark and generally lived the same way as the mass of other peasants. Yet they did not have full rights, partly because they were transient and not an indigenous element, and partly, which comes to the same thing, because their main business was not agriculture, which was then the center of gravity of economic life, around which public life and the laws and duties of the mark members revolved.[61] It was not possible, therefore, for just anyone to join the mark community. The acceptance of an outsider had to be unanimously approved by all of the members of the mark. Anyone who wanted to transfer their lot could do so only to another mark member, never an outsider, and only before the mark tribunal.

At the head of the mark community was the *Dorfgraf* or village mayor, in other places called the *Markmeister* or *Centener*. He was chosen for this position by the mark members. Not only was this an honor for the chosen individual, but

---

* The Wölpe is a tributary of the river Aller in the German state of Lower Saxony, which flows through woods, grassland, and farms.

also a duty; refusal would be penalized. With the passage of time, the office of mark president became hereditary in certain families, and because of its power and income, it was then only a small step before this office could be bought, with the land becoming a fiefdom, so that the position developed from that of a purely democratic elected leader of the community into a tool for its domination. In the heyday of the mark community, however, the mark president was simply the executor of the wishes of the collectivity. The assembly of the mark members regulated all communal affairs, reconciled disputes and imposed punishments. The entire system of agricultural work, paths and buildings as well as the field and village policing, were all decided by majority in the assembly. The assembly was also responsible for calculating from the "mark books," which had to be kept on the mark's business. Maintaining the peace and administering justice within the mark were carried out under the chairmanship of the mark president by those in attendance (the "court of jurisdiction"), who rendered judgments orally and publicly. Only members of the mark were allowed to attend the tribunal; outsiders were denied entry. The members of the mark were sworn to help and attest to one another, being generally required to assist one another in a brotherly and loyal manner in case of emergency, fire, or enemy attack. In the army, mark members formed their own battalions and fought side by side. No one was allowed to abandon his comrade to an enemy spear. When crimes and damages occurred in the mark or were committed by a member of the mark against an outsider, the whole mark banded together in solidarity. Members of the mark were also obliged to harbor travelers and to support the needy. Each mark originally formed a religious community, and after the introduction of Christianity—which in the case of the Germanic and Saxon peoples was quite late, only in the ninth century—the community was a religious congregation. Finally, the mark typically kept a schoolteacher for all the village youth.

It is impossible to imagine anything simpler and more harmonious than the economic system of the old Germanic mark. The entire mechanism of social life here is open to view. A strict plan and a tight organization cover everything each individual does and place him as a part of the whole. The immediate needs of everyday life, and the equal satisfaction of everyone, is the starting point and end point of the whole organization. Everyone works together for everyone else and collectively decides on everything. But what does this organization spring from, what is it based on, this power of the collective over the individual? It is nothing other than the communism of land and soil, that is to say, the common possession of the most important means of production by those who work. The typical characteristics of the agrarian-communistic economic organization can be brought out more easily if they are studied comparatively at an international level, so that it can be grasped as a global form of production in all its diversity and flexibility.

Let us turn to the old Inca Empire in South America. The territory of this empire, which consisted of the present-day republics of Peru, Bolivia and Chile, an area of 3,364,600 square kilometers with a present population of twelve million inhabitants,* was organized at the time of the Spanish conquest under [Francisco] Pizarro in the same way it had been for many centuries before. We find here right away the same arrangements as among the ancient Germans. Each clan community, around a hundred men capable of bearing weapons, occupied a particular area that henceforth belonged to them as their *marca*, even this term curiously resembling the German.† The mark's farmland was separated off, divided into portions and allocated annually to families by lot before the sowing of crops. The size of the portions was determined by family size, i.e. according to their needs. The village leader, whose position had already developed from an elected one into a hereditary one by the time of the formation of the Inca Empire in the tenth and eleventh centuries,‡ received the largest allotted share. In northern Peru, the male heads of household did not all cultivate their plots of land themselves, but worked in groups of ten under the direction of a leader— an arrangement that resembles certain aspects of the Germanic structure. This ten-man group cultivated in rotation the lots of all of its members, including those who were absent, on war service, or doing *corvée* labor for the Incas. Each family received the products that grew on its lot. Only those who lived in the *marca* and belonged to the clan had the right to a plot of land. Yet everyone was also obliged to cultivate his plot himself. Anyone who let his field lie fallow for a certain number of years (in Mexico, it was three) lost his claim to his land. The plots could not be sold or given away. It was strictly forbidden to leave one's own *marca* and settle in another one, this fact probably being connected to the strict blood ties of the village tribes.

Agriculture in the coastal regions, where there is only periodic rainfall, always required artificial irrigation by means of canals, which were constructed by the collective labor of the entire *marca*. There were strict rules governing the use of water and its distribution, both between different villages and within them. Each village also had "paupers' fields," which were cultivated by all the members of the *marca* and whose products the village leaders distributed among the elderly, widows, and other needy individuals. All land outside the tilled fields was *marcapacha* (common land). In the mountainous region

---

* Luxemburg left blank here the figures for area and population.

† Engels makes the same point in his *Origin of the Family, Private Property, and the State*: "Cunow has proved fairly clearly (in the journal *Ausland*, 1890, Nos. 42–44) that in Peru at the time of the conquest there was a form of constitution based on marks (called, curiously enough, *marca*), with periodical allotment of arable land and consequently with individual tillage." See Frederick Engels, *Origin of the Family, Private Property and the State* (New York: International Publishers, 1964), p. 52.

‡ The Inca Empire was actually formed several centuries later. Prior to 1438 Incan rule was restricted to the small city-state Kingdom of Cuzco.

of the country, where agriculture could not thrive, there was modest livestock farming, consisting almost exclusively of llamas, the basis of existence for these inhabitants, who periodically brought their main product, wool, down to the valley in order to trade it with the peasants for corn, pepper and beans. At the time of the conquest there were already private herds and significant differences in wealth in the mountain regions. An average member of the mark probably owned between three and ten llamas, while a chief might have between fifty and a hundred. Only the forest, soil and pasture were common property there, and as well as private herds there were village ones, which could not be divided up. At certain times, some of the communal herd were slaughtered and the meat and wool divided among the families. There were no specialized craftsmen; each family made the necessary household items itself. There were, however, villages with special skill in a certain craft, whether as weavers, potters, or metal workers. At the head of the village was the village leader, originally an elected office but later a hereditary one, who oversaw the cultivation, but in every important matter he consulted with the assembly of all adults, which was called together by sounding a conch shell.

Thus far, the ancient Peruvian *marca* offers a faithful copy of the German mark community in all essential characteristics. Yet it offers us more in our investigation of the essence of this social system by deviating from the pattern we already know, than it does in its similarities. What was unique in the old Inca Empire is that it was a conquered land on which foreign rule was established. The immigrant conquerors, the Incas, were indeed an Indian tribe, yet they were able to subjugate the peaceful Quechua* tribes who lived there because of the isolation in which these lived in their villages, concerned only with their own *marca* and its boundaries, unconnected to any larger territory, and uninterested in anything that existed or occurred beyond their own borders. This extremely particularistic social organization, which made the Inca conquest so effortless, was barely touched or altered by the Incas themselves. Yet they did graft onto it a refined system of economic exploitation and political domination. Each conquered *marca* had to give up a part of its own land for "Inca fields" and "fields of the sun." Though these continued to belong to it, their products had to be turned over to the ruling Inca tribe and its priestly caste. Similarly, they had to reserve a portion of their livestock in the mountainous *marcas* as "herds of the masters" and mark them as such. The protection of these herds as well as the cultivation of

---

* Luxemburg actually writes "Vechua" rather than "Keshua," the standard German for "Quechua," apparently transliterating directly from one of her principal sources, the Russian anthropologist Maksim Kovalevsky's book, *Obshchinnoe Zemlevadenie. Priciny, khod i posledstviia ego razlozeniia* (Communal Land Ownership: The Causes, Processes, and Consequences of its Disintegration) (Moscow, 1879). Marx knew Kovalevsky and made notes on his book shortly after it appeared. It is possible that Luxemburg was aware of this. A translation of most of Marx's notes can be found in the appendix to Lawrence Krader, *The Asiatic Mode of Production*; the full version appeared in Hans-Peter Harstick, ed., *Karl Marx über Formen vorkapitalischer Production*.

the fields for the Incas and their priests was based upon the compulsory labor of all members of the *marca*. On top of this there was compulsory labor for mining, likewise for public works such as road and bridge construction under the control of the rulers; a strictly disciplined military service; and finally a tribute of young girls, who were used by the Incas for ritual sacrifice or as concubines. This tight system of exploitation, however, did not interfere with the internal life of the *marca* and its communist-democratic organization; even the compulsory labor and dues were borne communistically as a collective burden of the mark. Yet what is remarkable is that this communistic village organization did not simply prove a solid and amenable basis for a centuries-long system of exploitation and servitude, as so often happens in history, but that this system was itself organized on a communistic basis. The Incas who ensconced themselves on the backs of the subjugated Peruvian tribes themselves also lived in clan groups with mark-type relations. Their capital, the town of Cuzco, was simply a combination of a dozen or two collective quarters, each the seat of a communistic household for a whole clan, complete with a communal burial area, and a common cult as well. Around these tribal houses lay the mark regions of the Inca clans, with unpartitioned forests and pastures and partitioned farmland, which was likewise cultivated in common. Being a primitive people, these exploiters and rulers had not yet renounced work themselves; they used their position of domination only to live better than the dominated and to make more opulent sacrificial offerings. The modern art of having one's food supplied by other people's labor and making refusal to work an attribute of domination was still foreign to the nature of this social organization, in which collective property and the general duty to work were deep-seated customs. The exercise of political domination was also organized as a collective function of the Inca clans. The Inca governors appointed to the Peruvian provinces, analogous in their role to the Dutch residents of the Malaysian archipelago, were seen as delegates of their clans in Cuzco, where they retained residency in the collective quarters and participated in their own mark community. Each year, these delegates returned home for the Sun Festival in Cuzco* to render an account of their official activities and to celebrate the great religious festival with their fellow clansmen.

What we have here, as it were, is two social strata, one above the other yet both internally communistic in their organization, standing in a relationship of exploitation and subjugation. This phenomenon may seem incomprehensible at first, being as it is in stark contradiction with the principles of equality, brotherhood and democracy that form the basis of the organization of the mark community. But we also have here living proof of just how little in reality the

---

* During each Winter Solstice in Cuzco, the residents gathered to honor the Sun God and plead for its "return" (the day before the Winter Solstice having the longest night of the year). The ceremony was banned by the Spanish in the 1570s, but it survives among many of the Quechua of modern Peru as the holiday of Inti Raymi.

primitive communist structures had to do with general freedom and equality. These expanded, generically valid "principles" applying to all abstract "human beings," or all people of the "civilized" countries, i.e., countries of capitalist civilization, were only a late product of modern bourgeois society, whose revolutions—in America as well as France—proclaimed them for the first time. Primitive communist society knew no such general principles for all human beings; their equality and solidarity grew out of the traditions of common blood ties and out of common ownership of the means of production. As far as these blood ties and common ownership reached, so too did the equality of rights and solidarity of interests. Whatever lay beyond these limits—which were no wider than the walls of a village, or at most the territorial boundaries of a tribe—was foreign and could even be hostile. Indeed, each community based on economic solidarity could and necessarily was periodically driven into deadly conflicts of interest with similarly constructed communities because of the low level of development of production, or because of the scarcity or exhaustion of food sources due to an increase in population. Brute struggle, war, had to decide, and its result often meant the eradication of one of the contending parties, or more frequently, the establishment of a system of exploitation. It was not devotion to abstract principles of equality and freedom that formed the basis of primitive communism, but the pitiless necessities of a low level of human civilization, the helplessness of humanity in the face of external nature, which forced them to stick closely together in larger alliances, and to act methodically and collectively with respect to labor and the struggle for life as an absolute condition of existence. Yet it was also the same limited control over nature that confined planning and action with respect to labor to a relatively quite small area of natural pasture or reclaimable village settlements, and made this unsuitable for collective action on a larger scale. The primitive state of agriculture at that time did not allow for any larger cultivation than that of a village mark, and for this reason presented strict limits to the solidarity of interests. And finally, it was the same inadequate development of labor productivity that also generated periodic conflicts of interest among the various social alliances, thereby making brute force the only means to solve such conflicts. War thus became a permanent method for solving conflicts of interest between social communities, a method that would prevail through to the highest development of labor productivity—the total domination of man over nature—that will put an end to material conflicts of interest between people. If clashes between different primitive communist societies were indeed a common occurrence, it was the development of labor productivity at the time that decided the outcome. When there was a conflict between two nomadic, herding peoples who had come into conflict over livestock pastures, only brute force could determine who would remain master of the land and who would be driven into drought-ridden, inhospitable regions or even be exterminated. Yet wherever agriculture was already sufficiently flourishing to nourish people well and securely, without taking up the entire labor force and the entire lifetime of these individuals, there was also the foundation for a systematic exploitation of these peasants by foreign conquerors. And this explains the relations that emerge, as in Peru, when one communistic community establishes itself as the exploiter of another.

The unique structure of the Inca Empire is important because it offers us the key to understanding a whole series of similar patterns in classical antiquity, especially those in the earliest period of Greek history. If, for example, we have a brief surviving account how on the island of Crete, which was ruled by the Dorians,* the subjugated people had to hand over their entire harvest, less the sustenance required for themselves and their families, to the community, to cover the communal meals of the free men (the ruling Dorians); or that in Sparta, likewise a Dorian community, there were "state slaves" or Helots,† who were given "from the state" to individuals to work their farmland, at first this kind of thing presents a puzzle. And a bourgeois scholar, Professor Max Weber in Heidelberg, proposes a curious hypothesis based on the standpoint of present-day condition and concepts, in order to explain these curious historical phenomena:

> The dominated population is treated here [in Sparta—R.L.] in the same manner as in state slavery or bondage. The sustenance of the warriors is deducted from agricultural production, partly in the collective manner that we have already mentioned, and partly in such a way that the individual is dependent on the yield of certain plots of land worked by slaves that are allocated to him, which are appropriated in one way or another, later increasingly through inheritance. New allocations of lots and other kinds of distribution were historically considered to be practicable and appear to have occurred. Naturally, they are not reallocation of *farmland* ["natural" is not something a bourgeois professor should concede, regardless of what it is about—R.L.] but rather a kind of reallocation of *ground rent*. Military considerations, especially a military population policy, determine all the particulars ... The urban-*feudal* character of this politics is characteristically expressed in the way that in Gortyn,‡ the plots of land occupied by serfs in the estate of a free man are subject

---

*   The Dorians were one of the four main subgroups of the ancient Greeks. It is disputed as to whether or not the distinctions were based on ethnicity. The earliest literary mention of the Dorians occurs in Homer's *Odyssey*, where they are held to inhabit the island of Crete. According to historical tradition, the Dorians invaded Greece from the north during the twelfth century BC and displaced the Mycenaeans, but there is little or no archeological evidence of this. The origin of the Dorians remains an issue of considerable scholarly controversy.

†   The Helots were a subjugated people who performed agricultural and domestic labor for the Spartans, who ruled over them. They may have been the native inhabitants of the area around Sparta; the name "Helot" derives from the Greek term "to be captured or made prisoner." As much as 90 percent of the Spartan kingdom consisted of Helots, who had no political rights.

‡   Excavation of this ancient town in Arcadia had begun in 1884, which was also when the Gortyn Code, the oldest survival of a Greek legal code, was discovered.

to military law: they form the *kleros*,* which is bound to the maintenance of the military family.

Translated from the academic into regular speech: the farmlands are the property of the whole community and thus may not be sold nor distributed after the death of the owner. Professor Weber explains this at another point as a wise measure "to prevent the fragmentation of wealth" and "in the interest of maintaining lots appropriate for the class of warriors."

> The organization culminates in a mess-like community dinner table of the warriors, the "syssities,"† and in the communal education of children by the state, in order to make them into warriors.[62]

In this way the Greeks of the heroic age, the age of Hector and Achilles—who happily possess the notions of annuities [*Rentenanstalten*] and the Prussian *Fideikommis*,‡ of officers' messes with their "class appropriate" champagne toasts—the blossoming, naked boys and girls of Sparta who enjoyed a national education, are all transformed into a jail-like institution for cadets such as that at Gross-Lichterfelde near Berlin.§

The relations described above will not present much difficulty for someone familiar with the internal structure of the Inca Empire. They are undoubtedly the product of a similarly blatantly parasitic dual structure that has emerged from the subjugation of an agricultural mark community by another communistic community. The extent to which the communistic foundation remains in the customs of the rulers as well as in the situation of the subjugated depends on the stage of development, the length and the environment of this pattern, all of which can offer a whole range of gradations. The Inca Empire, where the rulers themselves still labor, where the landownership of the subjects as a whole is not yet touched and each social stratum is cohesively organized, can indeed be viewed as the original form of such exploitative relations, which was only able to preserve itself for centuries thanks to the country's relatively primitive level

---

* At birth each Spartan was assigned a *kleros*, a piece of land, along with Helots to work it. This enabled Spartan males to concentrate all their time and energy on military exercises, training, and combat.

† The *sysities* were communal meals or messes, generally of ten to fifteen men at a time, which was a central obligation of social life among the Spartans.

‡ The *Fideikommiss* was a form of family wealth based on large-scale landownership, which was inalienable and could not be divided through inheritance. It was designed to preserve large landed property as the economic foundation of the Junkers' political power. *Rentenanstalten* were joint savings companies, which provided a lifetime annuity in return for an annual contribution or an investment of capital.

§ Gross-Lichterfelde was the main Prussian military academy, established in 1882. From 1933 to 1945 the grounds of the academy was the home of Adolf Hitler. During the Cold War it housed the US Army's Berlin Brigade.

of culture and isolation from the rest of the world. The historical information on Crete, drawn from traditional sources, suggests an advanced stage where the subjugated peasant community had to hand over all the fruits of its labor less what was needed for its own subsistence, where the ruling community lived not from their own labor in the fields, but from the dues paid to them by the exploited mark community, although this still had its own consumption in common. In Sparta we find—at a further stage of development—that the land is no longer seen as belonging to the subjugated community, but is rather the property of the rulers, being repartitioned and allotted by lot among *themselves* in the manner of the mark community. The social organization of the subjugated is shattered by the loss of its foundation, ownership of the land; they themselves become the property of the ruling community, who communistically, or "for the sake of the state," hand over the landless to individual mark members as laborers. The ruling Spartans themselves continue to live in strict relations characteristic of the mark community. And similar relations are supposed to have prevailed to a certain degree in Thessaly,* where the previous inhabitants, the *Penestai* or "poor people," were subjugated by the Aeolians,† or in Bithynia, where the *Mariandynoi* were placed in a similar situation by Thracian tribes.‡ Such a parasitic existence, however, constantly led to the seeds of disintegration being also brought into the ruling community. Conquest, and the imperative to establish exploitation as a permanent structure, already leads to a considerable development of the military apparatus, as we see in both the Inca state and the Spartan ones. This is the first precondition for inequality, for the formation of privileged classes, in the womb of the originally free and equal mass of peasants. It only requires favorable geographical and cultural-historical circumstances, which arouse more refined needs by contact with more civilized peoples and brisk trade, in order for inequality to make rapid progress even within the ruling classes, for the communistic cohesion to weaken, and for private property to enter the field with its division of rich and poor. The early history of the Greek world, after its contact with the civilized peoples of the Orient, is a classic example of such a development. Thus, the result of the subjugation of one early communistic society by another, whether sooner or later, is always the same: the unraveling of communistic, traditional social bonds among both the rulers and the ruled, and the birth of a totally new social formation in which private property along with inequality and exploitation, each engendering the other, enter the world right away. And thus the history of the old mark community in classical antiquity

---

*   A region of Greece, south of Mt. Olympus and bordering the Aegean Sea.

†   The *Penestai* were a class of people between slaves and freemen, much like the Helots in Sparta. They were essentially serfs attached to the land and could not be sold. They were allowed to serve on naval ships and to bear arms. They were descendants of the Aeolians, one of the four sub-groups of ancient Greeks, who were forced into servitude when the Thessalians conquered the area.

‡   Bithynia is in western Asia Minor. The *Mariandynoi*, subjected by Thracian invaders, had a similar social status as the *Penestai* of Thessaly and Helots of Sparta.

leads, on the one hand, to the opposition between a mass of indebted small peasants and an aristocracy that has appropriated military service, public offices, trade and the undivided communal lands as large-scale landed property; and on the other hand, to the opposition between this whole society of free people and the exploited *slaves*. It was only one step from this differentiated natural economy based on communal exploitation of a people subjected militarily to introducing the purchase of individual slaves. And this step was taken quickly in Greece by virtue of maritime and international trade, with its effects in the coastal and island states. [Ettore] Ciccotti also distinguishes between two types of slavery: "The oldest, most significant and most widespread form of economic servitude," he says,

> which we see at the threshold of Greek history, is not slavery, but a form of bondage that I would almost like to call vassalage. According to Theopompus [of Chios]: "Among all Hellenes after the Thessalians and the Lacedaemonians,* the inhabitants of the island of Chios in Asia Minor were the first to use slaves, but they did not acquire them in the same manner as others ... It is clear that the Lacedaemonians and Thessalians formed their slave class out of Hellenes who previously inhabited this part of the world they now owned, so that they forced the Achaeans, Thessalians, Perrebes† and Magnetes‡ into servitude and named these subjugated peoples Helots and *Penestai*. In contrast, the inhabitants of Chios acquired barbarian non-Greeks as slaves and paid a price for them."

And the reason for this distinction, Ciccotti correctly points out,

> lay in the different level of development of the inland peoples on the one hand and the island peoples on the other. Complete absence or a very low degree of accumulation of wealth, along with the weak development of commercial trade, in the one case excluded a direct and growing production on the part of the owners as well as their direct employment of slaves, leading instead to the more rudimentary form of tribute and to a division of labor and formation of a class system that created a body of armed soldiers out of the ruling class and a farming peasantry out of the subjugated peoples.[63]

The internal organization of the Peruvian Inca state reveals to us an important aspect of this primitive social form, indicating at the same time a particular historic process of its downfall. A different turn in the fate of this social form will appear when we trace the subsequent episode in the history of the Peruvian Indians as well as that of the other Spanish colonies in America. Here we

---

* Lacedaemonians is another word for Spartans.
† A people who lived in northern Thessaly.
‡ A people who lived in eastern Thessaly.

particularly encounter a completely new method of domination, which had no parallel with the Inca rulers, for example. The Spanish, the first Europeans in the New World, began their rule with the relentless extermination of the subjugated population. According to the reports of the Spanish themselves, the number of Indians exterminated in the space of only a few years after the discovery of America reached a total of between twelve and fifteen million. "We believe it justified to maintain," [Bartolomé de] Las Casas says, "that the Spanish, through their monstrous and inhuman treatment, have exterminated twelve million people, among them women and children." He further states, "In my personal opinion, the number of those natives murdered in this period exceeded even fifteen million."[64] "On the island of Haiti," says [Heinrich Gottfried] Handelmann, "the number of natives before the Spanish encountered them in 1492 was around one million; by 1508 only sixty thousand of these million people remained, and nine years later there were only fourteen thousand, so that the Spanish had to resort to introducing Indians from the neighboring islands in order to have enough working hands. In 1508 alone, forty thousand natives from the Bahamas were transported to the island of Haiti and made into slaves."[65] The Spanish regularly hunted down the redskins, as described for us by an eyewitness and participant, the Italian Girolamo Benzoni. "In part because of a lack of food, and in part out of fear following separation from their fathers, mothers, and children," says Benzoni after one such manhunt on the island of Kumagna, in which four thousand Indians were captured,

> the majority of the enslaved natives died on the way to the port of Cumana.[†] Each time that one of the slaves was too tired to march as quickly as his comrades, the Spanish stabbed him in the back with their daggers, inhumanly murdering him out of fear that he wanted to remain in order to lead a counterattack. It was a heart-breaking scene to see these poor souls, totally naked, tired, wounded and so exhausted from hunger that they could hardly stand on their feet. Iron chains bound their necks, hands and feet. There was not a virgin among them who would not be raped by these robbers, who were so addicted to this repulsive debauchery that many of them remained marred by syphilis forever ... All the natives taken as slaves were branded with hot irons. The captains then took a number of them for themselves, dividing

---

* In many places of the Americas, death rates for the indigenous inhabitants after the entrance of European conquerors and colonizers reached 90 percent. Many died from overwork and systematic oppression by the Europeans, though most died from the epidemic diseases that the Europeans brought with them.

† Luxemburg actually refers to the island of "Kumagna" and the port of "Kumani," transliterating both names directly from Kovalevsky (p. 51), who cites Girolamo Benzoni's *Storia del mundo nuovo* (History of the New World) (Venice: F. Rampazetto, 1565). Consulting Benzoni directly, we have identified "Kumani" as the port city of Cumana in present-day Venezuela, but were unable to identify "Kumagna." Cumana is the oldest European city in South America, founded in 1523.

the rest among the soldiers. They either gambled them away to one another or sold them to Spanish colonists. Merchants who traded this commodity for wine, flour, sugar and other daily necessities, transported the slaves to those parts of the Spanish colonies where there was the greatest demand for them. During their transport, a number of these unfortunates died from lack of water and the bad air in the cabins, which was due to the fact that the traders herded the slaves into the lowest level of the ship without giving them enough water to drink or enough air to breathe.[66]

However, in order to relieve themselves of the trouble of pursuing the Indians and the cost of buying them, the Spanish created a system known as *repartimientos* in their West Indian possessions and on the American mainland.* The entire conquered area was divided by the governors into districts, whose village leaders, *caciques*, were themselves obliged to supply on demand the number of natives for slavery requested by the Spanish. Each Spanish colonist periodically received the requested number of slaves that were delivered to him by the governor under the condition that he "take the trouble to convert them to Christianity."[67] The abuse of the slaves by the colonists defied all understanding. Suicide became a salvation for the Indians. "All of the natives captured by the Spanish," according to one witness,

> were forced by them to do hard and exhausting labor in the mines, away from their homes and families and under constant threat of beatings. No wonder that thousands of slaves saw no other possibility than to escape from their gruesome fate by not only violently taking their own lives, by hanging or drowning themselves or in other ways, but first also murdering their wives and children, in order to end an unfortunate and inescapable situation for everyone all at once. In other cases, women resorted to aborting their children in the womb or avoiding sexual contact with men so that they did not have to bear slaves.[68]

Through the intervention of the imperial confessor, the pious Father Garcia [Juan] de Loaysa, the colonists were finally able to have a decree issued by the Hapsburg emperor, Charles V,[†] summarily declaring the Indians to be hereditary slaves of the Spanish colonists. Benzoni in fact says the decree only applied to Caribbean cannibals,[‡] but was extended and applied to all Indians in general. In

---

*   The *repartimientos* was a colonial forced labor system imposed on the indigenous peoples by the Spanish. It was a tribute labor system, similar to the *mita* of the Inca Empire, though generally of a far more brutal character.

†   The decree was issued by Charles V in 1525.

‡   Although ritual cannibalism was practiced in some parts of the Caribbean, the claim by early European explorers and colonists that it was a widespread practice has no factual accuracy. For analyses of how the myth of Caribbean "cannibalism" became widespread, see *Cannibalism and the Colonial World*, edited by Francis Barker, Peter Hulme, and Margaret Iversen (Cambridge: Cambridge University Press, 1998).

order to justify their atrocities, the Spanish systematically spread dramatic horror stories about cannibalism and other vices of the Indians so that a contemporary French historian, Marly de Châtel, in his "General History of the West Indies" (Paris 1569)* could write of them: "God punished them with slavery for their evil and vice, since not even Ham sinned against his father Noah† to the degree of the Indians against the Holy Father."[69] And around the same time the Spaniard [José de] Acosta wrote in his *Historia natural y moral de las Indias* (Barcelona, 1591) about these same Indians, that they were a "good-natured people who are always ready to prove themselves of service to the Europeans; a people who, in their behavior, show such a touching harmlessness and sincerity, that those not completely stripped of all humanity could not treat them in any other way than with tenderness and love."[70]

Naturally, there were also attempts to stop the horror. In 1531, Pope Paul III published a bull decreeing that the Indians were members of the human race and therefore free from slavery. The Spanish Imperial Council for the West Indies also made a declaration against slavery, but the need for these repeated decrees testified more to the fruitlessness of these attempts than to their sincerity.

What freed the Indians from slavery was neither the pious actions of the Catholic clergy nor the protests of the Spanish kings, but rather the simple fact that the Indians' mental and physical constitution rendered them worthless for hard slave labor. Against this bare impossibility, the worst cruelty of the Spanish did not help in the long run; the redskins died under slavery like flies, fled, took their own lives—in short, the entire business was thoroughly unprofitable. And only when the warm and untiring defender of the Indians, Bishop Las Casas, hit upon the idea of importing the more robust Africans as slaves in place of the unfit Indians, were the useless experiments with the Indians immediately abandoned. This practical discovery had a quicker and more thorough effect than all of Las Casas's pamphlets on the cruelties of the Spanish. The Indians were freed from slavery after a few decades and the enslavement of the Negroes began, which would last for four more centuries. At the end of the eighteenth century a respectable German, "good old [Joachim Christian] Nettelbeck" from Kolberg, was the captain of a ship taking hundreds of Africans from Guinea to Guyana in South America, where other "good East Prussians" exploited plantations and sold slaves along with other goods from Africa, herding them into the lowest parts of the ship, as the Spanish captains had done in the sixteenth century. The progress of the humanitarian era of the Enlightenment showed itself in

---

* Marly de Châtel was the pen name of Martin Fumée, Lord of Marly-La-Ville. The book was actually by Francisco López de Gómara, a Spanish historian who never set foot in the Americas. Marly de Châtel was the translator of the French edition, published in 1569. For the original, see López de Gómara, *Historia general de las Indias* (General History of the Indies) (Saragossa: Edición Nucio Martin, 1554).

† A widespread prejudice among many Spanish commentators in the seventeenth century was that the Native Americans were descended from Ham, the cursed son of Noah.

the way that Nettelbeck, to alleviate their melancholy and to keep them from dying off, allowed the slaves to dance on the ship's deck with music and whip cracks every evening, something to which the more brutal Spanish traders had not yet resorted. And in 1871, in the late nineteenth century, the noble David Livingstone, who had spent thirty years in Africa searching for the sources of the Nile, wrote in his famous letters to the American [James] Gordon Bennett:

> And if my disclosures regarding the terrible Ujijian* slavery should lead to the sup-
> pression of the east coast slave trade, I shall regard that as a greater matter by far than
> the discovery of all the Nile sources together. Now that you have done with domestic
> slavery forever, lend us your powerful aid toward this great object. This fine country
> is blighted, as with a curse from above ...†

Yet the lot of the Indians in the Spanish colonies was not made significantly better by this transformation. A new system of colonization simply took the place of the old one. Instead of *repartimientos*, which were created for the direct enslavement of the population, the so-called *encomiendas*‡ were introduced.[71] Formally, the inhabitants were awarded personal freedom and full property rights to their land. But these areas were under the administrative direction of the Spanish colonists, in particular in the hands of the descendants of the first *conquistadores*, and these *encomenderos* were to be the guardians of the Indians, who were for their part declared to be legal minors. The *encomenderos* were supposed to spread Christianity among the Indians. To cover the cost of constructing churches for the natives and as compensation for their labor as guardians, the *encomenderos* legally acquired the right to demand "moderate payments in money and in kind" from the population. These provisions soon were enough to make the *encomiendas* hell for the Indians. The land was indeed left to them as the undivided property of the tribes, but the Spanish only under-stood, or only wanted to understand, this to be farmland, land that was under the plough. The undivided mark as well as unused lands, often even fields left to lie fallow, were taken over by the Spanish as "waste land." And they did this

---

* Ujiji is a city in western Tanzania, on the shores of Lake Tanganyika. Ujiji was a center of the slave trade in East Africa at the time, which David Livingstone vowed to eliminate. Henry Morgan Stanley and other European colonists subsequently used the excuse of wanting to eliminate the slave trade to brutally subjugate and control Central and Eastern Africa.

† Horace Waller, *Letze Reise von David Livingston in Centralafrika von 1865 bis zu seinem Tode 1873* (The Final Trip of David Livingston in Central Africa from 1865 to his Death in 1873) (Hamburg: Hoffmann & Campe, 1875), pp. 189, 209, 219. See *The Life and African Explorations of Dr. David Livingstone* (New York: Cooper Square Press, 2002 [orig. 1874]), pp. 328–9.

‡ In the *encomienda* system, the Spanish crown awarded Europeans with a specific number of Native Americans for whom they had to take responsibility. In exchange for educating and con-verting the Native Americans, the receiver of the grant could obtain tribute from them in the form of labor or gold. Although it was intended to alleviate the abuses of the *encomiendas*, it led to widespread and massive abuse of the indigenous population.

with such thoroughness and shamelessness that [Alonzo de] Zurita wrote on this subject:

> There is not a parcel of land, not a farm, that was not determined to be the property of the Europeans, without regard for the encroachments onto the interests and the property rights of the natives, who were thus forced to leave this land, which had been inhabited by them since ancient times. Cultivated land was often seized from them, under the pretext that this was being utilized only to prevent its acquisition by the Europeans. Thanks to this system, in some provinces the Spanish expanded their property so widely that the natives had no land left to cultivate themselves.[72]

At the same time, the "moderate" payments were increased so shamelessly by the *encomenderos* that the Indians were crushed under them. "All of the belongings of the Indian," Zurita says,

> are not enough to pay the taxes that are levied on him. You meet many people among the redskins whose assets do not even come to one *peso* and who live from daily wage-labor; these unfortunates, accordingly, having nothing left with which to support their families. This is the reason why so often young people prefer sexual relations out of wedlock, especially when their parents do not even have four or five *reales* at their disposal. The Indians can scarcely afford the luxury of clothing themselves; many who have no resources to buy themselves clothes are not able to take communion. It is no wonder, then, that the majority of them become desperate, since they cannot find any way to acquire the food needed for their families ... During my early travels, I discovered that many Indians hanged themselves out of despair, after explaining to their wives and children that they were doing this in the face of the impossibility of meeting the taxes demanded of them.[73]

Finally, in addition to increasing land theft and pressure of taxation, came forced labor. At the beginning of the seventeenth century, the Spanish openly returned to the system that had been formally abandoned in the sixteenth century. Though slavery was abolished for the Indians, in its place came a unique system of forced wage labor, which did not significantly differ from the system that preceded it. Already in the mid-sixteenth century, Zurita portrays for us the situation of the Indian wage laborers under the Spanish in the following way:

> The whole time, the Indians received no other nourishment than cornbread ... The *encomendor* has them work from morning to night, naked in the morning and evening frosts, in storms and thunder, without giving them any food other than half-spoiled bread. The Indians spend the night under the open sky. Because the wage is only paid at the end of their term of forced labor, the Indians have no means to buy the necessary warm clothing for themselves. It is no surprise that under such

circumstances, the work in the *encomenderos* is utterly exhausting for them and can be identified as one of the reasons for the Indians dying off so rapidly.[74]

This system of forced wage labor was introduced at the beginning of the seventeenth century by the Spanish crown, making it officially and universally legal. The stated reason for the law was that the Indians would not work voluntarily and that without them the mines could only be run with great difficulty, despite the presence of the African slaves. The Indian villagers were thus required to provide the number of workers demanded (in Peru, a seventh of the population, in New Spain, 4 percent), and these were at the mercy of the *encomenderos*. The deadly consequences of this system were immediately apparent. An anonymous memorandum sent to Philip IV, under the title "Report on the Dangerous Situation of the Kingdom of Chile from the Temporal and Spiritual Point of View," stated:

> The known cause of the rapid decrease in the number of natives is the system of forced labor in the mines and on the fields of the *encomenderos*. Although the Spanish have an enormous number of Negroes at their disposal, although they have taxed the Indians at a higher rate than they paid their leaders before the conquest, they nevertheless regard it as impossible to give up this system of forced labor.[75]

In addition, forced labor resulted in the Indians in many cases being unable to cultivate their fields, which the Spanish then used as a pretext to seize the land for themselves as "waste land." The ruin of Indian farming offered a fertile ground for extortion. "Among their native rulers," according to Zurita, "the Indians did not know any usurers."[76] The Spanish taught them very well these blessings of money economy and taxation. Eaten up by debt, huge lands owned by the Indians—those that had not already been simply stolen by the Spanish—fell into the hands of Spanish capitalists, with the assessment of their value forming a special example of European perfidy. Between them, the theft of land, taxation, forced labor and usury formed a tight circle in which the existence of the Indian mark community collapsed. The traditional public order and customary social bonds of the Indians were dissolved by the collapse of their economic base— mark community farming. For their part, the Spanish methodically destroyed it by disrupting all traditional forms of authority. The village and tribal chiefs had to be confirmed by the *encomenderos*, who used this prerogative to fill these positions with their own protégés, the most depraved subjects of Indian society. Another favorite method of the Spanish was the systematic instigation of the Indians against their leaders. Under the auspices of their Christian aims, of protecting the natives from being exploited by their chiefs, they declared them free from paying the dues that these had received since time immemorial. "The Spanish," writes Zurita, "based on what is happening in Mexico today, maintain that the chiefs are plundering their own tribes, but they bear the blame for this extortion, since they themselves and no one else robbed the former chiefs of their position and income and replaced them with ones from among their pro- tégés."[77] Likewise, they looked to instigate mutinies whenever village or tribal chiefs protested against illicit lands sales to the Spanish by individual members of the mark. The result was chronic revolts, and an endless succession of legal proceedings over unlawful land sales among the natives themselves. Along with ruin, hunger, and slavery, anarchy added to the mix that made the existence of the Indians hell. The stark result of this Spanish-Christian guardianship can be summed up in two phrases: the land going into the hands of the Spanish, and the extinction of the Indians. "In all the Spanish areas of the Indies," Zurita writes,

> either the native tribes disappear completely or they become much smaller, although others have claimed the opposite. The natives leave their dwellings and farms, since these have lost all value for them in the face of the exorbitant dues in money and kind; they emigrate to other regions, continuously wandering from one region to another, or they hide themselves in the forest and run the danger of becoming, sooner or later, the prey of wild animals. Many Indians end their lives by suicide, as I personally witnessed several times and learned from interviews with the local population.[78]

And half a century later, another high official of the Spanish government in Peru, Juan Ortiz de Cervantes, reported:

> The native population in the Spanish colonies grow ever more thin on the ground; they abandon the areas they formerly inhabited, leaving the soil uncultivated, and the Spanish have to struggle to find the necessary number of peasants and herds- men. The so-called Mitayos,* a tribe without whom work in the gold and silver mines would be impossible, either completely abandon the cities occupied by the Spanish, or if they stay, die out at an astonishing rate.[79]

We may truly wonder at the incredible tenacity of the Indian people and their mark community institutions, since remains of both persisted well into the nine- teenth century, despite these conditions.

The great English colony of India shows us another aspect of the fate of the mark community. Here, as in no other corner of the earth, one can study the most varying forms of property that represent the history of several millennia, like

---

*   In the Inca Empire the *mitayos* were not actually a tribe, but rather people who were mobilized to work for the *mita*, work groups organized by the state and paid in kind instead of in wages. The Spanish later made use of this system in order to force the indigenous peoples to work in the mines. Under Spanish rule, hundreds of thousands perished from overwork under this arrangement.

[William] Herschel's "star gages" model of the sky* projected onto a flat surface. Village communities alongside tribal communities; periodic repartitionings of equal portions of land alongside lifelong ownership of unequal portions of land; communal labor alongside private individual enterprise; equal rights of all villagers to community lands alongside the privileges of certain groups; and finally, beside all these forms of communal property, private property in land in the form of smaller subplots of rural land, short-term leaseholds, and enormous latifundia. All of this could still be observed in India, as large as life, a few decades ago. Indian legal sources attest that the mark community in India is an ancient system. The oldest common law, the Code of Manu† from the ninth century BC, contains countless ordinances concerning border disputes between mark communities, unpartitioned marks, and the new settlement of daughter villages on unpartitioned land of older marks. The code knows only ownership based on one's own labor; it mentions handicrafts only as a side-occupation of agriculture; it attempts to rein in the power of the Brahmins, the priests, by only allowing them to be granted moveable property. The future indigenous sovereigns, the rajas, appear in these codes still as elected tribal high chiefs. The two later codes, Yajnavalkya‡ and Narada,§ which are from the fifth century, recognize the clan as the social organization, with public and judicial authority lying in the hands of the assembly of mark members. These are, jointly and collectively, responsible for the misdeeds and crimes of individuals. Standing at the head of the village is the elected mark leader. Both legal codes advise electing the best, most peace-loving and most even-handed community member to this office and offering him unconditional obedience. The Code of Narada already distinguishes between two kinds of mark communities: "relatives" or clan-based communities, and "cohabitants" or neighboring communities as local associations of non-blood relatives. Yet, at the same time, both legal codes only recognize ownership based on individual labor. Abandoned land belongs to the person who takes it over for cultivation. Illegal occupation is still not recognized after three

---

* In 1785 William Herschel mapped out the Milky Way by using a series of measurements that he called "star gages." It actually failed to properly measure the size and shape of the Milky Way.

† The Code of Manu, also known as Manusmriti or Manusmruti, is one of the most important of the sacred texts of Hinduism in the Indian Brahmanical system. It is a long poem written in Sanskrit, divided into twelve chapters, dealing with law, politics, pleasure, and rules for regulating the caste system. It was composed much earlier than Luxemburg states, probably as early as the third century BC. See *Manu's Code of Law: A Critical Edition and Translation of the Manava-Dharmasastra*, translated by Patrick Olivelle (Oxford: Oxford University Press, 2006).

‡ The Yajnavalkya is a code of moral and ethical obligations, originally composed in Sanskrit and written around the fifth century AD. See *Yajnavalkya Smrte: Sanksrit Text, Transliteration and English translation*, translated by B.S. Bist (New Dehli: Chaukhamba Sanskrit Pratishthan, 2004).

§ The Code of Narada is one of the best known of the Dharmashastras—ancient Hindu collections of rules regulating personal and political life, especially criminal law. They were composed between the fourth and sixth centuries AD. See *The Narada Purana*, translated and annotated by G.V. Tagare, Ganesh Vasudeo Tagare, Hemendra Nath Chakravorty (New Dehli: Motilal Banarsidass Publishers, 2008).

generations if the individuals in question do not cultivate the land. Up to this point, we therefore see the Indian people still enclosed within the same primitive social groups and economic relations, as they existed for centuries in the Indus region and subsequently in the heroic period of the Ganges conquest, from which the great folk epics of the Ramayana* and the Mahabharata† were born. It is only in the commentaries on the old legal codes, which are always the characteristic symptom of deep social changes and aspirations, that one sees old legal views reinterpreted in the light of new interests. This is clear proof that up to the fourteenth century—the epoch of the commentators—Indian society went through significant adjustments in its social structure. In the meantime, an influential priestly class had developed, rising above the mass of peasants both materially and legally. These commentators—just like their Christian colleagues in the feudal West—seek to "explain" the precise language of the old legal codes in such a way as to justify priestly ownership of property and encourage the donation of land to the Brahmins, and in this way promote the division of the mark lands and the formation of clerical landed property at the expense of the mass of peasant farmers. This development was typical of the fate of all Oriental societies.

The life-and-death question for every form of developed agriculture in most parts of the Orient is irrigation.[80]‡ We see at an early date in India, just as in Egypt, large-scale irrigation systems as a solid foundation for agriculture, along with canals, streams and systematic precautionary measures to protect the land from periodic flooding. From the outset, all of these large undertakings were beyond the capacity of the individual mark community, in terms of the forces, initiative and planning they required. Their direction and execution were the work of an authority that stood above the individual village marks, one that could bring labor-power together on a larger scale. Also required was a mastery of natural laws greater than that available to the observational and experiential world of the mass of peasants, enclosed in the limits of their villages. Out of these needs arose the important function of the priests in the Orient, who were able to direct large public works such as irrigation systems by virtue of their observation of nature, this being an integral part of every nature-based

---

* The Ramayana is an epic poem composed in Sanskrit around the eighth or ninth century. According to tradition it was written by Valmiki. It focuses on the duties and responsibilities of relationships.

† The Mahabharata is one of the major Sanskrit epics of ancient India. It consists of a philosophic discussion of the main purposes of life dharma (right action), artha (purpose), kama (pleasure), and moksha (liberation).

‡ In referring to "the Muslim conquest and feudalization" in her marginal note to this sentence, Luxemburg is following Kovalevsky, who had argued that the Muslim conquest of North Africa and northern India introduced feudalism in land relations. Marx, who tended to avoid applying to non-European societies categories that were specific to Europe, rejected this claim of "Oriental feudalism" in his commentary on Kovalevsky's work. See "Karl Marx. Excerpts from M.M. Kovalevsky," in The Asiatic Mode of Production, pp. 370–83.

religion; the priests' exemption from direct participation in agricultural labor, a freedom that was the product of a certain stage of development, allowed them to direct the irrigation work. Naturally, over time, this purely economic function grew into a particular type of social power held by the priests. The specialization of these members of society, which emerged from the division of labor, turned into a hereditary, exclusive caste with privileges over the peasant masses and an interest in their exploitation. The pace and extent of this process for a particular people, whether it remained embryonic as in the case of the Peruvian Indians, or developed into official state rule by the priestly caste, theocracy, as in Egypt or among the ancient Hebrews, was always dependent on the specific geographical and historical circumstances. But it also depended on whether frequent contact with surrounding peoples allowed a strong warrior caste to emerge outside of the priestly caste, and raise itself up as a military aristocracy in competition with or indeed above the priests. In either case, it was the case again here that the specific, particularistic narrowness of the ancient communistic mark, with an organization unsuited for larger economic or political tasks, forced it to cede these functions to forces that dominated it from outside. These functions so surely offered the key to the political domination and economic exploitation of the peasant masses, that all barbarian conquerors in the Orient, whether Mongols, Persians, or Arabs, were forced, alongside their military power, to take control of the management and execution of the large public undertakings required for the agricultural economy. Just as the Incas in Peru regarded the supervision of artificial irrigation projects and of road and bridge construction as not only a privilege but a duty, so the various Asiatic despotic dynasties that succeeded one another in India applied themselves just as diligently. Despite the formation of castes, despite despotic foreign rule over the country, and despite political upheavals, the tranquil village pursued its existence in the depths of Indian society. Within each village the ancient traditional statutes of the mark constitution prevailed, continuing beneath the storms of political history its own calm and unremarked internal history, shedding old forms and adopting new ones, experiencing prosperity and decline, dissolution and regeneration. No chronicler ever portrayed these events, and when world history describes the bold campaign of Alexander [the Great] of Macedon all the way to the sources of the Indus, and is full of the battle sounds of bloody Timur and his Mongols,[*] it remains completely silent about the internal economic history of the Indian people. It is only from survivals of the various ancient layers of this history that we can reconstruct Indian society's hypothetical pattern of development, and it is the achievement of Kovalevsky to have unraveled this. According to Kovalevsky,

---

[*]   A reference to Timur (also known as Tamerlane), the fourteenth-century conqueror and founder of the Timurid dynasty who conquered much of the Middle East, southern Russia, and Central Asia. While he claimed descent from the Mongol warrior Genghis Khan, he was actually a Muslim Turk.

the various types of agrarian communities that were still observed in the mid-nineteenth century in India can be placed in the following historical sequence:

1) The oldest form is that of the pure clan community, comprising the totality of blood relatives in a clan or kinship group, which owns the land in common and cultivates it communally. Here the communal land is therefore unpartitioned, and it is only the products of the harvest, as well as those in communal storage, that are distributed. This most primitive type of village community survived only in a few districts of northern India, its inhabitants largely confined to a few branches (*putti*) of the old gens. Kovalevsky sees in this, by analogy with the *zadruga* of Bosnia-Herzegovina,* the product of a dissolution of the original blood relationship, which as a result of the growth of the population, broke up into a number of large families that withdrew from the community with their lands. In the middle of the previous century there were still a considerable number of village communities of this type, some of them with more than 150 members, while others boasted 400. More predominant, however, was the small village community, which came together in larger kinship groups on the area of the old gens only in exceptional cases, i.e. in connection with the sale of land. As a general rule, they led the isolated and strictly regulated existence that Marx, using English sources, portrays in a few short passages in *Capital*:[81]

> These small and extremely ancient Indian communities, for example, some of which continue to exist to this day, are based on the possession of the land in common, on the blending of agriculture and handicrafts and on an unalterable division of labor, which serves as a fixed plan and basis for action whenever a new community is started. The communities occupy areas of from a hundred up to several thousand acres, and each forms a compact whole producing all it requires. Most of the products are destined for direct use by the community itself, and are not commodities. Hence production here is independent of that division of labor brought about in Indian society as a whole by the exchange of commodities. It is the surplus alone that becomes a commodity, and a part of that surplus cannot become a commodity until it has reached the hands of the state, because from time immemorial a certain quantity of the community's production has found its way to the state as rent in kind. The form of the community varies in different parts of India. In the simplest communities, the land is tilled in common, and the produce is divided among the members. At the same time, spinning and weaving are carried on in each family as subsidiary industries. Alongside the mass of people thus occupied in the same way, we find the "*chief inhabitant*," who is judge, police authority and tax-gatherer in one; the *book-keeper*, who keeps the accounts of the tillage and registers everything relating to this; another official, who prosecutes criminals, protects strangers traveling through

---

* Similar to the Russian village commune, the *mir*, the *zadruga* of Bosnia-Herzegovina was a family or village community characterized by common possession and working of the land.

and escorts them to the next village; the *boundary* man, who guards the boundaries against neighboring communities; the *water-overseer*, who distributes the water
from the common tasks for irrigation; the *Brahmin*, who conducts the religious services; the *schoolmaster*, who on the sand teaches the children reading and writing;
the *calendar Brahmin*, or astrologer, who makes known the lucky or unlucky days
for seed-time and harvest, and for every other kind of agricultural work; a *smith*
and a *carpenter*, who make and repair all the agricultural implements; the *potter*,
who makes all the pottery of the village; the *barber*, the *washerman*, who washes
clothes, the *silversmith*, here and there the *poet*, who in some communities replaces
the silversmith, in others the schoolmaster. This dozen or so of individuals is maintained at the expense of the whole community. If the population increases, a new
community is founded, on the pattern of the old one, on unoccupied land... The
law that regulates the division of labor in the community acts with the irresistible
authority of a law of nature... The simplicity of the productive organism in these
self-sufficing communities which constantly reproduce themselves in the same form
and, when accidentally destroyed, spring up again on the same spot and with the
same name—this simplicity supplies the key to the riddle of the *unchangeability* of
Asiatic *societies*, which is in such striking contrast with the constant dissolution and
refounding of Asiatic *states*, and their never-ceasing changes of dynasty. The structure of the fundamental economic elements of society remains untouched by the
storms that blow up in the cloudy regions of politics.[82]

2) At the time of the English conquest, the original tribal community had
in most cases already been dissolved. From its dissolution, however, emerged
a new form, a kinship community with partitioned agricultural land, though
not equally divided. The unequal lots of land were given to individual families
and their size was based on the family's relationship to the tribal ancestors. This
form was prevalent in northwestern India as well as in Punjab. The lots here
were neither held for life nor were they hereditary; they remained in the family's possession until such time as the growth of the population or the need to
allocate a lot to a relative who had been temporarily absent made a repartitioning necessary. Frequently, however, new claims were satisfied not by a general
repartitioning, but by allocating new parcels of uncultivated communal land.
In this way, the familial lots of land were often—in fact, if not in law—theirs
for life, and even inheritable. Alongside this unevenly partitioned communal
land, forests, marshes, fields, and uncultivated land still belonged in common
to all the families, who likewise utilized them collectively. This unusual communistic organization based on inequality came into contradiction with new
interests. With each new generation, determining the degree of kinship became
more difficult, the tradition of blood ties faded, and the inequality of the familial
lots of land was increasingly felt as an injustice by those disadvantaged by it.
In many regions, on the other hand, a mixing of the population unavoidably

took place, whether because of the departure of some of the kinship group, because of war and extermination of another part of the population, or because of the settlement and acceptance of new arrivals. Thus, the population of the community, despite all the apparent immobility and immutability of their conditions, was indeed subdivided according to the quality of the soil into fields (*wund*), each family receiving a few strips of land both in the better, irrigated fields (which were called *sholgura* from *shola*, or rice) and in the inferior ones (*culmee*).* Reallocations were not originally periodic, at least before the English conquest, but took place each time population growth caused a real inequality in the economic situation of the families. This was especially true in communities rich in land, which had a supply of utilizable fields. In smaller communities, repartitioning occurred every ten, eight or five years, often every year. This was particularly the case where there was a lack of good fields, making equal distribution each year to all members of the mark impossible, so that only by rotating the use of the various fields could an equitable balance be achieved. Thus, the Indian tribal community ends, as it is disintegrating, by assuming the form that is historically established as the original German mark community.

With British India and Algeria,† we see two classic examples of the desperate struggle and the tragic end of the ancient communist economic organization through contact with European capitalism. The picture of the changeable fate of the mark community would not be complete if we failed to take into consideration the remarkable example of a country where history apparently took an entirely different course. In this case, the state did not seek to destroy the communal property of the peasants through force, but on the contrary, attempted to rescue and preserve it with all the means at its disposal. This country is tsarist Russia.

We do not need to concern ourselves here with the enormous theoretical debate on the origins of the Russian peasant commune that has gone on for decades. It was only natural, in complete accord with the general hostile attitude toward primitive communism among contemporary bourgeois scholarship, that the "discovery" by the Russian Professor [Boris] Chicherin in 1858, according to whom the agricultural commune in Russia was not an original historical product at all, but supposedly an artificial product of the fiscal policy of tsarism, should have achieved such a favorable reception and acceptance among German scholars.[83] Chicherin, who yet again provides proof that liberal scholars are, as historians, for the most part much more ineffectual than their reactionary

---

* The terms in parenthesis are drawn from Kovalevsky, pp. 84–5, who leaves them in the Western alphabet. He sources an 1845 British report on the Northwest Frontier Provinces, a Pashto-speaking area of present-day Pakistan and Afghanistan. In Pashto, *wund* also refers to the periphery of a village. *Culmee* refers to land that lacks natural or artificial irrigation and thus depends for its fertility upon rainfall.

† The discussion of Algeria is missing in the manuscript and may have been used in *The Accumulation of Capital*.

colleagues, still accepts the theory, which has already been definitively abandoned for Western Europe since Maurer, that the Russians settled in individual settlements from which communes developed, supposedly only in the sixteenth and seventeenth centuries.* In this connection, Chicherin derives collective farming and the imposition of plots of land from the crop rotation of strips of the common land, collective ownership of the land likewise from boundary disputes, and the public power of the mark community from the collective burden of the poll tax introduced in the sixteenth century. Thus, in a typically liberal fashion, he more or less turns all historical contexts, causes and consequences upside down.

Whatever one thinks about the antiquity of the peasant agricultural commune and its origins, it has, in any case, outlived the whole long history of serfdom as well as its dissolution, through to most recent times. We shall deal here only with its fate in the nineteenth century.

When Tsar Alexander II enacted his so-called "emancipation" of the peasants, their own land was sold to them by the lords—following completely the Prussian example—with the latter being well indemnified by the treasury in bonds for the worst areas of the land they allegedly owned, imposing a debt of 900 million rubles,† to be repaid at an annual rate of 6 percent within forty-nine years. This land was not, as in Prussia, assigned to individual peasant families as private property, but to whole communities as inalienable and unmortgageable communal property. The entire community took joint responsibility for the debt repayment, just as they had for the various taxes and dues, and had a free hand in assessing the shares of its individual members. This was the arrangement made for the entire massive area of the Great Russian peasantry. In the early 1890s, the distribution of landownership in European Russia (leaving out Poland, Finland, and the region of the Don Cossacks‡) was as follows: public domains, consisting mostly of enormous forest regions in the north and of wastelands, encompassed 150 million *dessiatines*;[84] imperial

---

*   Marx made a similar point in a letter to Nikolai Danielson of March 22, 1873: "The way in which that form of property was founded (historically) in Russia, is of course a secondary question, and has nothing whatever to do with the value of that institution. Still, the German reactionists like Professor A. Wagner in Berlin, etc., use that weapon put in their hands by Chicherin. At the same time all historical analogy speaks against Chicherin. How should it have come to happen that in Russia the same institution had been simply introduced as a fiscal measure, as a concomitant incident of serfdom, while everywhere else it was of spontaneous growth and marked a necessary phase of development of free peoples?" See *Marx-Engels Collected Works*, Vol. 44 (New York: International Publishers, 1989), p. 487.

†   Luxemburg left blank here the figures for area and population.

‡   The first Cossacks were free peoples with a tradition of making decisions based on a common assembly and who roamed the Russian steppes after it was depopulated by the Mongol invasions of the thirteenth century. Those who settled between the rivers Don and Donets became known as the Don Cossacks. From the sixteenth century they protected the border territories of Muscovy and became a major pillar of the tsarist regime. They were subject to a policy of repression and extermination after the Russian Revolution.

appanages, 7 million; church and municipal property, somewhat less than 9 million; in private ownership, 93 million (only 5 percent of this belonging to the peasants, the rest to the aristocracy), while 131 million *dessiatines* were communal peasant property. As late as 1900, there were 122 million hectares of communal peasant property, against only 22 million that were the property of individual peasants.[†]

Looking at the economy of the Russian peasantry in this enormous area, as it existed until recently and in part still exists today, it is again easy to recognize the typical structures of the mark community, as these existed in Germany and Africa, on the Ganges and in Peru. The mark's fields were partitioned, while forests, grasslands and bodies of water were undivided communal land. With the general prevalence of the primitive three-field crop rotation, summer and winter fields were divided according to soil quality into strips ("charts"), and each strip into smaller segments. The summer strips were distributed in April and the winter ones in June. With scrupulous observation of equal land distribution, the diversity of crops had become so developed that in the Moscow province, for example, there were in both the summer and winter fields an average of eleven strips each, so that each peasant had at least twenty-two scattered parcels of land to cultivate. The community usually reserved plots of land for emergency communal purposes, or laid up stocks for the same purpose, to which each individual member had to supply grain. The technical progress of the economy was ensured by each peasant family being able to keep their land for ten years on condition that they fertilized it, or each field being divided from the start into parcels of land that were fertilized from the outset and only repartitioned every ten years. Most of the flax fields and the fruit and vegetable gardens were subject to the same rule.

The allocation of various meadows and pastures for the community herds, the marking of herds, the fencing of meadows and the protection of fields, as well as decisions over system of rotation, the time for particular field work, and the date and method of repartitioning—all of this was a matter for the community, or more specifically, the village assembly. As far as the frequency of repartitioning was concerned, there was great diversity. In one particular province, for example, Saratov,[‡] nearly half of the 278 village communities studied in 1877 undertook a reallotment each year, while the remainder did this every two, three, five, six, eight or eleven years. At the same time, thirty-eight communities that practiced collective fertilization had given up repartitioning altogether.[85]

---

* Imperial appanages were portions of the royal domain granted to blood relatives of the sovereign.

† A large percentage of these communal lands were still in existence at the time of the 1917 Revolution. About 138 million acres of arable land, meadows and forest were communal and collective property by 1917.

‡ Saratov is a region southeast of Moscow, on the Volga River.

What is most remarkable about the Russian mark community is the method of land apportionment. The principle of equal lots common among the Germans was not prevalent in the Russian case, nor was a determination based on the needs of the particular family, as in Peru. Instead, the principle of taxability was the single determining factor. The government's concern with taxation continued to dominate the life of the commune after the peasants' "emancipation," and all the village institutions revolved around taxation. For the tsarist government, taxation was based on the so-called "audited souls," that is, all the male inhabitants of the community without distinction of age, as determined every twenty years, since the first peasant census under Peter the Great, by the famous "audits" that were the terror of the Russian people and tore whole communities apart.[86]

The government taxed the villages on the basis of the number of audited "souls." Yet the commune allocated the total amount of tax for which it was liable on peasant households according to their number of workers, and it was the tax capacity measured in this way that determined each household's portion of land. Rather than a basis of sustenance for the peasants, land allocation in Russia after 1861 was a basis of taxation. It was not a benefit to which each household was entitled, but an obligation imposed on every member of the commune as a state service. There was nothing more strange than the Russian village assembly for the partitioning of land. From all sides could be heard protests against the allocation of too large parcels of land—poor families with no real workers, made up predominantly of women or children, were generally spared from being allocated a parcel of land, on grounds of "powerlessness," while larger allotments were forced on wealthy peasants by the mass of poorer peasants. The tax burden that is so central to Russian village life is also enormous. On top of the debt repayments, there were also poll taxes, a village tax, church tax, salt tax, etc. In the 1880s, the poll tax and salt tax were abolished, yet the tax burden remained so enormous that it devoured all of the peasantry's economic resources. According to a statistic from the 1890s, 70 percent of the peasantry drew less than a minimum existence from their land allotments, 20 percent were able to feed themselves, but not to keep livestock, while only 9 percent had a surplus above their own needs that could be taken to market. Tax arrears were therefore a frequent phenomenon of the Russian village from the "emancipation" onwards. Already in the 1870s, an average yearly intake of fifty million rubles from the poll tax was accompanied by an annual deficit of eleven million rubles. After the poll tax was lifted, the poverty of the Russian village continued to grow, due to the simultaneous escalation of indirect taxation from the eighties onward. In 1904, the tax arrears amounted to 127 million rubles, a debt that was almost completely cancelled because collecting it had become totally impossible and because of the general revolutionary ferment. The taxes not only ate up all of the peasants' income, they also forced them to seek side occupations. One of these was seasonal farm labor, which brought whole migrations of peoples into the Russian hinterland, the strongest male villagers moving to the large aristocratic estates to be hired as day laborers, while their own fields back home were left in the weaker hands of older, female, and adolescent workers. The beckoning of the city with its manufacturing industries offered another possibility. In the central industrial region, therefore, a class of temporary workers formed who moved to the city only for the winter, mostly to textile factories, returning to their villages with their earnings in the spring to work in the fields. Finally, in many districts, there was industrial domestic work or occasional agricultural work on the side, such as transport or chopping wood. And even with all of this, the large majority of the peasant masses could hardly support themselves. Not only was the whole agricultural yield swallowed by taxation, but their extra earnings as well. The mark community, which was collectively liable for the taxes, was equipped with strong means of enforcement vis-à-vis its members. It could hire out those in arrears with their taxes for wage labor, and requisition their earned income. It issued or refused internal passports to its members, without which a peasant was unable to leave the village. Finally, it had the legal right to inflict corporal punishment on those whose taxes were intractably in arrears. Periodically, this made the Russian village in the enormous stretches of the Russian interior a horrific sight. Upon the arrival of the tax collectors, a procedure began for which tsarist Russia coined the term "flogging out those in arrears." The entire village assembly appeared, the "evaders" had to take off their trousers and lay down on a bench, whereupon they were brutally beaten with a birch by their fellow mark members, one after the other. The moaning and weeping of those being thrashed—most often bearded family fathers, even white-haired old men—accompanied the higher authorities, who, after they had completed their task with the ringing of bells, went off in their troikas to hunt in another community and carry out the same punishments. It was not uncommon for a peasant to spare himself this public punishment by committing suicide. Another unique product of those circumstances was the "tax beggar," an impoverished old peasant who took to begging as a tramp in order to cobble together the taxes due and bring them back to the village. The state watched over the mark community, which had been turned into a tax machine, with severity and persistence. A law of 1881, for example, decreed that the community could only sell agricultural land if two-thirds of the peasants made that decision, after which it was still necessary to get the consent of the ministry of the interior, the ministry of finance, and the ministry of crown lands. Individual peasants were allowed to sell their inherited lands only to other members of the mark community. Taking on a mortgage was forbidden. Under Alexander III, the village community was robbed of all autonomy and placed under the thumb of "land captains," an institution similar to the Prussian district administrators.* Decisions made by the

---

* "Land captains" were officials imposed on the *mir* by the state. They included clerks as well as policemen.

village assembly required the consent of these officials; repartitionings of land were undertaken under their supervision, as were tax assessment and debt collection. The law of 1893 made a partial concession to time pressure by declaring repartitionings permissible only every twelve years. Yet, at the same time, withdrawing from the mark community required the consent of the community and was allowed only on condition that the person involved contributed his individual portion of the repayment debt in full.

Despite all of these artificial legal binds that squeezed the village community, despite the guardianship of three ministries and a swarm of *chinovniks* [petty officials], the dissolution of the mark community could no longer be prevented. There was the crushing tax burden; the deterioration of the peasant economy as a result of the side activities in agricultural and industrial work; a shortage of land, especially pasture and forest, which had already been grabbed by the aristocracy at the time of emancipation, and a shortage of arable fields due to increasing population. All of this had two critical effects: the flight to the city and the rise of usury within the village. To the extent that the combination of peasant farming and outside work in industry or elsewhere increasingly served only to pay the tax burden, without ever providing a real subsistence, membership in the mark community became like an iron chain of hunger around the necks of the peasants. The natural desire of the poorer members of the community was to escape from this chain. Hundreds of fugitives were returned by the police to their communities as undocumented vagabonds, then made an example of by being beaten on a bench with rods by their mark comrades. But even the rods and the enforcement of passport controls proved powerless against the mass flight of the peasants, who fled from the hell of their "village communism" to the city under cover of darkness, to plunge definitively into the sea of the industrial proletariat. Others, for whom family bonds or other circumstances made escape inadvisable, sought to accomplish their exit from the agricultural commune by legal means. To achieve this, they had to contribute their share of the debt repayment, and were assisted here by moneylenders. Early on, not only the tax burden but the forced sale of grain on the most unacceptable terms in order to repay these debts exposed the Russian peasant to usurers. Every emergency, every bad crop made resort to them unavoidable. And ultimately, even emancipation from the yoke of the community was unattainable for most unless they put themselves under the new yoke of the usurer, paying dues and other services for an incalculable length of time. While the impoverished peasants sought to flee the mark community in order to free themselves from misery, many wealthy peasants simply turned their backs on it and left the commune in order to escape responsibility for the taxes of the poor. But even where there was less official departure of wealthy peasants, these individuals, who were in large part also the village usurers, formed a ruling power over the peasant masses, and knew how to extract decisions convenient to themselves from the indebted, dependent majority. Thus, in the womb of a village community officially based on equality and communal property, there grew a clear division of classes into a small but influential village bourgeoisie and a mass of dependent and effectively prole-tarianized peasants. The internal breakup of the village commune—crushed by taxes, eaten by usurers, and internally divided—eventually made waves outside as well: famine and peasant revolts were frequent occurrences in Russia in the 1880s, being put down by the provincial administrations with the same implac-ability as the tax executors and the military showed when coming to "pacify" the village. In many regions, Russian fields became the scene of horrific death by starvation and bloody turmoil. The Russian *muzhik* [peasant] experienced the fate of the Indian peasant, and Orissa[*] here is Saratov, Samara, and so on down the Volga.[87] When the revolution of the urban proletariat finally broke out in Russia in 1904 and 1905, the peasant insurrections, which had been chaotic up to that point, became a political factor by their sheer weight, tipping the scales of revolution and making the agricultural question a central issue. Now, as the peasants poured over the aristocratic estates like an irresistible flood, setting the "aristocrats' nests" on fire with their cry for land, while the workers' party formulated the distress of the peasantry into a revolutionary demand to expro-priate state property and the landed estates without compensation and to place them into the hands of the peasants, tsarism finally retreated from the centuries-old agrarian policies that it had pursued with such iron persistence. The mark community could no longer be resuscitated; it had to be abandoned. Already in 1902, the axe was taken to the very roots of the village community in its spe-cific Russian incarnation, with the abolition of collective liability for taxes. Of course, this measure was actively prepared by the financial policies of tsarism itself. The treasury could easily forgo collective liability when it came to direct taxation, now that indirect taxation had reached such a level that in the budget of 1906, for example, out of a total revenue of 2,030 million rubles, only 148 million came from direct taxes and 1,100 million from indirect taxes, including 558 million from the spirits monopoly alone, a tax that was implemented by the "liberal" minister, Count Witte, to combat drunkenness. The poverty, hopeless-ness, and ignorance of the peasants offered the most reliable form of collective liability for punctual payment of *this* tax. In 1905 and 1906, the remaining debt in repayment for emancipation was halved, and it was cancelled altogether in 1907. The "agrarian reform" implemented in 1907 then had the avowed aim of creating private peasant property.[†] The means for this were to come from the parceling of domains, appanages, and, in part, landed estates. Thus, the

---

[*]   Orissa is a state in northeast India.

[†]   In November 1906 the Tsar decreed a new agricultural policy, aimed at the destruction of the village communes, as a way to spur capitalist development in the countryside. As a result of the ensuing "reforms," between 1907 and 1915 about 25 percent of the village communities of Russia were eliminated.

proletarian revolution of the twentieth century, even in its first, incomplete phase, had already destroyed, at the same time, the last remainders of bondage and the mark community, which had been artificially preserved by tsarism.[*]

3

With the Russian village commune, the varied fate of primitive agrarian communism comes to an end; the circle is closed. Beginning as a natural product of social development, as the best guarantee of economic progress, and of the material and intellectual flourishing of society, the mark community ends here as an abused tool of political and economic backwardness. The Russian peasant, who is beaten with rods by his fellow community members in the service of tsarist absolutism, offers the most horrific historical critique of the limits of primitive communism and the most evident expression of the fact that even this social form is subject to the dialectical law that reason becomes unreason, a benefit becomes a scourge.[†]

Two facts spring to mind on close contemplation of the fate of the mark community in various countries and continents. Far from being a rigid, unchangeable pattern, this highest and final form of the primitive communist economic system displays above all endless diversity, flexibility and adaptability, as seen in its various forms. In each context, and under all circumstances, it undergoes a silent process of transformation, which, because of its slow pace, may be hardly apparent at first from the outside. Inside the society, however, new forms are always replacing old ones and it accordingly survives under any political superstructure of native or foreign institutions, its economic and social life constantly developing and decaying, advancing and declining.

At the same time, this social form shows an extraordinary tenacity and stability precisely because of its elasticity and adaptability. It defies all the storms of political history; or rather it tolerates them passively, lets them pass and patiently endures for centuries the strains of every form of conquest, foreign rule, despotism and exploitation. There is only one contact that it cannot tolerate or overcome—contact with European civilization, i.e. with capitalism. This encounter is deadly for the old society, universally and without exception, and it accomplishes what millennia and the most savage Oriental conquerors could not: the dissolution of the whole social structure from the inside, tearing apart

---

* Luxemburg is considerably overstating the case here, since the *mir* hardly went out of existence by the time of the end of the 1905 Revolution. Not only did it still exist, in some respects it rebounded in strength immediately following the 1917 Revolution, since government pressures and restrictions on the *mir* were lessened. The *mir* was actually dealt its death blow by Stalin's forced collectivization campaign of the 1930s. For a study of the persistence of the *mir*, see Pierre Pascal, *Civilisation paysanne en Russie* (Lausanne: L'Âge d'homme, 1969).

† "Reason becomes unreason, a benefit becomes a scourge" (*Vernunft wird Unsinn, Wohltat Plage*) is a quote from Goethe's *Faust*.

all traditional bonds and transforming the society in a short period of time into a shapeless pile of rubble.

But this deadly breeze from European capitalism is simply the last and not the sole factor that brings about the inevitable decline of primitive society. The seeds of this lie within the society itself. If we take the various paths of its decline together, those that we know from a number of examples, this establishes a certain historical order of succession. Communist ownership of the means of production, as the basis of a rigorously organized economy, offered the most productive social labor process and the best material assurance of its continuity and development for many epochs. But even the progress in labor productivity that it secured, albeit slowly, necessarily came into conflict with the communistic organization over time. After the decisive progress to a higher form of agriculture, with the use of the ploughshare, had been accomplished and the mark community had retained its solid form on this basis, the next step in the development of the technology of production after a certain amount of time necessitated a more *intensive* land cultivation, which could only be achieved at that stage of agricultural technology by more intensive smallholding and by a stronger and closer relationship of the individual laborer to the soil. Longer use of the same parcel of land by a single peasant family became the precondition for its more careful treatment. In both Germany and Russia, fertilization of the soil led to the gradual abandonment of land repartitioning. In general, we can identify a trait that is constant everywhere in the life of the mark community: the movement toward increasingly long intervals between land reallotments, universally leading sooner or later to a transition from allotted land to inherited land. In the same way that the transformation of communal property into private property keeps pace with the intensification of labor, it is noticeable that forest and pasture remained communal the longest, while intensively worked farmland led first to the partitioned mark and then to hereditary property. Establishing private property in parcels of arable land does not completely abolish the entire communal economic organization, which continues to be upheld by crop rotation and enforced in forest and pastoral communities. The economic and social equality at the heart of ancient society are still not destroyed by it either. Initially forms what comes into being is a mass of small peasants, equal in their living conditions, who can generally continue to work and live for centuries according to their old traditions. Yet the inheritability of property certainly opens the gates to future inequality, by the heritability of holdings and the primogeniture or other settlements that follow from this, subsequently by their salability or general alienability.

The undermining of the traditional social organization by the processes referred to above proceeds extremely slowly. There are other historical factors at work that accomplish this more quickly and thoroughly, in particular large-scale public works projects, which the mark community with its narrow limits is unable to tackle by its very nature. We have already seen the critical importance that artificial irrigation has for agriculture in the Orient. The great intensification of labor and powerful rise in productivity here led to quite different far-reaching results than the changeover to fertilization in the West. From the outset, artificial irrigation work is a mass work and a large-scale undertaking. Precisely because of this, there is no suitable institution for it within the organization of the mark community, so that special institutions standing above this had to be created. We know that the direction of public waterworks lay at the root of the domination by the priests and every Oriental power. But also in the West, and more generally, there are various public matters that, though simple in comparison to contemporary state organization, had nevertheless to be seen to in every primitive society. These grew with the development and progress of the society, therefore eventually requiring special organs. On all sides—from Germany to Peru, from India to Algeria—we can define the path of development as the tendency in primitive societies to transform elected public offices to inherited ones.

Initially, however, this turnaround, proceeding slowly and imperceptibly, is still not a break with the foundations of communistic society. Rather, the inheritability of these public offices is a natural result of the fact that here too, by the very nature of primitive societies, collective experience, tradition and personal, ensures the successful handling of such offices. Over time, however, the inheritability of the offices leads unavoidably to the creation of a small local aristocracy, former servants of the community becoming its rulers. The undivided mark lands, the *ager publicus* of the Romans,* to which power adhered, served as the economic basis for advancing the status of this aristocracy. Theft of the undemarcated or unused lands of the mark is the common method of all indigenous and foreign rulers, who vault above the peasant masses and subjugate them politically. If the people in question are isolated from the major centers of civilization, the aristocracy may not distinguish itself very greatly in its lifestyle from that of the masses, and may still directly take part in the production process, while a certain democratic simplicity of customs covers up differences in wealth. This is the case with the tribal aristocracy of the Yakut people, which is merely endowed with more livestock than the ordinary people, and more influence in public affairs. Following an encounter with more civilized peoples, however, and vigorous trade, refined taste and relief from labor are soon added to the privileges of the aristocracy, and a true class differentiation takes place in society. The most typical example is Greece in the post-Homeric period.

Thus the division of labor at the heart of primitive society unavoidably leads, sooner or later, to the breakup of political and economic equality from inside. One public undertaking, however, plays an important role in this process and

---

* The *ager publicus* is the Latin name for the public lands of ancient Rome. These public lands were often expropriated from Rome's enemies.

accomplishes the work more aggressively than do public offices of a peaceful nature. This is warfare. It is originally a mass affair of the society in question, subsequently turned, in the wake of advances in production, into the speciality of certain circles within primitive society in question. The more advanced, continuous and systematic the labor process of the society, the less it tolerates the irregularities and the drain of time and energy resulting from war. If occasional military campaigns are a direct result of the economic system of hunting and nomadic herding, agriculture goes together with a great peacefulness and passivity among the mass of society, so that a special caste of warriors is often needed for protection. In one way or another, the existence of war, itself just an expression of the limits of labor productivity, plays an important role for all primitive peoples and universally leads over time to a new form of division of labor. The separation of a military aristocracy or military leadership is the hardest blow that the social equality of the primitive society must endure. This is why, wherever we learn of primitive societies, either as survivals from past history or still existing today, we almost never come across any longer such free and equal relations as Morgan was able to convey to us with the serendipitous example of the Iroquois. On the contrary, inequality and exploitation are everywhere characteristics of the primitive societies we encounter, being the product of a long history of disintegration, whether it is a matter of the ruling castes of the Orient, the tribal aristocracy of the Yakuts, the "great clansmen" of the Scottish Celts, the military aristocracy of the Greeks, Romans and migrating Germans, or lastly, to the petty despots of the African empires.

If we look, for example, at the famous empire of Mwata Kazembe in south-central Africa, to the east of the Lunda empire,* into which the Portuguese penetrated at the beginning of the nineteenth century, we can see, right in the heart of Africa, in a region hardly touched by Europeans, primitive Negro social relations in which there is no longer much equality or freedom to be found. The 1831 expedition of Major [José] Monteiro and Captain [António] Gamitto, undertaken from the Zambezi into the interior for scientific and trading purposes, depicts this as follows. Initially, the expedition came into the land of the Marawi,† primitive hoe farmers living in small, conical palisade houses and wearing only a loincloth on their bodies. At the time that Monteiro and Gamitto

---

*   The Kazembe was a powerful kingdom of the Kiluba-Chibewa speaking peoples of south-central Africa, also known as the Lunda-Lunda. "Mwata" was the title given to its most powerful chiefs. The "Mwate Kazembe" to which Luxemburg refers is Mwata Kazembe III Lukwesa Ilunga, who repulsed Portuguese efforts in 1831 (led by Major José Monteiro and António Gamito) to conquer the kingdom. In 1867, David Livingston encountered the Lunda-Lunda, led at the time by Mwata Kazembe VII. Mwata Kzembe VII was later killed by traders. In 1894 the kingdom was divided up between the British (who took control of what is now Zimbabwe) and Belgium (who took control of what is now the Democratic Republic of the Congo).

†   The Marawi were a Bantu people living around Lake Malawi from the sixteenth century.

traveled through Malawiland, it was under the rule of a despotic leader who went by the title *nede*. He adjudicated all disputes in his capital city, Muzenda, and no disputing his decision was allowed. True to form, he convened a council of elders who were required, however, to agree with his opinion. The land was divided into provinces, which were governed by *mambos*, and these were then further divided into districts that were led by *funos*. All of these titles were hereditary.

> On the eighth of August we reached the residence of Mukanda, the powerful leader of the Chewa.* Mukanda, who had been sent a gift of various cotton goods, red cloth, a number of pearls, salt and cowries,† came on the following day, riding into the encampment on a black man. Mukanda was a man sixty or seventy years old, with a pleasant, majestic appearance. His only garment consisted of a dirty cloth that he had wrapped around his hips. He stayed for about two hours and, when he was leaving, asked everyone in a friendly and irresistible manner for a gift... The burial of the Chewa leaders is accompanied by extremely barbaric ceremonies. All of the wives of the departed are locked up with the corpse in the same hut until everything is ready for the burial. Then the funeral cortege moves... toward the crypt, and once it arrives, the favorite wife of the deceased, along with some others, climb into the crypt and sit down with their legs outstretched. This living foundation is then covered with draping and the cadaver laid on top of them, along with six other women who are thrown into the crypt after having their necks broken. Once the grave is covered, the terrifying ceremony ends with the impaling of two male youths, who are arranged on top of the grave, one at the head with a drum, the other at the feet with a bow and arrow. Major Monteiro, during his stay in Chewaland, was a witness to one such burial.

From here they went uphill into the middle of the empire. The Portuguese came to

> a barren region, situated high up and almost entirely lacking in foodstuffs. Everywhere can be seen the signs of destruction by previous military campaigns, and famine plagued the expedition to a disturbing degree. Messengers were sent with a few gifts to the next *mambo*, in expectation of guides, but the messengers returned with the dispiriting news that they had encountered the *mambo* and his family close to starvation and death, completely alone in the village ... Even before reaching the heart of the empire, samples of the barbarian justice that was part of everyday life

---

* The Chewa (sometimes referred to as the Nyanja) resides in central and southern Africa and is originally from the Congo. They are closely related to the Bemba. The Portuguese first made contact with them in the early 1600s. There are currently about 1.5 million Chewa, living primarily in Malawi and Zambia.

† Cowries are bits of porcelain that have long served as a form of money in India and Sub-Saharan Africa.

there could be seen. It was common to encounter young people whose noses, hands, ears and other appendages had been cut off as punishment for some minor offence. On the nineteenth of November we entered the capital city, where the donkey that Captain Gamitto was riding caused a stir. Soon we arrived at a road about forty-five minutes long that was fenced in on both sides by two or three meter-high fences made of interwoven poles so elaborately constructed that they looked like walls. In these straw walls there were small open doors spaced apart from each other. At the end of the road, there was a small square hut open only to the west, in the middle of which stood a human figure crudely carved out of wood, seventy centimeters tall, on a wooden pedestal. In front of the open side lay a heap of more than 300 skulls. Here, the road turned into a large square area, at the end of which was a large forest only separated from the square by a fence. On the outside of it, on both sides of the gate, was a line tied on either side of the gate with thirty skulls strung onto it by way of ornamentation ... Following this was the reception at Mwata's with all barbarian pageantry and surrounded by his army of between five and six thousand men. He sat on a chair covered by a green cloth spread over a pile of leopard and lion skins. His head covering consisted of a scarlet conical cap, which was composed of half-meter long feathers. Wrapped around his forehead was a diadem made of glimmering stone; his neck and shoulders were covered by a kind of necklace made of shells, square pieces of mirror, and faux gems. Each of his arms was wrapped in a piece of blue cloth, decorated with fur, and his forearms also had ornamental strings made of blue stones. A yellow-, red- and blue-fringed cloth held together by a belt covered his lower body. His legs, like his arms, were decorated with blue jewels.

Mwata proudly sat there with seven parasols protecting him from the sun and swung around the tail of a wildebeest for a scepter, while twelve Negroes armed with brooms were busy removing every piece of dust from the ground, every impurity from his holy vicinity. A rather complicated court surrounded the ruler. First, guarding his throne were two rows of figures, forty centimeters high, in the shape of the upper body of a Negro adorned with animal horns, while between these figures sat two Negroes who burned aromatic leaves in coal pans. The place of honor was occupied by the two main wives, the first dressed more or less like Mwata. In the background, the harem of 400 women was assembled, and indeed these women were completely naked, apart from the aprons on their lower bodies. In addition, there were two hundred black women who stood waiting for the slightest command. Inside the quadrangle built by women sat the highest dignitaries of the kingdom, the *kilolo*, sitting on lion and leopard skins, each with an umbrella and dressed similarly to Mwata. There were also several corps of musicians, who made a deafening noise with their strangely shaped instruments, while a few court jesters, dressed in animal pelts and horns, ran around completing the entourage of Kazembe who, armed in this dignified manner, awaited the Portuguese advance. Mwata is the absolute ruler of this people, his title meaning simply "lord." Underneath him are the *kilolo*, or the aristocrats, who are in turn divided into two classes. Among the more noble aristocrats are the crown prince, Mwata's closest relatives, and the high commanders of his army. But the very lives and property of these nobles exist only due to Mwata's absolute power.

If this tyrant is in a bad mood, he will have a person's ears cut off if he does not understand a command and asks for it to be repeated, "in order to teach him to listen more carefully." Every theft in his kingdom is punished by the amputation of the ears and hands; anyone who approaches one of his women or attempts to talk to her is killed or has all his limbs hobbled. The reputation he has among this superstitious people is that one cannot touch him without falling prey to his magical powers. Since it is impossible to avoid all contact with him, the people have discovered a means to avoid death. Anyone who has dealings with him kneels down before him, and the lord lays the palm of his hand in a mysterious manner on the kneeler and thereby absolves him from the death curse.[88]

This is a picture of a society that has moved a long way away from the original foundations of every primitive community, from equality and democracy. It should not, however, be a foregone conclusion that under this kind of political despotism, the relations of the mark community, the communal ownership of the land or communally organized labor cease to exist. The Portuguese intruders, who recorded precisely the superficial rubbish about costume and courtesans, have, like all Europeans, no eyes, no interest and no frame of reference when it comes to things that run counter to the European system of private ownership. In any case, the social inequality and despotism of primitive societies are completely distinct from the inequality that is common in civilized societies and transplanted now onto the primitive. The increase in status of the primitive aristocracy and the despotic power of the primitive leader are all natural products of this society, like all of its other conditions of life. They are only another expression of the helplessness of the society with respect to its natural surroundings and to its own social relations, a helplessness that appears both in magical cult practices and in the periodic famines that either partly or completely starve the despotic leader along with the mass of his subjects. This rule by an aristocracy and a chief is therefore in complete harmony with the other material and intellectual aspects of the society, as is clear from the significant fact that the political power of the primitive ruler is always closely bound up with the primitive nature religion, with the cult of the dead, and is sustained by it.

From this standpoint, Mwata Kazembe is the Lunda, whom fourteen wives follow alive into the grave and who rules over the life and death of his subjects according to his erratic moods, because he believes himself to be a magician, this being his people's rock-solid conviction. The despotic "Prince Kasongo" on the Lomami river who, forty years later, with great dignity among his noblemen and his people, performed, by way of greeting the Englishman [Verney Lovett] Cameron, a hopping dance with his two naked daughters in a woman's skirt braided with monkey skins and with a filthy handkerchief on his head, is in fact a much less absurd and insanely comical phenomenon than the ruler "by the grace of God" over sixty-seven million members of a people who produced the likes of [Immanuel] Kant, [Hermann von] Helmholtz and [Johann Wolfgang von] Goethe. And yet even the worst enemy of this ruler could not call him a magician.

Primitive communist society, through its own internal development, leads to the formation of inequality and despotism. It has not yet disappeared; on the contrary, it can persist for many thousands of years under these primitive conditions. Such societies, however, sooner or later succumb to foreign occupation and then undergo a more or less far-reaching social reorganization. Foreign rule by Muslims is of special historical significance, since it predated European rule in vast stretches of Asia and Africa. Everywhere that nomadic Islamic peoples— whether Mongol or Arab— instituted and secured their foreign rule, a social process began that Henry Maine and Maksim Kovalevsky called the *feudalization* of the land. They did not make the land their own property, but instead turned their attention to two objectives, the collection of taxes and the military consolidation of their domination over the country. Both goals were served by a specific administrative-military organization, under which the land was divided into several ethnic groups and given as fiefdoms of a kind to Muslim officials, who were also tax collectors and military administrators. Large portions of uncultivated mark lands were utilized for the founding of military colonies. These institutions, together with the spread of Islam, implemented a profound change in the general conditions of existence of primitive societies. Only their economic conditions were little changed. The foundations and the organization of production remained the same and persisted for many centuries, despite exploitation and military pressure. Of course, Muslim rule was not always so considerate of the living conditions of the natives. For example, the Arabs on the east coast of Africa operated for centuries from the Zanzibar sultanate* an extensive slave trade in Negroes, which led to frequent slave raids into the interior of Africa, the depopulation and destruction of whole African villages, and an escalation of despotic violence by the native chiefs, who found an enticing business venture in selling their own subjects or the subjugated members of neighboring tribes. Yet this transformation in conditions, which had such a profound effect on the fate of African society, was only accomplished as a further consequences of European influence: the slave trade in Negroes developed only after the discoveries and conquests of the Europeans in the sixteenth century, in order to service the plantations and mines exploited by the Europeans that were in full bloom in America and Asia.

---

* An island off the east African coast, Zanzibar was a possession of the Sultans of Omar on the Arabian peninsular until it was taken over by the British in 1890. For many years it was a center of the African slave trade.

The intrusion of European civilization was a disaster in every sense for primitive social relations. The European conquerors are the first who are not merely after subjugation and economic exploitation, but seize the very means of production, by ripping the land from under the feet of the native population. In this way, European capitalism deprives the primitive social order of its foundation. What emerges is something that is worse than all oppression and exploitation, total anarchy and that specifically European phenomenon of the uncertainty of social existence. The subjugated peoples, separated from their means of production, are regarded by European capitalism as mere laborers; if they are useful for this end, they are made into slaves, and if they are not, they are exterminated. We have witnessed this method in the Spanish, English, and French colonies. Before the advance of capitalism, the primitive social order, which outlasted all previous historical phases, capitulates. Its last remnants are eradicated from the earth and its elements—labor-power and means of production—are absorbed by capitalism. Early communist society fell everywhere, in the last instance, because it was made obsolete by economic progress, making room for new prospects of development. This development and progress are represented for a long time by the base methods of a class society, until this too is made obsolete and pushed aside by further progress. Here too, violence is merely the servant of economic development.

III. [COMMODITY PRODUCTION]

The task we have set ourselves is as follows. A society cannot exist without common labor, i.e. without labor with a plan and organization. And we have found various different forms of this, in all eras. In present-day society we hardly find it at all: neither rule nor law, nor democracy, no trace of plan and organization—anarchy. How is capitalist society possible?[*]

1

In order to trace the construction of the capitalist tower of Babel, let us imagine once again a society with a planned organization of labor. This may be a society with a highly developed division of labor, in which not only agriculture and industry are separate, but each particular branch of both has also become the speciality of a particular group of working people.[89] In this society there are for example agriculturalists and foresters, fisherfolk and gardeners, shoemakers and tailors, locksmiths and blacksmiths, spinners and weavers, etc. etc. This society, taken as a whole, is endowed with every kind of work and every kind of product.

---

[*] This introductory paragraph appears to be, like Luxemburg's marginal notes, a reminder to herself rather than part of the intended text.

These products are distributed in greater or lesser amounts to all members of society, as labor is communal; it is divided and organized from the start in a planned way by some kind of authority—whether this is the despotic law of the government, or serfdom, or any other kind of organization. For simplification, however, we assume that it is a communist community with communal property, as we are already familiar with from the Indian example. We only presuppose for the time being that the division of labor within this community is far more developed than was historically the case, and assume that one part of the members of the community devote themselves exclusively to agriculture, while other kinds of labor are all performed by specialist artisans. The economy of this community is quite clear to us: it is the community members themselves who possess the land and the means of production in common, and their common will also determines what, when and how much of each product is to be produced. The mass of finished products, moreover, since these belong equally to all, are distributed among everyone according to need. Now, however, imagine that one fine day, in the communist community with this arrangement, common property ceases to exist, and along with it also common labor and the common will that regulates this. The highly developed division of labor that has been attained obviously remains. The shoemaker still sits at his last, the baker has nothing and knows nothing except his oven, the smith has only his smithy and only knows how to swing a hammer, etc. etc. But the chain that formerly connected all these special labors into a common labor, into the societal economy, is broken. Each person is now on his own: the farmer, the shoemaker, the baker, the locksmith, the weaver, etc. Each is completely free and independent. The community no longer has anything to say to him, no one can order him to work for the whole, nor does anyone bother about his needs. The community that was previously a whole has been broken up into individual little particles or atoms, like a mirror shattered into a thousand splinters; each person now floats like a piece of dust in the air, as it were, and wonders how he will manage. What happens now to the community that has been struck overnight by such a catastrophe? What will all these people left to their own devices do the next day? One thing is certain right away—they will carry on working, exactly as they did previously. For as long as human needs cannot be satisfied without labor, every human society has to work. Whatever transformations and changes may take place in society, labor cannot cease for a moment. The former members of the communist community, therefore, even after the ties between them have been broken and they are left completely to themselves, will certainly each carry on working, and since we have assumed that all labor is already specialized, each of them will continue to pursue only that work that has become his speciality and for which he has the means of production: the shoemaker will make boots, the baker will bake bread, the weaver produce cloth, the farmer grow corn, etc. But a difficulty now immediately arises. Each of these producers, despite producing extremely important and immediately needed objects of use—each of these specialists, the shoemaker, the baker, the smith, the weaver—were until yesterday all equally esteemed useful members of society, and could not get by without society. Each had his important place in the whole. Now, however, the whole no longer exists, each person exists only for himself. But none of them can live alone, simply from the products of their own labor. The shoemaker cannot eat his boots, the baker cannot satisfy all his needs with bread, and even the farmer with the fullest barn of corn would die from hunger and cold if he had nothing but corn. Each person has many needs, and can only satisfy a particular one of these. Each accordingly needs a certain quantity of the products of all others. They are all dependent on one another. But how is this to be managed, since we know that no connections and ties between the individual producers exist any more? The shoemaker urgently needs bread from the baker, but has no means of obtaining this bread; he cannot force the baker to supply him, as both alike are free and independent people. If he wants to enjoy the proceeds of the baker's labor, this can evidently be based only on reciprocity, i.e., if he supplies the baker in turn with a product useful to him. But the baker also needs the products of the shoemaker, and finds himself in just the same situation as the latter. This indicates the basis for reciprocity. The shoemaker gives the baker boots so as to receive bread in return. Shoemaker and baker exchange their products, and both can now satisfy their needs. It turns out that, given a highly developed division of labor, a complete independence of the producers from one another and the absence of any kind or organization between them, the only way of making the products of different labors accessible to all is—*exchange*. The shoemaker, the baker, the farmer, the spinner, the weaver, the locksmith—all reciprocally exchange their products, and in this way satisfy all their various needs. Exchange creates in this way a new tie between the fragmented, individualized and separated private producers. Labor and consumption, the life of the shattered community, can start up again, as exchange has given them the possibility of once more all working for one another, it has again made possible social collaboration, social production, even in the form of fragmented private production.

But this is indeed a quite new and particular form of social collaboration, and we need to examine it more closely. Each individual person now works for himself, producing on his own account, on the basis of his own will and judgment. In order to live, he now has to produce products that he himself does not need but that others do. Each works accordingly for others. In itself, this is nothing special and nothing new. In the communist community, too, everyone works for everyone else. What is special now, however, is that each person now only hands over his product to others by way of exchange, and can only obtain the products of others likewise by exchange. Everyone must now, in order to obtain the products they need, produce by their own labor products designed for exchange. The shoemaker must continue to produce boots that he does not need himself, that are quite useless to him, a waste of labor. The only use and purpose they have for him is that he can exchange them against other products that he needs. He therefore produces his boots already with the purpose of exchange, i.e. he produces them as a commodity. Each person now can only satisfy his needs, only obtain products that others have produced, if he himself appears with a product that others need and that he has produced with his labor for this purpose; in other words, each obtains his share of the products of all others, of the social product, by himself appearing with a commodity. The product that he has made for exchange is now his right to demand a portion of the total social product. This total social product may well no longer exist in the earlier form it took in the communist community, where it directly represented in its mass and totality the wealth of the community, and was only then distributed. Everyone there worked in common on the account of the community and under the leadership of the community, so that what was produced already came into the world as a social product. The distribution of this total product to individuals occurred only subsequently, and only then did the product enter the private use of individual members of the community. Now things proceed the other way round: each produces on his own account as a private person, and it is only in exchange that the finished products together form a sum that can be viewed as social wealth. The share of each person, in both social labor and social wealth, is now represented by the special commodity that he has produced with his labor and brought for exchange with others. The share of each in the total social labor, therefore, is no longer represented in a certain quantum of labor that is allocated to him in advance, but rather in the finished product, in the commodity, that he supplies as he sees fit.[90] If he doesn't want to work, then he doesn't need to, he can just go out for a walk and no one will scold him in the street, as did indeed happen with refractory members of the communist community, where idlers were likely to be sharply reprimanded by the "chief inhabitant," the head of the community, or were liable to public contempt at the community assembly. Now each person is his own unrestricted lord and master, there is no community authority. But if he does not work, he also receives nothing in exchange for the products of work. On the other hand, however, today the individual is not even sure that, no matter how diligently he works, he will receive the means of subsistence he needs; for no one is compelled to give him these, even in exchange for his products. Exchange only comes about if there is a reciprocal need. If no one in the community needs boots at the moment, the shoemaker may work ever so diligently, and produce ever such a fine product, without anyone taking it and giving him bread, meat, etc. in exchange, so that he remains without what he most needs in order to live. Here again, we see a world of difference compared with the earlier communist relations in the community. The community maintained the shoemaker because there was a general need in the community for boots. He was told by the community authority how many boots he was to produce, and he worked as it were as a community servant, a community official, everyone being in exactly this same position. But if the community kept a shoe-maker, it obviously had to feed him. He received his share from the common wealth just like everyone else, and this share of his did not stand in any direct connection with his share in the total work. Of course he had to work, and he was fed because he worked, because he was a useful member of the commu-nity. But whether he had more or fewer boots to produce this particular month, even sometimes none at all, he still received the same means of subsistence, his share of the community's total resources. Now, however, he only receives to the extent that his work is needed, i.e. to the extent that his product is accepted by others in exchange, like for like. Everyone now works just as he wants, how he wants, as much as he wants, at what he wants. The only confirmation that he has produced the right things, what society needs, that he has indeed performed socially necessary labor, is the *fact* that his product is accepted by others. Not all labor, therefore, be it ever so diligent and solid, now has a definite purpose and value in advance from the point of view of society; only a product that is exchangeable has value; a product that no one takes in exchange, no matter how solid, is valueless work, work thrown away.

Now, therefore, each person, in order to participate in the fruits of social production, must also participate in social labor, must produce *commodities*. But the fact that his labor actually is recognized as socially necessary labor is not something anyone tells him, but rather something he learns from his com-modity being taken in exchange, being exchangeable. His share in the labor and product of the whole is thus only assured by his product's receiving the seal of socially necessary labor, the seal of exchange-value.[91] If his product remains unexchangeable, he has then created a worthless product, and his labor was socially superfluous. Then he is only a private shoemaker, cutting leather and cobbling boots for his own amusement, standing outside society, as it were, for society has no interest in his product, and so the products of society are una-vailable to him. If today our shoemaker has been fortunate enough to make an exchange, and obtained means of subsistence in return, he can not only eat his fill and be properly clothed, but also pride himself on his way home that he has been recognized as a useful member of society, his labor recognized as necessary labor. If on the other hand he returns home with his boots, as no one wanted to relieve him of them, he has every reason to be melancholy, as he not only remains without soup, but on top of this it has more or less been explained to him, if only with a chilly silence: Society has no need of you, my friend, your labor was just not necessary, you are a superfluous person and can happily go and hang yourself. A pair of exchangeable boots, or more generally, a commod-ity with exchange-value, is thus all that is needed each time for our shoemaker to be a member of society. But the baker, the weaver and the farmer—everyone— also find themselves in the same position as our shoemaker.[92] The society that sometimes recognizes the shoemaker, and sometimes rejects him with coldness and disdain, is no more than the sum of all these individual commodity producers who work for reciprocal exchange. The sum of social labor and social product that comes into being in this way is therefore not at all the same as the sum of all the labor and products of individual members, as was earlier the case in the communistic, communal economy. For now certain individuals can work diligently, yet their product, if it finds no one to take it in exchange, is something to be thrown away and does not count at all. Only exchange determines what were necessary labors and necessary products, those that count socially. It is the same as if everyone initially worked blindly at home, in any way they chose, then brought their finished products to a place where they were inspected and received a stamp: these labors were socially necessary and are accepted in exchange, but those ones were not necessary and so are completely worthless. The stamp says: these ones have value, those are worthless and remain private pleasures—or sufferings—of the people concerned.

If we summarize the various aspects, it turns out that, by the mere fact of commodity exchange, without any other ingredient or regulation, three important relationships are determined:

1) The *share* of each member of society in social *labor*. This share, in kind and measure, is no longer allocated to him in advance by the community, but only post festum, depending on whether the finished product is accepted or not. Previously, each individual pair of boots that our shoemaker produced was immediately and in advance social labor, even when still on the last. Now his boots are initially private labor, and no one else's concern. Only subsequently are they viewed on the market, and only to the extent that they are taken in exchange is the labor spent by the shoemaker acknowledged as social labor. Otherwise they remain his private labor and are valueless.

2) The *share* of each member in social *wealth*. Previously, the shoemaker received his share of the community's finished products by way of a distribution. This share was assessed, firstly according to the general prosperity of the community, its level of wealth at this particular time, and secondly according to the needs of the members. A numerous family necessarily received more than a less numerous one. With the partitioning of conquered lands among the Germanic tribes, who arrived in Europe in the era of the great migrations and settled on the ruins of the Roman Empire, family size also played a role. The Russian commune, which still carried out redistributions of its common property here and there in the 1880s, took into consideration the number of "mouths" in each household. Under the general rule of exchange, however, any relationship between the need of a member of society and his share in wealth disappears, as does any relationship between this share and the size of the society's total wealth. Now, only the product that each member offers on the commodity market decides his share in the social wealth, and only in so far as it is accepted in exchange as socially necessary.

3) Finally, the *social division of labor* is itself regulated by exchange. Previously, the community decided that it needed so and so many farm workers, so and so many shoemakers, bakers, locksmiths and blacksmiths, etc. The correct proportion between the different trades was the responsibility of the community and its chosen officials, as it also was to make sure that all branches of labor needed were practised. They were certainly familiar with the famous case in which the representatives of a village community asked that a locksmith condemned to death should be reprieved and a blacksmith hanged instead, as there were two blacksmiths in the village. This is a striking example of public concern for the proper division of labor in a community. (We saw, moreover, how in the Middle Ages,* Charlemagne expressly prescribed the kinds of artisans for his estates, and their numbers. We also saw how in medieval towns the guild regulations made sure that particular trades were practiced in the right proportions, and artisans whom it lacked were invited in from elsewhere.) With free and unrestricted exchange, this matter is settled by exchange itself. Now no one tells our shoemaker to work. If he wants, he can produce soap bubbles or paper dragons. He can also, if he likes, abandon shoemaking for weaving, spinning, or goldsmith's work. No one tells him that society needs him in general, and needs him as a cobbler in particular. Naturally, society does have a general need for shoemaking. But no one now decides how many shoemakers will meet this need. No one tells this particular shoemaker whether he is necessary or not, whether it is not rather a weaver or a smith who is needed. But what he is not told, he learns once more simply and solely on the commodity market. If his shoes are accepted in exchange, he knows that society needs him as a shoemaker. And conversely. He can produce the best commodity, but if other shoemakers have sufficiently met the demand, his commodity is superfluous. If this happens repeatedly, he has to abandon his trade. The redundant shoemaker is expelled from society in the same mechanical way as superfluous material is expelled from the animal body. Since his work is not accepted as social labor, he is en route to extinction. The same compulsion to produce exchangeable products for others as one's own condition of existence will eventually lead our expelled shoemaker into another trade, where there is a stronger and insufficiently met demand, for example weaving or haulage, and in this way the shortage of workers here is filled. But not only is a correct proportion maintained in this way between different trades, entire trades are abolished and new ones created. If a certain social need ceases or is met by other products than previously, this is not decided by the members, as in earlier communist communities, and workers accordingly withdrawn from one trade and moved into another. It happens simply by the unexchangeability

---

*   Luxemburg is referring to the chapter of the manuscript on the Middle Ages that has unfortunately not been found. Several chapters that she drafted for the *Introduction to Political Economy* have never been found. For more on this, see the Editor's Introduction to this volume. For her notes on the Middle Ages, see this volume, pp. 339–419.

of the obsolete product. In the seventeenth century, wig making was still an essential trade in every town. But after fashions changed, and people stopped wearing wigs, this trade died a natural death, simply by the unsalability of wigs. With the development of modern urban water supply, and pipes taking water mechanically to each dwelling, the profession of water-carrier—*Wasserer* as it was known in Vienna—generally disappeared.

We can now take an opposite case. Let us assume that our shoemaker, made to feel socially unnecessary in no uncertain terms by the systematic spurning of his commodity, imagines that he is despite this an indispensable member of humanity and still wants to live. In order to live, he must, as we know and he knows, produce commodities. And he now invents a new product, let us say a beard-cover or a wonderful boot-wax. Does this mean he has created a new socially necessary branch of labor, or will he remain unrecognized, like so many great inventors of genius? Again, no one tells him, and he learns this only on the commodity market. If his new product is accepted for long enough in exchange, then this new branch of production has been recognized as socially necessary, and the social division of labor has experienced a new expansion.[93]

You see how in our community, which, following the collapse of the communistic regime and common property, the disappearance of any kind of authority in economic life, any organization and planning in labor, any kind of connection among the individual members, initially seemed quite hopeless in the wake of this catastrophe, we gradually see the rise again of a certain connection, a certain order, and how this happens in a completely mechanical way. Without any understanding among the individual members, without the intervention of any higher power, the individual fragments form up into a whole, as best they can. Exchange itself now regulates the whole economy mechanically, just like a kind of pump mechanism: it creates a link between the individual producers, it forces them to work, it governs their division of labor, determines their wealth and its distribution. Exchange governs society. It is of course a somewhat strange order that has now arisen before our eyes. Society now looks completely different from how it did previously under the regime of the communist community. At that time it was a compact whole, a kind of big family, whose members had all grown up together and stuck closely together, a firm organism, even perhaps an ossified one, rather immovable and rigid. Now we have an extremely loose structure, in which the individual members keep falling away and then reassembling. We have seen, in fact, how no one tells our shoemaker *that* he should work, *what* he should work at, or *how much* he should work. On the other hand, no one asks him whether he needs sustenance, what he needs, or how much he needs. No one bothers about him, he does not exist for society. He only informs society of his existence by the fact that he appears on the commodity market with a product of his labor. If his commodity is accepted, then so too is his existence. His labor is acknowledged as socially necessary, and himself thereby acknowledged as its representative, only in so far as his boots are taken in exchange. He obtains means of subsistence from the social wealth only in so far as his boots are accepted as a commodity. He becomes a member of the society only in so far as he produces exchangeable products, commodities, and only so long as he has these and can dispose of them. Each exchangeable pair of boots makes him a member of society, and each unsalable pair excludes him once again from society. Thus the shoemaker has no connection with society as a human being, only his boots allow him to adhere to society, and they do so only in so far as they have exchange value, are saleable as a commodity. This is therefore not a permanent membership, but one that keeps on being dissolved and renewed. But as well as our shoemaker, all other commodity producers are in the same situation. And there is no one in this society but commodity producers, for it is only in exchange that one receives the means to live; in order to receive these, each person must therefore appear with commodities. Commodity production is the condition of life, and a state of society thereby comes into being in which people all lead their particular existence as completely separate individuals, who do not exist for each other, but only through their commodities attain a constantly fluctuating membership of the whole, or are again excluded from membership. This is an extremely loose and mobile society, caught up in the ceaseless whirl of its individual members.

We see that the abolition of a planned economy and the introduction of exchange brought about a complete transformation in people's social relations, turning society around from top to bottom.

2

There are great difficulties, however, with exchange being the only economic tie between the members of society, since exchange does not run as smoothly as we have just assumed. Let us look at the matter more closely.

So long as we only considered exchange between our two individual producers, the shoemaker and the baker, things were quite simple. The shoemaker cannot live from boots alone, and needs bread; the baker cannot live from bread alone, just like the Bible says, though what he needs in this case is not the word of God, but rather boots. Since there is complete reciprocity here, exchange happens easily: the bread moves from the hands of the baker, who doesn't need it, into those of the shoemaker; the boots move from the shoemaker's workshop into the bakery. Both have their needs satisfied, and both private labors have been confirmed as socially necessary. But let us assume that this happens not just between the shoemaker and the baker, but between all members of society, i.e. between all commodity producers at once. And we have the right to assume this, indeed we are compelled to make this assumption. For all members of society have to live, they must satisfy their various needs. The production of a society, as we already said, cannot stop for a moment, since consumption does not stop for a moment. And we must now add that since production is now split into individual independent private labors, none of which is alone sufficient to satisfy a person, exchange too cannot stop for a moment—unless consumption does as well. Everyone thus continues exchanging, with all their products. How does this come about? Let us return to our example. The shoemaker not only needs the product of the baker, he would like a certain quantity of every other commodity as well. As well as bread, he needs meat from the butcher, a coat from the tailor, the material for his shirt from the weaver, a top hat from the hatter, etc. All these commodities he can only obtain by way of exchange, but all that he can offer in return is boots. For the shoemaker, accordingly, all products that he needs for his life initially have the form of boots. If he needs bread, he first makes a pair of boots; if he needs a shirt, he makes boots; if he needs a hat or a cigar, he makes boots. In his special labor, the whole social wealth accessible to him has the form of boots. It is only by exchange on the commodity market that his work can be transformed from the confined form of boots into the diverse form of means of subsistence. But in order for this transformation to actually take place, for all this diligent work of the shoemaker, which promised him every kind of life's enjoyments, not to be stuck in the form of boots, one important condition is needed, which we already know: it is necessary for all the other producers, the product of whose labor our shoemaker needs, also to need his boots and be ready to take them in exchange. The shoemaker then only obtained all these other commodities if his product, boots, was a commodity desired by all other producers. And at any particular time he only obtained the quantity of all these other commodities that he could exchange by way of his labor, if his boots were a commodity that everyone wanted at any time, i.e. a commodity desired without limit. Already in the case of the shoemaker, it was obviously quite a presumption, and unfounded optimism, to believe that his special commodity was so absolutely and unrestrictedly something indispensable for the human race. But the matter gets much worse when not just the shoemaker, but all other particular producers, find themselves in the same position: the baker, the locksmith, the weaver, the butcher, the hatter, the farmer, etc. Each of them desires and uses the most varied products, but can only offer one single product in exchange. Each then could only fully satisfy his needs if his special commodity were constantly desired by everyone in society and taken in exchange. A brief reflection will tell you that this is pure impossibility. It is impossible for everyone to want all products equally at all times. It is impossible for everyone at all times, without limit, to be a taker of boots, bread, clothes, locks, yarn, shirts, hats and beard-covers. But if this is not the case, then these products cannot all be exchanged at any time against all others. And if exchange is not possible as a constant all-round relationship, this means that the satisfaction of all needs in society is impossible, consequently that all-round labor in society is impossible, the very existence of society is impossible. And we are again in a fix, and cannot solve the task we have set ourselves, i.e. to explain how, from the divided and fragmented private producers, who are not bound together by any social plan of labor, any organization, any tie, a social collaboration and an economy can none the less come into being. Exchange has indeed shown itself to be a means able to regulate all this, even if in strange ways. But for this to happen, exchange itself has to happen, it must function as a regular mechanism. We find already in exchange itself, however, at the very first step, such difficulties that we can not see at all how it is to develop into an all-round and permanent business.

Yet the means for overcoming this difficulty and facilitating social exchange have been found. True, it was no Columbus who discovered this, social experience and habit unnoticeably found the means in exchange itself; "life itself," as people say, solved the problem. As indeed, social life, along with all its difficulties, always does create the means for their solution.* It is clearly impossible for all commodities to be wanted by everyone all the time, i.e. to an unlimited extent. But at any time, and in any society, there is *one* commodity that is important, necessary and useful to everyone as a foundation of their existence, and is therefore wanted at any time. Boots could hardly be this commodity, people are not that vain. But cattle, for example, could be such a product. It is impossible to get by just with boots, nor even with clothes, hats or corn. But cattle as a foundation of economic life do secure a society's existence: they supply meat, milk, hides, plowing service, etc. Among many nomadic peoples, indeed, their whole wealth consists of herds of cattle. Still today, or at least until recently, there were African tribes that lived almost exclusively from cattle. Let us assume, then, that in our community cattle are a much-desired item of wealth, not the only one, but one preferred over many other products that are produced in society. The cattle-raiser here spends his private labor on the production of cattle, just as the shoemaker does on boots, the weaver on linen, etc. On our assumption, however, the product of the cattle-raiser enjoys a general unlimited popularity above all others, as it appears the most indispensable and important. Cattle are a welcome enrichment for anyone. Since we still assume that in our society nothing can be obtained by anyone except by way of exchange, it is clear that the much-desired cattle can also only be obtained from the cattle-raiser by exchange for another product of labor. But since, as presupposed, everyone would like to have cattle, this means that anyone would be happy at any time to part with his products against cattle. For cattle, conversely, it follows that at any time one can have any kind of product. Anyone who has cattle has only to choose, since everything is

---

* Luxemburg is here paraphrasing Marx's comment in the Preface to his *Contribution to the Critique of Political Economy* of 1859: "Mankind thus inevitably sets itself only such tasks as it is able to solve, since closer examination will always show that the problem itself arises only when the material conditions for its solution are already present or at least in the course of formation." See *Marx-Engels Collected Works*, Vol. 29 (New York: International Publishers, 1987), p. 263.

available for him. And it is precisely for this reason, conversely, that everyone is happier to exchange the particular product of his labor against cattle than anything else; if he has cattle, then he has everything, since everything is obtainable at any time in exchange for cattle. If after a while this has become generally clear, and become a custom, cattle then gradually become the universal commodity, i.e. the single commodity that is universally desired and exchangeable without limit. And as such a universal commodity, cattle mediate exchange between all other special commodities. The shoemaker is unwilling to directly accept bread from the baker in exchange for his boots, but he will accept cattle, as with cattle he can then buy bread and all possible things, whenever he wants. The baker, for his part, can pay for his boots in cattle, as he has received cattle in return for his own product, bread, as he also has from the locksmith, the stock-raiser and the butcher. Each of these accepts cattle from others for their own product, and pays again with the same cattle if he wants to have the products of others. The cattle thus pass from one hand to another, mediating every exchange and serving as the mental tie between the individual commodity producers. (And the more, and more frequently, cattle pass from one person to another as the mediator of business exchange, the more their universal unlimited desirability is reinforced, the more they become the only commodity desired and exchangeable at any time, the universal commodity.)

We have already seen how each product of labor, in a society of fragmented private producers without a communal plan of work, is initially private labor. Whether this labor was socially necessary, i.e. whether its produce has a value and secures the producer a share in the products of the whole, whether it was not rather wasted labor, all this is shown simply and solely by the fact that this product is accepted in exchange. Now, however, all products are exchanged only against cattle. Now, therefore, a product is socially necessary only in so far as it can be exchanged against cattle. Its exchangeability against cattle, its equivalence in value with cattle, is what now gives each private product the hallmark of socially necessary labor. We have further seen that it is only through commodity exchange that the individualized, isolated private person is confirmed as a member of society. We must now say more precisely that this is through exchange against cattle. Cattle are now the valid embodiment of social labor, and accordingly the only social tie between people.

You will certainly begin to feel at this point that we have rather got carried away. Everything was fairly straightforward and comprehensible up till now. But to conclude with cattle being the universal commodity, cattle as the embodiment of social labor, even cattle as the only social tie between people—isn't this a crazy fantasy, even an insult to the human race? And yet, if you think about it, there is no need to feel insulted. For no matter how superior you might feel to these poor cattle, it is clear at all events that they are much closer to humans—rather similar in a way, at least much more similar—than, let us say, a lump of earth picked up from the ground or a pebble or a piece of iron. You must admit that cattle are certainly more worthy of representing the living social tie between people than is a dead piece of metal. And yet humanity has precisely given preference here to metal. For the important role of cattle in exchange that we described above is in fact played by nothing other than *money*. If you cannot imagine money in any other way than in the form of coined gold or silver pieces, or even in paper banknotes, and you find this metal or paper money to be completely self-evident as the universal mediator in dealings between people, as a social power, but find my depiction of cattle playing this role absurd, this only shows how full your head is with the ideas of the present-day capitalist world.[94] A picture of social relations that is actually fairly reasonable strikes you as hare-brained, while you see as self-evident something that really is completely crazy. In actual fact, money in the form of cattle has exactly the same function as metallic money, and it is nothing more than convenience that has led us to make money out of metal. Cattle, of course, cannot be so easily exchanged, or their value so precisely measured, as can equal-sized metal discs, not to mention that storage of cattle-money requires far too big a purse, something like a stable. But before humanity hit on the idea of making money from metal, money had already long been the essential mediator of exchange. For money, the universal commodity, is precisely the indispensable means without which no universal exchange can get off the ground, without which the existing unplanned social economy of individual producers cannot exist.

We need only look now at the multifarious role of cattle in exchange. What made cattle into money in the society we were examining? The fact that they were a product of labor that was desired by everyone and at all times. But why were cattle desired in this way? We said that it was because they were an extremely useful product that could secure human existence as a many-sided means of subsistence. That was originally correct. But subsequently, the more that cattle were used as mediator in universal exchange, the more the immediate use of cattle as means of subsistence fell into the background. Anyone who receives cattle in exchange for their product will now make sure not to butcher them and eat them, nor to yoke them to the plough; cattle are more valuable to him now as a means for buying any other commodity he might want at any time. The receiver of cattle will therefore not now consume them as means of subsistence, but rather store them as means of exchange for future transactions. You will also note that the immediate use of cattle, in the context of the highly developed division of labor that we presuppose in this society, is also not easily feasible. What is the shoemaker, for example, to do with these cattle? Or the locksmith, the weaver and the hatter, who likewise do not have any land-holding? The immediate use of cattle as means of subsistence is therefore increasingly ignored, and the reason why cattle are then desired by everyone at all times is no longer because they can be milked, butchered, or yoked to the plough, but rather because they offer the possibility at any time of exchange for any commodity you like. It increasingly becomes the mission of cattle, their specific use, to facilitate exchange, i.e. to serve for the transformation at any time of private products into social ones, of private labors into social labors. Since in this way the private use of cattle, that of serving as means of subsistence, is increasingly ignored and they are instead devoted exclusively to their function of continuous mediation between the individual members of society, they gradually cease to be a private product like any other, and become from the start, by nature—right from the stable, as it were—a social product, and the labor of the cattle-raiser is now distinct from all other labor in society in being the only directly social labor. Cattle now are no longer raised just for their use as means of subsistence, but directly with the object of functioning as a social product, as the universal commodity. Of course, to some extent cattle are still butchered or yoked to the plough. But this so-to-speak private use and private character increasingly vanishes in the face of their public character as money. And as such, they now play a prominent and many-sided role in the life of society.

1) They definitively become the universal and publicly recognized *means of exchange*. No one any longer exchanges boots for bread, or shirts for horse-shoes. Anyone who tried this would be met with a shrug of the shoulders. It is only for cattle that anything can be bought. But in this way, the previous two-way exchange breaks down into two separate processes: selling and buying. Previously, when the locksmith and the baker exchanged their products with one another, each simultaneously with a handshake sold his own commodity and bought that of the other. Buying and selling were a single business. Now, if the shoemaker sells his boots, all he obtains and accepts in return are cattle. He first of all sells his own product. Then, when he wants to buy something, *what* he buys, and indeed whether he buys at all, is entirely up to him. It is enough that the shoemaker has got rid of his product, and transformed his labor from the form of boots into the form of cattle. The cattle-form, however, is as we have seen the official social form of labor, and the shoemaker can store labor in this form as long as he wants, as he knows that he has the opportunity at any time of exchanging the product of his labor again from the cattle-form into any other he wants—i.e. of making a purchase.

2) In the same way, however, cattle are now the means for storing and accumulating wealth, they become a *treasury*. As long as the shoemaker exchanged his product directly for means of subsistence, he also worked only as much as he needed to in order to meet his daily needs. What use would it have been to him to build up stocks of boots, or even large stocks of bread, meat, shirts, hats, etc.? Objects of daily use are generally damaged by prolonged storage, or even made unusable. Now, however, the shoemaker can store the cattle he obtains for the products of his labor as a resource for the future. Now, accordingly, a sense of thrift is aroused in our tradesman, he seeks to sell as much as possible, but

makes sure not to spend again all the cattle he has received; on the contrary, he seeks to accumulate them, since cattle are now good for anything at any time, so he saves and stores them for the future, leaving the fruits of his labor to his children as an inheritance.

3) Cattle become at the same time also the *measure* of all *values* and labors. If the shoemaker wants to know what his pair of shoes will bring him in exchange, what his product is worth, he says to himself, for example: I get half a cow for each pair, my pair of boots is worth half a cow.

4) Finally, in this way cattle become the *concept of wealth*. Now people do not say, this or that person is rich because he has a great deal of corn, flocks, clothes, jewelery or servants, but rather: he has a good deal of cattle. People say, hats off to that man, he's "worth" ten thousand oxen. Or they say, poor fellow, he doesn't have any cattle!

As you see, with cattle having become the universal means of exchange, society can only think in the cattle-form. People always talk about cattle, they even dream about them. A literal worship and admiration of cattle develops. A girl is most easily married if her attraction is increased by a dowry of large herds of cattle, even if her wooer is not a mere swineherd, but a professor, an intellectual or a poet. Cattle are the very concept of good fortune. Poems are written about cattle and their miraculous power, crimes and murders are committed for the sake of cattle. And people repeat, shaking their heads, that "cattle rule the world." If you are not familiar with this proverb, you can translate it into Latin; the old Roman word *pecunia*, meaning money, stems from *pecus*, meaning cattle.[95]

3

Our earlier investigation of how relations in the communistic community would be reshaped after a sudden collapse of common property and commonly planned labor, seemed to you no more than purely theoretical rumination, wandering around in the clouds. In actual fact, this was nothing other than an abbreviated and simplified depiction of the historical rise of the commodity economy, its basic features strictly corresponding to historical truth.

Yet a few corrections now need to be made to this depiction.

1) The process that we described as a catastrophe that happened suddenly, destroying the communist society overnight and transforming it into a society of private producers, in reality happened over millennia. The idea of a transformation of this kind as a sudden and violent catastrophe is certainly not pure fantasy. This idea does correspond to reality, everywhere that primitive communist tribes come into contact with other peoples already at a high capitalist stage of development. We see cases like this with most discoveries and conquests of so-called savage and semi-civilized lands by Europeans: the discovery of America

by the Spanish, the conquest of India by the English and of the East Indies by the Dutch,* and the same with the seizures of the English, Dutch and Germans in Africa. In most of these cases, the sudden arrival of Europeans in these lands was accompanied by a catastrophe in the lives of the primitive peoples who inhabited them. What we have assumed as a process of twenty-four hours, often needs no more than a few decades. The conquest of territory by a European state, or the mere settlement of a few European trading colonies in these countries, very soon results in a violent abolition of common property in land, the break-up and fragmentation of landownership into private property, the confiscation of herds of cattle, the reversal of all traditional social relations—with the difference that the general result here is not, as we assumed, the transformation of the communistic community into a society of free private producers with commodity exchange. For the dissolved common property does not become the private property of local people, but rather the stolen goods of the European encroachers, and the indigenous people themselves, robbed of their old forms and means of existence, are made either into wage-slaves, or slaves pure and simple, of European merchants, if they are not just exterminated, as happens when neither of these two options is feasible. For primitive peoples in colonized territories, therefore, the transition from primitive communist conditions to modern capitalist ones always does take place as a sudden catastrophe, an unforeseeable misfortune with the most frightful sufferings {as it is presently true of the Germans with Negroes of South West Africa}.† With the peoples of Europe, on the other hand, it was not a catastrophe but rather a slow, gradual and unnoticeable process, lasting for several hundred years. The Greeks and Romans still appear in history with common property. The old Germans, who spread from north to south soon after the birth of Christ, destroying the Roman Empire and settling in Europe, still brought with them the communistic primitive community, and maintained this for a good while. The developed commodity economy of the European peoples, as we described it, only came into being at the end of the Middle Ages, in the fifteen and sixteenth centuries.

---

    *   Luxemburg wrongly reversed the roles of the English and Dutch here.

    †   The bracketed expression, which was crossed out in the manuscript, does not appear in either the original 1925 edition of the *Introduction to Political Economy* (edited by Paul Levi) or in the edition contained in the German-language *Collected Works* (*Gesammelte Werke*, Band 5 [Berlin: Dietz Verlag, 1990]). On numerous occasions Luxemburg spoke out against Germany's genocide against the Herero and Nama peoples of modern-day Namibia from 1904–08. See especially *The Crisis in German Social Democracy* (1915): "The 'civilized world' that has stood calmly by when this same imperialism doomed tens of thousands of Hereros to destruction; when the desert of the Kalahari shuddered with the insane cry of the thirsty and the rattling breath of the dying..." See *The Rosa Luxemburg Reader*, p. 339. The German general who organized the genocide, Lothar von Trotha, later became an important mentor to the young Adolf Hitler. The German government did not officially accept responsibility for this genocide—which slaughtered at least 80 percent of the Herero people—until August 2004.

2) The second correction that has to be made to our depiction is a consequence of the first. We assumed that all possible branches of labor were already specialized and separate in the womb of the communist community, i.e. that the division of labor in society had reached a very high stage of development, so that with the occurrence of the catastrophe that abolished common property and introduced private production and exchange, the division of labor was already in place as the basis for such exchange. This assumption is historically incorrect. In the conditions of primitive society, so long as common property persists, the division of labor is very little developed, still embryonic. We have seen this in the example of the Indian village community. Only a dozen or so individuals had separated out from the mass of inhabitants to concentrate on special trades, no more than six of these being actual artisans: the smith, the carpenter, the potter, the barber, the washerman and the silversmith. Most handicraft work, such as spinning, weaving, making clothes, baking, butchery, sausage-making, etc., was all carried out by each family as a side occupation along with their main agricultural work, as is still the case even today in many Russian villages, in so far as the population have not already been drawn into exchange and trade. The division of labor, i.e. the separation of individual branches of labor as exclusive special professions, can only properly develop if private property and exchange are already in place. Only private property and exchange make possible the emergence of particular special trades. For only when a producer has the prospect of regularly exchanging his products against others does it make sense for him to devote himself to specialized production. And it is only money that gives each producer the possibility of storing and accumulating the fruits of his efforts, and accordingly also the impetus to regularly expand production for the market. On the other hand, however, this producing for the market and accumulation of money only has a purpose for the producer if his product and the receipts from it are his private property. In the primitive communist community, however, private property is precisely ruled out, and history shows us that private property only arose as a result of exchange and the specialization of labor. It turns out, therefore, that the emergence of specialist professions, i.e. a highly developed division of labor, is possible only with private property and developed exchange. It is conversely clear, however, that exchange itself is possible only if the division of labor is already present; for what purpose would there be in exchange among producers who all produce one and the same thing? Only if X for example only produces boots, whereas Y only bakes bread, is there a sense and purpose in the two exchanging their products. We thus come up against a strange contradiction: exchange is only possible with private property and a developed division of labor, but this division of labor can only come about as a result of exchange and on the basis of private property, while private property for its part only arises through exchange. This is even a double contradiction, if you examine it closely: the division of labor must exist prior to

exchange, even though exchange must at the same time exist prior to the division of labor; moreover, private property is the precondition for the division of labor and exchange, but the only way it can develop is from the division of labor and exchange. How is this tangle possible? We are clearly going round in a circle, and even the first step away from the primitive communist community seems an impossibility. Human society was apparently caught in a contradiction here, whose resolution depended on the further advance of development. But this inescapability is only apparent. A contradiction may well be something inextricable for individuals in everyday life, but in the life of society as a whole, you find contradictions of this kind everywhere you look. What today appears as the cause of a particular phenomenon is tomorrow its effect, and vice versa, without this continuous change in conditions of social life ever ceasing. On the contrary. The individual person cannot take a step further when he faces a contradiction in his private life. He will even accept in matters of everyday life that contradiction is something impossible—so that an accused person who gets tangled up in contradictions when he appears in court is thereby already found guilty of untruth, and in certain circumstances contradictions can lead him into prison or even to the gallows. But human society as a whole develops continuously in contradictions, and rather than succumbing to these, it only starts to move when it meets contradictions. Contradiction in the life of society, in other words, is always resolved by development, in new advances of culture. The great philosopher [G.W.F.] Hegel said: "Contradiction is the very moving principle of the world."* And this movement in the thick of contradictions is precisely the actual mode of development of human society. In the particular case we are concerned with here, i.e. the transition from communist society to private property with the division of labor and exchange, the contradiction that we found is also resolved in a particular development, a long historical process. But this process was essentially just as we originally depicted it, apart from the corrections we have just made.

Exchange initially begins already in primitive conditions with common property, and indeed, as we have assumed, in the form of barter, i.e. product for product. We already find barter at very early stages of human culture. Since exchange as we have depicted it, however, assumes the private property of both parties involved, and this is unknown within the primitive community, this early barter does not occur within the community or tribe but rather outside, not between the members of one and the same tribe, one and the same community, but rather between different tribes and communities when they come into contact with one another. And here it is not an individual member of one tribe who trades with someone from another tribe, but rather tribes and communities

---

* *Hegel's Logic: Being Part One of the Encyclopedia of the Philosophical Sciences,* translated by William Wallace (Oxford: The Clarendon Press, 1975), para. 119, *Zusatz,* p. 174. This is one of a very few direct references to a text by Hegel in Luxemburg's writings.

as a whole that enter into barter, represented always by their chiefs. The wide-spread idea held by scholars of political economy of a primitive hunter and fisherman who exchange their respective fish and game with one another in the first dawn of human culture in the primeval forests of America, is a double his-torical delusion. Not only were there in primitive times, as we saw, no isolated individuals living and working for themselves, but barter between individuals emerged only thousands of years later. Initially, history knows only tribes and peoples bartering with one another. As [Joseph François] Lafitau wrote in his book on the American savages,

> Savage peoples constantly pursue exchange. Their trade has in common with the trade of antiquity that it represents an immediate exchange of products against prod-ucts. Each of these peoples possesses something that the others do not, and trade conveys all these things from one people to the other. This includes corn, pottery, hides, tobacco, covers, canoes, cattle, household equipment, amulets, cotton—in a word, everything used for the maintenance of human life ... Their trade is conducted by the chief of the tribe, who represents the whole people.[96]

Moreover, if we began our earlier depiction of exchange with a particular case—exchange between shoemaker and baker—and treated this as something accidental, this again corresponds strictly to historical truth. In the beginning, exchange between particular savage tribes and peoples were purely accidental and haphazard; it depended on chance encounters and contacts. This is why we see regular barter emerge most early among nomadic peoples, since it is these, by their frequent change of place, who came most frequently into contact with other peoples.[97] As long as exchange remains a matter of chance, it is only the surplus products, what remains after meeting a tribe's or community's own needs, that are offered in exchange for something else. Over time, however, the more frequently such chance exchange is repeated, the more it becomes a habit, then a rule, and gradually people start to produce directly for exchange. Tribes and peoples thus increasingly specialize in one or more particular branches of pro-duction, with the object of exchange. A division of labor develops between tribes and communities. In this connection, trade remains for a very long while pure barter, i.e. direct exchange of product for product. In many regions of the United States, barter was still widespread in the late eighteenth century. In Maryland, the legislative assembly laid down the proportions in which tobacco, oil, pork and bread were to be exchanged for one another. In Corrientes [Argentina], as late as 1815, peddler boys ran through the streets with the cry: "Salt for candles, tobacco for bread!" In Russian villages until the 1890s, and in some parts still today, traveling peddlers known as *prasols* conducted simple barter with peas-ants. All kinds of knickknacks, such as needles, thimbles, belts, buttons, pipes, soap, etc. were exchanged for bristles, quilts, hare pelts and the like. Potters, plumbers, etc. traveled through Russia with their carts, exchanging their products for corn, linen, hemp, etc.[98] With the frequency and regularity of exchange transactions, however, it was not long before, in each district and tribe, one commodity separated out that was easiest to produce, and so could most frequently be given in exchange, or alternatively one that was most lacking and so generally desired. Such a role was played for example by salt and dates in the Sahara desert, sugar in the English West Indies, tobacco in Virginia and Maryland, so-called brick tea (a hard mixture of tea leaves and fat in the form of a brick) in Siberia, ivory among the black Africans, cocoa beans in ancient Mexico. In this way, the climatic and soil conditions in various regions already led to the separating out of a "universal commodity" that was suited to serve as a basis for all trade and a mediator of all exchange transactions. The same occurred with subsequent development from the particular occupation of each tribe. Among hunting peoples, game was naturally the "universal commodity" that they offered for all possible products. In the trade of the Hudson Bay Company, it was beaver fat that played this role. Among fishing tribes, fish are the natural mediator of all exchange. According to the account of a French traveler, on the Shetland Islands change was given in fish even on the purchase of a theatre ticket.[99] The necessity of such a generally desired commodity as universal mediator of exchange often made itself very perceptible. The celebrated African traveler Samuel [White] Baker, for example, described his exchange with tribes in central Africa:

> The difficulties of procuring provisions are most serious: the only method of purchasing flour is as follows. The natives will not sell it for anything but flesh; to purchase an ox, I require molotes (hoes): to obtain molotes I must sell my clothes and shoes to the traders' men. The ox is then driven to a distant village, and is there slaughtered, and the flesh being divided into about a hundred small portions, my men sit upon the ground with three large baskets, into which are emptied minute baskets of flour as the natives produce them, one in exchange for each parcel of meat.[100]

With the transition to stock raising, cattle become the universal commodity in exchange and the universal measure of value. This was the case among the ancient Greeks, as Homer describes it. In describing and valuing the armor of each hero, for example, he says that the armor of Glaucus was worth a hundred head of cattle and that of Diomedes nine.* As well as cattle, however, other products also served as money among the Greeks of this time. Homer again says that during the siege of Troy, wine from Lemnos† was paid sometimes in hides,

---

* In Homer's *Illiad*, Glaucus was a captain of the Lycian army, which was allied to Troy. In the epic he meets Diomedes, one of the greatest warriors of the Greeks, in the field of battle, but instead of taking up Diomedes' offer to engage in combat, Glaucus puts down his weapons and declares his friendship. Diomedes reciprocates by taking off his armor, worth ten oxen, and gives it to Glaucus.

† Lemnos is a Greek island in the northern part of the Aegean Sea.

sometimes in oxen, sometimes in copper or iron. Among the early Romans, as we said, the concept of "money" was identical with that of cattle; among the ancient Germans, too, cattle were the universal commodity. It was with the transition to agriculture that metals, iron and copper, acquired a surpassing importance in economic life, partly as material for producing weapons, but still more so for agricultural implements. Metal became the universal commodity as it was produced and used in greater quantities, expelling cattle from this role. Initially it was the universal commodity precisely because it was universally useful and desired for its natural use—as material for all kinds of tools. At this stage, it was also used in trade as raw material, in bars and only by weight. Among the Greeks it was iron that was in general use, among the Romans it was copper, among the Chinese a mixture of copper and lead. Only much later did the so-called precious metals, silver and gold, come into use, and also into trade. But for a very long time these were still used in trade in their raw state, uncoined and by weight.[101] Here, accordingly, we can still see the origin of the universal commodity, the money commodity, from a simple product with a particular use. The simple piece of silver that is given one day in exchange for flour might still be used directly the next day to decorate a knight's shield. The exclusive use of precious metal as money, i.e. coined money, was known neither to the ancient Hindus nor to the Egyptians, nor again to the Chinese. The ancient Jews likewise used metal pieces only by weight. Abraham, for example, according to the Bible, when he bought a burial plot for Sarah in Hebron,* paid 400 shekels in weighed-out trading silver.† It is generally assumed that coinage only appeared in the tenth or even eighth century BC, being first introduced by the Greeks. The Romans learned from them, manufacturing their first silver and gold coins in the third century BC.[102] With the coining of money from gold and silver, the long, millennial history of the development of exchange reached its fullest, most complete and definitive form.

As we have said, money, i.e. the universal commodity, was already developed before metals began to be used for monetary purposes. And even in the form of cattle, for example, money has precisely the same functions in exchange as gold coins do today: as mediator of transactions, as measure of value, as store of value and as embodiment of wealth. In the form of metallic money, however, the specific characteristic of money is expressed also in its outward appearance. We saw how exchange begins with the simple barter of any two products of labor. It comes into being because one producer—one community or tribe—cannot

---

* See Genesis, 23:16: "Abraham closed the bargain with him and weighed out the amount that Ephron had named in the hearing of the Hittites, 400 shekels of the standard recognized by merchants." *The Revised English Bible* (Oxford: Cambridge University Press, 1989), p. 17.

† The *shekel* was used as the unit of currency by the ancient Hebrews. *Shekel* is actually an Akkadian word; it was first used as a standard of measure in the Sumerian civilization of ancient Mesopotamia, around 3,000 BC. It originally referred to an amount of barley.

do without products of the other's labor. They assist each other with the creations of their respective labor by exchanging these. As such exchanges become frequent and regular, *one* product emerges as especially preferred, because universally desired, and this becomes the mediator of all exchange transactions, the universal commodity. Any product of labor has the intrinsic ability to become money: boots or hats, linen or wool, cattle or corn, and we also see that the most varied commodities have at times played this role. *Which* commodity is chosen simply depends on the particular needs or particular occupations of the people in question.

Cattle are initially preferred in this way as a useful product and means of subsistence. With the passage of time, however, cattle are desired and accepted as money. Cattle then make it possible for anyone to accumulate the fruits of his labor in a form that is exchangeable at any time for any other product of society's labor. Cattle, we said, as distinct from all other private products, are the only directly social product, the only one that is unrestrictedly exchangeable at any time. But in cattle, the dual nature of the money commodity finds strong expression: a glance at cattle shows how, despite being the universal commodity and a social product, they are at the same time a simple means of subsistence that can be butchered and eaten, an ordinary product of human labor, the labor of herders. In the gold coin, however, any memory of the origin of money out of a simple product has already quite disappeared. The coined piece of gold is inherently unsuitable for anything else, it has no other use but to serve as means of exchange, as universal commodity. It is only still value in so far as it is, like any other commodity, the product of human labor, the labor of the gold-miner and goldsmith, but it has lost any private use as means of subsistence, it is precisely nothing but a piece of human labor without any useful and consumable form for private life, it no longer has any use as private means of subsistence, as food, clothing, ornament or anything else, its only purpose being its purely social use, to serve as mediator in the exchange of other commodities. And it is precisely for this reason that it appears in this meaningless and purposeless object: in the gold coin, the purely social character of money, the universal commodity, finds its purest and most mature expression.

The consequences of the definitive development of money in the metal form are: sharp increase in trade, and decline of all social relations that were preciously geared not to trade but to self-sufficiency.[103] The ancient communistic community was shattered by trade, as this accelerated the disparity of wealth among its members, the collapse of common property, and finally the breakdown of the community itself.[104]

The free small peasant economy, which initially produced everything for itself and only sold its surplus, to put money under the mattress, was gradually forced, particularly by the introduction of monetary taxation, to sell its entire product, in order to buy not only food, clothing and household articles, but even grain for sowing. We have seen an example of such a transformation of the peasant economy, from one producing for its own needs to one producing for the market and being ruined in the process, with the last few decades in Russia. In ancient slavery, trade brought about a profound change. So long as slaves were used only for the domestic economy, for agricultural or artisanal tasks for the needs of the master and his family, slavery still had a mild and traditional character. Inhuman treatment of slaves began only when the Greeks, and later the Romans, developed the taste for money and started producing for trade, leading eventually to mass revolts by the slaves,* which although completely unsuccessful, were heralds and clear signs that slavery had had its day and become unsustainable.[105] Precisely the same situation was presented by the *corvée* in the Middle Ages. Initially this was a relationship of protection, with the peasantry owing the protecting lord a definite moderate sum, either in kind or in labor services, towards the lord's own consumption. Later, when the nobles learned the conveniences of money, these services and dues were steadily increased for the purpose of trade, the *corvée* relationship became one of serfdom, and peasants were driven to the utmost limits. In the end, the same spread of trade and the dominance of money led to dues in kind being commuted from serfdom into monetary payments. But this meant that the bell had tolled for the entire outmoded *corvée* relationship.[106]

Finally, trade in the Middle Ages brought power and wealth for the free towns, but in this way also led to the break-up and decline of the old guild handicrafts. Very early on, the appearance of metallic money made world trade possible. Already in antiquity, certain peoples like the Phoenicians devoted themselves to the role of merchants between peoples, attracting large sums of money in this way and accumulating wealth in the money form. In the Middle Ages, this role fell to the free towns, initially the Italian ones. After the discovery of America and of the sea route to the East Indies, at the end of the fifteenth century, world trade experienced a sudden great expansion: the new lands offered not only new products for trade, but also new gold mines, i.e. the money material.[107] Following the enormous import of gold from America in the sixteenth century, the North German towns—above all the Hanseatic League†—acquired immense riches, and in their wake so did Holland and England. As a result, in the European towns and to a large extent also the countryside, commodity trade, i.e. production for exchange, became the prevailing form of economic life. Exchange thus has its quiet and unremarked beginnings in grey prehistory on the frontiers of

---

*   One of the most famous of these slave revolts was led by the Thracian slave Spartacus in 73 BC. Marx considered him one of his greatest heroes. Luxemburg later named her revolutionary tendency that opposed World War I and fought to promote social revolution in Germany, the *Spartakusbund*, after him.

†   The Hanseatic League was an alliance of trading cities that dominated the Baltic and Northern Europe between the thirteenth and seventeenth centuries.

savage communist tribes, grows and develops alongside all successive planned economic organizations, such as free simple peasant economy, Oriental despotism, antique slavery, the medieval *corvée* and the urban guild regime, consuming these one after the other and helping to bring about their collapse and finally the dominance of the completely anarchic, unplanned economy of isolated private producers as the sole and universally prevailing economic form.[108]

4[109]

Once commodity economy had become the prevailing form of production in Europe by the eighteenth century, at least in the towns, scholars began to study the question as to what was the foundation of this economy, i.e. of universal exchange. All exchange is mediated by money, and the value of every commodity in exchange has its monetary expression. What then does this monetary expression mean, and what is the basis of the value that each commodity has in trade? These were the first questions that political economy investigated. In the second half of the eighteenth and the early nineteenth century, the Englishmen Adam Smith and David Ricardo made the great discovery that the value of each commodity is nothing other than the human labor it contains, so that with the exchange of commodities equal quantities of different kinds of labor are exchanged for one another. Money is simply the mediator here, and simply expresses in the price the corresponding amount of labor contained in each commodity. It does indeed appear rather remarkable to speak of this as a great discovery, since one might believe that nothing was more clear and self-evident than that the exchange of commodities depends on the labor they contain. It is just that the expression of the commodity value in gold, which had become the general and exclusive custom, concealed this natural state of affairs. At the time when the shoemaker and the baker exchanged their respective products, as I said, it was still obvious and visible that exchange came into being because, despite their different uses, each of these took the same amount of labor as the other, and each was therefore worth the same as the other in so far as they both took the same amount of time. But if I say that a pair of shoes costs ten marks, this expression is at first quite puzzling when examined more closely. For what does a pair of shoes have in common with ten marks, in what way are they equal, so that they can be exchanged for one another? How can such different things be compared with one another at all? And how can such a useful product as shoes be exchanged for such a useless and meaningless object as stamped gold or silver discs? Finally, how does it come about that precisely these useless metal discs possess the magic power of obtaining anything in the world by way of exchange? *All* these questions, however, the great founders of political economy, Smith and Ricardo, did not manage to answer. For the discovery that what is contained in the exchange-value of every commodity, even money, is simply human labor, and that the value of a commodity is therefore that much greater, the more labor its production requires, and vice versa, is only a half-truth. The other half of the truth consists in the explanation of how and why it is that human labor then assumes the strange form of exchange-value, and the puzzling form of money at that. The English founders of political economy did not even raise this question, since they considered it an innate property of human labor, given in the nature of things, that it created commodities for exchange and money. In other words, they assumed it was just as natural as that people have to eat and drink, that hairs grow on the head and that the face has a nose, that they have to produce with their hands commodities for trade. They believed this so firmly that Adam Smith, for example, raised the question in all seriousness whether animals did not already conduct trade, and he only denied this because at that time no such examples had yet been found in the animal world. He says:*

This naïve conception, however, simply means that the great creators of political economy lived in the rock-solid conviction that the present capitalist social order, in which everything is a commodity and produced only for trade, is the only possible and eternal social order, which will endure as long as there are people on this earth. Only Karl Marx, who as a socialist did not take the capitalist order to be the eternal and only possible social form, but rather a passing historical one, made comparisons between present relations and earlier ones at other times. He showed in this way that people had lived for thousands of years without knowing much about money and exchange. Only to the extent that any common planned labor came to an end in society, and society dissolved into a loose anarchic heap of completely free and independent producers with private property, did exchange become the only means of uniting these fragmented individuals and their labors into an integrated social economy. In place of a common economic plan that precedes production, money now becomes the only direct social means of connection, which it does because it represents the only thing in common between the many different private labors as itself a piece of human labor without any particular use, i.e. precisely because it is a completely meaningless product, unsuited for any kind of use in human private life. This meaningless invention is thus a necessity without which no exchange would be possible, i.e. the entire history of culture since the dissolution of primitive communism. The bourgeois political economists of course viewed money also as extremely important and indispensable, but only from the standpoint of the purely external convenience of monetary exchange. This can actually be said of money only in the same sense that one can say that humanity has for example invented religion for the sake of convenience. Money and religion are certainly

---

    * The intended quotation is missing in the manuscript, and does not seem to be the substance of Smith's remarks. Cf. "Nobody ever saw one animal by its gestures and natural cries signify to another, this is mine, that yours; I am willing to give this for that" (*The Wealth of Nations*, Book 1, Chapter 2).

two powerful cultural products, but they have their roots in quite particular and transient conditions, and, just as they arose, so they will become superfluous in due course. The immense annual expenses on gold production, just as the expenses on religion, not to mention those on prisons, the military or public welfare, which are a heavy burden on today's social economy, but are necessary costs given the existence of this economic form, will disappear with the abolition of the commodity economy.

The commodity economy, as we have got to know its inner mechanism, appears before us as a wonderfully harmonious economic order, based on the highest principles of morality. Firstly, complete individual freedom prevails. Each person works as he likes, on what he likes and as much as he likes; each is his own master and need only be governed by his own preference. Secondly, they all exchange their commodities, i.e. the products of their labor, for the products of other people's labor; labor is exchanged against labor, and moreover, on average in equal quantities. So there is also complete equality and reciprocity of interests. Thirdly, in commodity economy commodity is exchanged for commodity, one product of labor for another. Anyone therefore who does not have a product of his labor to offer, anyone who does not work, will also not obtain anything to eat. Here too we have the highest justice. In fact, the philosophers and politicians of the eighteenth century, who fought for the complete triumph of freedom of trade and the abolition of the last vestiges of the old relations of domination—the guild regime and feudal serfdom[110]—the men of the Great French Revolution, promised humanity a paradise on earth, in which freedom, equality and fraternity would rule.

A number of leading socialists in the first half of the nineteenth century were still of the same opinion. When scientific political economy was created and Smith and Ricardo made the great discovery that all commodity values were based on human labor, some friends of the working class hit on the idea right away that if commodity exchange were conducted correctly, there would necessarily be complete equality and justice in society. If labor was always exchanged for labor in the same quantities, it would be impossible for inequality of wealth to develop, at most just the well-deserved inequality between hard workers and idlers, and the whole social wealth would belong to those who work, i.e. the working class. But if despite this we see great differences in people's conditions in present society, if we see wealth alongside poverty and what is more, wealth in the hands of non-workers and poverty for those who create all values by their labor, this must obviously arise from something wrong in the process of exchange, owing to the intervention of money as mediator in the exchange of the products of labor.[111] Money conceals the real origin of all wealth in labor, provokes constant fluctuations of price and thus gives the possibility of arbitrary prices, swindling, and the accumulation of wealth at the cost of others. So, away with money! This socialism aiming at the abolition of money originated in England, represented there as early as the 1820s and 30s by such talented writers as [William] Thompson, [John Francis] Bray and others. The same kind of socialism was then rediscovered by [Johann Karl] Rodbertus, in a Prussia of conservative Pomeranian Junkers* and brilliant writers on political economy; and finally by Proudhon in France in 1849. Practical attempts in this direction were also undertaken. Under the influence of the above-mentioned Bray, so-called "bazaars" for "equitable labor exchange" were established in many English towns, to which goods were brought to be exchanged without the intervention of money, strictly in accordance with the labor-time they contained. Proudhon also proposed the foundation of a so-called "people's bank." But these attempts rapidly went bankrupt, along with the theory behind them. Commodity exchange without money is in fact inconceivable, and the price fluctuations that these people wanted to abolish are in fact the only means for indicating to commodity producers whether they are making too little of a particular commodity or too much, whether they are spending more or less labor on its production than it requires, whether they are producing the right commodities or not. If this sole means of communication between the isolated commodity producers in the anarchic economy is abolished, they are completely lost, being not only struck dumb, but blind into the bargain. Production necessarily comes to a standstill, and the capitalist tower of Babel shatters into ruins. The socialist plans for making capitalist commodity production into socialist simply by the abolition of money were thus pure utopia.

How do things really stand then in commodity production, as far as freedom, equality and fraternity are concerned? How can inequality of wealth arise in the context of general commodity production, where it is only for a product of labor that anyone can get anything, and where equal values can only be exchanged for equal values? Yet present capitalist society is precisely characterized, as everyone knows, by a glaring inequality in people's material condition, by tremendous accumulation of wealth in a few hands on the one side, and growing poverty for the mass of people on the other. The subsequent question that logically arises for us from all this is: *How is capitalism possible in a commodity economy, given that commodities are exchanged according to their value?*

IV. WAGE-LABOR

All commodities exchange against one another according to their value, i.e. according to the socially necessary labor they contain. The fact that money plays the role of mediator does not in any way change this basis of exchange: money itself is simply the bare expression of social labor, and the amount of value contained in each commodity is expressed in the amount of money for

---

* The Junkers were members of the landed nobility of Prussia.

which the commodity is sold. On the basis of this law of value, complete equality prevails between commodities on the market. And there would also be complete equality among the sellers of commodities, if there were not, among the millions of different kinds of goods coming onto the market for exchange, one particular commodity of a quite special character—labor-power. This commodity is brought to market by those who possess no means of production of their own with which to produce other commodities. In a society based exclusively on commodity exchange, nothing is obtained, as we know, except by way of exchange. We have indeed seen how the commodity that each person brings to market is this person's unique claim and title to a share in the mass of social products, and at the same time the measure of this share. Each person obtains, in whatever commodities he chooses, exactly the same amount of the mass of labor performed in society as he himself supplies in socially necessary labor in the form of any kind of commodity. To be able to live, therefore, each person must supply and sell commodities. Commodity production and sale has become the condition for human existence. Anyone who does not bring a commodity to market does not receive any means of subsistence. But the production of any kind of commodity requires means of labor, i.e. tools and the like, as well as raw and ancillary materials, not to mention a place of work, equipped with the necessary conditions of labor such as lighting, etc., and finally a certain quantum of means of subsistence, to keep life going until the process of production has been completed and the commodity is sold. Only a few insignificant commodities can be produced without an outlay on means of production: for example, mushrooms and berries that grow in the forest, or shellfish collected on the shore by inhabitants of the coast. But even here, certain means of production are always necessary, such as baskets and the like, as well as means of subsistence that make life possible during this labor. Most kinds of commodity, however, in any society with developed commodity production, require a quite significant outlay on means of production, sometimes a tremendous one. Anyone without such means of production, who is thus not in a position to produce commodities, has nothing for it but to bring himself to market as a commodity, i.e. to bring his own labor-power.

Like any other commodity, the commodity labor-power also has its definite value. The value of any commodity, as we know, is determined by the amount of labor required for its production. In order to produce the commodity labor-power, a particular amount of labor is likewise necessary, i.e. the labor that produces the requisites of life for the worker, food and clothing, etc. Whatever labor therefore is required in order to keep a person capable of labor, to maintain his labor-power, is also what his labor-power is worth. The value of the commodity labor-power, therefore, is represented by the amount of labor that is needed to produce the worker's means of subsistence. Moreover, as with every other commodity, the value of labor-power is measured on the market in terms of price, i.e. in money. The monetary expression, i.e. the price of the commodity labor-power, is called the wage. With every other commodity, the price rises when demand grows more quickly than supply, and conversely falls when the supply of the commodity is greater than demand. The same also holds for the commodity labor-power: with rising demand for workers, wages show a general tendency to rise, and if the demand falls or the labor-market is overfilled with fresh commodity, wages show a tendency to fall. Finally, as with every other commodity, the value of labor-power, and along with it ultimately its price as well, is higher if a greater amount of labor is required for its production: in this case, if the worker's means of subsistence require more labor for their production. And conversely, every saving on the labor required to produce the worker's means of subsistence leads to a reduction in the value of labor-power, and thus also in its price, i.e. in wages. As David Ricardo wrote in 1817:

> Diminish the cost of production of hats, and their price will ultimately fall to their new natural price, although the demand should be doubled, trebled, or quadrupled. Diminish the cost of subsistence of men, by diminishing the natural price of the food and clothing, by which life is sustained, and wages will ultimately fall, notwithstanding that the demand for laborers may very greatly increase.*

The only way, therefore, in which the commodity labor-power is initially distinguished from other commodities on the market is that it is inseparable from its seller, the worker, so that it cannot tolerate any long wait for buyers, otherwise it will disappear along with its bearer, the worker, for lack of means of subsistence, whereas most other commodities can tolerate a more or less long waiting-time quite well. The particularity of the commodity labor-power is thus not yet expressed on the market, where it is only exchange-value that plays a role. It lies elsewhere—in the use-value of this commodity. Every commodity is bought on account of the utility that its consumption can bring. Boots are bought in order to serve as clothing for the feet; a cup is bought so that tea can be drunk from it. What use then can labor-power serve when purchased? Obviously, that of laboring. But this scarcely says anything yet. People at every time could and had to work, ever since the human race existed, and yet whole millennia passed in which labor-power was completely unknown as a purchasable commodity. On the other hand, if we imagine that a person, with his full labor-power, was only in a position to produce the means of subsistence that he himself needed, then the purchase of such labor-power, i.e. of labor-power as a commodity, would be quite senseless. For if someone buys and pays for labor-power, puts it to work with his own means of production, and only obtains at the end of the day the

---

* David Ricardo, *Principles of Political Economy and Taxation* (London: John Murray, 1817), Chapter 23.

maintenance of the bearer of his purchased commodity, the worker, this means that the worker by selling his labor-power only obtains someone else's means of production in order to work with these for himself. From the standpoint of commodity exchange this would be a senseless deal, just as if someone were to buy boots simply to return them to the shoemaker as a present. If this were the only use of human labor-power, it would have no utility for the purchaser and accordingly could not appear on the market as a commodity. For only products with a definite utility can figure as commodities. If labor-power appears as a commodity, therefore, it is not enough that the person concerned can work, if he is given means of production, but rather that he can work more than is needed for the production of his own means of subsistence. He must be able to work not only to support himself, but also work for the buyer of his labor-power. The commodity labor-power, therefore, in its use, i.e. in labor, must not simply be able to replace its own price, i.e. the wage, but on top of this also supply surplus labor for the purchaser. And indeed, the commodity labor-power does have this convenient property. But what does this mean? Is it a kind of natural property of man, or of the worker, that he can perform surplus labor? At the time when it took people a year to make an axe out of stone, or hours rubbing two sticks of wood together to make a fire, when it took several months to make a single bow, even the cleverest and most unscrupulous entrepreneur would have been unable to press any surplus labor out of anyone. A certain level of productivity of human labor is therefore required in order for any surplus-labor at all to be provided. In other words, human tools, skills and knowledge, human domination over natural forces, must already have reached a certain level, not simply to be able to produce means of subsistence for the worker himself, but on top of this also to produce for others. This perfection of tools and knowledge, however, this degree of mastery of nature, was only acquired by human society through long millennia of painful experience. The distance from the first crude stone instruments and the discovery of fire through to today's steam and electrical machinery, represents humanity's whole course of social development, a development that was possible only within society, by people's social coexistence and collaboration. The productivity of labor, therefore, that endows the labor-power of the present-day wage-laborer with the convenient property of performing surplus labor, is not a physiological particularity of the human being, something given by nature, but rather a *social phenomenon*, the fruit of a long developmental history. The surplus labor of the commodity labor-power is simply another expression for the productivity of social labor, which manages to maintain several people from the labor of one.

The productivity of labor, however, particularly where it is assisted even at a primitive cultural level by fortunate natural conditions, does not always and everywhere lead to the sale of labor-power and its capitalist exploitation. Let us transport ourselves for a moment to those favored tropical regions of Central and South America that were Spanish colonies from the discovery of the New World until the early nineteenth century, and where bananas are the main food of the native population. "I doubt whether there is another plant on the globe which on so small a space of ground can produce so considerable a mass of nutritive substance," wrote Alexander von Humboldt:

> According to this last principle, and the fact is very curious, we find that in a very fertile country a demi hectare ... cultivated with bananas of the large species (*platano arton*), is capable of maintaining fifty individuals; when the same in Europe would only yield annually, supposing the eight-grain, 576 kilograms of flour, a quantity not equal to the subsistence of two individuals.*

Besides, bananas require for their production only the slightest human effort, needing only one or two light rakings of the earth around their roots. "At the foot of the Cordillera, in the humid valleys of the intendancies of Vera Cruz, Valladolid, and Guadalajara, a man who merely employs two days in the week in a work by no means laborious may procure subsistence for a whole family."†

It is clear that the productivity of labor here would certainly permit exploitation, and a scholar with a true capitalist soul, such as [Thomas] Malthus, could exclaim in tears at the description of this earthly paradise: "What immense powers for production are here described! What resources for unbounded wealth...!"[112] In other words, how splendidly gold could be beaten out of the work of the banana-eaters by zealous entrepreneurs, if these lazy-bones could only be harnessed to labor. But what do we actually see? The inhabitants of these favored regions did not think of accumulating money, but simply examined the banana trees, tasted their respective fruit, and spent a lot of free time lying in the sun and enjoying life. Humboldt says very pertinently of them:

> We hear it frequently repeated in the Spanish colonies, that the inhabitants of the warm region (*tierra caliente*) will never awake from the state of apathy in which for centuries they have been plunged, until a royal *cedula*‡ shall order the destruction of the banana plantations (*plantanares*).§

What from the capitalist standpoint is described as "apathy" is precisely the mental state of all peoples still living in relations of primitive communism, in

---

* A. Von Humboldt, *Versuch über den politischen Zustand des Königreichs Neu-Spanien*, Vol. 3 (Tübingen: J. G. Cotta, 1812), pp. 17–18; Alexander von Humboldt, *Political Essay on the Kingdom of New Spain*, translated by John Black (London: Longman, 1811), pp. 420, 426.

† Ibid., p. 22; English trans., p. 429.

‡ A royal *cedula* was an edict issued by the King of Spain.

§ Alexander Von Humboldt, *Versuch über den politischen Zustand des Königreichs Neu-Spanien*, pp. 23–4; *Political Essay on the Kingdom of New Spain*, p. 428.

which the purpose of human labor is simply to satisfy people's natural needs, and not the accumulation of wealth. But so long as these conditions prevail, then no matter how productive labor is, there can be no question of the exploitation of one person by another, the application of human labor-power for the production of surplus labor.

The modern entrepreneur, however, was not the first to discover this convenient property of human labor-power. We already see the exploitation of surplus labor by non-workers in ancient times. Slavery in antiquity, as well as the *corvée* relationship and serfdom in the Middle Ages, were both based on a level of productivity already attained, i.e. the capacity of human labor to maintain more than one person. Both are also simply different forms in which one class of society made use of this productivity in order to have itself maintained by another class. In this sense, the antique slave and the medieval serf are direct forerunners of today's wage-laborer. But neither in antiquity nor the Middle Ages did labor-power become a commodity, despite its productivity and despite its exploitation. What is particular in the present-day relationship between wage-laborer and entrepreneur, what distinguishes it from both slavery and serfdom, is above all the personal freedom of the laborer. The sale of commodities is the voluntary and private business of each person, based on complete individual freedom. An unfree person cannot sell his labor-power. A further condition for this, however, is that the worker possesses no means of production. If he did, he would produce commodities himself and not part with his labor-power as a commodity. The separation of labor-power from the means of production, accordingly, is another factor along with personal freedom that makes labor-power today a commodity. In the slave economy, labor-power is not separated from the means of production; on the contrary, it is itself a means of production and belongs together with tools, raw materials, etc. to the master as his private property. The slave is simply part of the indistinguishable mass of the slaveholder's means of production. In *corvée* labor, labor-power is legally tied directly to the means of production, to the soil, it is itself simply an accessory to the means of production. *Corvée* services and dues are not in fact the responsibility of individuals but of the plot of land; if the land is transferred to other hands, by inheritance or likewise, the dues go along with it. Today the worker is personally free, he is neither anyone's property nor is he tied to the means of production. On the contrary, the means of production belong to one person, labor-power to another, and the two owners face each other as independent and free, as buyer and seller—the capitalist as buyer of labor-power, the worker as its seller. Finally, however, neither personal freedom nor the separation of labor-power from the means of production always lead to wage-labor, to the sale of labor-power, even at a high level of labor productivity. We saw an example of this kind in ancient Rome, after the great mass of free small peasants were driven from their lands by the formation of large noble estates with a slave economy. They remained personally free, but no longer had any land, any means of production, so that they moved massively from the countryside to Rome as free proletarians. Here, however, they could not sell their labor-power, as there were no buyers to be had; the rich landowners and capitalists did not need to buy free labor-power, being maintained by the work of slaves. Slave labor at that time was completely sufficient to satisfy all the landowners' needs, as they had everything possible made by slaves. But labor-power could not be used for more than their own living and luxury, the very purpose of slave production being the owner's consumption rather than the sale of commodities. In this way, the Roman proletarians were excluded from all sources of wealth deriving from their own labor, and there was nothing left for them but to live from beggary—beggary from the state, from periodic distributions of means of subsistence. Instead of wage-labor, accordingly, what arose in ancient Rome was the mass feeding of property-less free people at the cost of the state, which led the French economist [Jean Charles Léonard de Sismondi] to say that in ancient Rome the proletariat lived at the expense of society, whereas today society lives at the expense of the proletariat.* But if today it is possible for proletarians to work for both their own consumption and that of others, if the sale of their labor-power is possible, this is because today free labor is the *sole* and exclusive form of production, and because as commodity production it is precisely not geared to direct consumption, but rather to the creation of products for sale. The slaveholder bought slaves for his own comfort and luxury, the feudal lord extracted services and dues from the *corvée* peasants for the same purpose: to live literally like a lord, along with his clan. The modern entrepreneur does not get workers to produce objects of food, clothing and luxury for his own consumption, but rather commodities for sale, in order to obtain money. And it is precisely this that makes him a capitalist, just as it makes the workers into wage-laborers.

We see, then, how the simple fact of the sale of labor-power as a commodity implies a whole series of particular social and historical relations. The mere appearance of labor-power as a commodity on the market indicates: 1) the personal freedom of the workers; 2) their separation from the means of production along with the accumulation of means of production in the hands of non-workers; 3) a high level of productivity of labor, thus the possibility of performing surplus labor; 4) the general prevalence of commodity economy, i.e. the creation of surplus labor in the commodity form as the purpose of the purchase of labor-power.

---

* Marx made a very similar statement in his 1869 "Preface to the Second Edition of *The Eighteenth Brumaire of Louis Bonaparte*": "People forget Sismondi's significant saying: The Roman proletariat lived at the expense of society, while modern society lives at the expense of the proletariat." *Marx-Engels Collected Works*, Vol. 21 (New York: International Publishers, 1985), p. 57. See Jean Charles Léonard Simonde de Sismondi, *Études sur l'économique politique*, Vol. 1 (Paris: Treuttel et Würtz, 1837), p. 24

Externally, from the standpoint of the market, the sale and purchase of the commodity labor-power is a completely ordinary business, one of thousands that take place every moment, like the purchase of boots or onions. The value of the commodity and its alterations, its fluctuating price, the equality and independence of buyer and seller on the market, the voluntary character of the deal—all this is exactly as with any other transaction. But owing to the particular use-value of this commodity, the particular conditions that create it as a use-value, this everyday market transaction becomes a new and quite particular social relation. Let us examine more closely what this market transaction leads to.

2

The entrepreneur buys labor-power and like any purchaser pays its value, i.e. its production costs, by paying the worker as his wage a price that covers the worker's maintenance. But this purchased labor-power is capable, with the average means of production used in society, to produce more than simply its own maintenance costs. This is already, as we know, a precondition of the whole business, which would otherwise be senseless; it is precisely here that the use-value of the commodity labor-power lies. Since the value of maintaining labor-power is determined, as with any other commodity, by the amount of labor required for its production, we can assume that the food, clothing, etc. that are needed for the daily maintenance of the worker in a condition capable of labor require, let us say for example, six hours' labor. The price of the commodity labor-power, i.e. its wage, must then normally come to six hours' labor in money. But the worker spends not just six hours working for his entrepreneur but longer, let us say for example eleven hours. In these eleven hours, the worker firstly spends six hours reimbursing the wage he receives, and on top of this provides five hours of labor for nothing, which the entrepreneur gets for free. The working day of each worker thus necessarily and normally consists of two parts: one paid, in which the worker simply reimburses the value of his maintenance, in which he works as it were for himself, and an unpaid part, in which he performs free or surplus labor for the capitalist.

The situation was similar in earlier forms of social exploitation. In the days of bondage, the labor of the serf for himself and his labor for his master were even distinct in time and space. The peasant knew exactly when and for how long he worked for himself, and when and for how long he worked for the maintenance of his noble lord, whether temporal or spiritual. He worked first for a few days on his own plot, then for a few days on that of the lord, or else he worked in the morning on his own plot and in the afternoon on that of the lord, or he worked continuously for some weeks on the one and then for some weeks on the other. In one particular village, for example, belonging to the Maurusmünster Abbey in Alsace,* *corvée* labor in the mid-twelfth century was laid down as follows: from mid April to mid May, each peasant household to provide three full days' labor per week, from May to Midsummer's day one afternoon per week, from Midsummer's day to haymaking two days per week, then three afternoons per week until harvest, and from Martinmas† to Christmas three full days per week. In the later Middle Ages, to be sure, with advancing enserfment, work for the lords increased steadily, so that almost every day in the week and every week in the year was taken up by *corvée*, and the peasants had scarcely any time left to cultivate their own fields. But in that era they knew quite precisely that they were working not for themselves but for someone else. Even the dumbest peasant could not possibly be mistaken on this score.

With modern wage-labor, matters are quite different. The worker does not produce in one part of his working day, as it were, objects that he needs himself: his food, clothing, etc., then in another part of the day other things for the entrepreneur. On the contrary, the worker in the factory or workshop spends the whole day producing one and the same object, which generally means an object that he needs only in very small amounts, if at all, for his own private consumption: for example, steel pens, or rubber bands, or silk cloth, or iron tubes. In the indistinguishable heap of steel pens or rubber bands or cloth that he has created in the course of the day, each piece looks just like any other, to a hair, there is not the slightest difference according to whether one part of this quantity is paid labor and the other part unpaid, whether one part is for the worker and the other for the entrepreneur. On the contrary, the product that the worker produces has no utility at all for him, and not a tiny bit of it belongs to him; everything that the worker produces belongs to the entrepreneur. Here we see a major outward difference between wage-labor and serfdom. The *corvée* peasant, in normal conditions, necessarily had to have some time on which to work on his own land, and the product of his labor there belonged to him. With the modern wage-laborer, his whole product belongs to the entrepreneur, and so it looks as if his work in the factory has nothing at all to do with his maintenance. He has received his wage and can do with it what he will. In return for the wage, he has to work at what the entrepreneur tells him, and everything he produces belongs to the entrepreneur. But the difference that is invisible to the worker is clear enough in the entrepreneur's accounts, when he calculates his receipts from the production of his labor. For the capitalist, this is the difference between

---

* The Maurusmünster Abbey in Alsace, a Benedictine monastery, was built in 590 and was rebuilt and expanded many times during the Middle Ages, especially in the twelfth century. It played an important economic role in the High Middle Ages, controlling a significant amount of territory. For a study of the Abbey, see August Hertzog, *Rechts-und Wirtschafts-Verfassung des Abteigebietes Maursmünster Während des Mittlealters* (Strassburg: Heitz & Mündel, 1888). Also see first footnote on page 347.

† Martinmas, or the Feast of St. Martin, is celebrated at harvest time. It is similar in some respects to the American holiday of Thanksgiving.

the sum of money he receives from the sale of the product, and his outlays both on means of production and on his workers' wages. What remains for him as profit is precisely the value created by unpaid labor, i.e. the surplus value that the workers have created. Each worker then produces, first of all his own wage, and then a surplus value that the capitalist gets for free. If he has woven eleven meters of silk cloth in eleven hours, then six meters of this may contain the value of his wage, and five meters are surplus value for the entrepreneur.

But the distinction between wage-labor and slave or *corvée* labor has still more important consequences. Both the slave and the *corvée* peasant performed their labor principally for their own private need and for the master's consumption. They produced for their master objects of food and clothing, furniture, luxury goods, etc. This was at all events the norm, before slavery and serfdom degenerated under the influence of trade, and were approaching their end. The ability of a person to consume, however, i.e. luxury in private life, has definite limits in each era. The antique slaveholder or the medieval noble could not consume more than full barns, full stables, rich clothes, richly appointed rooms, a sumptuous life for themselves and their household. Objects like these, which they needed for everyday life, could not even be stored in large quantities, as they would perish: grain easily succumbs to rot or is eaten by rats and mice; stocks of hay and straw readily catch fire, clothing is damaged, dairy products, fruit and vegetables are very hard to preserve. Even with a sumptuous lifestyle, therefore, consumption in both slave and *corvée* economy had its natural limits, and this also set limits to the normal exploitation of the slaves and peasants. It is different with the modern entrepreneur, who buys labor-power in order to produce commodities. What the worker produces in the factory or workshop is generally quite useless for himself, and equally useless for the entrepreneur. The latter does not put the labor-power he purchases to work at producing food and clothing, but has it produce commodities that he himself does not need. He only has silk or metal tubes or coffins produced so as to get rid of them by sale as quickly as possible. He has them produced in order to obtain money by their sale. And he receives back his outlays, as well as the surplus labor that his workers supply him with for free, in the money form. It is to this end, to turn the workers' unpaid labor into money, that he conducts his whole business and buys labor-power. But money, as we know, is the means for unlimited accumulation of wealth. In the money form, wealth does not lose value by lengthy storage. On the contrary, as we shall go on to see, wealth in the money form even seems to grow as a result of storage. And in the money form, wealth know no limits at all, it can grow endlessly. The hunger of the modern capitalist for surplus labor accordingly knows no limits. The more unpaid labor can be pressed out of the workers, the better. To extract surplus value, and extract it without limit, is the particular purpose and task of the purchase of labor-power.

The natural drive of the capitalist to expand the surplus value extracted from the workers takes two simple paths, which present themselves automatically, as it were, when we consider the composition of the working day. We saw how the working day of every wage-laborer normally consists of two parts: a part in which the worker receives back his own wage, and a further part in which he supplies unpaid labor, surplus value. In order to expand this second part as much as possible, the entrepreneur can proceed along two routes: either extend the whole working day, or shorten the first, paid part of the working day, i.e. reduce the wage of the worker. In actual fact the capitalist uses both methods at the same time, which gives the system of wage-labor a constant dual tendency: to the extension of working time, and to the reduction of wages.

If the capitalist buys the commodity labor-power, he does so as with any other commodity, in order to derive utility from it. Every commodity buyer seeks to get as much use as possible from his commodities. If we buy boots, for example, we want to wear them for as long as possible. The buyer of the commodity enjoys the full use and utility of the commodity. The capitalist, accordingly, who has bought the commodity labor-power, has the full right, from the standpoint of commodity purchase, to demand that the purchased commodity serve him for as long as possible and as much as possible. If he has paid for a week's labor-power, then the use of it belongs to him for a week, and in his capacity as purchaser he has the right to have the worker labor up to twenty-four hours for each of the seven days. The worker, on the other hand, as seller of the commodity, has a completely opposed position. While the capitalist does indeed have the use of his labor-power, this meets its limits in the physical and mental capacity of the worker. A horse cannot work for more than eight hours, day in, day out, without being ruined. A human being, likewise, in order to restore the energy spent in labor, needs a certain time for eating, clothing, rest, etc. If he does not have this, then his labor-power is not simply used, but destroyed. The worker is weakened by excessive labor and his life cut short. If each week the capitalist shortens the life of the worker by two weeks, by limitless consumption of his labor-power, this is the same as if he were appropriating three weeks for the wage of one. From the same standpoint of commodity exchange, this means that the capitalist is robbing the worker. In relation to the working day, capitalist and worker represent two diametrically opposed positions on the commodity market, and the actual length of the working day is decided only by struggle between the capitalist class and the working class, as a *question of power*.[113] Inherently, therefore, the working day has no definite limits; in different times and places we find working days of eight, ten, twelve, fourteen, sixteen and eighteen hours. And as a whole, the struggle over the length of the working day lasts for centuries. We can distinguish two major phases in this struggle. The first begins in the late Middle Ages, in the fourteenth century, when capitalism took its first hesitant steps and began to shatter the firm protective armor of the guild regime. The normal customary working time, in the golden age of handicrafts, amounted perhaps to ten hours,

with meal times, sleep, recreation, rest on Sundays and feast days being com-
fortably observed in all particulars. This was sufficient for traditional handicraft
with its slow methods of work, but it was not sufficient for the early manufacturing enterprises. The first thing that the capitalists required from governments,
accordingly, was the extension of working time. Between the fourteenth and
the late seventeenth centuries, we see in England, France and Germany specific
laws covering the *minimum working day*, i.e. bans on workers and journeymen
working less than a definite working time, which was generally twelve hours per
day. The great cry from the Middle Ages down to the eighteenth century is the
struggle against workers' idleness. But once the power of the old guild handicrafts
was broken, and a massive proletariat lacking any means of labor and forced to
sell its labor-power appeared, while on the other hand large factories with feverish mass production arose, the page turned in the eighteenth century. A sudden
consumption of workers of every age and both sexes began, with entire populations of workers being mown down in a few years as if by plague. A British
MP declared in Parliament in 1863: "The cotton trade has existed for ninety
years ... It has existed for three generations of the English race, and I believe I
may safely say that during that period it has destroyed nine generations of factory
operatives."* And a bourgeois English writer, John Wade, wrote in his book on
the *History of the Middle and Working Classes*, "The cupidity of mill-owners
whose cruelties in the pursuit of gain have hardly been exceeded by those perpetrated by the Spaniards in the conquest of America in the pursuit of gold."† In
the 1860s in England, in certain branches of industry such as stocking making,
children of nine or ten years old were occupied from two, three or four o'clock in
the morning until ten, eleven or twelve at night. In Germany, the conditions that
prevailed until recently, in mirror manufacture and in baking, for example, are
sufficiently well known. It was modern capitalist industry that first succeeded in
making the formerly quite unknown discovery of nightwork. In all earlier social
conditions, night was seen as a time determined by nature itself for human rest.[114]
The capitalist enterprise discovered that surplus value extracted from the worker
at night was in no way different from that extracted by day, and introduced day
and night shifts. Sundays, which in the Middle Ages were most strictly observed
by the handicraft guilds, were sacrificed to the capitalists' hunger for surplus
value, and equated with other working days. On top of this were dozens of little
inventions to extend working time: taking meals on the job without a pause,
cleaning machines after the regular working day ends, i.e. during the workers'
rest time, and so on. This practice of the capitalists, which prevailed quite freely

---

   * Cited in Karl Marx, *Capital* Vol. 1, p. 378. These comments by William Ferrand were made
in a speech to the House of Commons on April 27, 1863.
   † Cited in Karl Marx, *Capital* Vol. 1, p. 353, note 31. See John Wade, *History of the Middle
and Working Classes, with a Popular Exposition of the Economical and Political Principles which have
influenced the Past and Present Condition of the Industrious Orders* (London: E. Wilson, 1835), p. 114.

and unimpeded in the early decades, soon made necessary a series of new laws about the working day—this time not to forcibly extend working hours, but rather to curtail them. And the first legal restrictions on the maximum working day were not forced by the pressure of workers, but by capitalist society's own instinct for self-preservation. The first few decades of unrestricted operation of large-scale industry produced such a devastating effect on the health and living conditions of the mass of working people, with tremendous mortality, disease, physical crippling, mental desperation, epidemic disease and unfitness for military service, that the very survival of society seemed deeply threatened.[115] It was clear that if the natural drive of capital for surplus value were not reined in by the state, whole states would sooner or later be turned into giant cemeteries, in which only the bones of workers would be visible. But without workers there is no exploitation of workers. In its own interest, accordingly, in order to secure the future of exploitation, capital had to set some limits to present exploitation. The strength of the people had to be protected to a certain extent, in order to secure their future exploitation. A transition was necessary from an unviable economy of robbery to rational exploitation. This gave rise to the first laws on the maximum working day, along with bourgeois social reform in general. We can see a counterpart of this in the hunting laws. Just as game are protected by law for a definite time, so that they can multiply rationally and regularly as an object for hunting, in the same way social reform ensures the labor-power of the proletariat a certain time of protection, so that it can serve rationally for exploitation by capital. Or, as Marx put it, the restriction of factory work was dictated by the same necessity that forces the landowner to spread fertilizer over the fields. Factory legislation was born in a hard struggle of decades against the resistance of individual capitalists, initially for children and women, and in particular industries step by step. France then followed, where the February revolution of 1848, under the initial pressure of the victorious Paris proletariat, proclaimed the twelve-hour working day, this being also the first general law on the working time of all workers, including adult men in all branches of industry. In the United States, a general movement of workers for the eight-hour day began immediately after the Civil War of 1861[–65], which abolished slavery,* a movement that then spread to Europe. In Russia, the first protective

---

* The American Civil War of 1861–65, and especially the critical role of Black slaves in attempting to secure their emancipation, was an important impetus to the development of the US labor movement in the post-Civil War period. Shortly after the war, in 1867, the first US National Labor Union was formed to promote the fight for an eight-hour day. At its founding convention it declared, "The National Labor Union knows no north, no south, so east, no west, neither color nor sex, on the question of the rights of labor." See Timothy Messer-Kruse, *The Yankee International: Marxism and the American Reform Tradition, 1848–76* (Chapel Hill: University of North Carolina Press, 1998), p. 191. For a discussion of the impact of the US Civil War on both Marx's *Capital* and the struggle for the eight-day day, see Raya Dunayevskaya, *Marxism and Freedom, from 1776 Until Today* (Amherst. NY: Humanity Books, 2000), pp. 81–91.

legislation for women and minors arose from the great factory disturbances of 1882 in the Moscow industrial zone,* and a working day of eleven and a half hours for adult men was the result of the first general strike of 60,000 textile workers in St Petersburg in 1896–97.† Germany is now limping behind all other major modern states, with protective legislation only for women and children.

So far we have spoken only of one particular aspect of wage-labor, working time, and here we already see how the simple commodity transaction of buying and selling labor-power has many particular features. But it is necessary here to recall Marx's words:

> It must be acknowledged that our worker emerges from the process of production looking different from when he entered it. In the market, as owner of the commodity "labor-power," he stood face to face with other owners of commodities, one owner against another owner. The contract by which he sold his labor-power to the capitalist proved in black and white, so to speak, that he was free to dispose of himself. But when the transaction was concluded, it was discovered that he was no *"free agent,"* that the period of time for which he is *free* to sell his labor-power is the period of time for which he is *forced* to sell it, that in fact the vampire will not let go "while there remains a single muscle, sinew or drop of blood to be exploited."‡ For "protection" against the serpent of their agonies,§ the workers have to put their heads together and, *as a class,* compel the passing of a law, an all-powerful *social barrier* by which they can be prevented from selling themselves and their families into slavery and death *by voluntary contract with capital.*¶

Labor protection legislation is in fact the first official acknowledgement by present-day society that the formal equality and freedom on which commodity production and exchange is based already breaks down, collapses into inequality and unfreedom, as soon as labor-power appears on the market as a commodity.

---

* In response to agitation from the workers, on June 1, 1882 the Law of the Protection of Minors was passed in Russia, which prohibited children under the age of twelve from working in mills and factories. On June 3, 1885, an additional law prohibited night work for women and adolescents under the age of seventeen in the textile industry.

† On June 2, 1897 the Russian government agreed to enact legislation limiting the working day to eleven and a half hours per day. It took effect in early 1898.

‡ Marx quotes here from Engels's article, "The English Ten House Bill" (1850), in which Engels referred to "The callously brutal exploitation of children and women at that time—an exploitation which did not let up so long as there was a muscle, a sinew or a drop of blood left to extract profit from them." See *Marx-Engels Collected Works,* Vol. 10 (New York: International Publishers, 1978), p. 288.

§ The phrase "serpent of their agonies" is taken from the title of the poem by the German poet Heinrich Heine, "Der die Schlange meiner Qualen."

¶ Karl Marx, *Capital* Vol. 1, pp. 415–16. The emphases are Rosa Luxemburg's.

3

The capitalists' second method for expanding surplus value is the reduction of wages. Like the working day, wages also have no definite limits. Above all, if we speak of the wages of labor, we need to distinguish between the money that the worker receives from the entrepreneur, and the quantity of means of subsistence that he obtains for this. If all we know about a worker's wage is that he is paid, for example, two marks per day, we effectively know nothing. For when prices are high, the same two marks will buy much less in terms of means of subsistence than when prices are low. In one country, the same two-mark coin means a different standard of living than it does in another, and the same applies to almost every region within a country. The worker may even receive more money as his wage than previously, and at the same time live not better but just as badly, or even worse. The real, actual wage, therefore, is the sum of means of subsistence that the worker obtains, whereas the money wage is only the nominal wage. If the wage is then simply the monetary expression of the value of labor-power, this value is actually represented by the amount of labor that is spent on the worker's necessary means of subsistence. But what are these "necessary means of subsistence"? Aside from individual differences between one worker and another, which play no role, the different standard of living of the working class in different countries and at different times already shows that the concept "necessary means of subsistence" is very variable and flexible. The better-off English worker of today considers his daily intake of beefsteak as necessary for life, while the Chinese coolie lives on a handful of rice. In connection with the flexibility of the concept "necessary means of subsistence," a similar struggle develops over the level of wages as it does over the length of the working day. The capitalist, as buyer of commodities, explains his position as follows: "Is it not quite completely correct that I must pay its proper value for the commodity labor-power, just like any honest purchaser? But what is the value of labor-power? The necessary means of subsistence? Well, I give my worker exactly as much as is necessary for his life; but as to what is absolutely necessary to keep someone alive, this is a matter for science first of all, i.e. for physiology, and secondly a matter of general experience. And it goes without saying that I give exactly this minimum; for if I were to give a penny more, I would not be an honest purchaser, but rather a fool, a philanthropist, making a gift from my own pocket to the person from whom he has bought a commodity. I don't give my shoemaker or cigarette seller a penny extra, but try to buy their commodities as cheaply as possible. In the same way, I try to buy labor-power as cheaply as possible, and we are completely on the level if I give my worker the barest minimum that he needs to maintain his life." The capitalist here is completely within his rights, from the standpoint of commodity production. But the worker is no less within his rights when he responds to the commodity purchaser: "Of course I cannot claim more than the actual value of my commodity, labor-power. But what I demand is that you really do pay me its full value. I don't want anything more than the necessary means of subsistence. But what means of subsistence are necessary? You say that the answer to this is supplied by the science of physiology and by experience, and that these show what is the minimum a person needs in order to maintain life. What you refer to here, by the concept of 'necessary means of subsistence' is therefore the absolutely, *physiologically* necessary. But this is against the law of commodity exchange. For you know as well as I do that what decides the value of every commodity on the market is the labor *socially* necessary for its production. If your shoemaker offers you a pair of boots and asks 20 marks for them, as he has spent four days working on them, you will reply: 'I can get boots like this from the factory for only 12 marks, as they can be made in a day with machinery. Given that it is now usual to produce boots by machine, your four days' work was not necessary, from the social point of view, even if it was necessary for *you*, as you don't work with machines. But I can't help that, and will pay you only for the socially necessary labor, i.e. 12 marks.' If this is how you proceed when purchasing boots, you must then pay the socially necessary costs of maintaining my labor-power when you buy this. Socially necessary to my labor, however, is everything that in our country and in the present age is seen as the customary maintenance of a man of my class. In a word, what you have to pay me is not the physiologically necessary minimum that barely keeps me alive, as you would give an animal, but rather the socially customary minimum that ensures my habitual standard of living. Only then will you have paid the value of the commodity as an honest purchaser, otherwise you are buying it below its value."

We see here how the worker is just as much in the right as the capitalist, simply from the commodity standpoint. But it is only over time that the worker can get this standpoint accepted—as a social class, i.e. as a whole, as organization. Only with the rise of trade unions and a workers' party does the worker begin to sell his labor-power at its value, i.e. to insist on maintaining his life as a social and cultural necessity. Before the appearance of trade unions in a country, however, and before their acceptance in each particular branch of industry, what was decisive in determining wages was the tendency of the capitalist to reduce the means of subsistence to the physiological minimum, the animal minimum, i.e. to regularly pay for labor-power below its value. The time of unrestrained rule of capital, still not meeting any resistance on the part of workers' coalitions and organization, led to the same barbaric degradation of the working class in relation to wages as it did in relation to working time before the introduction of factory legislation. This is a crusade by capital against any trace of luxury, comfort and convenience in the life of the worker, as he was accustomed to in the earlier period of handicrafts and peasant economy. It is an attempt to reduce the worker's consumption to the simple bare act of supplying the body with a minimum of fodder, in the way that cattle are fed or machinery is oiled. In this connection, the lowest and least needy workers are presented to the spoiled worker as model and example. This crusade against the human maintenance of the workers began in England—along with capitalist industry. An English writer complained in the eighteenth century: "Simply consider the shocking quantity of superfluities that our manufacturing workers consume, for example brandy, gin, tea, sugar, foreign fruit, strong beer, pressed linen, snuff and smoking tobacco, etc."* At that time the French, Dutch and German workers were offered as a model of frugality to the English workers. An English manufacturer wrote: "Labor is a whole third more reasonable in France than in England; for the French poor"—this is how they referred to the workers—"work hard and are sparing on food and clothing, their main consumption being bread, vegetables, roots and dried fish, for they very seldom eat meat, and very little bread when wheat is dear."† Around the beginning of the nineteenth century, an American, Count [Benjamin Thompson] Rumford, produced a special "cookbook for workers" with recipes for cheaper food. One recipe from this famous book, for example, which was accepted with great enthusiasm by the bourgeoisie of several countries, went: "Five pounds of barley, five pounds of maize, 30 pfennigs worth of herrings, 10 pfennigs of salt, 10 pfennigs of vinegar, 20 pfennigs of pepper and vegetables—total 2.08 marks, provides a soup for sixty-four people, and with the average price of grain, the cost of food can be reduced to no more than 3 pfennig per head."‡ Of the workers in the mines of South America, whose daily work, perhaps the heaviest in the world, consists in carrying on their shoulders a weight of ore of between 180 and 200 lbs. from a depth of 450 feet, Justus Liebig relates that they live only on bread and beans.§

---

* This was written in an anonymous book entitled *An Essay on Trade and Commerce. By the Author of 'Considerations on Taxes'* (London: 1870), pp. 44, 46. It was quoted by Marx in *Capital* Vol. 1, p. 748.

† Ibid.

‡ Rumford's soup was invented by the American scientist Benjamin Thompson, Count Rumford, around 1800 as a ration for Bavarian workhouses, and acquired widespread use for military rations. Its basic ingredients are pearl barley, dried (yellow) peas and potatoes, with sour beer and salt being added. The corn and herrings are optional additions. Luxemburg is presumably quoting a German secondary source. Marx quoted Count Rumford's work on this same issue in his 1861–63 draft of *Capital*, but Luxemburg could not have known of this since the draft was unknown during her lifetime and was published only decades after her death. Marx wrote, "The cheapest meal which can be prepared, according to this 'philosopher,' is a soup of barley, Indian corn, pepper, salt, vinegar, sweet herbs and four herrings in eight gallons of water." See *Economic Manuscripts of 1861–63: A Contribution to the Critique of Political Economy, Marx-Engels Collected Works*, Vol. 30 (New York: International Publishers, 1988), p. 46. For Count Rumford's work, see Benjamin Thompson, *Essays Political, Economical and Philosophical*, Vol. 1 (London: T. Cadell and W. Davies, 1796–1802), p. 294.

§ See Justus von Liebig, *Die Chemie in ihrer Anwendung auf Agricultur und Physiologie* (Chemistry in its Application to Physiology and Agriculture), Vol. 1 (Braunschweig: Friedrich Vieweg, 1862), p. 194: "The workers in the mines of South America, whose daily task (the heaviest perhaps in the world), consists in bringing to the surface on their shoulders a load of metal

They would prefer just bread as their nourishment, but their masters, having found that they cannot work so hard on bread, treat them like horses and force them to eat beans, as beans contribute more to the building of bones than does bread. In France, the first hunger revolt of the workers took place already in 1831—that of the silk weavers in Lyon. But capital celebrated its greatest orgies in the reduction of wages under the Second Empire, in the 1860s, when machine industry proper took hold in France. The entrepreneurs fled from the towns to the countryside, where they could find cheaper hands. And they found women there who would work for one sou a day, about four pfennigs.* But this wonderful state of affairs did not last long, for such a wage could not sustain even an animal existence. In Germany, capital first introduced similar conditions in the textile industry, where wages in the 1840s were driven down even below the physiological minimum, leading to the hunger revolts of weavers in Silesia and Bohemia. Today the animal minimum subsistence remains the rule for wages where trade unions do not have their effect on the standard of living—for agricultural workers in Germany, in dressmaking, and in the various branches of domestic industry.

4[116]

In ratcheting up the burden of labor and pressing down the living standard of working people to as near as possible an animal level, if not sometimes indeed below this, modern capitalist exploitation is similar to that of the slave and *corvée* economies at the time of their worst degeneration, i.e. when each entered its respective phase of decay. But what capitalist commodity production is unique in having brought forth, quite unknown in all earlier epochs, is the partial non-employment and consequent non-consumption of working people as a constant phenomenon, i.e. the so-called reserve army of labor. Capitalist production depends on the market and must follow its demand. This however changes continuously and alternately generates so-called good and bad years, seasons and months of business. Capital must continuously adapt to the changing conjuncture, and accordingly employ either more or fewer workers. It must, accordingly, in order to have to hand at any time the labor-power needed for even the highest market demand, constantly keep available in reserve, on top of the workers actually employed, a considerable number of unemployed. These workers, not being employed, receive no wage, their labor-power is not bought,

---

weighing from 180 to 200 pounds, from a depth of 450 feet, live on bread and beans only; they themselves would prefer the bread alone for food, but their masters, who have found out that the men cannot work so hard on bread, treat them like horses, and compel them to eat beans; beans are relatively much richer in bone-ash than is bread." Marx quotes this in *Capital* Vol. 1, p. 718.

   *   Prior to the introduction of the Euro in 2001, a Deutschmark was comprised of 100 pfennigs. At the current rate of exchange, four pfennigs would be worth only a few cents.

it simply remains in store; the non-consumption of a section of the working class is thus an essential component of capitalist production's law of wages. How these unemployed live their life is no concern of capital, yet capital rebuffs any attempt to abolish the reserve army as a danger to its own vital interests. A striking example of this was offered by the English cotton crisis of 1863. When the spinning and weaving mills of England suddenly had to break off production for want of American raw cotton, and close to a million of the working population were workless, a number of these unemployed decided to emigrate to Australia in order to escape the threat of starvation. They asked the English Parliament to grant £2 million to facilitate the emigration of 50,000 unemployed workers. The cotton manufacturers, however, raised a storm of indignation against this suggestion from the workers. Industry could not do without machines, and like machines, the workers had to remain available. "The country" would suffer a loss of £4 million if the starving unemployed suddenly disappeared. Parliament accordingly refused the emigration fund, and the unemployed remained chained to the breadline so as to form the necessary reserve for capital. A still more dramatic example was offered by the French capitalists in 1871. After the defeat of the [Paris] Commune, when the butchery of the Paris workers, in both legal and extra-legal forms, was pursued to such an enormous degree that tens of thousands of proletarians, including the best and most capable, the elite of the working class, were murdered,* the satisfied sense of revenge on the part of the entrepreneurs was punctuated by an unease that a shortage of reserve "hands" might soon be painfully felt; it was precisely at this time, after the end of the war, that industry was experiencing a vigorous upswing. Several Paris entrepreneurs accordingly applied to the courts to have the persecution of Commune fighters moderated and thus save workers from military butchers for the arm o f capital.

For capital, however, the reserve army has a dual function: first, to supply labor-power for every sudden upswing in business, and second, to exert a constant pressure on the active workforce by competition from the unemployed, and so reduce their wages to a minimum.

Marx distinguished four different strata in the reserve army, with differing functions for capital and its conditions of existence. The topmost stratum is the periodically inactive industrial workers, who are present in all trades, even the best-situated ones. Their members constantly change, as every worker is unemployed at certain times and active in others; their numbers also fluctuate sharply with the course of business, becoming very high in times of crisis and low at the peak of the cycle; but they never disappear, and generally increase with

---

*   At least 20,000 people were murdered between May 21 and 28, 1871 by the counter-revolutionary forces that crushed the Paris Commune. Most were summarily executed by the government after the fighting was over. Tens of thousands of others who survived were imprisoned and banished.

the progress of industrial development. The second stratum are the unskilled proletarians who flood into the towns from the country, who appear on the labor market with the lowest demands, and as simple workers are not tied to any definite branch of industry, but are ready for employment in any branch as a reservoir. The third category is the lower order of proletarians, who have no regular employment and are constantly looking for one kind of casual labor or another. Here we find the longest working time and the lowest wages, and for this reason this stratum is quite as useful for capital, and as directly indispensable, as the former categories. This stratum is constantly recruited from the surplus numbers in industry and agriculture, but particularly from small-scale artisans who go under and from dying trades. It forms the broad basis for domestic industry, and acts as it were behind the scenes, behind the official showground of industry. And here it not only has no tendency to disappear, but actually grows both by the increasing effects of industry in town and country, and by the greatest production of children.

Finally, the fourth stratum of the proletarian reserve army are the direct paupers, the recognized poor, some of them capable of work, who in times when industry and trade are good are to a certain extent taken on, being then the first to be dismissed in times of crisis; others are incapable of work: older workers whom industry can no longer use, proletarian widows, orphans and pauper children, crippled and mutilated victims of large-scale industry, mining, etc., and finally those unaccustomed to work: vagabonds and the like. This stratum merges directly with the lumpenproletariat:* criminals and prostitutes. Pauperism, Marx said, is the disability home for the working class and the dead weight of its reserve army. Its existence follows just as necessarily and unavoidably from the reserve army as the reserve army does from the development of industry. Poverty and the lumpenproletariat are part of the conditions of existence of capitalism and grow together with it; the greater is social wealth, functioning capital, and the mass of workers employed by it, the greater too is the available stratum of unemployed, the reserve army; and the greater the reserve army in relation to the mass of employed workers, the greater is the lowest stratum of poverty, pauperism and crime. The number of unemployed and unwaged thus grows unavoidably along with capital and wealth, and so does the beggared stratum of the working class—official poverty. "*This is the absolute general law of capitalist accumulation*," wrote Marx.†

The formation of a constant and growing stratum of unemployed was, as we

---

*   *Lumpenproletariat* is generally a derogatory term to refer to those excluded from useful labor (the permanently unemployed, beggars, petty thieves, etc.) and therefore unlikely to develop class consciousness. It has connotations similar to the present-day term "the underclass." Although Marxists traditionally have looked upon the *lumpenproletariat* in disdain, in some of her writings— especially *Mass Strike, the Political Party, and the Trade Unions*—Luxemburg noted its capacity to sometimes play a relatively progressive social role, as in the 1905 Russian Revolution.

†   Marx, *Capital* Vol. 1, p. 798. Marx's emphasis.

said, unknown in all earlier forms of society. In the primitive communist community, it goes without saying that everyone works to the extent that is necessary to maintain their life, partly from immediate need, and partly under the pressure of the moral and legal authority of the tribe, the community. But *all* members of society are also provided with the available means to live. The standard of living of the primitive communist group is certainly quite low and simple, the conveniences of life are primitive. But to the extent that the means for life do exist, they are present equally for all, and poverty in the present-day sense, deprivation of the existing social resources, is at this time quite unknown. The primitive tribe sometimes goes hungry—even often, if it suffers from unfavorable natural conditions—but its lack is then the lack of society as such, whereas lack on the part of some members of society at the same time as a surplus is available for others, is something unthinkable; to the extent that the society's means of subsistence are ensured on the whole, so is the existence of each individual.

In Oriental and antique slavery we see the same thing. No matter how the Egyptian state slave or the Greek private slave was exploited and overworked, no matter how great the distance between his bare maintenance and the excess of the master might have been, his maintenance was at least ensured for him by the slave relationship. Slaves were not allowed to die of hunger, any more than a horse or a cow is today. It was the same with the *corvée* relationship of the Middle Ages: the chaining of the peasantry to the soil, and the solid construction of the whole feudal system of dependence, in which everyone had to be lord over others, or the servant of a lord, or both at once—this system ascribed everyone a definite place. No matter how bad the squeezing of the serfs might be, no lord had the right to drive them from the soil, i.e. rob them of their means of subsistence; on the contrary, the serf relationship obliged the lord in cases of distress, such as fire, flood, hail, etc., to support the impoverished peasants. It was only when the Middle Ages came to an end, with the collapse of feudalism and the entry of modern capital, that expropriation of peasant land got under way. In the Middle Ages, however, the existence of the great mass of working people was fully secured. To some extent, already at this time, a small contingent of paupers and beggars emerged as a result of the countless wars or of individual loss. But it was a duty of society to maintain these poor. Emperor Charlemagne already laid down expressly in his capitularies, "As for the beggars who wander around the countryside, we desire that each of our vassals should feed the poor, whether on the estate enfeoffed* to him or within his house, and he should not allow them to go and beg elsewhere." Later, it was a special vocation of monasteries to lodge the poor, and to provide them with work if they were capable of this. In the Middle Ages, therefore, any needy person was sure of reception in any house,

---

* In European feudalism, enfeoffment was the act by which an individual was provided with land in exchange for a pledge of service to the lord.

the feeding of those without means was seen as a simple duty, and was in no way linked with the stigma of contempt faced by a beggar today.

Past history knows only one case where a large stratum of the population was left unoccupied and workless. This is the already mentioned case of the ancient Roman peasantry, who were driven off the land and transformed into a proletariat, with no work to do. This proletarianization of the peasantry was of course a logical and necessary consequence of the development of great latifundia, along with the spread of the slave economy. But it was in no way necessary for the existence of the slave economy and large landed property. On the contrary, the unemployed Roman proletariat was simply a misfortune, a pure burden on society, and this society tried all available means to control the proletariat and its poverty, by periodic distributions of land, by distribution of foodstuffs, by organizing an immense food import and by subsidizing the price of grain. In the end, this great proletariat in ancient Rome was simply maintained by the state.

Capitalist commodity production, accordingly, is the first economic form in the history of humanity in which the lack of occupation and resources of a large and growing stratum of the population, and the direct and hopeless poverty of another stratum, is not simply a result of this economy but also a necessity for it, a condition of its existence. Insecurity of existence for the entire working mass, and chronic lack, in part direct poverty, of broad strata, are for the first time a normal social phenomenon. And the scholars of the bourgeoisie, who cannot imagine any other form of society than today's, are so imbued with the natural necessity of this stratum of unemployed and workless that they explain it as a natural law intended by God. The Englishman Malthus, at the beginning of the nineteenth century, constructed on this basis his celebrated theory of overpopulation, according to which poverty develops because humanity has the evil habit of multiplying children more quickly than means of subsistence.

As we have seen, however, it is nothing else than the simple effect of commodity production and exchange that led to these results. The law of commodities, which rests formally on complete equality and freedom, produces by iron necessity, without any intervention of statute or force, a glaring social inequality such as was unknown in all earlier conditions based on the direct rule of one person over another. For the first time now, direct hunger becomes a scourge inflicted daily on the life of the working masses. And this is also explained as a law of nature. The Anglican parson [Joseph] Townsend wrote as far back as 1786:

> It seems to be a law of Nature that the poor should be to a certain degree improvident, that there may always be some to fulfill the most servile, the most sordid, and the most ignoble offices in the community. The stock of human happiness is thereby much increased, whilst the more delicate are not only relieved from drudgery ... but are left at liberty without interruption to pursue those callings which are suited to their various dispositions ... [The Poor Law] tends to destroy the harmony and

beauty, the symmetry and order of that system which God and Nature have estab-lished in the world.*

The "more delicate," who live at the cost of others, had already seen the finger of God and a law of nature in every social form that secured them the joys of the exploiting life. Even the great minds of the past did not escape this histori-cal deception. Two thousand years before the English parson, the great Greek thinker Aristotle wrote:

> It is nature itself that has created slavery. Animals are divided into males and females. The male is a more perfect animal, and rules; the female is less perfect, and obeys. Similarly there are in the human race individuals that stand as much below others as the body stands below the soul or the animal below man; these are creatures that are fit only for physical work and are unfit to produce anything more perfect. These individuals are destined by nature for slavery, since there is nothing better for them than to obey others ... Does there exist so great a difference between the slave and the animal? Their works are similar, they are useful to us only by way of their body. We conclude from these principles, therefore, that nature has created certain men for freedom and others for slavery, and that it is accordingly useful and right that there should be slaves.†

"Nature," which is made responsible for every form of exploitation, must at all events have acquired a rather jaded taste over time. For even if it might still be worthwhile to demean a large mass of people with the shame of slavery, in order to raise a free people of philosophers and geniuses like Aristotle on their backs, the demeaning of millions of proletarians today to support vulgar factory-owners and fat parsons is a less attractive goal.

5

We have examined up till now what standard of living the capitalist commod-ity economy provides for the working class and its various strata. But we still know nothing precise as to the relationship between this living standard of the workers and social wealth in general. The workers may in one case, for example, have more means of subsistence, more nourishing food and better clothing than before, but if the wealth of the other classes has grown still more rapidly, then the *share* of the workers in the social product has grown smaller. The living standard of the workers in itself, in absolute terms, may thus rise, while their share relative

---

* Cited in Marx, *Capital* Vol. 1, p. 800. See Joseph Townsend, *A Dissertation on the Poor Laws* (London: V. Dilly, 1786), pp. 15, 38, 41.

† Aristotle, *The Politics* in *The Complete Works of Aristotle*, Vol. 2, edited by Jonathan Barnes (Princeton: Princeton University Press, 1984, p. 1990) [1254b22–1255a2].

to other classes falls. The living standard of each individual and each class, however, can only be correctly judged if the conditions of the particular time and the other strata of the same society are taken into account. The prince of a primitive, half-savage or barbaric African tribe has a lower standard of living, i.e. a simpler dwelling, poorer clothing, cruder food, than an average factory worker in Germany. But this prince lives in a "princely" fashion in comparison with the means and demands of his tribe, whereas the factory worker in Germany lives very poorly, compared with the luxury of the rich bourgeoisie and the needs of the present day. In order therefore to judge correctly the position of the workers in the present society, it is necessary not only to examine absolute wages, but also relative wages, i.e. the share that the worker's wage makes up out of the total product of his labor.* We assumed in our earlier example that the worker had to work the first six hours out of an eleven-hour working day in order to cover his wage, i.e. his means of subsistence, and then spend five hours creating surplus value for the capitalist for free. We assumed in this example, therefore, that the production of means of subsistence for the worker cost six hours' labor. We also saw how the capitalist seeks by all means to press down the living standard of the worker, to expand to the maximum the unpaid labor, surplus value. But let us assume that the worker's living standard does not change, i.e. that he is still in the position to obtain the same quantities of food, clothing, linen, furniture, etc. We assume, therefore, that there is no reduction in wages in absolute terms. If however the production of all these means of subsistence becomes cheaper, as a result of advances in production, and requires therefore less time, then the worker will spend a shorter time covering his wage. Let us assume that the quantity of food, clothing, furniture, etc. that the worker needs per day no longer demands six hours' labor but only five. Then the worker will not spend six hours out of his eleven-hour day replacing his wage, but only five hours, and he will have six hours remaining for unpaid labor, for the creation of surplus value for the capitalist. The share of the worker in his produce has been reduced by one-sixth, while the share of the capitalist has grown by one-fifth. There has however been no reduction in the absolute wage. It may even come about that the living standard of the workers is increased, i.e. that absolute wages rise, let us say by 10 percent, and indeed not just in money terms, but also the actual means of subsistence of the workers. But if the productivity of labor has risen in the same time by some 15 percent, then the share of the workers in the product, i.e. their relative wage, has actually fallen, despite the rise in absolute wages. The share of

---

* Luxemburg is arguing that relative wages can decline even as absolute wages increase, since the higher nominal wages obtained by workers tend to be offset by increased gains in productivity. The implication is that simply securing a higher nominal or absolute wage does not directly threaten the capitalist system. On the other hand, wage increases that challenge capital's ability to extract additional amounts of surplus value through technological innovation and increased labor productivity relative to workers' wages challenges the very basis of capitalist accumulation.

the worker in the product thus depends on the productivity of labor. The less labor it takes to produce his means of subsistence, the smaller his relative wage. If the shirts that he wears, his boots and his caps, are produced with less labor than before, due to advances in manufacture, then he may obtain with his wage the same quantity of shirts, boots and caps with his wage, but at the same time he now receives a smaller share of the social wealth, the total social product. The daily consumption of the worker, however, is made up of the same quantities of all the different products and raw materials. Not only do [advances in] shirt manufacture cheapen the worker's maintenance, but likewise in the cotton manufacture that supplies material for his shirts, the machine industry that supplies sewing machines, and the yarn industry that supplies yarn. Similarly, the worker's provisions are made cheaper not only by advances in baking, but also by American agriculture that supplies grain on a massive scale, by advances in railways and steam shipping that bring this American grain to Europe, and so on. Every advance in industry, every increase in the productivity of human labor, makes the maintenance of the workers cost ever less labor. The worker need therefore spend an ever smaller part of his working day on replacing his wage, and the part in which he creates unpaid labor, surplus value for the capitalist, becomes every greater.

But the constant and ceaseless progress of technology is a necessity for capitalism, a condition of its very existence. Competition between individual entrepreneurs forces each of them to produce their product as cheaply as possible, i.e. with the greatest possible saving on human labor. And if any one capitalist introduces a new and improved process into his own factory, this competition forces all other entrepreneurs in the same branch of production to improve their technology in the same way, so as not to be driven from the field, i.e. the commodity market. The visible outward form of this is the general introduction of machine power in place of manual, and the ever more rapid introduction of new and improved machines in place of old. Technical inventions in all areas of production have become a daily occurrence. The technical transformation of all industry, not only in production itself but also in means of communication, is an incessant phenomenon, a vital law of capitalist commodity production. And every advance in labor productivity is expressed in a reduction in the amount of labor needed to maintain the worker. In other words, capitalist production cannot take a single step forward without reducing the share of the workers in the social product. With each new technological invention, each improvement of machinery, each new application of steam and electricity to production and communications, the share of the worker in the product grows smaller and the share of the capitalist larger. Relative wages steadily fall lower and lower, without pause or interruption, while surplus value, i.e. the unpaid wealth of the capitalists squeezed out of the worker, grows just as steadily and constantly higher and higher.

We see here again a striking difference between capitalist commodity production and all earlier forms of society. In the primitive communist society, as we know, the product is distributed equally, directly after production, to everyone who works, i.e. to all members of society, as there is practically no one who does not work. Feudal relations are governed not by equality but by the exploitation of workers by non-workers. But it is not the share of the worker, i.e. the *corvée* peasant, that is determined by the fruit of his labor, rather the share of the exploiter, the feudal lord, that is fixed in terms of the definite dues and fees that he receives from the peasant. What remains over in working time and product is the share of the peasant, so that in normal conditions, before the extreme degeneration of serfdom, he has to a large extent the possibility of increasing his own share by exerting more labor-power. Of course, this share of the peasant was steadily reduced by the growing demands of the nobles and clergy for services and fees, over the course of the Middle Ages. But it was always definite, visible norms laid down by men, no matter how arbitrarily they were established, that determined the respective shares of the product of the *corvée* peasant and his feudal leech. For this reason, the medieval *corvée* peasant or serf could perceive and feel exactly when greater burdens were imposed on him and his own share was stinted. It was possible therefore to struggle against the reduction of this share, and such struggle broke out, when external conditions made this possible, as an open struggle of the exploited peasant against the curtailing of his share in the product of his labor. In certain conditions, this struggle was actually successful: the freedom of the urban burghers precisely arose by the way that the former bonded artisans gradually shook off the various *corvées—Kurmeden, Besthaupt, Gewandrecht,*[*] and the thousand other ways of bleeding of the feudal age—one after another, until they conquered the rest—political freedom[†]—by open struggle.

In the wage system there are no legal or customary determinations of the share of the worker in his product, not even arbitrary and forcible ones. This share is determined by the degree of productivity of labor at the time, by the level of technology; it is not the caprice of the exploiter but the progress of technology that steadily and relentlessly reduces the share of the worker. It is then a completely invisible power, a simple mechanical effect of competition and commodity production, that seizes from the worker an ever greater portion of his product and leaves him an ever smaller one, a power that has its effects silently and unnoticeably behind the back of the workers, and against which no struggle

---

[*] *Kurmade* (also *die kurmede*), *besthaupt* and *gewandrecht* (literally, "a right to the robe") refers to a manorial levy extracted from peasants upon the death of a lord or a change of ownership in the manor. Payment could be made in kind (through grain or cattle), money, or even by granting the lord of the manor allowance to sleep with a peasant's wife. It essentially served as an inheritance tax.

[†] The term "total personal freedom of property" was deleted in the manuscript in pencil in the margin and replaced by the term "political freedom."

is therefore possible. The personal role of the exploiter is still visible, whenever it is a question of the absolute wage, i.e. the actual standard of living. A reduction in wages that brings about a suppression of the actual living standard of the workers is a visible attack by the capitalists on the workers, and it is generally countered by immediate struggle when trade unions exist, in favorable cases even successfully. The fall in relative wages, in contrast to this, seemingly occurs without the least personal participation of the capitalist, and within the wage system, i.e. on the basis of commodity production, the workers have no possibility of struggle and defence against it. Workers cannot struggle against technical advances in production, against inventions, the introduction of machinery, against steam and electricity, against improvements in means of communication. The effect of all these advances on the relative wage of the workers thus follows quite mechanically from commodity production and the commodity character of labor-power. This is why even the most powerful trade unions are quite impotent against this tendency to a rapid fall in relative wages. The struggle against the fall in relative wages accordingly means also a struggle against the commodity character of labor-power, i.e. against capitalist production as a whole. The struggle against a decline in relative wages is thus no longer a struggle on the basis of the commodity economy, but rather a revolutionary, subversive initiative against the existence of this economy, it is the socialist movement of the proletariat.*

This explains the sympathies of the capitalist class for trade unions, which they originally fought furiously against, once the socialist struggle has begun— at least in so far as trade unions allow themselves be opposed to socialism. In France, all struggles of the workers to obtain the right of combination were in vain until the 1870s, and trade unions pursued with draconian penalties. Soon after, however, once the Commune uprising had put the whole bourgeoisie into a mad fear of the red specter, a sudden sharp transformation in public opinion began. The personal organ of President [Léon] Gambetta, *La République fran-çaise*, and the whole ruling party of "satisfied republicans," began to praise the trade-union movement, even to propagate it eagerly. In the early nineteenth century, the restrained German workers were pointed out to the English workers as a model, whereas today it is the English worker, and not even the restrained ones but the "covetous" beefsteak-eating trade unionist, who is recommended to the German worker as a model to follow. So true is it that the bourgeoisie finds even the most bitter struggle to increase the absolute wage of the workers

---

* The argument here provides a theoretical basis for Luxemburg's criticism of the conservative tendencies of the trade union movement, which is a persistent theme in her writings from *Reform of Revolution* onward. Trade unions, concerned with immediate bread-and-butter issues, tend to focus on increasing the workers' absolute wage while neglecting the tendency of their relative wages to decline. This by no means renders the role of trade unions superfluous, however, since as their struggles unfold in the context of a broader revolutionary challenge to the system, the need to challenge the decline in the relative wage can come increasingly to the fore.

a harmless triviality compared with an attack on what is most sacred to it—the mechanical law of capitalism to constantly suppress the relative wage.

6

Only if we bring together all the results of the wage relationship presented above, can we understand the capitalist law of wages that governs the material condition of life of the worker. What is most important is to distinguish absolute from relative wages. The absolute wage, for its part, appears in a double guise: first as a sum of money, i.e. the nominal wage, and second as a sum of means of subsistence that the worker can buy for this money, i.e. the real wage. The worker's monetary wage may remain constant or even rise, while his living standard, i.e. the real wage, falls at the same time. The real wage has the constant tendency to fall to the absolute minimum, the minimum of physical existence, in other words there is a constant tendency on the part of capital to pay for labor-power *below* its value. Only workers' organization provides a counterweight to this tendency of capital. The main function of the trade unions is that, by increasing the needs of the workers, by elevating their habits, they create in place of the physical minimum existence a cultural social minimum, below which wages cannot be reduced without immediately provoking a collective struggle in defense.* The great economic significance of Social Democracy, too, is particularly that by stirring the broad masses of workers intellectually and politically, it raises their cultural level and with it their economic needs. When such things as subscribing to a newspaper or buying pamphlets become part of a worker's everyday habits, his economic maintenance rises, and correspondingly so do wages. The effect of Social Democracy in this respect is a double one, if the trade unions of the country in question maintain an open alliance with Social Democracy, since opposition to Social Democracy drives even bourgeois strata to found competing unions, which in their turn carry the educational effect of organization and the rise in cultural level to broader strata of the proletariat. We see, therefore, how in Germany, besides the free trade unions that are allied with Social Democracy, a number of Christian, Catholic and secular trade-union associations are also active. The situation is similar in France, where so-called yellow trade unions were founded to combat the socialist unions, while in Russia the most violent outbreaks of the present revolutionary mass strike† began with

---

*   According to Marx, the value of labor power is not a given magnitude independent of contingent cultural, moral, and social considerations; it is instead directly dependent upon them. What is "necessary" to sustain a worker in one area or era is not the same as what is necessary in another. Luxemburg is showing that the class struggle itself determines the value of labor power. The subjective factor is integral to the objective determination of a central economic category of capitalism.

†   This reference to the outbreak of revolution in Russia shows that Luxemburg re-edited the text for publication as late as 1917–18, while imprisoned in the Wronke fortress.

the "yellow" unions' quiescent towards the government. In England, however, where the trade unions keep their distance from socialism, the bourgeoisie do not bother to spread the idea of combination in proletarian milieus.

The trade union thus plays an indispensable organic role in the modern wage system. It is only through the union that labor-power as a commodity is placed in a position where it can be sold at its value. The capitalist law of value, in relation to labor-power, is not abolished by the trade unions, as [Ferdinand] Lassalle misguidedly assumed; on the contrary, it is only by their action that it is realized.[†] The systematic giveaway price at which the capitalist seeks to buy labor-power is increasingly replaced by a more or less real price thanks to union action.

This function of theirs, however, is performed by the trade unions in the context of the pressure of the mechanical laws of capitalist production, first of all the constant reserve army of inactive workers, and second, the constant fluctuations of the trade cycle up and down. Both laws impose limits to the effect of trade unions that cannot be overcome. The constant change in the industrial trade cycle forces the unions, with every decline, to defend existing achievements from new attacks by capital, and with every upswing, once again to raise the level of wages that had been reduced back up to the level corresponding to the new situation. In this way, the unions are always placed on the defensive. The industrial reserve army of unemployed, however, puts what could be called spatial limits on the effect of the unions: only the upper stratum of the most well-situated workers are accessible to their organization and effects, those for whom unemployment is only periodic, "abnormal" as Marx put it. The lowest stratum of unskilled rural proletarians, on the other hand, constantly flooding into the town from the countryside, as well as from the various semi-rural irregular trades such as brickmaking and digging, are by the very spatial and temporal conditions of their occupation, as well as by their social milieu, less amenable to trade-union organization. Finally, the broad lower stratum of the reserve army: the unemployed with irregular occupation, domestic industry, as well as the sporadically employed poor, fall completely outside all organization. In general, the greater the need and pressure in a stratum of the proletariat, the less the possibility of trade-union influence. Trade-union action, accordingly, is very weak in the depths of the proletariat, while it is strong in the breadth—i.e.

---

[*]   A "yellow" union is a company union, generally formed by employers or the government in order to head-off independent working-class action and militancy. The color yellow was initially chosen for such unions in order to distinguish them from the socialist unions' embrace of red. The first yellow union was established in France in December, 1899 at Montceau-les-Mines.

[†]   Lassalle held that since the capitalist law of value is defined by paying workers according to the minimum necessary for their subsistence, the effort of trade unions to raise wages above this minimum "abolishes" the law of value. In contrast, Luxemburg holds that since the value of labor power is largely determined by the intensity of the class struggle, the efforts of trade unions to raise workers' wages instead *realizes* the capitalist law of value.

even if unions cover only a part of the topmost stratum of the proletariat, their influence extends to the whole stratum, as their achievements benefit the whole mass of workers employed in the trades in question. Trade-union action, in fact, leads to a stronger differentiation within the proletariat as a whole, by raising out of misery the upper advance detachment of industrial workers, those capable of organization, bringing them together and consolidating them. The gulf between the upper stratum of the working class and the lower strata thereby becomes that much greater. In no country is it as great as in England, where the additional cultural effect of Social Democracy on the lower strata, those less capable of organization, is absent, in contrast to the situation in Germany.

It is quite wrong in depicting capitalist wage relationships to focus only on the wages actually paid to industrial workers in employment, a habit of the bourgeoisie and its paid writers that has unfortunately been generally adopted even by the workers themselves. The entire reserve army of unemployed, from the occasionally unemployed skilled workers down to the deepest poverty and official pauperism, is a necessary factor in determining the wage relationships. The lowest strata of the needy and excluded who are employed only to a small extent or not at all, are not as it were a scum that does not form part of "official society," as the bourgeoisie very understandably present them, but are connected with the topmost, best-situated stratum of industrial workers by a whole series of intermediate steps. This inner connection is shown numerically by the sudden growth in the lower strata of the reserve army that occurs every time that business is bad, and the corresponding contraction at the peak of the business cycle, as well as by the relative decline in the number of those who resort to public assistance with the development of the class struggle and the related rise in self-consciousness of the mass of proletarians. And finally, every industrial worker who is crippled at work or has the misfortune of being sixty years old, has a fifty-fifty chance of falling into the lower stratum of bitter poverty, the "beggary stratum" of the proletariat. The living conditions of the lowest strata of the proletariat thus follow the same laws of capitalist production, pulled up and down, and the proletariat, along with the broad stratum of rural workers, the army of unemployed, and all strata from the very top to the very bottom, forms an organic whole, a social class, whose varying graduations of need and oppression can only be correctly grasped by the capitalist law of wages as a whole. Finally, however, no more than half of the law of wages is grasped if just the movement in absolute wages is taken into account. Only the law of automatic decline in relative wages that follows from the increase in labor productivity displays the capitalist law of wages in its full scope.

The observation that workers' wages have the tendency on average to stand at the minimum necessary means of subsistence, was made already in the eighteenth century by the French and English founders of bourgeois political economy. But they explained the mechanism by which this minimum wage was governed in a peculiar manner, i.e. by fluctuations in the supply of hands seeking work. If the workers obtain higher wages than are absolutely necessary for life, these learned men declared, then they marry more and bring more children into the world. In this way, the labor market becomes so overfilled again that it far surpasses the demands of capital. Capital then presses wages sharply down, taking advantage of the great competition among workers. But if wages do not suffice for the necessary maintenance of life, then workers die off on a massive scale, and their ranks are thinned out until only so many remain as capital has a need for, with the result that wages again rise. By this pendulum between excessive proliferation and excessive mortality in the working class, wages are always brought back again to the minimum means of subsistence. This theory, which prevailed in political economy until the 1860s, was taken over by Lassalle, who called it a "merciless iron law"[*] ...

The weaknesses of this theory are quite evident today, with the full development of capitalist production. Large-scale industry, with its feverish pace of business and competition, cannot wait to reduce wages until workers first marry too often, then have too many children, then until these children grow up and appear on the labor market, before it finds the over-supply it desires. The movement of wages, corresponding to the rhythm of industry, does not have the comfortable motion of a pendulum whose swing takes a generation, i.e. twenty-five years; wages are rather in a ceaseless vibrating motion, so that neither can the procreation of the working class govern the level of wages, nor can industry with its demand for the procreation of workers. Secondly, the industrial labor market is generally determined in its extent not by the natural procreation of the workers, but rather by the constant influx of freshly proletarianized strata from the countryside, from handicrafts and small-scale industry, as well as that of the workers' own wives and children. The over-supply of the labor market, in the form of the reserve army, is a constant phenomenon of modern industry and a condition of its existence. So it is not a change in the supply of labor-power, not the movement of the working class that is decisive for the level of wages, but rather change in the demand from capital, *its* movement. A surplus of the commodity labor-power always exists in reserve, and its payment is better or worse

---

[*] Lassalle's theory of the "iron law of wages" held that in capitalism wages tend towards the minimum requirements necessary to sustain the laborer. According to this alleged "iron law," wages can never drop below subsistence levels, since that would threaten the physical existence of the worker, but neither can they rise much above subsistence, given the competition among workers for employment. The logical implication of the theory is that the effort of trade unions to secure higher wages for its members is bound to prove ultimately fruitless. Although Marx is often associated with the idea, Lassalle's "iron law of wages" owes more to Malthus' theory of population than to Marx's work. Marx fervently opposed Lassalle's conception of the iron law of wages on both empirical and theoretical grounds; he argued that while there is a *tendency* for wages, at certain historic junctures, to gravitate towards subsistence, wages are dependent on the level of class struggle between workers and capitalists and therefore are subject to no "iron" laws at all.

according to whether capital moves to strongly absorb labor-power at the peak of the business cycle or to expel it again on a massive scale in the commotion of economic crisis.

The mechanism of the law of wages is thus quite different from how it was assumed by bourgeois political economy, and also by Lassalle. The result, however, i.e. the pattern of wage relations that actually arises from this, is still worse than it was according to that old assumption. The capitalist law of wages is certainly not an "iron" law, but it is still more relentless and terrible, being an "elastic" law that seeks to press the wages of employed workers down to the minimum in terms of means of subsistence, by simultaneously keeping a whole large stratum of unemployed squirming on a thin elastic tightrope between existence and non-existence.

The positing of the "iron law of wages" with its provocative revolutionary character was possible only at the beginnings of political economy, in its youthful years. From the moment that Lassalle made this law the axis of his political agitation in Germany, the lackeys of bourgeois political economy hastened to conjure away the iron law of wages, condemning it as a false and erroneous doctrine. A whole pack of regular paid agents of the manufacturers, such as [Léon] Faucher, [Hermann] Schulze von Delitzsch and Max Wirth, launched a crusade against Lassalle and the iron law of wages, in which connection they recklessly smeared their own predecessors: Adam Smith, Ricardo, and the other great creators of bourgeois political economy. Once Marx had shown the elastic character of the capitalist law of wages, under the effect of the industrial reserve army, in 1867,* bourgeois political economy finally went silent. Today, the official professorial science of the bourgeoisie has no law of wages at all, preferring to avoid this tricky subject and simply advance incoherent babbling about the lamentable character of unemployment and the usefulness of moderate and modest trade unions.

We have the same comedy in relation to the other major question of political economy, i.e. how is capitalist profit created, where does it come from? Just as on the subject of the share of the worker in the wealth of society, so on that of the capitalist, too, the first scientific answer was given already by the founders of political economy in the eighteenth century. This theory was given its clearest form by David Ricardo, who clearly and logically explained the profit of the capitalist as the unpaid labor of the proletariat.

7

In our consideration of the law of value, we started with the purchase and sale of the commodity labor-power. This already requires, however, a proletarian

---

* See *Capital* Vol. 1, pp. 781–94. 1867 was the year Marx published the first volume of *Capital*.

wage-worker without means of production, and a capitalist who possesses these on a sufficient scale to found a modern enterprise. How did these emerge on the commodity market? In our earlier presentation, we had only commodity producers in view, i.e. people with their own means of production, who themselves produce commodities for sale. How could capital on the one hand, and a complete lack of means on the other, arise on the basis of the exchange of equal commodity values? We have now seen that the purchase of the commodity labor-power, even at its full value, leads, when this commodity is put to use, to the formation of unpaid labor or surplus value, i.e. of capital. The formation of capital and inequality thus becomes clear, once we consider wage-labor and its effects. But this means that capital and proletarians must already be in existence! The question therefore is, how and from what did the first proletarians and the first capitalists arises, how was the first leap made from simple commodity production to capitalist production? In other words, how did the transition take place from small-scale medieval handicrafts to modern capitalism?

As to the rise of the first modern proletariat, the answer is given by the history of the dissolution of feudalism. In order for a worker to appear on the market, he had to have obtained personal freedom. The first precondition for this was therefore emancipation from serfdom and forced labor. But he also had to have lost all means of production. This was brought about by the massive "enclosure," through which the landholding nobility formed their present estates at the dawn of the modern age. Peasants by the thousands were driven from the land they had possessed for centuries, and communal peasant lands taken over by the lords. The English nobility, for example, did this when the expansion of trade in the Middle Ages, and the blossoming of wool manufacture in Flanders, made the raising of sheep for the wool industry a profitable business. In order to transform fields into sheep-walks, the peasants were simply driven off the land. These "enclosures" in England lasted from the fifteenth century through to the nineteenth. In the years 1814–20, for example, on the estates of the Duchess of Sutherland, no less than 15,000 inhabitants were evicted, their villages burned down and their fields converted into meadows, on which 131,000 sheep were kept instead of peasants.* In Germany, a notion of how this violent manufacture of "free" proletarians out of banished peasants was accomplished by the Prussian nobility, is given by [Wilhelm] Wolff's pamphlet *Die schlesische Millliarde* [The Silesian Billion].† These peasants, deprived of their existence, had nothing left

---

* Luxemburg's discussion of the Duchess of Sutherland closely follows Marx's critique of her policies in *Capital* Vol. 1, p. 891.

† Wilhelm Wolff's pamphlet *Die schlesische Milliarde*, on the weavers' uprising in Silesia, was first published as an article series in Marx's *Neue Rheinische Zeitung*. Exiled in Manchester, Wolff remained a staunch friend of Marx and Engels until his death in 1864, and Marx dedicated the first volume of *Capital* to "my unforgettable friend Wilhelm Wolff—intrepid, faithful, noble protagonist of the proletariat" (this dedication is unfortunately omitted in the Penguin edition). See Wilhelm Wolff, *Die schlesische Milliard mit einer Einleitung von Friedrich Engels* (Hottingen-Zurich: Verlag

but the freedom either to starve or to sell themselves, free as they were, for a hunger wage.*

VII. THE TENDENCIES OF THE CAPITALIST ECONOMY

1

We have seen how commodity production arose in the wake of the step-by-step dissolution of all forms of society with a definite planned organization of production—the primitive communist society, the slave economy, the medieval *corvée* economy. We have also seen how the present-day capitalist economy emerged out of simple commodity economy, urban artisanal production, quite mechanically at the end of the Middle Ages, i.e. without human will and consciousness. We initially posed the question: *how is the capitalist economy possible?* This is indeed the fundamental question of political economy as a science. And this science supplies us with an adequate answer. It shows how the capitalist economy, which in view of its total lack of planning, its lack of any conscious organization, is at first sight something impossible, an inextricable puzzle, can nevertheless exist and function at a whole. This happens:

By commodity exchange and the money economy, whereby all individual producers, and the most remote regions of the earth, are economically linked together, and a division of labor accomplished that spans the world;

By free competition, which ensures technological progress and at the same time constantly transforms small producers into wage workers, whereby capital is supplied with purchasable labor-power;

By the capitalist law of value, which on the one hand automatically takes care that wage workers never rise up from the proletarian state and escape labor under the command of capital, while on the other hand making possible an ever greater accumulation of unpaid labor into capital, and thereby ever greater concentration and extension of means of production;

By the industrial reserve army, which provides capitalist production with a capacity for extension and adaptation to the needs of society;

---

der Volksbuchhandlung, 1886). See also Engels's series of articles "Wilhelm Wolff" in *Marx-Engels Collected Works*, Vol. 24 (New York: International Publishers, 1989), pp. 129–71.

    * At the end of this chapter the following words were added to the manuscript in pencil: "Reformation! Bl. 293ff. Formation of the psychological *type* of the modern wage-slave out of the persecuted beggar, Bl. 350."

By equalization of the rate of profit, which governs the constant movement of capital from one branch of production into another, and thus regulates the balance of the division of labor; and finally

By price fluctuations and crises, which in part daily, and in part periodically, lead to a balance between blind and chaotic production, and the needs of society.

In this way, by the mechanical effect of the above economic laws, the capitalist economy arose and exists entirely by itself, without any conscious intervention of society. In other words, it becomes possible in this way, despite the lack of any organized economic connection between the individual producers, despite the completely planlessness in people's economic activity, for social production and its circuit with consumption to proceed, for the great mass of society to be put to work, the needs of society to be met one way or another, and economic progress, the development of the productivity of human labor, to be secured as the foundation of the progress of culture as a whole.

These however are the fundamental conditions for the existence of any human society, and as long as an economic form that has developed historically satisfies these conditions, it can claim to be a historical necessity.

Social conditions, however, are not rigid and immovable forms. We have seen how in the course of time they undergo many alterations, how they are subject to constant change, in which the progress of human culture beats a path for development. The long millennia of the primitive communist economy, which led human society from its first origins in a semi-animal existence to a high level of cultural development, with the construction of language and religion, stock-raising and agriculture, sedentary life and the formation of villages, is followed by the gradual demolition of primitive communism and the construction of antique slavery, which in turn brings with it major new advances in social life, to end again with the decline of the antique world. On the ruins of the antique world, the communist society of the Germanic peoples was the point of departure for a new form—the *corvée* economy, on which medieval feudalism was based.

Once again, development follows its uninterrupted course. In the womb of feudal society, germs of a completely new economic and social form arise in the towns, with the formation of guild handicrafts, commodity production and regular trade; it collapses and makes way for capitalist production, which arises out of artisanal commodity production thanks to world trade, the discovery of America and of the sea route to India.

The capitalist mode of production, for its part, is already right from the start, viewed in the quite immense perspective of historical progress, not something inalterable that exists forever; it is simply a transitional phase, a rung on the colossal ladder of human cultural development, in the same way as previous social forms. And indeed, the development of capitalism itself, on closer inspection, leads on to its own decline and beyond. If we have up to now investigated the connections that make the capitalist economy *possible*, it is now time to familiarize ourselves with those that make it *impossible*. For this, we need to trace the specific internal laws of capitalist supremacy in their further effect. It is these very laws that at a certain level of development turn against all the fundamental conditions without which human society cannot exist. What particularly distinguishes the capitalist mode of production from all its predecessors is that it has the inherent impetus to extend automatically across the whole of the earth, and drive out all other earlier social orders.* In the time of primitive communism, the whole world accessible to historical research was likewise covered with communist economies. But between individual communist communities and tribes there were scarcely any connections, or only weak ones between neighboring communities. Every such community or tribe lived a life closed in on itself, and if for example we find such striking facts as that the medieval Germanic communist community and the ancient Peruvian community in South America were almost identical, the "*mark*" in one being the "*marca*" in the other, this circumstance remains for us an unexplained puzzle, if not mere chance. At the time of the spread of ancient slavery, too, we find greater or lesser *similarity* in the organization and relations of individual slave economies and states of antiquity, but no common economic life between them. In the same way, the history of guild handicraft and its emancipation was repeated in more or less the same way in most towns of medieval Italy, Germany, France, Holland, England, etc., but for the most part the history of each town was a separate one.

Capitalist production extends itself to all countries, not just giving them a similar economic form, but linking them into a single great capitalist world economy.

Within each European industrial country, capitalist production ceaselessly drives out petty trade, handicraft and small peasant production. At the same time it draws all backward European countries, and all the lands of America, Asia, Africa and Australia, into the world economy. This happens in two ways: by world trade and by colonial conquests. Both began together with the discovery of America at the end of the fifteenth century, extended further in the course of the following centuries, and particularly in the nineteenth century experienced the greatest upswing and spread ever more widely. World trade and colonial conquest go hand in hand in the following way. First of all they bring the capitalist industrial countries of Europe into contact with forms of society of all kinds across the world that are based on earlier cultural and economic stages: peasant, slave economy, feudal *corvée*, but above all primitive communist. By drawing these into trade, they are rapidly shaken and destroyed. By the

---

* This is more exhaustively treated in Luxemburg's *Accumulation of Capital*.

foundation of colonial trading companies abroad, or by direct conquest, the land, and the most important foundation of production such as cattle where these are present, come into the hands of European states or trading companies. In this way, the indigenous social relations and mode of economy of native peoples are everywhere destroyed, whole peoples partly eradicated, partly proletarianized and placed under the command of industrial and commercial capital as slaves or wage-laborers in one form or another. The history of colonial wars lasting decades runs right through the nineteenth century: uprisings against France, Italy, England and Germany in Africa, against France, England, Holland and the United States in Asia, against Spain and France in America—a long and stubborn resistance by the old indigenous societies against their destruction and proletarianization by modern capital, a struggle in which eventually capital everywhere triumphs in the end.

First of all, this means a tremendous extension of the realm of capital, the construction of a world market and world economy, in which all inhabited lands of the earth are reciprocally producers and customers for products, working integrally together and participating in one and the same earth-spanning economy.

The other side, however, is the advancing immiseration of ever greater circles of humanity around the globe, and the increasing uncertainty of their existence. To the extent that in place of old communistic, peasant or *corvée* relations, with their limited productive powers and low standard of living, but with firm and secure conditions of existence for all, there appear capitalist colonial relations, proletarianization and wage-slavery, all the peoples affected in America, Asia, Africa and Australia come to experience bare misery, an unknown and unbearable burden of labor, and finally complete insecurity of existence. After fertile and rich Brazil had been transformed for the needs of European and North American capitalism into a gigantic wasteland of monotonous coffee plantations, and the indigenous people en masse into proletarianized wage-slaves on these plantations, these wage-slaves were suddenly exposed to a purely capitalist phenomenon: the so-called "coffee crisis,"* resulting in long-term unemployment and naked hunger. The rich and immense subcontinent of India was subjected by English colonial policy to the rule of capital after decades of desperate resistance, and since this time famine and typhus have been periodic guests in the Ganges region, to which millions have succumbed. In central Africa, English and German colonial policy over the last twenty years has transformed whole populations into wage-slaves and starved others, their bones lying scattered everywhere. The desperate revolts and famines in the Chinese empire[117] are the result of the crushing of the old peasant and artisan economy of this

---

* By 1900, 75 percent of world coffee production was in Brazil. In 1907, a fall in price on the international coffee market led to the first great coffee crisis in the state of São Paulo.

country by the entry of European capital. The arrival of European capitalism in North America was accompanied first by the extermination of the indigenous Amerindian population and the theft of their lands by English emigrants, then by the establishment at the start of the nineteenth century of a capitalist raw-materials production for English industry, and the enslavement of four million black Africans who were sold to America by European slave-traders, to be used as labor-power on the cotton, sugar and tobacco plantations under the command of capital.

In this way, one continent after another comes inextricably under the rule of capital, and on every continent one territory after another, one race after another, with ever new and uncounted millions succumbing to proletarianization, enslavement, insecurity of existence, in short, immiseration.[118] The establishment of the capitalist world economy brings in its wake the spread of ever greater misery, an unbearable burden of labor and a growing insecurity of existence across the whole globe, corresponding to the accumulation of capital in a few hands. The capitalist world economy increasingly means the yoking of all humanity to heavy labor with countless deprivations and sufferings, with physical and mental degeneration for the purpose of capital accumulation. We have seen how capitalist production has the peculiarity that consumption, which in every previous economic form is the purpose, is here only a means, simply a way of serving the real purpose: the accumulation of capitalist profit. The self-expansion of capital appears as alpha and omega, as the intrinsic purpose and meaning of all production. The craziness of this situation, however, only appears to the extent that capitalist production develops into world production. Here, on the scale of the world economy, the absurdity of the capitalist economy attains its true expression in the picture of all humanity groaning with frightful suffering under the yoke of a blind social power, capital, that it has itself unconsciously created. The underlying purpose of every social form of production, the maintenance of society by labor, the satisfaction of its needs, is placed here completely on its head, with production not being for the sake of people, but production for the sake of profit becoming the law all over the earth, with the under-consumption, constant insecurity of consumption, and sometimes direct non-consumption of the immense majority of people becoming the rule.

At the same time, the development of the world economy also leads to other important phenomena, important even for capitalist production itself. As we said, there are two stages in the intrusion of the rule of European capital into non-European countries: first the entry of trade, with the indigenous people being drawn into commodity exchange, and to some degree also the transformation of the existing forms of production of the indigenous peoples into commodity production; then the expropriation of these peoples from their land, in one form or another, i.e. from their means of production. These means of production are transformed into capital in the hands of the Europeans, while the indigenous peoples are transformed into proletarians. These two steps, however, are sooner or later followed by a third: the founding of capitalist production in the colonial country itself, either by emigrant Europeans or by enriched indigenous individuals. The United States of America, which was only populated by English and other European emigrants once the native redskins had been exterminated in a long war, first formed an agricultural hinterland of capitalist Europe, supplying raw materials such as cotton and grain for English industry, and customers for industrial products of every kind from Europe. In the second half of the nineteenth century, however, the United States developed its own industry, which not only displaced imports from Europe, but soon presented a tough competition to European capitalism in Europe itself, as well as on other continents. In India, English capitalism has similarly been faced with dangerous competition from an indigenous textile industry and others. Australia has embarked on the same path of development from a colonial country into a country of capitalist industry. In Japan, an indigenous industry developed already with the first step—under the impulse of foreign trade—and preserved Japan from partition as a European colony. In China the process of fragmentation and plundering of the country by European capitalism has been complicated by China's effort, with the aid of Japan, to found its own capitalist production as a defence against the European, though this attempt also leads to increased and complicated sufferings for its population. In this way, not only does the rule and command of capital spread over the whole earth by the creation of a world market, but the capitalist mode of production itself spreads steadily across the whole earth. This however means that the need of production to expand comes into an ever more unhappy relationship with its terrain of expansion, its outlet opportunities. It is the innermost need of capitalist production, as we have seen, the very law of its existence, that it should have the possibility of not remaining stable but extending ever more widely and ever more rapidly, i.e. producing ever greater masses of commodities, in ever larger factories, and ever more rapidly, with ever better technical means. This expansion possibility of capitalist production knows no inherent limits, since there are no limits to technological progress and hence to the productive powers of the earth. But this need for expansion does come up against quite particular limits, i.e. those of the interest of capitalist profit. Production and its expansion only have a sense if they yield at least the "customary" average profit. Whether this is the case depends on the market, i.e. on the relationship between effective demand on the part of consumers, and the amount of commodities produced along with their prices. The interest of capitalist profit requires on the one hand an ever more rapid and greater production, thereby creating of itself at each step market limitations that stand in the way of the impetuous expansive pressure of production. The result of this, as we have seen, is the unavoidability of industrial and trade crises, which periodically balance the relationship between the inherently unbounded, limitless capitalist pressure of production and the barriers to capitalist consumption, and make possible the continued existence of capitalism and its further development.

Yet the more countries develop a capitalist industry of their own, the greater is the need and possibility for expansion of production, while the smaller in relation to this is the possibility of expansion due to market barriers. If we compare the leaps by which English industry grew in the 1860s and 70s, when England was still the leading capitalist country on the world market, with its growth in the last two decades, since Germany and the United States have significantly displaced England on the world market, it is clear that growth has become much more slow in relation to the previous period. But what was the particular fate of English industry unavoidably faces German and North American industry too, and eventually the industry of the whole world. Incessantly, with each step of its own further development, capitalist production is approaching the time when its expansion and development will be increasingly slow and difficult.[*] Of course, capitalist development still has a good way to go, as the capitalist mode of production proper still represents only a very small fraction of total production on earth. Even in the oldest industrial countries of Europe, there are still alongside large industrial firms very many small and backward artisanal workshops, and above all, much the greater part of agricultural production is not capitalist but still pursued along peasant lines. There are also whole countries in Europe in which large-scale industry is hardly developed, local production still bearing a principally peasant and artisanal character. And finally, in the other continents, with the exception of the northern part of America, capitalist production sites are only small and scattered points, while whole immense expanses of land have in part not even made the transition to simple commodity production. Of course, the economic life of all these strata of society and countries that do not produce capitalistically, both in Europe and elsewhere, is dominated by capitalism. The European peasant may still conduct the most primitive economy on his holding, but he is dependent at every turn on the big-capitalist economy, on the world market, with which he has been brought into contact by trade and by the tax policy of the large capitalist states. In the same way, the most primitive countries outside of Europe have been brought by world trade and colonial policy under the sway of European and North American capitalism. The capitalist mode of production is still able to achieve powerful expansion by everywhere suppressing all more backward forms of production. In generally, the movement, as we have seen, is in this direction. But precisely through this development capitalism becomes caught in a fundamental contradiction. The more that capitalist production takes the place of more backward forms, the more tightly the limits placed on the market by the interest of profit constrict

---

[*]   This serves as the central argument of Luxemburg's *Accumulation of Capital*, which argues that the barriers to continued capitalist development lie in the failure to realize surplus-value.

the need of already existing capitalist firms to expand. The matter becomes clear if we imagine for a moment that the development of capitalism has proceeded so far that on the whole earth everything that people produce is produced capital-istically, i.e. only by private capitalist entrepreneurs in large firms with modern wage-workers. Then the impossibility of capitalism clearly appears.

Slavery

The tendency of the mark community* is to disintegrate and to make room for new relations, though always according to milieu or to other conditions and consequences.

The oldest form to establish itself after the mark, to a greater or lesser extent in the ancient world, is slavery, the oldest form of class domination and economic exploitation.

Engels says in his *Anti-Dühring* (pp. 162–93)† that after the emergence of private property, the opportunity to employ foreign labor arose. But war supplied them; prisoners of war who were, until this period, slain, and even earlier, eaten, were now used as laborers. (See *Anti-Dühring*, pp. 188–9.)‡

This explanation cannot, strictly speaking, satisfy us.

We are far too inadequately informed about the facts of the slave economy and its origins. Even until recently there have been disagreements among the bourgeois researchers about the meaning and the extent of slavery and the ways it emerged. We are more or less dependent on hypotheses.

It is necessary that one trace out the manner in which slavery emerged out of the mark and the gentile constitution.§ If we search for the point after which we see the mark and the gens exhibiting the oldest forms of exploitation and servitude, we will not immediately encounter slavery, but other forms, which might lead to slavery.

Unlike Engels, we do not need to place exploitation after the emergence of private property. The mark itself allows for exploitation and servitude. The grafting of a foreign mark onto another allows for and creates a relationship of exploitation and servitude *toward the outside*. (In fact, the mark ensured communism internally, but not externally.) An example of this is the *Inca Empire*. Moreover, the Inca Empire teaches us something else: although the conquerors, the Incas, themselves lived together in municipalities, we find in their case four ruling lineages, whose representatives governed the four provinces into which the country was divided. The Incas also had a standing army, necessary for

---

* The *Mark* was an ancient Germanic communal form of village organization that survived in modified form into modern times. Luxemburg subsequently uses the term more universally, applying to what she saw as similar forms in various societies around the world.

† Friedrich Engels, *Herrn Eugen Dühring's Umwalzung der Wissenschaft* (Stuttgart: Verlag von J.H.W. Dietz, 1894); *Anti-Dühring: Herr Eugen Dühring's Revolution in Science, Marx-Engels Collected Works*, Vol. 25 (New York: International Publishers, 1987), pp. 146–71.

‡ *Herrn Eugen Dühring's Umwalzung der Wissenschaft*; *Anti-Dühring: Herr Eugen Dühring's Revolution in Science*, pp. 168–9.

§ The *gens* (plural, *gentes*) was a clan or family group in ancient Rome that shared a common name, traceable to a common ancestor. Descent was through the male heir.

maintaining domination. Thus, there was already a certain aristocracy within the mark. How did this develop?

The four lineages would have taken control of the conquest. These four houses would have probably held an even greater position had the Spanish conquest not put an end to this process.

Similar examples that correspond [to] [*MS. Illegible*] the mark, [of which] there are many. E.g., the oldest historical reference from the island of Crete is that it was conquered by the Dorians.* The Dorians were one of the main tribes of Greece. The conquest took place in prehistoric times.† We do not know who lived on Crete. The conquered people on Crete must have handed over the yields from their crops, excluding the necessary sustenance for themselves and their families, to the conquerors. From these contributions from the subjugated people of Crete, the costs of the common meals of the free people were determined. This is due to the fact that the Dorians lived under communism. An example that the mark was compatible with the exploitation of other marks. The land continued to belong to the Cretan population; they only had to be able to afford the tribute. (The Greek legend of the Minotaur‡ that ate young boys and virgins can be explained by the fact that the subjugated had to hand over their young boys and virgins to the conquerors, similar to the Quechua tribes in the Inca Empire.)

Similar relationships existed elsewhere in Greece.

In Thessaly, the early inhabitants, who lived there before the Greeks, were conquered by the Aeolians and forced to become tenant farmers. They had a name that meant "poor people." Originally, this was one of their folk names. The [*MS. Illegible*] are from [*MS. Illegible*] wandered to Asia Minor, conquered Bithynia§ and similarly subjugated the people living there and forced them to pay tribute.

The most interesting and fruitful example is *Sparta* itself. In Sparta, we still find a strong tradition of gentile law. The Spartans used the peasant population

---

* The archeological discoveries of Arthur Evans from 1900 to 1905, which excavated the ancient Minoan city of Knossos, showed that Cretan history long preceded the "Dorian conquest" of 1,200 BC; literate Minoan civilization goes back to at least 2,700 BC.

† The notion that a "Dorian conquest" of Greece occurred around 1,200 BC that ushered in a "dark age" lasting until the ninth century was first formulated by German scholars in the early nineteenth century to explain the apparent sudden collapse of Mycenaean civilization in southern Greece and islands in the Aegean. There is no scholarly consensus, however, as to whether the collapse resulted from invasions by Greek-speaking Dorians who were initially external to the region. Some point to internal factors, such as ecological or social collapse, while others contend that the destruction of Myceanaean civilization may have been undertaken by the "sea peoples" who ravaged the eastern Mediterranean at the end of the second millennium BC.

‡ In Greek mythology the Minotaur is a creature with the body of a man and the head of a bull that resides in a maze-like construction, the labyrinth. The Minotaur feasted on human flesh; according to Greek mythology, custom demanded that seven Athenian youths and seven virgins be sent on a regular basis to be devoured by it.

§ Bithynia was a region in what is now northwest Turkey, close to the Bosporus straights.

of the Helots as state slaves. They were handed over by the state, that is, by the mark community, to individuals. The individuals were not allowed, however, to kill or sell them to the outside, because the slaves remained communal property. The Helots constituted the landless [agricultural workers] among the Spartans and had to relinquish a certain portion of their yields. Whatever they obtained beyond this amount belonged to them. The land still belonged to the Spartans. It was taken from [the Helots] by the Spartans, so that they now worked on a foreign land that had previously belonged to them. They also had military obligations.

The Spartans also married the Helots. The children of these marriages were, if they were raised as Spartans, not only free, but also citizens. For that reason, their education determined their fate. They were called *mothaken*: half-breeds.

Aside from the Spartans and the Helots, there was another population, that of the *Periokoi*, e.g. those that lived around the city (thus the word [related] word "periphery").* The *Periokoi* had no political rights, but were personally free.

The Spartans continued to live in the gens. Marriage was forbidden within the gens; the gentile law of inheritance was in effect, and thus the wealth remained in the gens. Marriage within the gens was only allowed to heiresses, in order that the wealth remain in the gens. From the dues of the Helots, the Spartans ran a communist economic organization. Bourgeois historians construe the communist meals in Sparta as militaristic club feasts.

WHAT IS THE DIFFERENCE BETWEEN CRETE AND SPARTA?

In Crete, the land remained the property of the inhabitants, even after the conquest by the Dorians, who only demanded tribute from the subjugated.

In Sparta, the Spartans took the land from the Helots and the Helots were forced to work this land for the Spartans. The Helots could therefore subsist only if they fed both themselves and their masters. They were dominated completely by the mark community of the Spartans and were assigned to individuals, that is, treated like objects. They therefore worked as labor power on foreign soil. They have no social cohesion of their own anymore; they are integrated into the mark of the Spartans. But they are not an active part of the mark of the Spartans, only the labor power for their subjugators. They have no more land, which was the basis of their social cohesion. They can only become Spartans if they are children of Spartans and Helots, and if they are in such a way raised as Spartans; apart from this, they can only become fully entitled members of the Spartan

---

* The *Periokoi* were mainly farmers and merchants who lived in the vicinity of Sparta. They were remnants of a conquered people who lived in the less fertile hills and along the coasts. Although they lacked citizens' rights, they were not slaves or Helots.

mark through distinction in military service. Thus they are already slaves; they live in a *class state.*

If we compare the Peruvians, Crete, and Sparta, we would have to locate the Peruvian and the Cretan forms as the older forms and the Spartan as the newer one. In Peru and Crete, the subjugated are not yet slaves. They are members of the mark as before. There is no class domination, no class society in effect here. A class society is the grouping of classes *within* a given society. In Peru and Crete, it is a matter of the exploitation of *one society by another society.*

However, the Helots form a *social bond* with the Spartans. Therefore, they live in a class society.

Slavery accelerates the dissolution of the communist association and goes hand in hand with the rise of private property. This stands in contrast to Engels, who saw slavery as arising only *after* the introduction of private property.

Slavery appeared naturally in several phases, depending on the level of development of the specific society.

The first beginning of slavery is a kind of tenant relationship. Communism is carried over, except that a certain tribiute has to be paid. This has a corrosive effect on the conquered, as well as the conquerors. In a later stage, the land is taken from the conquered, and already slavery has arrived. But the conquered are still being exploited communistically. Then the disintegration of communism. The rise of private property. Thereby the slaves also become private property. While before the slaves were not to be killed or sold, because they were communal property, once private property arose, the individual could do with the slave what he wanted.

The exploitation of one mark by another has a corrosive effect on the exploited [and the exploiting] mark, something we see already with the Incas. The disintegrative process is accelerated. First the conquest occurs and then a reconfiguration of the organization takes place. In order to fortify this, a specific class develops, the military, and thus inequality in the mark. Domination from above evolves faster when conquests and wars occur.

THE DEVELOPMENT OF SLAVERY AMONG THE GREEKS

At the moment the Greeks enter history, their situation is that of a disintegrated gens. Though there are strong vestiges of the gentile law remaining, nevertheless there already exists a *rural system of private property* and the free right to dispose of that land. The peasantry is already in a state of deep indebtedness. Along with them, there is an *aristocracy.* Its representatives can already be found in the gentile constitution. The aristocrats are the descendants of the public officeholders in the gentile constitution: chiefs of the mark, [chief] herdsmen, etc. In the mark, they generally emerge from the undivided mark and over time, they confiscate more and more from it. In this way, they obtain greater assets and with the advent of hereditary power, they develop more and more into a stratum that is supported by the peasantry. In this way, a minor aristocracy develops, one that already possesses privileges and goods. The earliest members of the mark are now the indebted peasants, who have to pay fees to the aristocracy.

These relationships were strongly influenced by the culture of the Orient, which was older and more prosperous. In order to be able to understand all the events of the ancient world in Greece and Rome, the influence of the Orient must, generally speaking, be taken into account, such as in the Near East, Assyria, Babylonia, Egypt, and Phoenicia. Historians and scholars of prehistory place great emphasis on the influence of the Near East. In particular, the oriental technologies of war were especially influential. The Greek war chariot originated in the Near East.

Exchange of goods with the Orient was critical. Luxury items were exchanged for the refinement of [the upper strata's] way of life. The reason for the exchange was in order to get their hands on these items. In the old empires, there was already a strong differentiation among classes and the upper strata lived quite luxuriously. Already in the ninth and tenth centuries before Christ, there existed a strong disintegration within the society.

Exchange with the Orient led to two things:

1. Provided an incentive to the [Greek] aristocracy to have *various products manufactured*, which could be exchanged for luxury items from the Orient. Among these items were oil, wine, and metals.

2. Spread, in association with exchange, the *money economy* in place of the earlier natural economy, since metal as a means of exchange comes from the Orient.[*] In a natural economy, all goods are produced only for subsistence and in fact mainly by the people who themselves consume, sell, or exchange them. The leader of the mark receives foodstuffs as income. Yet, once the leaders become an aristocracy and the money economy is in place, the fees had to be paid in money and in kind. This creates a situation wherein the peasantry falls increasingly into debt [to] the large landowners.

In Homer's time, around the same time as the great migration of the Germanic peoples,[†] raising livestock prevailed over agriculture, which was [already] important in this period. At this time, *the aristocracy* themselves took part in

---

[*]   The use of minted coin as money originated in Asia Minor, in the Kingdom of Lydia, around 650 BC.

[†]   Homer lived in the eighth century BC. Luxemburg's reference to a "great migration of the Germanic peoples" probably refers to a purported expansion of German-speaking tribes from southern Scandinavia to the Lower Rhine and Eastern Germany between 850 and 650 BC. The period is clouded in obscurity, however, and there is little scholarly consensus about the extent or nature of this migration; some argue that it actually occurred much later.

production, which ended after Homer. The aristocracy provided the fighters; *it had trade with the Orient in its hands.* This can also be deduced from the mark itself. The mark itself engaged in trade, but with the outside, not within its own borders. The mark as a *whole* was engaged in trade. Since the mark as such could not carry on trade, it came about that the natural or customary public officials became, at the same time, the natural public organs of trade. And it is from these public officials that the aristocracy was later derived.

As seats for the reigning military aristocracy, there were castles that served as permanent constructions of militarism. *Building the castles was a form of compulsory labor for the surrounding peasantry.* The more hereditary the mark's earlier leadership positions became, the greater the fees paid by the peasants. Instead of money, the only thing they could afford was compulsory labor. It was *compulsory labor* for them, because the peasants no longer paid their fees to an *elected* organization. An historically handed down inverted relationship from the past.

The refinement of the lives of the aristocracy led to an increasing division between them and the peasantry. It developed into, on the one hand, the mass of peasants, who bore the brunt of the work, and on the other hand, the small body of aristocratic families, who saw as their only occupations the conduct of war and trade, with the latter helping to enhance their way of life. *Eventually, the aristocracy ceased to participate in the production process.* This increased their standard of living even more. This increase resulted in an even greater trade, and in order to support it, production had to be adapted for trade.

Passive trade gave way to active trade. That is, while the aristocracy originally needed a surplus for trade, it later had goods manufactured for the sole purpose of exchange: oil, wine, and metals. These items were exchanged for fine linen, perfumes, purple robes, etc. With increasing trade came a growing use of precious metals. Increasingly, the peasants had to pay their fees in money; they fell more and more into debt.

This leads to the establishment of debt slavery. Peasants who cannot afford their fees are turned into slaves, who thus give over their life and death to the aristocracy. All of their labor is now performed for the aristocracy.

In conjunction with this, a new social form emerged, *the ancient city.* This was the area in which the aristocrats lived. Within the city they had their houses and outside of the city they kept their goods. Living in the city meant that one was not a participant in the production process, since the fields, the key source of production, lay further out.

In order to be able to live in the city, it was necessary for the aristocracy to have artisans living around them as well as city merchants, who acted as brokers for them, and in addition there were a whole series of personal servants. Here for the first time the foundations of a true slavery begin to take shape, one that we also see later in Greece.

Already during the time of Homer there were traces of slavery, though only in aristocratic families and in small numbers. *In this first phase of slavery, there was a preponderance of the female element.* Female slaves were used as concubines, wet nurses, and maids in the house, who worked next to the housewife and under her direction.

Then, adding to the decline of the peasant class, came *debt slavery.*

As early as the sixth century, these circumstances led to *revolutions* in Greece.

The ruined peasant class rebelled and called for new *allocations of land and soil,* a utopian demand to turn back the wheel of history. Although this call during the Solonian Revolution* of 594 would die away without being heard, the rebellion precipitated one thing: the *abolition of debt slavery.* (See "[Karl] Ploetz")† (Solon was the legislator, the Solonian Revolution is to be understood here as upheaval.)

The remarkable course of Greek history can be explained by these circumstances, where class domination took on the original form of *domination by the city over the land.*

Slavery *and trade* evolved at the same time as the aristocracy.

After slavery was initially adopted for personal service, the aristocracy reached the point where, in order to keep up with the increase in its living standards, it had to buy slaves in order to create products for exchange. For the first time, in Greece, we see workshops that are established specifically for slaves to produce goods for exchange. The use of slaves in oil and wine plantations and the massive use of slaves in mines. The slaves became direct competitors to the proletarianized peasants, and they eventually could be used by the aristocracy in their larger enterprises. In the mines, free labor was displaced *completely* by slave labor. Initially peasants doing compulsory labor carried out craft production for the aristocracy. As the needs of the aristocrats became more refined, however, the peasants were no longer adequate. Specialists emerged who could do much more refined work in their craft. In the end, the free artisans were largely replaced by slaves.

Thus we see in Greece, namely in Attica, that wealthy Greeks established *entire workshops* in which slaves manufactured products for exchange. Demosthenes, the father of the famous orator, had a workshop in which 30 slaves worked under supervision as sword-sharpeners and armorers.

---

* The Solonian Revolution refers to the series of reforms introduced by the Athenian statesman Solon in the sixth century BC. Central to these was the cancellation of onerous debts that the Athenian poor owed the aristocrats and large landowners. His reforms also lowered the property and financial qualifications for voting and holding public office, which served as an important foundation for the later emergence of Athenian democracy.

† See Karl Julius Plötz's *Auszug aus der alten, mittleren und neuren geschichte* (Abstract of Ancient, Medieval, and Modern History) (Berlin: A.G. Ploetz, 1895). The book has undergone dozens of editions since the nineteenth century; it is now published under the title *Der Große Ploetz—Auszug der Geschichte* (Göttingen: Vandenhoeck & Ruprecht, 2008).

As a result of the Solonian Revolution, not only was debt slavery abolished, but military obligations also came to affect the peasantry. They became, so to speak, full citizens. Under the circumstances, however, this contributed to an even more rapid disintegration of the peasantry. As a result of the development of trade, which in Greece was comprised of sea trade, a merchant fleet and a navy emerged. Thus there was a large military burden upon the entire people. The burden of the navy was one of the greatest burdens on the peasantry.

After debt slavery had been abolished, *prisoners of war* increasingly became *material for slavery*. Later, in the seventh century, slaves were increasingly *purchased*. The purchased slaves were the peoples who lived around the perimeter of the Black Sea. Some of them also came from less civilized regions in the West such as what is today Spain and the Gaul of that time. The Greeks kept *colonies* all around this region. *Colonization* was one of the causes of the disintegration of the peasantry. Wherever a group of Greeks conquered a speck of land, usually along the shoreline of the sea, they established themselves there with their facilities and it became a Greek city. This was the case with Chios, an island and a Greek colony, where there was a large slave market.

The slave trading economy was especially large in centers where the large mines and plantations were concentrated, such as Sicily and Attica (Attica is Athens with a certain perimeter), in Corinth and elsewhere.

Thus, after the Solonian Revolution, there were slaves who *were captured, purchased and who were born into the household.*

INDICATIONS ON THE SCOPE OF SLAVERY

The question of the size of the slave trade in Greece and in the ancient world is generally a point of contention among scholars, economists, and historians.

[Karl Johann] Rodbertus made himself well known for the portrayal of the ancient Greek *oikos* economy (*oikos* is the house, the family, together with the bondsmen, maidservants, and slaves).[*] With this description, he created the impression that the whole of economic life in the ancient world rested upon slavery. This view was accepted by Professor [Karl] Bücher,[†] for whom the first phase of economic development is the closed, household economy, based on

---

[*]   Karl Johann Rodbertus, a German economist and conservative socialist, rejected Eduard Meyer's contention that ancient Greek slavery represented a form of incipient capitalism. Max Weber later praised Rodbertus's studies on the ancient world as influencing his own approach to the understanding of this issue. Luxemburg is probably referring to Rodbertus's *Zur Frage des Sachwerths des Geldes in Altertum* (Or the Question of the Intrinsic Value of Money in Antiquity) (Jena: Druck und Verlag von Freidrich Mauke, 1870).

[†]   See Karl Bücher, *Die Aufstände der unfreien Arbeiter* (The Rebellions of Unfree Labor) (Frankfurt am Maine: Druck von C. Adekmann, 1874). Marx made notes of this work of Bücher's on slave revolts, which will appear for the first time in the forthcoming Vol. IV/27 of the *Marx-Engels Gesamtausgabe*.

slave labor. According to Bücher, this domestic economy predominated up to the Middle Ages.

Recently, Professor Eduard Meyer has strongly contradicted this view. Two works by him can be recommended:

1. *Die wirtschaftliche Entwicklung des Altertums. Ein Vortrag* [(The Economic Development of the Ancient World. A Lecture) (Jena: G. Fischer,] 1895).

2. *Die Sklaverei im Altertum* [(Slavery in the Ancient World) (Dresden: Zahn & Jaenisch,] 1898).

The first work was cited heavily by [Karl] Kautsky in *The Origin of Christianity.**

There are also numerous articles by Professor Eduard Meyer and his views (under "Population in Ancient Times") published in the *Handwörterbuch der Staatswissenschaften.*†

Unfortunately, Professor Eduard Meyer advocates the opposite extreme. He mainly demonstrates *that slavery played a rather marginal role in antiquity* and he bases his assessment on the fact that the number of slaves was either the same or smaller than the number of free laborers (with the exception of a few periods).

His rationale does not hold water. In contemporary society, capitalist production is dominant. Within it are the industrial workers. The farm laborers, the small craftsmen, the layers of educated professionals, etc., do not belong to it. But they, the industrial workers, stamp the conditions of their existence on the other classes. Contemporary society is formed by them although they are in fact a minority in the population.

It follows that the slaves may have been a minority of the population and yet all of the economic life in antiquity could have rested on them. It is not the numbers that are definitive, but the sum total of the tendencies that result from them that is definitive.

([...]‡ Eduard Bernstein came up with the idea, after the census of 1905, that there were thus so and so many craftsmen, tradesmen, etc. But that in no way disproves the fact that the proletariat is the foundation of today's society. It is not possible to arrive at that with numbers.)

The first detailed evidence concerning slave labor comes from the fifth century, the time of Pericles, who lived between 444 and 429 [BC].§ He was prom-

---

* See Karl Kautsky, *Der Ursprung des Christentrums: Eine historische Untersuchung* (Stuttgart: J.H.W. Dietz, 1908). For an English translation, see *Foundations of Christianity*, translated by Jacob Hartmann (New York: Monthly Review, 1972).

† See Eduard Meyer, "Die Bevölkerung im Altertum," *Handwörterbuch der Staatswissenschaften*, Vol. 2 (1886), pp. 674 ff. In this work Meyer took issue with the claim that ancient Greece suffered from a severe decline in population from the seventh century BC.

‡ In the original, the word "comrade" is crossed out.

§ Pericles actually lived from 495 to 429 BC. He led Athens from 461 to 429 BC.

inent in Attica and had a great influence. According to [Karl Julius] Beloch's[*] latest figures, in Attica, there were 130,000–150,000 freemen, 100,000 slaves at that time. The total population of Greece amounted to 2,250,000. Among them, Beloch counted 850,000 slaves in the same Periclean period.

Professor Meyer revised the numbers further. According to him, in the year 431, in the time of Pericles, there were 170,000 freemen, 40,000 *metics*,[†] descendants of mixed marriages of slaves and citizens, and 150,000 slaves. (Contemporary Greece has over two million inhabitants, remaining more or less stable.)

Afterwards, the worsening of conditions in Greece, after the turning point of Pericles' time. 431–404 BC, the *Peloponnesian War* between Sparta and Athens. In this war, a sizable number of free peasants perished because they formed the infantry. Later, slavery increased even further. For Attica in the fourth century, 317–307, the following statistics: 90,000 free citizens, 40,000 *metics*, and 400,000 slaves.

Professor Meyer does not dispute these numbers. They prove that after the war the number of slaves exceeded that of the rest of the population. He only claims that this was not the case before and, even then, not in all of Greece, but in a few centers. Furthermore, Professor Meyer speaks of industry and factories in Greece, a typically bourgeois bias.

Thus, where slaves predominated, they were not only used in crafts, mines, and on plantations, but also *very much in personal services*. Slaves were seen as belonging to the estate of a free citizen. Certain citizens owned 50, and others had 1,000. It became fashionable in the fourth century [BC] for free citizens to set foot in the city only with a drove of slaves in front and in back of them. When dandies appeared in Athens, slaves carried chairs for the dandies, letting the master sit down every few steps to shoo away the heat with fans (fanning cool air towards him).

Through Aristotle (born 384 BC, died 322 BC), we have a strong impression of the circumstances of this period. In his *Politics*, which comprises 8 books, he writes:

It is a complete household only if it contains slaves and freemen.[‡]

---

[*]   These figures, compiled by the German economic historian and demographer Karl Julius Beloch, are considered by today's scholars to be largely accurate. See his highly influential *Griechische Geschichte* (Greek History), three volumes (Strasbourg: Verlag von Karl J. Trubner, 1893–1904).

[†]   Metics were resident aliens who did not have citizen rights, although they served in the military and were subject to special tax burdens.

[‡]   Aristotle's *Politics*, in *The Complete Works of Aristotle*, edited by Jonathan Barnes, p. 1988 [1253b4].

From Book I of *Politics*:

> The essence of the science of being a master has to do with using his slaves correctly. He is the master, not because he is the owner of a person, but because he avails himself of it. The slave comprises a part of the wealth of the family.*

From Book III of *Politics*:

> Nature itself created slavery. Animals divide into male and female. The male is the more perfect one, it dominates. The female is imperfect, it obeys. Now, there are individuals in humankind who are just as subordinate to others, like the body to the soul, like the animal to man. These are those beings that are only good for manual labor, and are not suited for anything more perfect than that. These individuals are destined by nature to be slaves because there is nothing better for them than to obey. Is there then, in fact, any real difference between slaves and animals? Their services are similar to one another; they are only useful to us through their bodies. From these principles we can conclude that nature created some people for freedom and others for slavery, so that it is beneficial and just that the slave obeys.†

There is a complete split between mental and manual labor. According to Aristotle, nature created slaves; and physical labor, the basis of production, is according to him, the basis for bondage.

The free peasants were both members of society and citizens, and they took part in many aspects of public affairs.

With time, it transpired that every *aristocrat* lived in the city and his *main concern* became dealing with *affairs of state*, aside from the concern with science, art, and military service. *The peasants were proletarianized*, were unable to find work, since there were slaves everywhere. They became superfluous, did not count.

As a foreigner, the slave had no opportunity at all to take part in public life. He had no public obligations. Therefore, the master had the complete right to dispose of him, since there were no citizenship rights, no protection by the state.

Even if the slaves were the smaller group, they were nevertheless the principal focus. They proletarianized the peasants. The separation of intellectual life from the production process.

These are the fruits of slavery. This resulted in the disintegration of Greek society as well as the Roman one.

---

*   Ibid., p. 1982 [1255b30–32].
†   The statement is actually not from Book III but rather Book I of Aristotle's *Politics*. See Ibid., pp. 190–1 [1254b5–1255b1].

CONCLUSIONS

In Greece, slavery led to the *separation of knowledge from the process of production*. Before this, knowledge was not separate from productive labor. *Knowledge was collective and concentrated in production. Everyone* worked, and everyone worked *together*. Knowledge remained necessary. In order to cut a stone, in order to manufacture tools; for that, scientific understanding was necessary. In order to undertake the organization of the mark, quite a bit of knowledge was required.

The *next form* is that knowledge rested with the *priests*. As in India, they were not allowed to work in the fields. Because of this, they acquired time for extensive mental labor. This was necessary, for example, in the Orient, since organizing the construction of the large waterworks came to be carried out not only by the mark, but also by many others as well. The priests were in intimate contact with nature, because they had to support the cult, which at that time was a nature cult.

The *next form* in which knowledge was disconnected from production was *slavery*. And in fact, within slavery, total separation of manual and mental labor likewise took place.

This benefited science and art. Free from being bound to production, they could now float freely in the air, hurry ahead of time. Art succeeded in blossoming in Greece to a point that has not been reached in our time. Aristotle would not have been capable of becoming what he was without slavery. Everything that exists today is bound up with the ancient Greek world, with Aristotle. In this sense we could even say: *without slavery, there would be no socialism.*

Knowledge was also beneficial to the production process.

The exclusion of slaves from mental life led of course to *the rulers creating laws* that benefited their own interests, yet these also had to be honored by the slaves, although they did not take part in their enactment. It is not much different today. There were laws and a dominant class that did not take part in the production process. Those who created all the assets had to submit to them.

In socialist society, knowledge will be the common property of everyone. All working people will have knowledge.

THE HISTORY OF SLAVERY IN ROME

The history of Roman slavery is a later one than that of Greek slavery, just as Roman history as a whole is a later history. Rome was first founded in the eighth century BC.* In Greece, prehistory—that is, the era of Homer—reaches back to the tenth or eleventh century BC, in which slavery already existed, if only to a

---

*   By tradition, Rome was founded in 753 BC.

limited extent.* It was from Greece that Rome borrowed slavery, so to speak; from there it came to Rome in already finished form.

In general we distinguish *three periods of slavery in Rome*:

The *first* goes back to the Punic Wars,† that is, to the third century BC;

The *second* dates from the Punic Wars down to the era of the Caesars, that is, until shortly before and/or shortly after the birth of Christ (the first century AD);

The *third* dates from the first century AD, that is, from the time of Christ's birth, to the fall of the Roman Empire.

The First Period

In the *first period* the type of economic life in Italy was *peasant agriculture*. There was obviously a nobility already present, land ownership on a large scale by the nobility, [that is] differentiation is already present. The nobility and the peasantry we derive, as in Greece, from the mark; the peasants were previously members of the mark community; and the nobles were the ones who held public offices within the mark.

The *mode of production* on the estates owned by the nobility [at first] was hardly distinguishable from the mode of production on the property owned by the peasants; the difference was only in the size or scope of the landholding. There were no larger bases than these for an economic transformation.

Slavery in this first period has already been introduced, but still [only] to a limited extent. On the landholdings of the nobility the number of slaves was somewhat greater, and on peasant land, smaller. Many of the poorer peasant farmers had no slaves at all. Here [in this situation] slaves were still agricultural workers. Since peasant agriculture was the type of production that only met basic needs, a kind of patriarchal situation prevailed as a consequence for the slaves as well. They worked for the farmer alongside his family, and in the case of the nobles or the tenant farmers [they worked] alongside of other farm laborers. (The nobles leased out a great deal of land to tenant farmers, and that land was worked in the same way as the peasant farmers' own land.)

Thus the slaves were employed *as agricultural workers* next to the free peasants and together with the free peasants. For the most part they were slaves who

---

* Homer himself is reputed to have lived in the latter part of the eighth century BC, although the odes that came to become known as the *Iliad* may have been orally composed and transmitted as early as the tenth or eleventh centuries BC.

† The Punic Wars were fought between Rome and Carthage. Rome obtained Sicily as a result of the First Punic War (264 to 241 BC), southern Spain and much of the North African coast as a result of the Second Punic War (218 to 201 BC), and the remainder of Carthage through the Third Punic War (149 to 146 BC).

had been purchased. Most of them had been purchased for a period of twenty years; if they got old and/or sick, they were mostly sold at a low price. The land owned by a noble in the first period in Rome was called *villa rustica*, which meant an estate or manor. It consisted usually of a residence for the *villicus*,* the agricultural director of the operation, an official of the estate or manor. He had a dwelling place together with the slaves. Next to it were cowsheds, granaries, and so on. For the nobility a special [*MS. Illegible*]† was often built. All the slaves at such an establishment received their means of livelihood periodically and in a designated quantity. Clothing and shoes were usually purchased at a market. Every month they received a certain amount of wheat (rye and oats were not yet known at that time), and the recipients had to grind this themselves. In addition [there was] salt, olives, salted fish, wine, and cooking oil. That is how they lived in this first period. It was one and the same kind of life for the slave, the peasant farmer, and with minor differences, for the noble as well.

In addition to the *villicus* there was a *villica*, a female economic official, who prepared the food for the entire company, and they all had their meals together. Occasionally slaves suspected of [attempting to escape] or those who had committed serious offences were shackled and left in underground dungeons as punishment, but in the first period that was an exception and happened only in cases when the slave was guilty of a wrong. The son of the family was often punished in the same way as the slave. Both stood under the unlimited authority and domination of the paterfamilias.‡ For larger work operations, which required a larger accumulation of labor power in a short time, there were not enough slaves, and free wage laborers had to be hired, who performed the work together with the slaves, for example, during a harvest. Olive picking and the gathering of grapes were usually likewise entrusted to free employees, or free contractors together with slaves; that is, there were people who undertook to carry out that kind of work, and they brought their own slaves with them. For this they received compensation. In general the feeding and treatment of slaves were good. On holidays they were freed from labor obligations. And since they belonged to particular families in Rome, they took part in religious rites, including those of the family cult. (In Rome there were not only official gods of the Roman state as a whole, but each family had its own household gods§).

---

* The *villicus* was an estate manager.

† Several words are missing from the manuscript. Luxemburg appears to be referring to a manor house or villa.

‡ The head of a Roman family.

§ The gods that were held to watch over and protect the goods of a household were called *penates*. When Romans sat down for a meal, they would traditionally throw a bit of the food into the hearth to feed the *penates*. *Lares* were guardian deities that were held to watch over and protect people in a given location.

The Second Period

In the depths of Roman society radical changes began to take place around the third century BC. It began with Rome's struggle to establish an empire on a world scale. This struggle was initiated by an endless series of wars. The Punic Wars marked the turning point. Hardly a year went by without a war.

Finally came the Punic War with Carthage. This third Punic War, which ended in victory [for Rome], lasted until 146 B.C.

At the same time the wars with Macedonia began. (Macedonia was then a part of Greece, in the north.) There were three Macedonian wars:[*]

The first, 215–205 BC
The second 200–197 BC
The third 171–168 BC

Then almost simultaneously there was a war with Antioch and Syria, in Asia, to the southeast of Asia Minor, in the years 192–189 BC.[†]

Then the Greek war with the Aetolian League,[‡] in 146 BC, [which was] thus simultaneous with the third Punic War.

Then the war in Spain, the subjugation of Spain, 143–133 BC.

Then came the war with Numidia, which is located in Africa, in 111–105 BC.[§] (see the atlas of [Friedrich Wilhelm] Putzger, 1909, p. 3a[¶]), an eastern part of the ancient world.

---

[*]   There were actually four Macedonian Wars, the last being between 150 and 148 BC, in which Rome put down a Macedonian rebellion against Roman rule.

[†]   Antioch became the capital of the Seleucid Empire in the third century BC. Shortly after 197 BC, its ruler Antiochus III invaded Greece and came into conflict with Roman forces. He was defeated by the Romans and forced to sign the Treaty of Apamea in 188, which ceded Antioch and all of western Asia Minor to the Romans.

[‡]   The Aetolian League was a confederation of cities in central Greece established in the third century BC in response to pressure from Macedonians in the north and the Achean League (which included Thebes, Megara, and Corinth) in the south. It was the first Greek alliance to side with the Romans, fighting alongside them in the First Macedonian War of 215 to 205 BC. It later tried to maintain its independence from Rome, but was defeated (along with other Greek allies) by the Romans in the Achaean War of 146 BC.

[§]   Numidia was an ancient Berber kingdom in what is now eastern Algeria and western Tunisia. By the end of the Third Punic War it was allied with Rome and retained for a generation more its independence. The Numidians stubbornly resisted Rome's ultimately successful effort to conquer them from 111 to 105 BC.

[¶]   A reference to F.W. *Putzgers Historischer Schul-Atlas* (Putzger's Historical School Atlas) (Leipzig: Velhagen and Klasing, 1877). This historical atlas was widely used in schools at the time and it has appeared in many new editions since. It remains in print today. See *Putzger—Atlas und Chronik zur Weltgeschichte* (Berlin: Cornelius, 2002).

Then a war with the Cimbri and Teutones, in 113–101 BC.* (see Putzger's atlas, p. 9, on the northern part of the map).

A war with the kingdom of Pontus in Asia Minor, 69–64 BC.† (see Putzger's atlas, p. 9, in the eastern part [of the map]).

Then a war with the Celts, the Gallic war, in what is now France, 58–51 BC.‡

After that came the so-called Alexandrian wars in Egypt in 30 BC.§

Those are the times encompassed by the second period of Roman slavery.

A knotty tangle of wars in ever-wider scope, a collision of Greco-Roman culture with all the surrounding populations, which had remained on a more backward level.

All these wars were victorious for Rome. They ended with the founding of the Roman Empire, the transformation of all these lands into Roman provinces, obligated to pay tribute, and with the introduction of Roman law into those provinces.

The peasant farmers were the great raw material used in these wars. They were the *soldiers*. This brought with it the complete collapse of peasant agriculture, and yet that had been the cornerstone of the entire economic life of the country. Labor power was withdrawn from peasant agriculture, and it was encumbered with an enormous tax burden. Since the waging of war required monetary resources, which the Roman Empire obtained through taxes, these too fell upon peasant agriculture.

These two operating factors brought to maturity the *first phase of the second period, the ruin of peasant agriculture and the establishment of large landed estates.* The latter came into existence as a result of the fact that the large landed proprietors separated the peasant farmers from their property when they [the peasants] could not pay their debts.

Since the free peasant farmers had their own land taken out from under them, they could then serve as labor power for the large landed estates. But the peasant farmer was under the constant threat that he would be called up to fight

---

*   The Cimbri, by tradition from Denmark, were either a Germanic or Celtic people who migrated south in the second century BC and attacked the Roman Republic. They defeated the Romans in a series of battles between 109 and 103 BC, reaching as far south as northern Spain and Italy. The Romans finally defeated them at the Battle of Vercallae in 101 BC, after which the Cimbri were exterminated by the Romans. The Teutones, also originally from Denmark, were allied with the Cimbri. In 102 BC the Romans defeated them in the Battle of Aquae Sextiae, in modern-day France.

†   The kingdom of Pontus was a Persian state on the southern coast of the Black Sea in modern-day Turkey. It fought Rome in a series of three bitter wars between 88 and 63 BC, known as the Mithridatic Wars. It finally succumbed to Rome in the Third Mithridatic War, which ended in 63 BC.

‡   The Roman conquest of Gaul was led by Julius Caesar.

§   The Alexandrian wars of 30 BC represented the final chapter in Rome's effort to conquer Egypt. Alexandria (the most important city in Egypt at the time) was captured by Octavian, the future emperor of Rome, on August 1, 30 BC. To celebrate the victory, Octavian renamed himself Augustus ("The Great One") and changed the name of the month to August.

in a war. It was awkward for the great proprietor to hire him—even when he had the possibility of hiring such a free peasant farmer. Even in intervals between wars the peasant farmer faced the danger of being called up for military service.

On the one hand the peasant farmer lost his own land, and on the other he was too unsuitable for the great proprietor as hired labor power.

Besides that, the number of free peasant farmers was reduced significantly because of the wars, so that [for] the large landowner there were no longer enough of them by any means.

The great proprietors thus had to bring in more slaves. And the wars provided them in great quantities.

The incessant waging of war, without exception, led to the subjugation of large new provinces. The conquered populations were transformed into Roman subjects and had to pay tribute, partly in money and partly in kind. The latter consisted above all of grain. They began to import overseas grain. The granaries of Rome were Africa, Sicily, and Spain.

The Roman state used the grain above all to maintain the army; it was exclusively with foreign grain that the Roman army was fed. The plundering of foreign provinces brought ever more grain into the country [that is into Italy], as the army needed it. The state purchased this grain at ridiculously low prices. Soon the grain grown at home became superfluous, and the Roman farmer found no outlet for his grain. He became a proletarian. (The Latin word *proles* means "offspring.")

What could the peasants do? They had lost their own household plots, and the large landowners were employing slaves. The large landowners could obtain everything they needed either by having slaves produce it or by importing from the provinces.

The peasant farmers, being completely deprived of the means of existence, streamed into Rome, and at that time Rome was indeed *the* city, the center, and at the same time it was the political center. They flooded into Rome to demand the means of subsistence from the state. These peasant farmers were at the same time free citizens. (Rome was a republic. It had made the same kind of revolution as in Greece). The nobility made use of this proletariat in its own internal struggles. It had political rights and influence on the state. This proletariat had to be maintained, because otherwise it would become a constant danger to Rome. It slept overnight in the streets of Rome, literally.

Grain was distributed to the proletarians in the market of Rome at state expense, and this was precisely the same overseas grain.

Thus the importing of grain from the provinces had great significance.

On the basis of these [social and political] relations [Charles Léonard] Sismondi made the classical commentary in his writings dealing with social relations in Rome.

---

* That is, a proletarian was one who produced many offspring, hence "prolific."

"There was in Rome a proletariat as there is today. But whereas the proletariat today supports society, the Roman proletariat lived at the expense of society." That is the difference between the proletariat of today and of that time.*

Finally there comes an aspect in addition to the others [mentioned above] that closed in on peasant agriculture in such a way as to eliminate it —to wipe it off the face of the earth. That is the rapid development of the money economy. As a result of Rome's encounter with the countries of the Orient, the money economy in Rome developed very quickly. The Roman state promoted [the money economy] with all its might and in the process implemented all the greater opportunities the state had for various transactions, for example, the levying of taxes, using not only its own people [for this purpose] but also farming out the collection of taxes to rich people, who had to immediately pay the state a lump sum. They were allowed to raise taxes even higher as long as they also handed over the set sum to the state.

The money economy was at that time just as lucrative a source for rich people as government bonds are today. In the second century [BC] there already existed wealthy bankers who advanced funds to the state when it was necessary and who [generally] looked after and took care of money-related matters.

The ruining of peasant agriculture within a couple of centuries did not of course pass by without struggle and resistance by the peasants. In the second century BC there were *big revolutions by the peasants, a cry for a new distribution of the lands*, and indeed of *state lands*. (In the name of the state these lands were given the official names: "common estates," "undivided estates, or lands," and "common lands.")

By what means was this demand defeated? Not merely by the buying up of the household plots [of the peasants] by the nobles, but also as a result of the fact that the nobles had taken control of the state lands. The nobles began to transfer the state-owned domains to themselves at ridiculously low prices, and that was not impossible for them, because they were the rulers. These [state-owned] domains actually passed into their hands, and thus enabled their large landed estates to grow even larger.

Economic relations had advanced too far, and thus the demand of the peasants was retrograde, would have meant a step backward. They had exactly the same aspirations as present-day middle-class people.†

There were *earth-shaking revolutions of the proletarianized peasantry in*

---

*   See Marx's statement in his 1869 "Preface to the Second Edition of *The Eighteenth Brumaire of Louis Bonaparte*": "People forget Sismondi's significant saying: The Roman proletariat lived at the expense of society, while modern society lives at the expense of the proletariat." *Marx-Engels Collected Works*, Vol. 21 (New York: International Publishers, 1985), p. 57. See Jean Charles Léonard Simonde de Sismondi, *Études sur l'économique politique*, Vol. 1 (Paris: Treuttel et Würtz, 1837), p. 24.

†   Luxemburg is referring to the quest by many middle class people to return to an era prior to the ruination of their class.

Rome over the question of these lands. The most famous among these is the *revolution of the Gracchi* of 133–121 BC.* Tiberius and Gaius Gracchus, two brothers from the highest-ranking noble families, placed themselves at the forefront of this revolution. In this connection Tiberius Gracchus gave a famous speech before the senate:

> The wild animals of Italy have their places of refuge and their dens. But those who have fought and died for Italy have nothing that they can call their own except the air and the sunlight. Homeless, they must wander around with their wives and children, and the owners of the fields lie when they claim in front of their armies that they are fighting for their ancestral graves and sacred places. For no one anymore has a sacred place of their father's or an ancestral grave; no one from all the hosts of Rome's wars has those things. But rather these who are called the masters of the world fight for the wealth and privileges of strangers, while they themselves possess not even a clump of earth.†

The two Gracchi sought to improve the situation with specific reforms. They demanded that *the state lands be apportioned out to the peasants*, a purely utopian measure.

Tiberius Gracchus in 134 BC pushed through a *law*, which was intended to take the state domains back from the nobles and which stipulated that [the state domains] would be divided up into peasant household lots of thirty acres each; it also stipulated that large payments should be given to individual proletarianized peasants.

The result was that Tiberius along with 300 of his supporters were murdered by the nobles and their hangers-on. His brother Gaius then placed himself at the head of the movement and sought to carry the reforms still further, because the measure taken by Tiberius could not stop the colossal process of proletarianization. Even leased-out domains were turned into peasant colonies. He then introduced the free distribution of grain, so that the proletarians who were lying around (homeless?) could be fed. Peasant colonies were also established in the overseas provinces. The bankruptcy of the peasants can be seen in the fact that things could not be turned back even in their own country, where the peasants did not even have their own clump of earth.

---

* Tiberius and Gaius Gracchus were Roman social reformers who sought to give more power to the plebeian class by breaking up large landed estates and distributing land to soldiers, disenfranchised peasants and the poor. Tiberius Gracchus was elected tribune in 133 BC and appealed to the people to support his revolutionary proposals, which included limiting the amount of land that could be owned by any individual. Threatened by his proposals, Roman Senators had Tiberius and several hundred of his followers clubbed to death. Gaius Gracchus, his brother, was elected as tribune in 123 BC and pushed for land redistribution as well as extending citizenship rights to non-Roman Italians. Thousands of his followers were slaughtered by patrician forces.

† For the English-language text of Tiberius Gracchus's speech, see Plutarch, *The Parallel Lives*, translated by Bernadotte Perrin (Cambridge: Harvard University Press, 1921), p. 167.

[There followed] a powerful movement of resistance by the nobles; Gaius had to flee, and his flight ended in his own suicide. Thereupon the entire reform [movement] fell apart.

Professor Meyer states: This reform unfortunately led only to revolutions in which both Gracchi died and the reform was defeated.

The agrarian revolutions only led to upheavals in the state and did not bring about any changes.

There had been a struggle already for centuries to use laws to counter the fact that *free workers were more and more being pushed out by slaves.* A law of 367 BC that the owners of peasant households sought to establish stated that *the same number of freemen should be employed as the number of slaves.*

At the time of Caesar, in the first century BC, that is four centuries after the above-mentioned law, a new law was introduced according to which large landed proprietors were obligated to employ at least *one-third freemen.* That of course had no prospect of being carried out. Economic relations were more powerful than the law. The peasant was still a citizen with rights and duties, but the slave was purely and exclusively labor power.

That is how things went with laws in Rome, as with all laws that try to go against the tide of economic development: they remain a dead letter. Proof of that is that after four centuries this new law came.

In conclusion, we have the large number of proletarianized peasants in the state without any employment. And they remained up until the last period [of the Roman Empire.]

The next form to disappear was the small lease-holding. This was decisive in the sense that economically the large landed estate was still bound by the methods of peasant agriculture. Now we have *large-scale cultivation of crops,* and indeed this was possible because *employable labor power was present in large quantities.*

Since grain was imported from the provinces, *grain production [in Italy] shrank.* The cultivation of grain was forced out mainly by [the introduction of] *the raising of livestock (e.g., sheep and cattle),* and also by *the cultivation of vineyards and olive orchards.*

Things were *now produced for trade [purposes],* no longer for one's own use, as was previously the case on the peasant household plot.

The raising of livestock yielded wool; it was produced in the largest quantities possible, for trading purposes. Small plots of land, which earlier were intended for the production of grain, were transformed into large ranges for the raising of livestock. Vineyards and olive tree orchards were cultivated on exactly the same large scale.

Latifundia took shape. The opposite side of the coin was the collapse of peasant farming. It goes without saying that [the latifundia] were worked by slaves. Large columns of slaves were formed, under overseers, along with complete separation of their mode of life from that of their masters. The master lived in Rome, but he also had a villa out on the land.

On the rural estates [of the large landowners] the following items were developed: the cultivation of large gardens, and zoos, flowers being part of the luxurious lifestyle in Rome; the breeding of birds for purposes of luxury (peacock tongues and nightingale tongues); also, the cultivation of fruits in the most careful manner was pursued on a large scale and for personal consumption needs.

Chiefly, however, there occurred a depopulation and desolation of the entire land because of the widespread planting of vineyards and olive orchards. There was also a very unsatisfactory development of craft production, only for meeting immediate needs for tools and implements; other than that, everything was imported from Asia Minor; even the best tools and implements were brought from there.

Where earlier there had been 100–150 peasant farms, now there stood one latifundium, worked by 50 slaves. The slaves were not married and were not allowed to marry. The peasant farmers had either been sent off as soldiers to every possible foreign land or they lived as jobless proletarians in Rome.

Finally there remained the wealthy classes and the nobility. ([Theodor] Mommsen and Meyer always speak about Roman capitalists; but by that they understand simply wealthy people.)*

In Rome, in a later period than in Greece, there was so to speak no function for these classes. Greece had been subjugated politically by Rome, but spiritually and intellectually Greece dominated until the Middle Ages. Greek philosophy, art, and everything that could be achieved on the basis of the slave economy of antiquity had already been perfected by Greece. Rome merely had to borrow it, appropriate it, take possession of it. From then on Rome lived, one could say, as a sponger or freeloader.

For this reason the ruling classes in Rome separated themselves from mental labor as well [as physical]. In this second period the slaves represented not merely labor power on the landed estate, but they also undertook all functions in the city; thus there were slaves who performed mental labor. Slaves were bookkeepers, accountants, teachers, artists, actors, dancers, musicians, and architects. There was no sphere of public life that slaves did not engage in. That

---

*   At the time Luxemburg was composing this piece, a lively debate was taking place in Germany and within the German Social-Democratic movement concerning the existence of capitalism in the ancient world. On one side stood Karl Bücher and Eduard Meyer, who contended that a relatively modern form of capitalism existed in ancient Greece and Rome. This was contested by Guiseppe Salvioli, an Italian Marxist, as well as by Karl Kautsky. See Giuseppe Salvioli, *Der Kapitalismus im Altertum. Studien über die römische Wirtschaftsgeschichte* (Capitalism in Antiquity: Studies on Roman Economic History) (Stuttgart: J.H.W. Dietz Nachfolger, 1922 [orig. 1912]). Kautsky wrote the Preface to Salvioli's book and weighed in on the debate on other occasions. For a recent study of this debate, see Daniel Gaido, "Karl Kautsky on Capitalism in the Ancient World," in *The Journal of Peasant Studies*, Vol. 30 (2) January 2003, pp. 146–158.

they could carry out these mental and intellectual functions was due to the fact that in many cases they were prisoners of war who came from culturally developed lands and had previously been free citizens. There were, for example, a great many Greeks formerly of noble descent who later served as slaves in Rome. For work on the plantations [Rome] took from the backward populations, but for work in the cities it took from the intellectually developed populations.

Rome arrived at this conclusion: everything related to work is slave work, both physical and mental. In Greece only physical labor had been regarded as slave work.

The consequences of this development went so far that the following was true: on the one hand, *the masses of peasants were superfluous for the production process*, and on the other, *the ruling classes renounced all forms of labor*.

Thus in Rome the entire society lived exclusively on the slaves and the subjugated peoples.

Grain came from Sicily, and there the Carthaginians had already transformed the occupation of grain growing into slave work; the Romans carried this further, to the utmost extent.

Now of course the living conditions of the slaves had to undergo a change. *They were now completely reduced to the status of naked labor power*. In agriculture they were labor power that was applied for the purposes of trade. In this entire institution, or configuration, everything worked toward a single purpose: to extract the maximum possible from the slaves. A distinction must be made between the slaves in the mines and on the plantations and those in the city. Whereas in the city they represented the only intellectual activity and culture, in the outlying areas [MS. *Illegible*] on a regular basis they were chained and driven to work with whips and locked up at night in underground dungeons. They were branded on the forehead so that they would be recognizable and identifiable as slaves. They were released from detention only to be driven to work. They were not allowed to marry.

In that period they drove out free labor entirely and produced only for export. These relations inevitably led to *slave revolts*, particularly because the slaves had previously been free.

In the second century BC Rome was shaken by powerful slave revolts.

In 184 BC there was a slave revolt in *Apulia*.[*] In the suppression of this revolt 7,000 slaves were killed.

In 195 BC there was a large uprising in *Etruria*.[†] In this slave revolt there were pitched battles with the Roman armies.

---

[*]   Apulia is a region of southern Italy bordering the Adriatic Sea. It includes the "boot" of Italy. During the Roman Empire it was an important center for the growing of grain and oil. The slave revolt that Luxemburg refers to actually occurred in 185 BC.

[†]   Etruria, named after the Etruscans, is in northwest Italy. The slave revolt that Luxemburg mentions actually took place in 196 BC.

In 197 BC [there was a slave revolt] in *Latium*, where Rome is also located.

Later there began the most threatening of all: the *Sicilian* slave revolts.[*]

In 143–141 BC, another powerful uprising, in which 7,000 armed slaves took part. Here too there were pitched battles. After the rebellion was put down 20,000 slaves were crucified.

In 130 BC again there were a series of slave revolts in Italy in the course of which 4,600 slaves were executed. In 113 BC occurred the *second Sicilian slave revolt*, which lasted for two years.[†]

In 73 BC, *the third Sicilian slave revolt*, led by the famous *Spartacus*.[‡]

Then in *Greece, in Attica*, the slaves revolted. Here they were so rebellious that they could be driven to work only with the use of weapons.

Third Period

In the *first century AD* the third period in the history of Roman slavery begins. We need only draw the consequences from the development that has gone before in order to have a the necessary picture before us.

The slaves consisted of prisoners of war. But as a result of all the wars an empire had been founded on a world scale. Now a limit was placed on the wars. When this limit was reached the importing of prisoners of war from other countries dried up.

At the same time the peasant farmers, who had been the economic basis for Rome's world domination and who had been necessary for Rome's wars, had been annihilated or ruined. We have seen the collapse of peasant agriculture. The peasantry was transformed from a social stratum that sat on its own plot of land and had an interest in [the functionings of] the state, transformed into a mass that served only as cannon fodder for the interests of the nobility. For war it is not only necessary to have a certain number of soldiers with weapons but also the wars must serve their interests to some degree. The ruined peasant farmer lost his strength both morally and physically. With the downfall of the peasantry the level and quality of nutrition declined. In the second century [AD] meat and milk disappeared from the diet of the peasant farmers. As a result fewer and fewer of them were capable of bearing arms.

---

[*]   A series of slave revolts occurred in Sicily in the second century BC, especially from 135 to 132 BC and 103 to 101 BC. These were the "most threatening" of all the many slave revolts in ancient Rome because some of them led to the creation of temporary but relatively stable slave-run states. As many as a quarter of a million slaves took part in some of the Sicilian slave revolts.

[†]   113 BC appears to be a slip of the pen, since the second Sicilian slave revolt occurred from 103 to 101 BC.

[‡]   Spartacus was originally a shepherd from Thrace, to the north of Greece. After being captured by the Romans, he became a gladiator and a slave. After escaping from a gladiator school in 73 BC, he formed an army (numbering as many as 100,000) that defeated four Roman armies and controlled most of southern Italy. He was captured and crucified (along with 6,000 others) in 71 BC.

The rise of mercenary armies. Foreign, barbarian, mainly German people were recruited. And thus we see hired Germans being led against Roman citizens in time of [civil] war.

A combination of different lands and peoples came together in the Roman army. Only the officers were Romans. There were bound to be dire consequences from the fact that only foreign people who had come together accidentally were waging war. In the end they acquired great power and it was they who finally placed one or another Caesar [i.e., emperor] on the throne. They put one on the throne because he impressed them with his ability to sweat prodigiously. That is a fine illustration of the sanctity of the office of emperor. Those were the ultimate consequences of having foreign mercenary armies.

What results followed from all this for the economy of the latifundia and the slaves themselves?

Above all there was this: *a major change was introduced into slavery itself.* The mistreatment of slaves that had occurred in the second period was now impossible. Since slaves were no longer to be had freshly from each war, they had to be taken care of, treated differently. In the first century AD and thereafter a much milder form of slavery began. It is constantly maintained that Christianity brought this about. But it is exclusively the consequence of the fact that this labor power now had to be valued more highly, because there was no longer any surplus of it to be had.

Now slaves had to be permitted to marry so that they could reproduce. This fact alone meant a better living situation for the slaves. Also a slave had to be treated differently when he himself had a family, when he had children; he had to be paid as much as was necessary for him to maintain his children.

The more the proletariat gathered in Rome in large numbers, the more soldiers had to be richly rewarded for their services, and the more the proletariat had to be pacified with gifts—all the more had to be squeezed out of the foreigners in the subjugated provinces. That led to the decline of the subjugated populations, so that grain imports suffered.

Thus, *Rome had to return to the cultivation of grain.* The livestock pastures were turned back into grain fields.

The latifundia were operated with slave labor. However, grain growing was not possible with slave labor [in the form it had] up until then. First of all, the number of slaves was too small, and second, they had already been drilled and trained for work in the vineyards and olive orchards, but grain growing meant a return to a higher form of intensive agriculture.

And thus there came *a return to small peasant farming.*

The latifundia were broken up into individual parcels that were given partly to slaves with families and partly to free peasant farmers in return for certain payments or taxes, mainly payments in kind; because it was no longer possible to use money to pay farmers. For this purpose they leased land to those who had been hired as a protection against wars,* and so forth. Thus there was a return to a kind of *corvée* labor.†

In Rome this was called [land worked] by the *colonus*.‡ (From this we can derive the first beginnings of the corvée economy of the Middle Ages.)

There was one more necessity that forced the return to the colonus. The nourishment of the slaves was too inadequate. In the interests of the economy itself it had to be recognized that the slave took increasingly less interest in the work. Here again this is a very instructive example: It is a mistake to suppose that one needs only to have power and assert one's [military] might in order to exploit labor without there being any enticement for the exploited.

In Rome the result was a complete ruination of labor power.

E.g., slaves [working] in the mines [*MS. Illegible—several lines*]

The power of the exploited to do mental labor was also broken by exploitation.

Here the production process necessarily had to break down, because labor power was ruined by exploitation.

Such primitive labor by the slaves could never be carried out without tools. The relations were such that the slaves had a terrible hatred for the tools of their labor. They destroyed them along with the materials to be worked on. Such hatred between the living form of labor and the dead means of production had been created that a constant war between them prevailed.

The slaves gradually developed into the most expensive and least convenient force of production and for that reason there came to be fewer and fewer of them.

So then, to summarize:

The economy of slavery reached rock bottom of its own accord.

In the main, that is how the cycle of the historical development of slavery in the Roman Empire closed upon itself.

In general there was a return to the relations of old. This shows that it was not only the Germans who brought about the destruction [of the Roman Empire]. Rome was already ripe prey for foreign conquest after such consequences had been arrived at as a result of its own development.

---

*   Luxemburg is here probably referring to invasions by barbarian tribes.

†   A system of land tenure in which a tenant farmer was given land to work in return for a fixed payment or for certain stated labor services of a nonmilitary nature.

‡   *Colonus* (plural, *coloni*) is Latin for farmer or colonist, derived from *colo*, one who toils, cultivates, or worships the soil. In the Roman Empire the *coloni* were impoverished farmers who worked for landed proprietors, either for money, service, or labor. They often sought protection on the landed estates from invaders or government officials. In exchange for working the land, they were forbidden to sell or leave it. Their descendants became the serfs of the European Middle Ages.

WHAT ADVANCES ON THE WHOLE DID SLAVERY BRING ABOUT?

Greco-Roman culture is *something whole* even if we distinguish among particular configurations.

(1) *Slavery carried through [conclusively] the division separating mental and physical labor.* This has remained true to the present day, and is a fundamental fact, or reality, for the entire forward development of class society. Without it the mental-spiritual development [that we have] today would not have been possible.

In Greece this fundamental fact, or reality, was established as the distinction between freemen and slaves, and then took on various forms. But with the Roman Empire [this distinction] was transmitted to posterity.

Christianity emerged in the Roman Empire (here Rome being taken not as the state). It would not have arisen without Greek philosophy, which is one of the main roots of Christianity. And Greek philosophy rested upon—slave labor. But since Christianity is, so to speak, the legacy of the Roman Empire, it has come to dominate the entire modern era: Without Christianity, which was engendered by slavery, there could be no thought of the Middle Ages or capitalism, nor of the disposition of class forces in the modern world, and without the latter, socialism is inconceivable. The socialist revolution will be the first to eliminate this remnant of the legacy from Rome. (Christianity is one more proof, so to speak, that Rome based itself on Greece.)

The state as the coercive power in class society arose in Greece on the basis of slavery, and in Rome we see its continuation, carried to the utmost extreme. The state apparatus in Rome was much more extensive and more fully developed [than in Greece].

One proof of this is the *founding of the Roman world empire.*

In Greece, the leading states were Sparta and Athens, but they were cities, covering only a small area of the country.

In Rome, however, [we see] the gathering together of many lands, which as provinces of Rome came under the same binding laws as the Romans did. This was the first time that such a monstrously huge empire was brought together and ruled from a single center in a uniform manner. It was bound to fall apart because of economic reasons, not because of defects in its political institutions.

Such uniform political organization is a mighty step forward. Here too the Roman Empire had much more powerful consequences than Greece.[*]

---

[*]   At this point in the typescript, the following paragraph was heavily crossed out: In Greece, a refinement of craft production emerged as a result of slavery, without which this refinement would not have been possible. In Rome, the opposite is the case: there the work of craftsmen took a definite step backward. Only the crudest tools, for their own use, were produced by the slaves or

Why could the slaves not produce a higher culture, using the concept of culture in the broadest sense, as a whole, since they did constitute labor power?

Since the slaves were already destroying the crudest tools and implements, how could one give them better ones? In the end, the only means of production being used were utterly crude ones.

Slave labor itself was a fetter on technical progress.

The inner tendency of slavery is to develop into the self-destruction of labor power. This is also true today. The most drastic expression of this is the constant struggle to shorten the working day. But other circumstances also bring with them the fact that the condition of capitalist society itself ordains that this will happen.

Otherwise a deadly stagnation would set in that would destroy society.

In the southern states in North America, as a result of the introduction of cotton, sugar, and rice plantations, exploitation on a purely capitalist basis was driven so far and to such an extent that the slaves on average were worked to death in seven years. That is proof that capitalism too has the tendency to destroy labor power.

Since this tendency toward the destruction of labor power existed under slavery, it is therefore a given that economic development could advance no further.

The slave revolts were the first immense, world-historical class struggles against the exploiters. Not the free peasants, not the proletarians in Rome.

The slave revolts (including 70,000 slaves in Sicily) were completely without results. They were smashed by Rome [even though it was] ailing and rotten. The slaves wanted to return to their homelands; they wanted to break loose and get away from society entirely. They were only partly successful, to the extent that they escaped, some to their homelands, some joining robber bands or becoming pirates.

The slave revolts remained without consequence, because any further development of them was not based on any trend of economic development. The development of the economy at that point had ended in a blind alley.

The decline of the Roman Empire meant in the most precise sense that it was compelled to return to previously existing forms. Therefore, the uprisings of the slaves had been futile.

The economic form exhausted itself, it did not allow for a higher form of economic development.

One ought not to forget the great steps forward brought about by Rome, despite its fall.

---

peasant farmers; all more refined products [by skilled craftsmen] were imported from the subjugated lands. In this respect, then, Roman slavery brought no progress.

The entire mental-spiritual [aspect] of life was concentrated in Rome, as was the material [culture].

The gods of all the subjugated peoples* were dragged to Rome, so that a concentration of all the religious cults and observances were to be found there as well.

The Roman Empire fell back into barbarism, in the literal sense.

Only around the tenth century AD did commerce in Italy begin to rise again.

In the Middle Ages, as soon as dividing lines of class emerged in the new German society, they arose on the basis of those in Rome, [and as a result] when this new society began to flourish, it was receptive to and capable of responding to a higher form of mental-spiritual development, and thus people [readily] took to Greek culture [in] the Renaissance era, [and in] the time of the Humanists.

Nothing was lost from [the heritage of] mental-spiritual culture because of Rome.

Christianity tore the Germans out of barbarism. Despite the fact that the Germans broke the Roman Empire to bits—on the spiritual-intellectual level they adopted Christianity. And this Christianity was the product of the Roman Empire; it had prepared the ground politically for a world revolution.

In Greece, craft production experienced a refinement, which would not have been possible without slavery. In Rome, by way of contrast, it was forced backward by the pressures of world trade, reverting to a kind of lower form. Only the crudest articles for their own use were produced by the slaves or peasant farmers; all finer products were imported from the subjugated lands. In this respect Roman slavery brought no progress.

One forward step was the development of horticulture. Even today we still base ourselves on it. Even today the purpose of horticulture is, as it was in Rome, to provide a finer way of life for the rulers.

The raising of livestock began to take on wider scope. But the crudest elements among the slaves were assigned to it. They were also the first to start slave revolts, because they were left entirely to themselves. Livestock raising became very widespread, but was managed very crudely, mainly aiming at quantity.

Because of livestock raising, *agriculture* declined; that was a *step backward*. In Rome the economy of slavery began to have a distinctly reactionary effect.

Poultry farming, in contrast, represented a step forward.

The management of the large estates was exemplary. On the manorial estates of Charlemagne [modelled on those of Rome] we find products that show specifically what progress Rome had achieved in agriculture even with its economy of slavery.

Thus Rome had a progressive as well as reactionary impact.

---

* That is, their statues and other sacred objects, as well as those who worshipped them whom the Romans made slaves and prisoners.

In the Orient, there was also slavery, but there it remained more or less in the beginning stages. And to the extent that it flourished, it was soon destroyed by wars of conquest. Slavery became highly developed for the first time in Greece and Rome.

REFERENCES ON SLAVERY

Dietzgen: *Wesen der menschlichen Kopfarbeit*[*]
Vorländer: *Geschichte der Philosophie.*[†]
Engels: *Eugen Dührings Umwälzung der Wissenschaft.*[‡]
Eduard Meyer: *Die wirtschaftliche Entwicklung des Altertums. Ein Vortrag,* 1895.
Eduard Meyer: *Die Sklaverei im Altertum,* 1898.
Eduard Meyer: Several articles in *Handwörterbuch der Staatswissenschaften* on "Bevölkerung im Altertum."[§]
Kautsky: *Vorläufer des neueren Sozialismus.*[¶] Erster Band: Plato.
Kautsky: *Ursprung des Christentums*[**] (see note at bottom of page).[††]
Engels: *Feuerbach und der Ausgang der klassischen Philosophie.*[‡‡]
Beloch: *Griechische Geschichte.*[§§]

[*] See Joseph Dietzgen, *Wesen der menschlichen Kopfarbeit* (The Nature of Human Mental Labor) (Hamburg: O. Meissner, 1869)

[†] See Karl Vorländer, *Geschichte der Philosophie* (History of Philosophy) (Leipzig: Dürr'schen Buchandlung, 1908).

[‡] See Friedrich Engels, *Herrn Eugen Dühring's Umwalzung der Wissenschaft; Anti-Dühring: Herr Eugen Dühring's Revolution in Science, Marx-Engels Collected Works,* Volume 25.

[§] See Eduard Meyer, *Die wirtschaftliche Entwicklung des Altertums. Ein Vortrag* (Economic Development in Antiquity: A Lecture) (Jena: G. Fischer, 1895); *Die Sklaverei im Altertrum* (Slavery in Antiquity) (Dresden: v. Jahn & Jaensch, 1898); and "Die Bevölkerung im *Altertum,*" *Handwörterbuch der Staatswissenschafte,* Vol. II (3), pp. 674 ff.

[¶] See Karl Kautsky, *Vorläufer des neueren Sozialismus. Erster Band: Plato* (Forerunners of Modern Socialism: Vol. 1, Plato) (Stuttgart: J.H.W. Dietz, 1895); and *Der Ursprung des Christentums.*

[**] See Karl Kautsky, *Der Ursprung des Christentrums: Eine historische Untersuchung* (Stuttgart: J.H.W. Dietz, 1908). For an English translation, see *Foundations of Christianity,* translated by Jacob Hartmann (New York: Monthly Review, 1972).

[††] In the typescript at the bottom of this page a note appears, which was not written by Luxemburg; it reads: "In regard to Kautsky's *Foundations of Christianity:* In that work Kautsky elucidates the role of the slaves a little differently than does Rosa Luxemburg. He perceives slavery as exclusively a form of decline and retrogression; that is because his focus is on Roman slavery. But Greek slavery was decisive in world history. Roman history can be interpreted only as further development of Greek. Comrade Luxemburg, in her view of slavery, agrees with Marx and Engels, namely, with the view that slavery was a point of departure for important steps forward." Luxemburg must have emphasized her disagreement with Kautsky on this point, and the student or stenographer who wrote this is presumably echoing what Luxemburg said.

[‡‡] See Friedrich Engels, *Ludwig Feuerbach und der Ausgang der klassischen Philosophie* (Berlin: J.H.W. Dietz, 1886); *Ludwig Feuerbach and the End of Classical German Philosophy, Marx-Engels Collected Works,* Volume 26 (New York: International Publishers, 1990), pp. 353–98.

[§§] See Beloch's *Griechische Geschichte* (Greek History), four volumes (Strassburg: Verlag Karl J. Trubner, 1893–1904).

Prof. Bücher: *Entstehung der Volkswirtschaf.*[*]

Mommsen: *Römische Geschichte* (The fundamental work on the subject).[†]

Prof. Max   In the *Handwörterbuch der Staatswissenschaften*, see the article on
Weber: "Agrarian Relations."[‡]

Paul Ernst: Article on "Griechische Geschichte" or "Griechische Sklaverei" in der *Neue Zeit*, 11. Jahrgang, 2. Band (appeared in 1894 or 1893).[§]

Children's supplement to *Gleichheit* Nr. 13, 14, 15, Jahrgang 1908/09: "Aus der römischen Geschicht."[¶]

Children's supplement to *Gleichheit*: (?? Number): "Der Sklavenaufstand in Sizilien."[**]

---

[*]   See Karl Bücher, *Die Entstehung der Volkswirtschaft.*

[†]   See Theodor Mommsen, *Römische Geschichte* (History of Rome), 3 Volumes (Darmstadt: Wissenschaftliche Buchgesellschaft, 2010 [orig. 1854–56]). English edition, *The History of Rome*, volumes 1–5, translated by William Purdie Dickson (Piscataway, NJ: Gorgias Press, 2010).

[‡]   See Max Weber, "Agrarian Relations," *Handwörterbuch der Staatswissenschaften*, Vol. I (3), 1909, pp. 52–188. For an English translation, see *The Agrarian Sociology of Ancient Civilizations*, translated by R.I, Frank (Bristol: Classical Press, 1976).

[§]   This refers to a series of articles by Paul Ernest under the title "Die sozialen Zustände im römischcen Reiche vor dem Einfall der Barbaren" (Social Conditions in the Roman Empire Before the Invasion of the Barbarians)," published in Vol. XI of *Die Neue Zeit*, in 1893.

[¶]   See "Aus der römischen Geschichte" (From Roman History), *Gleichheit*, Nos. 13, 14, 15, 1908–09.

[**]   "Der Sklavenaufstand in Sizilien" (The Slave Uprising in Sicily), *Gleichheit*, 18 (1908), pp. 57–9. At this point at the end of the typescript, the following parenthetical comment, not by Rosa Luxemburg, appears: "(Both [or *all* the items referred to in the children's supplement] are either by Rosa or by Clara [Zetkin]." Rosa Luxemburg's close friend Clara Zetkin was the editor of the socialist women's paper *Gleichheit*, based in Stuttgart; and that the children's supplement was at that time being edited by Clara's son, Konstantin (Kostya) Zetkin, with whom Luxemburg was also closely associated.

Notes About the Economic Form of Antiquity/Slavery*

Eighty sheep one herdsman, for 50 horses, 2 persons.†

The price of slaves.

One can get some idea of the price of slaves in the Roman Empire from the fact that from 357 to 209 [BC] (148 years) the amount one had to pay to buy one's freedom was 4,000 pounds of gold.

PRICES

Cato (234–149 [BC]) said that he never paid more than [the equivalent of] 1,179 marks and that every slave under 20 years [of age] who cost more than 1,754 he regarded as a luxury item. Incidentally, prices reached such a low level that the slaves from among the spoils of war taken by Lucullus in Pontus (74–69 [BC])‡ were sold for [the equivalent of] 3.14 marks.

TECHNICAL ADVANCES IN ROME

They came mostly from the provinces: a better threshing tool (the *tribulum*) came from Africa.

From Gaul [came] a better way of grafting grapevines and a better way of mowing hay, as well as a new form of ploughshare with wheels. Also in Gaul, grain was harvested by a kind of machine pulled by draft animals and steered by a person, twice as fast as in Italy.

Pliny said that one could do worse than to turn over the cultivation of the fields to slaves from prison, because their work would at least be profitable, as was everything undertaken by desperadoes.

---

* The greater part of these "Notes About Slavery" seem to have been expanded more fully in Luxemburg's longer manuscript entitled "Slavery," which from the internal evidence (in the bibliography) was written in 1909 or after. However, there is some material here that does not appear in the longer manuscript, for example, Luxemburg's notes on the price of slaves at the beginning of this manuscript, and later on, her listing of what seem to be three proverbs showing the contemptuous attitude of the Roman rulers toward their slaves, and also her references to Gibbon and Blair on the number of slaves compared to the number of freemen.

† The "two persons" here may well refer to two slaves.

‡ Lucius Licinius Lucullus was a Roman politician and general who conquered much of Asia Minor in the Third Mithridatic War of 73 to 63 BC. He returned to Rome from the war with massive numbers of slaves and captured goods and became one of the wealthiest men in the Roman Republic.

(1) SLAVERY IN ROME (CRAFT PRODUCTION)

In Greece, the craftworks industry.

In Rome, large landholdings [predominated]. The free peasants were subject to military service, [but] *slaves had no military obligations.* (Hand in hand with that, agriculture was driven out by the raising of livestock {with corn (being imported) from Sicily, etc.}).*

The slave uprisings of the second and first centuries [BC].

The Gracchi,† second century (133–121 [BC]).

Rule by "kings," according to legend (753–570 [BC]).‡

The "Republic" (570 on).§

(1) The period up to the Punic wars, third century [BC].⁵

(2) The period up to the time of the Caesars, second and first centuries [BC].**

(3) The imperial period (from 31 BC on).††

Predominance of small and medium-sized land ownership and of peasant farming even on large landed estates (tenant farming).

Slavery on a small scale, slaves as family members engaged in agriculture.

I. Periods

Throughout the sixth and fifth centuries [BC], the struggle of the plebeians with the patricians.

---

    *   The passage in brackets is in the original typescript.

    †   The Gracchi refers to the brothers Tiberius and Gaius Gracchus, Roman plebeians who sought to limit the power of the large landowning patricians, at the end of the second century BC.

    ‡   According to tradition, Rome was founded in 753 and was led for the next centuries by kings who were chosen by the people of Rome. The end of Rome's "age of kings" was not 570 BC, as stated in the text, but rather 509 BC. In that year the last Roman king, Lucius Tarquinius Superbus, was overthrown in a popular uprising that led to the creation of the Roman Republic.

    §   The Roman Republic was formed in 509 BC, not 570 BC. It lasted until 31 BC.

    ⁵   The three Punic Wars between Rome and Carthage were fought in the years 264–241 BC, 218–201 BC, and 149–146 BC.

    **   Julius Caesar was undisputed ruler of Rome from 49 to 44 BC.

    ††   The Roman Empire lasted from 31 BC to 476 AD.

(1) The plebeians were drafted into military service in the second half of the sixth century [BC] (the Servian legislation'). (Protected relatives [*Schutzverwandte*] performed no military service).

(2) The struggle was carried further for political rights (the consulate, the tribunate), participation [by plebeians] in the Senate, and [the issue of the] *Ager publicus.*†

494 [BC], procession to the sacred mountain.‡ The struggle against debt slavery and for the distribution of the *Ager publicus*. A concession: tribunes of the people (distribution of grain from state reserves occurred as early as the beginning of the fifth century [BC]).

486 [BC] First proposal of an "agrarian law" (land distribution). Struggles without results.

455 [BC] Distribution of building sites to plebeians.

450 [BC] Laws of the Twelve Tablets§ (easing of debtor's law, on the Solonian model).

366 [BC] The winning of a consulate for the plebeians. Alleviation of the conditions of debtors. No one could own more than 500 morgen¶ of community land.

Toward the end of the fourth century [BC] the plebeians win political equality. [Ever] since then, the conflict between rich and poor.

326 [BC] Abolition of debt slavery. Land distribution.

---

*   This refers to a series of reforms initiated by the Roman King Servius Tullius in the sixth century BC, which undermined the power of the aristocrats in favor of the plebeians.

†   The *Ager publicus* were the public lands of ancient Rome, which were often obtained through the conquest of Rome's opponents.

‡   In 494 BC a group of Roman plebeians, deciding that they could suffer oppression and discrimination by the Roman state no longer, left Rome and occupied a hill on the banks of the A'nio River, a few miles outside of the city. They refused to abandon their occupation until Rome met their demands for greater economic rights and political participation. The patricians acceded to many of their demands by promising to release all plebeians imprisoned for non-payment of debts and to allow plebeians to veto decisions by magistrates.

§   The Law of the Twelve Tablets, formulated in the middle of the fifth century BC, was the foundation of Roman law during the Republic. The laws were adopted despite fierce opposition from the patricians due to the protests of plebeians, who threatened to leave Rome if their rights were not recognized. According to tradition, the laws were composed by a committee of ten men who traveled to Athens to study Solon's constitution of Athens.

¶   A morgen, a rough unit of measurement in medieval Germany, was equivalent to one-half to two-and-a-half acres. It was based on the amount of land one person could farm with an ox in a day.

Slavery in the first period. *Familia rustica**—agricultural slaves are under one manager [*Oekonomen*]; [there are] also slaves who direct the whole work operation. Slaves were bought at the age of plus or minus twenty and when they became old or sick were sold.

The *villa rustica*† [included] stables for livestock, a granary, and a dwelling house for the *villicus* and the slaves.

Often a special country house was built for the lords.

All slaves periodically received the means of subsistence in fixed amounts.

Clothing and shoes were bought at the market. Each month a certain amount of wheat [was distributed to the slaves]. (Rye and oats were not yet known‡—and the same with rice until the fifteenth century and corn [maize] until the seventeenth.) They all had to grind the wheat themselves, [and they also received] salt, olives, salted fish, wine, and oil.

The *villica* cooked for everyone, and mealtimes were held in common.

Slaves who had tried to escape or were being punished were sent to work in chains (but in earlier times, the sons of the family were treated the same way) and locked up in an underground dungeon at night.

For the harvesting work free contract laborers were also brought in—for the [reaping of the] sixth to the ninth sheaf.§

Harvesting of olives and grapes was usually contracted out to free entrepreneurs who supplied their own slaves.

The slaves were well fed, and on holidays were freed from work duties. But slaves were treated exactly like cattle.

"A watchdog should not get friendly with his fellow slaves." "A slave should either be working or eating." "So many slaves, so many enemies."

Peasant agriculture differed from that of the nobility only in its scope. The farming operation was the same, only with fewer or no slaves.

II—The coming of large-scale plantation agriculture (with wheat cultivation)

Large-scale influx of slaves ([from] wars: the Punic wars with Carthage, the Macedonian wars (the first being 215–205 [BC], the second, 200–197, the third, 171–169), wars with Greece, Spain, Numidia, the Cimbrii and Teutones, the Mithridatic war with the kingdom of Pontus in 68–64 [BC] for Asia Minor, wars with the Germans and Celts, the Gallic wars of 59–51, and with Egypt, the Alexandrian war of 30 [BC]).

---

*   *Familia rustica* is Latin for farm slaves.

†   *Villa rustica* is Latin for countryside villa, used for the purpose of agricultural production.

‡   Rye is native to central and eastern Turkey. Although it was cultivated in parts of northern and central Europe in the Bronze Age, it was not cultivated by Romans until the end of the Republic. It was often disparaged by Romans as an unappealing grain. Oats was also cultivated in the Bronze Age, but its use in southern Europe is not mentioned in extant literature until the first century AD.

§   A sheaf is a large bundle in which grain is bound together after reaping. In ancient Rome hired reapers were often paid in the sixth and ninth sheaf of grain instead of in wages.

According to the records of *Livy* (59–17 BC), the number of *prisoners of war* who were made slaves in the year 210 [BC] was 10,000; in the year 208, it was 4,000; in 202, 1,200; in 200, 35,000; in 197, 5,000; in 190, 1,400; and in the year 167, 150,000! Later it was even more.

(1) The tenant farming system was driven out [of existence], the peasant farmers being swallowed up by *military service*. From the time of Marius on (+/–110 BC) even the poorer *proletarians* served in the army.

(2) As early as 367 BC the *proletariat* tried to make it obligatory by law that land-owners had to employ freemen in agriculture in numbers corresponding to the number of slaves.

Capitalistic large landed property swallowed up the *domain lands* (mark community) and the peasant farms.

(3) (Tax) *indebtedness* of the peasant farms. Usurers and proletarians.

(4) Lowering of the price of grain in Italy because of the import of overseas grain. The grain trade run by the state.

In all of Italy the peasant farms driven out by large landed property, agriculture driven out by the raising of livestock, and free workers replaced by *slaves*.

Every kind of work became slave labor. Educated slaves. Slaves as stewards, educators, physicians, artists. Along with slave labor there were *luxury slaves*. The *slave trade*, the hunting down of slaves in all Mediterranean lands and the Near East.

The *treatment* [of slaves] in the second period [became] worse and worse: in *agriculture* [there was the use of] branding, leg irons, whips, nightly confinement in dungeons. Urban luxury slaves had it better.

Number [of slaves]: In the first century BC (the high point) there were ca. 1.5 million slaves in Italy (and 3 million freemen); in Sicily, 400,000 slaves (and ca. 400,000 freemen). According to [Edward] Gibbon, under Claudius (41–54 AD) the number of slaves and of freemen was the same. According to [William] Blair,* on the other hand, there were 7 million freemen and 20.8 million slaves in Rome [i.e., in the Roman empire].

(Second Period) State-run grain trade, massive import of overseas grain by the state, partly as tribute, partly at very low prices, from the provinces (Africa, Sicily, Spain). Grain from Sardinia, Africa, Egypt, Spain, Gaul, Boetia, and even,

---

* See William Blair, *An Inquiry into the State of Slavery Amongst the Romans; From the Earliest Period, Till the Establishment of the Lombards in Italy* (Edinburgh: Thomas Clark, 1833).

at the last, from Britain ([see the] Putzger [atlas, page] 9). The grain was used for the maintenance of the army and the civil service. From the time of the second Macedonian war (200–197 [BC]) the feeding of the army was permanently based on overseas grain. In addition, [there was] the government's price policy. Purchase of grain from other lands at cheap price and its sale in ...

Finally the government left it up to [tax farmers] ... [to collect] the very large grain tribute at very low pr[ices], and they could [then] sell it in Rome at giveaway prices.

In addition, transport to Rome from Sicily and Sardinia was cheaper than from Etruria and northern Italy.

Finally, all the subjugated provinces were forbidden to export grain to anywhere else but Italy, which also forced prices down.

Consequently: 1) The ruin of peasant farming; 2) With large landholdings [predominating] a transition [was made] to latifundia with slaves [as the workforce]. Grain production was reduced to the amount needed for the workers' own use, and in its place [came] *pastureland* [for livestock] and *olive plantations and vineyards*.

Likewise, [state] *domain lands* were converted by the nobility and the rich into latifundia.

The *money economy* develops strongly. As early as the second century BC there were already numerous bankers.

The state encouraged this because it leased out all its revenue and other major operations (the building of temples, aqueducts, military roads) to private entrepreneurs.

Craft production was developed only to provide tools and meet simple needs. Otherwise products were imported: linen from Egypt, royal purple from Miletus' and Tyre (Phoenicia and Palestine).[†]

Slaves were employed in all fields: commerce, banking, bookkeeping, as customs officials, architects, actors, musicians, and in mining. Their situation was *better* than on the plantations.

The general *buying up of peasant farms* and their conversion into plantations. Where 100–150 peasant families had formerly lived there now stood one latifundium worked by 50 slaves, most of whom were unmarried.

A *decline* in the second century [BC]: There were not enough men capable of bearing arms.[‡] Meat and milk disappeared from the diets of the people.

---

[*]   Miletus was an ancient Greek city on the western shores of modern Turkey. It was one of the wealthiest Greek cities, in part because of it was a center for extracting purple dye from sea snails.

[†]   "Royal Purple," the purple natural dye extracted from sea snails, was also known as Tyrian purple, from the city in Phoenicia in which much of it was produced. It was extremely expensive; it was worth its weight in silver.

[‡]   As a result, the vast majority of the soldiers in the Roman army in the third and fourth centuries AD were actually members of Germanic tribes.

Slave uprisings:

In 185 [BC] in Apulia, 7,000 slaves were killed (in a bacchanalia [of repression])[*]
  In 199 [BC], in Etruria, a battle of armies[†]
  In 198 [BC], [a slave revolt] in Latium.[‡]
  Slave hunting, in Asia Minor, mainly by pirates from Crete and Sicily (along the southern coast of Asia Minor). At the slave market in *Delos*, the number of slaves sold daily was often 10,000.[§]

(1) 135–132 [BC], the first slave war in Sicily, with 70,000 armed slaves; 20,000 were crucified.[¶]

In 130 [BC] in *Italy* 4,800 slaves were executed.

(2) 103–99 [BC], the second slave war in Sicily, lasting two years.[**]

In 73 [BC], Spartacus in lower Italy.[††]

In Delos, in Attica, and in ???[‡‡] the slaves had to be held down by armed force.

The proletariat and the Gracchi.

Tiberius Gracchus [becomes] tribune in 134 BC.

Agrarian law: State domains taken back from the nobles and divided into peasant plots up to 30 morgens in size with a moderate tax. Tiberius is killed with 300 of his supporters. But the law goes into effect.

---

[*] For a discussion of the slave revolt in Apulia, in southern Italy, in 185 BC, see Thomas Wiedemann, *Greek and Roman Slavery* (Baltimore and London: John Hopkins University Press, 1981).

[†] The battle was between Roman armies and rebel slaves, whose revolt was quickly suppressed.

[‡] The slave revolt in Latium was initiated by prisoners of war from Carthage, whom the Romans had enslaved during the Second Punic War.

[§] Delos, an island in the eastern Mediterranean, became a major market for the slave trade in the second century BC.

[¶] The leader of this slave revolt, known as the First Servile War, was Eunus, who was from the Middle East. He led the slaves of eastern Sicily in a major revolt, which at one point had over 200,000 participants. The Romans put down the revolt with great difficulty.

[**] The second slave war in Sicily actually lasted from 104 to 100 BC.

[††] For a recent study of the Spartacus slave revolt, which lasted from 73 to 71 BC, see Brent Shaw, *Spartacus and the Slave Wars: A Brief History with Documents* (Bedford: St. Martin's Press, 2001).

[‡‡] The question marks are in the original typescript.

Gaius Gracchus introduces the distribution of grain [to the proletariat in Rome] and takes leased state domains as the basis for founding peasant colonies, [which is] also done overseas (in Carthage).

Revolt of the nobility, revolution, Gaius is murdered while fleeing.

The whole reform [movement] is shattered.

The end: The third agrarian law, according to which *all community land taken into private possession* is transformed *into the tax-free private property of those making use of it up to that point.*

Third Period: Decline of the Latifundia Economy

(1) Exhaustion of the process of importing slaves, transition to the breeding of slaves, conservation of slaves [becomes] necessary, killing of slaves is forbidden.[*]

(2) Lack of profitability because of the bad [i.e., unproductive] work of slaves, transition to the leasing out of parcels of land to tenant farmers [becomes] necessary.

(3) End of grain imports, return to grain cultivation [in Italy becomes] necessary.

Result: Transition to a kind of serfdom and at the same time back to free tenant farming (transition from a *system of military draft* to a *mercenary army* from the time of Augustus—31 BC to 14 BC).

The *colonatum.*[†]

Economic progress [because] of slavery: *the large-scale enterprise*

(1) A) In Greece, separation of crafts.

   B) In Rome, large-scale cultivation of crops.

(2) *Division of labor.* Formation of the intelligentsia, the state, etc.

Economic *plan* under slavery.

---

[*]   Antonius Pius, Roman Emperor from 138–161 AD, made it illegal for a master to kill his slave.

[†]   The *colonatum* consisted of *coloni*, peasant farmers with a status similar to serfs.

The Middle Ages. Feudalism. Development of Cities

For the Middle Ages the point of departure is the communal society of the mark.*

Greek [civilization]† also began with the mark and ended with slavery. Then the barbarian Germans flooded over the Roman Empire, and from there a new point of departure began.

The decisive difference is that in antiquity [economic] development ran head-on into a blind alley, whereas the Middle Ages became the basis and point of departure for capitalist development, and thereby also became the point of departure for higher forms of development.

Now what we must keep our eyes on is the disintegration of the mark as the starting point for further development in the Middle Ages.

Briefly summarized, this is what led to that disintegration:

(1) *The right to bequeath and inherit landed property,*‡ out of which [there arose] inequality; either the property was bequeathed to one person, and thus others became dependent on that person; or the property was divided up among all heirs, and thus was fragmented.

The *ability to dispose of inherited property resulted in donations, sales, and purchases.* From this there arose the possibility of many properties being gathered into a few hands or of property being lost entirely. Donations [of land] to the Church; individual members of the mark made such donations, as did widows without children, and so forth; many also bequeathed [land] to their own descendants. Then, also, it was mainly the princes who bequeathed to the Church (they had gained their wealth through military campaigns and conquests) partly out of piety, partly for purposes of mutual support. The princes gave their support to the Church, and vice versa. It is characteristic that in almost every description of the lives of saints or holy persons (particularly in relation to the early Middle Ages) it is regarded as one of the greatest merits that the king or some other holy person decided to make such-and-such a very large donation to the church. For example, at the time of Charlemagne, the Abbey of St. Germain de Prés already owned 25 pieces of property, and indeed they covered 22,000 hectares of agricultural land [crop land], 427 hectares of vineyards, 503 hectares of meadowland, 92 hectares of grazing land, and 13,352 hectares of forest. The abbey of Denizel in western France counted [in its possession] 15,000 parcels of land. Those were the smallholdings of individual peasants. The cloister of

---

* See the first footnote on page 301.
† A word is crossed out here in the original typescript.
‡ The term given here for *Erbgut*, inherited property, can also be translated as ancestral estate.

Lorch near Worms had 2,000 such holdings; St. Gallen had 4,000; Gandersheim, 11,000; Tegernsee, 11,866; and Fulda had 15,000.

Further factors that led to inequality of land ownership included:

The relationship between protégé and patron. That meant: to give oneself *in commendation.* What this consisted of was that one placed oneself under the protection either of a larger landowner of the secular variety or, still better, under the protection of the Church. As a result in many cases it developed that the Church was already a member of the mark community as a result of donations [of land] and because of these, in the mark conflicts broke out. So that the peasant farmers could obtain friends rather than enemies, they placed themselves under the protection of the Church. This also happened out of religious devotion, piety. It was actually heaven under whose protection one stood and the lords of the Church were merely the representatives of that.

One other thing came up, which made the protectorate of the Church more desirable than a secular protectorate. The Lord Protectors of the Church were never as strict as the secular ones, because they never arrived at such a great concentration of property. The possessions of the Church were completely scattered about, and therefore things did not reach the point of such a system of punishments as arose under the secular "Lord Protectors." Additionally, the spiritual [i.e., ecclesiastical] lords were exempted from military service.

In addition to that there was another thing: the secular lords more and more acquired public power and authority over those under their protection. The power over life and death was separated very early from the public authority [structure in general] ... This had to be borrowed as an extra from the public authority and power of the emperor. It was forbidden for spiritual leaders to make use of the *Blutbann.*[*] They had to ... [submit to] the public authority of the emperor. Thus the Church to a certain extent was also under the power of the secular lords and rulers.

We must take some additional aspects into account, as a result of which the large landholding first took shape. To this category there belongs:

Formal separation from the mark. As long as rule over the land was still in the hands of the mark, that was the underlying factor in all the economic measures taken by the mark community.

Up to a certain point in time that could have been useful to the rising lords, as long as it gave them the opportunity to enrich the undivided mark and to force the peasant farmers to acquiesce.

Now there came *departures from the mark community.*

There was a name for one such type of departure: *emunitas.*[†]

---

[*]   The *Blutbann,* literally "blood spell," refers to the power of the Emperor of the Holy Roman Empire to impose capital punishment. Over time the power to impose the *Blutbann* became usurped by territorial nobles.

[†]   That is, immunity from taxation.

Anyone had the right to that who owned at least three *Hufen.*[*] One such domain could *fence in, or enclose, its land*; that meant: here was private property, and this had to do in particular with fencing off and enclosing the undivided mark, particularly the woodlands. This enclosure, or fencing off, of the woodlands was called *Einforstung*. The largest of all [privately owned] forests in Germany appeared in the twelfth and thirteenth centuries. That was one of the causes of the peasant war.[†] But emunitation had already begun at the time of Charlemagne. (He lived from 742 to 814, and came to the throne in 765.)

This emunitation provided the rulers with *complete domination of the mode of production*. In addition to that was *freedom from taxation*, because taxes for the mark were eliminated. In the seventh century AD the officials of the mark no longer had access to the manorial estates. That was even true when a mark constituted a manorial estate in its own right. Because no stranger had access to the mark without permission. In the mark that was called *the peace of the mark*. With this something was separated from the entire sphere of jurisdiction of the mark. Thus in place of the jurisdiction of the mark came the jurisdiction of the lords of the manors.

There was the same immediate result, even if this happened somewhat later, from the exemption for spiritual lords from military service. This is also an aspect of the reason why people preferred to place themselves under the protection of spiritual lords.

Also contributing to the breakdown of community ownership of landed property was the *Blutbann*, which indeed belonged solely to the princely power. Before the Carolingians the power of the princes was so extensive that they freely made use of the power over life and death through the *Gauverfassung*.[‡] A *Gau* encompassed several so-called hundredths and therefore also encompassed several marks and mark communities. The *Gau* had natural borders. At the summit of the *Gau* was the *Count of the Gau, who was installed by the princes*, and he had the power over life and death, or at least he was the chief judge of the *Gau* assembly or the court of the *Gau*, to which the members of the various marks belonged.

---

[*] A *Hufe* ("hide" in old English) were long strips of arable land, extending roughly 500 meters long and 200 meters wide. A *Hufe*, originally cultivated by one family, was often split into various sizes over the passage of time. It was also a term of taxation for the amount owed to the lord for using the particular strip of land. In medieval Germany, few peasant farms were larger than two or four *Hufe*, each *Hufe* being approximately 15 to 30 acres. The size of a *Hufe* varied widely, depending on geographical area and historical periods; its size would even vary within the same district (in some cases it consisted of 80 to 120 acres). In modern times a *Hufe* was established as 41.5 acres.

[†] This is a reference to the German Peasant wars of the early sixteenth century.

[‡] A *Gau* was a geographical region or district of German tribal organization that comprised two or more marks. The *Gauverfassung* was the constitution (i.e., the legal and administrative structure) of that region or district.

Even before Charlemagne these counts of the *Gau* sought to make themselves independent and to make their territories independent of the princely power so as to take it into their own hands. Charlemagne strove to introduce a strongly centralized power and authority and put a very tight rein on the counts of the *Gau*. (His inclination was to establish an empire on a world scale, following the example of the Roman Empire. But Charlemagne's empire fell apart, it was divided up among his sons, and its downfall proceeded ever further, so that the political attempt that he made proved to be purely ephemeral.)

The power of the count of the *Gau* came to represent the highest level of jurisdiction, [including possessing] the power to impose the *Blutbann*.

After the formation of the lords of the manors [as a class] they too sought to take the jurisdiction over life and death into their hands, and for this they had to present their request to the princes. This was achieved in particular by the ecclesiastical lords. In the tenth century most of the ecclesiastical landowners gained the power to impose the *Blutbann*.

There was one other aspect as a result of which landed property took shape among the Germans quite early.

In conquering the Roman Empire, the Germans encountered large landholdings as a finished product of Roman times, particularly in Gaul. Frequently they did not divide these up and turn them over to the mark communities, but kept them as they were. The princes distributed them to their friends and retainers.

There was another reason for the rise of landed property, namely that *during the conquests, entire mark communities were resettled onto fresh, new lands*, through colonization; from the outset, they were subordinate to and obliged to pay tribute to the lords.

In the year 846, the relationship between protector and protected became a binding obligation. There was a law that no small landowner could any longer exist without a lord protector recognized by the public authorities. That happened in order to ensure public order and the keeping of the peace. Since, at a later time, the individual mark communities had become too weak to maintain public order in times of constant warfare and to impose justice with a firm hand, they needed to have a lord protector. The same thing occurred in England as well, in the lands where German tribes had settled.

Thus there very soon arose two categories of the population:

(1) The *owners* of large *landed estates*.

(2) The great mass of the so-called *Hintersassen*˙—the smallholders, small farmers, who possessed only parcels of land for which they were obliged to pay a tax or fee and who were subject to the public authority.

On this basis by the time of Charlemagne the population was divided into *fully free persons* and *unfree persons*. The condition of being fully free with land

---

˙   Literally, those settled in the back or down below.

owned independently then became identical with the concept of nobility. (The lords of large landholdings called themselves *Adlige* or *Edlige* [nobles] as distinct from the unfree. At the time of Charlemagne the terms fully free, noble, and knights were used.)

Charlemagne specified that *military service on horseback* would be allowed for persons who owned at least 3, 4, or 5 *Hufen* of land. Whoever had less land than that had to work together and equip one [horseman] for all such persons combined.

And so, with regard to large landed estates, the Germans found models among the Romans.

They also found Roman models for dependent peasants—that is, the *colonatum*.* And it actually did serve as a model for that purpose.

METHODS OF MANAGEMENT

Now, on the large landed estates there were two types or methods of management.

(1) The estates [*Landereien*]† were managed from the manor house by an overseer, or as he was called earlier, a *villicus* (a term from Rome). Here the *Roman villa* [estate] served directly as the model for management. The largest part [of the land], however, was cultivated, not directly from the manor house, but by serfs, dependent persons, or free peasants serving on leased land or as tenants on land farmed in return for fixed payments. For the most part, the dependent persons, or bondsmen‡ were initially taken over from the Roman Empire. The same also applies to other conquered populations, the Wends§ and Slavs in Bavaria, in Carinthia, and so forth. They came directly into dependent status, bound to the land, under Germanic owners of large landed properties.

And then they [also] evolved from the former free mark communities that had placed themselves under protection [of a feudal lord], and out of mark communities that had been placed in the status of *coloni* from the outset.

For the management and direction of the large estates, the time of Charlemagne, with his constitution of *villas* on the Roman model, was particularly epoch-making. At the central point of such a *villa* stood the lord's manor house, [which was] in effect a royal palace, or king's court, and the operation of the farm was directed from there. One part of the lands was farmed by dependent people, bound to the estate, and they did this work on their own account. They were called *Ministerialen*.¶ Among them were laborers, craftsmen, women

---

* An institution consisting of *coloni*; singular, *colonus*.

† *Landereien* can also refer to parcels of land on an estate.

‡ These bondsmen were also referred to as *coloni*, peasants tied to the land.

§ *Wends* refers to an assortment of western Slavic peoples living close to areas of German settlement. In the Middle Ages, the term was often used for Slavs living within the Holy Roman Empire.

¶ The *Ministerialen* were people subject to the orders of the "ministers," that is, the officials of the estate.

employed in the workhouses, foresters, waiters [i.e., household servants], and so forth. Each branch or subdivision of economic activity was led by a particular official representing the lord of the manor, who stood at the head of that subdivision. Thus within the manor itself there were the following: upper-level officials, and lower officials subordinate to them, and—to say it again—each stood at the head of a single branch or subdivision of economic activity, and they all lived on the manorial estate, around or in the vicinity of the residence of the lord of the manor, inside the boundaries of the manor. Again, at the top, standing over them all, was a magistrate [or governor] of the estate, appointed by the king. He had full power of supervision over the craftsmen, the highest leadership authority over all the affairs of the estate, and in particular, judicial authority as well. Thus, the judicial authority is here [combined] together with the economic management of the manor. Later [this top official] was given such titles as *Schultheiss* [village mayor], *Ammann* or *Amtmann* [magistrate; bailiff], and *Burgvogt* [steward of a castle].

If the manorial estate was fortified, and at the same time served as a temporary residence for the king, it was called a castle, and such an official was then called the count of the castle. For the most part, however, the lands [of the estate] were turned over to bondsmen and to free peasant farmers in return for specified tax or rent payments and other obligations. These peasants also settled around the lord's manor, and all of this, taken together, constituted a *villa*.

Most of the *villas* of Charlemagne were located on state land, and the origin of that was—the undivided mark.* Other landowners, including monasteries, seminaries, and so forth, also managed their estates according to this model.

At that time the estates that were managed on their own account directly from the manor house were called manor lands [Salländereien].† *Great liberties were theirs to enjoy. For example, they were often free from having to pay a tithe to the Church. However, for the care of the poor and* [MS. Missing word] *they did have to pay a tithe, and that was called the manorial lord's tithe.*

(Indeed, it is well known that the income of the Church was apportioned as follows: one-third for charity, one-third for the maintenance of the Church, and one-third for the personal upkeep of the clergy. Naturally, after a while all three parts went to the clergy. Originally all [church] properties were for the care of the poor, but later that disappeared, and they became the private property of the clergy.)

The great mass of the peasants had to pay all three parts.

Where the lands were cultivated by peasant smallholders, *the mark* was typically [responsible] for management.

---

*   The undivided mark consisted of the lands held in common by the mark community.

†   That is, land partly cultivated by tenant farmers. *Salländereien* can also be translated as "manor hall lands."

Where the peasants constituted dependent colonies, one part [of the land] was left undivided, while on the other part lots were drawn for individual parcels.

Thus, on one part, the mark community was the model for economic management; on the other, the Roman villa was the model.

The only difference was that the peasants were headed not by a overseer elected by the mark [community], but by an official the village mayor. Such villages were called mayoral villages, of which there were many in Silesia and Brandenburg.

A picture of such a fully developed estate, and to be sure it was an ecclesiastical one, [is provided by] *the Maurusmünster Abbey in Alsace.**

Two original documents have been found in the archives [from that time]. They are financial records, belonging to the lord of the manor, recording what income the estate had and what it owed.

The documents were from the year: 1) 1120 2) 1144.

An immense territory belonged to this property, including a large number of villages. In addition the abbey owned a lot of properties in the Saargau [the Saar region], and besides that it collected tithes from the villagers as a representative of the ecclesiastical authority.

All the income of the property belonged to the abbey. In fact the various sources of revenue belonged collectively to the abbot.

He was obliged to provide lodging for the bishop of Metz and to the German emperor when they traveled, as well as similar services as their vassal.

The economic activity [of the estate] was directed by the abbot with the help of the following primary officials:

The overseer held a court of justice three times a year in the name of the abbot, at which all the subjects of the estate had to present themselves. Accordingly the overseer received one-third of all court penalties and specified goods in kind: one wild boar, 2 loaves of bread, 6 loaves of sugar, one measure of oats and 4 measures of wine. At Whitsuntide [he received] 6 yearling sheep and 4 loaves of bread, as well as oats and wine.†

The person in charge of the economic work was called a director. He directed all the work on the subordinate properties, which managed themselves. Every year on St. John's Day‡ it was his job to renew the contracts, or

---

* The Maurusmünster Abbey (also known as Marmoutier Abbey) in Alsace was founded in the sixth century AD by a community of Irish monks. In the eighth century it was reorganized as a Benedictine monastery under Maurus, from which its name derives. In the twelfth century it become extremely prosperous and controlled a large amount of surrounding territory. It began to go into decline during the late Middle Ages. Also see the first footnote on page 269.

† In some cases Luxemburg's typescript has Arabic numerals when enumerating something such as goods in kind (e.g., 6 loaves of bread) and in other cases it did not (e.g., three times a year). For the most part we have followed the usage in the typescript.

‡ St. John's Day was also known as Midsummer Day, the feast of St. John the Baptist. In many countries of Europe it is celebrated on June 24.

agreements, with those who were obligated to give service. He also set the day when the mowing of hay would begin, as well as deciding what the price of wine would be at the time specified for the subjects of the abbot to sell their wine. He [also] collected the taxes that were owed to the estate by the tenant farmers.

At the head of each village was a steward, who represented the lord of the estate. He had one *Hufe* of land for himself, but he was obligated to provide the abbot, when the latter came to the village to hold court, with bread, meat, 4 measures of wine, and so forth.

Six foresters were in charge of the forestry, each of whom had two *Hufen* of land and had the right to make use of the forest in several ways, but in return they had to provide the abbot annually with 1 suckling pig, 4 measures of wine, 8 loaves of bread, oats, and an axe. To the overseer: 6 measures of wine, 6 hens, and 6 loaves of bread. These primary officials had additional helpers under them with similar obligations.

The peasant population consisted of free peasants, peasants obligated to make regular payments, and bondsmen who belonged to the estate.

The first made a certain payment yearly for their parcels of land. Their number was small. On the abbey's entire property by 1144—in the second original document—there were only 80 free peasants, obligated to make regular payments, on such a gigantic estate.

The great mass [of peasants] consisted of dependent persons, bound to the land [*Hörigen*], who were obliged to make various payments to the abbot, and in addition they were obligated to give him three workdays per week. Each peasant household had to provide one man for the mowing of the hay, and all able-bodied men had to take part in the mowing. Each mower received one loaf of bread, and on one day would receive meat and beer in addition, and on another day would receive bread and wine. Each dependent person who possessed one *Hufe* of land had to work the lord's land for four days just as diligently as when he was working on his own property. He had to work the land for three days in the autumn and one day in the spring. Each agricultural worker during this labor received 3 loaves of bread and in the autumn received in addition some beer and in the spring some wine. Each peasant household had to provide one reaper. He received something to eat and to drink twice daily, and had the right to a loaf of bread in addition.

Besides that, they had to pay taxes to the abbot.

The dependent persons were obligated to perform personal services if they owned no land; they were called serving people, or porters. They received clothing, food, etc., from the estate. These serving people had to bind up the harvested grain, carry the sheaves into the barns, and thresh them. They brought the harvested grapes to the wine presses and pressed the grapes; they also split wood, heated the stoves and ovens, and helped with the baking of the bread and the brewing of the beer; they kept watch over the house and made everything ready when the abbot went on a journey.

They also had to clean the prison and empty the sewers and so forth.

Let us observe more closely the situation of the various categories on such a manorial estate [Fronhof].

(1) *The category of dependent persons who were not free.*

(2) *The category of personally free dependent persons.*

Those who were not free fell again into two separate categories:

(1) The lower serving people, especially field workers.

(2) Artisans, artists, actual servants in the manor house—engaged in personal service—and the actual officials.

The unfree thus were bound to the lord's estate and for the most part were propertyless.

Those in the second category mostly had possession of *Hufen* and were bound to the land.

The people in the first category were entirely subordinate to the lord and were not allowed to bear arms.

The dependent persons, or bondsmen who were personally free were the ones called up for military service.

Those in the first category, the unfree ones, were also not competent to claim any legal rights. Only their lord could demand revenge, or compensation, in their behalf.

The personally free had the right to demand blood vengeance [*Blutrache*].

(Those who owned no land and soil had no rights at all.)

Marriage between those in the first category and those in the second was at first prohibited on the pain of death. Later, when the practice had become so common and widespread that no one could forbid it any longer, the principle held throughout the Middle Ages that children "followed the angry hand." That meant that children who were descended from the unfree therefore always became unfree dependent persons themselves.

Thus eventually all were transformed into a mass of dependent peasants bound to the land. The personally free dependent persons more and more disappeared.

The personally free dependent persons stood between the fully free and the unfree, the fully free being the lords constituting the nobility. Marriage between the personally free and the fully free was not forbidden, but it would have been marriage between persons not of equal birth, and the children did not have the right of inheritance. An oath sworn by a dependent person, even one who was personally free, had only half the standing of an oath sworn by a fully free person.

The dependent persons were under the legal jurisdiction of their lord.

Following the model of Charlemagne's estate, every manorial estate owned by a lord, both secular and ecclesiastical, had a household of the lord of the manor house [*Hofstaat*] with its household retinue [*Hofgeleite*], and so there was a definite number of persons who always constituted the lord's retinue of household servants and household officials. The latter were called *Ministerien*. Those who served in the manor house were called *Ministerialen*.

In addition the following belonged to every manorial estate: the seneschal, who oversaw the kitchen staff; the chamberlain, who oversaw the stores of uniforms and the treasure vaults; the cup bearers; and the marshal, who oversaw the stables.

Those were the uppermost officials of the manorial estate.

In addition there belonged [to the estate] household servants of the lower rank; the master of the hunt, the forest master, the cook, the waiting staff, the steward, the overseers, and the craftsmen.

They all belonged to the estate and were under the legal jurisdiction of the lord of the manor. Thus what was later called service to the state was at that time service to the manorial lord.

The public officials were nothing but officials in service to the feudal lords until the late Middle Ages, and that was also true for those doing military service.

All of these *Ministerialen*,[*] from the topmost to those at the bottom, were under strict discipline and were even subject to corporal punishment. A special cane[†] [for beating errant servants] played a role right up until the seventeenth and eighteenth centuries, and in the nineteenth century we still find boxing of the ears.

Some of the officials of the estate were granted lands on lease by the lords. These were the so-called benefices, which the officials at first received as a lifetime benefit and in return for which they were obliged to make certain fixed payments or services. Later these leased lands became hereditary [property of the officials]. From these servants of the manorial estate there developed a feudal nobility, which later became the high nobility.

Thus the nobility had two sources, from below and from above; those from below originated from the old families, which had been members of the mark community; the upper nobility stemmed from those who belonged to the manorial estate.

The latter formation, which evolved from the manorial lord's household and from among the household servants in the lord's retinue, shows that large landed property had already entered the phase in which it *separated itself economically from its own labor.*

It is characteristic that in the eleventh century the Norwegian King Sigurd[‡]

---

* Service people under the officials of the manorial household.

† *Das spanische Rohr* in the typescript—that is, a cane originally from Spain.

‡ This is a reference to Sigurd Syr Halfdansson (died 1018), who was a king of northern Ostlandet, in modern Norway. He was renowned for eschewing royal prerogatives, preferring

managed and worked his lands himself and oversaw his own people.

However, the higher the manorial estates rose and the more they imposed themselves on the mass of the peasants as estates on which compulsory labor was required, the more the lords gave up the habit of doing their own labor. Their chief occupations became: military service, riding, hunting and other sports of the nobility, and drinking. (See Lassalle: Bastiat-Schulze.)*

At first there was only the seneschal, the marshal, the cook, and the baker; or seneschal, marshal, cupbearer, and majordomo (who was in charge of the household economy).

As early as the eighth century the latter had the chairmanship during judicial procedures at the manorial estate.

Later, each of these officials had an entire staff of lesser officials subordinate to him.

The craftsmen employed in the lord's household acquired an official for themselves, and standing at a higher point above them was an official of the manorial household [Hofbeamter], who prescribed the work they were to do and directed them.

Later, in addition, the scribe, or official secretary: the Kanzelarius. From which the [present-day public office of] chancellor is descended.

Later [there was also] a special patrimonial official [Hofrichter] or count palatine [Pfalzgraf].

Out of the counts palatine and so forth there developed the petty princes [rulers of small principalities], and Germany's numerous fatherlands [i.e., small separate states].

In many cases manorial estates became the large free cities, or imperial cities, of the Holy Roman Empire: Aachen, Mainz, Speyer, Regensburg, Worms, Ulm.†

Every larger manorial estate was managed according to the model of Charlemagne, with the only difference that...

In the ninth and tenth centuries supreme juridical power—above all the power over life and death—was transferred to the lords of the feudal estates. In particular, most of the bishoprics and a great many of the abbeys had the power of the Counts of geographic regions [Gaugrafs] transferred to them.‡

The upper echelons in each state originated from among the vassals of earlier times who had made themselves completely independent.

---

instead to carefully manage his rural property. His surname "Syr" may derive from the word for "sow," indicating that he was "rooted to the soil like a pig."

   * Ferdinand Lassalle, Herr Bastiat-Schulze von Delitzsch, der Ökonomische Julian, oder, Kapital und Arbeit.

   † The short paragraph is a repetition; the point made above is also made elsewhere in the typescript.

   ‡ That is, they were granted the same powers as the Gaugraffs.

On the one hand, the free service people elevated themselves *more and more to the rank of noble*. The earlier benefices,* granted for a lifetime, became hereditary landed property, independent of the lord's estate. Out of this the higher nobility took shape.

In the lower stratum the different categories disappeared into *one large mass of peasants in a position of complete economic dependence on the noble lord*.

Together with that the economic relationship naturally changes; taxes and other obligatory payments grow more and more.

And then we arrive at serfdom in its finished form.

Just as Charlemagne formerly provided the model for the manorial estates, so too in later centuries the ecclesiastical manors became the classic examples of the landholdings of the feudal lords.

The historical records from the Maurusmünster Abbey date from the twelfth century. But we have other examples as well.

And so, [here are] two examples from *earlier times*. [One is] From *France*, from the *second half of the eighth century*; according to other accounts, [it is] from the ninth century: [it is called] the benefices book-and-polyptych of the Abbot Eminont. [It is] from the Abbey of St. Germain de Prés.†

The second document is *the Polyptych of St. Emilius*‡ from the end of the ninth century from the hereditary archbishopric of Reims.

The land area of these two ecclesiastical estates was divided into two parts. One part was land belonging to the [ecclesiastical] lord and remaining at the personal disposal of the property owner, that is, the abbot. The other part was for the hereditary use of the smallholder peasants living in the area, both free and unfree.

Hence two methods of management. This was the consequence of very far-reaching historical factors.

On pieces of land that had been given away [as benefices], both free and unfree persons make their appearance in the oldest documents. The benefices book of Eminont at St. Germain mentions *entire settlements with only free peasants*. But they already have obligations to the lords. Annually each one had to work on the land of the manorial lord at two specified times of the year to the same extent as the unfree had to, and indeed they had to provide the equivalent of one grown man with a plough and two oxen.

---

*   A benefice is a reward obtained in exchange for services rendered (or to be rendered in the future) to a feudal lord. A benefice received from a king or nobleman was known as a fief. It generally took the form of a gift of land for services rendered to the lord.

†   The Abbey of St. Germain de Prés, on the outskirts of medieval Paris, was founded in the sixth century. Thanks to royal patronage, it became one of the richest abbeys in France during the High Middle Ages. In the eleventh century it became an intellectual center of the Benedictine order. The philosopher René Descartes is buried in one of its chapels.

‡   A polyptych is a painting divided into a series of sections or panels. This appears to be a reference to a painting in one of the Romanesque cathedrals in the French town of St. Emilion.

The elder in such a village is free from all obligatory payments; he has his own piece of land, like the others, and probably had official functions to perform in exchange for that, and probably we have here the elected village chief [*Vorsteher*] of a free community. Thus [we are talking about] communities that had placed themselves under protection [of a lord]. They are still personally free and their village chief is not yet an official of the manorial estate.

Individual peasants also have large pieces of land in their possession. From that it is necessary to conclude that they made the same obligatory payments in agricultural products (this is sufficient to make the supposition that this had been a mark community). Its inhabitants had to make no other payments to the lords aside from these [specified] services. They also did not have the freedom to live where they wished. That was in exchange for protection by the lords.

Thus [we are talking about] *half* the [peasant] farms, but still only as an exception.

The tax payments show how things were proceeding for people who had no plots of their own land at all.

It was the right of each free person to provide proof with the help of an oath [backed up] with seven [other] free persons that because of poverty...* one was allowed to relinquish one's claim to the land and was obligated from then on to do three days of compulsory labor during the harvest and to make other payments. In this way he [the free peasant] became a dependent person, or bondsman, belonging to the estate.

These free dependent persons [belonging to the estate] were still called *coloni* in the historical documents. A distinction was made between ... [(1)] *coloni* and (2) those who had placed themselves under a lord's protection of their own free will.

Both documents also mention unfree smallholders. Again, these fell into two categories. First were those who owned no land, [they were called] fellows and maids [i.e., farm laborers and farm girls], who did personal service at the [manor] house or who paid a yearly tax in kind or paid money. They received a house to live in from the lord's estate. In return they had to make certain payments to the lord's estate in the form of eggs and hens. Second were the fellows and maids who did agricultural labor in the fields. They possessed a house and a small plot of land, a portion of a field, if also [they were regarded] as free. They had to make the following payments: first, a contribution of 3 cooking chickens and 15 eggs annually, second, to put in 1 day's work per year in agricultural labor with a plough and two oxen. Those who did not have their own livestock were free from [the obligation] of performing agricultural labor with plough and oxen. [Maksim] Kovalevsky concludes from this that labor with plough and

---

* The passage suggests that the peasant had the right to provide proof that because of poverty he was unable to make his obligatory payments.

oxen was in return for the fact that the peasants could pasture their livestock on the fields belonging to the lord of the manor, on the lands lying fallow.

The field under cultivation had to be sown and harvested by the unfree peasants. They also had to do about 4 days labor per year at haymaking.

[There was] one category of obligatory payments for both free and unfree smallholder peasants: to provide 1 wagonload of wood from fallen trees annually; this was compensation for their use of the forest, [which had belonged] formerly to the undivided mark community. Posts for fences and wickerwork or reeds for roofs, as well as salt, had to be paid in return for the right to make use of the lord's property, the streams, lakes, and so forth.

All the needs of the lords' manorial estates were covered by the peasants' obligatory payments. They were not exacted by force, but for any use [of the lord's estate] the peasants had to make payments.

The later displacement is merely [the result of] this fact: Previously, when the mark community existed, the land and soil belonged to the peasants. Therefore they worked for themselves and the results [of their labor] belonged to them. The displacement consisted fundamentally in the fact that the owners of the ground and soil had changed; as a result of the dissolution of the mark, large tracts of land and finally all the land came under [the ownership of] the large landed proprietors. The peasants still lived by their own labor. But the lords of the manorial estates were maintained by the peasants, and the reason was that the ground and soil, which had previously belonged to them, had been lost to the peasants.

In these old documents the historical sources of the later [feudal] relations can be seen everywhere. But later, for example, at the Maurusmünster Abbey, relations have changed so that the law stipulates that the person to whom the land belongs [can] demand all possible taxes and obligatory payments from the small peasants. A relationship of lord to subject had developed in which the fact of rule by the lord comes first and the economic relations are merely the consequence of that.

The course of development proceeds from this starting point with the result, on the one hand, that whereas in the [early] Middle Ages there were various categories of the small peasantry, with the passage of time there was only *one large mass of unfree persons.*

In the beginning there were also large differences of nationality, but later on, all of that was mixed together into a uniform, homogeneous mass of unfree peasants, obligated to provide unpaid labor services to the lord of the manor [*fronpflichtige*]. The taxes and other payments kept growing more and more, to the outermost limit. In general, whatever could be gotten out of them was extracted from the peasants.

In the end, after the taxes and other payments had completely ripened, we arrive at the following categories:

Payments in kind. There were actually no items that were not demanded by the lords from the peasants. All types of livestock, poultry, milk, honey and beeswax, and fish. The [category of] honey and beeswax in particular [was] a characteristic form of taxation under the feudal relationship in which compulsory labor was required [*das Fronverhältnis*]. The church needed beeswax for candles, and honey for food. Then there were flax and hemp, as payments that had to be provided mainly by women. The peasants even had to provide leeches, and in addition, grain, wood, wine, [and,] all items required for the [lord's] household and kitchen, underwear in finished condition, handkerchiefs, linen cloths, other finished linen items, furs, towels, leather, and readymade gloves.

Obligatory payments on palace day at the estate of the Abbot of Corvey in Westphalia.

On palace day payments [in kind] were accepted from the peasants, court was held, and all the vassals of the abbot, who indeed were often landowners as well, had to make their appearance and take seats at the abbot's table.

On one such palace day on the estate of the Abbot of Corvey in 1187 the following were received: 6 fat hogs, 1 suckling pig, a large number of hens, geese, eggs, and fish, 30 cheeses, among which it was specified that there must be 2 quite large cheeses made from sheep's milk, as large as a woman's rear end or so large that if one placed one's thumb in the middle one's hand could reach the outer edge, a large quantity of fruits of every kind, salt, pepper, 1 pitcher [each] of mustard, honey, and beer, 33 kettles that could be used for cooking, 100 dishes or bowls, 10 pots, 2 casks for wine and 2 for other purposes, 2 large cans, 1 mortar made of wood, a large quantity of oats, and so forth.

At a palace day of the Archbishop of Cologne (in about the twelfth century) the following contributions were made: 24 large and 8 middle-sized hogs and especially for the major feast days another 12 middle-sized hogs, 24 hens, 230 eggs, 24 cheeses, 650 dishes and bowls, among which there also had to be [serving] plates, and so on.

The natural economy did not continue up until the end of the Middle Ages; there was a change to *payments in money, rental or tax payments made in money*. It was no longer necessary just to satisfy personal needs but also to make *money*. And that is when the real abuse and mistreatment began, just as it had under slavery. With the change from payments in kind to money payments the required contributions spiraled upward to a colossal extent.

Various forms of tax or rental payments [Zinses]

(1) A ground tax for the use of the land.

---

* The Abbey of Corvey in Westphalia, in northeast Germany, was founded in 815 as a Benedictine monastery. It was one of the most important monasteries in the Carolingian period. In the tenth century it became a major economic power when it was granted the power to obtain labor services and payments from the surrounding peasants. It also obtained the power to mint its own coins. The Abbey went into decline after the fifteenth century.

(2) A head tax, a personal tax that was also called a body tax.

(3) A household tax [*Rauchzins*] for the use of the [lord's] manor house and household; *Rauch* is just another name for the manor house.

(4) Money for watchmen, for the maintenance of public order.

(5) A milk tax and a grass fee for the [use of the] pastures for livestock.

(6) Spinning products money; the linens and other cloths had been changed into money.

(7) [Also there was] egg money, broom money, a hen tax, a tax on cotton thread or yarn, a wax fee, a tax on bees, and an oats tax, as well as marketing money, in return for the right of the peasants to take their goods to market; a water tax for the use of water [on the lord's land], and a tax for the windmills; earlier there were water mills, and then windmills developed, and the tax for the mills was transferred to the windmills, which has been maintained down to the present time. (One may read about this in the book *Die schlesische Milliarde* [The Silesian Billion] by [Wilhelm] Wolff. Wolff himself had been a serf subject to compulsory labor, and his father had to pay a large sum so that he could be allowed to learn [in school]. *The Silesian Billion* first appeared in the *Neue Rheinische Zeitung.* It was still a burning question at that time.)

The livestock tax represented the compulsory labor service by oxen which the poor peasants previously had to provide. [There were also] *taxes for practicing a craft, taxes for allowing one's children to learn any profession; [also] departure money had to be paid for moving to another village or to another district.*

Then there was *a third category*; it had three names [in German]: *Kurmade, Bestraub, Gewandrecht.*†

The *right of inheritance by the lords*; at first this had to do with the inheritance of a peasant or a peasant's wife. When a peasant died, the lord took the best from the peasant's herd or the best thing from his closet. Usually it was the best horse, the best ox, right on down to the best rooster. One document states the following: "No livestock should remain there, and no good clothing, and then the best featherbed, and if cushions or pillows are lacking, one takes the door

---

*   Wolff, who was from Silesia, became a close friend of Marx in 1846, to whom he dedicated Vol. 1 of *Capital*. During the 1848 Revolutions Wolff travelled to Silesia, where he fought for the abolition of feudal obligations that still prevailed among the peasantry. Marx published numerous articles by him on the campaign in the *Neue Rheinische Zeitung*, including a series of eight articles entitled "The Silesian Billion," from March 22 to April 25, 1849. In these influential and inflammatory writings Wolff calculated the amount of money, labor, and landed property that the Silesian aristocracy had robbed from the peasants through feudal dues since the beginning of the Middle Ages. The articles were reproduced as a book after Wolff's death, to which Engels wrote the Introduction. See *Die schlesische Milliarde* (Hottingen-Zürich: Volksbuchhandlung, 1886).

†   *Kurmade* (also *die kurmede*), *besthaupt* and *gewandrecht* (literally, "a right to the robe") refers to a manorial levy extracted from peasants upon the death of a lord or a change of ownership in the manor. Payment could be made in kind (through grain or cattle), money, or even by granting the lord of the manor allowance to sleep with a peasant's wife. It essentially served as an inheritance tax.

to the house, because it is also has four corners." A truly medieval touch, this combines naivety with gross bestiality.

Fourth category: the right of the lord and his guests to be boarded and fed while traveling. This has the following meaning: if the lord wishes to stay overnight, the master of the house must provide a bed for him, with sufficient pillows and cushions on it, and so forth. It was specified exactly what the bed had to be like. Even the *poorest* peasants had to do this, and it was prescribed how *they* had to make the bed. It was also prescribed what the lord had to be given to eat. The peasants at whose house the lord slept also had to take pains to ensure a good rest for the lord. They had to keep the frogs [in the vicinity] quiet, so that the lord could sleep peacefully. That was stipulated in a document of an old [*MS. Missing word*] near Trier. Indeed, this was one of the complaints of the French peasants at the time of the great revolution [of 1789]. They had to spend entire nights wading in the ponds and beating sticks so that the frogs would remain silent.

The category of weddings. For dependent persons belonging to the lord of an estate, a wedding permission was necessary from the overseer, and in addition a tax had to be paid, the so-called wedding money. It had various names, and as one approaches the vicinity of Germany some of the names are rather drastic: the petticoat tax, the bed tax, the nightgown shilling, and so forth.

Then there was the feudal right to the first night. A document about that belonging to a convent at Zurich, which was the estate of an ecclesiastical lord, dating from 1543, which means after the Reformation, states the following: "And so when the wedding is over, the groom must allow the steward of the estate to lie with his wife on the first night [thus the lord had transferred his right to the steward, one of his officials—R.L.]—or he must buy her out of this obligation with such-and-such an amount of money." The possibility of buying one's way out of this "pleasantry" was indeed a step forward.

Protection money paid by the poorest peasants, those who had no home or land of their own and who paid a tax only as people in a changed status as weavers (?), as people on their own, and so forth. These were the so-called enclosed ones, the poorest of the poor. The protection money had to be paid by them so that the lord, if a violation was committed, would have to come to their defense.

Protection money for prostitutes, for courtesans. These prostitutes lived in what were called women's houses in the Middle Ages and were subject to the jurisdiction of the manorial estate. Prostitution was regarded as one of the crafts [of the manor], a horizontal trade. Prostitutes were therefore called women of the estate [*höfische Frauen*], which meant that they were under the legal jurisdiction of the manor, women subject to the manorial ordinances, and they were classed as "dependent persons." (The term *höfisch* [of the manorial lord] was used in opposition to the term "*bäuerlich*" [of the peasants].) In the imperial cities and in other cities in Germany they [the prostitutes] were under the protection of the hereditary imperial marshal, Herr von Pappenheim.* This office was hereditary in the Pappenheim family. Until the year 1640 protection money had to be paid to them. Only then was it abolished.

The consumer use of prostitutes was very extensive in the Middle Ages. During a council [of the Church] in Basel in 1451, 700–1,500 prostitutes gathered there. At that time they were under the supervision of the [*MS. Missing word*] of Saxony. It was the same at public political events. When an Imperial Diet was held in Frankfurt in 1394, 300 prostitutes came there. In the capital city of each [German] state a *Landeshofmarschall* was in charge of the public houses. He was the marshal of the court in that state, also called lord chamberlain. It was also the same in Vienna. The court in Vienna obtained its revenue from all possible sources and did not disdain payments from the prostitutes. Only in 1558 did the emperor Ferdinand I abolish this in Vienna.

Hunting rights applied only to the lords. Hunting was forbidden to the peasants, who were defenceless against damage done by wild animals, and they were also obligated to provide compulsory labor service as beaters [for the hunters].

[This is] one of the most important categories: *payments in labor, compulsory labor services.* And indeed there were [such categories as] compulsory labor for a day, for a week, in the fields, at the lord's manor, and that included chopping wood and carrying water for the kitchen, for the cooks, and so forth, as well as cultivating the land, and [in general] everything that needed to be done.

Service as messengers on foot and on horseback.

In the state of Delbrück,† for example, there were special bearers of venison, fish, and crayfish.

Labor service with teams of horses, when the lords went to church or made other trips. There were special wine journeys [by the lords] for tasting the new, young wine. Compulsory service on boats or ships [*Schiffdienste*], rowing, and so forth.

Compulsory building services [*Baufronden*]: building the manor houses, building kitchens, and so forth.

Compulsory hunting and fishing labor services [*Jagd- und Fischerfronden*].

[And to repeat:] compulsory service as beaters [in hunting] [*Treiberdienste*].

Compulsory dancing [*Frontänze*], for the entertainment of the lords.

In the [regions of] Gera, Schwarzburg-Rudolstadt,‡ and the Palatinate,

---

* General Gottfied Henrich Graf von Pappenheim was a famous military commander and mercenary during the Thirty Years' War (1618–48), in which he was employed by the armies of the Holy Roman Empire. He became imperial marshal in 1632.

† Delbrück is a town in northeast Germany, in Rhine-Westphalia. The town was founded in 1219.

‡ Gera is a city in southwest Germany, in the state of Thuringia. It was founded in the ninth century AD. Schwarzburg-Rudolstadt is a state in Thuringia. It is named after the Schwarzburg family, which resided in the town of Rudolstadt.

and so forth, for example, there were special Whitsuntide* dances.

Then there was another important category:

Legal costs for violations of the law. Fines often had to be paid in kind. If there were squabbles between women they had to pay with eggs and cheese. There was a regulation stating: "Where two women were having a scrap, pulling out each other's hair, or hitting each other, each one must pay our gracious lord one basketful [*Malter*]† of cheese or eggs."

The transformation of compulsory payments and contributions into money began as early as the *twelfth century*.

Lassalle in his book *Capital and Labor* (pages 118–80)‡ describes the medieval economy. Lassalle derives the status of dependency [bondspeople belonging to a lord's estate] from serfdom; but [actually] it's the other way around; first there was dependency, and then serfdom.

Slavery and the feudal economy were both at first for the purpose of covering one's own needs. But in both of them the money economy arose [and became increasingly important]. Because of that the [previously existing] form of society began to fall apart—the form in which work was done only to satisfy one's own needs—and the new [form of society] emerged, which produced for trade. Under slavery this led to [economic] collapse, the decline and fall [of the system].

In the feudal economy the result would have probably been the same as under slavery if a *new starting point* had not arisen. *And indeed [that starting point was] in the cities.* The beginning of the city is the village and the manorial estate [*Fronhof*].§

The decline of productivity became evident [which meant] the economic disintegration of the economy. The peasants more and more had to neglect the cultivation of their own land. The decline of the land became ever greater, and the physical incapacitation of the peasants grew ever greater. This reached its sharpest point in France; the French Revolution did away with this. In France

---

*   Whitsuntide (also known as Witsunday) is the Christian festival of Pentecost that falls on the seventh Sunday after Easter. It commemorates the descent of the Holy Spirit upon Christ's disciples.

†   A *Malter* is literally a "corn-measure"—an ancient measurement of corn that varies in different locations. In some parts of Germany, a *Malter* was a basket or container that held about 150 liters.

‡   The reference is to Lassalle's book, *Herr Bastiat-Schulze von Delitzsch, der Ökonomische Julian, oder, Kapital und Arbeit*, pp. 118–80. Marx was much more critical of this work by Lassalle than Luxemburg seems to have been. See his letter to Engels of June 3, 1864, where he accuses Lassalle of having "cribbed" much of the work from his *Wage Labor and Capital*. In response, Marx planned at the time to reprint *Wage Labor and Capital* "without any mention of Izzy [Lassalle]. He won't enjoy it in the least."

§   The manorial estate was that part of the manor directly controlled by the lord and used for the benefit of his household and dependents. Compulsory labor was required of those belonging to it.

this was expressed much more thoroughly than in Germany. Because in Gaul, which means in France, the Germans had taken over large landed property in finished form from the Roman Empire. But in today's Germany that was not so; in general it remained a backward country, that is, up until the present. In France [there was] unproductive agriculture, population increase became minimal (that is even so today and it dates from that time), and there was a high mortality rate, including among children. The peasants in France, according to descriptions by writers at that time, were scarcely human any longer; they could barely speak a few words, dressed in rags and working their land by primitive methods; they were like wild animals. In France [there was] the great revolution; in Germany, the peasant war. These ended, however, in complete fiascos. They had a reactionary program, wanted to divide up the land. This was stated by Lassalle.*

A new path was opened that, as we can see in retrospect, brought freedom to the peasants and unfolded entirely new prospects of development for the future.

[This was] another aspect of development in the Middle Ages:

THE DEVELOPMENT OF THE CITIES

To begin with, [there was] an epoch of retrogression.

The development of cities is a later phenomenon. Between the Roman city and the medieval one lies an interval of several centuries.

The opinions of scholars on this matter are quite divergent.

An earlier, older trend among scholars traces the origins of the medieval city directly from the Roman city.

Only in the second half of the nineteenth century did there occur the unearthing of the old original records, etc. As long as these were not known, it was natural to think that the medieval city was derived from the Roman city.

The medieval cities in many cases began to flourish at the same locations where earlier there had been Roman cities. Cologne, Basel, Aachen, and a large number of others had been Roman cities. Therefore, without looking into it further, people assumed that the medieval French and Italian cities were a direct continuation of the Roman cities.

Two French researchers, [François] Guizot, a reactionary but a serious historian, and [Augustine] Thierry are both adherents of this theory. Also subscribing to it are the following German scholars: [Friedrich Carl von] Savigny (a knowledgeable authority on law and the history of law), [Karl Friedrich] Eichhorn, [Ernest Theodor] Gaupp, and [Heinrich] Leo. The following works by these authors come into consideration with regard to this question:

---

* Luxemburg is again referring to Lassalle's *Herr Bastiat-Schulze von Delitzsch, der Ökonomische Julian, oder, Kapital und Arbeit.*

Guizot, *Geschichte der Zivilisation in Frankreich* [History of Civilization in France], first published in 1830–32.[*]

Thierry, *Betrachtungen über die Geschichte Frankreichs* [Reflections on the History of France]. 1840.[†]

Thierry, *Geschichte des 3. Standes im Mittelalter* [History of the Third Estate in the Middle Ages].[‡]

Savigny, *Geschichte des römischen Rechts* [History of Roman Law].[§]

Eichhorn, *Über den Ursprung der Städteverfassung in Deutschland* [On the Origin of the Constitution of the Cities in Germany].[¶]

Gaupp, *Über deutsche Städtegründung* [On the Founding of the German Cities]. 1824.[**]

Leo, *Entwicklung der Verfassung der lombardischen Städte* [Development of the Constitution of the Lombard Cities].[††]

[There are] researchers who derive the medieval cities from the craft guilds [*Zunft* was the earlier German word for a "guild"; later the term *Gilde* was used]. ???????[‡‡] [I refer you to] The following scholars; they are definitive authorities in the field of city structure.[§§]

[Wilhelm Eduard] Wilda, *Über das Gildenwesen im Mittelalter* [On the Guild System in the Middle Ages], 1831.[¶¶]

---

[*]   Guizot's book was actually first published in French between 1828 and 1830. See François Guizot, *Histoire de la civilisation en France depuis la chute de l'empire romain jusqu'en 1789* (History of Civilization in France from the Fall of the Roman Empire to 1789) (Paris: Pichon et Didier, 1828–30).

[†]   See Augustin Thierry, *Erzählungen aus den merovingishcen Zeiten: mit einleitenden Betrachtungen über die Geschichte Franksreich* (Stories of Merovingian Times, Preceded by Reflections about the History of France) (Elberfeld: Friderichs, 1855). The book originally appeared in French as *Récits des temps mérovingiens, précédés de considerations sur l'histoire de France* (Paris: Furne et Cie, Éditeurs, 1851).

[‡]   See Augustin Thierry, *Recueil des monuments inédits de l'histoire du Tiers Etate* (Unpublished Collection of Documents of the History of the Third Estate) (Paris: Didot, 1850–53).

[§]   See Friedrich Carl von Savigny, *Geschichte des römischen Rechts* (History of Roman Law), six volumes (Heidelberg: J.C.B. Mohr, 1815–31).

[¶]   See Karl Friedrich Eichhorn, *Über den Ursprung der Städteverfassung in Deutschland* (On the Origin of the Constitution of the Cities in Germany) (Berlin: Nicolai, 1815).

[**]   See Ernest Theodor Gaupp, *Über deutsche Städtegründung, Stadtverfassung und Weichbild im Mittelalter, besonders über die Verfassung von Freiburg im Breisgau verglichen mit den Vergassung von Cöln* (On the Founding of the German Cities, The City Constitution, and the City Precincts in the Middle Ages, Especially the Constitution of Frieburg in Breisgau Compared with that of Cologne) (Jena: F. Frommann, 1824).

[††]   See Heinrich Leo, *Entwicklung der Verfassung der lombardischen Städte bis zu Ankunft Kaiser Friedrich I* (Development of the Constitution of the Lombard Cities to the Rise of Emperor Friedrich I) (Hamburg: Perthes, 1824).

[‡‡]   These question marks are in the original manuscript. It is probable that the secretary or student recording Luxemburg's lecture did not understand what she said at this point.

[§§]   *Städtewesen*; a term that might also be translated as "the nature and condition of the cities."

[¶¶]   See Wilhelm Eduard Wilda, *Über das Gildenwesen im Mittelalter* (On the Guild System in the Middle Ages) (Halle: Rengerschen Buchhandlung, 1831).

Karl Dietrich Hüllmann, *Städtewesen im Mittelalter* [City Structure in the Middle Ages], 1827.*

A different tendency: this one derives the development of cities from the constituents of the mark community. This theory is represented by Professor L[udwig] von Maurer.[†]

Then [there appeared] yet another tendency: This tendency traced the development of cities from the manorial constitution [*Hofverfassung*], from manorial lands on which peasant farmers performed compulsory labor service. This tendency was represented by Professor [Wilhelm] Arnold, a legal scholar who taught at Basel in the 1860s.[‡]

From this material we are likely to conclude that these theories collectively are not entirely wrong, but they are also not entirely correct. They all contain a kernel of truth.

Cologne, Strasbourg, and Aachen [Aix-la-Chapelle] had undoubtedly been Roman cities. However, while this theory was flourishing, there were two circumstances that had not yet been clarified, and they are decisive in this case.

The Roman city was fundamentally different from the medieval one. It had been an extraordinarily strictly organized body, or corporation, which was run by state officials from Rome, with a certain amount of participation by the ruling classes of the city, but without any participation by the masses.

In this regard the medieval city represents something fundamentally different from the Roman one.

In the medieval city nothing has remained of Roman municipal law; none of it had been utilized. That is the legal side, [having to do with] the organization of the city.

But there was something that belonged to the essential nature of the city, both under Rome and in the Middle Ages, distinguishing it from the villages, an external characteristic, the walls that surrounded the city. That was the first true sign of a city.

It is a fact that when the Germans conquered the Roman Empire, they destroyed all the conquered cities, and in particular they tore down the walls. After the conquest by the Germans, several centuries went by in Rome [i.e., in the Roman Empire] during which absolutely no walling of the cities took place, and a retrogression in agricultural relations occurred.

As soon as the Germans had conquered the Roman Empire they settled

---

* See Karl Dietrich Hüllmann, *Städtewesen im Mittelalter* (City Structure in the Middle Ages) (Bonn: Adolph Marcus, 1829).

† See Georg Ludwig von Maurer, *Einleitung zur Geschichte der Mark-, Hof-. Dorf- und Stadtverfassung und der öffentlichen Gewalt.*

‡ See Wilhelm Arnold, *Das Aufkommen des Handwerks in den deutschen Städten* (The Rise of Craft Production in the German Cities) (Basel: H. George, 1861).

down in their old mark communities. [This is] a sign that a people does not by any means leave the external product that it has conquered as it was, but [such change] occurs only when that fits in with their social relations. To the Germans the city was an alien product. They had no use for it.

One Roman author wrote: "The Germans are people who love unlimited freedom. They cannot bear to have walls around them and therefore they tear them down." That was not, however, the real reason for the tearing down of the walls. The fact that the Germans had no need for walls or for the city as a whole was decisive for them.

It was only at the time of Charlemagne, in approximately the eighth century, that the building of walls around cities was begun again. This is not yet the city in final form. However it was, so to speak, the formation of the cells from which the city would develop.

The building of walls around all such manors became necessary in particular because of the Viking raids in the ninth century.

Most of the former Roman cities did later become medieval French and German cities. But why?

In the formation of the later city it was not only the king's palaces or castles but also the seats of the bishops that became the central point of the city's development. According to canon law only the seat of the bishop [i.e., the diocesan town] could be surrounded with walls. The churches and the valuables possessed by the churches were to be protected; that was stipulated under canon law; and therefore the building of the walls took place. Those Roman cities in which the palaces of kings as well as the seats of bishops had been introduced by the Germans became the largest imperial cities.* In contrast to those, the locations that did not have walls built around them were transformed by the Germans into rural communities. Many [so-called] Roman cities are Roman cities that once again became cities after a long time as villages.

The first beginnings of the walling-in of cities occurred as early as in the sixth century, and in particular under Charlemagne [in the eighth century].

What was it that was walled in?

The lord's manor together with everything that belonged to it. Buildings and lands that belonged directly to the manor.

It constituted a village if it was not walled in, and a city if it was. That is the earliest distinction.

Frankfurt was walled in, in the ninth century, Zurich in the tenth, Ulm in the eleventh, and Aachen in the twelfth.

It was not merely the villas [manors] of the kings and bishops, but also those of the secular and spiritual princes of the realm who had their manorial estates walled in, the manors becoming cities. Thus, for example, Heidelberg, where

---

* Imperial cities were free cities of the Holy Roman Empire.

the counts who had palaces on the Rhine* lived. They turned it into a city in the twelfth century. Apparently most of the cities of Brandenburg have the same origin.

Even the small landowners had their fortified manors, and from that there developed a city, for example, Brakel.

In the same way, non-secular institutions, monasteries, abbeys, and seminaries, often developed into cities when they were walled in. Münster, for example. The same was true of Bremen, which was given as a gift by Charlemagne when it was only a village to the bishopric of Bremen. Hamburg likewise was a village belonging to the parish of St. Peter, and the streets in Hamburg still show where the formerly dependent persons were located; for example, Bakers Street and Cutlers Alley.

Likewise, Hildesheim and Bamberg were all formerly villages and manorial estates of the clergy.

[Among the cities] arising from walled-in monasteries [are] Eichstadt, Buxtehude, St. Gallen, Fulda, and Schaffhausen.

Only those could undertake to establish a city, that is, to wall in their manorial estates, who had public power and the authority to levy troops.

But only the free lords of manors had this power. For example, in the ninth century the diocesan towns collectively already had the same power and authority as the counts of geographical regions. Thus they had the possibility of developing into cities.

[This was] the first beginning after a long period of purely agricultural work being done ... on the manorial estates.

That was a confirmation of Arnold's theory.

But who was to be found inhabiting the manorial possessions? Who was numbered among the population of the walled-in city?

First of all the rulers: the ministerial officials, the vassals, then the dependents belonging to the manor, as well as those doing personal service such as the craftsmen. In particular, however, in most such cities destined for significant development, there also were present several communities of old-time free residents. They had placed themselves under the protection of the regional counts, that is, under the protection of the public authority. At the same time, however, they had avoided becoming personally dependent. In many regions of Germany entire communities as free members of the mark avoided becoming dependents, but they had to place themselves to a certain extent under the protection of the great lords [of the region], and from this there arose the small country squires in cases where a lesser nobility did not exist.

In cases where they found themselves in the walled-in center of a manorial possession, they preserved their personal freedom and had to recognize only the

---

*   The counts that had their palaces on the Rhine were called Counts Palatinate.

public authority. From these arose a class of patricians as soon as the development of the city began.

In this respect there is truth in both Arnold's view and in Maurer's, but not in that of either of them alone.

With the further development of these manorial possessions which were becoming cities the existence of the free mark community within it played a role of prime importance.

(1) The manorial estate as a center of economic, social, and political life; a free community of persons who had been free since olden times, who had preserved their personal freedom and who constituted a decisive element of the city population in subsequent times.

To begin with, after being walled in, the city still remains a village. The primary [economic] activity in the city was crop cultivation inside the walls. This work was done by part of those who belonged to the manorial estates, that is, by the dependent serfs, and in part it was done by the free members of the old mark communities, on their own account. Thus, for example, in Munich there were city dwellers who still engaged in agriculture in the sixteenth century. The raising of crops and livestock, then, was pursued at first within the city walls. And only bit by bit, as development continued, were the raising of crops and livestock banned within the city walls and removed step by step to the area outside the city walls. This also shows that the Roman tradition was taken up again, only much later.

The gradual rise of *trade* brought about changes here. Trade began to flourish only around the ninth and tenth centuries. The natural economy did advance during those centuries—and that was why trade eventually arose, though belatedly.

A social differentiation had to occur first: a breaking away from doing one's own labor and the elaboration of a mode of life on a higher level.

Now it was natural that old Roman relationships should be taken up again. Where old trade routes existed they were put to use again. Since the Roman cities, such as Cologne and others, already had roads formerly used for trade, they were put to use again. Trade tended to flow to the cities because the people who had settled there were the ones who had needs and requirements on a higher level.

The items of trade were luxury goods. They came mainly from the Orient and from the south, and for Germany that meant in particular from Italy. Foreign traders came with their goods into the country [of Germany], where the rulers then acquired the goods.

Given the insecurity and uncertainty on the main trade roads at that time and the difficulties of transportation, trade was not brisk. The traders brought large quantities of goods and sought to defend themselves along the way, making use wherever possible of the protection provided by the rulers to whom the land they were passing through belonged. In the manorial estates they had to receive permission from the lords to have land allocated for them to settle on. Thus they soon had the protective hand of the rulers over themselves. And the trader had a judge* in the event that he was robbed while inside the city.

In short, a certain legal foundation connected the relations that arose at that time. The trader had no rights at all unless he became a settler [on the manor].

Thus, in the walled-in manorial estates entire settlements of foreign merchants arose. For example, in Mainz in the year 886 merchants from Frisia inhabited the best part of the city. In Lübeck as early as the thirteenth century many visitors from foreign cities had settled, and among those who appeared at the market were Normans, Russians, Swedes, and Ruthenians. In Magdeburg as early as the tenth century there was a separate church for the foreign merchants, which was called the Market Church.

In Regensburg the merchants built a special separate new city, which was called the merchant city. It had a street called Welschstrasse.† And one part of the city was called Little Rome, which was the section where the merchants from Rome lived. There was also a Jewish quarter.

In Worms and Speyer there were many merchants from Friesland, who came to the city bringing their wine, salt, pitch, etc.

Where did the land come from that was used for the settlements of these merchants?

Above all the common lands were taken for this purpose, lands from the undivided mark community.

The first step then was the gradual dividing up of the commons into allotments [Aufteilungen] for foreign merchants. From that it soon followed that the raising of livestock had to be conducted outside the city, and later on, the raising of crops also had to be done outside the city, because it was not possible at that time to raise crops without also raising livestock.

The raising of crops was done in part by dependent people [serfs] and in part by the free peasant farmers. The dependent persons of course engaged in agriculture for the benefit of the lords.

The main emphasis was placed on direct contribution from the small farmers of the villages.

But what happened with the free peasant farmers who engaged in agriculture on their own account? The land and the soil remained theirs, but they could no longer support themselves on it. Trade was the only thing that remained for them. These patricians were the first to become home grown merchants. They were also competent, qualified, and capable for that purpose. A tradesman must

---

* That is, a judicial authority that he could appeal to.
† The word element *Welsch* refers to Romance-speaking persons from southern Europe.

first of all be a free person, and among the entire population, the old free ones [*Altfreie*]* were the only free persons. Second, a certain economic foundation was necessary for trade. And again, the old free ones had this. They still had a certain modest prosperity left over from earlier times; some of them even possessed a few dependent persons and possessed some feudal lands on a small scale. They also had avoided the paying of taxes. In addition, they preserved all the qualities that at that time were necessary to constitute a merchant. The dependent persons [serfs] by then had become too crude. For these free persons a perceptible enrichment resulted from this transformation [their engagement in trade]. Trade generally was on the upswing at that time. Thus a rapid upward movement for these patricians also occurred. Who were the main customers of this [rising] trade?

First there was the abbot with his entire large household. It added to *his* lustre if his vassals lived in a more refined way than the rest of the population. In his entourage especially noteworthy were the higher officials and the personal attendants. These began as dependent persons of the court, but they belonged to the personal retinue of the lord, the ruler. They were very often also provided with certain benefits by their lords. They sought to make themselves more or less free, and when they reached the heights they themselves became lords of the manor [*Fronherren*], and thus they obtained a certain amount of personal freedom.

They had a similarity most of all with the old free ones. Even now these could be observed living amidst the population of manorial dependents—living as nobles and persons of noble lineage [*Geschlechter*].†

In addition there were certain liegemen or vassals of the lord of the manor, who likewise occupied a position between the rulers and the masses of dependent people. These vassals owed military service to the manorial lords.

Thus, two social estates, so to speak the upper ten thousand, took shape during the first development of the cities. On the one hand, as vassals or ministerial officials, they constituted the knighthood; on the other hand, there were the old free families who made up the greater part of the merchants.

This coming together of two elements, both of which traced their line back to the mark community, the knights from the manorial estates and the old free

---

*   According to Luxemburg's interpretation, the *Altfreie*, or old free ones, were descendants of the former free members of the mark community.

†   The term *Geschlechter* has a number of different meanings, depending upon the historical context. It originally referred to persons of noble lineage, or "those of well-born families." Over time, such persons tended to engage in trade and commercial activity. In the High Middle Ages, therefore, *die Geschlechter* came to denote a merchant or an elite family of merchants. It often occurred, however, that subsequent to engaging in trade and commerce these families withdrew from such activities and invested their capital in farmland, banking, or urban real estate, using these to claim noble status. Patricians and Junkers (the so-called "best citizens") could therefore also be referred to as *die Geschlechter*.

ones from the mark—the presence of these two social estates was decisive for the development of the cities in the first epoch.

In the twelfth and thirteenth centuries occurred the first revolutions aimed at liberation from the rule of the landlords. First the merchants and second the vassals played a role in these.

Historical and political circumstances additionally contributed to the revitalization and upturn of trade. In particular there was the period of the Crusades. The first Crusade took place in 1096–99, and the last one in 1270. The Crusades brought people into contact with the Orient. They engaged in plunder there; and this happened with the express permission of the Pope [who stated] that the liberators of the Christian faith were allowed to plunder all unbelievers. Actually they behaved like robber bands, with the result that the population fled at word of their approach.

In this connection travel in ships also became important, because the Crusades needed communication services across the water. After the Third Crusade, Venice and Genoa had entire fleets such as the Mediterranean had never seen before. Related to this was the first court of maritime law, established in Barcelona.

Three classes took part in the Crusades, including craftsmen, among others. They learned many skills from the Greeks and Arabs—in Damascus, for example, fine metalworking and weaving; and in Greece, silk weaving—and they transplanted these to Italy. From the city of Tyre in Palestine they brought glass-making to Venice.

Cane sugar was brought from Tripoli to Sicily then. At the same time there was increased trade in spices, such as pepper, cinnamon, etc., which played a big role in the Middle Ages, and an extensive spice trade resulted.

In the cities trade was carried on by both domestic and foreign merchants. For us special note must be taken with regard to the domestic, or home grown, merchants. First there were the old free people, who to begin with engaged in trade along with agriculture and then exclusively in trade as agriculture was driven from the city. They carried out their public obligations as they had before in the mark community by serving in the assembly and as chairpersons of the assembly.

We actually see, in addition, a transformation of this rural mark into an urban mark. That is the central point of Maurer's theory.

To begin with, the urban mark was a mark community inside city walls. It carried out its public duties through elected representatives, but now these are city councils. But this relationship could not last forever; it did not have a stable equilibrium. After all, it was located inside a walled-in manorial estate. The lords of the manors had already acquired all public power and authority for themselves including the power over life and death. Rising above these urban marks with their city councils was the manorial estate, representing public power and authority, and it also rose above the free persons from times of old. Thus there arose a natural conflict between the urban marks with their city councils on the one hand, and the power and authority of the lords of the manor, on the other, particularly in all of the cities that were later called bishopric cities, or bishop's cities.

To begin with, there was a tendency for the following to occur: everywhere the lords of the manors grouped themselves together in order to subject these old free people and turn them into dependent persons on their estates or manors, and indeed since they wanted to deal with the city council as a public body directly subordinate to themselves they tried at first to put one of their vassals in charge of the city council as its chairperson. In many cases the lords of the manors succeeded. In many, however, they did not—that is, in cities that were later to be called free cities of the Holy Roman Empire. That was prevented by the merchants as a group which already had some economic power to back itself up.

In all places where they managed to form a social estate consisting of the merchants with increasing wealth, matters developed into large conflicts within the city walls and led to the first urban revolutions. (The twelfth and thirteenth centuries are the period when the free knights and persons of noble lineage dominated). That was the first rebellion against feudalism.

[Here we see] the center of the first conflict, so to speak.

The persons of noble lineage actually had the material force to bring the laws over to their side. The battles were fought simply with fists and other means of violence, and these battles took the form of street fighting.

The chief *dramatis personae* in these conflicts were, on the one hand, feudalism represented by the lords of the manors and, on the other, the merchants. On the one hand, some of the latter had already become nobles of some kind, and on the other, [many] merchants were at the same time knights, or people of noble lineage.

The merchants brought the craftsmen out to fight on their side, as well as those vassals or liegemen in service to the feudal lord who aspired to become free from the manorial system. In all the bishop's cities, where the people of noble lineage and merchant families opposed the lord of the manor, we see the knights taking their side and fighting along with them. They were of the upper classes, but the great mass [of the fighters] consisted of craftsmen.

The craftsmen to begin with were dependent persons. This is shown to be so by Charlemagne's *Capitularies*. Then there were those who belonged to the mark community, and in the mark they were personally free, and there they worked for the mark community as a whole, but on the manorial estates they worked for the lords of the manors. From this it came about that the craftsmen were able to do better and more refined work as a result of their subjection to the lords. It was a step forward in craft production that the craftsmen worked for the rulers.

On the lands outside the city each man made his own tools as much as possible. As a result there were *fewer* craftsmen in the rural mark. On the manorial estate, from the outset, a differentiation of craft production advanced further. Goldsmiths and others who did fine, highly skilled work with metal were found only on the manorial estates, not in the rural mark. On the manorial estate there were several people engaged in each craft. Because a large number of people were now in the entourage of the manorial lords, the entire retinue of the lord of the manor also had to live in a more refined way than the rest. The mark community, however, found itself under maximum limitation when it came to the allotment of craftsmen, because the mark community had to support the craftsmen itself.

On the manorial estate, however, the economic possibility of maintaining a larger number of craftsmen existed thanks to the labor of others. The *possibility* of having several craftsmen resulted from the lord of the manor's having the manorial ordinances [*das Hofrechts*] at his *disposal.*

In addition to that there were ever increasing needs. Thus craft production became differentiated and refined.

In what way, however, did this refinement take place?

Through example and emulation ... through the working together of a number of craftsmen. An official of the manor stood over them, prescribing their work for them. Thus there developed a division of labor, and from that there came refinement and improvement.

Out in the countryside, in the rural mark community, there were fewer and fewer craftsmen, and for centuries they had worked in the same old way, using the same old methods. In Greece slavery had provided the possibility of bringing together the labor power of many foreigners and of their being led and managed in a uniform fashion, resulting in a division of labor and a refinement and improvement in the work.

Now we see the same thing again, on the basis of the manorial estate.

The relationship of domination thus brought about a certain amount of economic progress even if for the craftsmen it was a reduction in status, a social degradation.

The more feudalism developed, the more the number of craftsmen increased. For example, in Hamburg there were entire streets inhabited by certain types of craftsmen. The craftsmen were placed entirely under the legal power of the lord of the manor and were supported by the manor; it was from there that they received their work assignments, and that was the authority they worked for.

In this way [there occurred] a greater and greater gathering together of skilled workers on the manorial estate.

Thus more products accumulated gradually, both with the growing productivity and the coming together of labor power from various places—more products than the manorial estate itself could consume. The economic possibility arose for still others to work in the city. In the case of a serf, a dependent person who worked only for his lord, there was the additional possibility that with his lord's permission he might begin working for others as well. The lord of the manor granted the permission, but the craftsman had to pay some compensation for it. By this means the craftsmen gained the possibility of supporting themselves. For that reason the rulers quite readily granted this permission.

It was the free persons from olden times in the city who purchased what the craftsmen produced. Both pomp and pageantry, were part of feudalism. And the wealthier the serfs became, the swankier, the more luxuriantly they could live. And yet these serfs remained serfs with unpaid labor services to the lord [fronpflichtige Knechte].

Thus the *craftsmen* were at first [to be found] on the manorial estates of the feudal rulers. The craftsmen at first were supported as dependent persons together with all the other dependent persons on the feudal manor. The craftsmen worked exclusively to meet the needs of the manorial lords. They were organized in the sense that all the craftsmen of a certain trade were under one official. A single such branch of craft production was called an *Amt* at first and later an *Innung.** At the top of such an *Innung* was a *master craftsman.* The master craftsmen thus had earlier been dependent persons on the feudal manor. The artisans who worked under the master craftsman were called *Diener* [servants]. That is the first point of departure for the further development of craft production in the Middle Ages: a certain gathering together of craftsmen ...

What is most decisive is that they are organized into guilds, whose leaders are called master craftsmen and whose workers are called servants. Only when craft production was freed entirely from the power of manorial law did the craftsman gain the right to become a master craftsman. Earlier only an official of the manor could do that. Thus it was only in the city that the craftsman could become a master craftsman.

The point of departure for this development was that a larger and larger gathering-together of craftsmen took place, which led to a certain liberation of labor time from the immediate needs of the manor. The craftsmen came to be in a situation in which their labor time was no longer overwhelmingly taken up by the needs of the manor. On the other hand they had already become specialized. They themselves had the need to work for others. The people who purchased their products in the cities were the persons who had been free in older times, that is, the people of noble lineage, the merchants, and the freed vassals and ministerial officials of the manor, who formed a class in between the lords of the manors and the dependent persons [bondsmen and serfs]. The lords allowed the craftsmen to work for others, [first,] because thereby the craftsmen became able

---

*   An *Innung* was a professional organization of crafts at the local or regional levels in which self-employed craftsmen came together to promote their common interests. In Germany and Austria the *Innungs* was succeeded by the guilds, in the twelfth century.

to support themselves, and second, because they had to make a certain payment for this permission to work for others, and this payment was *in money*, which came in very handy for the lords, as the money economy was on the rise; thirdly, the craftsmen still had to provide a certain number of products regularly for the use of the rulers.

As soon as the craftsmen became more and more freed from the feudal manor, they acquired the urge more and more to free themselves entirely from the power and authority of manorial ordinances. First of all they purchased their freedom from manorial ordinances. That was advantageous for the lords of the manor. Second, they were helped by an unbroken series of revolutions in the streets of the cities, in which one manorial law after another was abolished.

The money economy was developing more and more, and the lords of the manors had a good source of money right there in the craftsmen. Material interests and psychology went hand in hand in this case.

The craftsmen had to pay a certain sum to buy their freedom, but they also had to provide a certain quantity of products.

For example, as early as the thirteenth century in Halberstadt the shoemakers had to provide the bishop with shoes and boots both winter and summer, and the bakers had to provide the officials with bread, and so forth.

The craftsmen's purchase of their freedom was a first step, which at the same time became an economic basis for further development. The craftsmen, step by step, began to free themselves from the manorial estate. This struggle for liberation filled the entire twelfth and thirteenth centuries.

The rights of personal freedom and freedom of marriage were introduced in Worms in 1114 and 1180. (Sometimes the introduction of such a law had to occur four different times, because the rulers, again and again, rendered the right that was granted illusory.)

Personal freedom was achieved with difficulty in Freiburg in 1120, in Bern 1218, in Vienna 1238, in Eisenach 1283, in Wesel 1277, and in Brakel 1322 (that was a small city, and therefore the craftsmen won freedom there only later). In Vienna the right to marry freely was won in 1221, in Winterthur in 1264, and in Bregenz in 1409. Where the right to marry freely was not granted entirely, a prohibition against unequal marriages remained in force.

The abolition of forced marriages (the lord of the manor had been able to force dependent people to marry) was abolished in Munich in 1294, in Hagenau 1257, in Vienna 1221, in Freiburg 1120, and in Nuremberg 1257.

Abolition of *das Besthaupt, die Kurmede* (?????)* (those were rights of inheritance for the lords)—they were abolished in Speyer in 1117 and 1182, in Worms 1180, in Augsburg 1276, in Ulm 1290, in Frankfurt 1291, and in Münster 1309.

Personal freedom of movement was fought for and won in Freiburg in 1120,

---

* The question marks are in the original typescript.

in Kolmar 1293, in Winterthur 1297, in Basel 1542 (century-long struggles took place here against the bishop), and in Bregenz in 1409. These numbers [i.e., dates] apply only to the craftsmen. The vassals did not need to fight for these rights because they were not *personally* subordinate to the manorial estate.

Not all such rights, taken together, were won at the same time. The south German cities at this time come to our notice because of the battles going on there. They happened there because south Germany was a cultural ground of long standing from Roman times, a linkage point of the cities [with Italy], and an area where Christianity had been propagated most widely.

Each city had to fight these battles for itself alone. At the same time, however, we see a current of motion flowing from one city to others. However, there were very large intervals in the process. The movement began in the twelfth and thirteenth centuries. The result everywhere was freedom from dependency on the feudal manor and the manorial ordinances.

Each craft, each guild came forward in its own behalf.

Just as the capitalists today crowd and shove the workers together into one factory and thereby give them the possibility of organizing and agitating, in the same way the lord of the manor gave the craftsmen the possibility of fighting through the existing craft organization.

Manorial ordinance was an organizing power oriented toward higher needs and therefore raised production to a higher level. One may simply compare the mark community to the manors of Charlemagne to see the progress of the manorial estates as against that of the mark community.

The craftsmen had arrived at a higher level of technology and technique as a result of manorial ordinance. But social relations had changed and grew up over the head of manorial ordinance. Craft production was the first branch of production that outgrew manorial ordinance; manorial ordinance ceased to be a progressive factor of production; it became a fetter on production. And also for craft production.

Now the other two classes: the merchants [*die Geschlechter-Kaufleute*]* and the vassals, who also fought against manorial estates. They preserved all the benefits that they had from the old mark community and the new economic ones they had as merchants. They are the ones who established the city councils, while the lords of the manors wanted to subject the city councils to themselves. From that arose a conflict. It broke out in confrontations in which on the one side stood the merchants originally from the mark community and on the other stood the feudal economic system [*Fronwirtschaft*]. The merchants and the vassals persisted and engaged in intrigue, but the craftsmen served as cannon fodder. Thus, again, on the one side we have the feudal economic system and

---

*   Here, and throughout much of the rest of the piece, *die Geschlechter* refers to merchants or merchant families that descended from people of noble lineage.

on the other the merchants and vassals in the foreground and behind them the artisans and craftsmen, who were not fighting for the rights of the city councils but for their own demands. All of them taken together constituted the population of the cities.

The merchant families wanted the city council to be elected by the urban population, with the manorial estate being totally excluded, because it wanted to control the leadership of the city council. The merchant families wanted to give shape to the city council on their own. Meanwhile the craftsmen were fighting for their personal freedom. What fused them all together was the common enemy. The merchants fought to defend the freedoms of the craftsmen at the same time in order to win the latter over to their side. The craftsmen could expect that the city council of the merchants would confirm and validate their personal freedoms.

(This disposition of fighting forces is reminiscent of the great French Revolution. The following is characteristic: in the great French Revolution we see the entire Third Estate uniting against the old feudal powers. At the summit stands the bourgeoisie, and behind them the peasants, craftsmen, etc. After the victory this camp of allied forces falls apart along the natural default lines of class interest. The workers could not yet gather up the fruits of the victory.)

Now comes the contradiction between the patricians and the craftsmen. That is the signature of the struggles of the fourteenth and fifteenth centuries.

The chief objective of the uprisings ...

In addition, the freeing of the craftsmen from legal obligations to the manorial ordinances.

The merchants promised and delivered to the craftsmen the right to freely practice their trades, in return for their help against the common enemy [the feudal lords].

In the first [period of this historical] epoch the free rights of the independent city population and the liberation of the craftsmen from the manorial ordinances were won by force.

And so, after that, we see the rights of a free city and the personal freedom of the population living in that city. But at the same time there were big differences in the political situation. The city council was elected by merchant families, and they are the ones who passed the laws and held legal jurisdiction. The craftsmen, who had previously been subordinate to the law and the courts of the lord's feudal manor, were now under the jurisdiction of the free city's court and legal system. In this law court, however, as in the city council, only the merchant families had the leading role and functioned as the rulers.

Thus the merchant families gained political domination in the cities; the craftsmen [gained] only personal freedom without any part in political rule.

From this there arose new conflicts between the craftsmen and the merchants over political rights.

It turned out that the city now represented the only center within the entire feudal society in which one could win civic freedom from manorial ordinance. Previously the only person who was free was the one who had landed property and was not obliged to make any compulsory payments.

Now something occurred that had world-historical significance; a new type of personal freedom emerged: the craftsmen were now personally free citizens on the basis of the craft they pursued.

Thus the city became a point of attraction for dependent persons from the surrounding area, because one could gain personal freedom there. The city was glad to offer refuge to those fleeing from feudal rule, because all of these new arrivals were born enemies of the feudal legal system, the common enemy of all.

The free city council of the merchants offered protection to such newcomers within the city walls. There soon arose a law stating that a dependent person who had run away [from the manorial estate to which he belonged] and who had lived inside the city walls for a year and a day could no longer be forced by the feudal lords to go back. If a feudal lord discovered a runaway dependent person after a few months in the city, the city had to let the dependent person be taken away. However, if a feudal lord' discovered him after a year and a day, he [the lord] did not get him back. A saying developed out of all that: City air makes you free.

The city laws of Basel state: "If the lord finds him during the course of the first year, he must be allowed to go follow [i.e., go back to the lord]. But if this does not happen within the year, the manorial ordinance is no longer in effect."

City law in Saxony also states: "Whichever man has settled within the city precincts for a year and a day without a claim by anyone [being made against him] that person may fully keep his freedom, together with his immediate family (next of kin)."

Besides that, the dependent persons in the city had the prospect of acquiring property through free labor, either by practicing a craft or working for the merchants.

Thus the cities became colossal points of attraction for those living in the surrounding areas. A very strong influx began. Many times the walls had to be rebuilt so that they extended farther out.

Growth of the city, and together with it also the growth of crafts, trade, and so forth, and the expansion of political rights.

The gaining of freedom from feudal manorial law was thus decisive for the dependent persons.

Now began the struggle of the craftsmen against the merchants. Most of the dependent persons from the surrounding areas naturally took up a craft, not going to work for the merchants. Thus the craftsmen increased their numbers,

---

*   Luxemburg here uses *Hofherr* as a synonym of *Fronherr*.

becoming the great mass of the city population. Because everywhere where the city became victorious matters ended with the expulsion from the city of the manorial estate.

Crop cultivation and livestock raising were driven out of the city; craft production and trade remained. As a result there was a wider differentiation.

The vassals, who in the earliest epoch had fought on the side of the merchants, were now to a certain extent placed in an awkward position. Economically their status was on the wane. After all, they did represent the agricultural economy.

Among the persons of noble lineage there was also more and more a transition to full merchant status or else a move backward from the city to the villages.

At this point after the crafts had defeated the merchant families ... [the process] came to completion. The merchant families removed themselves from the city.* And toward the end of this epoch, in the fourteenth and fifteenth centuries, we see the craftsmen as the dominant mass in the city. That is the completion of the process of development of the cities, which at the start had been under manorial ordinance.

The organizations of the craftsmen in their struggle for political rights were called *Innungen*. They changed their name to *Zünfte* [guilds] as soon as they had freed themselves from manorial ordinance.

Thus, in the second epoch we see the following: the guilds struggle with the merchants over [control of] the city council. The guilds would be the organizations that would take the city council into their hands. In the twelfth and thirteenth centuries the merchants owned the city councils; in the fourteenth and fifteenth centuries, the guilds owned them. These are two clearly distinct periods of history. But historically these two periods were interwoven. A few examples of this [follow].

Strassburg. The struggle with the bishop over the rights of the city begins there in the tenth century. The struggle breaks out as early as 906. Strassburg was a former Roman city, where the traditions of trade and commerce quickly began to bloom again. This struggle lasted from 906 to about 1100. And once again, at the beginning of the thirteenth century, the struggle began anew because the bishop constantly made encroachments, over and over again. Only in the years 1214–19 did a new, free city come into existence in Strassburg, and indeed it was the result of an understanding reached between the burghers and the bishop. Thus it was a compromise. As early as 1261 the struggle began again because the new bishop refused to recognize the concessions made by the old bishop. Nevertheless the city forged ahead, electing *Meister*'s [city officials] and raising taxes, and so the bishop left the city along with the other clergy and placed the city under a ban. The struggle continued until a new agreement in 1263. In that

---

*   This is a reference to the fact that in response to these struggles, a number of merchant families (*die Geschlechter*) withdrew from direct commercial activity and invested their capital in farmland, banking, or urban real estate, using these to claim noble status.

year the city won the right to freely elect the city council, and the rights of the bishop sank to the merely symbolic function of taking oaths. The freely elected city councils swore an oath [of allegiance] to the bishop.

In *Worms* the bishop originally chaired the city council as the lord of the domain. The city council was constituted from four free mark villages. However, the city councils soon sank to the level, just as in other cities, of being mere couriers [*Boten*], that is, servants of the bishop. Then the city's fight against the bishop began.

Now a third power stepped in, the emperor. He took the side of the city, because at that time the imperial power was fighting against the papacy. In return the cities provided him with taxes in money form. The emperor's troops were recruited from among the masses of the city population; they were no longer feudal [troops]. That was decisive.

This process took particularly sharp form in France. In Germany the emperors sometimes interceded on behalf of the bishops and sometimes on behalf of the cities. They played a very ambiguous role. They sought to squeeze what they could out of the cities, but they sympathized more with the enemies of the cities.

Thus Emperor Friedrich I intervened in Worms. According to him, the city council in 1156 ought to consist of 28 burghers who were merchants and 12 knights or ministerial officials of the bishop's. But the bishop did not accept this, and the struggle continued. At the beginning of the thirteenth century the bishop tried to reduce the size of the city council from 40 to 12 members, in order to reduce its importance. The burghers did not accept this, and the emperor supported them. In 1220 a new city council of 40 members was once again elected.

In the same year the bishops in all of Germany had their rights confirmed by the emperor. And at the Diet of Worms in 1231*—that was [the term used for a] gathering of all secular and ecclesiastical princes in the Middle Ages—and also at the Diet of Ravenna in 1232,† they even voted for the abrogation of all city councils that had been elected without their approval. And so all the concessions were taken back.

The burghers and the city council of Worms energetically registered their protest. At that point Emperor Heinrich VII once again changed his attitude and in 1232 allowed the "dear" burghers of Worms, and especially their city council, to again have their rights, which had been taken away from them. With that, in 1233, things reached the point where there was fierce fighting in the city. Since Bishop Heinrich‡ did not want to accept this [decision of the emperor], a com-

---

* At the Diet of Worms in January 1231 the ecclesiastical princes forced the emperor of the Holy Roman Empire to outlaw town-leagues and other associations of the burghers.

† The Diet of Ravenna in January 1232 outlawed all statues made by the town burghers that were opposed by the bishops.

‡ This is a reference to Bishop Henry II of Saarbrücken, who served as Bishop of Worms from 1217 to 1234.

promise was reached again, and the emperor confirmed this one as well. The agreement was as follows: the bishop recognized the city council, but the latter was organized in the following way: the bishop named 9 burghers as council members for life and replenished their number each time one of them died [*MS. Missing words*] The bishop was supposed to have the chairmanship, but when taxes were to be raised or [important] consultations or discussions to be held, 16 burghers and 4 priests were to be added to the council.

This agreement, however, was not actually put into practice. As early as 1235 this arrangement was cancelled by Emperor Friedrich II. Since the burghers did not want to drive the bishop out [of the city], as the emperor wanted, the emperor set up a new city council consisting of 4 knights and 7 burghers and installed one of his own ministerial officials over them. The burghers fought against this arbitrary action, and in 1236 the emperor once again confirmed their old freedoms and a city council of 40 members.

1238 [*MS. Illegible words*] the history of all this back and forth [is] in Maurer's book *Geschichte der Stadtverfassung* (History of the City Constitution). Probably there are two or three volumes. [According to] him the conflict was extraordinarily dispersed [over time]. In 1238 full authority was also assigned to the bishop by the emperor ... The struggle was dragged out for so long that in the struggle between [*MS. Missing words*]

Several examples from the winning of freedom by the cities.

The second period.

Guilds with old burghers [*Altbürger*].*

Strassburg. [I refer you to the] Two volumes of the history of the city constitution by Maurer.

Beginning of the fourteenth century. The cause of a conflict between craftsmen and merchants in 1308 [was] a mayor from the Zorne clan.† This time the merchant families won, and many of the craftsmen were killed, others fled and were then banned and declared outlaws. Many merchants behaved with arrogance, which led to a new uprising. The merchants let the craftsmen know and feel [in no uncertain terms] that they held the power in their hands.

That lasted however only as long as the merchants remained united.

Conflicts among the people of noble lineage.

Romeo and Juliet.‡

Even today [of course] there are conflicts within the ruling classes.

---

* The *Altbürger*, or old burghers, were members of the urban middle class in the towns of the early Middle Ages that were originally descended from serfs who had fled the manorial estates.

† Zorne (also spelled Zorn) was a name of a group of families that played an influential political and economic role in such cites as Strassburg and Innsbruck in the Middle Ages.

‡ This is a reference to the feud between the Montagues, who were aristocrats, and the Capulets, who were merchants, in Shakespeare's famous play.

The struggle had to do with maintaining the economic base, which was common to all, on which they all depended for their livelihood, and which stood in contradiction to the mass of the people.

In the ranks of the merchant families there were always two families or clans who stood out above all the others in the course of the struggle [as in Strassburg].

In 1332 these two clans engaged in a fight in a garden. One side had strengthened itself by newcomers from the countryside, while the other side allied itself with the craftsmen. That brought about the collapse of the [previously existing] constitution, and the craftsmen were victorious.

The first phase, in which *public taxes* were introduced. In the manorial estate the public upkeep was provided for by the dependent persons.

City taxes. When the burghers [had achieved] a certain level of organization. What kind of taxes were being paid?

[There was] the land tax [*Grundzins*],* the land still belonging to the lords.

The merchant families in the cities at first introduced *indirect* taxes in the twelfth and thirteenth centuries as a measure toward bleeding the craftsmen and as an obligatory contribution toward military defence of the city.

See Lassalle: [his book on] indirect taxes.†

Indirect taxes rose at that time as prosperity grew. They were imposed arbitrarily to the point of impoverishment.

Then [there were] commissions for control [to check up and monitor taxes] and the guilds were also brought in to take part in that.

The wool weavers wanted to break the power of the rich people's organization. The wool weavers stood at the forefront of the struggle of the craftsmen in Cologne.

In other cities [there was] the merchant's guild.

Compromises always brought about a retrogression, and that led as a result to a new and more violent revolution.

Wherever the guilds had been victorious, everyone had to belong to a guild. The guild as ruler [*Herrenzunft*]. The guilds had their own specific governing bodies, and elected masters [heads of the guilds].

They also had to provide the militia for the city.

Whoever [did not] belong to a guild could have no political rights.

They [the guilds] lived entirely for politics, as did the craftsmen.

---

* *Grundzins* is here rendered as land tax, but it can also be translated as ground rent.

† Luxemburg is referring to Ferdinand Lassalle's *Die indirekte Steuer und die Lage der arbeitende Klassen* (Indirect Taxation and the Position of the Working Classes) (Zurich: Verlag von Meyer & Zeller, 1863). Marx had a far less favorable view of this book than Luxemburg. As Marx wrote to Engels on June 12, 1863, "One or two individual bits are good, but for one thing it is, on the whole, *written* in an unbearably officious, chatty style, with absurd pretensions to scholarship and consequentialness. In addition, it is *essentiellement* the confection of a '*pupil*' who cannot wait to make a name for himself as a 'thoroughly learned' man and original scholar. Hence the abundance of historical and theoretical blunders."

In other cities the rulers were all thrown together into one guild, for example, the shoemakers' guild, and so forth.

Also in Speyer ...

In Augsburg the struggle began in 1303.

The starting point was a dispute over the spending of public resources after taxes had been introduced.

The craftsmen were armed. They had taken up arms as guilds and had even been obliged to do that by the council of merchant families, because, after all, they had to take part in the struggle against the manorial estate.

Later the weapons were turned precisely against the merchant families, for whose rights they [the guilds] had fought in the first place.

[Here are] three more examples of the struggle of the guilds against the merchant families.

In particular the history [of this struggle] in Basel is typical because it was stretched out for such a long time, with many vicissitudes and changes of fortune ...

Regensburg ...

The cities at that time had about 10,000 inhabitants, going up into the hundreds of thousands.*

In Germany in particular matters often were blunted by compromise, but not in France and Italy.

Earlier theories derived the guild from Rome. In particular Gaupp on the founding of German cities.†

In the last phases of the Roman Empire there did outwardly exist craft guilds, but those were bodies organized for service to the state, and one could neither leave them or marry outside of them.

All traces of those old Roman guilds disappeared.

We derive the medieval guilds from the manorial constitution.

The craftsmen [on the manors] had been supervised by ministerial officials of the manorial estate. The latter appear subsequently as masters and the ordinary craftsmen as servants. They had to make payments in kind. They continued even after the craftsmen had freed themselves from the manorial estate.

In Regensburg the obligation to pay a land tax to the feudal lord [*Zinspflichtung*] was not abolished until 1486.

In the manorial estate the craftsman had stood under the legal jurisdiction of the estate. Later they were under the legal jurisdiction of the city.

---

*   Luxemburg is here considerably exaggerating the size of medieval cities. The largest city in the Holy Roman Empire in the fourteenth century was Cologne, with about 40,000 inhabitants.

†   See Ernst Theodor Gaupp, *Über deutsche Städtegründung* (On the Founding of German Cities).

In Germany the freeing of the craft organizations [*Innungen*]* was completed at the earliest time in Magdeburg and Cologne. In Magdeburg as early as 1147.

In 1202 the archbishop [of Magdeburg] granted permission for a sign-makers' guild [*Schilderinnung*] and at about the same time for a tailors' guild [*Schneiderzunft*], and so on. Thus [we see that] each guild had to win its freedom for itself alone.

In Cologne the guilds, which were called *Ämter*, rather than *Innungen*, at that time, freed themselves as early as the twelfth century.

In Basel it was only in the middle of the thirteenth century, the furriers being the earliest.

What attitude did the imperial power in Germany take toward this movement? Here too it was ambivalent, and actually opposed to the upward-striving guilds. The emperors repeatedly banned the organizations of the craftsmen, as Heinrich VII did in Worms in 1237. In Goslar they were forbidden by the emperor in 1219, in Esslingen in 1275, in Frankfurt in 1366, in Freiburg in 1454 (already the fifteenth century), [and] in Ulm in 1312; in Würzburg they were forbidden by the bishop in 1279, [and] in Erfurt in 1264; in Regensburg they were forbidden by the dukes of Bavaria in 1384, and in Vienna by Rudolph von Habsburg in 1278. These prohibitions characterized the trend of imperial policy in the first stage. It was a direct statement of position against the upward-striving craftsmen. The prohibitions continued for centuries, but they remained entirely unsuccessful.

The earliest guilds in the cities generally were those of the merchants, and also of the garment workers, the tailors, and the cloth workers.

The merchants needed a guild to protect themselves. They were able to constitute the first guilds because they were personally free. They had formerly been the so-called patricians.

The forming of guilds in the textile industry occurred so early because for the most part it satisfied a great need. They were the wealthiest and therefore the earliest to free themselves from the manorial estate.

THE NATURE OF THE GUILD SYSTEM

What distinguishes the guild from the craft organization on a manorial estate is this: *the guild itself elects its own master*. In addition, all craftsmen can now become free masters themselves and may employ apprentices and journeymen themselves.

The guild organization is an organization of *free masters*.

---

* The *Innung* was the earlier form of the guilds when they were still subject to the manorial estate of the feudal lord.

Each guild has an executive committee, which it elects freely. This is a left-over from an earlier time; it stems from the fact that the craft organization was still entirely under the legal jurisdiction of the feudal estate, and it had a master who supervised the workers.

Then came a time of transition. The craft organizations freed themselves, but certain obligatory payments still remained, and they were paid by part of the group of masters in the name of the guilds. These masters ...

Thus the executive committee, in the beginning, was still named by the [lord of] the manor.

The development proceeded to the point where this executive committee was also freely elected, and it looked out for the interests of the free guild.

The guild leaders were originally elected for one or several years, but later for life. It was even permissible for people who were not guild masters to be elected to the executive committee.

The investiture, or act of installing a guild master in his office, usually took place in a festive manner, with great ceremony and celebration. He concerned himself with the business of the guild and with the provision of food and drink to traveling craftsmen [i.e., journeymen]. When important matters came up, they had to be decided by the guild as a whole. These guild assemblies had such names as Morning Speech, and so forth.

Guild assemblies [occurred] from one to three times a year. They made accountings, accepted delivery of goods, and enacted craft regulations. The building in which guild assemblies were held was called the guildhall. In Berlin it was called the Convent [place for convening], and the term *Stube* was sometimes used for it also. In the case of wealthy guilds the guildhalls were veritable palaces. At times of conflict the guildhalls were places where armed men gathered. They were often fortified as well, so that they could withstand a real siege. But at the same time they were drinking houses and houses for social activities: baptisms, funeral services, and so on.

Only members of the guild, along with their wives, had access [to the guildhall].

The main powers held by the guild assemblies were the following: legal jurisdiction over all business or trade affairs, and all disputes among guild members. However, the power of life and death belonged only to the city council.

In addition the guilds had vice squads. They had jurisdiction over such things as indulgence in luxuries, fraud, adultery, and prodigality.

In Strassburg there was in each guild a secret group of censors, who were called reprimanders [*Rüger*], appointed to ensure good morals.

Finally, as the fundamental basis for a free guild, there was the guild's power to enforce compulsory membership in the guild [*Zunftzwang*]; that is, the exclusive right to conduct the business of the craft inside the city, and the compulsory obligation for every person pursuing that craft to belong to that guild. In every city there were craftsmen who earned their livelihoods outside of the guild. The guilds had the right to prosecute such persons.

The guilds were ecclesiastical associations. Each had its own special saints, [religious] banners, and many had their own special chapels. In addition, emblems and coats of arms. Guild members were mutually obligated to help and protect one another, obligated to provide last honors to one another, that is, to take part in funerals and burials, and so forth.

Lastly, they also formed military detachments. Each craftsman had to do real military service with his guild, as well as guard duty in the city.

When there were uprisings and similar events in the city; all those belonging to the guilds had to arm themselves and gather immediately as soon as the alarm bell had rung. In the event of war each guild had to provide one or more men on horseback for the city. (The knights were personally obligated to perform duty on horseback, but the craftsmen only had to provide several horsemen.) On the other hand, the craftsmen constituted the entire infantry. They were the first foot soldiers.

They were armed with halberds, battleaxes, pikes, crossbows, and primitive guns [Büchsen]. They wore iron helmets, collars, suits of armor, aprons, gloves, armor for the legs called greaves, and so forth. The way in which they were to be armed was prescribed for them very exactly.

In Frankfurt the arming of the craftsmen depended on their ability to pay, and so in the case of the bakers it depended on the number of pigs [they owned].

In the guild, apprentices were under strict subordination of the journeymen under the master and the chief master of the guild.

In the guild there was strict subordination, which was later to be particularly bitter for the apprentices; in the era when medievalism flourished there was a strong basis for this. It was the reason for the extraordinary efficacy of the city armies ...

Nevertheless there were many regulations that [governed] existence in the cities, particularly in other lands [other than Germany]

The decree of King Edward [III] in the years 1322–77 for the guilds of London.

It was decreed that all crafts in the city of London should be regulated by law and supervised ... In each craft, according to need, 4 or 6 would be sworn in and given authority by the mayor to carry out the supervision well.

The guild made sure that the work of the craftsmen was carried on in an orderly way, that it participated in the waging of war, and had political rights.

After its victory the guild became the political organization of the burghers.

In some cities where the fighting was especially sharp the merchant families were driven out. In others, they withdrew of their own accord, and in still others they blended in and merged with the guild regime.

Actual withdrawal of the merchant families from the city occurred after the victory of the guilds in Speyer, Strassburg, Augsburg, Regensburg, Osnabrück, Dortmund, and other cities.

They were actually driven out of the city in Bremen, Zürich, Basel, Cologne, and Magdeburg.

In some cities full-fledged rule by the guilds was achieved. Subsequently, for example, in Cologne, Speyer, Zürich, Schaffhausen, Basel, Konstanz, Halle, and Magdeburg.

There were shared regiments in Frankfurt, Vienna, Augsburg, and other cities.

People belonged to the guild who did not practice its trade at all. [For example] belonging to the merchants' guild in Basel were the renters, officers, and jurors and the physicians belonged to the blacksmiths' guild.

As Ludwig von Maurer states, as a result of the victory of the guilds the mark community, or previously existing community [*Realgemeinde*], became a community of individual persons [*Personalgemeinde*]. The difference between the mark community and the community of individuals is that in the latter there is no land involved, as there is in the mark community; other means of production become decisive.

The special economic conditions of the rule of the guilds in relation to the mode of production.

Compulsory membership in the guild. No one could practice a craft outside of the guild. No one could bring their goods into the city without the permission of the guild. No one in the city could offer their goods for sale other than through the guild.

Along with that there was a direct prohibition against outsiders offering their goods for sale in the city, with the exception of certain annual markets or fairs, which were usually connected with one or another church festival, held at specified locations and with specified taxes or fees being paid to the city.

[There was] a regulation specifying the number of masters in each guild, and [*MS. Missing words*] so that each could make a livelihood.

A regulation specifying the number of journeymen and apprentices under each master craftsman.

This had the consequence that all journeymen and apprentices had approximately the same amount of work, and it also meant that not too many master craftsmen would emerge.

A regulation about the division of labor among separate crafts. That meant that the field of operation for each guild was sharply delimited from the neighboring guild, so that no disputes over the fields of operation of the individual guilds would arise. This resulted in the technical improvement and refinement of the craft.

The hat makers alone were divided into five separate guilds. The knife makers could not make handles for the knives, and the handle makers could not make blades. Candles from old wax were strictly distinguished from candles made from new wax, and the makers belonged to two different guilds. A sharp line was drawn between two types of carpenters, the *Zimmerleute* and the *Schreiner.*

Since such encroachments on these restrictions were to be found at every turn, *guild trials* were constantly taking place.

If there were not enough people in one craft, or too few master craftsmen, people could be brought into the city from outside, but only by permission of the city council with the consent of the leaders of the guilds.

Regulation of production within each craft. The total number of orders that a guild could obtain in the city had to be distributed equally among the individual master craftsmen, so that all the masters could live equally well. It was forbidden for any master craftsman to undertake more than one job at any one time, so that his neighbor could also earn a living. It was forbidden for craftsmen to take customers away from each other or to undercut prices.

Then there were regulations on the *purchase of raw materials*, so that no individual master could gain special advantage. For example in Lübeck every cutler was obligated, when he wanted to purchase raw materials outside the city, to inform the guild three days in advance ...

The craft obtained its raw materials from the countryside. At first by the city and later by the guilds *firm prices were set for all raw materials and craft products.*

Prescriptions concerning production technique or technology.

Prescriptions concerning the length of apprenticeship.

Regulations concerning the period when journeymen could travel about learning their craft.

Regulations governing *how masterworks were to be made.*† This was necessary to obtain the right to be recognized as a master craftsman.

Regulations concerning the *production process.*

For example, for candle makers it was specified exactly how much fat was to be used and how it was to be processed, and so forth.

In general the guild regulations had the purpose of both *assuring the necessary actual amount of production* for the customers in the city as well as *assuring the existence of the craftsmen themselves* and preventing *people in need and people without work* from coming into existence in the city.

The guild was from the outset a *progressive phenomenon*. Production was firmly organized and regulated through the guilds. New crafts were created directly as the result of guild regulations. The division of labor, with the crafts being separated into sharply delineated branches of production, brought with it great technological advances. Because of the regulations concerning the way

---

* A *Schreiner* was a maker of fine woodwork, such as a cabinetmaker. A *Zimmermann* (plural, *Zimmerleute*) was a carpenter who constructed houses and buildings.

† A masterwork was a special work done to qualify as a master craftsman; it was also called "masterpiece."

production was carried out, the technology of the craft was also advanced. This was based on the experience of previous times and also on present-day experience. Apprenticeship, the travels of journeymen, and the making of masterworks were also means of advancing progress in the technology of the craft.

Furthermore: *at all times a specific total number of workers and labor time was necessary in order to satisfy the needs of a specific community.*

The satisfaction of these needs was guaranteed by the guild regulations. The number of master craftsmen, journeymen, and apprentices was set in advance. Labor time was regulated; one worked only to a certain extent, so that exhaustion of one's capacity for labor was avoided.

In every society a certain total amount of time and labor are employed to produce the means of production. That was also regulated in a planned way. One worked only after the extent of [the community's] needs was established, thus [work was done] in accordance with demand.

That has been the case up until now with all forms of economic production. But now the way in which needs are to be satisfied becomes completely different, of an entirely new kind.

The mark community regulated the satisfaction of needs by dividing up the land [among the peasant farmers] and by calculating the yield from the lands of the undivided mark, and this was done by the members of the mark as a whole. The extent of the needs [of the community] was ascertained in advance.

In the feudal economy there occurred the division of the means of livelihood [and this was done] by the lord of the manor on the basis of his rights as lord of the manor. The total amount of the needs [of the feudal manor] was known in advance.

This was not true of the crafts, organized by the guilds. Here the total amount of the needs did not determine production. Each person ordered what he needed as a single individual from an individual master craftsman. Whereas in all previous forms of economic production the product was *divided up*, now for the first time products were *purchased*. Craft production is the first *commodity production*.

It developed slowly and gradually within the feudal economy, grew further in the struggles against the manorial law, and found its finished form in the guild. Thus the struggles of the guilds against manorial law was the struggle and the victory of an entirely new economic epoch.

But now the satisfaction of needs could not be regulated, for the most part, as it had been in earlier forms [of economic production]. The meeting of needs is now connected to purchasing power. The mass of those having purchasing power consisted, however, of the city dwellers who belonged to the guilds, and their purchasing power was assured by the regulation of production. The producers were at the same time, on the reverse side of the coin, the consumers.

Up to this point the mode of production had been a regulated one. But the regulation was limited only to a craft, to *one branch* of production. The production of raw materials, and agricultural production, took place outside the city, and those were not regulated by the guild system.

This division between agriculture and craft production is an important historical fact in which capitalism has its roots. The city of the Middle Ages has now become one more element causing a split in the economic community as a whole. The city by itself is no longer an economic unit in the true sense. Therefore it also does not represent a mode of production that is regulated in a planned way. It encompasses only one branch of planned production. An actual city economy never did exist. (Professor [Karl] Bücher claims that it did exist. See his book on the origins of the national economy.)*

For development to go further, the guild was of great significance. Modern machinery would not have been possible if the guild had not brought craft production up to the highest conceivable level. Development was achieved through the division of labor in the guild. Among the important inventions of the era of craft production are the compass, the pocket watch, the tower clock, gunpowder, the making of paper, and the printing of books.†

The guilds made it possible for many craftsmen in a single branch of production to unite in a single space and thus create the preconditions for manufacture. As time went by the number of journeymen became more than was needed. They began to work on the side and settled in the country, because there they were freed from guild restrictions.

Also the second precondition for manufacture, the capital in the hands of craftsmen, originated in the cities through trade. Here the forces were organized that made a mass market possible.

The outlying lands around a city could not serve as a [sufficient] area for the sale of its products. The feudal economy dominated there, and it continued to hold its own until the nineteenth century. The *development of capital in the cities paved the way for the victory of the bourgeoisie*, which succeeded in the eighteenth and nineteenth centuries.

The consumers in the city were increased in number by the plentiful inflow of peasants fleeing from the land.

Capitalism rested upon the machine and on wage labor. The latter is only conceivable when the worker is personally free. This freedom was won in the struggles of the guilds against manorial ordinances. The commodity economy, the chief foundation for the capitalist mode of production, originated in the city.

---

* Karl Bücher, *Die Entstehung der Volkswirtschalt.*

† All of these "inventions" actually arose outside of Europe, in China, and were adopted by Europeans through the impact of increased contact with Asia. Paper, for instance, first came to Europe after the eleventh century through contact with Muslims, who had earlier learned the art of papermaking from the Chinese.

Thus all the preconditions for capitalism were prepared in the cities.

Eventually development had to break out of the form taken by the guilds in order to make room for capitalist industry.

This new form had to be a world economy from the very outset.

Historically the most important fact is that here for the first time the division of agriculture and industry into two separate entities appeared, and the connection between these two parts was provided by the exchange of commodities.

The machine brought many different tools together in a single organized system. This still required a driving force that would exceed human power. At first there were attempts to drive machines with human power. But that did not provide any economic advantages. First, the strength of the human body did not extend that far, and second, human strength did not have the mechanical evenness and regularity that was necessary to power a machine.

The machine would not have been possible if craft production had not flourished through the activity of the guilds.

The compass.

Gunpowder.

The tower clock and the pocket watch, products that were purely the result of labor by craftsmen, invented by craftsmen.

The making of paper, which began to flourish as early as the fourteenth century.

The art of printing books.

The production of steel, the blending of cast iron with wrought iron.

Without all these inventions modern capitalist development would have been impossible. It was only the work of craftsmen that made today's discoveries and inventions possible.

The preliminary stage for today's mode of economic production is that a large number of craft workers was brought together for the first time in a single workplace.

Manufacture:

The workforce consisted of people from the countryside and journeymen who could no longer become master craftsmen.

As a result, the first instances of manufacture were in the countryside.

The raw labor power that poured into the city from the countryside could only be put to use later on.

Manufacture was organized by the merchants. It was because of [increased] trade that the merchant class rose; *in the city* trade played the main role, along with the guilds.

A *mass market* for goods was still necessary; otherwise manufacture would have been superfluous.

It was not possible to have a market for goods in the outlying areas around the cities.

Manufacture found its market in the city ...

In the cities for the first time the conditions were created for *the free disposal* of labor power.

Today the entire economy is based on an ever-expanding production of commodities.

The commodity economy, or the money economy, which is only its reverse side, and therefore the driving out of the natural economy, or subsistence economy—this commodity economy arose inside the city. Thus all the foundations, taken together, for modern development arose inside the city.

In the Middle Ages the cities were isolated, separate points ... each city lived its own life [separately], both economically and politically.

However, the waves [emanating from the city] rebounded against the outlying countryside, and feudalism was [eventually] defeated everywhere.

Internationally the development of cities proceeded in the same way, in England, Italy, France, everywhere there were the same basic lines of development, and therefore we take an example from France.

Amiens in northern France. (In the Putzger [atlas] it is on page 12, and there it is called Samarobriva.) The present name comes from ... these were formed for defense against the Romans. Caesar defeated its army with 10,000 men. He installed his garrison there.

The city was placed under the rule of Roman city officials, and at first it got a magistrate with political power and legal jurisdiction, a *curia* with police and local authority, which also had legal jurisdiction, but all this was chosen [all these officials and official bodies] by the central Roman power and was dependent on that to the greatest degree. That was the typical Roman city constitution.

In the fourth century Amiens became a city of respectable size, a juncture point for trade, located on a major trade route.

A bishop was [there], who wanted to teach Christianity. He was killed and in this way earned a place among the saints.

In 406 the city was destroyed by the Germans, Swabians, Vandals, and Burgundii. In this military campaign by the Germans, Speyer, Strassburg, and Worms were also destroyed, all of them Roman cities.

In 428 the Franks arrived, although at first they were driven back. In 436 they pressed their way in under [Clodion the Hairy]* and destroyed all the cities on their way. The Roman municipal constitution was completely altered at that point, and a Carolingian count was installed as the highest authority. Next to him stood what was called the people's assembly of the fully free, the said assembly being convoked by the count, who also chaired the assembly. It should be understood that the people's assembly was [actually] the mark community, and thus there was a regression of the Roman city into a mark.

---

* The name does not appear in the typescript, a blank space appearing instead.

From the seventh century to the tenth all traces of a city constitution disappeared in Amiens. The Frankish kings began to appoint bishops and install them in the city. In 779 Charlemagne released the abbey of Amiens from all taxes, with the right to trade freely. He also introduced for the first time the institution of jurors; these were [the equivalent of] judges elected by the people, who carried out judicial functions under the chairmanship of the count.

In the ninth century [there were] unceasing raids by the Norsemen [Vikings] and wars among the rising counts. All power and authority in the city came into the hands of the counts, and in the tenth century the city was made a feudal manor, with barbarian practices being followed, that is, the predominance of natural economy. The city's land belonged at that time in part to the count and in part to the bishop. The castle with the manor house belonged to a third lord, namely the king. Thus three feudal lords were established in the city, and three forms of manorial ordinance.

In the twelfth century a series of revolutions began in the cities of northern France. In the period from 1100 to 1112 social explosions ensued in all the cities of northern France, resulting in incendiarism and looting; in one of the cities the bishop was even killed.

In 1113 Amiens followed with a revolution. Here what was called a commune was established for the purposes of the revolution. That meant a federation,* an alliance [of city dwellers] joined in the common struggle to win their freedom. The commune was formed in opposition to the manorial ordinances; and the bishop, whose status as a ruler was much lower, sided with the commune. At the same time it negotiated with the king, Ludwig the Fat, who for a large sum of money took the side of the commune and recognized it: with an elected council, its own legal jurisdiction, and the abolition of the manorial ordinances and law of the count. The count thereupon attacked the city with arms in hand, and the fight lasted for three years. The fighting went on from street to street and barricades were thrown up. The bishop withdrew from the city at that time.

In the year 1115 at the request of the bishop, the king came with his army to Amiens. He attacked the castle, but was wounded and driven off. The count with his army was in the castle. Then began a siege to starve out the castle, and the siege lasted two years. In 1117 the count and the count palatine surrendered, and the castle was razed to the ground.

The count was deposed, and the countship as an official office was transferred to another family. These people united themselves with the burghers of the city in an agreement whereby the city annually elected a council and a director, or steward (French, *Maire*).

Taxes to be paid to the count remained as a burden on the territory of

---

*   *Eidgenossenschaft* is more literally, a fellowship of the oath.

the city, and later on, the city had to buy out the title to this right in a special procedure.

In 1190 the constitution of the commune [of Amiens] was confirmed and expanded by King Philipp August.

On the whole, then, [this was] enormously early by comparison with the German cities.

The history of this city is typical for France. But the overall course of development, looking at it more broadly, is exactly the same as in Germany. And indeed the history of this city is especially characteristic because Amiens was a former Roman city.

In *Italy* the city structure had a prominent development very early.

The Italian cities are especially interesting because the Renaissance starts with them.

The center of the Renaissance in Italy was Florence. The chief supporter of this movement was the Medici family. This family is a merchant clan [by origin] [*Kaufmannsgeschlecht*].

The first to come to prominence is Ardingo de Medici. He was a guild master in Florence, and [it was he mainly] who brought about the victory of the guilds in Florence in the year 1291.

Then we meet a certain Averardo [de Medici]. In 1314 he is the standard-bearer for the guilds.

In the same century, in an urban revolution in which the lower mass of guild members gained the victory, Francesco de Medici was elected.

In 1360 Bartolomeo de Medici led an uprising to overthrow the lords of high finance among the merchants.

In 1378 a certain Silvestro de Medici carried out a new uprising of the same kind.

Giovanni de Medici became an ambassador, who was sent out by the city of Florence to represent its interests. He was three times the chief elder of the guilds [*Zunftältester*] and the standard-bearer of the guilds. His son Cosimo de Medici the sponsor of the Renaissance, was leader of the people's party. Because of that he was banned from the city for ten years. He was called back as early as one year later and dominated the city because of his wealth. He was the true leader of the Renaissance.

Another one after him [Lorenzo de Medici]* founded libraries and erected public buildings [*Beute*] in the city. Michelangelo worked under him.†

The patrician merchant families and the bishop made a conspiracy against

---

* The name is not given in the manuscript, the space here being left blank.

† While the typescript has *Beute*, Luxemburg probably said *Gebäude* (which means "buildings"). The two German words are pronounced quite similarly, and a stenographer listening to Luxemburg speaking this text could have easily heard *Beute* when Luxemburg said *Gebäude* (or even *Bäude*, which means the same).

him. His brother was murdered. The people rose up against that, and the arch-bishop was hanged at his own window. At that point the pope sent an army against Florence.

In the end his [Lorenzo de Medici's] son became Pope as Leo X.

From the same family, came Catherine de Medici, a queen of France, and then an illegitimate son of the Medici family became Pope.

This merchant family [*Geschlecht*], which is so completely connected with the Renaissance, is [also] inseparably linked with the rise of the cities.

The city of Florence was founded two centuries before the birth of Christ. In 82 BC it was destroyed by a Roman military leader. Caesar revived the city as a colony, that is, as a military colony. In the fourth century [AD] Florence became the seat of a bishop. In the eleventh century it really came up in the world as a result of [increased] trade, and in the twelfth century the city fought its way free of manorial ordinance and gained its own legal jurisdiction. Thus it was far in advance, compared to the German cities, in the process of liberation.

In 1185 the German Emperor Frederich I [Frederick Barbarossa] took away this freedom, because at that time these cities had come under the rule of the German Empire.*

In 1197 Florence regained its own legal authority and joined with other cities in an alliance against German rule.

In the twelfth and thirteenth centuries there was a great increase in trade and commercial activity, primarily wool weaving and banking. From 1115 on, Florence had its own money, which was called the florin.

As early as 1193 the heads of seven guilds took the side of the burgomaster [mayor of the city]. Now there began a prolonged struggle with the merchant clans. In 1206 [there was] a revolution. The people fought alongside of the bur-gomaster, who had [actually] originated from among the merchant families; [he had become] a representative of the people, the community. [There was a] col-legium of the twelve chief elders. The merchant families were driven out of the city, and then they organized a conspiracy and went to war against Florence. In 1260 the Florentines suffered a severe defeat in this war, and the merchant families marched into the city again, whereupon the constitution of 1250 was abolished.

The craftsmen's party was at that point supported by the Pope against the merchant families, and in 1267, on a night in April, all the merchant families were driven out of the city. But through the mediation of a papal cardinal the merchant families were allowed to re-enter the city in 1280. Thus the popes played a major role.

In 1282 [the constitution] was again abolished by the Pope, and power

---

*   That is, the so-called Holy Roman Empire.

passed directly to the more highly placed guilds, to the merchants and wool weavers. The nobles and the aristocracy of money also maintained a certain participation in the regime.

In 1293 [there was another] uprising, and the merchant families were completely excluded from the city council and placed under strict legal control. To hold the merchant families in check, a special standard-bearer of justice was established in coordination with the city council. But in 1316 [there was] another revolution, and the wealthy merchants seized the power for themselves. And yet in 1328 the guilds carried out a revolution and took the rule of the city back into their own hands. In 1341 and 1343 there were new revolutions, in which the lower guilds came to power. But the nobles and the aristocracy of finance soon regained the upper hand. In 1378 there was an uprising, which was called the revolution of the wool carders. But this revolution failed. There were further struggles by the craftsmen in 1387, 1393, 1397, and 1400, but the merchant families managed to remain at the helm. At the same time Florence attained an ever-higher stage of wealth and power.

In 1405 the city of Florence purchased the city of Pisa for 200,000 gold florins and subjugated it by force. That happened because of the harbor and because Pisa was a competitor.

In 1491 the harbor of Livorno* was purchased [by the Florentines] from the Genoese.

In the meantime the Medicis had arrived at the head of the people's party. They took part in all the revolutions. Under Cosimo de Medici the famous age of the Renaissance, the age of the Medici, began. In 1494 the Medici were driven out of the city, and a new republican constitution was introduced, with the leading role played by the party of Savonarola, against whom the Pope imposed a ban and who was killed in 1498. Again there was further unrest until 1502, when a lifelong standard-bearer [of the guilds] came to the top. But in 1512 he too was overthrown, and the Medicis were called back. In 1527 an uprising of the republican party under the merchant clan of the Strozzi† [took place] and the Medicis were again driven out. In 1530‡ Florence was taken by the [Holy Roman] Emperor Charles V.

Florence is typical of the development of the cities. We see that the city did not go to rack and ruin because of the unrest, but rather it bloomed and flourished. The fairy tale about the eternal peace that is supposedly necessary for culture is not confirmed by the actual development and rise of the modern bourgeoisie.

---

*   This town was called Leghorn by the English.

†   The Strozzi was the name of a noble family of Florence that played an important part in the city's affairs in the thirteenth and fourteenth centuries. The Strozzis founded the first public library in Florence.

‡   Luxemburg mistakenly gives the date as 1503.

The most outstanding feature of the medieval *Italian cities* [is] in particular the overweening influence and later the rule of the merchants.

That came about because the Italians were the intermediaries in trade with other countries bordering on the Mediterranean. And indeed trade developed [substantially] in the cities. The merchant families experienced an upsurge [economically] and at the same time rose to political power, and nowhere did the cities achieve such complete independence as in Italy. The cities were independent republics. They came into conflict with feudalism.

Indicative for the Italian cities was the struggle against the German emperors.

In Germany itself the emperors attempted to support the cities here and there, but in Italy the emperors turned directly against the cities and waged an unceasing struggle against them.

Consequently, two large alliances were formed in Italy.

The Lombard League was politically the most important, because it was the most extensive and was located in the north. The chief city for that League was Milan.

Florence tended more to pursue commercial interests. Belonging to the Lombard League, for example, in addition to Milan, were the following: Pisa, Arenza, Como, Lugano, Novi, Parma, Bologna, Pavia, and Genoa.

The city of *Milan*. In the year 569 it was taken by the Langobardi.* They were Germans, and then came the Franks. Under them Milan was the center of a count's domain. In the eleventh century the counts were from the house of Este. In 1056 a movement broke out in Milan that is known to history as the Partarser (?).† It was named after the rag-and-bonemen's quarter of the city (a derisive term). [It was] directed against the rule of the archbishop and indeed was favored by the Pope. The papacy was striving for greater political power and sought with strict discipline to make the bishops concentrate on spiritual matters in order to leave the secular rule of the church in its own hands [that is, in the hands of the papacy]. Therefore it supported the cities in their struggle against the bishops.

Pope Gregory VII opposed certain marriages. He ...

The conflict with Frederick Barbarossa. Milan was besieged many times [during this conflict] ... but in spite of it all the development of the city did not come to an end.

... Two clans came to the forefront: Della Torre and Visconti. They established a veritable dynasty, as the Medici had done in Florence ...

---

*   The Langobardi is another name for Lombards, a Germanic tribe that ruled much of Italy from 567 to 774 AD.

†   This is a reference to the Pataria (or Patarines), a religious movement in Milan in the eleventh century, led mainly by traders, that sought to reform the clergy by ending simony and clerical marriage. *Patarini* derives from the word for "ragpickers," which they were called by their upper-class adversaries.

The conclusion was that in the sixteenth century Milan was subjugated by Charles V of Spain in the War of the Spanish Succession. It then passed to Austria.

The rise of the merchants led to a great flourishing of spiritual life. This in turn led to the Renaissance. It came about because there had been stagnation in all spiritual life here for centuries, since antiquity. Whoever observes the reality of the Renaissance with a critical eye will soon see proof in it that our present-day culture is not a continuation from the ancient world, but that after undergoing a real retrograde movement, lasting roughly from the eighth to the tenth centuries, all science ended up at that time in the hands of the Church and the monks. Science was restricted almost entirely to theology.

The spiritual life of the times was concentrated there [in the Church], but in part some traditions from the ancient world were handed down through the various doctrines and tendencies in the Christian religion, but they had almost completely lost their original form.

The language of the Christian Church was Latin. Through knowledge of this language [*MS. Missing words*]

Theology was the positive science of that time. It was a consistently thought-out structure.

Contained in it, in part, were traditions handed down from Greek culture, but entirely remolded and adapted to the doctrines of the Christian Church.

In the philosophy and science of antiquity everything rested on research and investigation, while afterward faith was the only thing that remained, because all of science was subordinated to firmly fixed schematic doctrines [by the Church]. The more absurd something was, the more one was supposed to believe in it, the more it proved that we were not created to inquire into things.

All arts became, as it were, slaves of the church: painting was holy pictures; architecture was building churches.

This stagnation of culture was conditioned by the regression to the older economic forms of the mark constitution with the collapse of slavery. [There was] a turn backward to methods in which science was superfluous, primarily to agriculture, and thus, since life was devoted entirely to the production process, that meant the natural economy.

Art and science develop when there is an inclination toward them.

The nobility in Germany in the Middle Ages lived mainly on the land.

A new form of production had to arise in order for art and science to flourish again; [there had to be] new historical perspectives, new classes and class struggles, and then the accumulation of wealth in the cities. And it was possible for this wealth to be accumulated by the people of noble lineage who were up and coming as merchant clans.

The culture of antiquity had its roots in the ancient city, which represented the center of class rule. Also in the Middle Ages the city had to re-emerge, deep-going class differences had to develop, new social problems had to arise, and the wealth of the merchants had to be present as a material basis before art and science could again come into bloom. At that point the city signified, in different form, the same thing it had signified in antiquity.

The Renaissance gave a new start to the pagan art of antiquity. People began digging out the treasures of antiquity and reacquainted themselves with them. There was a revival of pre-Christian science of the pagan variety. The printing of books* was the precondition that made the flourishing of humanism possible.

Great names are connected with this epoch. Names linked with the Renaissance are the best known.

Chronologically:

Dante	1265–1321
Petrarch	1304–1374
Boccaccio	1313–1375

They were the first who wrote in so-called "kitchen Latin," that is, Italian.

The first beginnings of the Italian Renaissance.

The whole trend toward the readoption of the languages and science of antiquity was called humanism. Its expansion was helped along in particular by the definite results achieved in the development of the cities and the crafts in the Middle Ages: the printing of books was a genuine product of the development of cities and the skilled crafts.

Humanism expanded from Italy first to France. Greek began to be taught at the University of Paris for the first time in 1430. The universities are also a purely urban phenomenon. However, they were entirely under the spell of theology at first. All the chairs at the university were occupied by churchmen, and Latin was the ruling language. But now there was the beginning of an opposition at the universities.

The gymnastics of the spirit.

That was mocked by [Ulrich von] Hutten in his letters about the obscurantists.†

Then [humanism spread to] Spain and England (Sir Thomas More, one of the noblest representatives of humanism).

Then to Holland (Erasmus of Rotterdam, 1466–1536), and the humanist movement came to Germany from Holland.

[Johann] Reuchlin, 1455–1522. He had a famous dispute with the theological faculty of Cologne. It was then that [Ulrich von] Hutten (he lived from 1465

---

*   The printing of books as a skilled craft was begun by Gutenberg in 1436.

†   Ulrich von Hutten's *Epistolae obscurorum vivorum* (Letters About Obscurantist Men), written in 1520, was a famous attack on monkish life. He was a follower of Martin Luther.

to 1517) wrote his famous letters about the obscurantists. Then came [Philip] Melanchthon (in German the name means "black earth.").[*] He lived from 1497–1560, and then came Zwingli, from 1484 to 1533.[†]

This last name, along with the name of Hutten, shows that in Germany humanism was intertwined with the Reformation. ([See] Conrad Ferdinand Meyer, *Huttens letzte Tage* [Hutten's Last Days].[‡] Extraordinarily easy to read and also giving a very accurate picture historically.)

Humanism was expressed in the readoption of the artistic explorations made by the artists of antiquity, and then in the special flowering of painting, sculpture, and architecture. And everywhere this was sponsored by wealthy patrons. The rich made themselves the protectors of medieval artists, kept them at their palaces, and allowed them to do their work as artists as they saw fit. Thus, once again, this was an achievement made by a court [*Hof*] but not only a manorial estate. The ... of Goethe is highly characteristic in that regard ...

The dynasty of the Medici in Florence is especially famous in this connection, because they spent large sums on the splendid buildings, paintings, etc., in Florence. The great edifices were intended to win the favor of the people. Job opportunities became available to the people through these projects.

All the cities were united against external powers, but they fought bitter struggles against each other, especially over the Mediterranean and the Black Sea. That meant trade with the Orient.

After Constantinople fell to the Turks [in 1453] the powerful drive to find a sea route to the East Indies had its origins especially in the Italian cities.

Two factors that promoted the development of the cities in the north.

The liberation of the Netherlands from Spain and the *Hanseatic League.*

The Netherlands, its history and its population.

[The Netherlands, or Low Countries, were conquered] first by German tribes ... and Frisia in Roman times. They were subjugated by the Romans until the beginning of the fifth century AD.

Then came the Franks. In the eighth century, after long resistance, they were converted to Christianity and subjugated by the Carolingians. Bishoprics and abbeys and the domains of counts were established.

After the collapse of Charlemagne's empire, a decline in France, Germany, and [the duchy of] Lorraine was named after Lothar.[§] In the fourteenth century it came through marriage to the duchy of Burgundy with the seat of the duchy

---

[*]   His original name was Schwarzerd, which in German meant "black earth."

[†]   Zwingli actually died in 1531, not 1533.

[‡]   A reference to Conrad Ferdinand Meyer's poem, *Huttens letzte Tage* (Hutten's Last Days) (Leipzig: H. Haeffel, 1891). The poem was one of Luxemburg's favorites.

[§]   The duchy of Lorraine was originally called Lotharingia after Lotha I, one of Charlemagne's grandsons who obtained control of Alsace, Lorraine, Burgundy, northern Italy, and parts of modern-day western Germany after the death of his father, Louis the Pious.

in Brussels. In 1477 the Low Countries passed through marriage to the house of Hapsburg and thus belonged to Austria. After Emperor Charles V withdrew from power the Low Countries fell to Philip II of Spain.

In the meantime there was a great flourishing of the cities in the Low Countries in the twelfth and thirteenth centuries. The struggle of those cities against the counts for city freedoms began, and in the thirteenth and fourteenth centuries they had free city constitutions everywhere.

The time when the cities of the Netherlands reached their peak was a few centuries later than that of the German cities, whose time of blossoming was, in turn, later than that of the Italian cities.

Antwerp. Its trade flourished from the fourteenth to the sixteenth centuries. A large foreign colony existed there, that is, foreign merchants, and [there was] mutual trade with Germany. Antwerp conducted a worldwide trade and possessed its own commercial fleet.

The trade link with the Orient as a result of the land route to the East being replaced [by the sea route] ...

There was also a shift of a major route for world trade to northern Europe as a result of which the Baltic and the North Sea came to the fore.

The previous culture.

As a result, first Holland and then England reached a high point.

Amsterdam at the beginning of the thirteenth century was still a fishing village and a feudal possession of the lord of Amstel (the river there is called the Amstel.) The entire city is built on dams along this river.

The lords of Amstel were vassals of the seminary at Utrecht. But as early as the beginning of the fourteenth century the city got rid of manorial ordinances and won its own constitution. In the fourteenth and fifteenth centuries Amsterdam's trade with the Baltic flourished. In the sixteenth century Amsterdam was the number one city of the Netherlands, as far as trade was concerned. But the actual flourishing of Amsterdam dates from the downfall of Antwerp. The Dutch East India Company was founded in 1602. In 1622 Amsterdam had a hundred thousand inhabitants. That was its highest peak.

Bruges. It was walled in as early as the seventh century. In the ninth century it received a castle and became a count's city, and thus a feudal possession. In the twelfth century Bruges was the largest trading city in Flanders. The largest battles between guilds, those of the weavers and the fullers, were played out here, with bloody street battles. Later Bruges flourished to the greatest extent as part of the Flemish textile industry, and the city had the wool trade with England [entirely] in its hands.

In connection with all this a brilliant artist's colony arose there in the sixteenth century. Rubens, Rembrandt, and so forth, on the basis of the development of the city.

Brussels. In the eleventh century it was a fortified town belonging to the counts von Löwen (?). It was at about the halfway point on the trade road from Cologne to Bruges, and it became the center of a flourishing textile industry. In the fourteenth century the fiercest constitutional battles were fought out in Brussels.

Ghent. It was first a fortified castle of the counts of Flanders, founded in 1180.†

It rose to prominence from the thirteenth to the fifteenth centuries. During this time the fiercest battles of the guilds against the merchant families were fought out in Ghent. A merchant clan was at the head of the struggle against the manorial ordinances of the counts, the Artevelde family. In 1345 there was a conspiracy of the weavers against the rule of the merchants and a violent uprising in which Artevelde, the main leader, was murdered.‡ In the fourteenth and fifteenth centuries there were as many as 40,000 linen weavers and wool weavers in the city. This shows that matters had already gone beyond the handicraft form of production here; this was already manufacture. The work methods were still of the handicraft kind, but a huge number of craftsmen had been brought together, and they were exploited by the merchants.

All these flourishing cities entered into a major historical conflict after they came under the rule of the Spanish crown in 1455, a conflict with the Catholic Church and Spanish despotism, which had risen to its highest level of power in Spain. That was where the Inquisition reigned.

It waged the fiercest fight against the Renaissance.

And now the merchants in Holland made themselves the champions of free trade and freedom of thought and belief.

Commerce needed free trade, and business freedom was needed for industrial activity, but Spanish policy prevented all that.

At the same time humanism had come from Italy by way of France. In Holland [there was] the earliest acceptance of Calvinism.

In reality underlying the struggle between Holland and Spain was an economic and social conflict, *the conflict between the natural economy of feudalism and a new development, manufacture*, which was on the rise.

---

*   In Dutch, the name of the town is Leeuwen. The question mark is in the original typescript.

†   Ghent's origin can be dated earlier, to the seventh century, when two abbeys were built there, around which the town developed. After the town was destroyed by a series of raids by Vikings in the ninth century, it was rebuilt. By 1100 it was already a thriving city. The fortified castle that Luxemburg mentions was built in 1180, replacing the wooden fortifications of an earlier castle. The fortified castle was called Gravensteen Castle ("castle of the count"). From the eleventh to the thirteenth century Ghent was the largest city in Europe after Paris, with a population of about 60,000.

‡   In 1338, Jacob von Artevelde (1290–1345) led a revolt of the weavers of Ghent against the count of Flanders and France, because of restrictions placed upon Ghent's trade with England. The revolt expelled the count from Ghent and Artevelde took over as head of the city council. After allying Ghent with England during the Hundred Years' War, he was killed as a result of an uprising of the artisans who came to oppose his policies.

[At the same time] the rising force of absolutism needed gold in order to fight against feudalism, to maintain armies, and so forth.

The policy of the Dutch merchants in the colonies went in the direction of importing raw materials from those foreign lands as well as labor power—the slave trade.

When Holland came under Spanish rule these two [forms] came into conflict.

All the flourishing Dutch cities, after Spanish rule was imposed on them, engaged in constant conflict with the Catholic Church, which had achieved its highest level of power in Spain. The Inquisition tried to drown the upcoming new era in blood. Thus the Dutch cities became the foremost champions of commercial freedom, freedom of thought, and freedom of belief, and they won those freedoms in the struggle against Spain. The rising force of humanism strengthened the struggle, but it alone was not the determining factor. Rather it and these struggles were products of the economic revolution that was beginning.

The Dutch were the first to establish modern colonies (Indies!).* While the early colonial policy of *Spain* knew only the quest for gold as its sole aspiration, *Dutch colonial policy* culminated in efforts to promote the development of trade with the processing of raw materials and the production of finished goods. Holland came under Spanish domination, and the two [divergent] tendencies were bound to come into conflict. Struggles erupted that lasted eighty years; the first period was from 1565 to 1598 and the second from 1621 to 1648. The result of the first phase was the secession of Netherlands from Spain and the founding of a republic. Only after the second phase of struggle did the defeated Spanish recognize the [Dutch] republic and its independence.

Then the House of Orange rose to power in the Netherlands holding the office of *stadtholder*† as a hereditary right.

Schiller [in his *Revolt of the Netherlands*] gave a literary depiction of this struggle. In addition, [see] Goethe's drama *Egmont*.‡

In the midst of this desperate eighty-year struggle, in the course of which the cities were plundered many times by the Spanish, the Netherlands reached its highest point, flourishing in all fields. [This serves] again as proof of how very much the Middle Ages was developing on ground that was truly volcanic.

At the same time the colonial conquests of the Dutch proceeded apace. It

---

*   The reference is to the Dutch East Indies, today's Indonesia.

†   A *stadtholder* was chief magistrate of the Dutch republic in the sixteenth and seventeenth centuries.

‡   Friedrich Schiller's book was first published in 1800. For an English translation, see *Revolt of the Netherlands* (Whitefish, MT: Kessinger Publishing, 2004). Goethe wrote his drama *Egmont* in 1788. For an English translation, see *Egmont*, translated by Anna Stanwick (New York: Bartleby, 2001). This work is perhaps best known from Beethoven's overture of the same name.

[Holland] conquered the Sunda Islands[,]* Ceylon, the Cape region [around South Africa's Cape of Good Hope], and Brazil.†

Holland's trading fleet numbered 35,000 ships, and the Bank of Amsterdam had 300 million gold florins lying in its vaults.

The enormous costs of war with Spain, thanks to this flourishing [of commerce], were easily borne, along with high taxes.

The Netherlands also became at that time a place of refuge for the victims of feudalism: craftsmen and merchants, learned men from Spain, from France, from Italy, all fled to the Netherlands. The Netherlands at that time, thanks to its geographical location, was the only country in Europe where the mode of life in the cities was entirely oriented toward the interests of the burghers, while elsewhere the latter were defeated by a rising absolutism.

In addition, modern philosophy also arose in Holland: Spinoza.

Both the later artistic Renaissance of Holland and the modern [*MS. Missing words*] show the contrast between the Dutch Renaissance and the Italian. The Italian: churchly in character; the Dutch [showed]: burghers and the life of the burghers.

As a result of all this flourishing, which at the same time in economic areas was passing over from the forms of craft production to those of manufacture, trade had already become genuine world trade. In this way Holland then came into conflict with England. The struggle between those two is, so to speak, the boundary line between the true modern era and the last phase of the Middle Ages.

Holland, with the flourishing of its Renaissance, with its victorious struggle against Spain, and with its colonial policy, is the last blossoming of medieval city development.

England already represents the beginning of the capitalist phase. Both of them are linked by the textile industry.

[It was first in Holland] that textile manufacture arose.

England still played a passive role then, providing the raw materials. That resulted in agriculture being pressed back by stock raising, and in that connection a large number of peasant households were forced out of existence. In their place came pastureland for sheep, driven by capitalist impulses. From that came the modern proletariat and modern capital in England, which opened a new period of economic production.

We must look at *the Hanse* [*the Hanseatic League*] in order to make clear the contradictory role of Germany [i.e., of the German cities].

History of the Hanse. The word *Hanse* [*Hansa*] means "chief alliance." And the word *hänseln* [to make a fool of; to hassle] is derived from *Hanse*. That was the method of the Hanse.‡

---

*   These are the islands of present-day Indonesia.

†   The Dutch held northeast Brazil from 1630 to 1654.

‡   The verb *hänseln* appears to have a different etymology from the one given by Luxemburg.

The formal coming together of the Hanseatic League in 1354 followed in the wake of the Cologne Confederation.* The origin of the Hanseatic League in an earlier, looser form goes back to the beginning of the thirteenth century. The beginnings consisted in separate groups of cities with special relations among one another and with the outside world. And the latter was the point from which the Hanse actually emerged. It was necessary at that time to take special measures to ensure the protection of trade caravans, expeditions, and the like, in order to conduct an extensive trade with other areas and countries. Given the situation at that time it was necessary for merchants in foreign trading centers to establish their own settlements. Today it is not necessary because freedom of commerce exists, but at that time it did not.

At that time the protection of one's rights was based on a person's being connected to manorial ordinances or, in a city, belonging to a guild. The protection of one's rights depended on belonging to a particular social group, whereas today it depends on being a citizen of a particular country.

The oldest German trade settlement abroad was that of the Cologne merchants in *London*. It was called the *Steelyard*. It was started in the thirteenth century, beginning on such a small scale that its actual point of origin cannot be established exactly. It became the central point for all trade with England. (See page 17b in the Putzger atlas.)

The second trading settlement of the Germans was at *Wisby on the island of Gotland*.† (See page 17b in the Putzger atlas.)

The third settlement, which went out from there, was in Novgorod (court of St. Peter). (See page 17b in the Putzger atlas.)

In connection with all this, *three alliances of cities* were formed, and they were called the "three thirds" of the later Hanseatic League. Then there came a *"fourth third" of the Hanse*.

The first alliance was concluded between *Hamburg und Lübeck* in 1241 to ensure the security of the trade between the Baltic and the North Sea. Grouping itself around these two main cities was: the *Wendish Third*. It was founded in 1285. Here the leading city was Lübeck. It concluded an alliance with the cities of Wismar and Rostock, and later Stralsund and Greifswald also joined. A number of small cities in Pomerania and the Mark [of Brandenburg] soon joined as well: Stargard, Stendhal, Salzwedel, Brandenburg, Berlin, Frankfurt-on-the-Oder, and others.

On the other hand, *Hamburg* made an alliance with a series of towns in the Lower Rhineland; this part of the Hanse was called the *Lower Rhineland-Prussian*

It appears to have originally referred to an initiation rite.

   * The Cologne Confederation was a military alliance forged by the Hanseatic League in 1367 for purposes of waging war against Denmark. It led to the Second Danish-Hanseatic War of 1367–70, in which the Hanseatic League was victorious. The Cologne Confederation was disbanded in 1385.

   † Wisby is in the Baltic Sea between Sweden and the Danish peninsula.

Third. Belonging to this part were the cities of: Cologne, Dortmund, Soest, Münster, Herfurt, and Minden, as well as some Netherlands cities such as Bruges, etc. At the other end some Baltic cities also belonged, such as Torun, Kulm, Danzig, and others.

Wisby was the center of a third group, including cities of Estonia and Livonia in the Baltic. This group was called *the Gotland Third.* Those belonging here included Reval, Pernau, Dorpat, Riga ...

They also had branches in the Russian cities of Novgorod, Pskov, Polotsk, and Vitebsk.

The "fourth third" grouped itself around *Bremen.* This group of Hanse cities was called *the Saxon Third.* Belonging to this were the cities of Göttingen, Halle, Halberstadt, Hildesheim, Braunschweig [Brunswick], Hannover, Lüneburg, and later also Magdeburg, which gained a leading role.

Thus the separate groups had their origins, and in 1367 all of them together signed a *joint constitution* in Cologne. They formed what was called the Cologne Confederation.

The aim of this formal agreement was to win commercial freedoms at home and abroad, to secure the trade routes against attacks by robbers, and so forth, settlement of all disputes among one another by a court of arbitration, and joint regulation of commercial law. And such regulation has also come into existence now, with the development of international trade, and has become an established norm.

The safeguarding of maritime travel, the regulation of coins and weights, the joint organization of commercial fleets and crews, and indeed of navies as well, in order ultimately [to protect] the rights of the Hanse with [*MS. Missing word(s)*]

There was also a registration list for purposes of war, which defined the part each separate city would have in outfitting [the League for war]. Keeping the peace in the cities was also a joint obligation. The point of this regulation, as of the entire organization of the Hanse, was directed internally against the guilds. The joint keeping of the peace in the cities meant: keeping the guilds down.

The aim was to establish the dominance of the merchants in a way analogous to the Italian cities.

The entire practical activity of the Hanse involved measures against the guilds and against unrest stirred up by the guilds.

The Hanse had assemblies [*Bundestage*] to which each city sent a representative.

By itself this assembly was rather a loose arrangement, but each of the four "thirds" had its own assemblies. Also, the individual cities remained independent in all their internal affairs. Only when common interests involving trade came up was it necessary to directly force some cities into obedience, using the method of harassment, which ultimately meant laying siege and waging war.

Thus the Hanse, because of its fleet and the power that backed it up, won great privileges in England.

Then it dealt with Denmark in particular. In 1362 Denmark had taken Wisby on the island of Gotland, and with that began a bloody war with Denmark. Under the leadership of the burgomaster of Lübeck, the Hanseatic navy sailed against Copenhagen. It was taken and plundered by the Hanseatic League. Then an armistice was concluded with Denmark. In 1367 in Cologne 77 cities declared war against Denmark. A powerful Hanseatic navy occupied the Norwegian coast and again besieged Copenhagen and the Danish islands. In 1370 a peace treaty was signed in Stralsund with the Danish king. The Hanse had achieved complete victory and assured itself exclusive trade rights in all of Denmark.

By 1397 it had the same rights in all the Scandinavian lands. That meant that no merchant was allowed to go there if he was not a member of the Hanseatic League. Fish from the North Sea and the Baltic constituted the main item of trade. This favorable situation for the League in the North Sea and the Baltic lasted for a century. Merchants of the Hanse in the Nordic cities had ...

Danzig then replaced Wisby in the leading position in the Baltic, and this had to do with the grain trade from the east, from Poland and Russia. At the same time trade with Russia kept increasing, and here timber and furs played the main role.

The Hanse also conducted extensive trade with England, with France, and with Portugal. It had its [own] settlements everywhere. Also there was a lively trade with Venice.

The main trading offices were Bruges, Bergen, and Novgorod, as well as Schonen,* and indeed the last-named city served as a trans-shipping location.

The chief objects of trade were [as follows]: from France, salt and wine; from Flanders, textiles; from England, wool and other kinds of cloth; from Sweden, wax, furs, and ore; from Russia, grain, furs, and timber; and from Nordic waters, fish.

These, then, were no longer luxury items, but objects of daily use on a mass scale, which went mainly to the cities. Here one senses already a transition to a new era in which trade is no longer meant only for the rulers.

The high point of domination by the Hanse was in the fourteenth, fifteenth, and sixteenth centuries. At that time the Hanse represented a power that was also highly respected politically. It waged war on its own account and concluded treaties with foreigners. And it seemed that the prospects for the Hanse's further development were very great. But it turned out otherwise. Signs of decline began to appear.

As early as the year 1423 the revolt of the Dutch cities is to be noted, and they allied themselves with Denmark against the Hanse.

---

*   This was also called Skane, or Scania.

That came about because the Netherlands cities already aspired to become an independent power [in their own right]. A new form of production had already begun to develop in them. By contrast, the German cities pursued trade interests exclusively on the basis of the old form of production.

In particular in the sixteenth century the sea route for trade with the Orient shifted to the north.* And now the cities of the Netherlands were geographically more favorably located for this new commercial sea route than Germany. Thus we see that the flourishing of the Hanse occurred between that of the Italian cities and that of the Netherlands cities.

With the opening of the trade routes to the East Indies prospects for trade expanded enormously. The cities of the Netherlands were the first to pursue a colonial policy. The Hanse, on the other hand, stuck firmly to the old trade routes and the old items of trade and did not want to know anything about distant overseas trade. That is why the Hanse became outdated, and for that reason cities gradually, one after another, dropped out of the Hanse.

In the first half of the sixteenth century the Hanse, under the leadership of the burgomaster of Lübeck, Jürgen Wollenweber,† became involved in a new war with Denmark with the aim of excluding the cities of the Netherlands from the right to trade [in the Baltic]. Thus the war with Denmark was at the same time a war with the Netherlands cities. The Hanse was defeated and its domination in Scandinavia was broken. It is no accident that the first war [against Denmark] was won and the second was lost. It was a sign, a symbol that [*MS. Missing words*]

In the sixteenth century England emancipated itself from the Hanse. Because the latter had often forced the English kings to grant trade advantages to the Hanseatic cities, so that England was condemned to an entirely passive role in trade. [At the end of] the sixteenth century, under Queen Elizabeth, England began to free itself from the Hanse. The rights of the Hanse began to be restricted in England. Lübeck tried with the help of the German Diet‡ to forbid all entry to Germany for trade from England. Queen Elizabeth replied by confiscating 60 Hanseatic ships, shutting down the Steelyard, and abrogating all the privileges of the Hanse in England.

As a result the interests of the city of Hamburg were harmed to such an extent that Hamburg dropped out of the Hanseatic League and made a trade treaty with England on its own account.

At approximately the same time, in 1553, the English discovered a sea route

---

* Since the time of John Cabot at end of the fifteenth century, English explorers were interested in finding a way to Asia by sailing northeast, through the Arctic. In 1552 English explorer Richard Chancellor penetrated the White Sea and arrived at the port of Archangel in Russia, the first Englishmen to do so. As a result of his voyage, a sea trading route was opened up between England and Russia.

† His last name means "wool weaver."

‡ That is, the Diet of the Holy Roman Empire.

to Russia by way of the White Sea, in the north, and they were likewise emancipated from the Hanse in that way, since they could now trade directly with Russia.

And in the fifteenth century the cities of the [Brandenburg] Mark dropped out of the Hanse, and actually this came about under the influence of the rising landlord class, the power of the Electors [of the Holy Roman Empire].

Likewise in the fifteenth century Novgorod was destroyed by the rising power of the tsarist regime, by Ivan the Terrible, and it was stripped of its independence entirely. Thus the cities fell away one after the other, so that at the beginning of the seventeenth century only 14 cities still remained in the Hanseatic League.

After the Peace of Westphalia, in 1648,* the Hanse fell into decline completely.

Unfortunately there are not many studies of the Hanse. There are modern ones, but none of them are as good as the old one by *Sartorius von Waltershausen*, three volumes (cheap in used bookstores). The book contains no critique; one must provide that oneself; but it does contain the material.†

The Hanseatic League represented trading interests exclusively, and consequently it rested on outdated forms and methods of trade. That was expressed in the fact that the Hanse cities did not want to participate in the founding of colonies, as England and the Netherlands did.

Here their *geographic position* was decisive.

On the one hand the cities in Germany did not acquire sufficient power so that on their own accord they could carry out centralization on a large scale. The superiority of landed property in feudalism was too great for that.

It was the small landowning princes that were the cause of Germany remaining backward. They had the power to hold the cities down, but not enough power to lay the groundwork for a new period.

On the one hand, it [the Hanse] was too conservative to help build the new mode of production. On the other, it was already oriented against the guilds, and would not allow them to gain as much strength as they had in Italy, and so forth.

It was only a structure for exploiting trade at a certain historical period. Novgorod is characteristic. It was destroyed by a single tsar [Ivan the Terrible]. That was one of the phenomena that led to the decline of the Hanse.

Why was Novgorod destroyed? In its internal life it had raised itself to the level of a republic, just as cities elsewhere had done. But at the same time, tsarist absolutism was on the march in Russia, and the freedom of the city, which had only begun a weak, unsteady growth, was bound to give way.

---

* The Peace of Westphalia, in 1648, concluded the Thirty Years' War and proved instrumental in the emergence of the modern nation state.

† See George Friedrich Christoph Sartorius von Waltershausen, *Urkundliche Geschichte des Ursprung der deutschen Hanse* (Documentary History of the Origin of the Hanseatic League) (Hamburg: J. Perthes, 1830).

The Hanse represented a line of development that remained backward in comparison to the forward-moving tendencies [of its time].

It shoved itself in between the Italian Renaissance cities and the period of [rising] manufacture in Holland.

Even when particular phases of history occur in succession, there is a single line of development [persisting] in the connection between them, and the one [phase] would not be possible without the other.

From what has been said we may conclude that the following was characteristic [of the Hanse]:

The Hanse was bound to go under. Trade outgrew the limits of the Hanse. New discoveries had brought world trade into being; colonial policy was now possible. The Hanse represented trading interests exclusively; it did not take into account the drastic change in the form of production and trade. Because of its geographical location it could not assume its share [of the new possibilities]. The Netherlands and England were the first countries to gain some benefits from this shift [in world trade]. Production had already grown beyond the limits of the small [trading] centers of the cities. However, the Hanse arose basically as a unification of a number of small trading-center cities. On the one hand, the development of the cities in Germany had not succeeded in growing to a high enough level so that the [Hanseatic] cities could establish a firmly consolidated alliance. On the other hand, in Germany absolutism did not become a powerful formation, as it did elsewhere, in order to become the vehicle for a new age of production as opposed to feudalism. It was particularism, [the existence of many] small states not strong enough to form a greater whole, but strong enough to hold back the development of the cities.

With the development of the cities, commodity production gradually rose higher. It established itself first in the cities, while feudalism reigned all around. Thus all around [the cities] there still remained a form of organized economic production that was controlled by the feudal lords.

Internally the Hanse was directed against the aspirations of the guilds. It [the Hanse] was such a truly German product, a wavering, contradictory structure between two epochs. To be sure, it was a powerful tool for the development of trade, but from the outset it was encumbered with a reactionary tendency. The Hanse was, just like Germany as a whole at that time, inserted parenthetically between two epochs. Novgorod, an important point of support for the trade of the Hanseatic League, was destroyed by tsarism. That was no accidental event. Novgorod represented city autonomy as against the rising aspirations of tsarist absolutism; the upward striving freedom of the city necessarily had to give way [in the face of tsarist absolutism], and that meant the destruction of Novgorod. The development of cities in Russia was thereby annihilated. In this downfall the even greater backwardness of Russia played its role.

The Hanse was shoved in between the flourishing of the cities at the time of the Renaissance in Italy and [the rise of] manufacture in Holland, which again was just a prelude to the further development taken over by England.

The value of the Hanse is that it promoted the powerful upward surge of the Netherlands cities and of trade. Without the Hanse the further development in England of manufacture that had its origins in Flanders would not have been possible.

The study of economic history has shown us that, as far as we have come, all economic forms have been *organized* in one way or another, were *planned*. Now in our studies we have come to the threshold of a society that is not ruled by any organization.

To understand this, let us take an example.

We imagine a primitive-communist mark community. Only yesterday it was living according to its planned and regulated relationships, but today all of a sudden all organization has ended.

The foundation of every society is labor.

Exchange

In all previous societies production was organized in a planned way, and the same was true of the distribution of products.

Where organization is lacking, exchange is necessary and serves as the only connecting link of human society.

In an organized society it is not exchange that takes place, but rather distribution. Each member from the outset contributes socially necessary labor. Before products are made there is an order for them by the society as a whole. Everyone receives what he or she needs, and what the individual receives is the result of a division of the social wealth. (In a society that is wealthier the individual receives more than one would in a society that is poorer.) In an organized society the contribution of the individual cannot serve as a measure of what he or she will receive.

Where organization is lacking each works for himself. He engages in private labor. Only when the finished product is exchanged for another does the labor of the individual change into socially necessary labor.

For exchange a finished product is necessary, as well as a need for that particular product. Products that are exchanged must contain the same amount of labor. A product that is exchanged thereby becomes socially necessary. It has value.

The number of products needed arises out of the experience of one exchange after another. Only after an exchange does it become clear whether a product is socially necessary. From one exchange to another, demand may alter. Since it is possible only after exchange [*MS. Missing words*] only after exchange is it regulated [*MS. Missing words*]*

As a result, at one moment there will be too many products and at another moment too few.

Uncertainty of the position of the individual.

Exchange is regulated by the division of labor.

Exchange is a substitute for economic planning.

In a socialist society there will be no exchange, but only distribution of the products.

The formation of a money economy

In the course of history a whole series of the most varied forms of economic production have followed one after another, but they always had a definite plan as a basis.

What we know about the capitalist economy is that it is unplanned. Thus the question arises: how is the existence of such a society possible, one that operates without any plan?

It is assumed that a communist society with a very highly developed culture and wide-ranging division of labor would suddenly collapse for any number of reasons if such an indescribable lack of regulation were to occur.

Only one thing is constantly, irreversibly, and fixed firmly: *everyone must work*. Without labor a human society is not conceivable.

The division of labor exists. With his or her labor each produces only one kind of product. Where there is no work plan—and here that would be the case—the only bond available would be *exchange*. Exchange takes place only where the organization of labor does not exist. In a planned economy mediation of products occurs not through exchange but through *distribution*.

Example: a shoemaker now works as an individual without connection to the society. He delivers his shoes to this person today and to that person tomorrow. That is how he earns his livelihood. In a communist society the shoemaker's production would be based on the total need of society. He would receive everything he needs from the society. That would be governed by the average wealth of the society at any given time.

Now [i.e., under capitalism], in contrast, the products exchanged on all sides represent the sum total of the labor that is put into each product. When two producers have a mutual exchange of products they are still completely independent of one another and [usually] don't even know one another. It is irrelevant if one receives less than he gives.

---

*   In this incomplete sentence, Luxemburg may have intended something like: "Only after exchange has taken place is it possible to attempt regulating the number of goods to be produced."

In an organized society that need not be the case. A shoemaker produces boots according to the orders placed by society. In return he receives his means of livelihood, not as a reward for his labor, but as a *fully entitled member of society*. That is governed more or less by the average social wealth. The labor expended to produce his means of livelihood is once again determined by the needs of the society as a whole. In an organized society the contribution of one and the return contribution of another are not measured against each other. A rich harvest, which also provides the shoemaker with a richer quantity of means for his livelihood, does not require more shoes. Here there is no exact reciprocal relationship. Thus in this case exchange is not taking place.

In a communist society each person receives what he or she needs as a member of that society.

In a slave economy [he receives] because he must be maintained [i.e., kept alive to work].

In an unplanned economy each produces as much as is necessary in order to exchange that for the means of livelihood. The volume of one's production determines the needs [that will be met].

In an organized society all labor would be, from the outset, *socially necessary labor*.

In an unplanned economy every product, from the word go, from the first foothold represents *private labor*. Labor is transformed into socially necessary labor only *after exchange.* Something is first produced and then is regulated by demand. No one can be sure immediately whether he will receive the share of the social wealth due to him in return for his labor.

Exchange thus becomes the substitute for planned organization of labor. In an unplanned economy socially necessary labor, which must exist always and at every time, is no longer the sum of the labor of those who are working. Every instance of labor is first of all private labor, and it becomes socially necessary labor only after exchange, but that comes into the picture only after production has been completed. Socially necessary labor is now the sum total of the products that have been exchanged.

Only those products that are needed [i.e., that can be used] succeed in being exchanged. The exchange value of a product is its capacity to be used. Because

---

* Luxemburg's claim is questionable. As she here emphasizes, in capitalism labor assumes a social form only *indirectly*, through the medium of *money* in exchange relations. However, the ability of labor to assume such an indirect character is a result of specific relations of production, in which concrete labor is subsumed by abstract labor. The exchange process is therefore not the decisive issue; instead, the peculiar form of capitalist *production* relations is decisive. See Marx's *Capital* Vol. 2, p. 196: "In the relation between capitalist and wage laborer, the money relation, the relation of buyer and seller, becomes a relation inherent in production itself. But this relation rests fundamentally on the social character of production, not on the mode of commerce; the latter rather derives from the former." For more on this, see Peter Hudis, *Marx's Concept of the Alternative to Capitalism* (Leiden: Brill, 2012), pp. 92–182.

only when it is used does a product become socially necessary labor; only then does it have exchange value. Until then every product is valueless private labor.

Exchange is thus the distinguishing characteristic of unplanned production.

That is why in a socialist society no exchange will be able to exist. Exchange is only possible if a society lacks organization.

For each individual labor is the precondition for his or her existence. Without labor one cannot exist.

How much labor is necessary for the maintenance of the society, and what kind of labor? That is [now] determined in the process of exchange. What is produced in excess of that will remain on the market [unsold]. It remains valueless private labor.

The experience gathered from previous instances of exchange serves as the guiding measure for further production.

In the unplanned economy therefore that which is socially necessary is always determined after the fact.

The means of regulation will now be a rough approximation constantly either above or below the actual volume of existing needs.

The tendency of private labor to come close to this approximation is bound to be more or less unsuccessful. Exchange is the only regulating factor.

In an organized society the distribution of products is regulated in a planned way. The amount of total needs is known in advance.

Now one's share in the social wealth depends on exchange. Complete uncertainty prevails.

Even the way in which the division of labor occurs is now regulated by exchange. The number of workers in each branch of production is regulated independently.

It is left up to each individual to bring new products to the market. Exchange will show him whether a need had been served or not. In this way exchange determines the appearance of new trades or professions.

To repeat: exchange presents itself as the regulating factor in an economy where the planned organization of labor is lacking.

Each person can satisfy their own needs only by exchanging the product of their labor. Thus people produce their vital needs themselves. But their means of livelihood can be gained only through exchange, when someone else has a need for their product. All individual members of society find themselves in the same situation.

Since exchange is the only intermediary for the meeting of needs, all the needs of an individual can only be met if all members of society have the same need for the product of each individual [worker].

Example: the cobbler can meet all his own needs only if all those who make products that he requires for the satisfaction of his manifold needs continually have the same strong need for the product of his labor, boots, for example.

Since this target will never be met, a difficulty arises which an organized society does not know. There the need of the society as a whole is a known factor. Now what exists are a large number of individual, independent needs.

Such an unlimited need by all for all products has never existed. But as a historic fact it has occurred that one particular product, for example, cattle, was a universal need that was felt by everyone at all times, was desired to the same strong degree. We would use one term here for the purpose of our subsequent discussion: that is, a *concrete* need or product.

This concrete product will be taken by anyone at any time in exchange for any other product.

The precondition is that in the society under consideration there is a general consumer need for this product.

It is precisely through exchange that each one is in a position to gain possession of this product. To begin with, he exchanges something for it in order to consume this product.

Soon, however, he arrives at the conclusion that he can also use this product to exchange for other things that he needs.

It now turns out that one such product has a dual function.

Example: the product of the cobbler's labor, that is, boots, must now be transformed into the concrete product. Then he can use this concrete product to exchange it for products that he requires in order to satisfy his needs.

Each person makes products with his own labor. It becomes socially necessary labor only through exchange. The only form [this can take] is when the product of his labor can be transformed into the concrete product.

Now a product must exist that is known in advance to be a social need. Only for such a product will private labor immediately become socially necessary labor. Every [instance of] private labor now becomes socially necessary labor if it is transformed into this concrete product of exchange. This concrete product is now the only connecting element within this loosely structured society. This concrete product is now the commodity that will be accepted by anyone at any time. This concrete product has now become *the means of exchange*.

The means of exchange is therefore a product that from the outset embodies socially necessary labor, and it gives, to every individual who possesses it, access to the social wealth.

This concrete product performs a dual function: as a means of consumption and as a means of exchange. Thus a certain part of this product might not be consumed. That part will be designated in advance as a means of exchange.

For example, [at one time] cattle were a means of exchange. Thus when an exchange took place one or some of the cattle would be marked separately, stamped or branded to distinguish them from the cattle designated for consumption. All the qualities that were valued and required in the cattle designated for consumption were unnecessary and superfluous in the cattle designated as a means of exchange. These cattle now are only a means of exchange.

However, the type of exchange product (for example, cattle) is bound to run into difficulties, such as how they are to be safeguarded, circulated, etc., and these difficulties tend to hinder the cattle's usability as a means of exchange. Now only one more step is necessary for this problematic means of exchange to be replaced by another that will not be burdened by these difficulties, for example, metal.

This corresponds to what actually happened. The selection of this exact new means of exchange is not mere speculation, however; it is historically determined. The transition from cattle as means of exchange to metal as means of exchange occurred simultaneously with the transition from herding to agriculture.

Agriculture needed metal. Its usability increased with the development of tools and weapons and the technology of their production. Metal became a universally desired item of consumption.

This course of development was reflected in words. In Latin, money was called *pecunia*, but this term was derived from *pecus*.* It is interesting furthermore that the first coins very often had the image of an ox or a sheep—that is, the type of animal that had previously served as the universal means of exchange.

Cattle and metal were not the only products that had significance as means of exchange. For example, for the Arabs it was dates, and for many primitive peoples of Africa it was cowrie shells.

These latter items also were included in the ranks of universally desired means of consumption. They served as jewelry that had significance as a means of distinguishing different tribes, ranks, and classes of seniority.

There is nothing at all exceptional about this. In our society also, despite an incomparably higher level of culture, symbols that are worthless or of very little worth have great meaning as distinguishing marks of a certain rank or standing for those wearing them or carrying them.

But the significance of cattle and metal became predominant. Their range of dominance was much wider than anything else. As we have already said, cattle as a means of exchange were pushed out with the transition from herding to agriculture. This process, in which the one superseded the other, was not completed quickly, nor did it occur everywhere at the same time; it happened gradually, at the same kind of pace that occurs in any transition. For a long time they both served side-by-side as means of exchange of equal worth.

In the poetry of Homer (eighth century BC) oxen and copper and iron were all named side-by-side as means of exchange.

It was possible for metal to become the most significant of all other [means

---

* *Pecus* is Latin for cattle.

of exchange] because it possessed physical qualities in a higher degree than all others that made it especially appropriate for that purpose.

One can remove all the consumer qualities from metal, and yet at any time it can be turned back into its former condition as a means of consumption. That is its greater advantage.

Metal became the means of exchange that dominated trade and exchange in general.

Indeed the extent of trade and exchange is variable. It goes up and down and cannot be determined in advance. Thus it lends itself also to a great many different means of exchange that may be used in trade at any particular time and that can never be set in advance.

Money is now the only product that represents socially necessary labor from the very outset.

It can possess this characteristic only when all other labor represents only private labor. Hidden behind that is an entire epoch in which the organization of labor was totally lacking.

Money is necessary in an unplanned economy.

Money is only the expression of commodity production.

With that we have also answered the question of whether a socialist society will need money. It does not need it.

The development of money, briefly then, is as follows:

Gold is to begin with a product of social labor that is universally desired.

Money is at one moment a product of exchange and at another a product of consumption.

Part of this product is designated only for consumption and another part exclusively as a means of exchange.

This latter part was deliberately distinguished by stamping it.

Now money took on a form in which it could not be consumed. Now it is only money. But it serves as a means by which every need without exception can be satisfied.

Now the only thing that remains is to *investigate whether the premise of a sudden collapse of a form of economy is justified.*

It is, because it is a historical fact.

A catastrophe cannot be measured during the time when it is happening. The nature of a catastrophe consists above of all in the fact that in a short span of time it brings with it in a forceful way entirely new forms, a transformation that was prepared for a long time during peaceful development. It is a further development, accelerated by revolution, of a particular line of previous development.

Example: the French Revolution of 1793. [With that came] the introduction of private property in Algeria, and all colonial policies in general.

The premise is historically grounded.

However, it is not the only form that development must necessarily take.

Example: the development of Germany. One stage passes gradually over into another, supported by revolutions, which do not however appear here as catastrophes or have catastrophic effects.

Further, is it possible for exchange to spring up suddenly?

Exchange does not need to be invented suddenly at a critical moment. Exchange exists at every time. Even peoples who are by no means organized into firmly fixed associations know exchange.

Example: during excavations in northern France stone tools were found made from a kind of stone that did not exist in that region.

We do not know of any epoch [in human development] without exchange; and even less so now does any separate people live without exchange.

Exchange was the mechanism by which cultural advances spread far beyond the region of their origin; at every time it contributed to the advancement of culture.

Exchange was possible as soon as the productivity of labor had reached a certain high level at which labor produced surpluses, quantities of goods greater than absolutely necessary. As far as knowledge of the history of culture has been able to conclude, this precondition [i.e., exchange] has been present everywhere.

Thus it is justified to introduce [the subject of exchange] into our investigation [of the Middle Ages].

Exchange always begins where organized production reaches its limit in time or space.

The economic foundation for exchange is the productivity of labor and the surplus produced by it. The expansion of exchange occurs to the same extent that it becomes habitual.

From the outset* it [exchange] is limited to individual instances and to certain objects that, because of favorable conditions, are more abundantly available. That which succeeds in becoming the possession of another tribe or people soon becomes a need there. Thus exchange becomes a necessity, and production for this exchange becomes a rule.

This exchange also stimulates the production of other goods. It spreads further. There are more and more objects that are produced in advance for exchange, that is, as commodities.

To the extent that more products are brought within the sphere of the exchange process, as exchange spreads wider, the greater the need grows for a designated means for exchange.

---

* At this point in the typescript, the following typewritten note appears in the margin: "'from the outset' obviously means 'in the beginning.'"

An example of the difficulties for the exchange process when such a universal means of exchange is lacking is as follows: [Jérome] Becker found a Black African tribe at the headwaters of the Nile* which would exchange only meat for other products. In order to obtain flour, hammers (or spades) were offered in exchange, along with cloth. For the hammers an ox was offered in trade, which was then slaughtered and cut into pieces. Only in exchange for these pieces of meat could the desired flour then be obtained from the tribe in question.

For us, cattle are the most important of all the means of exchange because it became the means of exchange for the peoples who were the ancestors of our culture.

Metal money later took the place of cattle. From the outset it represented socially necessary labor.

Gold is the highest form of money because consumption value is attached to it only to a very small extent. It is precisely for that reason that it represents socially necessary labor in its purest form. It possesses hardly any everyday usefulness.

The outer aspect of the social development of money reaches its peak in gold. Money did not develop originally in the Middle Ages, but had its origins in the early ancient world, in the Orient.†

In the early Middle Ages, in contrast, the natural economy predominates. Only with the development of commodity production does the money economy reappear here. Thus, the development [of the money economy] had to become so widespread it was necessary to represent social labor in a form that had no consumption value. The development of money thus recurs many times.

And each time the development of money is nothing more than a reflection of the development of the relations of production within a specific cultural area or region.

The capitalist form of economy endeavors to spread commodity production over the entire globe. With that it also spreads the money economy to the same extent. The world economy has turned money into world money.

Commodity production and the money economy form the basis on which the capitalist economy is built.

With the elimination of this economic form these two fundamental pillars [on which it rests] must also disappear.

They are the foundation and characteristic feature of this unplanned mode of economic production, namely, the capitalist mode of production.

---

* Jérome Becker was a Belgian explorer who searched for the origin of the Nile River, reaching Lake Albert in 1864. Luxemburg may have known of his book, *La Vie en Afrique ou Trois Ans dans l'Afrique* (Life in Africa, or Three Years in Africa) (Paris: J. Lebéque et Cie, 1887).

† By "the Orient" Luxemburg seems to mean the civilizations of Egypt, Mesopotamia, Persia, and other regions to the east and south of the Mediterranean.

Capitalism develops within itself the preconditions for a new mode of production, which through historical necessity must surely replace it.

That is the socialist economy, organized on a planned basis.

With that we end these investigations [into the Middle Ages], at the point where Marx steps in with his investigation into and critique of the capitalist mode of production.

REFERENCES

Statistisches Jahrbuch für Deutschland [Statistical Yearbook for Germany]*

Putzger: *Geschichts-Atlas.* [Historical Atlas][†]

Perthes: *Taschen-Atlas.* [Pocket Atlas][‡]

Plötz: *Auszug aus der Geschichte.* [Excerpt from History][§]

Bücher: *Entstehung der Volkswirtschaft.* [Origin of Economics][¶]

Engels: *Die Lage der arbeitenden Klassen in England*
              [Condition of the Working Class in England]

Engels: *Die Entwicklung des Sozialismus von der Utopie zur Wissenschaft.*
              [Socialism, Utopian and Scientific][**]

Lippert: *Kulturgeschichte, I. Band.* [History of Culture, Vol. 1])[††]

Ratzel: *Völkerkunde.* [Ethnology][‡‡]

Engels: *Der Anteil der Arbeit an der Menschwerdung des Affen*
              [The Part Played by Labor in the Transition from Ape to Man], *Neue Zeit*, Year 14, Vol. 2, p. 545.[§§]

Weitling: *Garantien der Harmonie und Freiheit.* [Guarantees of Harmony and Freedom][¶¶]

---

* The *Statistisches Jahrbuch für das Deutsche Reich* was published yearly, beginning in 1880, by Puttkammer & Mühlbrecht (Berlin).

† *F.W. Putzgers Historischer Schul-Atlas.*

‡ Justus Perthes, *Taschenatlas der ganzen Welt* (Pocket Atlas of the Entire World History) (Hamburg: J. Perthes, 1896). This popular atlas has appeared in many editions since the nineteenth century.

§ See Karl Julius Ploetz, *Auszug aus der alten, mittleren und neuren Geschichte.*

¶ Karl Bücher, *Die Entehung der Volkswirtschalt, Vorträge und Aufsätze.*

** Engels's *Condition of the Working Class in England* was first published in Leipzig in 1845. *Socialism, Utopian and Scientific* was first published in 1880 in the March, April and May issues of *Revue Socialiste.*

†† Julius Lippert, *Kulturgreschichte der Menschheit in ihrem organischen Aufbau* (The Cultural History of Humanity in its Organic Structure) (Stuttgart: F. Enke, 1886).

‡‡ Friedrich Ratzel, *Grundzüge der Völkerkunde* (Fundamentals of Ethnology) (Leipzig: Bibliographisches Institut, 1895).

§§ Engels first wrote this in 1876, as part of a planned work entitled *Die drei Grundformen der Knechtschaft* (The Three Basic Forms of Bondsmanship). It was never completed in this form, however, and Engels later included it in *Dialectics of Nature*, in 1896. It was originally published in *Die Neue Zeit* in 1895.

¶¶ Wilhelm Weitling, *Garantien der Harmonie und Freiheit* (Guarantees of Harmony and Freedom) (Hamburg: Im Verlag des Verfassers, 1842). The work was referred to several times by the young Marx, who initially had a favorable impression of Weitling.

Morgan: *Die Urgesellschaft.* [Ancient Society]*

Maurer: *Einleitung zur Geschichte der Mark-, Hof-, Fron- und Dorfverfassung.* [Introduction to the History of the Mark, Court, Village and Town Constitution]

Caesar: *Der gallische Krieg.* [The Gallic Wars]†

Cunow: *Die soziale Verfassung des Inkareiches.* [The Social Constitution of the Inca Empire]‡

Macaulay: Warren Hastings.

Macaulay: Lord Clive.§

Haxthausen: *Studien über die inneren Zustände usw. in Russland.* [Studies on Internal Conditions, etc., of Russia]¶

Plekhanov: Chernyshevsky.**

Engels: *Internationales aus dem Volksstaat. Soziales aus Russland.* [International Material from *Der Volkstaat.* Social Material from Russia]††

Tschuproff: *Die Feldgemeinschaft.* [The Rural Community]‡‡

             Handwörterbuch der Staatswissenschaften. [Concise Dictionary of the Political Sciences], article on the "Mir" (this is the Russian Mark)§§

---

* Lewis Henry Morgan's book first appeared in English in 1877, under the title *Ancient Society, or: Researches in the Lines of Human Progress from Savagery Through Barbarism to Civilization* (London: MacMillan & Co., 1877). Luxemburg made use of the German edition, *Die Urgesellshaft oder Untersuchung über den Fortschritt der Menschheit aus der Wildheit durch die Babarei zur Zivilisation* (Berlin: J.H.W. Dietz Verlag, 1891).

† Luxemburg was using the German edition of Julius Ceaser's *De bello Gallico,* his commentaries on the Gallic Wars. For a modern English translation, see *The Conquest of Gaul,* translated by S.A. Handford (New York: Penguin, 1983).

‡ Heinrich Cunow, *Die Soziale Verfassung des Inkareiches: Eine Untersuchung des altperuanischen Agrarkommunismus* (The Social Constitution of the Inca Empire: An Examination of Ancient Peruvian Agrarian Communism) (Stuttgart: J.H.W. Dietz Verlag, 1896).

§ Thomas Babington Macaulay's "Lord Clive" was an essay written in January 1840. Clive was a British officer who established England's control over India following the Battle of Plassey in 1757, which drove French forces from the country. "Warren Hastings," first published as an essay in 1841, discussed British colonial policies in India. Hastings served as the first Governor-General of India, from 1773–85. A supporter of British colonialism, Macaulay helped govern India from 1834–38. See his *Essays on Lord Clive and Warren Hastings* (Whitefish, MT: Kessinger Publishing, 2005).

¶ See August Freiherr von Haxthausen, *Studien über die Innern Zustände, des Volksleben und Insbesondere die ländlichen Einrichtungen Rußlands* (Studies on the Internal Conditions of Russia, the Life of its People and Especially its Rural Institutions) (Hannover: Hahn, 1847–52).

** See G.V. Plekhanov, *N.G. Chernyshevsky* (St. Petersburg: Shipovnik Publishing House, 1910). This book contains a series of articles on Chernyshevsky written by Plekhanov in *Sotsial-Democrat* in 1890 and 1892.

†† Engels's essay on "Russia and the Social Revolution" was first published in *Volkstaat* on April 21, 1875. It was reprinted in the booklet *Internationales aus dem 'Volksstaat'* (1871–75) (Berlin: J.H.W. Dietz Verlag, 1894). An English translation can be found in *Marx-Engels Collected Works,* Volume 24 (New York: International Publishers, 1989), pp. 39–50.

‡‡ See Aleksandr Alexandrovich Chuprov, *Die Feldemeinscaft, eine morphologische Untersuchung* (The Field of Community: A Morphological Study) (Strassburg: K.J. Trübner, 1902). The Russian last name Чупров is transliterated into English as Chuprov, but into German as Tschuproff.

§§ See Eduard Meyer's article on the Russian mir (a peasant community owning and working land in common), in the *Concise Dictionary of the Political Sciences.*

Parvus: *Das hungernde Russland.* [Starving Russia]*

Engels: *Anti-Dühring.*[†] Theory of Violence

Engels: *Ursprung der Familie.* [Origin of the Family, Private Property, and the State][‡]

Kautsky: *Ursprung des Christentums;* die Sklavenwirtschaft. [Foundations of Christianity; The Slave Economy][§]

Eduard Meyer: *Geschichte des Altertums.* [History of Antiquity]

Eduard Meyer: *Sklaverei im Altertum.* [Slavery in Antiquity]

Eduard Meyer: Entwicklung des Wirtschaftslebens im Altertum. [Development of Economic Life in Antiquity][¶]

Handwörterbuch der Staatswissenschaften [The Concise Dictionary of Political Sciences]: articles "Bevölkerung im Altertum," [Population in Antiquity] "Agrarverhältnisse im Altertum." [Agrarian Relations in Antiquity][**]

Beloch: *Griechische Geschichte.* [Greek History][††]

Ernst: *Neue Zeit,* 11. Jahrgang, 2. Band.[‡‡]

Kautsky: *Vorläufer des Sozialismus; Plato und der griechische Staat.* [Forerunners of Socialism: Plato and the Greek State][§§]

Mommsen: *Römische Geschichte.* [History of Rome]

Lassalle: *Kapital und Arbeit.* [Capital and Labor] (Description of feudal economy)

---

* Alexander Parvus (Israel Lazarevich Helphand), *Das hungernde Russland. Reiseeindrücke, Beobachtungen und Untersuchungen* (Starving Russia: Travel Impressions, Observations, and Investigations) (Berlin: J.W.H. Dietz, 1900).

† Friedrich Engels, *Herrn Eugen Dühring's Umwalzung der Wissenschaft; Anti-Dühring: Herr Eugen Dühring's Revolution in Science, Marx-Engels Collected Works,* Vol. 25, pp. 146–71.

‡ Frederick Engels, *Origin of the Family, Private Property and the State* (New York: International Publishers, 1964)

§ Karl Kautsky, *Der Ursprung des Christentrums: Eine historische Untersuchung.* For an English translation, see *Foundations of Christianity,* translated by Jacob Hartmann (New York: Monthly Review, 1972). "Slave Economy" appears to be a reference to the fourth section of Part I of this book, entitled "Die technische Rückständigkeit der Sklavenwirtschaft" (The Technological Backwardness of the Slave Economy).

¶ See Eduard Meyer's *Geschichte des Altertums* (History of Antiquity), five volumes (Stuttgart and Berlin, J.G. Cotta, 1884–1902) and *Sklaverei im Altertrum* (Slavery in Antiquity) (Dresden: v. Jahn & Jaensch, 1898). Luxemburg provides a somewhat inaccurate title of the third work; it is actually *Wirtschaftliche Entwicklung des Altertums* (Economic Development of the Ancient World) (Jena: G. Fischer, 1895).

** The *Handwörterbuch der Staatswissenschaften* (Jena: G. Fischer), edited by Johannes Conrad, Wilhem Lexis, L. Elster, and Edgar Loening, appeared in four editions between 1890 and 1928. "Population in Antiquity" was an article by Eduard Meyer. See *Handwörterbuch der Staatswissenschaften,* second edition, Vol. II (1899), pp. 674 ff. "Agrarian Relations in Antiquity" was an article by Max Weber. See Max Weber, "Agrargeschichte. I: Agrarverhältnisse im Altertum," in *Handwörterbuch der Staatswissenschaften,* second edition, Vol. 1, Jena 1898, pp. 69 ff.

†† Karl Julius Beloch, *Griechische Geschichte* (Greek History), four volumes (Strassburg: Verlag von Karl J. Trubner, 1893–1904).

‡‡ This refers to a series of articles by Paul Ernst under the title "Die sozialen Zustände im römishcen Reiche vor dem Einfall der Barbaren" (Social Conditions in the Roman Empire Before the Invasion of the Barbarians), published in Vol. XI of *Die Neue Zeit,* in 1893.

§§ Karl Kautsky, *Vorläufer des neueren Sozialismus. Erster Band: Plato* (Forerunners of Modern Socialism: Vol. 1, Plato) (Stuttgart: J.H.W. Dietz, 1895).

Lassalle: *Indirekte Steuern.* [Indirect Taxes]
Willibald   *Der Roland von Berlin.* [Roland of Berlin]*
Alexis:
Professor   *Das Aufkommen des Handwerks in den deutschen Städten.* [The Rise of
Arnold, Basel: Craft Production in the German Cities]
Schiller: *Der Abfall der Niederlande.* [Revolt of the Netherlands]
Goethe: *Egmont.*
Sartorius von   *Geschichte der Hansa* [History of the Hanse]
Waltershausen:
Marx: *Das Kapital.* [Capital]

Literature on Feudalism and on the Development of Cities:†

Ludwig von   *Einleitung zur Geschichte der Mark-, Hof-. Dorf- und Stadtverfassung*
Maurer:‡   [Introduction to the History of the Mark, Court, Village and Town
                 Constitution (Publisher Ignaz Brand, Vienna, cost 6.50 Marks)
Ludwig von   *Geschichte der Städteverfassung* (Many volumes) [History of the City
Maurer: Constitution]
Engels: *Die Lage der arbeitenden Klassen in England.* [The Condition of the
                 Working Class in England]
Engels: *Bauernkrieg.* [The Peasant War in Germany]
W. Wolff: *Die schlesische Milliarde.* [The Silesian Billion]
Willibald   *Der Roland von Berlin* (and other novels by him).
Alexis:
Fr.v. Schiller: *Abfall der Niederlandeo* [Revolt of the Netherlands]
Goethe: *Egmont.*
Guizot: *Geschichte der Zivilisation in Frankreich* [History of Civilization in
                 France], first published in 1830–32.
Thierry: *Betrachtungen über die Geschichte Frankreichs* [Observations on the
                 History of France] 1840.
Thierry: *Geschichte des 3. Standes im Mittelalter.* [History of the Third Estate in
                 the Middle Ages]
Savigny: *Geschichte des römischen Rechts.* [History of Roman Law]

---

   *   Willibald Alexis was the pseudonym of Georg Wilhelm Heinrich Häring, who in the mid-nineteenth published a historical novel of the Middle Ages entitled *Der Roland von Berlin* (Leipzig: Brockhaus, 1840).
   †   The following note appears right before this subhead; it is not by Luxemburg, but apparently by a student who had attended her course: "This lengthy listing of references, before it can be used, must be checked for accuracy. Some information about the books listed is deficient and obviously not precise. As I recall, and as can be deduced from a hint in the 'stenogram' [i.e., the typescript], I received it [this listing] from another student. Both of my own listings on page 28 and page 100 are, I believe, more precise, but some of the books mentioned here are lacking there. And it is possible that in my text, too, deficient information about the books listed may be scattered about even more widely, and that needs to be checked." The page numbers "28" and "100" do not seem to refer to anything in Luxemburg's typescript. This suggests that Luxemburg distributed copies of these typescripts to the students attending her courses (no more than 30 per year, according to her own report). That may help explain how this damaged copy of a typescript survived when so much of Luxemburg's written material was destroyed.
   ‡   Most of the authors and titles in this list repeat what was contained in the earlier list of literature immediately above, or elsewhere in the typescript.

Lassalle: *Kapital und Arbeit.* [Capital and Labor]
Eichhorn: *Über den Ursprung der Städteverfassung in Deutschland.* [On the
                   Origin of the Constitution of the City in Germany]
Lassalle: *Indirekte Steuern.* [Indirect Taxes]
Gaupp: *Über deutsche Städtegründung* [On the Founding of German Cities]
                   1824.
Leo: *Entwicklung der Verfassung der lombardischen Städte.* [Development of
                   the Constitution of the Lombard Cities]
Wilda: *Über das Gildenwesen im Mittelalter* [On the Guild System in the
                   Middle Ages] 1831.
Hüllmann: *Städtewesen im Mittelalter* [City Structure in the Middle Ages] 1827.
Arnold [in]   *Das Aufkommen des Handwerks in den deutschen Städten.* [The Rise of
Basel: Craft Production in the German Cities]
Putzger: *Geschichts-Atlas.* [Historical Atlas]
Perthes: *Taschen-Atlas.* [Pocket Atlas]
Bücher: *Entstehung der Volkswirtschaft.* [Origin of Economics]

Literatur zur Hansa (Literature on the Hanseatic League):

Sartorius von   *Geschichte der Hansa.* (History of the Hanse)
Waltershausen

Practical Economics:
Volume 2 of Marx's *Capital**

Volume 2 is rather divergent in character from Volume 1. *Volume 2 has more of a theoretical and scientific character*. It deals with problems that do not lend themselves to immediate application for use in practical life, for example, in agitational work. *On the other hand, it is especially important for solving the problem of economic crises*. Other than that, unfortunately, Volume 2 is [like] a quantity of capital that has not yet been put to use, that has not shown a profit.

If we want to read the whole of *Capital*—this is what Comrade Luxemburg recommends to us†—we can "with a clear conscience" skip over Volume 2, to begin with, in order to [go ahead and] read Volume 3. Volume 3 deals with problems that coincide more directly with the observations made by an ordinary person in practical life.

Volume 2 deals with the process of circulation of capital. The circulation of capital is the total process that capital as a whole goes through. This encompasses the purchase of raw materials, and of means of production, the actual production process itself, and the sale of the goods produced. The circulation process is the entire circuit completed by capital.

Volume 1 deals with the middle phase, which is the decisive one, the most important, because it shows where surplus value comes from.

It is not only the individual phases that belong to the overall process of circulation, but also certain periods of time that depend on the conditions of commodity exchange on the market.

Depending on the branch of production in which a [particular quantity of] capital is employed, and depending on the state or condition of the market [in general], these time periods may be longer or shorter, [that is,] the time periods that are used for the purchase of raw materials, the production of the commodities, and then their sale.

To begin with, [let us consider] the acquisition of the means of production. There are branches [of the economy] in which the raw materials and tools are

---

    * It is not entirely clear why the heading "Practical Economics" appears at the top of this typescript about Volume 2 of *Capital*, since as Luxemburg noted in the first paragraph, Volume 2 "deals with problems that do not lend themselves to immediate application in practical life, for example, in agitation." However, since most of the manuscript is not directly on the content of Volume 2 but on the history of actual capitalist crises, Luxemburg may have intended her discussion here to be more directed towards the "practical" application of *Capital* to the history of political economy.

    † The student or secretary who transcribed Luxemburg's lecture on this subject, presumably Rosi Wolfstein at the SPD Party School in Berlin, refers to her here in the third person, as "Comrade Luxemburg." This will occur several times in the transcript.

present right there on the spot. *In mining, for example, the time [necessary] for the acquisition of raw materials drops out of consideration entirely.* In other branches, where materials are worked up, [the time necessary for] the acquisition of the materials has to be added. Depending on whether these raw materials need to be brought from far away or are produced nearby, the time necessary for getting hold of them will be longer or shorter.

Depending on *where the markets for the sale of the commodities are located,* the time necessary to reach the market will of course be longer or shorter. In the food industry, for example, the realization of the commodities [must] take place immediately after they are produced and in a continuous, unbroken process. On the other hand, in the clothing industry, which is put to work at particular times, production is linked with longer time intervals, in [a situation in] which larger quantities of goods are placed on the market at the appropriate "season." Here the realization of the commodities takes a longer time.

Also in the phase of actual production we see greater differences, depending on the state of the technology and the particular characteristics of the production process. To a certain extent it can be said that the length of the production process is shortened by advances in technology. For example, today in contrast to former times, it is possible for products that have to be dried before they are completely finished to be *dried by chemical processes.* Previously one had to rely on natural drying.

The means of transport and their development can enormously reduce the time that capital needs to get hold of goods and get rid of them.

The development of production *on the world market* gives capital the possibility of making it easier to obtain raw materials.

In addition there occurs the building up of the credit system, which accelerates commodity production in general.

The development of technology contributes to shortening the turnover time for capital. But there are quite large differences among the various branches of production. An important consequence follows from this for the production of surplus value:

The amount of surplus value that one quantity of capital obtains depends on the size of the variable capital during a certain time span. One may take three equal quantities of capital, with the same amount of variable capital, and the same degree of intensity of exploitation. All three will have a different turnover time. One quantity of capital will turn over in all of three months (that is, after three months the capitalist will have turned everything back into money); another capital will require all year, and the third all of two years. Given that the law of value remains in full force and that surplus value is fully calculated and its derivation fully ascertained, it is only from the variable capital, on the basis

---

*   This is because in mining the raw materials are right there at the mining site.

of different turnover times, that a great disparity would necessarily arise in the surplus value of the individual quantities of capital.

We come now to questions that Volume 1 of *Capital* dealt with, questions such as: *How is surplus value divided up among the individual capitalists so that, on the one hand, the law of value is not violated* (that is, the law according to which commodities are bought or sold in accordance with the amount of labor that has gone into them), *and so that, on the other hand, each individual quantity of capital earns an equal profit?*

If no equalization [of profits] takes place, then the capitalists would invest their capital in *those* branches of industry that have the shortest possible turnover time. That would have [the following] effect on the production process: prices would be reduced and therefore so would surplus value.

How far down would surplus value go? Down to the amount that is produced in the next [longest] category [in terms of turnover time], that is, in the category of capital that turns over in one year.

In the latter category, however, an outflow of capital has taken place, back into the first category [where] the turnover time is only three months. Thus there is reduced production, from which there follows a rise in prices and because of that, a rise in the rate of surplus value. As a result there is again an inflow of capital, because to capital it is all the same whether it is employed in businesses that turn over four times a year or in businesses that turn over only once a year, as long as the latter yield the same amount of surplus value as those that turn over four times a year.

The difference in turnover times brings about a movement of capital from one branch of production into others. The purpose of this process of equalization is to arrive at [roughly] the same amount of surplus value [for all capitalists]. And this goes on in such a way that the production that is put to work for society is always subject to fluctuation. *But this coincides with the needs of society, with social demand.* That is the other aspect which determines how far the overfulfillment of production can go.

The satisfaction of needs in the various spheres of society is regulated by the movement of capital. On the other hand, by the same token, this movement of capital represents a dividing-up of the total capital among the various branches of production, a division that corresponds to the needs of society.

Volume 2 of *Capital* breaks down into two parts.[*] It[†] gives special treatment to the conditions [necessary] for the realization of the commodities produced by capital to be carried out smoothly.

---

[*]   Volume 2 actually has *three* parts: (1) "The Metamorphoses of Capital and their Circuit"; (2) "The Turnover of Capital"; and (3) "The Reproduction and Circulation of the Total Social Capital."

[†]   This is a reference to the third part of Volume 2 of *Capital*.

It turns out that the content of this volume mainly provides material for solving the question of crises, although Marx seldom mentions the term "crisis" in this volume.[*]

As an introduction to Volume 2, then, [I will say] a few words about the history of *crises* and an overview of the crises that happened in the nineteenth century.

The economic crisis of 1815 in England provided the impetus for a theory of economic crises to be developed.

That crisis is not a characteristic crisis of modern society; it does not belong among the crises that grew out of economic conditions. The series of [periodical] economic crises in modern times therefore is usually dated from 1825.

The crisis of 1815 was the consequence of [Napoleon's] Continental System, and thus it came about for political reasons. The Continental System was imposed in 1806 against England. It lasted until 1812–13. It was supposed to destroy England. It forbade the import of English goods into any country on the Continent of Europe. English subjects living in countries that were part of the Continental System were declared to be prisoners of war and their fortunes were confiscated.

Actually the result of this blockade was the following: it gave rise to a huge smuggling industry. America brought in English goods under the American flag. Also, industry in Europe developed as a result of the absence of English competition. The spinning mills in Vogtland date from this time.

During the blockade England calculated that after the lifting of the blockade a huge new market would open up. For this reason it built up large stocks of goods. *When the blockade was lifted, however, things turned out differently* from what England thought.

Demand was not as large as England had expected. This resulted in 1815 in the first crisis to occur in England, mainly in the cotton industry.

This occurrence in and of itself provided the impetus for a major disagreement and dispute between English and French economists.

The theories of *Malthus, Say,* and *Sismondi* now come under consideration.

The first person who looked into the question of economic crises from the standpoint of the working class was Robert Owen. In his writings of 1815, 1818, and 1823[†] he sought to explain the crises by the contradiction between rising

---

[*]   For Marx's discussions of crisis, see *Capital* Vol. 2, translated by David Fernbach (New York: Vintage, 1981), pp. 153–7, 391–3 and 486–7 especially. Marx's theory of crisis, however, is delineated not in Volume 2 but in Volume 3 of *Capital*, in his discussion of the tendency of the rate of profit to decline. Luxemburg tended to deny the relevance of Marx's theory of tendential decline in profit rates, on the grounds that it contradicted empirical capitalist reality.

[†]   This is a reference to Owen's works, *Observations on the Effect of the Manufacturing System* (London: R. & A. Taylor, 1815); *Two Memorials on Behalf of the Working Classes* (London, Longman, Hurst, Orme & Brown, 1818); and *An Explanation of the Cause of Distress which Pervades the Civilized Parts of the World* (London: British Philanthropic Society, 1823).

productivity from the introduction of machinery and the lowering of wages, which was also caused by the introduction of machinery. This explanation is very interesting. Owen derived it independently of Ricardian theory. *As a remedy for the crises Owen called for employment of the workers by the state.*

That was the first democratic and socialist theory about economic crises.

Malthus came out against that and Sismondi followed along with him.

Malthus derived the source of crises primarily from the division of income and the urge to economize on the part of the industrial capitalists. He saw as the reason for the crises the fact that, owing to the capitalists' drive to economize, consumption did not increase satisfactorily, which produces nothing. *As a remedy Malthus called for an increase in the large number of unproductive consumers (the nobility, the court, etc.) and a higher level of expenditures for the military, the navy, the bureaucracy, and so forth.*[*]

The theory of [Max] Schippel shows up as a minor reflection of this theory [of Malthus].[†]

According to Malthus, improving the conditions of the workers is not a remedy for the crises. Because, as Malthus explains, the workers consume only as much as they earn in wages. Thus they can only replace capital with capital.

Sismondi takes the same point of departure as Malthus.[‡] However, he also sees the remedy as being to increase the purchasing power of the working masses. Thus he finds himself in a contradiction from which he cannot extricate himself. This is shown by the fact that he himself concedes: if one increases purchasing power and improves the condition of the workers, that will have a blunting effect on the capitalists' drive for accumulation. And then production will not be able to expand. He seeks the middle ground in his truly petty bourgeois approach:

---

[*] See Thomas Robert Malthus, *An Essay on the Principle of Population* (London: Johnson, 1803) and *Definitions in Political Economy; Preceded by an Inquiry into the Rules which Ought to Guide Political Economists in the Definition and Use of their Terms; With Remarks on the Deviation from these Rules in their Writings* (London: John Murray, 1827).

[†] Luxemburg is especially referring to Schippel's articles, "War Friedrich Engels milizgläubisch?" (Did Friedrich Engels Believe in the Militia?), in *Sozialistischen Monatsheften* (November 1898) and "Friedrich Engels und das Milizsystem" (Friedrich Engels and the Militia System), in *Die Neue Zeit*, Nos. 19–20 (1898/99). Luxemburg replied to Schippel in articles in the *Leipziger Volkszeitung*, Nos. 42–44, 47 (February 20–22, 25, 1899), which she incorporated as an appendix to her *Reform or Revolution*. See Rosa Luxemburg, *Gesammelte Werke*, Band 1/1 (Berlin: Dietz Verlag, 2007), pp. 446–66. For an English translation of two of these four articles by Luxemburg, see "Militia and Militarism," in *Rosa Luxemburg, Selected Political Writings*, edited by Dick Howard (New York: Monthly Review, 1971), pp. 135–58. See also Schippel's *Hochkonjunktur und Wirtschaftskrisis* (Boom and Economic Crisis) (Berlin: Vorwärts, 1908). Schippel, a right-wing revisionist who supported German imperialism, used this argument to defend the necessity of a standing army and militarism.

[‡] See Jean Charles Léonard Simonde de Sismondi, *Nouveaux principes d'économie politique, ou De la richesse dans ses rapports avec la population* (New Principles of Political Economy, or Wealth in its Relationship with Population) (Paris: Delaunay, 1819).

not such a rapid accumulation of capital, but on the other hand an improvement in the condition of the workers.

Say came out in opposition to all of these. He attached himself likewise to the theory of value of the classical political economists. But he applied the theory in such a way that it was a slap in the face to the Smith-Ricardo school. This is what Say said:

Exchange consists of exchange between economies of equal value. Money is only an intermediary. How can one speak of the possibility of a crisis when each commodity represents nothing other than a demand for other commodities, but rather also [*MS. Missing words*]

According to Say's theory, a general condition of overproduction is impossible; only a partial overproduction.* If overproduction begins [in one area], that is only proof that there is underproduction in other branches [of the economy]; therefore the remedy for crises is an increase of production in those branches of the economy where underproduction exists.

The critique made by Say is based on a misjudgment about the actual conditions, which made universal barter† impossible and made the development of money necessary.

After Say came the agrarian reformers. They derived the causes of crises from private ownership of the land.

Thus we see, on the one hand, the derivation of crises from the unequal distribution of income.

The democratic trend sees, as the means for eliminating crises, increasing the purchasing power of the masses.

The other trend hopes to eliminate crises by increasing capitalist production.

Then came Marx. He said that crises are a result of the unregulated mode of production that is capitalism.

Professor [Heinrich] Herkner at Zurich University has learned a lot from Marx. In the fifth volume of the *Handwörterbuch der Staatswissenschaften* there is a treatment and discussion of crises by him. But in this treatment he introduces other conceptions as well.‡

---

*   See Jean-Baptiste Say, *Traité d'économie politique, ou simple exposition de la manière dont se forment, se distribuent ou se consomment les richesses* (Treatise on Political Economy, or a Simple Exposition to Show How Wealth is Created, Distributed, and Consumed) (Paris: Horace Say, 1803). Say argued that crises of overproduction are impossible, on the grounds that production creates its own market.

†   That is, the direct exchange of commodities.

‡   See Heinrich Herkner, "Krisen," in *Handwörterbuch der Staatswissenschaften*, edited by J. Conrad et. al, second edition, Vol. 5 (Jena: G. Fischer, 1900), pp. 413–33. Herkner was initially known as a "socialist of the chair" and close enough to the Social Democratic movement to be praised by Karl Kautsky and invited for a discussion with Friedrich Engels. By 1907, however, he became a political conservative. Herkner had an eclectic explanation of crises, attributing them not to any single phenomena but to a diverse array of factors. However, he was close to Sismondi in emphasizing underconsumption as a prime determinant. As one recent study notes, "Herkner

In 1866 a special inquiry was authorized to investigate economic crises in America. This investigation named 180 causes of crises.[*] Numerous individual factors were named that certainly were correct. But only when the particularities are all brought together can we see where the responsibility lies for crises: namely the entire unregulated system of capitalist production.

[Mikhail Ivanovich] *Tugan-Baranovsky*, who had earlier been a Marxist and is now a revisionist, once commented as follows on Marx's theory of crises:

The breeding grounds from which crises originate are in the so-called heavy industries: the iron, coal, and machine industries. These industries are the direct producers of means of production. According to Tugan-Baranovsky, crises originate out of a disproportion, that is, the lack of a proper ratio, or relationship, between the different branches of industry in which the means of production are made and those in which the means of consumption are produced.

As far as recent years are concerned, what Tugan-Baranovsky said is right. But what does this deficient relationship signify? If Baranovsky wants nothing more than to particularize it more exactly and establish it more precisely, he is right. But that does not bring us one single step further. However, if Baranovsky wants to say by this that on the basis of present-day society a means exists for the establishing of a correct relationship between these branches of industry, that is a purely utopian bit of imagining.

Thus Baranovsky's attempt is quite equivocal and unclear.

Despite its fuzziness this theory has been welcomed by the world of learned German gentlemen. In particular Professor [Werner] Sombart dealt with it in a lecture he gave in 1903 at the Thirtieth General Assembly of the Association for Social Policy.[†] In this lecture he accepted Tugan-Baranovsky's theory on behalf of German science. But he did try to modify it. He said that crises actually arise from a deficient relation between branches of production that produce inorganic materials, on the one hand, and the branches that produce organic materials on the other. By organic materials Professor Sombart apparently means

---

also points to increases in the productivity of labor, which are linked to technological change. As a consequence of the new, more efficient techniques, the price of commodities declines, which leads to their greater saleability. However, expansion of the market very often cannot keep abreast of an increase in production because price decreases come into force only incompletely and with delay." See Harald Hagemann, "Heinrich Herkner: Inequality of Income Distribution, Overcapitalization and Underconsumption," in *Crises and Cycles in Economic Dictionaries and Encyclopedias*, edited by Daniele Besomi (London: Routledge, 2012), pp. 361–73.

[*] See *Industrial Depressions: The First Annual Report of the Commission of Labor* (Washington, DC: Government Printing Office, 1886), especially Chapter 1, "Modern Industrial Depressions," pp. 61–3, for its list of 180 causes of crises, which range from "planless production" and "speculation" to "lack of interest of the laborer in his work." We wish to thank Daniele Besomi for drawing our attention to this document.

[†] Sombart's lecture was delivered in two parts, on September 14 and 16, 1903. For a fuller discussion of Sombart's speech on Luxemburg's part, see "Im Raten der Gelehrten," in *Gesammelte Werke*, Band 1, Zweiter Halbband (Berlin: Dietz Verlag, 2000), pp. 382–90. Her essay first appeared in *Die Neue Zeit*, Year 22, 1903/04, Band 1 (1), pp. 5–10.

food products, and by inorganic he means coal, etc. This attempt of Sombart's is not to be taken seriously because it is no longer in the realm of political economy.

The Succession of Crises

1. 1815 in England
2. 1825 in England
3. 1836–39 in England and the United States (some call this the Panic of 1837, but it actually lasted three years)
4. 1847
5. 1857
6. 1864–66
7. 1873
8. 1882
9. 1891–92
10. 1893 (this was especially an American crisis)
11. 1895
12. 1900/1901
13. 1907

Crises are a fundamental ailment of present-day society. And no cure for them has been cultivated in present-day society.

The question, however, arises of *how* one is to understand this theory [of crisis]. One may draw different conclusions from it.

In our agitation [in the SPD] one argument is used very widely—that crises arise as a result of insufficient purchasing power among the workers, because of low wages.

It is not only that this argument does not belong to Marx's theory, which is that crises are the result of the present-day mode of production; it is not only that but also the *way* in which this theory is presented.

Marx begins first of all with the fact that he envisions a society that does not produce on a capitalist basis.

In earlier years one of the most important aspects of crises had to do with the building of railroads.

Let us imagine therefore a society based on planning. It adopts an undertaking similar in kind to the large-scale building of railroads. (This is historically valid: for example, in Egypt the building of the pyramids and canals, also in Peru the building of roads, and so forth. It is not relevant whether the project is useful, but simply that it is a large-scale project in which large numbers of people work together and are concentrated in one place.)

Such an undertaking requires large quantities of labor power to be brought together in one arena of labor, and the society does not have the use of that labor for a longer stretch of time. During this whole time, however, this many-headed workforce has to be maintained. This implies that food, and other means of subsistence, as well as the means of production and [appropriate] management have to be provided.

Such an undertaking, in a society based on planning, cannot come into existence if society does not have excess labor power, labor power that can satisfy needs above and beyond current, day-to-day needs. Therefore in the past we see such large-scale undertakings only by way of exception.

A primitive communist society can only put such an undertaking into operation if it is actually in a position to assign a portion of its workers [to this task] and to maintain them regardless of [the amount required for] their daily consumption.

In cases where a class society already exists, no consideration will be given to this. A large mass of workers will be gathered together and thrown into a task even at the expense of a lowering of their living standards, and they will be maintained by the labor of others, for example, in Egypt.

In both cases, an approximate calculation of the labor power that society can spare and the quantity of means of subsistence necessary to maintain such masses of workers—such calculation would have to be done in advance.

The result of this would be a reduced standard of living and [greater] suffering for the masses of the population ...

For the workforce assigned to such a large-scale project, there is an unusually hard and heavy burden of labor. The result might perhaps be that in the course of a year a product has come into existence that is of absolutely no use to society, such as the pyramids.

After the completion of this project, the living labor power would be sent back to its old work assignments, and so nothing like a [modern-day economic] crisis would result from that sort of event.

When the undertaking had ended the earlier standard of living, with living conditions at the same level as before, would be resumed.

Now let us imagine such an undertaking in a capitalist country, for example, the building of railroads.

As soon as the decision is made to found a railroad company, the first necessity is a relatively large quantity of money capital. In order for this to be possible, it is necessary that the prospects exist for capital to obtain a high profit [from investment] in railroad construction.

Capital flows in from all possible spheres of production, and in particular this is done on an international basis. The building of a railroad has never been carried out exclusively, with the *national* capital of *one country alone.*

The very fact that the resources for building a railroad in one country flow in from another country shows that there is no precise [i.e., planned] coordination here. This fact completely excludes the general assumption that can be made when we view any primitive society.*

As soon as capital flows in and concentrates at one particular point, the immediate result is that a large quantity of labor power, plus means of subsistence and means of production, follow along in the wake of that capital.

When there is a demand for money it will be impossible to control all the means that might be available for obtaining money.

As soon as a relatively large mass of workers finds in one location a relatively large availability of employment then wages consequently go way up, this labor power represents a large demand for means of subsistence. The further consequence is a rise in prices in agriculture. Agriculture [in one country] is not in a position to satisfy such a growing demand.

Consequently, the strong demand results in intensified importing of food from other countries. This massive influx of food and other means of subsistence from other countries causes a substantial rise in prices in those other countries, along with an increased desire to export [from those countries].

This results in a boom even in countries that, to begin with, had nothing to do with the railroad construction.

Now the project is carried out. The masses of employed workers disappear. In the meantime a whole series of branches of production have been established on the basis of the railroad construction and alongside of it. They bring their supplies to market at a time when the demand has already disappeared.

From this there arises a crisis. The large market has now been cut off. Then comes a crisis in the countries that were providing goods for the construction of railroads, and then a collapse on the money market and in credit relations on an international basis.

That is approximately a schematic outline of the crises that occurred in the first half of the nineteenth century, which were played out back and forth between England and America.

In the old days people said that crises were the result of overproduction. That is merely a description of the state of affairs. The real answer is: since no one knows how much society needs, too much is produced.

But the correct answer is this: Every relatively large undertaking in society must inevitably bring a crisis in its wake. Because branches of industry have been built up, which then become superfluous after the project is over.

Why is production not expanded to an extent sufficient to meet the demand—why doesn't that take place? Because, after all, it is known that the undertaking will come to an end some day.

---

* Luxemburg is here operating on the assumption that in primitive communal society, economic activities are planned.

Once production has been expanded it cannot just shrivel up artificially. Or if it does, the result is a crisis.

If production is expanded [to a large extent], and then a transition is made [back] to a smaller basis—that will mean a crisis in capitalist society.

Such a state of affairs is inevitable nowadays.

The only means for raising profits is progress in technology, increasing productivity. Raising the level of technology is linked with the expansion of production facilities.

How do the capitalists operate in response to a campaign for wages to be raised, and so forth? With an expansion of technology. And this [in turn] finds expression in an expansion of production.

Again, capitalist production responds to the discovery of new markets with expansion of production.

Its perennial method is the expansion of production.

From this it becomes clear that the actual feature of capitalism that contributes toward crises is that the capitalist mode of production has an inherent tendency toward the constant expansion of production.

What has now happened to the assumption that underconsumption by the masses is to blame for crises, and that therefore the purchasing power of the masses must be increased? What is incorrect about that?

Let us assume that the workers manage to keep their wages at a very high level. The result would again be a large-scale expansion of production. To satisfy the higher level of demand, supply would be raised to an even higher level.

The capitalist mode of production has the tendency to hastily pass beyond every limit, because profit is the only thing it takes into consideration.

What about the assumption that if unproductive expenditures are increased, crises can be avoided—what happens to that assumption? The same thing would then occur as with the raising of wages. The supply would then be increased much more than the higher level of demand by unproductive consumers.

Russia shows that it is precisely very large orders by the state that can immediately call forth a colossal expansion of production, which has the tendency to go speeding past and beyond the increased demand.

The number one necessity for the worker is to make use of every boom in order to get prepared and fitted out as well as possible for the next crisis.

Here is another example of how capitalist society creates crises out of everything and anything, whereas in some other society there would not be the remotest chance that such things would cause a crisis.

What used to happen in any society based on natural economy in the past when an especially rich harvest occurred? Consumption could be increased, depending on the make-up of society. If it were communist, an equal raising of the standard of living for all members would be the consequence, and at the same time a building up of reserves, that is, raising the capacity for maintaining the means of subsistence in the future.

Or if it were a class society: taxes would reach an especially high level [and there would also be] a certain, even if small, increase in the standard of living of the peasants.

In 1906 and 1907 Brazil had a colossal coffee harvest.* The effect was that from month to month the alarming news spread, and panic occurred on all the stock exchanges. Instead of prosperity being increased, the cries of woe in Brazil rose higher because its capital was mainly invested in coffee plantations and now there was a plunge in prices. In order to try to prevent this, the capitalists forced the Brazilian government, at its own expense, to buy up huge quantities of coffee, to hold it in reserve, to withdraw it from the market in order to keep prices at a high level. That was called an act of valorization. This sounded quite outlandish, and was deliberately meant to [do so]. The ordinary person would be unable to make any sense of it.

The state had to buy the coffee. It gave the capitalists a large quantity of money in return for the coffee it was forced to buy up. Naturally this was mainly in government bonds or securities. But interest had to be paid on these securities. Where would the government get the money for that? Naturally from taxes. A monstrous tax burden was placed on the middle class and on the working classes, and the result was a general depression in the country, a colossal wave of layoffs, the firing of workers in Brazil, and businesses in Europe were [also] drawn in [to the crisis] because they had made it possible for the Brazilian government to obtain loans.

In general Brazil was shaken to the core, and that situation has continued up to the present. Sooner or later the government will have to sell the coffee. And then the sword of Damocles will fall, sooner or later the crisis will occur. Or else: voices are already being raised suggesting that the government dump the coffee in the ocean. That is the same method that grain dealers used in the Middle Ages in order to prop up grain prices. Bourgeois historians usually cite this as an example showing how high we have risen above the ancient world and the Middle Ages.

In capitalist production every unusual turn of events in production— whether it be a bad harvest or a bountiful one, whether there is railroad construction going on or stagnation and absence of any such undertakings—all of it leads equally to a crisis.

Marx speaks out strongly against the concept that overproduction or

---

* In 1906 Brazil produced 80 percent of the world's coffee, a total of 22 million sacks. Output so much exceeded demand that the price of coffee immediately fell. World War I stimulated an increase in the demand for coffee; Brazil's harvest of 1917 was 1.6 billion pounds, the largest on record up to that point.

underproduction is to blame for crises. See Volume 2 of *Capital*, page 385 [of the first German edition].*

The first effects of any crisis are always felt in the luxury industries and by their workers.

Robertus derives the source of crises mainly from the underconsumption of the masses. He proposed that profits be shared with the workers engaged in production.

If the raising of wages was an effective means against crises, then no crises would happen. Because the fact of the matter is that in every boom wages go up, and every crisis is preceded by a boom.

The crisis of 1815 was characterized by the destruction of machinery and great tumult.

The first periodic crisis was in 1825. It was preceded by a strong economic upturn in England after the crisis of 1815. There was a big upswing of business activity: the building of canals, the building of roads, installing gasworks for the purpose of lighting (as early as 1814 gas was used for lighting in the streets in the cities of England), and then the founding of banks and speculation in securities.

England's relations with South America played a large role in all of this. Many of the countries there had recently won their independence. Argentina, Brazil, Central America, and so on had constituted themselves as independent states. This was important in part because some of those countries were major suppliers of gold and silver.

The new states began taking out large loans. The [corresponding government bonds] were mainly bought up on the London Stock Exchange. In 1824–25 the governments of South and Central America paid out more than 20 million pounds sterling [in interest on loans]. In addition a large number of shares were traded on the London Stock Exchange, in particular those of mining companies. The stocks, or shares, of joint English-Mexican companies for the exploitation of mines rose in price by 2,500 pounds sterling from December 1824 to January 1825. The shares of another mining company went up 800 pounds. Everything

---

* See Marx, *Das Kapital*, Band 2 (Hamburg: Otto Meissner, 1885), p. 385. Marx writes in *Capital* Vol. 2: "Considered from the standpoint of the whole society, there must be a constant overproduction, i.e. production on a greater scale than is needed for the simple replacement and reproduction of the existing wealth" (pp. 256–7). Since "the periods in which capitalist production exerts all its forces regularly show themselves to be periods of overproduction" (p. 390), the latter cannot be construed as the principal cause of crises. At the same time, Volume Two also argues against the claim that crises are caused by *underconsumption*. Marx writes, "It is a pure tautology to say that crises are provoked by a lack of effective demand or effective consumption. The capitalist system does not recognize any forms of consumer other than those who can pay ... If the attempt is made to give this tautology the semblance of greater profundity, by the statement that the working class receives too small a portion of its own product, and that the evil would be remedied if it received a bigger share, i.e. if wages rose, we need only note that crises are always prepared by a period in which wages generally rise, and the working class actually does receive a greater share in the part of the annual product destined for consumption" (pp. 486–7).

was thrown into speculation on these mining shares. This was facilitated by the fact that payment of only 5 or 10 percent was sufficient to buy a share. Thus even the poorer classes could participate in this giddy craze.

That was the first great speculative craze in paper securities on a stock exchange.

The nominal capital of the stock exchange at that time supposedly amounted to 372 million pounds sterling.

But companies only worth a total of 102 million were present on the stock exchange. Everything else was pure speculation.

Together with this speculation, prices of goods rose to a very high level. Cotton prices rose by 109 percent, prices of pig iron by 77 percent, and sugar by 99 percent ... In connection with all this there was a hasty rush to build new cotton mills in Lancashire, along with the expansion of old mills using bank credit.

Also in South and Central America a large increase in demand for commodities arose.

In 1821 England's exports to those [countries was] ... 2.942 million pounds sterling; in 1825 it was 6.442 million ...

The main export was cotton fabrics.

But these goods were purchased with English money, because that money traveled from the London Stock Exchange to the Americas, and there it was used to buy English goods.

The enlivening of the cotton industry and the raising of prices attracted massive imports from the European countries to England. There was a rapid outflow of gold.

Then suddenly there was a backlash. Prices fell very quickly in London, and the South American countries provided the impetus for the crash by the fact that they did not pay the hoped-for interest on their bonds. They were entirely incapable of doing so.

At that point a panic broke out. The joint-stock companies and the mining industry were not paying the expected dividends, and that spread such a panic that the Bank of England itself in London had to post an extraordinarily high bank rate and refuse to grant credit. That intensified the general turmoil even further, and within six weeks 70 provincial banks crashed, and a whole mass of smaller entrepreneurs and speculators went down with them.

The consequences of the crisis of 1825 are also characteristic. It led to a general cleaning-out, or purge, of industry in the sense that an entire large number of backward manufacturing techniques were abandoned.

Soon after 1825 [there occurred] the universal introduction of the steam-powered loom, along with drastic changes in [the technology of] the iron industry.

After ten years came the crisis of 1836. Extraordinarily good harvests from 1832 to 1836, four years in a row, provided the impetus. Grain imports to

England dropped off, because England was able to get by with its own grain. England ended up with 4 percent of its former exports.* The cheapness of food lowered the price for labor.

Together with this there was an external phenomenon: a strong outflow of English capital to North America. Investments of capital were traveling on a massive scale to America, and consequently a demand for English goods arose there, so that those in turn were paid for with English gold.

In North America [there was] intensive economic activity involving means of transport and [new] industrial enterprises. The shares, or stocks, for these companies were for the most part sold in England.

New banks were founded, 61 of them with a capital totalling 52 million dollars. At the same time as this animated activity involving industrial enterprises there arose a large demand for government-owned land for expanding agriculture, but even more than that for speculation based on the rising prices of land.

All this gave rise to highly intensive demand in America for European goods. England in particular exported to America [on an increasingly large scale].

English Exports to:	1832	1836
America, the United States	5,468†	2,486
Northern European countries	9,897	10,000
Southern European countries	5,867	9,001
Asia	4,235	6,751
Central and South America	4,272	5,955

That is all in thousands of pounds sterling.

In 1833 and 1834 Spain and Portugal became heavily indebted by taking out loans from England. As a result the prices on the stock exchanges rose to an extraordinarily high level.

In 1836, 48 banks were founded in England. The nominal capital of the banks founded between 1832 and 1836 in England amounted to 105.2 million pounds sterling. Of that 69.6 million [was invested] in railroads; 23.8 million [went to] institutions connected with banking; 7.6 million to insurance companies; 7.0 million to mining enterprises; 5.4 million [was invested in] canal building, and so forth.

The impulse that set off the crisis came from the United States. Speculation in land had gone so far in that country that the government at that time had to impose some regulation. It was forbidden to purchase land in any other way than by cash payment. Of course a panic broke out on the stock exchanges in

---

* Luxemburg probably meant to say *imports* here.

† The figures in the table are in thousands of pounds sterling.

America as a result. The American banks frantically sought to obtain gold from England, and consequently panic broke out in England as well.

In 1837,* there were 618 bank failures in the United States ... In England there were no bank failures, it's true, but there were great difficulties, and it was the cotton industry that suffered most from this economic collapse, because it was the main industry exporting to the United States. Great unemployment resulted, with downward pressure on wages, and this crisis contributed very strongly to the activation of the Chartist movement.

Ten years later there followed a third crisis, the crisis of 1847.

A very bad harvest was the initial impulse [for this crisis].

After the crisis of 1837 a depression lasted and reached its bottom in 1842; then the depression tapered off and an upturn began. In 1843 and 1844 there were two good harvests [which meant] cheap food and [increased] demand for manufactured goods. In addition, 1842 saw the opening of the Chinese market. This was connected with the opium war [of 1839–42]. The main [economic] result was that five Chinese ports were declared open to free trade, without any customs duties having to be paid; also the island of Hong Kong was surrendered to England.

In 1844–45 boom times prevailed in England. The cotton industry once again took first place. Large numbers of new cotton mills were founded, very high wages. In addition, there was massive railroad construction in England.

[The following table shows the value of] the total number of licenses for railroad construction granted by Parliament, up through December 1849 [with figures in millions of pounds].

	Licenses granted	Railroads built
1843	81.9	65.8
1844	20.4	6.7
1845	60.5	16.2
1846	131.7	37.8
1847	44.2	40.7
1848	15.3	38.2
1849	3.9	29.6

This railroad construction created a huge demand for workers as well as for goods. Prices for iron increased enormously. From 1844 on, there was madder and madder speculation on railroad construction. In 1845 and 1846 two bad years occurred in agriculture. The potato crop failed. So did the grain crop.

---

*   In the original typescript the year is given as 1834.

In Ireland universal famine broke out, so that Parliament had to send relief [payments] to Ireland [of] 8 million [pounds sterling].

The rise in prices led to wild speculation by grain dealers. That is, massive amounts of grain had to be imported from abroad, and prices rose steeply.

In the United States the cotton crop failed. From 1844 to 1847, prices rose by 65 percent.

In spite of this, the prices of cotton yarn and cotton goods did not go up at all.

The consumption of cotton fabrics in England in 1845 fell by [a quantity worth] 21 million pounds sterling, and in 1846, by 13 million pounds sterling.

Cutbacks in the cotton industry were the necessary consequence. On top of that came business failures on a large scale as a result of grain speculation.

In April and May 1847, English grain traders had purchased enormous quantities of grain in European countries at the very highest prices, grain meant for England. It was delivered in July and August. But meanwhile, in England a very good harvest had come in. Prices fell, and the grain speculators saw themselves ruined. Their bankruptcies brought bank failures in their wake, [including] many banks in Liverpool, and after those a general panic broke out. Then the prices of railroad stocks fell, very suddenly and steeply. A few figures will show this [as follows]:

	In December 1845	In December 1849
Capital invested in railroad construction:	100 million pounds sterling	230 million pounds sterling
The stock exchange price that could actually be obtained for RR shares amounted to:	160 million pounds sterling	110 million pounds sterling
Profits and losses amounted to:	Profits in 1845: 60 million pounds sterling.	Losses in 1849: 120 million pounds sterling.

This meant ruin for the owners of stocks in railroad companies, followed by a general collapse of prices.

The cotton industry suffered the most from this.

Among others, coal and other mining companies suffered in particular.

The Crisis of 1857. The First Big Worldwide Crisis.

In 1854 and 1855 [there was] the first big Australian crisis—a consequence of the feverish gold rushes of 1850–51. [There was also] colossal emigration from Europe to Australia, [along with a colossal] demand for goods, and speculation in mining.

The factors that paved the way for the 1857 world crisis were the following:

A large role [was played by] the abolition of the corn laws* and of other [protective] tariffs; in short, England's transition to free trade.

The assumption that the elimination of tariffs would slow down or eliminate crises corresponded to the theories of Say.

The English advocates of free trade said that if the corn laws and other tariffs were eliminated, crises would end. In 1844, England began to eliminate the corn laws. England abolished almost all protective tariffs. With that, economic activity in England was enlivened in every area, all products became cheaper, and there was a colossal upturn in production.

As a recoil there came the worldwide crisis of 1857. [Leading up to it was] the discovery of gold in California and Australia. In 1850 the annual average extraction of gold in the whole world was worth 150 million marks. In 1853, thanks to the new discoveries, it was 760 million marks.

For the entire world in 1909, the annual extraction of gold amounted to [only] 420 million dollars.

The end of the Crimean War coincided with the crisis of 1857. The holding back of Russian exports of hemp and flax products created the possibility for the crisis to be prolonged.

The era of free trade, the building of railroads, and the profusion of liberal reforms in Russia—all opened the way for the inflow of English products into Russia.

After 1848, France and Germany became powerful participants in the capitalist mode of production. Also contributing to that was: The bourgeoisie [was] on the upswing, [and] the proletariat had been beaten down.

There was a flow of European capital to the United States, which seemed to be the safest place for investments.

According to an estimate by Professor [Albert] Schäffle, in the years 1849–54, a thousand million guilders, that is, one billion, were invested in American securities. A guilder at that time was worth about two marks, and so this was approximately two billion marks.

In 1857, England had possession of American securities worth 80 million pounds sterling.

The Crimean War very much suited the United States. It interrupted the ... At the same time, in the late 1840s and early 1850s, there was massive emigration to the United States from Germany and from Russian Poland.

In the United States, in connection with grain exports, there began a colossal speculation in government-owned lands. In 1852–53 in the United States, public lands worth 1.7 million dollars were purchased as pieces of land to be used for the cultivation of grain. Because America was now exporting grain to Russia.

---

*   The corn laws imposed high tariffs on imported grain.

In the years 1852–54, the value of the public lands that were purchased was 20.4 million dollars.

Along with that, [there was] an impressive amount of railroad construction. In 1856, the rail network in the United States was enlarged by 4,250 miles. A mile is approximately 1.6 kilometers.

The prices of goods rose rapidly, which attracted imports from Europe. In 1857, the import of goods into the United States increased by 32 million dollars. At this same time there was a failure of the cotton crop, and [therefore] very high cotton prices. In spite of that, the cotton industry was greatly expanded. In addition, American banks and import-export dealers engaged in colossal speculation on imports from Europe.

In 1857, [there was] an exceptionally good grain harvest in Europe.

That caused a series of bankruptcies among grain-exporting businesses in America. These bankruptcies brought bank failures in their wake. The failure of one small bank gave the signal for a general panic among all the banks in America.

In December 1857 in America, prices plunged universally by 20 to 30 percent.

The bankruptcy of America meant the immediate bankruptcy of England.

In October, there was a suspension of payments by one Liverpool bank. Thereupon, universal panic [broke out] in England.

From there the crisis was transplanted to France. During the entire nineteenth century [until then] the bank rate of the Bank of France had stood at 4 or 5 percent, but in December 1857 it soared to 10 percent.

The higher a bank rate goes, the harder the bank has to work. An increase in the bank rate is a storm signal.

Then Germany followed, Hamburg in particular.

The bankruptcy of several German commercial firms in England, which engaged in business with Sweden and Denmark, had repercussions in Hamburg. From Hamburg the crisis spread to the main centers of Prussia and at the same time to Sweden and Denmark, as well as to South America.

The collapse in Sweden and Denmark had a recoil effect on Hamburg. And Hamburg is the place in Germany where world trade had its earliest foothold.

Almost all commercial activity in Hamburg came to a stop. Only through some desperate salvation attempts, some very strained efforts by the banks, was a little bit of help forthcoming [for the economy].

The "Cotton Famine" of 1861. This crisis only affected the cotton industry; it was not a general crisis. And indeed it was mainly a local crisis, an English crisis. [This is] an indication that not only worldwide crises come along now.

[Let us take] *a closer look at this crisis, because it is very important.* The cotton famine began with the breaking-off of the import of raw cotton [from] the United States as a result of the Civil War.

In 1860, the cotton industry in England consumed 1,840 million tons of cotton; in 1862, this consumption fell to 452 million tons.

There was a corresponding drop in overall exports from England to the United States, also because of the Civil War.

In 1861, such exports were worth 23 million pounds sterling; in 1862, 11 million pounds sterling.

The cotton shortage meant tremendous enrichment for the industrialists.

According to a calculation that was made in England, the factory owners and cotton traders earned over 19 million pounds sterling from the raw cotton they had previously stored up. And from [the sale of] cotton fabrics [they made] over 16 million pounds sterling. In total, they gained more than 35, almost 36 million pounds sterling.

Certainly a painful blow was also struck internally, inside the cotton industry: that is, the small manufacturers immediately went kaput.

	Number of cotton mills in England	Number of spindles in England
1862	2,887	30,387
1867	2,549	32,000

This means [that] a big concentration of production [took place].

The only ones who suffered from the crisis were the workers. For the industrialists this crisis meant big business. The workers had to bear all the costs of the crisis.

The county of Lancashire*

Manchester

The workers of Lancashire stood at the highest point among workers generally. They had the highest wages, and were the most intelligent and best-organized workers. In the whole region, working conditions were held to firmly established standards. Many workers were so well off that they even had some savings and owned their own small houses.

The percentage of those on relief was lower than anywhere else in the entire country. That is attributed not only to their prosperity but also to the pride of the workers in Lancashire.

This was the flower of the English working class. But because of the cotton famine it was denied the very means of existence for several years and was ruined completely.

Joblessness grew so much in the fall of 1861 that charity, both public and private, had to step in strongly and take a hand.

---

*   The county of Lancashire is in the northwest of England, adjacent to the Irish Sea.

In January 1862 the spread of joblessness became [truly] menacing. Cutbacks in production in the spring of 1862 were so large that by April, out of the 47,504 workers who had earlier been employed in the cotton industry in Manchester, only 23,722 remained fully employed, as against 15,393 on half-time, and 8,369 completely unemployed. These figures apply only to the city of Manchester.

In another center of the cotton industry, in Blackburn and its surrounding areas, 8,459 were completely unemployed out of 40,000 workers, and most of the rest worked only two, three, or four days a week. The workers had to sell their furniture, including their beds, and the wives and children of these very proud working-class men had to go begging from house to house.

All of this was described in workers' letters published in the bourgeois newspapers.

In May of 1862 the number of jobless workers in the county of Lancashire had reached 58,000, but according to others, the number was as high as 100,000.

After the workers the small shopkeepers in the entire district were also ruined, since they were linked with the workers for their existence. The local relief effort was inadequate. A central relief committee was set up in London under the chairmanship of the Lord Mayor.

At the same time there began a highly characteristic struggle by the jobless workers with the local officials in charge of charity for the poor. Relief was provided only if the recipient submitted to work out of a workhouse. This meant the most demeaning and crudest kind of dirty work: sweeping the streets and breaking rocks. It is very interesting and instructive for us to follow the course of this struggle through the length of the crisis. The Lancashire workers did not want to submit to this condition. They explained that they did not want to be reduced to performing this kind of work, for which they were not suited. The greatest physical strength was required for such work, and that was not the kind of work they did in a spinning mill.

The workers engaged in a bitter struggle with the local poor-relief officials. The outcome was this: (1) Relief was paid in money, not in goods. The workers said, "We are not beggars, asking for food." They wanted the right to dispose of their money as they saw fit. (2) Forced labor from workhouses was abolished.

The workers were so stiff-necked and persistent about this that they developed a magnificent plan of action. In one city after another they held huge gatherings at which the question of jobless relief was discussed. At these they always explained that they were not beggars, that they had been removed from their jobs by the actions of others. They wanted assistance for the unemployed to be organized on a public basis, corresponding to their own sense of honor and self-worth. They demanded that, instead of forced labor, workers' schools should be established so they could study during their time of unemployment. And they won this demand. Schools and courses for the workers were set up.

They marched in the streets, and in a number of cities they began doing some vandalizing. They won their demands all along the line.

Especially characteristic throughout this crisis was the behavior of the free-trade advocates, those widely renowned gentlemen, Mr. [Richard] Cobden and Mr. [John] Bright. As early as the 1840s they had been in the forefront of agitation for free trade, and at that time had turned to the workers [for support].

Now [let us look at] the behavior of these gentlemen in the big cotton crisis [of the early 1860s]. Mr. Bright was concerned above all to minimize the extent of the disaster. They lied [outright] about its extent. The explanation for their taking this position was that the real state of affairs dealt a stunning blow to the whole free-trade movement. He [Bright] said that the impoverishment was much less than it would have been if free trade had not existed. He defended the local poor-relief officials with whom the workers were embroiled. While the workers were demanding public assistance, Parliament and the central authorities urged the workers to exert pressure on the local authorities. Bright said that it would be wisest for the central government to undertake the least possible interference in the sphere of jurisdiction of the local authorities. He opposed all large-scale relief action, because in his view that would only increase poverty.

The free-trade advocates actually represented the mill owners. Cobden and Bright were mouthpieces for the cotton mill owners of Lancashire.

The only ones who spoke up for the workers in this crisis were members of the landowning nobility, who had also pushed through the demands of the movement for the ten-hour day. They did what they could for the workers. This was an expression of the old battle between rent for land and profit for capital.

The landowners, particularly in the House of Lords, that is, in their own chamber of Parliament, defended quite warmly the demand of the workers for the elimination of forced labor.

The workers' struggle with the local poor-relief authorities continued. In Blackburn a thousand unemployed workers refused to work at breaking up rocks.

In July [1862], out of the 355,000 workers in the textile mills of the county of Lancashire, 80,000 were completely unemployed, and the others were employed only part of the time. Charity contributions however flowed in abundantly from all directions.

The behavior of the workers, their stiff-necked, proud, and stubborn struggle, and their rampaging, caused the government and society as a whole such great anxiety that they took action at least to appease the hunger of these people.

The entrepreneurs, the millionaires in Lancashire, for the most part refused to give any relief payments. Even in the [main] conservative newspaper, *The Times*, they were often stigmatized.

In Parliament, Cobden spoke out very sharply against the formal proposal that relief in the counties of England be organized on a broader basis so that one community could send aid to another, to wherever the need was greatest.

In his speech he spoke as though the most unfortunate people in the crisis were the mill owners. [He argued that] relief should not be organized on a wider basis, because then the mill owners would have to pay the most, and that should not happen, because then the mill owners would not have enough money when the upturn came. Lord Palmerston, who spoke against Cobden in parliament said: "In reality they want to shift the entire burden from the wealthy to the poor." Palmerston was the leader of the land-owning nobility.

At that point the free traders and the mill owners were victorious. The proposal was changed, despite the greatest protests of the House of Lords that relief payments did no harm to the mill owners.

Meanwhile poverty and need were such that in Manchester the mortality rate was 60–70 percent higher than in the rest of the country.

At the same time, however, *through their struggle* the workers achieved [victory] in the fall of 1862. By means of the most energetic struggle, they won their demands *that relief was to be paid entirely in money and not in kind. Forced labor was also replaced by instruction at schools.*

Special schools were established for the workers, where they learned reading, writing, and arithmetic. Sewing schools were established for women, and it was precisely this latter development that the factory inspectors mentioned as being especially healthy for the living conditions of the workers. Most of the wives and daughters of the workers, in particular those who were still employed, had not actually been able up until that time to take needle in hand [and learn how to sew].

December 1862 was the high point of the crisis. In Lancashire and Cheshire [counties] at that time 271,983 persons were receiving public assistance. Out of those 271,983 relief recipients, only 12,500 were working. All the others had been let go.

[Here are] *statistics for joblessness at the end of January 1863.* In the cotton-industry districts the total number of those completely unemployed was 247,230, of those who were employed part time the number was 165,600, and those employed full time, 121,129.

After the mill owners had enriched themselves enormously by raising the prices for raw cotton and cotton fabrics, they took the opportunity to drive wages down in Lancashire by 10–20 percent, and in this way again were able to put enormous profits in their pockets.

At the end of 1862 a remarkable movement for emigration began. This is also of great interest in that it shows the proud spirit of the workers at that time.

They made the simple decision to emigrate en masse. It happened that at that time offers had come from Australia and in particular from New Zealand to accept emigrating workers from England. Of course the best conditions were promised. One province in New Zealand even offered 10,000 pounds sterling for emigrants from England, to cover the costs of emigration by English workers.

Again large gatherings of workers began to be held, where they discussed the question of emigration. It was from these meetings that the decision was reached to emigrate en masse [first of all] and second to demand that Parliament provide the means to cover the expenses of emigration. They demanded this on the basis that it was rightfully due to them. Since England was not able to employ them, England should provide the means for them to go elsewhere to work. The large landowners also supported this emancipatory movement, but the factory owners did not. They were overcome by terrible fears, and at that time produced the memorable document in which the workers were described as living machines, [and they argued that these machines] should not be allowed to go wandering off. You will find this document quoted in Volume 1 of Marx's *Capital*.*

When the mill owners saw that in spite of everything the workers were emigrating, they demanded that Parliament take out a public loan to initiate a program of public works. Parliament gave in on this point also.

On the front line of opposition to the movement for emigration and in support of the demand for public works there once again appeared Mr. Cobden. Under pressure from the mill owners the government provided credit amounting to 1.2 million pounds sterling to provide work for the unemployed.

These public works consisted included road building, canal building, the building of aqueducts, and the laying out of parks, all of this being mainly in the provinces. In this way the English provinces of that time acquired the most beautiful parks. But these public works came into existence at a time when the greatest need had already passed. In this way England, at ridiculously low wages, had an entire range of public labor performed. Nevertheless, this did contribute to the well-being of the workers.

A laughable number of workers were employed on these public works—8,324. Counting their families that meant 30–40,000 persons benefited somewhat from that.

Toward 1864 the economic conjuncture gradually made an upward turn again, and the workers again found employment.

The reserve stocks of raw cotton and woven goods had long since been sold off, and cotton was being imported from India and Egypt. A few statistics about that:

---

* This is a reference to a letter published in *The Times* of March 24, 1863 by Edmund Potter, a President of the Manchester Chamber of Commerce, that referred to the workers as "the machinery." Marx discusses Potter's letter at length in *Capital* Vol. 1, pp. 720–3.

Value of imports to England:
In 1860, from India 15 million pounds sterling
    from Egypt 10 million pounds sterling
In 1864, from India 52 million pounds sterling
    from Egypt 20 million pounds sterling

There then began a boom for the cotton industry, and as early as in the following year complaints could be heard from the mill owners of Lancashire about the shortage of labor power.

That was how the crisis of 1861 was overcome.

Scarcely had the upturn begun, however, than *a new crisis, that of 1866,* made its appearance.

A severe monetary crisis in England. It was the consequence of the powerful influx of imports from the Orient, the main element being cotton. [There was] a colossal inflow from the East, from India. In exchange for this inflow England was not immediately paid in cash, but with an exchange of goods, and so forth. On the other hand, however, England was paying in cash.

Currency based on the silver standard prevailed for the most part in India and the East, and consequently there was a massive outflow of silver from England to India and the East. Thus by 1864 there was a colossal emptying out of the coffers of the Bank of England, which caused great turmoil on the money market, so that the Bank of England found it necessary to sharply raise the bank rate in order to attract money to England.

This did not affect commerce and industry [at first]. In 1864 a major upturn [in the economy] set in. Once again the founding of joint-stock companies flourished.

From 1863 to 1865 the joint-stock companies founded in England had a total nominal capital of 582 million pounds sterling. (Nominal capital is what is printed on paper. On the money market this capital is worth much more.)

The founding of these companies shows that even then speculative fever existed in England.

A new impetus to England's industry resulted with the end of the Civil War in the United States in 1864. There was a new demand for English goods and therefore a new upswing in English industry.

England's exports to the United States rose as follows:
In the year 1864 exports were worth 16.7 million pounds sterling.
In 1866 they were worth 28.5 million pounds sterling.

The following table shows the prices of commodities during the boom and during the bust:

	Increase in prices as of January 1, 1866 (compared to the previous year)	Decrease in prices as of January 1, 1867 (compared to the previous year)
Coffee	+11%	−17%
Sugar	+11%	−9%
Tea	+31%	−23%
Silk	+27%	−9%
Flax and Hemp	+ 6%	−17%
Copper	+21%	−20%
Cotton	+15%	−28%

By 1866 all this led to a crisis in England, and the high point of the crisis was 1867.

An outbreak of panic followed, as ever, from some particular event, and indeed in this case it was a bankruptcy of Overend & Co.* The consequence of this bankruptcy was a frightful panic. In two weeks the reserves of the Bank of England were almost completely emptied.

Banks that functioned as joint-stock companies failed massively, as did railroad companies.

(From now on the railroads played a huge role in crises generally.)

Those hit hardest by the crisis were the iron industry, the machine industry, and shipbuilding.

(From now on, after the second half of the nineteenth century, so-called heavy industry took the dominant position, which up until then had been held by the cotton industry. That came about as a result of constantly expanding progress and technology; more and more machines and means of transport were being used.)

In 1869 there was a severe money and credit crisis in the United States.

A second world crisis in 1873.

Germany played the leading role in this [crisis].

The years 1871–73 were an era of extraordinary upswing in industry throughout Europe. This came after the end of the Franco-Prussian War and the suppression of the Paris Commune. After its suppression a feeling of calm and reassurance set in [for the bourgeoisie], and of *joie de vivre.* Especially for Germany there came into consideration the influx of war reparations, which France had to pay, [5] billion [francs].† The elimination of the

---

*   Overend, Gurney & Co. was a London wholesale bank, founded in 1800, which collapsed in 1866, after speculating heavily in railroad stocks. Its losses were the equivalent of about $2 billion in current prices. More than 200 companies were forced out of business as a direct result of the failure of the bank.

†   In the typescript the number is given as 14 instead of 5 billion.

national debt, and as a result the freeing up of a large amount of capital, now searching for investment opportunities, and consequently the striving for the founding of new companies, and in addition the establishment of freedom of trade, standardization of bourgeois laws, and of the tariff structure, and so forth. All of this was conclusively accomplished by the political unification of 1870–71.

Along with this there was an upturn in Austria. The end of the War of 1866* and the beginning of the constitutional era in Austria in 1867 contributed to the fact that a great enlivenment [of economic activity] began in Austria. Germany and Austria in those years constituted the main arena for stock market speculation. There was the construction of new railroads, feverish housing construction, in particular in Vienna, and in connection with that [extensive] real estate speculation.

In Germany there was a fever for the founding of new companies:

According to the statistics of [Ernest] Engel,[†] in *Prussia* alone:

From 1800 to June 30, 1870, 410 joint-stock companies were founded with a total capital of 1,026,172,455 talers; [in contrast,] from July 1, 1871 to 1874, 857 joint-stock companies were newly founded, with a total capital of 1,429,925,925 talers.

According to [Richard] Vanderborght,[‡] in all of Germany:

	Number of newly founded joint-stock companies	Capital worth (in millions of marks)
1871	207	757
1872	479	1478
1873	242	544
1874	90	106
1875	55	46
1876	42	18
1877	44	43
1878	42	13

From here on the figures are in *five-year* periods

---

* A reference to the Prussian-Austrian war of 1866, in which Prussia decisively defeated Austria.

† Engel published his statistical surveys in a number of journals edited by him, such as *Preuss Statistik* and *Zeitschrift des Statischen Bureaus.*

‡ See Richard Vanderborght, *Die wirtschaftliche Bedeutung der Rhein-Seeschiffahrt* (The Economic Importance of the Rhine-Maritime Region) (Köln: Selbstverlag der Handelskammer, 1892).

	Number of newly founded joint-stock companies	Capital worth (in millions of marks)
1871–75	1073	2,931
1876–80	270	223
1881–85	620	595
1886–90	1061	1,100
1891–96	814	824.8

The table above is based on data from the Imperial Statistical Office for *1906*.[*]

	Amount (in start-up companies)	Equity in Millions of Nominal Capital
[1906]	5050	13,767.7
1907	5147	14,218.3
1908	5184	14,634.6

In England the capital worth of joint-stock companies amounted to 2 billion pounds sterling.

The building of railroads played a big role.

The following table shows the length (in kilometers) of standard-gauge railroads in *Germany*.

	Total length in kilometers
1845	2,143
1855	7,826
1865	13,900
1875	27,981
1880	33,645
1890	41,818
1904	53,822

In *Austria*, in the years 1867–73, among the newly licensed businesses were 175 [regular] banks, 34 railroad enterprises, 645 industrial companies, 104 banks [*Baubank*][†] concerned only with lending for [home] building purposes, 39 insurance companies, and 8 shipping companies, with a total amount of capital involved, all together, of 4 billion guilders.

---

[*]   The Kaiserliches Statistisches Amt (Imperial Bureau of Statistics) published a series of journals and monographs of statistical information on industry, agriculture, and the overall economy from 1872 to 1918.

[†]   A *baubank* generally funds construction and housing projects.

Indicative of the craze for founding new companies and the speculative fever in general is the fact that out of all this, only 682 companies actually came into existence, with joint-stock share capital worth 2,577 billion guilders. A large number of these of course went bankrupt later in the crash [of 1873].

The craze for the founding of new companies also spread to the *United States*, where a new economic upturn had followed the end of the Civil War. This was also expressed in the founding of new railroad companies, in other words, the most modern means of transport. In the years 1870–73, in the United States, a network of new railroad lines of 23,406 miles was built. (An English mile is about 1.6 kilometers.)

A new era began in 1864 after the Civil War in the sense that the expansion of indirect taxes was undertaken on a colossal scale, along with [the imposition of] high protective tariffs. That led to the amassment of substantial resources by the government and to colossal undertakings [such as railroad building].

In England at the same time there was an unheard-of prosperity, which was expressed especially in the upturn of the iron, steel, and coal industries, which were necessary for the building of railroads in other countries.

[The value of] exports from England to the US:

1870   28.3 million pounds sterling
1872   40.7 million pounds sterling
1873   14.6 million pounds sterling (showing the
          effects of the crisis [of 1873].)

Total exports of iron, steel, and hard coal from England:

1868   Iron and steel together   17.6 million pounds sterling
1868   Exports of hard coal   5.4 million pounds sterling
1873   Iron and steel   37.7 million pounds sterling
1873   Hard coal   13.2 million pounds sterling

Total exports from England of cotton, wool, and linen fabrics:

	Cotton	Wool	Linen fabrics
1868	53 million pound sterling	19.6	7.1
1873	81.5 million pound sterling	25.4	7.3

Statistics on pig iron production in England:

	Production of pig iron in millions of tons	Median price for pig iron
1867	4.7	52 shillings, 6 pence
1868	4.9	52 shillings, 9 pence
1869	5.4	53 shillings, 3 pence
1870	5.9	54 shillings, 4 pence
1871	6.6	59 shillings
1872	6.7	101 shillings, 10 pence
1873	6.8	117 shillings, 3 pence

(The price rose so high because the expansion of production could not keep pace with the growing demand, caused by the increasing needs of railroad construction.)

Speculation on foreign loans also developed on the London Stock Exchange.

Again this gives us an overview of the international connections [existing at that time] and the role of the state.

In the years 1870–75, foreign loans taken out in London amounted to a value of 260 million pounds sterling. Oriental governments played the main role in this. Since they needed money to finance their military establishments, and the like, they promised to pay high interest rates, but in the meantime it turned out that these governments did not yet have a sufficiently solid foundation. Therefore [there was] only partial repayment of the loans, and bankruptcy followed.

In the 1870s [MS. *Missing words*] Turkey, Egypt, Greece, Bolivia (South America), Costa Rica, Ecuador, Honduras (Central and South American states), Mexico, Paraguay, Uruguay, Peru, Venezuela, and Santo Domingo [took out loans].

And the capitalists in London went along with that.

The following figures give us an overview of [capital] movements [involving] government loans, and what a very lively effect they had upon the playing that took place on the stock exchanges:

The total value of securities issued on American and European stock exchanges:

1870	4,560 million marks
1871	12,560 million marks
1872	10,110 million marks
1873	8,722 million marks
1874	3,368 million marks

The years 1871 and 1872 were the two high points in the issuing of securities. These are not exact statistics, [merely] estimates, but the estimates were made by recognized statisticians, so that they do have great significance.*

Then came the crash [of 1873], although the crashes in the United States and in Europe occurred independently of one another. [In Europe] this time the panic hit the Vienna stock exchange first, and spread out from there. In the United States, the collapse began with a company that had invested in the building of railroads. Then the crisis transmitted itself further, of its own accord. In Europe the crash came to the Vienna† stock exchange on the memorable day of May 3. By May 28 there were already 100 bankruptcies in Vienna. And by then, shares [on the stock exchange] in Vienna alone had lost 300 million guilders in value. In June the panic was transplanted from Vienna to Berlin. The value of securities suddenly fell by 30–50 percent. The American crash had a reciprocal effect on Germany and Austria, naturally, and that intensified the general collapse.

Then England followed [with] a severe commercial crisis. In the years 1873–75 and even beyond that, bankruptcies kept increasing more and more. The crisis of 1873 was notable for its long-lasting effects. As late as 1878, banks of the top rank continued to fail in England, as an effect of the crisis [of 1873]. In 1878 in particular a very severe crisis developed in England for the cotton industry, the iron industry, and coal mining. The crisis reached its high point in England only in 1879. Then, until 1880, it spread little by little across Italy, Russia, Holland, Belgium, South America, and Australia to all the major branches of industry.

That is the picture of the crisis of 1873.

Not even a decade had gone by when a large-scale crisis broke out in France. This was the *French crisis of 1882*. France had overcome the crisis of 1873 earlier than all the other important countries. It had not been disturbed very greatly by that crisis. After the reestablishment of the bourgeois republic an economic upturn had begun in France. The Paris Commune had been suppressed in 1871. The war [with Prussia] had ended, and war reparations were paid. Then there began an upturn. Here as everywhere, together with that upturn, there was a great craze for founding new companies on the stock exchange. Joint-stock companies, the founding of new banks, the most daredevil and foolhardy ventures, [anything] in order to put new capital to use.

Central to all this was the founding of a company with the name Union Générale. At the head of the founders of this company stood a certain [Paul

---

*   Prior to about 1900, statistics did not show the proportion of government securities (as opposed to those of private companies) that were traded on stock exchanges.

†   In the typescript this is erroneously given as Berlin instead of Vienna.

Eugene] Bontoux.* The crisis in France [of 1882] is often also called the Bontoux crisis. Bontoux headed a group of capitalists. They had declared that they wanted to bring Christian-Catholic capital properly to the fore, in order to drive Jewish capital from the field, Jewish capital being to blame for all troubles. By Jewish capital they meant the Rothschild group.

The Bontoux group also found protection from various dukes and duchesses in Austria from the royal house of the Hapsburgs. As an expression of this movement there occurred in Vienna the founding of *the Vienna Agricultural Bank*, which worked with Catholic capital and knew how to obtain great privileges from the government for the Bontoux group. The activity of the Union Générale was expressed in two ways. First, it stepped up its activity on the stock exchange in order to drive the value of its own capital upward, [that is,] to drive up the value of its own shares on the stock exchange. They purchased their own shares in order to create an [artificial] bull market. French legislation allowed joint-stock companies to periodically purchase their own shares. Thus they created an artificial demand for their own securities, and the value of their shares was driven up. In this way they enticed money out of various hiding places, particularly from among the petty bourgeoisie.

Now they had to employ this capital. A massive craze for founding new companies began, with immediate undertakings. New enterprises were founded on such a massive scale: gas works, coal mines, insurance companies, railroads, and so on and so forth. It was characteristic that the Union Générale also provided itself with a string of newspapers in order to systematically influence public opinion.

In 1882 there followed the collapse of this entire operation. To begin with, the crisis broke out in Lyon, then a sudden plunge in stock prices on the stock exchanges both in Paris and in Vienna by way of the agricultural bank, and on January 29, 1882, the bankruptcy of the entire Union Générale occurred. Monsieur Bontoux was at first imprisoned, because there was dreadful fury among the petty bourgeoisie over the fact that Catholic capital had let them down. The authorities had to set Bontoux free, however, because he had not in any way violated the laws governing joint-stock companies.

Among the newly founded companies were total phantasms, figments of the imagination, for example, coalmines that hardly existed in the real world. Some name would be announced, but no one knew where in the world this mine might be located.

This crisis had an echo in other countries, especially where there had been speculative crazes on stock exchanges.

---

* The Union Générale was a French Catholic Bank founded by Paul Eugene Bontoux in 1878.

Scarcely had this crisis been overcome when again the build-up to a new economic upturn began. In some countries the new upturn started as early as 1879. In the United States at the beginning of the 1880s there was a railroad fever once again. In the years 1880–82 the railroad network of the United States was enlarged by an additional 28,240 miles.*

As a result, there was increased exports from England to the United States and in 1878 the value of such exports was 14.6 million pounds sterling. In 1882 the value was 31.6 million pounds sterling. That refers to total exports from England to the United States.

The following table shows the role of heavy industry [in these exports]
Exports from England to the United States:

Iron and steel   1878   18.4 million pounds sterling
Machines   1878   7.5 million pounds sterling

Exports from England, in general:

Iron and steel   1882   31.6 million pounds sterling
Machines   1882   11.9 million pounds sterling

Exports of England's Textile Industry, in general (in millions of pounds sterling):

	Cotton fabrics	Woolen fabrics	Linen fabrics
1878	52.9	16.7	5.5
1882	62.9	18.8	6

As a result of this situation, in 1884 there was again a severe crash in the railroad industry in the United States. There naturally followed from that a general collapse of prices in England of 15–20 percent. Here, however, we must direct our attention to a particular phenomenon, which had *general significance*. The general collapse of prices in England is not merely a consequence transmitted from the crash in the United States; rather, it was a sign of an overall drop in prices, first of all a drop in the price of grain on the world market. This decline of prices, especially of the price of grain, has brought an enormous literature into existence, both in England and in other countries. In this literature people take up this question: Where does the explanation lie for why prices fell?

---

*   There seems to be an error in the typescript: the phrase 28,240 *million* appears rather than 28,240 *miles*.

What phenomenon was it in Western Europe and especially in Germany, dating from this time of the sharp plunge in grain prices, about which people have spoken so much? [It was] *the so-called agrarian crisis.* That refers to nothing other than the sharp drop in prices for agricultural prices. What were the causes? The main cause was the import of American grain. Why did that bring about a sharp fall in prices? It was incomparably cheaper to grow grain in America. Not that the fertility was so great. Not at all. Agriculture was not even half as productive as in Germany. The intensity of agriculture [in Germany] was the reason for that.

Another reason was the great extent of railroad construction. It was not the result of economically necessary factors, but on the contrary there was great activity in founding new companies for the benefit of rising industrial capital, especially English capital. The result was the building of railroads across the West [of the United States] on a colossal scale. Along with that, the flood of emigration pushed westwards. This led [eventually] to the flooding of American grain onto the European market.

When a great hue and cry about a sharp drop of prices in England was raised, the calculation was made that income from agriculture in England in the 1880s had been reduced by 42.8 million pounds sterling.

The Agrarian Crisis

Comrade Luxemburg read aloud[*] from a book by Tugan-Baranovsky about commercial crises in England,[†] quoting some statements made by a commission that was assigned to investigate this phenomenon in England. Tugan-Baranovsky ascribes these crises to intense competition, the large-scale founding of new joint-stock companies, and the creation of new means of transport.

But the main cause of the crisis [of 1884] *had to do with agriculture.*

Below are some *statistics for Prussia.* By the term world market the entire world is meant here. But in the narrower sense it means the English market.

The table shows average prices on the most important markets for agriculture (Danzig, Königsberg, Mannheim). The prices are shown per ton (1,000 kg.) and in marks. These statistics were assembled by Professor [Heinrich] Dade and published by the Association for Social Policy.[‡] This table covers *four eight-year periods.*

---

  *   This is a further indication that these notes were taken down by one of Luxemburg's students, in this case most likely Rosi Wolfstein.

  †   The following passage refers to "Comrade Luxemburg" in the third person, indicating that someone present was transcribing, or taking notes on her lecture about Volume 2 of *Capital.* The book referred to by Mikhail Ivanovich Tugan-Baranovsky was *Studien zur Theorie und Geschichte der Handelskrisen in England* (Studies in the Theory and History of Commercial Crises in England) (Jena: Fischer, 1901).

  ‡   Heinrich Dade published a series of four essays on "Agrarzolle" (Agricultural Tariffs) in *Beiträge zur neuesten Handelspolitik Deutschlands herausgeben von Verein für Socialpolitik* (Essays

	1868/69–75/76	1876/77–83/84	1884/85–91/92	1892/93–99/00
Wheat	223 marks	207 marks	181 marks	155 marks
Rye	173 marks	166 marks	156 marks	131 marks
Barley	165 marks	158 marks	148 marks	138 marks
Oats	160 marks	148 marks	142 marks	138 marks
Potatoes	56 marks	59 marks	53 marks	49 marks
Straw	46 marks	50 marks	48 marks	43 marks
Hay	72 marks	65 marks	60 marks	59 marks

This shows a steady fall in prices. After that [came] a rise in prices, inflation. *After 1886 a new industrial upturn begins.*

In this upturn *South America* plays a big role, especially Argentina.

This [leads to] a peculiar crisis, mainly played out between England and South America.

After 1886 England's exports increased *in general*, above all iron, machinery, and coal.

In 1886 England's exports of iron were worth 21.8 million pounds sterling, of machinery, 10.1 million pounds sterling, and of coal 9.8 million pounds sterling.

In January 1890, England's exports of iron were worth 31.6 million pounds sterling, of machinery, 16.4 million pounds sterling, and of coal, 19 million pounds sterling.

[Now let us look at] the exports of the three most important textile industries: cotton, wool, and linen fabrics. In 1886, England's exports of cotton fabrics had a value of 57.4 million pounds sterling, of wool fabrics, 19.7 million pounds sterling, and of linen fabrics, 5.3 million pounds sterling.

In 1890, England's exports of cotton fabrics had risen to 62.1 million pounds sterling, its exports of woolen fabrics was now worth 20.4 million pounds sterling, and its exports of linen fabrics, 5.7 million pounds sterling.

The textile industry was making smaller and smaller leaps forward, as the figures show. This applies in particular to the cotton industry, because this is the industry that was most successful in finding its way into other countries. The wool industry still maintains itself for the most part. That is because, to this day, English sheep breeding plays a foremost role on the world market, especially for the finer types of wool.

Argentina plays a special role. At the end of the 1880s a mad craze for founding new companies developed in Argentina. In the years 1887–89, 250 joint-stock companies were founded in Argentina with a nominal capital of 764 million dollars. In addition to that there was also Argentina's government debt. In 1874 it amounted to 10 million pounds sterling, but in 1890 [it had risen to]

59.1 million pounds sterling. We speak in terms of pounds sterling because it was English capital that financed Argentina's national debt.

From government loans and the founding of new joint-stock companies the main investments of capital in Argentina shifted to the building of railroads. In 1883, the railroad network in Argentina amounted to 3,123 kilometers; in 1893, it was 13,691 kilometers. That was how much was actually built at that time. But much more was licensed, and that also became the object of speculation. In 1889 [new] railroad construction was licensed for a total length of 12,000 kilometers. Of course these licensed railroad lines were not built [because] the crash came the following year.

Thus, in 1890 [there was] a tremendous crash, accompanied by a civil war in Argentina.* Upheavals of this kind are very characteristic for the situation in newly established countries. The crash in Argentina was immediately echoed in England. The impetus for this came in November 1890 with the collapse of the largest English private bank: Baring & Co. This collapse naturally brought a whole series of further business failures in its wake.†

After that the crisis spread outward from England, resulting in a crash in Transvaal [South Africa], one in Mexico, and one in Uruguay.

In connection with all this there was a severe cotton crisis in England in 1890, because the countries involved [in the crisis] did not yet have their own cotton industries.‡

Barely three years went by, and *in 1893 there was a huge crash in the United States and in Australia.*

The immediate cause in both countries was a railroad-building frenzy.

In Australia, for example, it was again primarily English capital that was at work. The investment of this capital was first of all in government loans. English capital was tied up in Australian government loans to the sum of 112 million pounds sterling. Of that, 81 million pounds had been put into the building of railroads and streetcar lines. The following statistics show how the railroad network in Australia took shape.

In 1880, it was 4,900 miles long; and in 1895 it was 15,600 miles long.

Along with that there was a wild craze for investing in real estate and housing construction in all these new countries. As early as 1891 the collapse of the housing bubble began, and that was followed in 1895 by a general collapse

---

* Argentina's crisis of 1890 was precipitated by a surge of inflation in its over-heated economy. In response to the crisis, the army attempted a coup against President Miguel Juárez Celman, who was replaced by Carlos Pellegrini.

† English capital was heavily invested in Argentina, and the crisis almost caused the collapse of Baring & Co., which had extensive holdings in that country. Baring was saved only after obtaining a significant bailout from the British government, to the tune of about $2 billion in today's currency.

‡ That is, they had been importing cotton from England but now imported less because of the crisis.

in Australia. Almost all the states of Australia stopped making any further payments.

At the same time things were developing in the United States, although along different lines. The main problem was overly rapid railroad construction. In addition, *trusts* were already playing a role, which contributed to price increases, speculation, and so forth, in the most varied spheres of the economy.

There were scandals involving trusts, especially the whisky trust, which bought up the entire reserve supply of grain in order to drive prices up extravagantly.* There were also battles over currency in the United States, because at that time the advocates of placing currency on a silver standard [rather than the gold standard] came to the helm.

The approximate cause of the crash [of 1893] that took place generally was the collapse of the "wheat ring" on the stock exchange.†

A massive quantity of bankruptcies followed in the United States, and commerce came to a complete standstill. In August 1893 there were 600 bank failures in the United States.

In 1890 there had been a total of 7,538 bankruptcies with liabilities amounting to a total of 93 million dollars.

In 1893 there were 11,174 bankruptcies with liabilities totalling 324 million dollars.

Seventy-four railroad companies collapsed with 29,000 miles of railroad still under construction.

Pig iron production declined in the United States as follows: in 1892 it amounted in total to 9,157,000 tons, but in 1893 it was only 7.124 million tons.

In May 1893 shares in trusts lost 25–50 percent of their value in general.

There now took place something that was very characteristic of the crisis. There was a colossal amount of unemployment, and poverty was rampant. Then the unemployed from different regions decided to submit a so-called living petition to the American Congress, that is, to set out on a journey together and march on foot to Washington. And that is what they did. They demanded that Congress provide jobs through public works, road building, and so forth. This march was led by a certain [Jacob] Coxy, a farmer.‡ He was not lacking in all

---

*   The "Whisky Ring" was a conspiracy of 1875 on the part of government bureaucrats and distillers to drive up the price of liquor and siphon off the proceeds of federal taxes on liquor. It was one of the major scandals of the presidency of Ulysses S. Grant.

†   It is not clear what Luxemburg is referring to here, since the Panic of 1893 was precipitated by overcapacity in the railroad industry. "Wheat ring" probably is how the person taking down these notes heard "whiskey ring," but the latter took place two decades earlier and had nothing to do with the economic crisis of 1893.

‡   The transcript erroneously gives the name as Cozy. Coxey was not a farmer, but a businessman, politician, and social reformer. Coxey's Army was a protest march on Washington by unemployed workers. The movement was popularly known as Coxey's Army, but it also called itself by the name Army of the Commonweal of Christ. A number of different marches by unemployed "armies" in different parts of the US also set out for Washington to demand jobs around

sorts of mystical accessories; his movement took the name of something like Christian Brothers (perhaps that was the name).

The first troops [of Coxey's Army] set out on Easter Sunday in 1894. Twenty marches met up [or were supposed to] and arrived in Washington on May. When they arrived they demonstrated in Washington in front of Congress.* This march caused a big sensation throughout Europe because for the first time the bourgeoisie in Washington were stricken with great fear. Also the unemployed had to make great sacrifices along the way; it was a difficult journey. Naturally they did not have any results [from their protests]. They had to wait until an economic upturn came again. According to Rosa Luxemburg's personal recollection, the newspapers [in Europe] at that time estimated that there were half a million people involved.[†]

The [1893] crash in the United States and the one in Australia had a combined effect and gave rise to a major depression for the world economy as a whole.

As early as 1895 there was another new crisis. Again this was a crisis that occurred mainly on the stock exchanges, resulting not from the conditions of production, but from *speculation on South American gold mines.* (The beginning of gold extraction [on a really large scale] dates from the mid-1880s.)

A postlude [to all this] was the Boer war [in South Africa][‡] and the taking of the gold mines by the British.

How intense the speculation was at that time is shown by the fact that in the year [*MS. Missing* words] In the case of 25 mining companies that paid dividends, the face value of their shares amounted to 6.55 million pounds sterling, but the market value was 38.52 million. If this increase in value is calculated as a percentage—it is an increase of 588 percent. In the case of the 133 mining companies that did not pay dividends, because they were not yet profitable, the face value of their shares amounted to 27.73 million pounds sterling, but the market value was 113.23 million. Calculated as a percentage, this was an increase of 409 percent.

The Land Speculation Company and others [like it] in Transvaal were likewise able to increase the value of their shares by speculative operations. The nominal value was 15.87 million pounds sterling, but the value of those shares

---

the same time as the one led by Coxey, who predicted he would bring 100,000 to the capitol. If all the other "armies" and marchers of that time are counted, as well as their numerous supporters, they probably numbered several hundred thousand. L. Frank Baum, author of *The Wonderful Wizard of Oz*, participated in Coxey's march on Washington and later incorporated it in his story, in which the scarecrow symbolizes the impoverished farmer and the tin woodman the industrial worker. For more on Coxey's movement, see D. L. McMurry, *Coxey's Army* (Seattle: University of Washington Press, 1970 [1929]) and Carlos Schwantes, *Coxey's Army: An American Odyssey* (Lincoln: University of Nebraska Press, 1985).

* Coxey and other leaders were arrested, and the marchers dispersed without achieving their goals.

† Luxemburg is here referred to again in the third person by Wolfstein, the likely transcriber.

‡ The first Anglo-Boer war in South Africa was fought in 1880–81; the Second Boer War was fought from 1899 to 1902.

increased above the nominal value by a factor of 401 percent. Some shares on the stock exchange stood at a level 600 percent or even 900 percent above their nominal value.

The collapse of prices on the stock exchanges: On October 1, 1895, the market value for the shares of 146 gold trusts was *5,095 million marks*. On February 28, 1897, in contrast, their market value was only *1,960 million marks*.

After the crisis of 1895, a general economic upturn began. A role in this was played by the ending of the Sino-Japanese war, which expanded the market and then [brought] European exports [to Asia], followed by Siberian railroad building, which opened up Russia's North and East, [and led to] trade treaties with Russia.

After this economic upturn [after 1895] there followed the crisis of 1900–01. Then the crisis of 1907, and so forth. We have the most precise data about these [most recent] crises from the trade unions. Up until then, we never had such [exact] material.

With regard to the upturn that began after 1895, there is a good pamphlet by Comrade Parvus [Alexander Helphand], published in Dresden in either 1896 or 1897. Its title is something like *Aufschwung und Gewerkschaften* (Economic Upturn and the Trade Unions).[*]

Statistics on the [number of] bankruptcies in Germany from 1896 through 1909 [are] in the pamphlet by [Max] Schippel, *Hochkonjunktur und Wirtschaftskrise* (Economic Boom and Economic Crisis).[†] There are also good numbers in that pamphlet.[‡]

Bankruptcy Statistics, 1898–1909:

1898	7,364
1899	7,220
1900	8,547
1901	10,566
1902	9,801
1903	9,609
1904	9,499
1905	9,329
1906	9,388
1907	9,886
1908	11,581
1909	10,998

---

[*] Luxemburg appears to have in mind Parvus's pamhlet, *Die Gewerkschaften und die Sozialdemokratie.* (The Trade Unions and Social Democracy) (Dresden: Verlag der Sächsischen Arbeiter Zeitung, 1896).

[†] See Max Schippel, *Hochkonjunktur und Wirtschaftskrise* (Boom and Economic Crisis). Luxemburg is probably using a later edition than the original of 1908 in order for her to cite it as a source for statistics on bankruptcies in 1909.

[‡] That is, helpful statistical data for use in the practical work of the SPD.

Nowadays the distinction between boom and bust is much less sharply defined than before, because no uninterrupted boom can occur anymore, and thus we no longer experience an actual boom in the earlier sense of the term.*

---

* That Luxemburg cites statistics covering the entire year of 1909 indicates this typescript dates from at least 1910, perhaps even from the autumn of 1911. The latter supposition is reinforced by Luxemburg's letter of November 21, 1911, to Kostya Zetkin, which discusses economic crises and Tugan-Baranovsky's (inadequate) analysis of them, as well as Karl Kautsky's inadequate treatment of crises. This letter also indicates that by November 1911 Luxemburg was working on a problem she had encountered in Volume 2 of Marx's *Capital*—a problem that prompted her, beginning in January 1912, to start writing her major work, *The Accumulation of Capital*. See *The Letters of Rosa Luxemburg*, pp. 315–16.

History of Crises[*]

History of Theories of Economic Crises
Impetus given by the crisis of 1815

(1) *Robert Owen* in his writings of 1815, 1818, and 1823 [gave an] explanation of crises [as coming] from the contradiction between increased productivity because of machinery [on the one hand] and the reduced wages and intensified exploitation of the workers because of these same machines [on the other]. [His] demand: employment of the jobless by the state, and a greater share of the product to go to the workers.

(2) *Malthus* and *Sismondi* derive crises from the distribution of income. Malthus (1820)[†]: thrift and the drive for capitalization [i.e., accumulation] must lead to crises, unless consumption is expanded by *unproductive* consumption ([on the part of] the nobility, the military, government officials, etc.). [That is] according to Malthus. [But] *according to Sismondi*, mass consumption through the improvement of the workers' conditions [can expand consumption]. The more evenly income is distributed, according to Sismondi, the smaller the danger of crises.

(3) *Say* polemicizes against Malthus and Sismondi, because [according to Say's theory,] a general condition of overproduction is impossible. Overproduction in one sector only means underproduction in another. Supply is demand, and vice versa.[‡] This theory was enormously successful and had great influence, particularly on the liberal school of political economy.

(4) *Marx*

---

* This typescript consists of notes or rough drafts that were developed further in the expanded version that appears in the typescript entitled "Volume 2 of *Capital*." Most of that latter typescript (all but the first five pages) discusses precisely the history of crises and follows this outline version quite closely. Sometimes gaps in the later typescript can be filled in by looking at this earlier typescript, and vice versa. The later typescript, in which about 55 double-spaced pages are devoted to "the history of crises," was probably transcribed by a secretary or student from a lecture or lectures Luxemburg gave at the SPD's Party School in Berlin (possibly in 1911, since the typescript includes a reference to statistics from 1911).

† See Thomas Malthus, *Principles of Political Economy* (London: W. Pickering, 1820).

‡ Therefore, according to Say, the remedy for crises is an increase of production in those branches of the economy where underproduction exists. See Jean-Baptiste Say, *Traité d'économie politique, ou simple exposition de la manière dont se forment, se distribuent ou se consomment les richesses*.

SUNSPOTS

In 1886 in the United States an investigation undertaken into [economic] crises came up with 180 causes! [See the article] by Herkner entitled "Causes" in the *Handwörterbuch der Staatswissenschaften.*

   (5) Tugan-Baranovsky[.] Disproportion between production and consumption

   (6) Sombart[.] Disproportion between lack of organization and organization

CRISES

   1815 England. [Aftermath of Napoleon's] Continental System
   1825 England. Exports to South America and Speculation
   1836/37 England and the United States
   1847
   1857
   1861
   1866/7
   1873
   1882
   1890/2
   1893
   1895
   1900/1
   1907/08

CRISES [DISCUSSED IN DETAIL]

1815

The Continental System. November 21, 1806 to 1812/1813. The entire coast of the European Continent [was affected]. Unworkable because of smuggling. Effects: rise of the cotton industry in *Saxony*. Here in the eighteenth century there were 25,000–30,000 spinners working by hand. Ruinous competition by imports from England forced a transition to spinning machines. In 1800 there

---

   * Luxemburg's typescript mistakenly gives "Ursachen" (Causes) as the title of Herkner's article, when actually it was "Krisen" (Crises). See Heinrich Herkner, "Krisen," in *Handwörterbuch der Staatswissenschaften*, edited by J. Conrad et. al, second edition, Vol. 5 (Jena: Verlag von Gustav Fischer, 1900), pp. 413–33. For the 1886 study of the causes of economic crises in the U.S. cited by Herkner, see *Industrial Depresssions: The First Annual Report of the Commission of Labor* (Washington, DC: Government Printing Office, 1886), especially Chapter 1, "Modern Industrial Depressions," pp. 61–3. This lists 180 causes of crises, which range from "planless production" and "speculation" to "lack of interest of the laborer in his work."

were already 2,000 spinning jennys* (hand-operated) in Saxony, and more than 150 mechanics were making them. Until 1798 these machines were used in small-scale production, in the cottage industry. In 1798 in Chemnitz a business-man [*Verleger*] for the first time brought many spinning machines together in one workroom. Now there soon came onto the scene a spinning jenny driven by *water*-powered machinery as in a water mill, and that wiped out small-scale production. The first "spinning mills" were introduced in Saxony in 1800. One started out with 620 spindles, the others with 432 each. This form of manufac-ture spread quickly then, and thanks to the Continental System, by 1813 there were more than 256,000 spindles in operation in the cotton industry. Around this time the (hand-operated) jenny disappeared completely. In 1813, the last uprising by 1,100 hand spinners in Vogtland [occurred].

Also, there was constricted purchasing power in the countries on the Continent. In 1815 in England, a crash, factory disturbances, destruction of machinery.

1825

After 1815, soon [there was economic] recovery and a sharp upturn. Canal building, road construction, gas works for street lighting, banks, speculation. Particularly [with regard to] *South America*. Independence of the South and Central American countries (Argentina, Brazil, Mexico, Colombia, Ecuador, Peru, Chile). Gold and silver mining in *Mexico* and *Peru* (Potosi, now in Bolivia [formerly "Upper Peru"]). Beginning in 1824, the London Stock Exchange was flooded with South American securities. In 1824–25 countries of South and Central America issued government bonds in London worth more than 20 million pounds sterling (at 7–8 percent [interest rates]). In addition, [there was] an enormous quantity of shares, mainly in mining companies, part of which were completely imaginary. The [price of the] shares of the English-Mexican Company rose in the first month (December 1824 to January 1825) by 125 pounds sterling; those of the Real del Monte company, by 800 pounds sterling; those of the United Mexican Company, by 120 pounds sterling, and so forth. Everything was thrown into speculation on the stock exchange. Only a partial payment (of 5–10 percent) was enough for the purchase of shares, so that even poor people could participate. "Princes, aristocrats, politicians, officials, lawyers, physicians, clergy, philosophers, poets, maidens, wives, and widows—all threw themselves upon the stock exchange, in order to invest part of their fortune in enterprises of which nothing was known but the name" (the *Annual Register* of 1825[†]).

---

*   A jenny is a machine for spinning cotton.

†   *The Annual Register: A Review of History, Politics, and Literature of the Year* is a reference work that has been published in England yearly since 1758. Its first editor was Edmund Burke.

The nominal capital of companies that were founded or projected in 1824–25, according to some estimates, reached 372 million pounds sterling. Of these, the companies that still remained, later on, had a nominal capital of 102 million pounds sterling.

Prices went sky high (cotton prices rose by 109 percent; pig iron, 77 percent; sugar, 39 percent). In 1825 [the prices of] cotton fabric went up by 23 percent. Rapid construction of new factories [took place] in Lancashire, as well as the expansion of existing factories, using credit from banks.

Export of British goods to Central and South America in 1821 was 2,942,000 pounds sterling; in 1825, it was 6,426,000 pounds sterling. The main product was cotton fabric. But part of this came back to Europe or went on to North America. The high prices in England were a strong attraction for *imports*. A rapid outflow of gold from England resulted. A backlash followed. Prices fell suddenly in London. The South American countries were not paying interest. The mining companies were paying no dividends. The Bank of England raised its bank rate sharply and refused to pay the best rate of exchange. A panic resulted. Within six weeks, 70 provincial banks collapsed, and a large number of small entrepreneurs and speculators were ruined along with them. The crisis of 1825 led to the universal introduction of the *steam-powered loom* and to a major technological upheaval in the *iron foundries*, along with major advances in technology in general.

1836

In 1833–36, there were extraordinarily good harvests in England, and grain imports declined almost completely. As a result, a new upturn. At the same time strong exports of English capital to the *United States*: railroads, canals, industrial enterprises, the shares being sold in England for the most part. In 1835–36, new banks founded in the United States had a [total] capital of 52 million dollars. At the same time, the purchase of public lands in the West and speculation on those. In 1833, 4 million dollars were spent on public lands; in 1836, 24.8 million dollars.

All of this: a surplus of capital, a boom in trade and industry, [and] rising prices for goods and land created strong demand for European goods. In particular, English exports to the United States increased.

English exports [in general, are shown in the following table, the numbers being in thousands of pounds sterling:]

English Exports to	1832	1836
United States	5,468	12,486
Northern European countries	10,000	9,897
Southern European countries	5,867	9,001
Asia	4,235	6,751
Central and South America	4,272	5,955

In addition it happened that in 1833 and 1834 Spain and Portugal took out a large number of loans from England. Prices on the stock exchange [in England] rose swiftly. Likewise the prices of goods. Speculation began on *English* securities: railroad shares and bank shares. In 1836, 48 banks were founded in England (with low share prices, of [only] 10 or 5 pounds sterling).

NB: The nominal capital of the joint-stock companies founded between 1834 and 1836 [in England] amounted to 115.2 million pounds sterling. Of that, 69.6 million [was invested] in railroads; 23.8 million [went to] institutions connected with banking; 7.6 million to insurance companies; 7.0 million to mining enterprises; 3.7 million [was invested in] canal building, and so forth.

The high prices of goods in England quickly promoted *imports* into England.

In the United States a panic broke out: because of an 1836 restriction on land speculation (cash only). The American banks frantically sought to obtain gold from England, and consequently panic broke out in England as well, because of the strong outflow of gold. In 1837 there were 618 bank failures in the United States. [The panic in the U.S. had a] recoil effect on England: a run on the banks of south England. Bankruptcies of export houses, with the cotton industry suffering the most. (*No* bank failures [in England].) Unemployment—the *Chartist* movement.

1847

The immediate cause: a bad harvest.

The depression reached its bottom in 1842. In 1843 and 1844 there were two good harvests, [which meant] cheap food and [increased] demand for manufactured goods. Then the opium war [of 1839–42]. 1842 saw the opening of the *Chinese market* (five [Chinese] ports were declared open to free trade, and the island of Hong Kong was surrendered to England). In 1844–45 boom times prevailed [in England], particularly in the cotton industry. A large number of [new] cotton mills were founded, with very high wages. Then [came massive] *railroad construction*.

[The following table shows the value of the] licenses for railroad construction granted by Parliament, and the value of those actually built [with figures in millions of pounds]:

(Through December)	Licenses granted	Railroads actually built
1843	81.9	65.8
1844	20.4	6.7
1845	60.5	16.2
1846	131.7	37.8
1847	44.2	40.7
1848	15.3	38.2
1849	3.9	29.6

This railroad construction created a huge demand for products and for labor (200,000 workers). Prices for iron increased enormously. From 1844 on, there was madder and madder speculation on railroad construction.

Then in 1845 a potato blight struck in Ireland and England, and the entire crop was destroyed. There were also bad grain harvests in 1845 and 1846. *Famine in Ireland.* Parliament had to authorize relief payments of 8 million pounds sterling. At the same time, however, there was mad speculation by the grain dealers. Then the *cotton crop* failed [in the United States]. In spite of this, the prices of cotton yarn and cotton goods did not go up at all, because demand went down. (Consumption of cotton fabrics in England in 1845 fell by [a quantity worth] 21 million pounds sterling, and in 1846, by 13 million pounds sterling.) Thereupon, there were cutbacks in the cotton industry. On top of that came business failures on a large scale among the grain speculators. In April and May 1847, English grain traders had purchased enormous quantities of grain [abroad] at the very highest prices. This grain was delivered in July and August (it took two months to transport it!) just as prices dropped because of the very good prospects for the harvest [in England in 1847]. The bankruptcies of the grain speculators brought bank failures in their wake: the Royal Bank in Liverpool, the Liverpool Credit Company, etc. After that a general panic broke out. Then the prices of railroad stocks fell. [A few figures will show this, as follows]:

	In December 1845	In December 1849
Capital invested in railroad construction:	100 million pounds sterling	230 million pounds sterling
The stock exchange price that could actually be obtained for railroad shares amounted to:	160 million pounds sterling	110 million pounds sterling
Profits and losses amounted to:	Profits in 1845: 60 million pounds sterling	Losses in 1849: 120 million pounds sterling

Ruin of many shareholders. In 1848 a general fall in prices. *The cotton industry suffered the worst*, and then the mining industry, coal and iron ore in particular.

In 1854–55, a crisis in Australia ([involving the newly discovered] gold deposits)

1857. First worldwide crisis.

Abolition of the corn laws in 1846 and from then on England's transition to free trade. The free trade advocates prophesied that [with free trade] crises would not happen any more.

The discovery of *gold deposits* in California and Australia opened new markets for English industry. Until 1850 and 1851 gold production was mainly in Brazil and Siberia, the annual average extraction of gold in the whole world then being worth 150 million marks. By 1853, it had risen to 760 million marks (now, in 1909,* it is 460 million dollars). The ending of the *Crimean War* in 1856 gave English industry new [opportunities for] expansion.

Meanwhile, however, capitalist industry in other European countries had also developed after the revolutions of 1848. Therefore the crisis now affected Germany, Sweden, Denmark, and above all, the United States.

Under the impact of political unrest (1848) European capital had flowed massively to the United States. According to an estimate by [Albert] Schäffle, during 1849–54, 1,000 million guilders (a guilder = +/–2 marks) were invested in American securities. There was an enormous boom in the United States. The Crimean War had interrupted the export of grain from Russia, which America took advantage of. The purchase of and speculation on public lands, and at the same time massive emigration to the United States from Germany, Russia, and Poland. In 1852–53 in the United States, public lands worth 1.7 million dollars were purchased, but in 1852–54, the figure was 20.4 million dollars. Along with that, a tremendous amount of railroad construction. In 1856, the rail network in the United States was enlarged by almost 4,500 miles and even more was projected. The prices of goods rose, which attracted imports. In 1857, the import of goods [into the United States] increased by 32 million dollars. A failure of the cotton crop, and [therefore] high cotton prices, but in spite of that, enormous expansion of the demand for cotton. American banks and import-export dealers engaged in colossal speculation on the import of goods from Europe.

In 1857, [there was] an exceptionally good grain harvest in Europe. That caused a series of bankruptcies among grain-exporting businesses in America. The failure of one small bank gave the signal for a panic on all the American stock exchanges. In December 1857, prices [in the United States] plunged by 20 to 30 percent.

---

* Although Luxemburg refers to "now" as 1909, she also gives statistics for 1911 near the end of this typescript. The notes in those last few pages are not expanded on in her lengthy discussion of the history of economic crises in her typescript entitled "Volume 2 of *Capital*."

The American crisis was immediately transmitted to England. In October, there was a suspension of payments by one Liverpool bank. Thereupon, panic in all of England.

From there the crisis was transplanted to France (where the bank rate had always been 4 percent, and only in 1847 went up to 5 percent; but in November 1857 it rose to 10 percent!).

There immediately followed a collapse in *Hamburg*, from which the crisis spread to Prussia and at the same time to Sweden and South America, with which Hamburg had strong trade relations.

1861–65

The price of cotton per kilo rose from [the equivalent of] 60–80 pfennigs to 4–5 marks!

[Total] exports from England to the United States
  In 1861, 23 million pounds sterling
  In 1862, 11 million pounds sterling.

[Drop in the value of] Consumption of cotton in England
  In 1860, 1,084 million pounds sterling
  In 1862, 452 million pounds sterling

The cotton shortage brought about a general slowdown in English industry. To be sure, the cotton mill owners and cotton dealers not only did not suffer from this crisis but even gained from it. The blow fell mainly on the small manufacturers, who were ruined.

	Number of cotton mills in England	Number of spindles in England
1862	2,887	30,387
1867	2,549	32,000

On the other hand, the cotton shortage led to the enrichment of the big cotton mill owners. In mid-1861 very substantial stocks of unsold raw cotton and cotton goods had been built up. A consequence of the breaking-off of imports from the United States [because of the Civil War] was that prices for these stored-up goods experienced an extraordinary increase. According to one calculation, the mill owners and cotton traders gained more than 19 million pounds sterling from the [sale of the stocks of] raw cotton, and 16 million pounds sterling from the cotton goods, for a total of more than 36 million pounds sterling. Mainly the Lancashire capitalists.

It was different for the workers! By the 1860s the workers of Lancashire had reached the highest level within the English working class. They had the highest wages, and were the most intelligent and best-organized workers. Wages and working conditions were held to firmly established standards. Many workers had some savings. The percentage of those on relief was lower than anywhere else in the country. And it was precisely these workers who for several years were robbed of the very means of existence. Beginning in autumn 1861 unemployment grew so much that charity, both public and private, had to step in to an extraordinary extent. By January 1862 unemployment reached threatening dimensions. Cutbacks in production in the spring of 1862 were so large that by April, out of the 47,504 workers who had earlier been employed in the cotton industry in Manchester, only 23,722 remained fully employed, as against 15,393 on half-time, and 8,369 completely unemployed. In Blackburn and its surrounding areas, out of 40,000 workers, 8,459 were completely unemployed and most of the rest worked only 2–4 days a weeks. The workers had to pawn or sell their furniture, beds, etc., and the wives and children went begging. In May of 1862 the number of jobless workers in the county of Lancashire reached 58,000; according to some sources, the number was as high as 100,000. Large numbers of small business owners were [also] ruined. A relief committee was founded in London. The workers of Lancashire engaged in a struggle with local charity officials, who wanted to force the cotton mill workers to perform the crudest kinds of labor [at workhouses].

The behavior of the *free-trade advocates* was characteristic. [John] Bright was concerned above all to minimize the extent of the disaster. He claimed that impoverishment had been much worse under the Corn Laws in the early 1840s. He also defended the local charity officials energetically and demanded the least possible interference by the central government in the sphere of jurisdiction of the local poor-relief authorities. He opposed all large-scale relief action, because in his view that would only increase pauperism in Lancashire

The *Tories*, as always, did more for the workers than the liberal factory owners. In the House of Lords they defended quite warmly the demand of the workers for the elimination of forced labor. Meanwhile, the workers' struggle with the local poor-relief authorities continued. In Blackburn a thousand unemployed workers refused to work at breaking up rocks.

In July [1862], out of the 355,000 workers in the textile mills of the county of Lancashire, 80,000 were completely unemployed, and the rest were employed only part of the time. Charity contributions however flowed in abundantly. The government and society feared social unrest, and that was the reason for charity action on a large scale. But it was precisely the cotton mill owners who were least inclined to make sacrifices, and complaints were printed [even] in the conservative newspapers that they [the mill owners] did not want to sign the lists [for charity donations]. In Parliament, Cobden spoke out sharply against the proposal that relief in the counties of England be organized on a broader basis. That would mean the ruin of the mill owners, said Cobden. He advocated a public loan that would provide relief [through a public works program]. Lord Palmerston stated publicly: "In reality they want to shift the entire burden from the wealthy to the poor." However, the mill owners won.

In Manchester the mortality rate rose to a level 60–70 percent higher than in the rest of the country.

By an energetic struggle, the workers won their demands: [first,] that relief was to be paid entirely in money, instead of half of it being paid in kind; second, that forced labor be replaced by instruction at schools. Special schools were established for the workingmen, and sewing schools for their wives.

December 1862 was the high point of the crisis. In Lancashire and Cheshire [counties] 271,983 persons were receiving public assistance, [and] 236,310 were receiving [other types of] assistance. Out of those 271,983 on public relief, only 12,500 were at workhouses.*

At the end of January 1863, in the cotton-industry districts the number of those completely unemployed was 247,230, of those who were employed part time the number was 165,600, and those employed full time, 121,129. Wages were driven down by 10–20 percent! The mill owners once again walked off with the winnings!

At the end of 1862 a movement for emigration began. The best workers emigrated. Invitations came from New Zealand. One province in New Zealand offered 10,000 pounds sterling for emigrants from England. Large gatherings of workers began. They demanded public support to cover the costs of emigration. On top of that, there were storms of indignation against the mill owners.

In March 1863, in a number of small factory towns of Lancashire, workers began to engage in public disorders because public relief had been reduced. Stores were looted, etc. The Tories supported the emigration movement. However, the government, under pressure from the mill owners, provided credit amounting to 1.2 million pounds sterling for a public works program. *Cobden* defended this in order to counteract emigration. But these public works came into existence after the greatest need had already passed. The work consisted of road building, canal building, labor on aqueducts, the laying out of parks, etc. Thus public works were constructed at ridiculously low wages. A laughable number of workers were employed on these public works—8,324. Counting their families that meant 30–40,000 persons benefited somewhat from that.

By 1864 there was an upturn in the economic conjuncture. Cotton was being imported from India and Egypt, to replace American cotton, and soon the mill owners were complaining about the shortage of work hands.

---

*   These workhouses were established by the Poor Law Amendment of 1834.

English Imports of Raw Cotton:

In 1861, from India 15 million pounds sterling
   from Egypt 10 million pounds sterling
In 1864, from India 52 million pounds sterling
   from Egypt 20 million pounds sterling

Crisis of 1866/67

The enormous amount of cotton imported from the Orient caused a severe monetary crisis in England.

There was a rapid outflow of silver to India and the East. The Bank of England tried to counteract this by frequently raising the bank rate. But trade and industry remained undisturbed. The founding of new companies flourished. In 1863–65 the joint-stock companies founded in England had a total nominal capital of 582 million pounds sterling. Speculative fever.

The end of the American Civil War gave new impetus to English industry.

England's exports to the United States [increased as follows:]
   1864 [exports were worth] 16.7 million pounds sterling.
   1866 [exports were worth] 28.5 million pounds sterling.

[The following table shows the prices of goods during the boom and during the bust:]

	Increase in prices 1866	Decrease in prices 1867
Coffee	+11%	−17%
Sugar	+11%	−9%
Tea	+31%	−23%
Silk	+27%	−9%
Flax and Hemp	+6%	−17%
Copper	+21%	−20%
Cotton	+15%	−28%

All this led to a crisis in 1866. There was a sudden outbreak of panic in May as the result of the bankruptcy of a big firm, Overend & Co. In two weeks the reserves of the Bank of England were almost completely emptied. Banks that functioned as joint-stock companies failed, as did railroad companies. Those hit hardest by the crisis were the iron industry, the machine industry, and shipbuilding.

In 1869, a money and credit crisis in the United States.

Second worldwide crisis, *1873.*

The years 1871–73 were a time of extraordinary industrial growth in all of Europe. Billions of francs as payment of war reparations from France poured into Germany. The founding of many new companies.

Statistics on joint-stock companies.

Germany and Austria become the main arena of stock market speculation. The building of new railroads, home building, real estate speculation, particularly in Vienna.

[The following table shows] the length of standard-gauge railroads in Germany:

	[Total length in kilometers]
1845	2,143
1855	7,326
1865	13,900
1875	27,881
1880	33,645
1890	41,818
	53,822

In Austria, in the years 1867–73, among the newly licensed businesses were 175 [regular] banks, 34 railroad enterprises, 645 industrial companies, 104 housing and construction banks [*Baubanken*], 39 insurance companies, and 8 shipping companies, with a total amount of capital involved, all together, of 4 billion guilders. Only 682 [of these] companies actually came into existence, with joint-stock share capital worth 2,577 billion guilders.

The craze for the founding of new companies spread to the United States, where an enormous economic upturn had followed the end of the Civil War. Railroads: in the years 1870–73, in the United States, a network of new railroad lines of 23,406 miles was built. In 1864 there also began the system of high indirect taxation and high protective tariffs.

In England, unparalleled prosperity in the iron and coal industries.

Total value of exports from England to the US:

1870	28.3 million pounds sterling
1872	40.7 million pounds sterling
1873	14.6 million pounds sterling (showing the effects of the crisis [of 1873]

Total exports of iron, steel, and hard coal from England [to all the world]:

1868	Iron and steel together	17.6 million pounds sterling
1868	Exports of hard coal	5.4 million pounds sterling
1873	Iron and steel	37.7 million pounds sterling
1873	Hard coal	13.2 million pounds sterling

Total exports from England of cotton, wool, and linen fabrics:

	Cotton	Wool	Linen fabrics
1868	53 million pound sterling	19.6	7.1
1873	81.5 million pound sterling	25.4	7.3

Statistics on pig iron production in England:

	Production of pig iron in millions of tons	Median price for pig iron
1867	4.7	52 shillings, 6 pence
1868	4.9	52 shillings, 9 pence
1869	5.4	53 shillings, 3 pence
1870	5.9	54 shillings, 4 pence
1871	6.6	59 shillings
1872	6.7	101 shillings, 10 pence
1873	6.8	117 shillings, 3 pence

The price rose so high because the expansion of production could not keep pace with the growing demand, caused by the increasing needs of railroad construction. In this connection, very heavy speculation on foreign loans developed on the London Stock Exchange.

In the years 1870–75 foreign loans taken out in London amounted to a value of 260 million pounds sterling! Most of these were Oriental governments, but they did not pay back the loans. At the end of the 1870s the following governments did not pay the interest on their loans or made only partial payments: Turkey, Egypt, Greece, Bolivia, Costa Rica, Ecuador, Honduras, Mexico, Paraguay, Uruguay, Peru, Venezuela, and Santo Domingo.

Total value of securities issued on American and European stock exchanges:

1870	4,560 million marks
1871	12,560 million marks
1872	10,110 million marks
1873	8,722 million marks
1874	3,368 million marks

In general: great technological changes in the United States, England, Germany, etc.: machinery, steam power, railroads!

The crash began separately in the United States, with the collapse of speculation on the railroads, and in Europe, in Vienna on May 3, 1873.

By May 28 in Vienna there had already been 100 bankruptcies and shares had lost 300 million guilders in value. In June there was a panic in Germany. The value of securities suddenly fell by 30–50 percent.

The American crash intensified the general collapse.

Then a severe commercial crisis followed in England. There were more and more bankruptcies from 1873 to 1875 and even later. In 1878 some top-ranking banks failed. In England in 1878 there was a major crisis in the cotton industry and also in the iron industry and coal mining. The high point was 1879.

From 1873 to 1880 the crisis spread across Italy, Russia, Holland, Belgium, South America, and Australia and affected all the major branches of industry: iron and coal, textile, the chemical industry, the food industry, the railroads, and shipbuilding.

The Crisis of 1882 and the Depression of 1883–86

In France, recovery after the [Franco-Prussian] war, the Third Republic, and also the subsidence of Communism.* In 1875 an upturn begins. Founding of the Union Générale and the Banque de Lyon by Bontoux, supported by the Catholic party in France and Austria—in opposition to the Rothschild group. Also the founding of the Vienna Agricultural Bank. [The Bontoux group] bought up its own shares, to make the house look more prosperous. To put their capital to use, new enterprises were founded on a massive scale: gas works, coal mines, insurance companies, railroads, etc. Newspapers were purchased in order to influence public opinion. The first collapse came in Lyon. A sudden plunge in the value of shares. Also in Vienna. On January 29, 1882, bankruptcy of the Union Générale.

Also in other countries: After 1879 a new upturn began. In the United States, the feverish building of railroads: in the years 1880–82, 28,240 miles [were added to] the railroad network.

[The value of] exports from England to the United States was:

| In 1878 | 14.6 million pounds sterling |
| In 1882 | 31.0 million pounds sterling |

---

*   That is, after the crushing of the Paris Commune of 1871.

[The value of] exports from England in general [was as follows (in millions of pounds sterling):]*

	Iron & Steel	Machinery	Cotton fabrics	Wool fabrics	Linen fabrics
1878	18.4	7.5	52,9	16.7	5.5
1882	31.6	11.6	62.9	18.8	6

In 1884 in the United States there was a severe economic crash involving the railroads. A general fall of prices in England followed, about 15–20 percent. The drop in prices [of agricultural products] on the world market has given rise to an entire body of literature. In particular, grain prices fell ([because of cheaper] transport, and American grain!). According to the *price charts* recorded in Hamburg, from 1884 to 1886 prices fell by 31 percent for agricultural products, by 7 percent for industrial products, and by 12 percent for products from colonies.

The crisis of 1890 (South America and England)

After 1886 [there was] a new industrial upturn.

Exports from England:

	Iron	Machinery	Coal	Cotton fabrics	Wool fabrics	Linen fabrics†
1886	21.7	10.1	9.8	57.4	19.7	5.5
1890	31.6	10.4	19.0	62.1	20.4	5.7

Exports to *Argentina* were especially strong.†

At the end of the 1880s a mad craze for founding new companies developed in Argentina.

In the years 1887–89, 250 joint-stock companies were founded in Argentina with a nominal capital of 764 million dollars.

The national debt of Argentina was:

In 1874   10 million pounds sterling
In 1890   59.1 million pounds sterling

---

* In the longer typescript, "Volume 2 of *Capital*," the figure for "1882, Machinery" is given as 11.9 instead of 11.6 pounds sterling.

† In the longer typescript on "Volume Two of *Capital*," the figures for "1886, Iron" is given as 21.8 instead of 21.7, and "1890: Machinery" is given as 16.4, instead of 10.4.

London was the main source [of funding for Argentina]
The railroad network in Argentina:

In 1883   3,123 kilometers
In 1893   13,691 kilometers

This was the amount actually built. Much more was projected. In 1889 alone, [new] railroad construction was licensed for 12,000 kilometers.

In 1890 in Argentina there was a tremendous economic crash, and a revolution.* As a result, there came a crisis in England. The largest English private bank, R. Baring & Co., collapsed in November 1890.

Then a crash in Transvaal followed, and in Mexico, Uruguay, etc.

A severe commercial crisis in England.

1893 The United States and Australia

Railroad construction at a furious pace in both countries.

In the United States, in addition, the confused uproar of the "silver party" over currency policy; also, trust scandals (the "Whiskey Trust,"† the cornering of the wheat market, etc.). Bankruptcies on a massive scale in the United States. Trade grinds to a halt completely. Failure of 600 banks in August 1893.

Total number of bankruptcies:

1890   7,538 with liabilities worth 93 million dollars
1893   11,174 with liabilities worth 324 million dollars

Among these, 74 railroad companies, with 29,000 miles of track, went bankrupt. In May 1893, the shares of the trusts fell in value by 25–50 percent.

Pig iron production:

1892   9,157,000 tons
1893   7,124,000 tons

---

* The 1890 revolution in Argentina was named "the Revolution of the Park," and took place on July 26 of that year. It was against the presidency of Miguel Juárez Celman, who was accused of corruption and abuse of power. The main impetus behind the revolt was the rising cost of living. Though Celman was forced from power as a result of the revolution, it failed to achieve its aims of transforming Argentinian government or society.

† The Whiskey Trust was the nickname of the Distiller's Security Corporation. It was founded by Julius Kessler in the 1870s and cornered the market on distilled liquor.

March on Washington by the unemployed.[*] Demand for public works (road building). On Easter Sunday in 1894 the first march began, and arrived in Washington on May 1. In Australia, the government had borrowed 112 million pounds sterling from English capitalists. Of that, 81 million pounds sterling went into railroad and streetcar construction.

Length of the railroad network in Australia:

1880   4,900 miles
1895   15,600 miles

Real estate and construction craze.

In 1891 the construction companies began to collapse. In 1893 a general crash. Almost all the Australian banks stopped payments.

In 1895 a *stock exchange crisis.*

In 1895 *a crisis in* the value of South African mines (extraction of gold began in Transvaal in 1882–85). The market value and assets of 146 gold trusts on October 1, 1895, were 5,095 million marks; on February 28, 1897, they were 1,960 million marks.

Beginning in 1896, an unparalleled *upswing.*

The Sino-Japanese war.

The Trans-Siberian railroad.

Trade treaty between Germany and Russia, upsurge of electric power technology, [an upsurge in] gold production in South Africa, Australia, and the Klondike (and Alaska).

NB: orders [and contracts] given out by the army and navy!

(Parvus's pamphlet)[†]

1898 Bernstein![‡]

The World Crisis of 1900–01

Terrible unemployment in Germany, Austria, England, Russia, France, Italy, Belgium, and East Asia. It first appeared in Russia.

In *England* imports fell by [the equivalent of] about 35 million marks, and exports by about 235 million marks, particularly the import of raw materials

---

[*]   A reference to Coxey's Army and its march on Washington in 1894.

[†]   Most likely a reference to Parvus' *Die Gewerkschaften und die Sozialdemokratie. Kritischer Bericht über die Lager u. die Aufgaben der deutschen Arbeiterbewegung* (The Trade Unions and Social-Democracy: Critical Report on the Position and Tasks of the German Workers' Movement) (Dresden: Sächsischen Arbeiterzeitung, 1896).

[‡]   A reference to Eduard Bernstein's articles that sparked the revisionist controversy which were published in *Die Neue Zeit* in 1897–98. Luxemburg responded to them in her *Reform or Revolution.*

(cotton, etc.) and the export of coal and iron. — In *Austria*, an enormous drop in prices for iron goods and machinery, a colossal decline in exports, business cutbacks and unemployment.

In *Russia* the iron and coal industry as well as the oil industry suffered the most. Prices and [*MS. Illegible—single word*] fell, in part, by a third.

In *China* the Boxer Rebellion and the campaign by "the Huns" brought about a severe general crisis. Commerce was laid low completely. As a result *Japan* was also drawn into the crisis, because China, particularly its southeastern coastal districts, was a significant customer for Japan.

The *United States* remained unaffected. Indeed, it was registering great prosperity: there was full employment in the textile and iron industries, and strong demand on the railroads. As a result new trusts were formed and new businesses started. [All] that would contribute to the next major world crisis.

1907

[The crisis of 1907] started out precisely from the United States.

In the years 1903–06 [there was] a boom. The military and the navy, high protective tariffs, high prices. Then a panic and the collapse of prices on the New York Stock Exchange, which spread to London, Berlin, etc. Almost all countries were affected.

In Germany in 1908 [there were] 11,581 bankruptcies (even in [the crisis of] 1901 there had been only 10,566).

The world crisis was most clearly reflected in the downturn in maritime shipping, which was unparalleled. The two largest shipping firms, H.A.S. and North German Lloyd, had *none at all!*[*]

[This was the] consequence of overproduction in shipbuilding during the boom. In north German harbors even at the beginning of 1909, ships with a capacity of two million freight tons were lying at anchor, unused. *Trade unions.*

NB: emigration!

Number of between-deck passengers from Hamburg and Bremen to New York:

1907   268,000
1908   77,000 (???Is that correct?)[†]

---

[*]   That is, they did no business at all.

On the North German Lloyd line alone:[*]

1908   to America: 59,000
       from America: 89,000
1909   to America: 151,000
       from America: 35,000

Crises in *particular economic sectors!*
  Prices fall universally
  Three sets of index numbers

	According to the "Economist"	Acc. to Palgrave	Acc. to Sauerbeck
1865–69	100	100	100
1870–79	93	97	97
1880–87	77	82	78

(different types of goods [calculated, using] different methods)

In 1886 a commission was established in England to investigate the causes of the economic slowdown. Various causes were explained: (1) increased cost of gold; (2) depreciation of silver; (3) protective tariffs by many countries as an obstacle to trade. But the explanations agreed mainly on two things: (1) radical changes in production technology; and (2) radical changes in the means of transport. The report of the commission states, among other things: "In recent years with the help of science, and with the application of machinery to the production and transport of goods in all countries of the world, a revolution of the greatest significance has been enacted in the vital relations of the entire civilized world. The quantity of labor that is required for the accomplishment of a particular result in the sphere of production or transport has diminished to an extraordinary extent and continues to diminish."[†]

Technology: The total number of steam engines (in the *world*), expressed in *horsepower* amounted to: 6.3 million in 1850; 11.4 million in 1860; 19.5 million in 1870; 28.9 million in 1880; and 35 million in 1885. Of these: 10.5 million were in the United States; 9.7 million in England; and 14.8 million in the heartland of Europe.

---

[*]   The question marks within the parentheses are in the original typescript.

[†]   See *Final Report of the Royal Commission Appointed to Inquire into the Depression of Trade and Industry (With minutes of evidence)* (London: Eyre and Spottiswoode, 1886), p. lvii. Curiously, Luxemburg does not mention one factor that the report mentions: "The fall in the rate of profit which is the natural tendency of the accumulation of capital" (p. lxii).

Just one example:

Steam engines in Prussia

	Number of Steam Engines	Horsepower
1837	437	7,514
1840	634	12,279
1843	1,090	27,241
1846	1,491	41,130
1849	1,969	67,150
1852	2,833	92,476
1855	4,085	161,774
1861	8,685	365,631
1878	37,320	2,891,867
1885	48,868	1,426,739
1889	58,782	1,773,454
1901	99,096	4,328,778

(The figures for 1837–78 do not include locomotives or steam engines used on ships. The figures for 1885–1901 do not include locomotives or steam engines used on naval vessels.)

Transport: (1) railroads in the United States, Russia, India; (2) the Suez Canal (1869); (3) steamships replace sailing ships; (5) ships built of steel instead of wood; (5) enormous increase in the power of the machinery.

Freight costs become cheaper in the 1880s. The freight cost for [approximately] one quarter [ton] of grain (217.7 kilograms) from New York to England was: in 1874, 10.5 shillings; in 1884, 4 shillings; and from Odessa to England: in 1874, for one ton (1,000 kilograms), 40 shillings; in 1884, 16 shillings.

The steep drop in prices on the [world] market for agricultural products lowered the purchasing power of the rural population with regard to industrial products. According to one estimate, during the 1880s agricultural income in England declined by 42.8 million pounds sterling. In the United States in the 1880s the ruin of millions of [family] farmers occurred. They lost their farms on a massive scale or became tenant farmers instead of farm owners.

Statistics on the agricultural crisis[*]

[The table below shows] average prices on the most important markets for agricultural products in Prussia. [This table covers] four eight-year periods.

---

* The table presented at this point by Luxemburg also appears in her longer typescript "Volume 2 of *Capital*." We have used the same format as in the translation of the longer typescript, which appeared with the following statement by Luxemburg: "The statistics [in the table below] were assembled by Professor [Heinrich] Dade and published by the Association for Social Policy."

	1868/69–75/76	1876/77–83/84	1884/85–91/92	1892/93–99/00
Wheat	223 marks	207 marks	181 marks	155 marks
Rye	173 marks	166 marks	156 marks	131 marks
Barley	165 marks	158 marks	148 marks	138 marks
Oats	160 marks	148 marks	142 marks	138 marks
Potatoes	56 marks	59 marks	53 marks	49 marks
Straw	46 marks	50 marks	48 marks	43 marks
Hay	72 marks	65 marks	60 marks	59 marks

Cotton crisis in Egypt

The Civil War in the United States and the [resulting] high prices for cotton provided the impetus for the expansion of cotton production in Egypt on an enormous scale. Cotton cultivation was introduced in Egypt under Mohammed Ali in the beginning of the nineteenth century, but not on a large scale. Now speculation enters in. The khedive Ismael Pasha stole land and converted it into cotton plantations. There was an entire revolution in crop cultivation, the irrigation system, deep ploughing, steam engines for pumping water, steam-driven ploughs (machines from England), and [the employment of] serf-type forced labor. Loans from English and French capitalists. In 1865, a collapse. In [???]* in Egyptian cotton.

Cotton Cultivation in 1900:

	Area	Yield
United States	25 million acres	9 million bales (500 lbs. per bale)
India		1.5 million bales
Egypt		1.3 million bales
World production		14 million bales

But Egyptian cotton, because of its quality, brings a higher price and is even imported by the United States in substantial amounts.

Bank rates in the 1860–80s:

London	1861–70	4.3%
	1871–75	3.5%
	1876–80	2.9%
	1885	2.5%
Amsterdam	1884–87	2.5%
Berlin	1870s	4.5%
	1884–87	3–3.5%

---

* The question marks are in the original typescript.

The strong expansion of joint-stock companies also intensified competition in industry. Industry developed in a series of new countries: Germany, Austria, the United States, Russia. As a result of all this, an intensified competitive struggle on the world market. And from that, the strong efforts to form monopolies.

(1) Long-term *protective tariff policies*
(2) *Cartels and trusts*

BIBLIOGRAPHY ON THE THEORY OF CRISES AND HISTORY OF CRISES

[Eugene von] Bergmann[,] *Geschichte der [Nationalökonomishen] Krisentheorien* [History of the Political Economy of Theories on Crises], Stuttgart[:Kolhammer, 1895].

Max Wirth[,] *Geschichte der Handelskrisen* [History of Commercial Crises], Frankfurt[:J.D. Sauerländer,] 1858 (fourth edition, 1890).

Herkner's article [entitled "Crises"] in the *Handwörterbuch der Staatswissenschaften*

Tugan Baranowsky[,] *Studien zur Theorie und Geschichte der Handelskrisen in England* [(Studies in the Theory and History of Commercial Crises in England)], Jena[: G. Fischer,] 1901.

Parvus[,] *Die Handelskrisis und die Gewerkschaften* [The Trade Crisis and the Trade Unions], Munich: Verlag M. Ernst, 1907.

[Parvus,] *Der wirtschaftliche Aufschwung und die Gewerkschaften* [The Economic Boom and the Workers' Movement], Dresden 1896(?)[†]

Georg Bernhard[,] *Krach–krisis und die Arbeiterklasse* [Crash—Economic Crisis and the Working Class], Berlin: Vorwärts, 1902.

PROBLEMS

Do cartels and trusts regulate production? (The crises since 1880)
Can cartels and trusts arbitrarily set prices?
Can cartels and trusts be expanded to include all [spheres of] production?
Cartels, trusts, and the working class.
Cartels, trusts, and tariff policy.

International contradictions
Legislation against cartels and trusts
Raw materials and processing

---

[*]   Heinrich Herkner, "Krisen," in *Handwörterbuch der Staatswissenschaften*, edited by J. Conrad et. al, second edition, Vol. 5 (Jena: G. Fischer, 1900), pp. 413–33.

[†]   The question mark is in the original typescript. This appears to be a reference to Parvus' *Die Gewerkschaften und die Sozialdemokratie. Kritischer Bericht über die Lager u. die Aufgaben der deutschen Arbeiterbewegung.*

In 1911 [*even*] *without [counting] the world market!*

Chemical industry	156, 405
Textile industry	922,817
Metal and machine industry	1,657,863
Timber industry	429,975
(timber for building)	
(and for commercial use)	

Gold and *silver* as *monetary material*
Do cartels represent progress?

(2)[†] *"Regulation of Industry"* — Crises

[Crises] since the 1880s[:] 1893 in America, *1900* in Europe, *1907* in America and Europe—the ups and downs are extremely sharp, as before. Other methods [are necessary.]

The trade unions suffer the least; those that are weaker suffer the most.

(3) *Price policy.* (1) on occasion [i.e., conditionally there might be?]: a trust [limited to?[the "homeland"; (2) competition from "outsiders"; (3) on the world market (export premiums, giveaway prices); (4) competition through surrogates; (5) all-sided? struggle among cartels [producing] finished goods, semi-finished goods, and raw materials.

(4) Can a "universal cartel" come into existence?

(5) [General] Trends: 1) Conglomeration ????[‡] the smaller [swallowed up] by the larger, elimination of the middleman; 2) High protective tariffs, international conflicts; 3) Subjugation of the state!; 4) Exhaustion of the mass of the people, and of the petty bourgeoisie.

(6) The position of the workers

In general: sharpening of the contradictions, greater anarchy [of production], acceleration of development.

(7) Trusts and tariff policy. [See] Table 59, Liefmann, page 5

(8) Do cartels and trusts represent progress?

[A list of] crises [beginning with] 1815.[§] [mention] Robert Owen

1815, 1825, 1836/9, 1847 *England* (South America, the United States)

Canal building, railroad construction, *speculation,* exports [from England] to America.

---

*   Luxemburg does not make clear what the numbers in the following table refer to. Perhaps she meant the number of persons employed by cartels and trusts in 1911.

†   There is no number 1 listed in the typescript. It is possible that the first on the list of 8 points was intended to be the earlier sentence reading "Do cartels represent progress?"

‡   The question marks are in the original typescript.

§   The following seem to be incomplete notes for material already written about in greater detail earlier in the manuscript.

After 1825, the *steam-powered loom* and radical change in the smelting of iron.

1842 Opening of the Chinese market.

1857 world crisis (abolition of the corn laws in 1846; gold deposits in California and Australia in 1850 and 1851; the Crimean War in 1855. After the *1848 revolutions:* [economic expansion in] France, Germany, Sweden, Denmark, the United States. The crisis breaks out in America, then [spreads to] England, France, Hamburg.

1861–65 the "cotton famine".

In 1863 250,000 totally unemployed; 170,000 partly; only 122,000 fully employed.

1867 enormous imports to England from the Orient (cotton). After the American Civil War, an upturn.

1873 Second worldwide crisis: [involving] the United States, Germany, Austria, England, Italy, Russia, Holland, Belgium, South America. *The iron industry.*

Practical Economics: Volume 3 of Marx's *Capital*

The content of Volume 3 of *Capital* breaks down into two parts:

(1) The development of the rate of profit; and

(2) How it is divided up into different parts: entrepreneur's profit; commercial profit; interest on loan capital; and ground rent. Most important and decisive is the development of the rate of profit. Once again, this is specifically Marx's scientific explanation of the profit rate, and to this day it remains the only one.

Volume 3 is the most important and interesting [part of *Capital*] after Volume 1.

It is written clearly in its theoretical aspect, and if we study it on our own, it will not cause us any special difficulties. To be sure it requires effort in order to follow the how the profit rate develops. But it is not as difficult as the theory of value in Volume 1.

The third volume is especially important because after its publication, great confusion arose. [In some circles] people had the impression that the content of the third volume disproved teachings presented in the first volume.* As a result there was uncertainty in the circles indicated, which found expression in the allegation that Marx's theory did not have a solid footing despite the fact that in particular areas it was capable of achieving a great deal.

And so, first of all, *development of the rate of profit*.

Everyone probably had the impression that the theory of value [in general], not just Marx's, is the cornerstone of economic life.

Marx's [theory of value] is, however, distinct from all others. It makes a distinction between two things:

(1) the hidden laws that operate invisibly behind the scenes in the bourgeois economy; and

---

* This is a reference to Eugen von Böhm-Bawerk's *Zum Abschluß des Marxschen Systems* (Karl Marx and the Close of His System) (Berlin: von Otto von Boenigk, 1896) and Ladislaus von Bortkiewicz's "Wertrechnung und Preisrechnung im Marxschen System: ein Übersicht über die Marx-Kritlk" (Value and Price in the Marxian System: An Overview of the Critique of Marx), *Archiv für Sozialwissenschaft*, 23 (1906) pp. 10–50, 445–488, which argued that Marx's discussion of the transformation of values into prices in Chapter 9 of Volume 3 of *Capital* is internally inconsistent with his presentation of the theory of value in Volume 1. For a recent refutation of these criticisms of Marx's theory, see Andrew Kliman, *Reclaiming Marx's Capital: A Refutation of the Myth of Inconsistency* (Lanham, MD: Lexington Books, 2006). For an English translation of Böhm-Bawerk's work, *Karl Marx and the Close of his System: A Criticism* (London: Unwin, 1898); for an English translation of Bortkiewicz, see "Value and Price in the Marxian System," *International Economic Papers*, No. 2, 1952, pp. 5–60.

(2) the outward forms in which those laws reach the consciousness of human beings.

The main thing is the great conversion of the objective laws of the capitalist economy into pictoral representations [*Vorstellungen*] [showing] how those laws prevail on the surface of that economy: i.e., the way in which the rate of profit is formed.

The value of a commodity is represented by the amount of socially necessary labor embodied in it. How is that represented in capitalist terms?

In a capitalist enterprise how does the value of a commodity arise?

The value of a commodity contains: constant capital[;] The value of labor power: variable capital[;] surplus value.

Those are the distinctions we Marxists make.

Is this representation of value meaningful for the entrepreneur? No. What sticks in his mind as value is what he can stick in his pocket, what he has gained [in profit].

For the *capitalist a different way of dividing up the value of the commodity* is important, one different from the method of scientific inquiry.

From the capitalist's point of view we can break down the value of each commodity into the *cost price of the commodity*, that is, into constant and variable capital, [on the one hand,] and into *surplus value* [on the other]. That expresses the capitalist point of view. For the capitalist, everything that he has laid out are on one sheet of paper, and on the other, everything he has taken in as an increase [of his capital].

Surplus value in this way has been separated from capital outlays, because the capitalist has put all his outlays together [in one place], and as a result surplus value is viewed in connection with cost price as a whole.

Surplus value, when viewed in connection with total cost price, appears to him to be profit.

What follows from this? That the capitalist has placed surplus value, which he has also placed in his pocket, in a proportional relationship with all the outlays he has made in the production of a commodity. *From this it follows [in his view] that surplus value is a result of the application of [his] capital, i.e., that it comes equally from all parts of his capital.* Its [real] origin is [thus] veiled. Profit as a *fruit produced by capital* is the result of this conception.

What strengthens the capitalist in this conception? First, he has the experience that he can never produce without means of production. Then there is an additional appearance, that his outlays for wages are placed in the same category with [outlays for] the various other means of production.

Among the means of production are those from which only a small portion goes into the commodity and those that enter into the commodity entirely: that is, raw materials.

For the capitalist, all the costs of the means of production have now been accounted for.

The capitalist probably makes a distinction between the expenditures whose value goes completely into the product and the expenditures he has made that last for a longer period of time. He distinguishes between *fixed and circulating capital*, that is, between that which is stationary and that which moves around.

Raw materials belong to circulating capital, as do wages.

From the standpoint of this distinction, the [real] origin of surplus value is obscured all the more. The capitalist is reinforced in the conception that the surplus value he obtains has no connection with any *one* part of his capital. He thinks it comes from the capital as a whole.

What happens when machines are introduced?

Their application means that living labor is displaced. *The capitalist shifts part of his variable capital over to constant capital. His surplus value does not become smaller. To the contrary, at first it is even larger.* At first he obtains an extra amount of surplus value.

This strengthens him in his conception *that profit comes from all the various parts of capital.*

Profit [in the view of the capitalist] is that part of the commodity that is obtained over and above the cost price. *Only after the sale of the commodity does the capitalist see whether he has obtained a profit. On the market what happens for him is that, depending on supply and demand, he obtains a larger or smaller profit. From this he derives the conception that the profit is the result of the circulation of the commodity, because depending on the conditions of the market he obtains a larger or smaller profit.*

The average capitalist receives more profit, the more he succeeds in reducing the cost price. The capitalist makes savings if he succeeds *in driving down the wages of the workers, but also if he buys raw materials more cheaply.* Thus the more he can drive down the cost price, the more profit he has. This strengthens him in his false conception.

It seems as though the profit of the capitalist is the result of the *activity of the capitalist.*

Capital appears here as a self-fructifying relationship.

But this is more like the illusion of the capitalist's thinking.

If I, for example, with a capital of 100 marks, 80 of which go into constant capital and 20 of which go into variable capital, at the same time obtain 20 marks [profit], *then it makes no difference, to begin with, whether or not I imagine that I obtained them by means of the entire capital or just the variable capital.*

But there is indeed a difference if I express the profit as a percentage.

The rate of surplus value is never the same as the rate of profit. The latter will always be smaller than the rate of surplus value.

This is also not true in reality, as we shall see.

Examples:

Let us imagine: 5 capitals. Each would amount to 100 marks. These 5 capitals break down in different ways into constant capital [c] and variable capital [v].

1: 80 c + 20 v. Surplus value 100% The surplus value amounts to 20 marks. The value of the products comes to 120 marks, and the rate of profit 20%.

Tables:

In the tables below, it is assumed that the *entire constant capital* passes over into the new products. This is seldom or never the case [in reality].

1st capital:	80c + 20v, with the rate of surplus value at 100%. Thus surplus value is 20 marks and the value of the products, 120 marks, but the rate of profit is only 20%.
2d capital:	70c + 30v, the rate of surplus value 100%. Surplus value is 30 marks, the value of the products is 130 marks, and the rate of profit, 30%.
3d capital:	60c + 40v, with the rate of surplus value 100 %. Thus surplus value is 40 marks, the value of the products is 140 marks, and the rate of profit, 40%.
4th capital:	85c + 15v, with the rate of [s] 100%. Thus surplus value is 15 marks, the value of the products is 115 marks, and the profit rate 15%.
5th capital:	95c + 5v, with the rate of surplus value 100%. Thus surplus value is 5 marks, the value of the products is 105 marks, and the profit rate 5%.

The larger the constant capital and the smaller the variable capital, the smaller the rate of surplus value and the rate of profit will be.

First, the size of the constant capital in the various steps [represented by the 5 different capitals in the above tables] depends on advances in technology in one and the same branch of production. Only after that do other, *different* branches of production come into consideration.

There are in reality no two enterprises in which the distribution of constant and variable capital is the same.

From this it follows, however, that the various capitalists, depending on which branch of production they invest their capital in and depending on what the level of technology is in that branch of production (with all other things being equal—that is, the degree of intensity of exploitation, the rate of surplus value, etc.) the result comes out differently, depending on the distribution of capital. The different capitalists receive quite different rates of profit.

Even with completely equal rates of surplus value, quite different rates of profit will result.

For the capitalist the rate of surplus value does not exist at all—only the rate of profit.

And so he encounters the following result: the more varied his capital investments are, he finds himself in the peculiar situation of obtaining quite different rates of profit.

But he derives his profit unalterably from the investment of capital.

These dissimilar, or uneven, profit rates would be an abnormality, however, from the standpoint of the capitalist mode of production [as a whole]. To understand how this situation is amended, let us imagine the following:

The 5 different capitals [in the table] belong to one and the same capitalist. What would happen to him when he saw the result [in the form of these] disparate profit rates?

If, for example, a capitalist owns a rolling mill* and a coal-mining operation, he would by no means get rid of the rolling mill just because he doesn't make as much profit from it as he does from the coal-mining operation. Because he needs the rolling mill for his coal mining.

And so the capitalist will view his 5 capitals as a single unit of capital and will calculate an average profit from it. He will then observe whether this average profit is as high as that of his colleagues and competitors.

Thus the individual, private capitalist will calculate an average rate of profit. He will regard his separate units of capital as a single whole, see them all together as a single whole, a collective quantity of capital.

How does capitalist society as a whole act [in this regard]?

It acts exactly the same way, except that it does not calculate everything as a collective owner, but it does view itself as equally justified, like every individual capitalist does.

The capitalist will seek to withdraw his capital from the investment that does not bring in as much profit. Other capitalists will do that too. They put their capital into businesses that earn a higher profit. This results in an inflow of capital to those businesses and an outflow from the old businesses from which the capitalists are turning away, and as a result there is a rise in the rate of profit.

A capital inflow results in an increase in production, and therefore a larger market is needed. However, the market is not guided by the amount of capital investment, and hence the capital inflow leads to a lowering of prices.

What will happen in the areas from which there is a capital outflow? A shrinking of production will result. Production will drop, and then there will be an onset of increased demand [because these goods are now in short supply]. Prices will climb, and [with that] the rate of profit will rise.

How far will the rise and fall of the profit rate go on in the two businesses? Until it reaches a middle level.

What helps decide this middle level?

---

* A rolling mill is a process for producing certain forms of metal, such as sheet metal, in which stocks or ingots of molten metal are shaped as they pass through a series of rollers.

Social demand, and social need. In either case it must be satisfied.

Must we assume that things will constantly go as follows: after prices are driven down in the most profitable branches so that they [no longer] earn abnormally high profits, will the capital flow go back into the old businesses?

In certain branches of production prices must constantly be higher than their value, because otherwise the law of the equal rate of profit would be cancelled out.

The law of the rate of profit or the law of value? That is the chief difficulty to which the various critics of Marx take exception. Certainly Smith and Ricardo were unable to solve this problem.

Is it possible for commodities to be sold at their real value and for everyone to indeed obtain an equal rate of profit? (After all, every commodity requires a different labor input and therefore has a different value.)

To be sure, in every single, separate branch of production upward or downward deviations occur.

But if we take all branches of production together, it turns out that prices all come out in the same way, so that the law of value really does hold true so that prices coincide with value.

The law of value holds true for the system of capitalist production as a whole.

Is this a violation of the law of value? Not at all. Those who take that position obviously proceed from the following [mistaken] conception of the law of value:

[They think it means that] *each individual commodity ought to be sold at its value.* But can the law of value hold true for anything other than the total amount of social labor?

How could one think, after absorbing the first volume of *Capital*, that the law of value means that each individual commodity is exchanged in accordance with the amount of labor that was necessary for its production?

The concept of socially necessary labor is the result of the most varied branches of production and individual enterprises conceived of as acting in combination.

It is as if society is an entirety that hangs together despite the anarchy [of production]. The law of value is precisely what holds it together.

The total amount of social labor is decisive in determining the prices of the total number of commodities.

The law of the equal rate of profit is nothing other than the law of value transformed capitalistically.

Postscript on the development of the rate of profit.

The rate of surplus value is the relation of surplus value to variable capital.

The rate of profit is the relation of surplus value to total capital.

Surplus value is the relation of unpaid labor to paid labor.

In the concept of profit the concept of unpaid labor disappears.

The rate of profit blurs over and obscures the source of surplus value.

The concept of *the rate of surplus value* is the formulation of the relation between capital and labor. The *rate of profit* is the relation of capital to itself. According to that conception, capital fructifies itself and produces a surplus of its own accord.

Is the transformation of the rate of surplus value into the rate of profit something more than a mere illusion of the capitalists? Yes, it is:

From the concept of the rate of profit it follows as a law for the capitalist mode of production that all capitals of the same size must bring in the same profit.

What practical actions are linked to the various concepts? The capitalists derive profit from the application of capital as a whole. From this it follows that: If it is capital that produces profit, then each individual quantity of capital of the same size must produce the same profit. For [the concept of] surplus value this is incorrect, because it [profit] comes from variable capital. Depending on the size of the latter, the size of the surplus value will vary. The distribution of capital into constant and variable differs depending on the branch of production and the individual business operation. One branch of production will use more dead means of production and less living labor, while for another the opposite is true. That depends on the technological composition of the business in question. The distribution of capital into constant and variable is not exactly the same in one business as in another.

In practice the equal rate of profit for all [individual capitals] holds true. A capital of 100 marks, for example, will bring in as much profit as another capital of 100 marks that is invested in another branch of production and whose division into constant and variable capital differs from the first.

This carrying through [of the equal rate of profit for all units of capital] happens in the following way (see above): one quantity of capital produces more profit in a business than the same amount of capital in another business, and so the second quantity of capital will flow away from the second business and turn its flow toward the first business. And it is not only this one quantity of capital that will do this, but all other capitals of the same size that are earning less profit than the first. As a result, in the business to which the flow of capital is turning, production will rise, and as a result supply will again become greater than demand, and because of that, once again, many goods will not be sold or will be sold at a lower price. In both cases the rate of profit falls. Meanwhile in the second business, which has experienced an outflow of capital, demand becomes greater than supply, and as a result prices rise and the rate of profit becomes higher.

As a result of this constant movement of capital an equal rate of profit is obtained.

This brings about the fact that in some particular branches of production goods are sold regularly at prices below their value and in others they are sold regularly above their value.

The average rate of profit for all capitals thus signifies that the following phenomenon will occur:

Some capitalists, in the rate of profit they obtain, receive less surplus value than they have actually extorted.

Other capitalists receive more surplus value than they have actually extorted.

With each *individual* capitalist and in each individual branch of production there is thus a distortion of the real state of affairs, which not only results in a different designation but also in a different quantity.

If one views the capitalist class as a whole and the working class as a whole, the law of value applies exactly.

Practice contradicts the theory of value, as long as we have our eyes fixed on the *individual* enterprise and the *individual* branches of production. But that is not so when we look at all enterprises as a whole and the working class as a whole.

In practice vulgar economics seems to be right when it says that it depends on the market prices how much surplus value one will receive, not the number of workers [employed].

In the law of the generally equal rate of profit, we find the formulation, or expression, of the class solidarity of the employers as opposed to the workers.

Joint stock companies have created the possibility for capital to flow back and forth with insane speed. On the stock exchange everything can change in a few hours. The quicker that happens, the more rapidly the rate of profit evens out.

The development of the credit system also contributes to the rapid evening out of the rate of profit.

Capitals	Rate of surplus-value	Surplus-value	Rate of profit	Used up c	Value of commodi-ties	Cost price	
I. 80c + 20v	100%	20	20%	50	90	70	
II. 70c + 30v	100%	30	30%	51	111	81	
III.60c + 40v	100%	40	40%	51	131	91	
IV. 85c + 15v	100%	15	15%	40	70	55	
V. 95c + 5v	100%	5	5%	10	20	15	
390c + 110v	—	110	110%	—	—	—	Total
78c + 22v	—	22	22%	—	—	—	Average

Capitals	Surplus-value	Value of commodities	Cost-price of commodities	Price of commodities	Rate of profit	Divergence of price from value
I. 80c + 20v	20	90	70	92	22%	+2
II. 70c + 30v	30	111	81	103	22%	−8
III. 60c + 40v	40	131	91	113	22%	−18
IV. 85c + 15v	15	70	55	77	22%	+7
V. 95c + 5v	5	20	15	37	22%	+17

From Volume 3 of *Capital* by Marx, pp. 134, to the end of 136, 176, 178.[*]

Does what we have said about socially necessary labor still remain valid or not?

The raw materials that pass over completely into a commodity cost as much as the socially necessary labor put into them. This is expressed in the form of money.

Thus, if the capitalist calculates that he paid so-and-so much for raw materials, for tools, and so on, he is only totalling up the social labor that was necessary to produce those things.

The new value that has been put into the product is always larger than wages. That will also be true in a socialist society. Every human being can create more [*MS. Missing words*]

Then comes the new value—the human labor that has entered into the product. The new value that has been put into the product is always higher than wages. That will also remain true in socialist society. Most human beings are capable of creating more than is necessary to maintain them.

So the capitalist calculates in addition to his expenditures for raw materials, and so on. [He says to himself:] "I have spent so-and-so much on wages." In so doing, he is adding a calculation for a part of the surplus value that has been created.

If he now finishes his calculations and gives an expression to the commodity in the form of its price, would he have summed up the real value of the commodity?

No, because an additional portion of human labor has been put into the commodity that was not paid for.

In order to express the real value of the commodity, the capitalist must add to his calculation all the unpaid labor as well, even though he did not spend anything for it.

How does he express this part? What point of departure does he have for doing that?

---

[*]   Luxemburg largely reproduces these tables from Volume 3 of *Capital*. See Karl Marx, *Das Kapital*, Band III (Hamburg: Otto Meisner, 1894), pp. 134–6; *Capital* Vol. 3, translated by David Fernbach (New York: Vintage, 1981), p. 256.

For this [part] there does not exist any subjective experience [on the part of the capitalist]. It is only from common sense that he has any concept of this. He knows: in his branch of production, one gets a return of 10 percent or 20 percent on what one lays out. He says to himself, "If I did not fight for that percentage, I would be a fool."

But we know that he is merely adding to his calculations the part of the labor that was not paid for. The value of the commodity now represents socially necessary labor.

What does this average profit have to do with the size of the unpaid labor which has been put into the commodity and which still needs to be taken into account? Does it correspond to the part of the unpaid labor that is still stuck inside the commodity?

Does profit match up with the sum total of unpaid labor?

Not in all cases. Only in those where by chance the rate of profit an individual receives happens to agree with the average rate of profit.

For every individual business the profit will not correspond, but for all commodities taken together it will. If we calculate all commodities together, what is calculated as profit will coincide with the part of socially necessary labor that is unpaid.

This fact is confirmed even if we take into account the fluctuations in prices in a given branch of production.

One question that especially interests us is this: How do wages affect the way prices of commodities may move?

What impact does the movement of wages have on the value and price of commodities?

If food becomes cheaper, wages drop: the employers is then in a position to put more surplus value into his pocket.

That is, the movement of wages affects only the rate of surplus value. That rate changes, or moves, in an opposite way in relation to wages. It rises when wages fall and falls when wages rise.

According to the theory of value, the level of wages does not affect the value of commodities at all.

The capitalist knows what his capital outlays are, and he knows the profit that he is entitled to fight for. Of surplus value he knows absolutely nothing.

Let us assume that we have a branch of production in front of us in which the combination of constant and variable capital coincides with the average [rate of profit].

The average rate of profit would be as follows:

C	V	Rate of Surplus Value	Profit Rate	Price of Commodity
80	20	100	20	120

Wages rise 25 percent, and the rate of surplus value drops to 75 percent. The rate of profit will now come to 15 percent instead of 20 percent. The composition of the price [of production is now]: 80c, 25v, and 15 for the rate of profit. Thus it amounts to 120, as before.

C	V	Rate of Surplus Value	Profit Rate	Price of Commodity
92	8	100	20	120

[Let there be] an increase in wages of 25 percent. The variable capital would now amount to 10 instead of 8. The cost price would now be 102. Add to that 14 2/7,* and the price of the commodity will amount to 116 2/7. Thus prices have been influenced by the level of wages. A lowering of the prices has been the outcome.

C	V	Increase in Wages	Profit Rate
50	50	25%	20%

The cost price [now amounts to] 112 and ½, [and the rate of profit is] 16 ⅞ percent. When added up, the price of the commodities would come to 129 ⅜. And so [in this case too] prices have risen.

In those branches of production where outlays for wages are higher than the outlays for constant capital, the prices of commodities rise. But in those branches where the outlays for variable capital are lower than the outlays for constant capital, prices fall.

The lowering of prices [in one part of the economy] is counteracted by the raising of prices [in another].

For the totality of all branches of production the rise in prices in one case and the fall in prices in another compensate for one another, and as a whole the outcome will be what theory has shown us. Marx: *Capital*, Volume 3, page 181, Part I.†

If the capitalists say to us in each particular case: Every rise in wages must invariably have the consequence that prices will rise, that would be wrong in that

---

*   That is, the rate of profit would now be 14 2/7, instead of 20.

†   Marx discusses this in Chapter 11 of Part 2 (not Part 1, as stated in the typescript) of Volume 3, entitled "The Effects of General Fluctuations in Wages on the Prices of Production." Marx writes, "The conclusion is that a general fall in wages leads to a general rise in surplus-value, in the rate of surplus-value, and with other things remaining equal, also in the profit rate, even if in a different proportion; it leads to a fall in production prices for the commodity products of capital of lower than average composition and a rise in production prices for the commodity products of capitals of higher than average composition." See *Capital* Vol. 3, p. 305.

general form. In one case the price rises, but in another it does not. In the one case prices went higher, but in the other they fell.

For capital as a whole there is only one consequence: if wages rise, profits will be smaller.

C	V	Profit Rate	Price
50	50	20%	120

Wages rise by 25 percent.
Now:

C	V	Profit Rate
50	62 ½	14 2/7%

Added all together, this comes to 16½ percent, and the price of the commodities will be 128 7/12. Thus, the price of the commodities have increased. But not as much as the wages, 25 percent, but only by 6½ percent. Wages have here increased by 25 percent, the prices from 120 to 128 7/12, that is, by 6½ percent.

This is proof that the capitalists do not have to increase prices to the exact same extent as the rise in wages. Here the rise in wages was 25 percent, but the increase in prices was only 6½ percent. [This shows] that after all wages are only part of capital.˙

C	V
92	8

A wage increase of 25 percent. The cost price, 92 plus 10, would come to 102. On top of that we add a profit rate of 14 2/7 percent, which gives a price of production amounting to 116 2/7.

That is, the price of production has fallen 3 percent. Wages went up 25 percent, and prices fell 3 percent.

The rate of profit has taken away approximately as much as corresponds to the average variable capital, but here the variable capital is smaller than the constant capital.

˙   Luxemburg's arithmetic here is in error. 6½ percent of 120 (the original price) is 7.8, not "8 and 7/12." The new price should therefore be 127.8. It appears that the 7 and 8 in this number was mistakenly transposed. Also, it should read 7/10, not 7/12.

These are the results if there is an *overall* rise in wages or if a general falling-off of wages occurs. Only a general rise or fall can have a standardizing, or regulating, effect on the average rate of profit.

How do things stand if the workers have imposed a wage increase in a particular branch of production? The employer says he will now have to raise prices by such-and-such an amount. Can he really do that? No, [because] for him the average rate of profit is the determining factor as a rule. In order to charge for the wage increase, he would have to push prices way up. The consequence would be that he would price himself out of the market. And the result of that would be that, in order to stick with the old prices, he would have to pocket a smaller profit.

That is the outcome, just as the theory of value has shown. *An increase in wages brings with it a reduction in profit.*

For society as a whole, what we have learned from the law of value holds true completely.

Let us assume for a moment a case where along with a rise in wages prices also rise. We are taking only *one* branch of production.

C	V	Average rate of profit
92	8	20

Wages rise by 25 percent. In this case the average rate of profit is 14 ²/₇ percent.

Now the capital outlays are 102. To that we add the old rate of profit: 20. The result is that the prices of the commodities are 122. Prices have risen exactly as much as wages.

Can this branch of production deal with wages in such a way that it grabs approximately 6 percent more in prices? No, the average rate of profit comes into play. If that did not happen, there would be an immediate inflow of capital into this branch until the rate of profit dropped back down to the average.

[Let us consider another case:]

C	V	Average rate of profit
50	50	20

An increase in wages of 25 percent. As a result the average rate of profit drops. Capital outlays, taken altogether, are now 112 ½. If the *old* rate of profit were added to that, it would give 132 ½.

[But] if the old profit rate really was added, again an inflow of capital would take place until the average rate of profit was again established.

The movement of prices does not happen at the will of the capitalists. In setting prices they have to stick with those that correspond by and large to the value of all commodities.

Average:

C	V	Average rate of profit
80	20	20

Wages have increased by 25 percent. And so capital outlays of 80 plus 25 = 105.

We assume that profit will be calculated at the old rate, and this gives 125 for commodity prices.

[But what] for example, if this should happen in all of Germany? The consequence would be that it would be hit hard on the world market. Because other countries would not accept this price increase, Germany would have to back down. Or else we would experience this phenomenon: To the extent that the German producer found it possible to pursue a dual policy, he would do the following: Inside the country he would charge extra high prices, but on the world market his prices would be as low as possible. That corresponds to the actual policies of the cartels.

C	V
60	40
70	30
80	20
85	15
95	5

This table above shows an increase in constant capital and a decline in variable capital. This corresponds to the reality. With the increasing productivity [of labor] constant capital rises at the expense of variable capital.

This succession [the series of numbers, in the table above] is the *capitalist* expression of the growing productivity of labor.

In general the productivity of labor expresses itself in the fact that less human labor is necessary to produce something. This is expressed in capitalist terms in the fact that constant capital rises at the expense of variable capital.

That is how we arrive at the historical succession showing the development of capital.

The average rate of profit is the [same as] total surplus value, [that is,] as a total amount that is thrown together and then divided up among capitals of equal size.

What movement of the rate of profit is to be expected with the progressive development of capitalist production? Does it indeed proceed in the order of succession shown in the table above?

With the development of capitalist production variable capital becomes smaller and smaller. Surplus value is calculated on the basis of an ever-increasing amount of capital. If productivity rises, surplus value also must rise. But then the increasing productivity of labor results in a decline in the cost of maintaining the existence of the workers.

Variable capital increases absolutely. It declines only relatively to constant capital. The total number of workers increases. For that reason alone the total amount of surplus value must grow.

With regard to the rate of surplus value: the productivity of labor rises as the number of employed workers increases, because technology is also advancing. The rate of surplus value, that is, the relation between surplus value and variable capital, is bound to increase. *At the same time it turns out that the rate of profit falls.*

Here it becomes evident that the rate of profit is nothing other than a misleading and indeed falsifying way of calculating surplus value.

The general law of the fall in the rate of profit was already known to the classical authors of bourgeois political economy. They could not explain it because they had not calculated surplus value correctly.

Calculated as a percentage, the rate of profit declines.

From this the capitalists draw the conclusion that they will constantly obtain less profit.

But this is [also] true: The rate of surplus value constantly rises.

The first explanation of this phenomenon, so filled with contradictions, was given by Marx. [See] *Capital*, Vol. 3, Part 1, p. 192 [of the first German edition].*

All roads in political economy lead to the law of value.

It is the cornerstone of [Marxist] *political economy. If this [the law of value] is left out, nothing remains of Marx's doctrine.*

By this one can measure the worth of [Eduard] Bernstein's statement in his *Prerequisites of Socialism* to the effect that Marx's doctrine would be very good if only the law of value wasn't so bad.†

---

* The passage Luxemburg is referring to appears in Chapter 13 of Part 3 of Volume 3 of *Capital*, entitled "The Law Itself." Marx writes, "The hypothetical series we constructed at the opening of this chapter therefore expresses the actual tendency of capitalist production. With the progressive decline in the variable capital in relation to the constant capital, this tendency leads to a rising organic composition of the total capital, and the direct result of this is that the rate of surplus-value, with the level of exploitation of labor remaining the same or even rising, is expressed in a steadily falling general rate of profit." (pp. 318–19).

† For Luxemburg's repudiation of Bernstein's rejection of Marx's value theory (which was

[See Volume 3 of *Capital* by Marx, Part I,] p. 199.* From this passage it follows that Marx assumed the number of capitalists would grow in absolute terms even if capital was being concentrated more quickly. [See] pp. 227, 228 until the end of the chapter. [See] pp. 229 ff.†

The growing productivity of labor, on the other hand, has the consequence of *a constant devaluation of capital*. That is, machines are made obsolete by new ones and then have to be reappraised as though they were cheaper.

That is an aspect that tends to stop the falling rate of profit, that is, slows it down.

(Final Section)‡

Is it not strange that someone invests his capital and gets back only part of the profit, instead of supplying all of the capital himself and obtaining the entire profit?

Answer: First, if someone lends his capital, it is guaranteed that he will receive a specified [rate of] interest. But if he invests it himself, he does not know whether [or not] he will receive surplus value, or how much surplus value he will receive.

Second, smaller capitals are completely insufficient for making [big] profits. The basis for that becomes constantly larger.

Third, small amounts of capital have the possibility, through the system of interest payments, of becoming profitable. By themselves they were to small to make a profit.

According to what laws is the level of interest determined?

Is interest determined according to some laws based in the production process, for example, the rate of wages, or is it there no definite determining factor?

---

largely inspired by Bernstein coming under the influence of bourgeois marginal utility theory), see chapter 9 of her *Reform or Revolution*.

   * See *Capital* Vol. 3, p. 322: "The law of the falling rate of profit, as expressing the same or even a rising rate of surplus-value, means in other words: taking any particular quantity of average social capital, e.g. a capital of 100, an ever greater portion of this is represented by means of labor and an even lesser portion by living labor. Since the mass of living labor added to the means of production falls in relation to the value of these means of production, so too does the unpaid labor, and the portion of value in which it is represented in relation to the value of the total capital advanced." This is discussed in Part 3 of Volume 3, not Part 1, as indicated in the typescript.

   † See *Capital* Volume 3, Chapter 15, "The Development of the Law's Internal Contradictions," p. 354: "It also leads to the centralization of this capital, i.e. the swallowing-up of small capitalists by big, and their decapitalization. This is simply the divorce of the conditions of labor from the producers raised to a higher power, these smaller capitalists still counting among the producers, since their own labor still plays a role." For Luxemburg's reference to "the end of the chapter," see pp. 359–75.

   ‡ In this part of the course Luxemburg discusses Marx's theory of credit and interest-bearing capital.

For relations, or conditions, within the realm of production it makes absolutely no difference whether the capital is one's own or someone else's. It is thus a private matter between the two people to whom the given amounts of capital belong. But of course it is not an entirely arbitrary matter.

The demand for capital at any given time and the [available] supply of loan capital determine the level of interest.

What course of motion does interest take from the very outset?

The colossal piling up of capital is what constantly expands the supply on the capital market. That is why the rate of interest is bound to fall. Mark my words: [we are talking about] interest on loans to capitalists.

Ground Rent Theory

Until now we have had two major theoreticians who have expanded [the theory of] ground rent: (1) Ricardo, who was the dominant figure up until Marx; (2) Rodbertus.

What Marx gives us goes beyond them both.

Ricardo knew only differential ground rent. Rodbertus knew only absolute ground rent.[*]

Marx was the first to distinguish two types of ground rent: (1) absolute ground rent; and (2) differential ground rent.

Conditions in England:

How high must the profit be that a quantity of capital seeks to obtain in agriculture? For example, a tenant farmer.

The profit must be at least as high as the average rate of profit. But in addition, it must also include the ground rent due to the capitalist.

The price of the products from the land must be high enough that, over and above profit, the ground rent can also be paid.

---

   [*]   Ricardo argued that ground rent and the value of land have a tendency to continuously increase, providing important (albeit unjustified, in his view) benefits to landowners. The rent obtained from land, for Ricardo, is therefore always *differential* instead of *absolute*. As Marx put it in Chapter 39 of Volume 3 of *Capital*, "[Ricardo] assumes that no other rent but differential rent exists" (p. 788). In contrast to Ricardo, Marx held that the value of land and ground rent is impacted by the productivity of labor as well as the fertility of the soil; on these grounds, he argued that rents appropriated by the landlords are often a burden for industrial capitalists. Rodbertus argued that since the fertility of the soil determines agricultural output, mortgage indebtedness should be replaced by a permanently fixed (or *absolute*) rent. Although Marx acknowledged the importance of Rodbertus' theory of rent, he argued, in Chapter 46 of Volume 3 of *Capital* that he erred in viewing the growth of profit on land as necessarily correlating with a growth in the value of capital. Marx held that absolute rent cannot exist where the organic composition of capital in agriculture is at a higher level than in the economy as a whole.

In reality there are also a large number of possibilities that allow, sometimes temporarily, sometimes [*MS. Incomplete*]

Differential Ground Rent. This results from the differences in fertility of the various pieces of land that are put to agricultural use by various private land-owners. The level of the prices for food is so great in agriculture that a certain [amount of] rent must be deducted from it.

Differential ground rent provides extra income for the class of landowners who happen to possess the worst land.

This differential ground rent is naturally subject to a certain amount of fluctuation. If an entirely new [quantity of] land suddenly appears on the world market, so that an entire large quantity of products at a quite insignificant price are thrown [onto it.]

The costs of production are governed at any given time by the poorest type of land. Prices on the world market have fallen.

In the 1880s we experienced a drop in food prices, but on the other hand, since then, food prices have constantly risen. And if we look more closely, we have to say: This is based on the general trend of capitalist society. We will have to expect, unfortunately, that things will be no different [in the future], that prices will continue to rise. The capitalists will hold the line on wages and will want to push them down. That is important for the union movement. From this standpoint, our prospects are not at all rosy. But as realistic politicians, we have to take this into account.*

---

* Two paragraphs appear at the end of the original typescript that were not written by Luxemburg. This further confirms that the typescript was a stenographic record of a lecture by Luxemburg at the SPD's Berlin party school, with a listener (or the stenographer) commenting at the end on some final remarks by her. It is also possible that the typescript was prepared by Luxemburg *before* her lecture, for use in it or as a handout to help students follow it, and that the paragraphs about Kautsky's book might have been added or inserted into the manuscript by a listener. The two paragraphs read:

In conclusion, with regard to ground rent theory, Comrade Luxemburg recommends that we read [Karl] Kautsky's book *Die Agrarfrage* (The Agrarian Question). It is going to be reprinted.

This book also explains why the general development, which nowadays has entered the stage of [capital] concentration, becomes blurred and obscured to some extent in agriculture. This is, so to speak, an optical illusion, which results from the fact that people apply to agriculture very mechanically the same methods they have for viewing industry.

History of Political Economy

There is no decent book on political economy. Only a good Marxist could write a history of political economy.

The fundamental aspects are in Marx's *Theories of Surplus Value*. But [to read] that is very heavy going, except for the first part.

The least demanding small book that I can recommend to you as a reference work [is]: [John Kells] Ingram, History of [*Political Economy*]. A very superficial presentation, but useful as a reference work.*

By and large, we can distinguish the following schools of political economy.

The oldest are the *mercantilists*. The mercantile system had already developed in the sixteenth century, with the [growing] money economy in the cities, and absolutism's great need for money. The first issue they dealt with was: "Wealth equals gold." Hence [they wrote] inquiries into the question of money.

The very titles of [the first mercantilist] writings are indicative: [Gaspero] *Scaruffi, "About Money,"* written in 1582.† The second is: [Bernardo] *Davanzati, "Lectures on Money,"* 1588.‡

Then an interesting work: *Antonio Serra, "Brief Treatise Concerning the Basis on Which States Possessing No Mines Can Obtain Gold and Silver,"* written in 1613. This book title is typical of the mercantilists.§

The primary thought content of the [mercantilists'] school is: "wealth equals gold." Their main concern: "How to bring gold into a country?" The balance of trade [was the answer]: to trade so that more was imported than exported. To pay premiums for exports and to embargo imports or impose tariffs on them.

Anyway, the [key question for the mercantilists [was]: the question of [foreign] trade.

The most important English mercantilists are:

Thomas Mun, A Discourse of Trade from England unto the East Indies, 1621.¶

---

* Luxemburg is referring to John Kells Ingram's book, *History of Political Economy* (Edinburgh: Adam & Charles Black, 1888). Some 55 editions of Ingram's book, in eight different languages, were published between 1888 and 2008. Luxemburg was using the German edition of the work, *Geschichte der Volkswirtschaftslehre*, translated by E. Roschlau (Tübingen: H. Laupp, 1905). Some of Ingram's earlier work was known to Marx, who read and made excerpts of his writings.

† In the manuscript, Luxemburg gives the name as "Scaruff." The actual title of Scaruffi's work is *Discurso sopra le monete e della vera proporzione tra l'oro e l'argento* (Discourse on Money and on the True Proportions between Gold and Silver) (Milan: Destefanis, 1804 [1582]).

‡ The actual title of Davanzati's book is *Lezione delle monnete* (Lessons About Coins) (Milan: Destefanis, 1804 [1588]).

§ The title given for Serra's work is translated from the German wording used by Luxemburg. In the original Italian it was *Breve trattato delle cause che possono far abbondare li regni d'oro e d'argento dove non sono miniere* (Brief Treatise on the Causes Which Can Make Gold and Silver Abound in Kingdoms Where There Are no Mines) (Milan: Destefanis, 1803 [1613]).

¶ Adam Smith considered Mun to be the most outstanding proponent of the mercantilist

[Josiah] *Child, "On Trade and Interest on Money,"* 1668.*

[William] *Temple, Observations upon the United Provinces of the Netherlands,* 1672.†

(At that time the Netherlands had come up in the world,‡ and was England's biggest competitor.)

All the economists of Germany in the seventeenth and eighteenth centuries were mercantilists. But not outstanding, just parroters of the Italians.

The *physiocrats* were the second school. Marx dates the history of political economy from them. France is the place of their birth. They stand in sharp opposition to the mercantilists. They explain: What is wealth? Land and the soil, nature and labor. [They hold that] only agriculture is productive. Why? Because here labor provides more in quantity of output than labor itself costs. In contrast, trade and industry are unproductive.

At first glance this seems to be a feudal theory. In outward appearance, a purely reactionary school.

However, they draw the following conclusion: Since agriculture is the only productive branch of the economy, it is therefore fair and just that all taxes be applied to agriculture and that industry and trade be left entirely free from taxation.

In the first part of *Theories of Surplus Value*, Marx wrote very beautifully on this subject.§ Until then one could not tell whether this theory [of the physiocrats] was reactionary or revolutionary. Marx showed that with this theory the bourgeoisie made its appearance, though still under the wing of feudalism.

They [the physiocrats] demanded personal freedom and equality for the people working on the land, so that this branch of the economy could develop sufficiently for it to bear all the burdens placed upon it. Therefore a fight against feudal burdens. And thus it was a highly revolutionary school of thought.

The main founders of this school were:

[First, Pierre Le Pesant de] Boisguilbert: 1. *"Treatise on Grain and the*

---

system. See Mun's *Discourse of Trade from England unto the East Indies* (London: Nicholas Okes, 1621).

   * The actual title of Child's book is *Brief Observations concerning Trade and the Interest of Money* (London: Elizabeth Calvert, 1668).

   † Temple's book was actually first published in 1673. See William Temple, *Observations upon the United Provinces of the Netherlands* (London: J. Maxwell, 1673).

   ‡ That is, reached a high point of economic development.

   § See "The Physiocrats," in *Economic Manuscript of 1861–1863, Marx-Engels Collected Works,* Vol. 30 (New York: International Publishers, 1988), pp. 352–76. The material contained in what has became known as *Theories of Surplus Value* was originally part of the 1861–63 draft of Volume 1 of *Capital*. After 1863 Marx decided not to include the material (which he called "History of Theory") in Volume 1, intending instead to issue it as a separate Volume Four of *Capital*. It was first published separately by Karl Kautsky under the title *Theories of Surplus Value* between 1905 and 1910.

Grain Trade." 2. "*On the Nature of Wealth, Money, and Taxes*"† He died in 1714. Second was the official founder of this school, *Fr[ancois] Quesnay, personal physician of the king [Louis XV]*. He [Quesnay] lived from 1694 to 1774. His chief work is his famous *Tableau Économique*.‡ In it he portrayed the society as a whole. The book had as its motto: "Poor farmers, poor kingdom; poor kingdom, poor king."

Third: [Anne-Robert-Jacques] *Turgot*, finance minister under Louis XVI. His main activity was to carry out reforms and take measures that were in the spirit of this school. His chief written work was "*Reflections on the Formation and Distribution of Wealth.*"§

This school had a colossal influence on thinking people. Above all, it had a retroactive effect in relation to Italy.

The names of the most prominent Italian physiocrats, who all lived in the eighteenth century [are]: [Antonio] Genovesi, [Pietro] Verri, [Giovanni Rinaldo] Carli, [Cesare] Becarria (author of a brilliant book against the death penalty).¶

The German physiocrats, who lacked all significance, [included]: *Karl*

---

* Boisguilbert is widely considered to have been a *precursor* of the physiocrats. This was also Marx's view. He writes in *Theories of Surplus Value*, "Ideas related to those of the Physiocrats are to be found in fragmentary form in older writers who preceded them, partly in France herself, for example Boisguilbert. But it is only with the Physiocrats that these ideas develop into an epoch-making system." See *Economic Manuscript of 1861–1863, Marx-Engels Collected Works*, Vol. 30, p. 359. The actual title of Boisguilbert's book, first published in 1704, is *Traité de la nature, culture, commerce et intéret des grains* (Treatise on Nature, Culture and Interest of the Grain Trade). It can be found in *Pierre de Boisguilbert ou la naissance de l'économie politique*, 2 volumes (Paris: Institut National d'Etudes Démographiques, 1966). For an English translation, see *A Treatise of the Nature of Wealth, Money and Taxation*, translated with an introduction by Peter Groenewegen (Sydney: Centre for the Study of the History of Economic Thought, 2000).

† The title of the book in French, first published in 1707, is *Dissertations sur la nature des richesses, de l'argent et des tributs*. It can be found in *Pierre de Boisguilbert ou la naissance de l'économie politique*, 2 volumes (Paris: Institut National d'Etudes Démographiques, 1966).

‡ The *Tableau économique* (The Economic Picture) was first published in France in 1759. For an English translation, see *Tableau économique*, edited by Marguerite Kuczynski and Ronald Meek (London: Macmillan, 1972).

§ In the original French, *Réflexions sur la formation et la distribution des richesses*. It was first published in 1769 in the journal *Ephémérides du citoyen, ou Bibliotheque Raisonnée des Science Morales et Politiques*.

¶ Antonio Genovesi was primarily a philosopher who wrote on logic and metaphysics. His *Lezioni di commercio* (Lessons on Commerce) (Naples: Appresso I Fratelli Simone, 1765) is considered the first systematic work on economics in Italian. Pietro Verri is primarily known for his *Meditazioni sulla economia politica* (Mediations on Political Economy) (Genoa: Livornio, 1771). Giovanni Rinaldo, Count of Carli, is author of *Della Monete, e della instituzione delle zecche d'Italia dell'antico e presente sistema di esse* (Of Coins, and the Establishment of Mints in Italy and the Ancient and Present System) (Pisa: G.P. Giovennelli, 1751–59) Cesare Becarria first argued against the death penalty in his treatise, *Dei delitti e delle pene* (On Crimes and Punishments) (Harlem: Dal Molini, 1764). Although his economic writings are today not as well known in the English-speaking world as his contributions to political thought, Joseph Schumpeter referred to him as "the Italian Adam Smith."

*Friedrich Margrave of Baden.** He wrote his book in French, so that Germans would not be able to learn the principles he advocated.

THE CLASSICAL SCHOOL

[Among the French authors in] the classical school Marx counts the physiocrats, from [*MS. Illegible*]† to [Jean Charles Léonard de] Sismondi.‡

[Englishmen of this school were:]

[David] Ricardo: 1772–1823.

His main work was:§ His most famous pupils were John Stuart Mill and the latter's father, James Mill.

Adam Smith, 1723–90. His main work, about the "wealth of nations," appeared in 1776.¶

Among Smith's followers in Germany, only two became more or less well known, although they were entirely lacking in independent significance and merely parroted Smith:

Prof. [Karl Heinrich] *Rau* and Prof. [Heinrich von] *Storch*.** The latter lived in St. Petersburg [in Russia], although he was a German.

Thus it may be said that until then Germany did not exist as far as political economy is concerned.

The only [German economic school] is the so-called *historical school*. Its founder is Professor [Wilhelm Georg Friedrich] *Roscher*, but Professor[s] [Bruno] *Hildebrand* and [Karl] *Knies* [were] together with him.

---

*   Karl Friedrich, Grand Duke of Baden was one of the few European monarchs to support the physiocrat's promotion of free trade. Luxemburg is referring to a précis that he wrote on the phsyiocrats, entitled *Abrégé des principes de l'économie politique* (Abstract of the Principles of Political Economy) (Baden: Grossherzog, 1772).

†   Luxemburg most likely had in mind Boisguilbert.

‡   Marx tended to use the term "classical political economy" to refer to the English political economists, from William Petty to David Ricardo, as well as to the French economists, from Boisguilbert to Sismondi.

§   The title of the work is not given in the manuscript. Luxemburg is referring to Ricardo's *On the Principles of Political Economy and Taxation* (London: John Murray, 1817).

¶   The reference is to Smith's, *An Inquiry into the Nature and Causes of the Wealth of Nations*, first published in 1776.

**   Storch was economics tutor to Tsar Nicholas I of Russia.

From the historical school, [German] *Kathedersozialismus** developed. It was founded in 1872 at Eisenach.

This school wants to gloss over class conflicts entirely.

Its main representatives are: [Albert] *Schäffle, [Adolph] Wagner, [Gustav von] Schönberg*, all of them professors.

Kathedersozialismus has long since passed away, having been absorbed into the camp of the employers.

One of these professors even voted for the anti-socialist laws.

FURTHER READING (AN INCOMPLETE LIST)

Volume 2 of Marx's *Capital.*

Volume Five of the *Handwörterbuch für Staatswissenschaften;* the essay on crises by Prof. [Heinrich] Herkner of Zurich.[†]

Volume 3 of Marx's *Capital.*

Parvus [Alexander Helphand], *Aufschwung und Gewerkschaften*, published in Dresden.[‡]

[Max] Schippel, *Hochkonjunktur und Wirtschaftskrise.*[§]

---

*   Kathedersozialismus refers to "academic socialism" or "socialism of the chair"—a relatively conservative socialist tendency among German economists and sociologists of the late nineteenth and early twentieth century that opposed laissez-faire and supported state intervention in the economy while opposing the revolutionary aims of the workers' movements. Almost all of its adherents were professors at German universities. In Luxemburg's era it was virtually unheard of for a revolutionary socialist or Marxist to have a position at a German university.

†   Heinrich Herkner, *Krisen* (Crises), in *Handwörterbuch für Staatswissenschaften* (Dictionary of the Social Sciences), second edition, Vol. 5 (Jena: G. Fischer, 1900).

‡   Luxemburg appears to have in mind Parvus' book, *Die Gewerkschaften und die Sozialdemokratie* (The Trade Unions and Social Democracy) (Dresden: Verlag der Sächsischen Arbeiter Zeitung, 1896).

§   See Max Schippel *Hochkonjunktur und Wirtschaftskrise* (Boom and Crisis) (Berlin: Vorwärts, 1908).

Appendix: Theory of the Wages Fund

(1) Content of the Wages Fund Theory. How it is usually linked with population theory.[*]

(2) Dissemination of the Theory. Adam Smith—[Jeremy] Bentham[†] ([Jean-Baptiste] Say).[‡]

(3) Its Historical Justification (small-scale producers, the Middle Ages)

(4) Its True Social Roots (the fate of workers being dependent on capital)

(5) (a) The Iron Law of Wages of [David] Ricardo–[Ferdinand] Lassalle[§]

   (b) Bentham

(6) Critique of the Theory of the Wages Fund

   (a) [William] Thompson[¶]

---

[*] According to the classical theory of the wage fund, the wages of workers are determined by the proportion between the total amount of capital and the population of available workers. If the total amount of capital in a given society remains given but the population increases, wages will decline; if population decreases, wages will rise. The implication is that class struggle, trade unions, or social resistance cannot affect wage rates, since the wage fund is presumably a fixed amount dependent on the ratio between the volume of capital and the size of the laboring populace.

[†] In *A Manual of Political Economy* (1795), Bentham provided the first quantitative formulation of the theory of the wage fund. He wrote, "But the rate of wages depends upon, and is necessarily governed solely and exclusively by, the degree of opulence in the country at the time: that is by the proportion of the quantity of wealth in readiness to be employed in the shape of capital in the purchase of labor to the number of persons for whose labor there is a demand." See *Jeremy Bentham's Economic Writings*, Vol. 1 (London: Allen and Unwin, 1952–54), pp. 247–8.

[‡] J.B. Say argued in *Traité de l'Economie politique ou simple exposition de la manière dont se forment, se distribuent et se consomment les richesses* that as workers' wages increase above subsistence, family size grows and the supply of labor eventually outstrips the demand for labor, which in turn compels wages to return back to their "natural" level.

[§] Lassalle's theory of the "iron law of wages" held that in capitalism wages tend towards the minimum requirements necessary to sustain the laborer. According to this alleged "iron law," wages can never drop below subsistence levels, since that would threaten the physical existence of the worker, but neither can they rise much above subsistence, given the competition among workers for employment. The logical implication of the theory is that the effort of trade unions to secure higher wages for their members is bound to prove ultimately fruitless. Although Marx is often associated with the idea, he fervently opposed Lassalle's conception of the iron law of wages on both empirical and theoretical grounds.

[¶] In *Inquiry into the Principles of the Distribution of Wealth* (London: Hurst, Rees, Orme, Brown & Green, 1824), William Thompson, a socialist neo-Ricardian, rejected the wages fund theory on the grounds that workers are entitled to the entire value of their labor.

(b) [Friedrich Benedict Wilhelm] Hermann*

(c) [Johann Karl] Rodbertus†

(d) [William Thomas] Thornton‡

(e) [Jean Charles Léonard de] Sismondi§

(f) Professor [Julius] Wolf¶

(7) Critique of These Critiques

(a) Individually

(b) In General: They cannot be refuted by abstracting from currently existing institutions. The opposite is true.

---

*   Hermann was the first German economist to criticize the wages fund theory of the
British economists in his *Staatswirtschaftliche Untersuchungen* (Inquiries into Political Economy)
(München: A. Weber, 1832). He argued that the actual consumer of labor power is not the capitalist
(as Smith and Ricardo contended) but the consumers who purchase the laborer's products. Since
the consumer is the buyer of labor, the capitalist, in his view, simply pays out in wages the price of
the goods made by labor.

†   Rodbertus rejected the idea that wages are paid out of capital on the grounds that workers
are bound to receive a progressively smaller proportionate amount of wages as production increases.
Luxemburg took issue with him in *The Accumulation of Capital*: "Since the 'laws of exchange value'
determine the wage, an advance in labor productivity must bring about an ever declining share
in the product for the workers. Here we have arrived at the Archimedean fulcrum of Rodbertus'
system. This 'declining wage rate' is his most important 'original' discovery on which he harps from
his first writings on social problems (probably in 1839) until his death, and which he 'claims' as his
very own. This conception, for all that, was but a simple corollary of Ricardo's theory of value and
is contained implicitly in the wages fund theory which dominated bourgeois economics up to the
publication of Marx's *Capital*. Rodbertus nevertheless believed that this 'discovery' made him a
kind of Galileo in economics, and he refers to his declining wage rate as explaining every evil and
contradiction in capitalist economy." See *The Accumulation of Capital* (New York: Modern Reader,
1951), p. 244. See also Rodbertus' *Die Forderungen der arbeitenden Klassen* (The Claims of the
Working Classes) (Frankfurt am Main: V. Klostermann, 1946 [1837]).

‡   Although not as radical as Thompson in his approach, Thornton's *On Labor: Its Wrongful
Claims and Rightful Dues, its Actual Present and Possible Future* (London: Macmillan and co., 1869),
took sharp issue with the wages fund theory, which led John Stuart Mill to abandon his earlier
defence of it. Mill recanted the theory of the wage fund in a letter of April 9, 1869 to J.E. Cairnes. See
Later Letters of John Stuart Mill, 1849–73, edited by Francis Mineea and Dwight Lindley (Toronto:
University of Toronto Press, 1972), p. 1587.

§   Sismondi was one of the first economists who took issue with the claim of the classical
political economists that wages are advanced by the capitalist in proportion to the amount of the
accumulated capital, on the grounds that the increasing productivity of labor and the divorce of
workers from control over the means of production actually leads to a decline in their relative wage,
and indeed to their ultimate impoverishment. See his *Nouveaux Principes d'Economie politique ou
de la richesse dans ses rapports avec la population.*

¶   For Luxemburg's discussion of Julius Wolff's critique of the theory of the wage fund, see
below.

(8) Marx on the wages fund theory.* Marx on the "Iron Law of Wages."†

(9) Prof. [Julius] Wolf's criticism in regard to Marx.

(10) Reply [to his criticism].

One can say that up to now economic science has put forward only two theories of wage labor: the theory of the wages fund and the theory of the industrial reserve army,‡ the first a product of bourgeois economics and the latter, of socialist economics. Obviously it should not be said therefore that all economics theoreticians without exception have sworn by one or the other of these theories. There have also been writers who took a very critical attitude toward the wages fund theory without at the same time showing any awareness of the industrial reserve army theory, which of course had not yet been put forward.§ In the most recent period on the other hand a [new] theory has been advanced which subjects both of the above-named theories to thorough criticism and regards both of them as mistaken—we have in mind the theory of Professor Julius Wolf, which quite recently has been adopted and reiterated by some German economists, such as [Adolph von] Wenckstern.¶ However, if we leave aside these products of the most recent times—which we will go into in more detail further below—we find, during the entire lengthy period from the beginning of classical political

---

*   Marx discusses the wages fund theory in *Capital* Vol. 1, Chapter 24. He writes: "Classical political economy has always liked to conceive social capital as a fixed magnitude of a fixed degree of efficiency ... Variable capital in its material existence, i.e. the mass of the means of subsistence it represents for the worker, or the so-called labor fund, was turned by this fable into a separate part of social wealth, confined by natural chains and unable to cross the boundary to the other parts ... The facts on which the dogma is based are these: on the one hand, the worker has no right to interfere in the division of social wealth into means of enjoyment for the non-worker and means of production. On the other hand, it is only in favorable and exceptional cases that he can enlarge the so-called 'labor fund' at the expense of the 'revenue' of the rich." (pp. 758–60).

†   In many of his writings Marx took strong exception to the theory of the "iron law of wages," which Lassalle had attributed to him. Marx heaped scorn on the theory as representing little more than an application of Malthus' theory of population to the determination of the value of labor power. See especially Marx's critique of this Lassallean notion in his *Critique of the Gotha Program*: "The nonsense is perpetrated of speaking of the 'abolition of the wage system' (it should read: system of wage labor) '*together with* the iron law of wages.' If I abolish wage labor, then naturally I abolish its laws too, whether they are of 'iron' or sponge. But Lassalle's attack on wage labor turns almost solely on this co-called law ... But if this theory is correct, then again I can *not* abolish the law even if I abolish wage labor a hundred times over, because the law then governs not only the system of wage labor but every social system." *Marx-Engels Collected Works*, Vol. 24, p. 91.

‡   In the manuscript the first several lines of this paragraph were crossed out (through the phrase "industrial reserve army"), but we have preserved these lines since there is no alternative wording for the beginning of this long sentence.

§   This is especially the case with such socialist neo-Ricardians like Thompson, whose criticism of the wages fund theory pre-dates Marx's development of the concept of the industrial reserve army.

¶   See Adolph von Wenckstern, *Marx* (Leipzig: Duncker & Humblot, 1896).

economy to our own times, only the two above-named theories about the wages paid for labor—the wages fund theory and that of Marx.

As early as Adam Smith we find the wages fund doctrine stated clearly and explicitly. In his [*Wealth of Nations*,] Book 1, Chapter 8, "On Wages," he comments approximately as follows: The natural wage is the product of the amount of labor expended. However, this wage is paid only in primitive social conditions. With the accumulation of private capital, wages are determined by a struggle between capital and labor. The result of this struggle depends as a rule on the relation between supply and demand for labor. By "demand for labor" Smith understands the [size of the] *capital fund* at any given moment. In Adam Smith we also find the inseparable addition to the hypothesis of the "wages fund"—population theory: the labor supply, says Smith, depends in turn on the frequency of births [i.e., the birth rate] among working people at any given time—but this in turn is precisely geared at every moment to capital's demand [for labor]. (Unless we are mistaken, Smith used that very word— "precisely.")*

The same propositions are put forward by David Ricardo, the last classical author of the bourgeois school of political economy, in another connection— namely, in his theory of ground rent. In the chapter† where he deals with wages *ex officio* we read only that wages—like the prices of all other commodities—are determined according to relative supply and demand. But what Ricardo means by this he tells us in a different place—in his ingenious explanations about ground rent. Here the theory of the wages fund serves him naturally as a logical link for constructing a connection between rent and the movement of capital. Rent, he tells us, rises with the growth of capital. How so? Through the intervention of the working class. Capital consists at any given time of a *wages fund of a determinate size*. With the growth of capital or, which amounts to the same thing, with the growth of the demand for labor, *the number of workers increases* (through natural increase!), but with that the demand for the means of subsistence also grows, above all for the products of agriculture. The growing demand increases the price of these products, and as a direct consequence ground rent increases.

---

*   Luxemburg here gives the English word "precisely," along with its German equivalent *genau*. Luxemburg is apparently referring to the following passage in Chapter 8 of Volume One of Smith's *The Wealth of Nations*: "In Great Britain the wages of labor seem, in the present times, to be evidently more than what is precisely necessary to enable the laborer to bring up a family. In order to satisfy ourselves upon this point it will not be necessary to enter into any tedious or doubtful calculation of what may be the lowest sum upon which it is possible to do this. There are many plain symptoms that the wages of labor are nowhere in this country regulated by this lowest rate which is consistent with common humanity." See Adam Smith, *An Inquiry into the Nature and Causes of the Wealth of Nations* (London: Metheun & Co, 1904), Vol. 3, p. 27.

†   This is discussed in Chapter 5 of *The Principles of Political Economy and Taxation*, second edition (London: John Murray, 1819). Luxemburg most often refers to the second edition of the work, which originally appeared in 1817.

Both above and below when we refer to statements by the theoreticians we are discussing, going by memory, we are not in the least disregarding the demand for exactness in *one's mode of expression*. Turns of phrase such as "he said," serve merely to distance ourselves from unpleasant association.*

Thus we find in Ricardo as well [as in Smith] the same linking of the wages fund theory with population theory, or to put it more exactly, the same mediation of the wages fund theory by the population theory: the latter is the medium through which the domination of the wages fund over wages themselves is made a reality.

It would take us too far afield if we were to follow in the same detail the course of thought among the other adherents of the wages fund theory. This would also be superfluous because the theory was neither carried further nor even modified by the other representatives of classical political economy. Among them we encounter the same formulations as were once given by Adam Smith and David Ricardo, with almost the exact form of expression, and this is true of both the epigones of classical political economy and the founders of vulgar economics: James Mill (*Defence of Commerce*, 1808), J.B. Say (*Traité de l'Economie politique*, 1803), [Antoine Comte de] Destutt de Tracy (*Traité de la volonté et de ses effets*, 1821), John Stuart Mill (*Principles of Political Economy*, 1856), [and] [Henry] Fawcett (*The Economic Position of the British Laborer*, 1865),† and finally this applies as well to "old man" [Karl Heinrich] Rau, and [John Ramsey] MacCulloch, and all the others.‡

In economics as in all social sciences [*MS. Missing word(s)*] two kinds of criticism are possible: (1) One may criticize the content of a given theory *in and of itself*, to reveal its inconsistency, its logical insufficiency; (2) One may,

---

* This paragraph was a marginal notation in the manuscript.

† James Mill was one of the most important advocates of the classical theory of the wage fund. He argued that wages are advanced by the capitalist out of the funds that would otherwise be constituted as capital. See James Mill, *In Defence of Commerce* (London: C. and R. Baldwin, 1808). Destutt de Tracy's *Traité de la volonté et de ses effets* (Treatise on the Will and its Effects) (Paris: Courcier, 1821), argued that since wages are a deduction from the value of capital, an increase in workers' wages would lead to social impoverishment. On these grounds he declared that "in poor nations the people are comfortable, in rich nations they are generally poor." John Stuart Mill's *Principles of Political Economy* was actually first published in 1848 (London: Longmans, Green and Co.). It strongly defended the classical theory of the wage fund, a theory that Mill repudiated two decades later. For Marx's critique of Mill, see the "Introduction" to the *Grundrisse* and Chapters 15, 16 and 24 of *Capital* Vol. 1. Henry Fawcett's *The Economic Position of the British Laborer* (London: Macmillan and Co., 1865) is discussed by Marx in *Capital* Vol. 1, in the section on "The So-Called Labor Fund." See *Capital* Vol. 1, pp. 758–61.

‡ Karl Heinrich Rau's *Lehrbuch der politischen Ökonomie* (Textbook of Political Economy) (Heidelberg: Winter, 1826–37) was the first work in Germany to articulate and defend the theory of the wages fund. He argued that wages are but a special form of price—the latter in his view, being determined by the value of the commodity, the cost of exchanging the commodity, and competition. John Ramsey MacCulloch argued in his *The Literature of Political Economy* (London: Brown, Greens, and Longmans, 1845) that wages are necessarily dependent on the proportion between the total amount of capital and the size of the laboring population.

on the other hand, also deal with the object of criticism in its historical connection to the social realities of its time, the basis on which the criticized theory first arose. Here the objective material basis of the theory must be revealed, and the latter must be viewed not in and of itself, not on a logical-theoretical basis, but from a material-historical standpoint. The first critical method passes judgment absolutely, like the members of a jury: either "guilty" or "not guilty" (or more exactly, either "true" or "false"). The second method takes into account the relativity of truth, that is to say, that truth is conditioned by the times. It does not condemn the theory in question, but only shows that the theory eventually became outdated. We believe that there is no effective refutation other than the one that demonstrates the social context in which a doctrine [at one time] represented "reason," [a refutation] that makes it possible to follow the [emergence of a] changed social context in which the doctrine has becomes "meaningless." Obviously this method cannot be applied in all cases: that which, in the case of Adam Smith or David Ricardo at the turn of the century [between the 18th and 19th centuries] was a historically determined error is in the case of [Lujo] Brentano at the end of the [19th] century merely apologetics, and although perhaps in both cases "material relations" are to blame for the theory, that is true in two entirely different senses ...

Before we criticize the wages fund doctrine from a theoretical standpoint, we want to examine it briefly from a historical one.

So what, in short, do we have to say about the theory?

There is at any point in time a quantitatively specific amount of capital that represents the demand for hired hands. As a result, in relation to this capital there arises a larger or smaller number of hands for hire [to be paid with] a larger or smaller amount in wages. It is obvious that, if this theory is to have some justification, *a single* basic determining element in [the existing] social relations is necessary: [i.e.,] a certain degree of stability in the conditions of production, so that, first of all, [there would be] a technically given relation between a specific amount of capital and the number of workers employed by it; and secondly, that because of market conditions a definite relation could be observed as a *constant factor* between the time required for production and exchange and the time required for the reproduction of human beings. Both of these are conditions that our present-day capitalist economy would look down on with a supercilious smile. They would appear to it as something like "a fairy tale from days of yore." First of all, depending on the level of productive technology and exploitation (length and intensity of the working day in connection with the wage form), at any moment one and the same quantity of capital can harness the labor power of a highly variable number of workers; not only that, but this relationship is altered at every moment by advances in technology, so that both in time and space the concept of a constant [fixed] proportion (a coefficient) between capital and labor can only be a fiction. Secondly, the time spans required for modern production no longer correspond in any way with the amounts of time necessary for human reproduction. During the last twenty-five years, speaking approximately, the modern production cycle takes up not even half of that time.* If we take into account only the biggest economic crises in our century, we see the following: 1825, 1836, 1847, 1857, and finally 1867.† Thus, almost exactly in ten-year intervals, there has been an economic cataclysm, and after each one a convulsive contraction of capital, then a gradual expansion, followed by a sudden unrestrained boom until once again the wings of capital are clipped by the next crisis. Given the short and—as we will show—constantly shorter length of the production cycle, given this tendency of capital toward sudden contractions and expansions, [the notion] that the size of the population can be regulated by the amount of available capital in relation to the natural amount of time necessary for the propagation of a new generation of workers once again becomes nothing but a fiction. Obviously one can say that capital reigns over the death of the worker, but not that it is a dominant influence in the number of workers who are born. It is well known that three or four days of not eating (that is, of joblessness) are enough to cause death; but to give birth to and raise a human being requires many long years.

All this was quite different in Ricardo's time and even more so in that of Adam Smith. Machinery was just beginning to revolutionize the relations of production, and generalized economic crises were still in the offing. To be sure, Ricardo experienced the first significant economic crisis in England, which followed after the establishment of Napoleon's continental system. However, in that case the capitalist hoof was concealed behind historical "accident," and it was easy to conceive of this crisis as a quite specific consequence of the machinations of "that fiend Napoleon." In general the predominant mode of production—manufacture—was still based on manual labor, trade relations were still dominated almost exclusively by England, and hence were fairly stable and easy to observe, the time periods necessary for production were relatively

---

* That is, the time necessary for a new generation of workers to be raised.

† The economic crises of 1825 resulted from a stock market crash arising from speculative investments by English investors in Latin America. It is considered the first modern economic crisis. In referring to "1836," Luxemburg is probably thinking of the financial crisis of 1837 in the US, which occurred after President Andrew Jackson refused to renew the charter of the Second Bank of the US. The crisis of 1847 refers to the collapse of British financial markets after the bursting of a bubble in the railway industry. The Panic of 1857, which greatly drew Marx's attention, is considered to have been the first worldwide economic crisis in human history. It resulted, in part, from a run on stocks following the British government's decision to withhold the release of hoards of gold and silver to back up its currency. The reference to 1867 is the crisis in England of 1866–67. In her discussion of the history of crises in her manuscript "Volume 2 of *Capital*" in this volume, Luxemburg noted: "By 1866 all this led to a crisis in England, and the high point of the crisis was 1867. An outbreak of panic followed, as ever, from some particular event, and indeed in this case it was a bankruptcy of Overend & Co. The consequence of this bankruptcy was a frightful panic. In two weeks the reserves of the Bank of England were almost completely emptied."

lengthy and slow, and the technical proportionality between capital and labor power was up to [a point] a given.* Here lies the relative justification for the classical theory of the wages fund, but here at the same time lies [the basis for] its condemnation by history. Gone are the lovely days of peaceful, phlegmatic, seemingly patriarchal capital. Today [it is] nervous, constantly stirred up, at one moment "storming the heavens," at the next "in the depths of depression"; today one can calculate neither how much labor power capitalism will need at the next moment nor even the number of workers to be supplied. With capital on its wild chase the workers, waiting upon its command, have time enough only to die, but not to be born. And it is well to note that the time when the wages fund theory had its relative justification was extremely short. Before Ricardo's very eyes the mighty process of industrial transformation in England took place. The second edition of Ricardo's main work already contains a section about machinery (and this is already characteristic), a section in which he himself refutes his "theory of compensation," and thus indirectly and unconsciously throws out the very proposition he himself put forward about the wages fund.† And if today, in the age of [the monopoly capitalists] Krupp and [Carl Ferdinand] Stumm,‡ German economists put the old theory of the wages fund back on the table and seek to cover up the modern phenomena of capitalism with shreds and tatters from the old classical theory, it is the kind of work that Heine knew only too well.

> They plug up the holes in the universe
> With bits of old dressing-gown and nightcap.§

Incidentally the old theory of the wages fund served not only for plugging the holes in the capitalist universe. In it there also lay a real kernel [of truth], independent of its specifically historical justification: it was the first general theoretical formulation of the social dependency of the working class on capital. But now it became possible for two different kinds of conclusions to be drawn

---

* Three question marks in place of a word appear in the manuscript here. We have provided what we take to be the meaning of the missing word in brackets.

† Ricardo discusses this in Chapter 31 of the second edition of his *Principles of Political Economy and Taxation*. In the Preface (p. 3), he noted: "To determine the laws which regulate this distribution, is the principal problem in Political Economy: much as the science has been improved by the writings of Turgot, Stuart, Smith, Say, Sismondi, and others, they afford very little satisfactory information respecting the natural course of rent, profit, and wages." Shortly thereafter the critique of the wages fund theory was carried further by such neo-Ricardian socialists as William Thompson in his *Inquiry into the Principles of the Distribution of Wealth*.

‡ Alfred and Friedrich Krupp were one of Germany's most important steel and armaments manufacturers (see the second footnote on page 114 of this volume). Karl Friedrich Stumm at the time was the most important employer in mining and iron and steel industries in Saarland, in western Germany.

§ *Des Weltbaus Löcher verstopfen sie/Mit alten Schlafröcken und Mützen.* These lines are from Heine's famous work, *Buch der Leider* (1827), or *Book of Songs*.

from this. In the hands of *Lassalle* the wages fund theory became a revolutionary lever for the emancipation struggle of the working class. Jeremy Bentham, father of utilitarianism, knew how to "utilize" this theory in a different way: from it he concocted a dogma, which entirely removed any social responsibility from the capitalist and against which all the demands of the working class were intended to bounce off as though from a suit of armor.

Ricardo's work, containing the clearest and most decisive formulation of the wages fund theory, appeared in 1817. As early as seven years later it ran into criticism. *William Thompson*, in his *Inquiry into the Principles of the Distribution of Wealth* (1824), pointed out that this theory was thoroughly one-sided, that it only took into account the quantity of accumulated capital, but that the productive forces of the nation (potentially) at any moment and even the yearly consumption by the nation at any moment were illimitably greater than this.[*] It is obvious that a comment like this, even if it is quite correct in and of itself, could not touch a hair on the head of the theory being criticized, because in any discussion of wages it is not the existing wealth of the world, past or future, which comes under consideration, but unfortunately the portion of that wealth which at any given time the worker encounters in the form of capital. Between the overall wealth of the productive forces of the society and the working class stands precisely the individual capitalist with his demand [for labor]; and here we run into a wall. Thompson's critique might seem quite incomprehensible if we did not know that he belonged to that utopian school of older English socialists who wanted to reshape capitalist reality so thoroughly, wanted to eliminate capitalist reality so badly, that they abstracted [from that reality] in their economic theory. Thompson had such a great desire to cancel the dependency of the workers on capital, as formulated in the wages fund doctrine, that in his criticism he abolished the very existence of the private capitalist.

The later critics of the wages fund theory are the Germans Hermann and Rodbertus.

Hermann, in his *Staatswirtschaftlichen Untersuchungen* (1832), puts forward the proposition that the worker is paid not from the employer's capital but by the consumers of the commodities produced. The employer is presented here in the innocent and at the same time noble role of a personally disinterested inter-mediary between the worker and the consumer, as though he were a mere clerk. The only problem is that in one way or another it is notoriously well known that the worker receives his wages *before* the sale of the products of his labor, and indeed he receives them directly from the employer out of that person's private capital, and thus the actual question that was raised has not been touched on at all.

---

[*]   That is, greater than the quantity of accumulated capital.

Rodbertus is no more fortunate in his criticism. In his work *Zur Erkenntnis unserer staatswirtschaftlichen Zustände* he held that the wages for labor are not paid out of the capital already accumulated before the production period began but out of the product of that same period. This consoling notion, derived from a bizarre disregard for the elementary phenomena of the capitalist mode of production, needs no further refutation. Any child knows that the production period in most realms of economic activity—from the beginning of production through the sale of the goods on the market—takes half a year or a full year, but workers receive their wages every two weeks or even every week, and so the employer must have a reserve supply of capital in advance; wages cannot be taken, bit by bit, out of current production.

Here, as in so many other fields of economics, Marx provided the first true criticism. Above all he knew—in accordance with his dialectical method—that there cannot be any general law of wages that is absolutely applicable in all cases. Every mode of production has its own law of population and its own special law of wages.

He went on to outline the law of wages for the production period in large-scale industry. This consists of two aspects: on the one hand, the existing *reserve supply of capital*; and on the other, the existing *reserve army of workers*. The accumulation of capital, on the one hand, and the proletarianization of the middle layers of the population, the small producers, on the other, have already advanced so far, he held, that the needs of production today cannot be squeezed into any natural, or so to say, physical, limits, neither on the side of capital nor on the side of the workers: the expansion of production in and of itself could be unlimited, but it would always find enough capital and "*Arme*" (in the dual sense).† In reality then what does the mass of employed workers depend on and what does the amount [size] of their wages depend on? Solely and exclusively on the interests of the capitalist at any given moment, on his *need for the utilization of capital*.‡ However, this depends, on the one hand, on the market, but today the market has become a world market, where hurricanes rage on a world scale, and so the market is at any given moment a totally variable quantity, because of changes in production technology, which at every moment change the need for the utilization of capital. Thus today the so-called demand for labor depends neither on the quantity of someone's capital nor on the number of [available] workers, but on the market and production conditions taken as a whole, which constantly fluctuate and the sum total of which actually constitutes the entire modern mode of production. The law of wages today—Marx cries out!—is

---

* See Rodbertus's *Zur Erkenntnis unserer staatswirtschaftlichen Zustände* (Contribution to the Knowledge of Our Economic Conditions) (Neubrandenburg: Friedland, 1842).

† Here *Arme* means the "poor," but Luxemburg intends it also to mean *Armée*, that is, the reserve army of the unemployed.

‡ That is, for his capital to make a profit.

worse than an "iron law"; it is "elastic"! Today it can be given neither the name of "wages fund" nor that of any special law, [it can be given] no name other than that of the modern economy as a whole, [no name] other than that of capitalism itself!

We mentioned at the beginning that a new theory, that of *Prof. J[ulius] Wolf*, rejects both theories—the wages fund theory as well as Marx's theory of the industrial reserve army. Prof. Wolf says that the theory of Ricardo-Lassalle is false because, first of all, an increased wage does not necessarily cause a greater number of children to be born; and secondly, the demand for workers may also increase with their [increased] number. Both of these arguments concur essentially with the criticism that Marx directed at the wages fund theory, and thus to a certain extent it may allow a common theory [to be stated].* Matters stand otherwise with regard to the positive assertions of Marx's theory of wages. The extensive expansion of production—says Prof. Wolf—rushes forward more quickly than the intensive development of production as a result of the advance of technology, and therefore the reserve army does not grow but gradually diminishes. On these questions it is difficult, we must concede, to offer direct proofs. If the school of Marx were to cite a series of statistical data in support of its assertion, Prof. Wolf would present a series of statistical results in opposition to those. Given the present-day condition of statistics, it can provide proof, as is well known, in the same degree either for or against any assertion. Nevertheless we think that proofs may be sought precisely in an indirect way, in such social phenomena as can be explained for us only by accepting the notion of an advancing proletarianization. Thus, for example, the [constant] overseas emigration, as well as the dubious attempts of all governments to "save the middle class" (see the recent proposal for a government organization to promote German handicrafts!); and also the ease with which even the largest industrial actions of the working class can be broken by "reservists" from the industrial reserve army (see the recent strike in Hamburg); and likewise the unceasing "de-specialization" (to make up a word ad hoc) of the workers and with that the fact that skilled workers are increasingly being rendered superfluous; and also, finally, the growing dissatisfaction among the masses of the people and consequently the growth of the workers' movement. These are all facts with which a theory of wages must deal in one way or another, and all of them seem to lead to the conclusion that there is an increasing proletarianization of the middle classes, and with that comes the growth of the reserve army. Without going into these questions any further we want to restate in its essentials the unique wages theory put forward by Prof. Wolf. In reality—says Prof. Wolf—the level of wages at any given time depends on (1) the supply of workers available for hire; (2) their wages policy—an aspect which, as far as we know, no other German bourgeois economist has brought up

---

* The common theory would be one that reflected the views of both Marx and Julius Wolf.

with such emphasis, and among English economists was raised only by Thornton in his work *On Labor* (1869); and (3) on the prosperous condition of business in general; and lastly (4) it depends on the effect of prices on consumption as well as the share that wages have in the costs of production.[*]

---

[*]   The manuscript breaks off at this point.

Notes

THE INDUSTRIAL DEVELOPMENT OF POLAND

1 See O. Flatt, *Opis miasta Lódzi pod wzgledem historycznym, statystycznym i prze-myslowym* (Historical, Statistical and Industrial Description of the City of Łódź) [(Warsaw: Drukarnia Gazety, 1853)], pp. 133–42; Witold Zalęski, *Statystyka porównawcza Królestwa Polskiego* (Comparative Statistics of the Kingdom of Poland) [(Warsaw, 1876)], pp. 170–1; *Diplomatic and Consular Reports. Foreign Office.* [Annual Series: On the Trade of Warsaw (London: Her Majesty's Stationary Office, 1888),] No. 321, p. 5; and T. Rutowski, *W sprawie przemyslu krajowego* (On the Question of the Country's Industry) [(Kraków: Drukarnia Zwiazkowa, 1883)], p. 34 ff.

2 See I.S. Poznanskii, *Proizvoditelnye sily Tsarstva Polskogo* (Productive Forces of the Kingdom of Poland) [(St. Petersburg: Tsederbauma i Goldenbliuma, 1880)], pp. 67, 106; also, Zalęski, *Statystyka porównawcza Królestwa Polskiego*, p. 71.

3 See Poznanskii, *Proizvoditelnye sily Tsarstva Polskogo*, p. 140.

4 Raw materials from Russia and Poland were declared to be duty-free; a tariff of 1 percent was levied on goods manufactured from either country's own raw materials and one of 3 percent ad valorem on goods manufactured from the raw materials of a foreign country. Sugar and raw cotton were exceptions; duties of 25 percent and 15 percent, respectively, were placed on them. From Russia's standpoint the tariff on raw cotton was quite senseless, but for Poland, which had been importing this cotton from Russia in large quantities, the tariff was extremely favorable because it protected the Polish cotton industry from Russian competition, but at the same time it encouraged the export of Polish woolen materials to Russia.

5 Flatt, *Opis miasta Lódzi pod wzgledem historycznym, statystycznym i przemyslowym*, p. 62; K. Lodyshenski, *Istoriia russkogo tamozhennogo tarifa* (The History of the Russian Tariff) [(St. Petersburg: Balashev, 1886)], pp. 217 and 218.

6 Zalęski, *Statystyka porównawcza Królestwa Polskiego*, p. 47.

7 Source of above figures: Lodyzhenskii, *Istoriia russkogo tamozhennogo tarifa*, p. 218. According to F. Rodecki in *Obraz geograficzno-statystyczny Krolestwa Polskiego* (Geographical-Statistical Depiction of the Kingdom of Poland) [(Warsaw: Drukarni Antoniego Gałęzowskiego i Kompanii, 1830)], Table III, the export of products of the Polish wool industry to Russia in 1827 amounted to 13.2 Polish guilders (one guilder being worth 15 kopecks).

8 Source of above figures: K. Lodyzhenskii, *Istoriia russkogo tamozhennogo tarifa* (History of the Russian Tariff). St. Petersburg, 1886, p. 219.

9 Flatt, *Opis miasta Lódzi pod wzgledem historycznym, statystycznym i przemyslowym*, p. 61.

10 Lodyzhenskii, *Istoriia russkogo tamozhennogo tarifa*, p. 223. Raw materials were still imported duty-free, as before, and duties on many manufactured goods increased by a factor of between three and five, but the duty imposed on the chief export item from Poland, woolen goods, was raised to the same high level paid for Russian woolen goods imported into Poland, that is, 15 percent *ad valorem*.

11 See I[van] I[vanovich] Ianzhul, *Istoricheskii ocherk razvitiia fabrichno-zavod-skoi promyshlennosti* (Historical Sketch of the Development of Factory Industry) [(Moscow, 1887)], p. 32.

12   Rutowski, *W sprawie przemyslu krajowego*, p. 241.
13   Ibid., pp. 250, 251; see also J[an] Bloch, *Przemysl fabryczny Królewstwa Polskiego 1871–1880* (The Factory Industry of the Kingdom of Poland, 1871–1880) [(Warsaw: Drukarni Cotty, 1884)], pp. 29–31, 111–12, 12–13, and 58.
14   W. Zalęski, *Statystyka porównawcza Królewstwa Polskiego* (Comparative Statistics of the Kingdom of Poland), Warsaw, 1876, p. 172.
15   Lodyzhenskii, *Istoriia russkogo tamozhennogo tarifa*, p. 252.
16   One result of the formation of a tariff zone including Poland was that an innovation was now made in the Russian tariff system: the introduction of a so-called differential tariff. Since Poland had pursued significantly more of a free-trade policy toward Western Europe, a new distinction was made after the Russian tariff boundary was extended to include Poland—a distinction between the land border and the maritime border. A lower tariff was set for goods being shipped by sea.
17   *Istoriko-statisticheskii obzor promyshlennosti Rossii* (Historico-Statistical Review of the Industry of Russia), D. A. Timiriazev, ed. 2 vols. [(St. Petersburg: 1883)], Vol. 2, p. 95.
18   [For the source of the following figures, see] Rutowski, *W sprawie przemyslu krajowego*, p. 241.
19   Ivan I. Ianzhul, *Istoricheskii ocherk razvitiia fabrichno-zavodskoi promyshlennosti* (Historical Sketch of the Development of Factory Industry), Moscow, 1887, p. 36
20   The total length of the railroad network in Russia was as follows:

In 1838	25 versts [one verst = 3,500 feet]
In 1850	468 versts
In 1860	1,490 versts
In 1865	3,577 versts
In 1870	10,090 versts

Let us, while we are at it, review the data from later years as well:

1875	17,718 versts
1880	12,226 versts
1885	24,258 versts
1890	28,581 versts
1891	29,156 versts

[Source:] *Gornaia Promyshlennost Roissii. Vsemirnaia kolumbbova vystavka v Chikago 1893* (Russia's Mining Industry. Report for the Chicago World's Fair 1893), [Rossiia, Departament Gornog Dela, Ministervo Gosudarstvennykh imushchestv (issued by the Mining Department of Russia's Ministry of State Properties), St. Petersburg, 1893], p. 61. From 1891 to 1896, 10,625 versts of new railroad lines were opened to traffic, and another 10,000 versts are now under construction, according to *Trudy Imperatorskogo Svobodnogo Ekonomicheskogo Obshchestva* (Proceedings of the Imperial Free Economic Society) [published twice monthly], 1897, No. 6, p. 132.
21   See G. Simonenko, *Sravnitel'naia statistika Tsarstva Pol'skogo i drugikh evropeiskikh stran* (Comparative Statistics of the Kingdom of Poland and Other European Countries) [(Warsaw: Tipografiia Meditsinskoi gazety, 1879)], p. 127; and W. Zalęski, *Statystyka porównawcza Królestwa Polskiego*, pp. 172 and 273.
22   *Fabrichno-zavodskaia promyshlennost i torgovlia Rossii. Vsemirnaia kolumbova vystavka v Chikago 1893* (Factory Industry and Trade of Russia. Chicago World's Fair 1893), [by Departament Torgovli i Manufaktur Ministerstvo Finansov (Department

of Trade and Manufactures of the Ministry of Finances), St. Petersburg, 1893,] XIX, pp. 156–83.

23 [On the source of the figures in the above table] see ibid., XX, p. 185.

24 *Petitions by the Imperial Free Economic Society. Review of Russian Custom-Tariffs* [St. Petersburg: 1890], p. 116.

25 *Trudy Imperatorskogo Svobodnogo Ekonomicheskogo Obshchestva*, No. 6, pp. 129 and 127 [1897].

26 [On the source of the data in the table above see] *Petitions by the Imperial Free Economic Society. Review of Russian Custom-Tariffs*, p. 150.

27 *Vestnik Finansov*, No. 17, May 9, 1897.

28 *Trudy Imperatorskogo Svobodnogo Ekonomicheskogo Obshchestva*, No. 6, p. 134.

29 *Diplomatic and Consular Reports.* [*Foreign Office. Annual Series: On the Trade of the District of the Consulate-General at Warsaw* (London: Her Majestry's Stationary Office, 1894),] No. 1449 (1894), p. 14.

30 Ibid., No. 461, p. 3.

31 On the development of the metal and coal industries, see below, pp. 14–18, 23, 37–40 [in this volume.] The table above was compiled from Zalęski, *Statystyka porównawcza Królestwa Polskiego*, pp. 172 and 246; Bloch, *Przemysl fabryczny Królewstwa Polskiego 1871–1880*, p. 151; *Factory Industry and Trade of Russia*, p. 33; Rutowski, *W sprawie przemyslu krajowego*, p. 241; *Materials on Trade and Industrial Statistics of Russia*, [*Data on the Factory Industry in Russia for the Year 1890* [(St. Petersburg: Department of Trade of the Finance Ministry, 1893)], pp. 158–82; *Materials* [*on Trade and Industrial Statistics of Russia, Data on the Factory Industry in Russia*] *for the Year 1891* [(St. Petersburg: Department of Trade of the Finance Ministry 1894),] pp. 124–44. The data cited about total production are only approximately accurate, because they are significantly lower than the actual volume of production. For the most part we compiled the data from reports by the entrepreneurs, who notoriously gave too low a figure for the volume of business at their factories, in order to avoid higher taxes. Thus, J[an] G. Bloch considered it necessary, in order to obtain an accurate conception of the volume of industrial output, to tack on about 25 percent to the official data. Another Polish statistician, J. Banzemer, in his *Obraz przemyslu w kraju naszym* (A Picture of Industry in Our Country) [(Warsaw: Drukarni Noskowskiego, 1886)], showed with numbers, that the before-tax value of total industrial production for the year 1884 was not 182 million rubles, as the official reports state, but 199 million rubles. On the grounds of similar considerations we have come to the conclusion that production in Poland in the year 1890 represented a value not of 240 million rubles, but at least 300 million. — We arrived at the figure of 240 million for total production in 1890, since for the sake of uniformity [i.e., consistency] we increased the figure of 210 million rubles, given in the report to the 1893 Chicago World's Fair (the volume on *Factory Industry and Trad of Russia*, p. 33), in order to take account of the increased excise tax on alcohol, etc. These excise taxes were included in the data for previous decades, and they should not be left out. — The figure concerning total production of the cotton industry in 1891 is only approximately correct. Here we have, again for the sake of consistency, added an amount for dyeing and finishing, which although it is not a large amount, was included for other branches of the textile industry. In the year 1891, cotton weaving and spinning alone show up as having 86 factories, with 21,229 workers, and production worth 36.8 million rubles. In the above table, we took this year into account, because it was not appropriate to treat the Polish cotton industry as an exception.

32   [On the source of the data in the above table] See *Reports of the Members of the Commission for Investigation of the Factory Industry in the Kingdom of Poland* (St. Petersburg, 1888), Vol. 1, p. 84.

33   Bloch, *Przemysl fabryczny Królewstwa Polskiego 1871–1880*, p. 142–3. Bloch included many small businesses in his calculations, which to a certain extent distorted the general picture of the concentration of industry.

34   *Factory Industry and Trade of Russia*, p. 33; and *Materials on Trade and Industrial Statistics of Russia ... for the Year 1890*, p. 134. With regard to the value of production for one firm in 1890, we have been able to determine that only for branches of industry not subject to excise tax (that is, for all industries except mining, distilling, tobacco processing, and sugar refining). In terms of earnings in that year, the branches on which excise taxes were not imposed certainly accounted for 74 percent of all industry. For other branches of production, exact data about the number of businesses is lacking.

35   [On the sources of the data in the last line of the above table:] The figures "1,612" and "5,303" are from Bloch, *Przemysl fabryczny Królewstwa Polskiego*, pp. 14–15; and the figure "139,298" is from *Materials on Trade and Industrial Statistics of Russia ... for the year 1890*, pp. 158–95.

36   [On the sources of the data in the last line of the above table:] The figures "994" and "7,950" are from Bloch, *Przemysl fabryczny Królewstwa Polskiego*, pp. 14–15. According to Rutowski, the value of cotton production in 1880 was 33 million rubles. The figure "291,736" is from *Materials on Trade and Industrial Statistics of Russia ... for the year 1890*, pp. 124–45.

37   [On the source of the data in the above table] See A.S., *Bor'ba mezhdu Moskvoi y Lodzem* (The Conflict between Moscow and Łódź) [(St. Petersburg, 1889], p. 17.

38   See *Factory Industry and Trade of Russia*, Vol. 1, pp. 11 and 13. The figures for the Russian cotton industry refer to the Russian Empire not including Finland and Poland.

39   [On the figures in the above table:] The figure "1,803" in the last line is from *Materialy po statistiki parovykh mashin v rossiiskoi imperii* (Materials for Statistics on Steam Engines in the Russian Empire), [Rossiia, Tsentral'nyi statisticheskii komitet (Central Statistical Committee of Russia), St. Petersburg, 1888], pp. 158 and 163. In the column under "1890," the first two figures are from *Materials on Trade and Industrial Statistics of Russia ... for the Year 1890*, pp. 134 and 158–94, the top figure referring only to coal mining and to branches of industry to which no excise tax applied. The last figure, "10,497," refers to coal mining alone, and is from *Russia's Mining Industry*, p. 74.

40   *Reports of the Members of the Commission for Investigation of the Factory Industry in the Kingdom of Poland*, Vol. II, pp. 1–2.

41   In making this assumption [of 120 million] we base ourselves on the growth of the city of Łódź, [about which] see the following page(s). But since Ianzhul [in his *Historical Sketch of the Development of Factory Industry*], p. 48), and after him [W.] Sviatlovskii, *Fabrichnyi rabochii (iz nabliudeniia fabrichnogo inspektora)* (The Factory Worker [Warsaw, 1889], p. 23) both consider the figure for 1885 too low—a figure we have taken from the official data—and since they estimate the value of this region's production as already 70 million rubles as early as 1886 and 1883, respectively, the present-day value of the region's production may be significantly higher than our estimate.

42   Ianzhul, *Istoricheskii ocherk razvitiia fabrichno-zavodskoi promyshlennosti*, pp. 44–6;

Flatt, *Opis miasta Lódzi pod wzgledem historycznym, statystycznym i przemyslowym,* pp. 47, 71, and 110.

43   [On the sources for the data "in 1860" and "in 1878" in the above table:] Ianzhul, *Istoricheskii ocherk razvitiia fabrichno-zavodskoi promyshlennosti,* pp. 44–6; and Flatt, *Opis miasta Lódzi pod wzgledem historycznym, statystycznym i przemyslowym,* pp. 47, 71, and 110. [On the source for the data "in 1885" see] *Reports of the Members of the Commission for Investigation of the Factory Industry in the Kingdom of Poland,* Vol. II, p. 1. According to other sources, in 1886 the proceeds from production in Lódż already amounted to 40–46 million rubles. (*Diplomatic and Consular Reports.* [*Foreign Office. Annual Series: On the Trade of the Kingdom of Poland* (London: Her Majesty's Stationary Office, 1887)], No. 128, p. 4.) [On the source for the number of inhabitants "in 1895" see] *Vestnik finansov,* No. 21, June 6, 1897. This number actually refers to January 1897. [On the source for the value of production in 1895 see] *Gazeta Handlowa* [Warsaw], December 1, 1896.

44   *Reports of the Members of the Commission for Investigation of the Factory Industry in the Kingdom of Poland,* Vol. II, p. 23.

45   [On the source of the data in the following table see] A. S., *The Conflict between Moscow and Lódż,* p. 51.

46   *Reports of the Members of the Commission for Investigation of the Factory Industry in the Kingdom of Poland,* Vol. II, p. 25.

47   Ibid., p. 46.

48   See "Stan historia I terazniejszosc Miasta Lódż" (The History and Present Condition of the City of Lódż), *Gazeta Handlowa* (Newspaper of Poland), December 3, 1896.

49   See *Reports of the Members of the Commission for Investigation of the Factory Industry in the Kingdom of Poland,* Vol. I, p. 33.

50   [On the source of the data in the following table see] Ibid., p. 38.

51   Ibid., p. 87.

52   Sviatlovskii, *Fabrichnyi rabochii,* p. 24.

53   [For the source of] "78.4," see Timiriazev, *Istoriko-statisticheskii obzor promyshlennosti Rossii,* Vol. 1, Tables XIV–XV. [The source for the figure "150.8" is] *Russia's Mining Industry,* p. 91. The above figures refer only to private industry. Production from state-owned mines in 1860 was 7.2 million poods, and in 1870, 6.3 million poods. Since 1878, coal extraction from state mines has stopped completely.

54   [On the source of the above data see] *Russia's Mining Industry,* p. 72.

55   Ibid., p. 92.

56   See *Proizvoditel'nye sily Rossii* (The Productive Forces of Russia. [For the regional industrial exhibition at Nizhny Novgorod), Rossiia, Ministerstvo Finansov (issued by the Ministry of Finance), St. Petersburg, 1896], Vol. VII, p. 39.

57   *Gazeta Handlowa,* December 14, 1896.

58   The average annual import of foreign coal into Russia was as follows: 1866–70: 70 million poods; 1871–75: 605 million poods; 1876–80: 971 million poods; 1881–85: 1,122 million poods; 1886–90: 1,097 million poods. [Source:] *Russia's Mining Industry,* p. 75.

59   *Prawda* (Truth), No. 52, December 26, 1896

60   *Russia's Mining Industry,* p. 57.

61   Ibid., pp. 58 ff.

62   Ibid., p. 5; [see] also *Factory Industry and Trade of Russia,* Vol. XIX, p. 181.

63   [On the source of data in the following table see] *Russia's Mining Industry,* pp. 65 and 66. The percentage of imported foreign metal used annually in Russia, as against domestically produced metal, was as follows:

	Pig Iron		Iron	
	(total used)	(foreign)	(total)	(foreign)
1866–70	106 mln poods	8%	97 mln poods	12%
1871–75	133 mln poods	11%	122 mln poods	31%
1876–80	171 mln poods	26%	132 mln poods	35%
1881–85	220 mln poods	32%	135 mln poods	26%
1886–90	256 mln poods	21%	146 mln poods	19%
1891–95	402 mln poods	9%	159 mln poods	23%

[Source:] *Vestnik finansov*, No. 21, June 6, 1897.

64 [On the sources of the data in the following table see] Timiriazev, *Istoriko-statisticheskii obzor promyshlennosti Rossii*, Vol. 1, Tables viii–ix and x–xi; *Russia's Mining Industry*, pp. 58 and 60. The figures above refer only to the private sector. Production of pig iron at state-owned plants in 1860, 1870, and 1880, respectively, was 0.65, 0.47, and 0.29 million poods; and for iron and steel the corresponding figures are 0.33, 0.1, and 0.1 million poods.

65 *Encyklopedia Rolnicza* (Agricultural Encyclopdia), Vol. 3 [(Warsaw: Drukarnia Artystyczna Saturnina Sikorskiego, 1894)], p. 15. According to Orlov (in *A Register of the Factories of European Russia, [including the Kingdom of Poland and the Grand Duchy of Finland* (St. Petersburg, 1881)], p. 620), there were already 66 machinery factories in 1879 with production amounting in value to 6.7 million rubles.

66 *Encyklopedia Rolnicza*, Vol. 2 (1891) [(Warsaw: Drukarnia Artystyczna Saturnina Sikorskiego, 1891)], pp. 530 ff.

67 *Factory Industry and Trade of Russia*, Vol. XIII, pp. 6–7.

68 Ibid., p. 7.

69 *Diplomatic and Consular Reports. [Foreign Office. Annual Series: On the Trade of the District of the Consulate-General at Warsaw* (London: Her Majestry's Stationary Office, 1894),] No. 1449, p. 7.

70 [On the source of the data in the following table see] *Factory Industry and Trade of Russia*, Introduction, pp. 32–3. The Moscow region, i.e., central Russia, includes the following provinces: Moscow, Vladimir, Kaluga, Kostroma, Nizhny Novgorod, Smolensk, Tver, and Yaroslavl; within the St. Petersburg region are the provinces of St. Petersburg, Pskov, Novgorod, Courland, Livonia, and Estonia.

71 See *Vestnik finansov*, No. 8, March 7, 1897.

72 See *Factory Industry and Trade of Russia*, Vol. I, p. 11.

73 See *Materials [on Trade and Industrial Statistics of Russia, Data on the Factory Industry in Russia] for the Year 1892* [(St. Petersburg: Department of Trade of the Finance Ministry 1895),] pp. 192–204.

74 *Reports of the Members of the Commission for Investigation of the Factory Industry in the Kingdom of Poland*, p. 18.

75 [On the source of the data in the following table see] Ibid., Appendix I, pp. 41–3. According to English sources, the export of products from the textile industry of Łódź to Russia in 1886 was 970,791 poods, while 229,900 poods remained in Poland; in 1887, 264,665 poods stayed in Poland, and 721,115 poods went to Russia (*Diplomatic and Consular Report: On the Trade of Warsaw*, No. 321, p. 7).

76 Ianzhul, *Istoricheskii ocherk razvitiia fabrichno-zavodskoi promyshlennosti*, p. 63.

77 On the source of the data in the following table see] *Ateneum*, 1890, Vol. I, No. 2, pp. 294–6. In particular, the market in the Caucasus for Polish iron was as follows:

in 1887, 310,500 poods; in 1888, 299,044 poods; in 1889, 340,905 poods; and in 1890, 398,210 poods (*Ateneum*, 1891, Vol. III, No. 3, p. 612).

78 *Ateneum*, 1891, Vol. III, No. 3, p. 611.

79 *Kraj* (Our Country), 1889, No. 43.

80 Ibid., 1888, No. 21.

81 *Prawda*, 1893, No. 3.

82 Ibid., 1894, No. 51.

83 Ibid., 1896, No. 5.

84 For a brief history of this reform and of the relations between landowners and peasants in Poland, see the English [*Foreign Office. Miscellaneous Series Reports. On the Peasantry and Peasant Holdings in Poland* (London: Her Majesty's Stationary Office, 1895)], No. 355.

85 See J[an] Bloch, *Landed Property and Its Indebtedness* [(Warsaw, 1890)]. (Note also this statement:) "There is no doubt that the great majority of the landowners in Poland live under the most difficult conditions" [*Foreign Office. Miscellaneous Series Reports. On the Position of Landed Proprietors in Poland* (London: Her Majesty's Stationary Office, 1895)], No. 347, p. 11). Some related material is also in J[an] Bloch, *The Peasants' Bank and Parcelization* (Warsaw, 1895), pp. 1 and 16.

86 Bloch, *The Factory Industry of the Kingdom of Poland*, p. 181.

87 *Factory Industry and Trade of Russia*, pp. 32 and 33.

88 Cf. J[an] Bloch, *O Selskokhozaistvennom Melioratzionnom Kreditye v Rossi i Inostrannykh Gosudarstvakh* (Agricultural Amelioration Credit in Russia and Foreign States) [(Warsaw, 1892)]; also, L. Górski, *Our Mistakes in Agriculture* (Warsaw, 1874).

89 "The encouragement thus given to foreign immigrants and to local industry and trade in general has caused a very remarkable industrial development, especially in that part of Poland which is nearest to Germany, whence the vivifying element came; but the policy which had been followed uninterruptedly for 73 years, and by which the industries of this country had been built up, was suddenly reversed on March 14, 1887, by the well-known imperial ukase forbidding foreigners from acquiring real property in the kingdom of Poland and in the Baltic provinces."—"Another measure which will seriously affect the industries of this country is the new regulation prohibiting the erection of buildings within a quarter mile of the frontier."—"This and the other measures in contemplation are attributed to the jealousy of the Moscow manufacturers, who at the last fair of Nizhny Novgorod addressed a memorial to the Government asking for protection against the Polish industries." (*Diplomatic and Consular Reports. Foreign Office. Annual Series: On the Trade of Warsaw*, No. 321, pp. 6 and 7). Further, [see Gerhart von] Schulze-Gävernitz, "Der Nationalismus in Russland und seine wirtschaftlichen Träger" (Nationalism in Russia and Its Economic Spokesmen), *Preussische Jahrbücher* (Prussian Yearbooks), Vol. 75, Jan.–March, 1894. See also *Blue Book: Royal Commission on Labor, Foreign Reports, Vol. X, Russia* (London: 1894), p. 9. The extracts quoted here from the latter publication are based on the English consular reports from Poland, which on this particular subject have not always remained free of one-sided influence from the local [Polish] capitalist press.

90 Lodyzhenskii, *Istoriia russkogo tamozhennogo tarifa*, pp. 220, 218, and 222.

91 A.S., *The Conflict between Moscow and Łódź*, p. 22.

92 [Sergei Fedorovich] Sharapov, *Sobranie sochinenii* (Collected Works) (St. Petersburg: 1892), Vol. 1, pp. 70–94.

93 A.S., *The Conflict between Moscow and Łódź*, p. 22.

94   *Reports of the Members of the Commission for Investigation of the Factory Industry in the Kingdom of Poland*, "Introduction," pp. 1 and 2.

95   Ibid., Vol. 1, p. 101, and Vol. 2, pp. 101–7.

96   Ibid., Vol. 1, pp. 102, 103, and 104.

97   *Diplomatic and Consular Reports. Foreign Office. Annual Series: On the Trade of Warsaw*, No. 321, page 7; A. S., *Moscow and Łódź*, p. 23.

98   On the basis of what has been said before, it is easy to judge how far these two figures were below the real profits.

99   *Diplomatic and Consular Reports. Foreign Office. Annual Series: On the Trade of Warsaw Diplomatic and Consular Reports*, No. 321, page 7.

100 Ibid., p. 6.

101 A. S., *Moscow and Łódź*, p. 23.

102 Ibid., pp. 29, 32–5, 40–2, and 60.

103 *Ateneum*, 1891, Vol. III, p. 609.

104 *Diplomatic and Consular Reports. [Foreign Office. Annual Series: On the Trade of the District of the Consulate-General at Warsaw* (London: Her Majestry's Stationary Office, 1893)], No. 1183, pp. 5 and 6.

105 *Reports of the Members of the Commission for Investigation of the Factory Industry in the Kingdom of Poland*, Vol. 1, p. 30.

106 Ibid., pp. 30–1.

107 Ibid., pp. 32–3.

108 [The figures in the following table are from] *Factory Industry and Trade of Russia*, Vol. 1, pp. 16–17.

109 See Schulze-Gävernitz, "Der Nationalismus in Russland und seine wirtschaftlichen Träger," p. 359.

110 For the price of coal, see *Reports of the Members of the Commission for Investigation of the Factory Industry in the Kingdom of Poland*, Vol. II, p. 104 and Vol. I, p. 33. The price of one pood of naphtha coal is arrived at in the following way: "For the equivalent of 100 units of weight of coal," writes [Dmitri Ivanovich] Mendeleyev, "only 67 units of weight of naphtha residue are required." But according to the same source, the price of naphtha residue has varied "in recent years ... in Moscow between 20 and 30 kopecks per pood." (*Factory Industry and Trade of Russia*, Vol. XII, pp. 311–12.

111 Ibid., Vol. I, p. 17, note; Vol. XXII, p. 264; and "Introduction," p. 21.

112 Ibid., Vol. XII, p. 310.

113 Ibid., [Vol. XII,] p. 312.

114 Ibid., pp. 312–313.

115 *Vestnik Evropy*, No. 21, June 2, 1895

116 R. Mikhailov, "Investigation of Naphtha Residue," *Zapiski Imperatorskogo russkogo tekhnicheskogo obshchestva* (Reports of the Russian Imperial Technology Society) (St. Petersburg), No. 1, January 1898.

117 *Reports of the Members of the Commission for Investigation of the Factory Industry in the Kingdom of Poland*, Vol. 1, p. 35.

118 "[W]eekly wages are higher in Poland than in Russia ... [but] the workday in Russia is so much longer," etc. See Schulze-Gävernitz, "Der Nationalismus in Russland und seine wirtschaftlichen Träger," p. 359; similarly, see S. G., "Die Industrielle Politik Russlands in dessen polnischen Provinzen" (Russia's Industrial Policy in Its Polish Provinces)," *Neue Zeit*, 1893–94, Vol. 2, No. 51, p. 791.

119 [On the source of the data in the table below see] *Reports of the Members of the*

Commission for Investigation of the Factory Industry in the Kingdom of Poland, Vol. 1, p. 39.

120   Ibid., p. 41.

121   Ibid., pp. 42 and 43. Cf. Sviatlovskii, *Fabrichnyi rabochii,* p. 39.

122   Sviatlovskii, *Fabrichnyi rabochii,* pp. 59–60.

123   *Reports of the Members of the Commission for Investigation of the Factory Industry in the Kingdom of Poland,* Vol. 1, p. 71.

124   [On the source of the data in the following table see] Ibid., p. 39.

125   Sviatlovskii, *Fabrichnyi rabochii,* p. 47. — [K.V. Davydov,] *Report of the Factory Inspector for the St. Petersburg Region* [(St. Petersburg: 1886),] p. 11. — In three industrial districts of Moscow province, where the relevant investigations were made, 56.8 percent of all the male workers lived in factory barracks; among spinners and weavers this figure rose to 66.8 percent. See Y[evstafy] M[ikhailovich] Dement'ev, *Fabrika: chto ona daet naseleniiu i chto ona u nee beret* (The Factory: What It Gives to the Population and What It Takes Away) [(Moscow: 1893)], p. 42. According to the same investigations, 22.2 percent of those living in the barracks were not included in the total number of workers living there. These were members of workers' families who were not themselves employed at the factory (ibid., p. 44).

126   See I.I. Ianzhul's article "The Factory Worker in Central Russia and in the Kingdom of Poland," *Vestnik Evropy* (European Herald), February 1888, p. 794.

127   Ibid., p. 792.

128   Out of all the workers in the three above-mentioned industrial districts of Moscow province, the number of grown men who left the factory in the summer amounted to 14.1 percent, and for the textile workers the figure was 19.7 percent (Dement'ev, *Fabrika: chto ona daet naseleniiu i chto ona u nee beret,* p. 4).

129   [I.I. Ianzhul,] *Report of the Factory Inspector for the Moscow Region* [(St. Petersburg, 1884)], p. 81.

130   [Dr. Peskov,] *Report of the Factory Inspector for the Vladimir Region* [(St. Petersburg, 1886)], p. 68.

131   Cf. Thomas Brassey, *Work and Wages* [London: Bell and Daldy, 1872]; see also [Lujo] Brentano, *Über das Verhältnis von Arbeitslohn und Arbeitszeit zur Arbeitsleistung* (On the Relation of Wages and labor Time to Productivity) (Leipzig: Duncker & Humboldt, 1893).

132   "In countries where capitalist production stands at different levels of development and between which the organic composition of capital consequently varies, the rate of surplus value (one factor that determines the rate of profit) may be higher in a country where the normal working day is shorter than in one where it is longer. Firstly, if the English working day of 10 hours, because of its higher intensity, is equal to an Austrian working day of 14 hours, then, given the same division of the working day, 5 hours' surplus labor in the one country may represent a higher value on the world market than 7 hours in the other. Secondly, a greater part of the working day in England may form surplus labor than in Austria." See Marx's *Das Kapital,* Band 3 (Hamburg: Otto Meisner, 1894), Part I, pp. 195–6 [*Capital* Vol. 3, translated by David Fernbach (New York: Vintage, 1981), pp. 321–2.]

133   See Ianzhul, "The Factory Worker in Central Russia and in the Kingdom of Poland," p. 791. — According to Sviatlovskii, *Fabrichnyi rabochii,* p. 61, only the work of weavers is cheaper in Poland; in contrast, the work of spinners is more expensive than in Russia. — According to *Factory Industry and Trade of Russia,* Vol. 1, p. 17, the cost of production of one pood of cotton in Poland and in Russia is on the whole approximately the same, and in this situation the Polish factory

owner, even if he pays about 52 kopecks less [per pood] for fuel, nevertheless pays *more* for labor power than the Moscow factory owner, and that amounts to 33 kopecks [per pood of cotton]. We consider more reliable the data on wages that we have cited in the text, which were obtained as a result of Ianzhul's personal investigations. As a former factory inspector in the Moscow region and as leader of the [1886] commission investigating industry in Poland, he had the opportunity to become acquainted with both Polish and Russian industry from his own observations. — "Despite the lower wages, labor in Russia is very expensive. In England three workers can operate 1,000 cotton spindles; in Russia, according to Mendeleyev, [the corresponding number is] 16.6 [workers]. Thus even if the English worker earns four times more in wages than the Russian, he still works far more cheaply. But in addition to wages [in Russia] there are also the high costs for supervision, passports, workers' housing, hospitals, etc., which are not present at all in England, and for the most part are absent in Poland as well." (Schulze-Gävernitz, "Der Nationalismus in Russland und seine wirtschaftlichen Träger," p. 361.) All this, however, does not prevent the selfsame Professor Schulze-Gävernitz from citing the higher weekly wage, as we have seen, as a disadvantage offsetting the advantage of cheaper fuel. —The point is made clearly, on the other hand, in the English Royal Commission's *Blue Book*: "Although the Russian manufacturer appears to have an advantage in these respects (i.e., "the extraordinarily low rate of wages"—R. L.), the cost of production is greater for him than for the Polish manufacturer" ([*Blue Book:*] *Royal Commission [on Labor, Foreign Report,]* Vol. X, [*Russia* (London: Eyre and Spottiswoode, 1894)], p. 9). Furthermore: "There is a still more striking difference between the Polish and Russian work-people. The latter, although now nominally free, are but little removed from their former condition [of serfdom], and have small ambition to improve their position. The Poles have a far higher standard of comfort, and since they depend entirely upon their wages for their support, they are not contented with low earnings, but still their work is found to be less expensive than that of the Russians" (*ibid.*). By the way, this characterization of the Russian workers is highly antiquated: the big strikes that have continued unceasingly in Russia since 1896 show that the workers there too "have ambition to improve their position." The *Neue Zeit* article entitled "Russia's Industrial Policy in its Polish Provinces," p. 791, contains this statement: "Labor power in Russia is also cheaper than in Poland ... Labor time in Russia is much longer than in Poland ... *But as far as the intensity of labor is concerned, as the above-mentioned factory inspector Svyatlovsky assures us, it is the same in both countries.*" (Emphasis added—R. L.) Actually, not a trace of such "assurance" is to be found in the writings of Sviatlovskii. By the way, it would be difficult for Sviatlovskii to give the kind of assurance that has been put in his mouth [by the author S. G.], first, because in no instance does he [Sviatlovskii] betray any inclination to assure the reader of anything that does not exist, an inclination that is strongly inherent in the author of "Russia's Industrial Policy in its Polish Provinces"; and second, because on the question of the intensity of labor in Poland he [Sviatlovskii] rather "assures us" of the exact opposite. See Sviatlovskii, *Fabrichnyi rabochii*, pp. 59–61.

134   *Reports of the Members of the Commission for Investigation of the Factory Industry in the Kingdom of Poland*, Vol. 1, p. 10.

135   The cost of 1,000 bricks, for example, was 14–15 rubles in Łódź in 1876; in Moscow in 1874, it was ca. 32 rubles; in Łódź in 1886, 8–9 rubles; in Moscow in 1887, ca. 22 rubles. Ibid., p. 13.

136   The cost of construction of barracks and the like, for example, for two of the larger Russian factories, was as much as 400,000 rubles each, or ca. one-sixth of the total fixed capital. Ibid., p. 12.

137   Ibid., p. 36.

138   [On the sources of the data in the following table see] *Materials on Trade and Industrial Statistics of Russia ... for the Years 1885–1887*, pp. vi and xi; *Materials on Trade and Industrial Statistics of Russia ... for the Year 1888*, pp. 106 and 126; *Materials on Trade and Industrial Statistics of Russia ... for the Year 1889*, pp. 134 and 158; *Materials on Trade and Industrial Statistics of Russia ... for the Year 1890*, pp. 110 and 131. The figures for Russia, here and further on, at pp. 169 and 174, unless more details are given, refer only to European Russia, without Finland and Poland. The Asian part of Russia does not come into consideration at all on the question of competition, and citing that data for comparison would only make the picture more unfavorable to Russia. [The author of an article cited earlier, S. G.,] "Die industrielle Politik Russlands in dessen polnischen Provinzen" (The Industrial Policy of Russia in Its Polish Provinces), p. 791, asserts the following: "Lastly, capital in Russia is more concentrated. The average gross profit of a factory in Russia is 45,898 rubles, in Poland 35,289 rubles." This assertion, as well as the figures he quotes, are simply made up out of whole cloth.

139   *Russia's Mining Industry*, pp. 71 and 73.

140   *Productive Forces of Russia*, Vol. 7, p. 39.

141   [The sources of the data in the following tables are] Compiled from *Materials on Trade and Industrial Statistics of Russia ... for the Year 1890*, pp. 172–9, with reference only to cotton spinning and cotton weaving. Here and in the next table, below, we compare only the steam power in the two countries, because water-power plays only a miniscule part in the Russian cotton and wool industries, while in those of Poland it is infinitesimal.

142   Ibid., pp. 160–3. In the [following] table above we compare wool spinning and wool weaving especially, which in Poland represented 72 percent of all profit of the wool industry for that year (1890).

143   *Russia's Mining Industry*, p. 75.

144   Ibid., pp. 71, 73, and 74.

145   *Vestnik finansov*, No. 29, July 28, 1895.

146   *Factory Industry and Trade of Russia*, Vol. XIII, p. 13.

147   Ibid., p. 11.

148   Ibid., p. 16.

149   "Thus all the conditions of production are more favorable for Russia than for Poland." This upside-down conclusion is drawn by [the author of an article cited earlier]: S. G., "Die industrielle Politik Russlands in dessen polnischen Provinzen" (The Industrial Policy of Russia in Its Polish Provinces), p. 791. He derives this from his data about the relations of production between Russia and Poland, data that are twisted upside down in every respect, and in the process he has entirely forgotten two "minor" points—production technology and the type of fuel used as a heat source. However, since it is an undeniable fact that in the real world Polish goods are driving Russian goods from the battlefield [i.e., outselling them in the market] and therefore with one good sweep the assertion about "all the unfavorable conditions of production" must be tossed in the dump, the author tries to get himself out of this difficulty by referring to the individual abilities of Polish manufacturers: "The only (!) reason for this state of affairs is the greater commercial skill of the Polish industrialists and especially the better educated upper-level factory

personnel, who consist mainly of *Germans and Austrians*." (Emphasis added—
R. L.) The author apparently does not know that we live in an age when the decisive
factor on the capitalist battlefield is steam power, and that among those standing
before the countenance of Mercury [the god of commerce], there are no chosen
people. [On the sources of the data in the tables below see] Bloch, *The Factory
Industry of the Kingdom of Poland,, op. cit*, pp. 14–15, 86–7, 102, 126–7; *Materials
on Trade and Industrial Statistics of Russia, [Data on the Factory Industry in Russia
for the Years 1885–87* (St. Petersburg: Department of Trade of the Finance Ministry,
1889)], p. x; *Materials [on Trade and Industrial Statistics of Russia, Data on the
Factory System in Russia for the Year 1888* (St. Petersburg: Department of Trade of
the Finance Ministry, 1891)], p. 126; *Materials [on Trade and Industrial Statistics
of Russia, Data on the Factory System in Russia for the Year 1889* (St. Petersburg:
Department of Trade of the Finance Ministry, p. 1891)], p. 158; *Materials on
Trade and Industrial Statistics of Russia ... for 1891*, p. 146; *Materials on Trade and
Industrial Statistics of Russia ... for 1892*, p. 164 (the volumes of this publication
for more recent years have not yet appeared in bookstores); *Istoriko-statisticheskii
obzor promyshlennosti Rossii*, Vol. 1, Tables VIII–IX, X–XI, and XIV–XV; *Russia's
Mining Industry*, pp. 58–60; *Vestnik Finansov*, No. 52, January 5, 1896 and No. 8,
March 7, 1897.

150 Respectively it was about 26 percent for this branch of industry (textiles) if we
compare the period of 1871 to 1886 (fifteen years) with the period 1885–92 (six
years)—because the year 1885 was especially unfavorable for the textile industry
in view of the economic crisis of 1884.

151 Lodyzhenskii, *Istoriia russkogo tamozhennogo tarifa*, p. 294.

152 *Petitions by the Imperial Free Economic Society. Review of Russian Custom Tariffs*,
p. 21.

153 A. S., *The Conflict Between Moscow and Łódź*, p. 32.

154 The quotation is from *Novoe vremia* as translated in *Kraj*, No. 51, 1894. The cited
article's headline was characteristic: "How Central Russia Was Neglected."

155 *Kurjer Warszawski* (Warsaw Courier), November 5, 1894.

156 "The increase in the sharply differentiated railroad rate (for grain) ought to meet
with no difficulties because of the alleged (!) interests of the lower classes in Poland
... (The difficulty is) the impoverishment of the landowning population of Poland
(as a result of the increased differential rate on grain), which also brings with it a
worsening of the material situation for the textile industry and only benefits the
entrepreneurs in large-scale industry. They alone reap benefits in the midst of the
general disaster because of the lower wages that result from lower grain prices ...On
the basis of all that has been stated above it cannot be doubted that *in the interests
of the landowners* of both the regions located near the internal market, [i.e.,] *of
the Polish and the northern Black Earth regions, as well as all the landowners in
the regions located near harbors*, it seems desirable that the railroad rate on grain
should be revised along the following lines ..." (*Memorandum of the Warsaw Stock
Exchange Commission [About the Railroad Tariffs for Grain]*, pp. 31, 32, and 37).

157 *Sankt-Peterburgskie Vedomosti* (St. Petersburg News), 1896, Nos. 242 and 243;
Gazeta Handlowa, September 21, 1896.

158 *Gazeta Handlowa*, October 8, 1896.

159 *Kurjer Warszawski* (Warsaw Courier), November 7, 1894.

160 *Gazeta Handlowa*, November 30, 1896.

161 "This development of the economic and commercial forces of Poland is attributed by the same authority (the Russian-language organ of the Polish government,

Varshavskii Dnevnik [Warsaw Journal]) to the establishment of branch agencies by the principal Russian banks, among others the 'Azov-Don,' which disposes of considerable capital, and has representatives at all the Black-Sea ports, besides being in direct commercial relations with Bukhara and Teheran. It is, says the 'Warsaw Journal,' through this and other Russian banks, which have established branch houses at Warsaw and Lodz, that the manufacturers of Poland have opened up new channels of trade and strengthened the already existing ones." (*Diplomatic and Consular Reports: On the Trade of the District of the Consulate-General at Warsaw*, No. 1183, p. 4.)

162   See *Kraj*, August 1888.

163   *Ibid.*

164   See *Ateneum*, November issue, 1894, p. 378. Anti-German bias exists, it should be noted, not only in a certain stratum of the Polish bourgeoisie. Compare [for example] the weekly *Rola* (Plowland), organ of the "Christian landowners," which has a regular headline, "Jews, Germans, and Us." See also the petty bourgeois publications *Gazeta Polska* (Polish Gazette), *Niwa* (Field), etc.

165   The constantly growing demand in Poland for iron ore from southern Russia is reported, among others, by *Vestnik Finansov*, No. 52, January 5, 1896. As early as 1893, in relation to the total amount of raw cotton processed, the use of Central Asian cotton in the main centers of the Polish textile industry was as follows: in Pabianice and Zgerz, 30 percent; in Łódź, 40 percent; and in Bedzin, 45 percent (*Przeglad Tygondniowy*, No. 49, 1894]. — The government, for its part, favors this shift by Polish industry toward the use of Russian raw materials by a corresponding policy on the railroad system. In 1895 it established a special low railroad rate from the Donets Basin to Poland in order to make cheaper the delivery of southern Russian coke to Polish iron works (*Vestnik Finansov*, No. 27, July 14, 1895). Likewise, the Polish owners of iron and steel works were promised a reduction in transport costs for southern Russian iron ore in 1897 (*Gazeta Handlowa*, December 11, 1896). In 1893 the Polish spinning mills were provided with a reduction of about 20 percent on the freight costs for wool from southern Russia (*Diplomatic and Consular Reports: On the Trade of the District of the Consulate-General at Warsaw*, No. 1183, p. 4). On the raising of sheep in southern Russia especially for the Polish spinning mills, see *Diplomatic and Consular Reports. [Foreign Office. Annual Series: On the Trade of the District of the Consulate-General at Warsaw* (London: Her Majestry's Stationary Office, 1891), No. 863, p. 2. — On the other hand, the government is promoting the expansion of Polish coal into Russia. In 1895, for example, as part of a general revision of railroad rates for coal, lower terms were set for the transport of Polish coal into Russia than for coal from southern Russia, and the motivation for this was that "an evening-up of the sales opportunities for Polish coal should be introduced, because in terms of average heat-producing capacity, coal from the Donbas performs less well" (*Vestnik Finansov*, No. 27, July 14, 1895).

166   How much the production and exchange of the two countries complement one another and are interconnected, precisely because they have a market in common and can establish a division of labor between them, is shown by the fact that in 1897 a cartel between Moscow and Łódź was projected, with the types of goods to be produced by each of the parties to be determined, so that they would jointly regulate the market (*Torgovo-Promyshlennaya Gazeta*, July 31, 1897). Even if this plan falls through, nevertheless the very idea [of such a cartel] remains strikingly indicative of the relations that actually exist.

167   Since we have set ourselves the task of probing this question thoroughly, we want, additionally, to shed some light on a few relevant statements that we did not have the opportunity to take up in the body of our text.

1) What belongs here, first of all, are the remarks made by Professor Schulze-Gävernitz ("Der Nationalismus in Russland und seine wirtschaftlichen Träger," p. 344) regarding Russia's *tariff policy*. "Even the tariffs on coal, which make fuel more expensive for the western border regions, serve Moscow's interests." Professor Schulze-Gävernitz is so mistrustful about all of Russia's measures in trade policy that he has come to a conclusion here that is the exact opposite of what he should have come to, based on all the evidence. If coal tariffs make fuel more expensive for Polish *factories*, they benefit Polish *coal-mining businesses* to the same extent. At any rate, the tariff is not aimed against Poland as such, but against one group of capitalists—to the benefit of another group. But how the tariff on coal could serve Moscow's interests remains obscure. As an industrial region that has to obtain its coal from elsewhere—because naphtha fuel for the time being, as has been shown, can meet only a small part of the demand—Moscow can scarcely derive any advantage from more expensive coal. That is obvious. Also, the result of the "coal crisis," as we have seen, was that the central region saw itself forced to obtain fuel from Poland, and the corresponding prices were of course higher. Thus the Polish coal industry began massive sales of its product in the interior of Russia.

2) Mr. S. G., in his article in *Neue Zeit* on Russia's industrial policy in Poland ("Die industrielle Politik Russlands in dessen polnischen Provinzen," p. 790), asserts, among other things, that the government of Russia "did not keep people waiting for long" before it took measures against Polish industry. "First it raised the tax on trade and industry in the Polish provinces ..." This assertion is once again, to put it mildly, unfounded. In 1887 the distribution of government taxes in the various regions [of the Russian empire] was as follows:

Regions	Percentage of all government taxes	Taxes as a percentage of total turnover	Public taxes per capita (in rubles)
St. Petersburg and Moscow gubernias (provinces)	13.16%	4.26%	26.75
Southwestern region	8.10%	8.47%	6.56
Little Russia [Ukraine]	5.49%	6.25%	5.78
Black earth region	17.80%	7.73%	6.66
Central industrial region	9.12%	5.99%	5.38
Baltic region	2.26%	3.50%	6.28
Northwestern region	6.08%	7.84%	4.59
Southern region	8.43%	4.39%	
Eastern region	11.30%	5.22%	5.05
Northern region	3.20%	6.51%	5.51
Caucasus	1.20%		
Russia in Asia	6.60%		
Poland	6.05%	6.01%	5.64

[Source:] (Sibir' I sibirskaia magistralopolskii, [*Geographic Distribution of Government Revenue in Russia*], Vol. 1, pages 131 and 236.)

As is evident from the above table, the distribution of the public tax burden among the various regions is highly uneven; in many regions it is significantly lower than in Poland, but in others much higher, so there can be no question of a special tax policy toward Poland. Certainly Polish landed property has a significantly heavier tax burden than its Russian counterpart, but that is connected with causal factors of an entirely different nature—among others, with the Polish nobility's battles in the past for freedom from Russian rule. In any case, it has no connection with the question of present-day Russia's industrial policy toward Poland. As far as the special taxing of industry goes, and in the given instance this is relevant, in 1887 it was significantly lower in Poland than in the two main industrial regions of Russia, as was shown in *Reports of the Members of the Commission for Investigation of the Factory Industry in the Kingdom of Poland*, Vol. 1, p. 47, which shows the ratio of taxes to value of production in 1887 [in the table below]:

	Poland	Moscow province	St. Petersburg province
Cotton industry	0.33%	6.64%	0.78%
Linen industry	0.27%		0.59%
Wool industry	0.28%	0.50%	1.00%
Metal industry	0.35%		0.61%

The higher percentages of taxation in Russia can certainly be explained by various special circumstances, e.g., the ownership by Russian entrepreneurs of forests, peat bogs, workers' barracks, factory-linked inns or taverns, etc.

With the constant swelling of the Russian budget, taxes on industry were also raised in 1893, but this was done throughout the empire without exception and on an equal basis. In all the materials that have been at our disposal we found no trace of any special taxes whose aim was to place Polish industry in a less favorable position than Russian industry.

3) Lastly, this same author of the *Neue Zeit* article about Russia's industrial policy toward Poland (S.G., "Die industrielle Politik Russlands in dessen polnischen Provinzen," p. 790) reports that the Russian government "introduced the so-called *differential tariff*, which means that goods going from Russia to Poland pay lower railroad rates than those which are transported from Poland to Russia. By this last measure the customs border between Poland and Russia was reestablished." Once again this tale is a figment of the author's imagination. This person had apparently heard something about the introduction of a differential railroad rate in Russia, but had no opportunity to find out what that actually was. This terrible measure, however, simply meant that the railroad charge for goods transported over longer distances would be calculated at a lower rate than goods going shorter distances, and this had not the slightest thing to do with special treatment of Poland.

There is one fact, or circumstance, that plainly lies at the basis of the uninformed assertion made above by Mr. S. G., and that is the following: As long as the policy for railroad rates in Russia was made by the railroad companies on their own initiative, there existed on the railroad lines going from the

European border to the interior of Russia a special lower rate for foreign goods. In 1891, when uniform regulation of the transport system was introduced, the government regarded these lower railroad rates from the border primarily as a direct violation of the protective tariff wall, a violation that benefited foreigners, but also as "an unjustified preferential treatment in railroad rates for the industry of the border region (Poland and the Baltic provinces) relative to the industry of central Russia" (with regard to the purchase of foreign goods). (See *The Agriculture and Forest Industry of Russia*, p. 478.) The freight charges in dealings with foreign countries were also brought into line with those of domestic commerce (ibid.). The above-mentioned reform did not apply especially to Poland, as one can see, but to all of Russia's border regions, to areas on the Black Sea as well as on the Baltic, and it conformed in its purposes with the general aims of [the government's] protective tariff policy. The mutual exchange of goods between Poland and Russia, whose tariff reform Mr. S. G. is discussing, was not even remotely an issue in this case, because what the government was dealing with was direct trade by parts of the empire with the outside world.

By the way, it ought to be pointed out that the "differential tariff," which Mr. S. G. knows how to report on in such a confident tone, is purely fictional, [as is shown by] the exposition of the entire actual course of events, which we have laid out for the detailed information of the reader. The following figures suffice to refute the assertions made by Mr. S. G.: The tariff on products of the textile industry (and of course this industry is the one under discussion above all) "from Łódź to Moscow *or from Moscow to Łódź* amounted to 60 kopecks per pood (and under the new tariff of 1893, 91 kopecks per pood), from *Moscow to Odessa* (that is, inside Russia itself) it was 86 kopecks (in 1893, 105 kopecks), and from Łódź to St. Petersburg *or in the reverse direction* it was 62 kopecks (in 1893, 79 kopecks)." (See *Novosti*, August 1893.) Thus the tariffs today, just as before, are calculated in exactly the same manner for goods being transported from Poland to Russia as for the same kind of goods going from Russia to Poland. All of Mr. S. G.'s argumentation, including his grandiose conclusion about the "reestablishment of the customs border between Poland and Russia," must therefore be thrown out onto the garbage heap.

One parting comment about this author [S. G.] who we have cited so many times. In addition to those we have criticized here, most of the other assertions and details in his article are either made up out of whole cloth or turned upside down [*verkehrt*]. Thus, for example, he manufactures some information about the establishment of the Russian-Polish customs border, which as any third-grader in Poland knows, was done in 1851, but S. G. declares that it was the direct result of the Polish uprising of 1863 ("Die industrielle Politik Russlands in dessen polnischen Provinzen," p. 789). And so on. This and all the other topsy-turvy assertions were obviously meant to demonstrate that Polish capitalism was being destroyed by Russian persecution, and from this [supposedly] a material basis could be derived for Polish national aspirations. This method of basing a political programme on statistical inaccuracies is in and of itself undoubtedly wrong, but let it not be disputed that in the given instance one may sympathize very much with the motivation behind these distortions—namely, the sincere desire on the part of the author to contribute to the best of his ability to the liberation of his country.

168   Lodyzhenskii, *Istoriia russkogo tamozhennogo tarifa*, p. 220.

169   Ibid., p. 245.

170   *The Factory Industry and Russian Trade*, "Introduction," p. 29.

171   This side of the question, which we cannot go into in more detail here, has been dealt with by us quite thoroughly in a number of essays related to the political development of Polish society. See "Der Sozialpatriotismus in Polen" (Social Patriotism in Poland), *Neue Zeit* (Stuttgart), 1895–96, No. 41, pp. 37–51; "Von Stufe zu Stufe. Zur Geschichte der bürgerlichen Klassen in Polen" (Step by Step: Toward a History of the Bourgeois Classes in Poland), *Neue Zeit*, 1897–98, No. 6, pp. 94–111; and "La questione polacca al Congreso internazionale di Londra" (The Polish Question at the International Congress in London), *Critica sociale, Revista quindicinale del Socialismo Scientifico* (Milan), 1896, No. 14.

172   See the decrees of December 1892 concerning repayment of customs duties on exported products of the textile industry, and later on exported sugar.

173   [The names of these banks were] Deutsch-Asiatische Bank; Comptoir National d'Escompte de Paris; Hong Kong and Shanghai Banking Corporation; Chartered Bank of India, Australia, and China; Chartered Mercantile Bank of India, London and China; Bank of China, Japan and the Straits.

174   *Vestnik Finansov*, No. 52, January 5, 1896.

175   [On the source of the data in the following table see] *Sibir' i sibirskaia magistral'. Vsemirnaia kolumbbova vystavka v Chikago 1893* (Siberia and the Great Siberian Railroad. [Report for the World's Fair in Chicago), Rossiia, Departament Torgovli, Ministervto Finansov (issued by the Department of Trade of Russia's Finance Ministry), St. Petersburg, 1893], p. 246.

176   [On the source of the data in the table above see] *Productive Forces of Russia*, [section on] "Foreign Trade," p. 26.

177   [On the source of the data in the following table see] *Vestnik Finansov*, No. 44, November 11, 1894.

178   [On the source of the data in the following table see] *Vestnik Finansov*, No. 44, November 11, 1894. In Bukhara, from 1890 through 1893, total sales of products from the textile industry of Russia averaged 140,000 poods per year.

179   This was the year of the cholera outbreak.

180   The figure for 1893 is also from *Vestnik Finansov*, No. 44, November 11, 1894.

181   *Productive Forces of Russia*, Vol. VII, p. 5. According to *Vestnik Finansov*, No. 44, November 11, 1894, it was 120,000 poods yearly.

182   [On the source of the data in the following table see] *Vestnik Finansov*, No. 52, January 10, 1897; also, *Productive Forces of Russia*, [section on] "Foreign Trade," pp. 25–6.

183   One [researcher] who says this is B. H. Kuhn in his 1892 book *Die Baumwolle, ihre Cultur, Structur und Verbreitung* (Cotton: Its Culture, Structure, and Distribution) [Vienna: A. Hartleben, 1892)]: "Russian products show to advantage with respect to their durability ... For the most part only small quantities have been produced, but with these Russia can compete successfully even with England." [Quoted in] (*Productive Forces of Russia*, Vol. I, p. 23).

184   *Vestnik Finansov*, No. 44, November 11, 1894.

185   As was stated by the government, many sugar shipments gave their destination as Central Asia merely for the sake of appearances, in order to have the excise tax reimbursed, and taking advantage of the deficient functioning of the border guards, simply sent the shipments "back to the Fatherland." Many shipments made the trip several times before they actually reached their sales destination in Persia. This led the government to temporarily suspend reimbursement of the excise tax

on sugar and to reorganize border guard operations (*Vestnik Finansov*, No. 15, April 25, 1897).

186   The newspaper *Sibir* (Siberia), January 8–20, 1897, reports: "Some Moscow factories, in their relations with Siberia, have finally decided to resort to the system of *commis voyageur* [traveling agent], but because of our clumsiness more confusion and misunderstanding than necessary has arisen from this. In the summer the Konshin Company sent its agent to Siberia with samples of goods, and not long ago he obtained two orders from Vladivostok, but the company has already refused to fill them exactly, because they are no longer able (they say) to produce goods corresponding to the sample."

187   The same issue of *Sibir* reports the following: "The firm Pyotr Vereshchagin & Co. in Hankow, which intends to devote itself exclusively to the sale of Russian goods in China, sent messages to 14 Moscow factories on September 6 (in 1896) requesting samples and above all the initiation of regular relations, but to date (January 1897) only a single reply has been forthcoming."

188   *Vestnik Finansov*, No. 44, November 11, 1894.

189   Thus the newspaper *Sibir* wrote on January 20, 1897: "Protected by nearly prohibitive tariffs and all sorts of other government measures, the apathetic Moscow entrepreneurs do not feel any need for new markets."

190   *Vestnik Finansov*, No. 52, January 10, 1897.

191   Cited in *Gazeta Polska*, December 3 and 5, 1894.

192   *Vestnik Finansov*, No. 44, November 11, 1894.

193   *Diplomatic and Consular Reports. Foreign Office. Annual Series: On the Trade of Warsaw*, No. 321 [1888], p. 5: "In consequence of some important orders for carriages and linen which the Shah of Iran had given to the manufacturers of those articles in Poland, the attention of the mercantile community in this country was called to the possibility of establishing direct commercial relations with Persia; ... with this object in view a [major] commission agent proceeded to that country about the end of last year for the purpose of making himself thoroughly acquainted with its markets, taking with him a considerable quantity of samples of different kinds of goods, and it is said that, if his journey is attended with favorable results, a wholesale depot and commission agency will be opened at Teheran."

194   *Vestnik Finansov*, No. 44, November 11, 1894.

195   Ibid.

196   Ibid.

197   *Diplomatic and Consular Reports. Foreign Office. Annual Series: On the Trade of Warsaw*, No. 321, p. 4.

198   *Gazeta Handlowa*, November 25, 1896.

199   *Ateneum*, Vol. IV, No. II, pp. 241–2.

200   Diplomatic and Consular Reports. Foreign Office. Annual Series: On the Trade of Warsaw, No. 321, p. 5.

201   *Novosti*, November 4, 1893.

202   We have taken this excerpt [from the Russian-language "Warsaw Journal"] as quoted in Diplomatic and Consular Reports. Foreign Office. Annual Series: On the Trade of the District of the Consulate-General at Warsaw, No. 1183, p. 4.

BACK TO ADAM SMITH!

1   This conception appeared even more crassly in, for example, Ad[am] Smith, who in fact declared the "inclination to exchange" a distinctive feature of human nature, after having sought it in vain among animals, such as dogs, etc. As is well known, this, like so many other passages, provided later bourgeois economists much occasion for superior smiles and shoulder shrugs. Smith's sassy young followers had no idea that his "classical deduction" was most classically expressed precisely in the old master's much-mocked naïveté and that they, the bourgeois economists, irrecoverably lost, along with that naïveté, their Samson's hair, the source of their research strength.

2   In this light, the fact that attempts have conversely been made in our ranks (recently and in all seriousness, and especially by those who prolong their professional existence by discretely living on Marxian treasures) to renovate and to "advance" this very same Marxian doctrine by borrowing from the young bourgeois economists seems especially tragi-comic. This procedure vividly reminds us of the drunk who *partout* wants to fetch a pinch of snuff from his own shadow.

INTRODUCTION TO POLITICAL ECONOMY

1   Gustav Schmoller, "Volkswirtschaft, Volkswirtschaftslehre und-methode" (Economics, Economic Doctrine, and Method), in *Handwörterbuch der Staatswissenschaften*, Vol. 7, edited by Johannes Conrad, et al. (Jena: G. Fischer, 1901), pp. 546–7.

2   See Eugen Dühring, *Kritische Geschichte der Nationalökonomie und des Sozialismus von ihren Anfängen bis zur Gegenwart* (Critical History of Political Economy and Socialism from its Beginnings to the Present) (Leipzig: C. P. Naumann, 1899), p. 16.

3   See Eugen Dühring, *Kritische Geschichte der Nationalökonomie*, pp. 20–6.

4   Gustav Schmoller, "Volkswirtschaft, Volkswirtschaftslehre und-methode," p. 546.

5   Karl Bücher, *Die Entstehung der Volkswirtschaft; Vorträge und Versuche* (The Emergence of Economies: Lectures and Investigations), fifth edition (Tübingen: H. Laupp, 1906), p. 85.

6   Ibid., pp. 141–2.

7   W[erner] Sombart, *Die deutsche Volkswirtschaft im Neunzehnten Jahrhundert* [The German National Economy in the Nineteenth Century], second edition [Berlin: Georg Blondi Verlag,] 1909, pp. 400–20.

8   Hermann Schulze-Delitsch, *Capitel zu einem deutschen Arbeiterkatechismus. Sechs Vorträge vor dem Berliner Arbeiterverein* (Leipzig: E. Keil, 1863), p. 15.

9   Ferdinand Lassalle, *Herr Bastiat—Schulze von Delitzsch*, pp. 72–5.

10 Gottfried August Bürger, *Leonore*, in *Bürgers Werke in einem Band* (Weimar: Volksverlag, 1962), p. 67.

11 Background in India: the "national economy" of the peasant community is breaking up. Industry ... The crude figures of imports and exports give telling information on this. [Marginal note by R.L.]

12 Karl Bücher, *Die Entstehung der Volkswirtschaft*, p. 142.

13 Nikolai Sieber, *David Ricardo und Karl Marx*, Moscow 1879, p. 480. [N. J. Siber, "David Rikardo i Karl Marks v ish obstchestvenno—ekonomitcheskich

issiedowanijach" in *Isbrannyie ekonomitscheskiye proisvedenija v dvuch tomach*, Vol. 1, Moscow, 1959, pp. 448-9.]

14 D., p. 245. [Charles Darwin, *Reise eines Naturforschers um die Welt*, second edition (Stuttgart: E. Schweizerbart, 1899), p. 245. Charles Darwin, *Journal of researches into the natural history and geology of the various countries visited during the voyage of H.M.S. Beagle under command of Captain Fitz Roy RN* (London: John Murray, 1902), pp. 213-14.]

15 Karl Bücher, *Die Entstehung der Volkswirtschaft; Vorträge und Versuche*, p. 135.

16 Ibid., p. 136.

17 Ferdinand Lassalle, "Die Wissenschaft und die Arbeiter," in *Ferdinand Lassalle's Reden und Schriften. Neue Gesammtausgabe. Mit einer biographischen Einleitung hrsg. von Ed. Bernstein*, Vol. 2 (Berlin: Verlag der Expedition Vorwärts, 1893), p. 83.

18 Cited in Maksim Kovalevsky, *Obshchinnoe Zemlevadenie. Priciny, khod i posledstviia ego razlozeniia* (Communal Land Ownership: The Causes, Processes, and Consequences of its Disintegration), Volume 1 (Moscow, 1879), p. 81.

19 Ibid., p. 78.

20 Ibid.

21 Ibid., pp. 81-2.

22 Information from [Heinrich] Cunow [*Die Soziale Verfassung des Inkareichs. Eine Untersuchung des altperuanischen Agarkommunismus* (The Social Constitution of the Incas: An Investigation of Ancient Peruvian Agrarian Communism) (Stuttgart: J.H.W. Dietz Verlag, 1896)], p. 6.

23 C.N. Starcke, *Die Primitive Familie in ihrer Entstehung und Entwicklung* (The Primitive Family in its Origin and Development) (Leipzig: F.A. Brockhaus, 1888), p. 221.

24 The critiques and theories of Starcke and Westermarck were subjected to a fundamental and devastating examination by von Cunow in his *Verwandschaft-Organisationen der Australneger* [Kinship Organizations of the Black Australians (Stuttgart: J.H.W. Dietz Verlag, 1894)], to which the two gentlemen, as far as we know, have not answered with a single word. This does not however prevent more recent sociologists, such as von Grosse, for example, from being unashamedly celebrated as refuters of Morgan and prime authorities. The same is more or less true for Morgan-refuters as Marx-refuters: bourgeois science is content with tendentious treatment of the hated revolutionaries, and good intent substitutes here for any scientific achievement.

25 Lippert, *Kulturgeschichte der Menschheit in ihrem organischen Aufbau*, Vol. 2, Part 1, p. 40.

26 Karl Bücher, *Die Entstehung der Volkswirtschaft*, pp. 8-9.

27 Professor E[duard] Meyer, likewise, writes in his introductory *Geschichte des Altertums* [History of Antiquity (Stuttgart: J.G. Cotta, 1884-1902)], (p. 67): "The assumption of G. Hansen, well-founded and generally accepted, that private ownership of land was everywhere preceded originally by a common ownership, as Caesar and Tacitus describe it among the Germans, has been strongly challenged in recent years: the Russian *mir*, at least, only arose in the seventeenth century." This latter contention Professor Meyer takes over uncritically from the old theory of the Russian Professor [Boris] Chicherin.

28 Ernst Grosse, *Die Formen der Familie und die Formen der Wirtschaft* (The Forms of the Family and Forms of the Economy) (Freiburg and Leipzig: J.C.B. Mohr, 1896), p. 3.

29   Ernst Grosse, *Die Anfänge der Kunst* (The Beginnings of the Arts) (Freiburg and Leipzig: P. Siebeck, 1894), pp. 34–5.

30   Ibid., p. 35.

31   Ernest Grosse, *Die Formen der Familie und die Formen der Wirtschaft*, pp. 4–5.

32   Collect material and "observed facts," just like the Verein für Sozialpol [Association for Social Politics] with monograph. [Marginal note by R.L.]

33   [Ernst] Grosse, *Die Anfänge der Kunst*, p. 34.

34   H. S. Maine, *Village-Communities in the East and West* (London: J. Murray, 1913), p. 7.

35   Grosse, *Die Anfänge der Kunst*, pp. 35–7 and 38.

36   Grosse, *Die Formen der Familie*, p. 238.

37   Ibid., pp. 215 and 207.

38   Grosse, *Die Formen der Familie und die Formen der Wirthschaft*, pp. 38–9.

39   Ibid., p. 57.

40   Grosse, *Die Formen der Familie und die Formen der Wirthschaft*, p. 137.

41   Ibid., pp. 30–1.

42   [Alfred William] Howitt, cited in [Felix] Somló [*Der Güterverkehr in der Urgesellschaft* (Social Intercourse in Primitive Society) (Brussels, Leipzig and Paris: Misch et Thron, 1909)], pp. 44–5. [See Alfred William Howitt, *The Native Tribes of South-East Australia* (Canberra: Aboriginal Studies Press, 1996) (first pub. 1904), p. 767.]

43   Friedrich Ratzel, *Völkerkunde* [Ethnology], 2 vols. [(Leipzig: Verlag des Bibliographie Institute, 1886)], p. 64.

44   [Alfred William] Howitt, cited in [Felix] Somló [*Der Güterverkehr*], p. 42 [*The Native Tribes of South-East Australia*, p. 756. Emphases by R.L.].

45   See Howitt [*The Native Tribes of South-East Australia*, p. 759], cited in Somló [*Der Güterverkehr*], p. 43.

46   See Ratzel, [*Völkerkunde*, Vol. 1], p. 333.

47   William John McGee, *The Seri Indians*, p. 190. Cited in Somló, *Der Güterverkehr*, pp. 124–5.

48   Karl von den Steinen, *Unter den Naturvölkern Zentral-Brasiliens. Reiseschilderung und Ergebnisse der zweiten Schinu-Expedition 1887–1888* (Among the Primitive Peoples of Brazil. Travel Narrative and Results of the Second Xingu Expedition) (Berlin: D. Reimer 1894), p. 491.

49   Karl von den Steinen, *Unter den Naturvölkern Zentral-Brasiliens*. p. 502.

50   Report of the 8th session of the International Congress of Americanists in Paris, 1890, account of M. G. Marcel, Paris, 1892, p. 491. [Gabriel Marcel, *Les Fuégiens à la fin du XVIIe siècle. D'après des documents français inédits. Congrès international des Américanistes. Compte-rendu de la 8ème session, tenue à Paris en 1890* (The Fuegians in the Late Seventeenth Century, According to Unpublished French Documents. International Congress of Americanists. Proceedings of the Eighth Session held in Paris in 1890)].

51   See Man, cited after Somló, pp. 96–9. [E. H. Man, *On the Aboriginal Inhabitants of the Andaman Islands* (London: Bibling & Sons, 1932), p. 26.]

52   Siegfried Passarge, *Die Buschmänner der Kalahari*, (Berlin: D. Raiser, 1907), p. 54.

53   Ibid., pp. 57–8.

54   See Somló [*Die Güterverkehr in der Urgesellschaft*], pp. 116.

55   Peruvians—but of course they're not nomads. Arabs, Kabyls—Kirghiz, Yakuts. Examples from [Émile Louis Victor de] Leveleye! [Marginal note by R.L.]

56   Ernst Grosse, *Die Formen der Familie*, p. 158.

57   See Somló [*Die Güterverkehr in der Urgesellschaft*], pp. 155–77.

58 [Karl] Bücher, *Die Entstehung der Volkswirtschaft*, pp. 86–8.

59 Ibid., p. 91.

60 See Georg Ludwig von Maurer, *Geschichte der Markenverfassung in Deutschland* (Erlangen: E. Enke, 1856), p. 119.

61 This was also the position of craftsmen in the Greek communities of the Homeric age: "All these people (metal worker, carpenter, musician, doctor—R.L.) were *demiurgoi* (from *demos* = people—R.L.), i.e. they worked for the members of the community rather than for themselves, they were personally free, but were not accepted as full members, standing below the real community members, the small farmers. They may well have not been sedentary, but moved from place to place, or even, if they had made a name for themselves, be called away." (Eduard Meyer, *Die wirtschaftliche Entwickelung des Altertums: ein Vortrag* [The Economic Development of Antiquity: A Lecture] [Jena: G. Fischer, 1895], p. 17.)

62 [Max Weber, "Agrargeschichte. I:] Agrarverhältnisse im Altertum" (Agrarian History, I: Agrarian Relations in Antiquity). [In] *Handwörterbuch der Staatswissenschaften*, 2nd edn, Vol. 1, [Jena 1898], p. 69.

63 C., pp. 37–88. [Ettore Cicotti, *Der Untergang der Sklaverei im Altertum* (The Decline of Slavery in Antiquity) (Berlin: Vorwärts, 1910)]

64 *Brevissima Relación de la destruycion de las Indias* [Brief Account of the Destruction of the Indies) (Sevilla: Sebastián Trugillo), 1552), cited in [Maksim] Kovalevsky, [*ObshchinnoeZemlevadenie. Priciny, khod i posledstvija ego razlozenija* (Communal Land Ownership: The Causes, Processes, and Consequences of its Disintegration), Vol. 1 (Moscow 1879),] p. 47.

65 Heinrich Handelmann, *Geschichte der Insel Hayti* [History of the Island of Haiti (Kiel: Schwers, 1856)], p. 6.

66 Girolamo Benzoni, *Storia del mundo nuovo* [(History of the New World) (Venezia: F. Rampazetto], 1565), cited in Kovalevsky, pp. 51–2.

67 [Pierre François-Xavier] Charleroix, *Histoire de l'Isle Espagnole ou de St. Dominique* [(History of the Island of Hispaniola and Santa Dominica) (Paris: F. Barrois], 1730), part 1, p. 228, cited in Kovalevsky, *Obshchinnoe Zemlevadenie*, p. 50.

68 [José de] Acosta, *Historia natural y moral de las Indias* [(Natural and Moral History of the Indies) (Barcelona: I. Cendrat,] 1591), cited in Kovalevsky [*Obshchinnoe Zemlevadenie*], p. 52.

69 Cited in Kovalevsky, *Obshchinnoe Zemlevadenie*, p. 49.

70 Kovalevsky, *Obshchinnoe Zemlevadenie*, p. 49.

71 Relations here similar to those in India, Algeria (Russia), Java, etc. [Marginal note by R.L.]

72 Zurita, [*Rapport sur les différentes classes de chefs dans la Nouvelle-Espagne*], pp. 57–9, cited in Kovalevsky[, *Obshchinnoe Zemlevadenie*,] p. 62.

73 Zurita, [*Rapport sur les différentes classes de chefs dans la Nouvelle-Espagne*,] p. 329, cited in Kovalevsky, [*Obshchinnoe Zemlevadenie*,] pp. 62–3.

74 Zurita, [*Rapport sur les différentes classes de chefs dans la Nouvelle-Espagne*,] p. 329, cited in Kovalevsky, *Obshchinnoe Zemlevadenie*,] p. 65.

75 Cited in Kovalevsky, [*ObshchinnoeZemlevadenie*,] p. 66.

76 Cited in Kovalevsky, *Obshchinnoe Zemlevadenie*, p. 68.

77 Zurita, [*Rapport sur les différentes classes de chefs dans la Nouvelle-Espagne*,] p. 87, cited in Kovalevsky, [*Obshchinnoe Zemlevadenie*,] p. 69.

78 Zurita, [*Rapport sur les différentes classes de chefs dans la Nouvelle-Espagne*,] p. 341 [cited in Kovalevsky, *Obshchinnoe Zemlevadenie*, p. 60].

79 *Memorial que presenta a su Magestad el licenciado Juan Ortez de Cervantes, Abogado*

y Procurador general der Reyno del Peru y encomenderos, sobre pedir remedio del daño, y diminución des los Indios [Memorial Presented to His Majesty the Lawyer and Attorney General Juan Ortez de Cervantes on the Encomenderos of the Kingdom of Peru on the Request for the Remedy of the Damage and Diminution of the Indians], [Madrid:] 1619, cited in Kovalevsky, [*ObshchinnoeZemlevadenie*,] p. 61.

80   1. Canal building (division of labor). Despite this, mark community. 2 Several types (Kovalevsky) of society. 3. All this remains despite the Muslim conquest and feudalization. 4. English! [Marginal note by R.L.]

81   James Mill!! [Marginal note by R.L.]

82   Karl Marx, *Das Kapital*, Vol. I [(Hamburg: Verlag von Otto Meissner, 1867)], p. 321. [*Capital* Volume One (New York: Penguin Books, London 1976), pp. 477–9. Emphases by R.L.]

83   The new edition of the *Handwörterbuch* on Plekhanov and Russian Social-Democracy. However, Engels in "Afterword [1894] to Social Relations in Russia" [See *Marx-Engels Collected Works*, Vol. 27 (New York: International Publishers, 1990), pp. 432–3].

84   1 *dessiatine* = 1.09 hectares [about two and a half acres].

85   See [W. G.] Trirogov, [*Obstschina i podat*, St. Petersburg: Suvorina, 1882,] p. 49.

86   The first "audit," which Peter enacted by ukase in 1719, was organized like a kind of penal expedition on foreign soil. The military was ordered to handcuff defaulting governors and place them under arrest in their own office, leaving them there "until they improve." Clerics who were assigned the task of implementing the peasant list and allowed the concealment of "souls" to go on, were relieved of their positions and "after being subjected to a relentless beating upon the body, had to submit to penal servitude, even if they were advanced in age." People who were suspected of hiding "souls" were placed on tenterhooks. The later "audits" continued to be just as bloody, though they were carried out with decreasing stringency.

87   See C[arl] Lehmann and [Alexander] Parvus [*Das hungernde Russland. Reiseeindrücke, Beobachtungen und Untersuchungen* (Stuttgart: J.H.W. Dietz, 1900)].

88   *Stanleys und Camerons Reisen durch Afrika* [Richard Oberländer, *Livingstones Nachfolger. Afrika von Osten nach Westen quer durchwandert von Stanley und Cameron. Nach den Tagebüchern, Berichten und Aufzeichnungen der Reisenden* (Livingston's Successor, Across Africa from East to West, Travels of Stanley and Cameron. According to the Diaries, Reports, and Records of the Travelers) (Leipzig: Otto Spamer, 1879)], pp. 74–80.

89   We shall go on to examine whether, or how far, such a hypothesis is justified. [Marginal note by R.L.]

90   Now however it is no longer the community as a whole that he deals with and that always has a need for his product, but rather the individual community members. [Marginal note by R.L.]

91   Social labor 1) as sum of the labors of the members of society for each other, 2) in the sense that the product of each individual is itself a result of the collaboration of many (raw materials, tools), even the whole society (science, need). In *both* cases, the social character is mediated by exchange. Knowledge in the future community, in slave society and today. [Marginal note by R.L.]

92   NB. Overproduced, unexchangeable commodities and unconsumable stocks in an organized society: commercial community (Indian rice), slave and *corvée* economy. Relationship between "need" (incalculable need on the one hand and overproduction of unsalable commodities on the other), overproduction in socialist society. [Marginal note by R.L.]

93   Cotton drove out linen in the nineteenth century. [Marginal note by R.L.]
94   Aristotle on slavery. [Marginal note by R.L.]
95   The discarding of use-value is complete in metallic money. [Marginal note by R.L.]
96   [Joseph François Lafitau], *Mœurs des sauvages américains comparées aux mœurs des premiers temps* [Habits of the American Indians Compared with the Morals of the Early Times) (Paris: Saugrain laîné, 1724)], Vol. 2, pp. 322–3, cited in [N.J.] Sieber ["David Ricardo i Karl Marks b ich obstchestvenno—ekonomistcheskich issledovaniach," in *Isbrannyie ekonomistcheskie orisuvedenia v dvuch tomach*, Vol. 1, Moscow, 1959], p. 245.
97   NB. Prehistoric discoveries! *First* of all, nomadism. [Marginal note by R.L.]
98   Sieber, ["David Ricardo i Karl Marks b ich obstchestvenno,"] pp. 245–6.
99   Sieber, ["David Ricardo i Karl Marks b ich obstchestvenno,"] p. 246. [Marginal note by R.L.]
100 *Reise zu den Nilquellen* [*Der Albert Nyanza, das große Becken des Nil und die Erforschung der Nilquellen*, t. 1 (Jena: Costenoble, 1867)], p. 326. [Samuel Baker, *The Albert N'Yanza Basin of the Nile; and Exploration of the Nile Sources* (London: Macmillan and Co., 1866), p. 380.]
101 Why did precious metals keep this role? [Marginal note by R.L.]
102 Sieber, ["David Ricardo i Karl Marks b ich obstchestvenno,"] p. 247. [Marginal note by R.L.]
103 NB. Replacement of useful metals by precious metals, particularly gold. [Marginal note by R.L.]
104 More detail. [Marginal note by R.L.]
105 Karl Marx, *Das Kapital*, Vol. 1, p. 197. [Marginal note by R.L.] [*Capital* Vol. 1, p. 345.]
106 Karl Marx, *Das Kapital*, Vol. 1, pp. 198–200. [Marginal note by R.L.] [*Capital* Vol. 1, pp. 346–8.]
107 NB. *Faux frais* [incidentals] of unplanned society; this must as it were produce once more its total wealth. [Marginal note by R.L.]
108 NB. Cultural importance of trade from prehistory on. *International* connection! [Marginal note by R.L.]
109 NB. Money illusions: hunt for gold—discovery of America. Charles V's mercantile policy. Alchemy (gold). [Marginal note by R.L.]
110 Natural economy. [Marginal note by R.L.]
111 Cf. John Bellers, [Eduard] Bernstein, *Engl[ish] Rev[iew]*, p. 354. [Marginal note by R.L.] [See "John Bellers, Champion of the Poor and Advocate of a League of Nations," in Eduard Bernstein, *Sozialismus und Demokratie in der grossen englischen Revolution* (Socialism and Democracy in the Great English Revolution) (Stuttgart: J.H.W. Dietz, 1908). For an English translation, see *Cromwell and Communism*, by Eduard Bernstein (London: George Allen & Unwin, 1963), chapter 17.]
112 Thomas Robert Malthus, *Principles of Political Economy Considered. With a View to their Practical Application* (chapter 7, section 4) (London: John Murray, 1820), p. 383.
113 Interests of capitalist production itself? [Marginal note by R.L.]
114 Egyptian slavery. [Marginal note by R.L.]
115 Since the introduction of general military service, the average height of adult men has steadily declined, and with it the legally prescribed size for enlistment. Before the great Revolution, the minimum height for infantrymen in France was 165 cms, then a law of 1818 reduced this to 157 cms, and it was further reduced to 156 cms in 1852, while on average, over half of men called up in France are rejected on

account of insufficient height or weakness. In Saxony, the military height in 1780 was 178 cms, whereas by the 1860s it was only 155 cms, and 157 cms in Prussia. In 1858, Berlin could not supply its replacement contingent, being 156 men short.

116   Rise of the reserve army. [Marginal note by R.L.]
117   Typhus in India due to hunger. [Marginal note by R.L.]
118   Extermination of primitive peoples. [Marginal note by R.L.]

A Glossary of Personal Names

Abamelik-Lazarev, Semyon Semyonovich (1857–1916), Russian industrialist, wrote a number of works on the mining industry and Russia's economy. He was also an archaeologist and scholar of ancient societies.

Acosta, José de (1539–1600), Spanish Jesuit and traveler, arrived in Peru in 1571 founded a number of colleges and universities in South America. He wrote an important study of the Native Americans of South America and Mexico, *Historia natural y moral de las Indias,* which is one of the most accurate depictions of the New World produced at the time.

Alexander II (1819–81), Tsar of Russia from 1855 to 1881; in response to Russia's defeat in the Crimean War, initiated a series of reforms, the most important being the abolition of serfdom, in 1861; also reorganised the military, state bureaucracy, and penal code. Brutally suppressed the Polish uprising of 1863 and banned the use of Polish, Lithuanian and Ukrainian languages. He was assassinated by a revolutionary in 1881.

Alexander III (1845–1894), Tsar of Russia from 1881 to 1894, extremely conservative and reactionary ruler who reversed many of the reforms of his assassinated predecessor, Tsar Alexander II. Insisted on the suppression of the languages and cultural heritage of non-Russian peoples of the Empire and severely persecuted the Jews. He severely weakened the power of the *zemstvo,* the elected local councils, in favor of the "land captains" appointed by the central government.

Alexis, Willibald. See **Häring, Georg Wilhelm Heinrich**

Allart Rousseau, Léon (1837–1906), Belgian entrepreneur and industrialist; founded a textile factory in Roubaix, France, near the border with Belgium, in 1849. In the 1870s his company built a large textile factory in Łódź, Poland, becoming one of the largest textile producers in the country.

Arkwright, Richard (1732–92), English inventor who is credited with devising the spinning frame and carding machine (to convert cotton into yarn), which helped launch the industrial revolution. His mill at Cromford helped create the modern factory system.

Arnold, Wilhelm (1826–83), German legal scholar and economic historian; a follower of Leopold von Ranke, wrote extensively on constitutional history and the political economy of the Middle Ages.

Artevelde, Jacob von (1290–1345), Flemish statesmen, became the ruler of the city of Ghent (one of the largest in Europe in the Middle Ages) following a revolt in 1338 by merchants and weavers opposed to the alliance between the Count of Flanders and France, which had impoverished many of them by denying them access to the English market. Artevelde ruled all of Flanders for a short time after leading the revolt but he was killed in an uprising of artisans opposed to his pro-English policies.

Babeuf, François-Noel (Gracchus) (1760–97), French revolutionary and journalist, member of the "Conspiracy of Equals" of 1796 that sought to replace the Directorate with a radical regime committed to the eradication of poverty and inequality. Participated in the Revolution of 1789, was initially close to the Jacobins, but went on to advocate a more radical program of income redistribution and equality of property.

Baker, Samuel White (1821–93), English explorer, explored the Upper Nile and was the first European to reach Lake Albert, in 1864. He was also an Abolitionist who strongly opposed slavery.

Beccaria, Cesare (1738–94), Italian philosopher and politician who is best known for writing *On Crimes and Punishments*, a passionate attack on torture and the death penalty that advocated a radical reform of the penal system; his books were an important influence on such US thinkers as Thomas Jefferson.

Becker, Jérome (1850–1912), Belgian explorer who traversed the course of the Nile to Lake Albert, in 1884. He wrote about his travels in *La Vie en Afrique ou Trois Ans dans l'Afrique Central* in 1887.

Bellers, John (1654–1725), English educational theorist, argued that it was the responsibility of the wealthy to provide for the education of the poorer classes of society. A Quaker and friend of William Penn, he lived for a time in Pennsylvania. He was a fervent opponent of capital punishment and advocated a unified European state. Some of his ideas were influential upon such utopian socialists as Robert Owen.

Beloch, Karl Julius (1854–1929), German economic historian, spent much of his life at the University of Rome; authored a number of important studies of Greek and Roman history, foremost of which is the four-volume *Griechische Geschichte*.

Bennett, James Gordon Jr. (1795–1872), American journalist, publisher of the *New York Herald*; provided the financial backing for Henry Morton Stanley's trip to Central and East Africa in 1869 in pursuit of David Livingston, which eventually led to the brutal opening up of the Congo basin to European imperialism.

Bentham, Jeremy (1748–1832), English philosopher and economist, one of the leading figures in the development of modern utilitarianism; defended free trade, usury, and unrestricted free markets and formulated the first quantitative formulation of the classical theory of the wage fund; a liberal social reformer, he founded (along with James Mill) the *Westminister Review*, a leading journal of the "philosophical radicals."

Benzoni, Girolamo (1520–1570), Italian adventurer and historian, spent fifteen years traveling through Spanish America; recorded his observations in a series of works in which he sharply attacked the Spanish for their repressive policies against the Native Americans.

Bernier, François (1625–88), French traveler and physician, lived in India for twelve years, during which time he was the personal physician of the Mughal Emperor Aurangzeb. Author of *Travels in the Moghul Empire*, one of the earliest accounts of Mogul India by a European. He helped promote the (erroneous) view that the Moghul Emperors owned all of the land, which became an important cornerstone of the theory of "Oriental Despotism."

Bernstein, Eduard (1850–1932), German socialist politician and theoretician, initially a follower of Lassalle, joined the "Marxist" Eisenachers in the 1870s; 1890–1901 lived in exile in London; appointed literary heir of Marx's archives by Engels; regular contributor to *Die Neue Zeit*; from 1896 on, one of the major theoreticians of "revisionism," the view that Marxism should be revised and "modernized"; subject of Luxemburg's polemic in her *Reform or Revolution*; member of the German Reichstag 1902–06 and 1912–18; in 1906, became a teacher at the SPD's party school in Berlin; resigned from the SPD on pacifist grounds in 1914 and became a leading member of the USPD; rejoined the SPD in 1919.

Bismarck, Otto von (1815–98), Prussian-German statesmen and first Chancellor of Germany from 1871 to 1890. A member of the Junker landowning class and extreme nationalist and authoritarian, he was instrumental in Prussia's (and later Germany's) military expansion. He imposed the anti-Socialist Laws against the workers' movement while trying to buy off sections of it by providing some social welfare protections.

Blanc, Louis (1811–82), French journalist, historian, and politician; reformist socialist who advocated national workshops, under government control, to ameliorate poverty and unemployment; in 1848, member of the Provisional Government; 1848–70, lived in England as an émigré; in 1871, elected to the French National Assembly; supported the reactionary regime of Thiers and took a position against the Paris Commune of 1871; in 1876, became a member of the Radical Party.

Blanqui, August (1805–81), French revolutionary, joined the conspiratorial society, the Carbonari in 1824 and later other groups, including the League of the Just; devoted himself to various schemes for insurrection with the aim of liberating society from oppression by bringing to power a cadre of professional revolutionaries who would rule on behalf of the masses; spent the bulk of his life in prison; he was an uncompromising revolutionary who spent little time or effort on theory or in developing a conception of the future social relations that could replace capitalism.

Blanqui, Jérome-Adophe (1798–1854), French economist, brother of famous revolutionary Louis August Blanqui. Made important discoveries in economic history and labor economics. An advocate of improved conditions for workers, but a supporter of free market capitalism.

Bloch, Jan Gotlib (1836–1901), Polish banker and financier who helped develop the railway industry in Poland. In 1877 he was appointed a member of the Russian Foreign Ministry's Scientific Committee. He also wrote a number of works on the Polish and Russian economy. Although he converted to Christianity as a young man he did not deny his Jewish roots and was an early supporter of Zionism. Near the end of his life he turned his attention to the need to avoid future European wars, arguing (in his six-volume study *Is War Now Impossible?*) that technological developments ensured future wars would lead to entrenchment and stalemate without clear victors.

Boccaccio, Giovanni (1313–1375), Italian poet and writer, author of the *Decameron*, a highly influential work of Renaissance humanism; also authored *On Famous Women*; emphasized a return to classical Greek and Latin sources, stimulating the rediscovery of ancient texts and ideas that proved of critical importance in the Renaissance.

Böhm-Bawerk, Eugen von (1851–1914), Austrian economist and leading figure in the conservative Austrian school of economics; served as Minister of Finance of Austria from 1895–1904 and afterwards was professor of economics in Vienna and Innsbruck; best known for his criticism of Marx's economics, arguing that Marx's discussion of value in Volume 1 of *Capital* was internally inconsistent with his theory of prices in Volume 3 and that the labor of workers is not the sole source of value. His work proved highly influential on such right-wing thinkers as Ludwig von Mises.

Boisguilbert, Pierre Le Pesant Sieur de (1646–1714), French economist, one of the earliest theorists of the virtues of a free market; opposed mercantilism (the notion that the wealth of nations consists in their possession of precious metals) on the grounds that wealth depends on the level of production and exchange; considered a major precursor of the Physiocrats. Marx, who often discussed his work, favorably quoted his comment that social wealth depends not on the level of coinage but on the enjoyment of human capacities.

Bontoux, Paul Eugene (1820–1904), industrialist and banker in the Austro-Hungarian Empire, invested heavily in railroads and mining; founded the General Union in 1878, an association of conservative bankers that sought to limit the economic power of Jews; he was arrested for participating in a banking scandal that helped precipitate the economic panic of 1882. After being sentenced to prison, he fled to Spain.

Borght, Richard van der (1861–1926), German jurist and statistician, taught economics at the University of Aachen from 1892 to 1900, served as a member of the Prussian lower house and in the Council of the Ministry of the Interior after 1898; published a book in 1892 on *The Economic Importance of the Rhine-Maritime.*

Börne, Ludwig (real name, Löb Baruch) (1786–1837), German author of imaginative literature and political journalism; a radical democrat in the period after the July Revolution in France of 1830; *Briefe aus Paris* (Letters from Paris) is his most famous work.

Bortkiewicz, Ladislaus von (1868–1931), Russian-born economist and statistician of Polish origin who spent much of his professional life in Germany; best known for his criticism of Marx's theory of reproduction, in which he claimed that Marx failed to adequately transform values into prices in Volume 3 of *Capital.* Bortkiewicz's criticism of Marx's alleged inconsistency in determining how values become transformed into prices, which has since been seriously challenged, was largely accepted by a number of left-wing economists, such as Paul Sweezy and Piero Sraffa.

Bray, John Francis (1809–1897), English economist and utopian socialist, a follower of Robert Owen who developed the theory of "labor money"—the idea of replacing money with notes or chits denoting hours of labor that could be exchanged for commodities.

Brentano, Lujo (1844–1931), German economist; "socialist of the chair" associated with the historical school of economics and member of the Association for Social Policy; studied under Adolph Wagner and later worked with Ernest Engel in studying the role of British trade unions. A moderate socialist, he was a strong supporter of German militarism in World War I and briefly served as Prime Minister in Kurt Eisner's Bavarian Socialist Republic of 1918.

Bright, John (1811–89), British politician and social reformer; strongly opposed protectionism, becoming one of the best-known opponents of the Corn Laws; a strong advocate of free trade, he opposed capital punishment, restrictions on religious and political liberty, and British colonial policy in Ireland, Egypt and India. He became known as one of Britain's greatest orators.

Bücher, Karl (1847–1930), part of the "Young German" historical school of economics that emphasized statistical and sociological analysis as against classical economists' emphasis on deductive reasoning. Criticized unregulated free markets and defended Germany's authoritarian welfare state.

Buckle, Henry Thomas (1821–1862), English historian and sociologist, author of *History of Civilization in England* (1857–1861).

Bürger, Gottfried August (1747–94), German poet and writer, author of *Lenore* (1773); his popular ballads are considered among the outstanding works of German literature.

Caesar, Julius (100 BC–44 BC), Roman general and statesmen who served as dictator of Rome from 49 BC to 44 BC. His early military career was defined by the conquest of Gaul (modern France), which he recorded in an important historical work. He effectively put an end to the phase of republican government of ancient Rome.

Cameron, Verney Lovett (1844–1894), English explorer, traveler and opponent of slavery who sought to suppress the East African slave trade; embarked on an expedition to East Africa in 1873 to assist the explorations of David Livingston; traversed the Congo-Zambezi watershed, becoming the first European to cross equatorial Africa from coast to coast; his reports on his travels, first published in 1877, helped open up the African interior to European colonization.

Cartwright, Edmund (1743–1823), English inventor of the power loom, which played a critical role in the industrial revolution; mechanical spinners were in use prior to his inventions, but his work improved the speed and quality of mechanical weaving.

Celman, Miguel Juárez (1844–1909), President of Argentina from 1886 to 1890. A liberal who favored the separation of church and state, he was forced to resign in 1890 after the "Revolution of the Park" took issue with his increasingly autocratic policies.

Cervantes, Juan Ortiz de (birth date unknown; died 1629), Spanish lawyer, judge, and Attorney General of Upper Peru, who wrote a book on the destruction of the South American Indians.

Chancellor, Richard (birth date unknown; died 1556), explorer and navigator. He was the first Englishman to explore the White Sea and establish direct commercial relations between England and Russia. At the time, England did not have access to the Baltic Sea, so his journeys established a new market for English wool for the countries of the East.

Charlemagne (742–814), King of the Franks from 768–814, greatly expanded the Frankish Kingdom into an Empire that incorporated much of Western and Central Europe. His Empire ranged from northern Spain to Croatia.

Charles V (1500–1558), ruler of the Spanish Empire (as Charles I) from 1516–56 and of the Holy Roman Empire (as Charles V) from 1519–56; presided over a massive empire that included Spain, Austria, The Netherlands, parts of Italy and the Spanish Americas; her was a fierce opponent of Protestantism and helped foster the Counter-Reformation.

Charlevoix, Pierre François-Xavier (1682–1761), French Jesuit traveler and historian, considered the first historian of New France; arrived in Canada in 1705, where he served for four years in Quebec as Professor; visited North America again in 1720–22 and explored the Great Lakes, Mississippi River, and the Caribbean; in addition to his history of New France and Hispaniola, he also wrote a history of Paraguay.

Châtel, Marly de see **Fumée, Martin.**

Chicherin, Boris Nikolaievitch (1828–1904), Russian jurist and political philosopher, strong supporter of the liberal reforms of Tsar Alexander II; influenced by Hegel's political philosophy, he supported a constitutional monarchy.

Child, Josiah (1630–99), English economist and proponent of mercantilism; Governor of the East India Company from the 1680s until his death; author of *Brief Observations Concerning Trade and the Interest of Money* (1688) and *A new Discourse on Trade* (1690).

Chuprov, Aleksandr Alexandrovich (1874–1926), Russian statistician and demographer; he argued for the use of statistics in analyzing and resolving social problems. A follower of Ladislaus Bortkiewicz, he taught at St. Petersburg Polytechnic Institute until 1917, when he went into exile following the Russian Revolution.

Ciccotti, Ettore (1863–1939), Italian teacher, historian and politician, wrote several influential works on ancient history; an active socialist, he also sponsored a number of translations of Marx's and Engels's works into Italian; best known for his studies of women and politics in ancient Rome and on the decline of slavery in ancient society.

Clodion the Hairy (392–448), King of the Franks who invaded the Roman Empire in 428, defeating the Romans at Cambrai; by 431 he extended his kingdom from northern Gaul south to the Somme River; defeated and killed in battle in 448 by the Roman general Flavius Aëtius. His name probably derives from wearing his hair long, a custom among many Frankish rulers of the time.

Cobden, Richard (1804–65), British liberal politician who worked closely with John Bright in leading the Anti-Corn Law League. A firm supporter of free trade, he opposed both the conservative landlords and the radical Chartist movement. He was a sharp critic of British foreign policy, arguing against excessive military spending and colonial domination; he especially opposed Britain's role in the First Opium War against China.

Cockerill, John (1790–1840), British industrialist who was born in Belgium, built wool processing machinery and founded an ironworks and mechanical engineering company; after his company went bankrupt in 1839, he traveled to Congress Poland and Russia, where he established several business ventures.

Cölln, Friedrich von (1777–1831), German writer and politician; served as an official of the Prussian government during the Napoleonic Wars primarily responsible for formulating taxation policy. After the Battle of Jean he became a strong supporter of the Stein–Hardenberg reforms.

Conrad, Johannes (1839–1915), German political economist, co-founded Verein für Sozialpolitik with Gustav von Schmoller. Co-edited the influential *Handwörterbuch der Staatswissenschaften* (Concise Dictionary of Political Sciences).

Coxey, Jacob S. Sr. (1854–1951), American politician and populist; in 1894 and 1914 led tens of thousands of unemployed on a march on Washington, DC demanding that the government initiate a job creation program; it became the inspiration for later marches on Washington. He began his career as a businessman and in the 1870s and 1880s became a leading member of the Greenbacks, which demanded that the government print additional money to stimulate the economy; in the 1890s was a leader of the People's Party; in 1932 ran for President of the US on the Farmer-Labor Party.

Cunow, Heinrich (1862–1936), German economist, historian, sociologist, and ethnographer; one of the leading theoreticians of the Second International, edited the main theoretical journal of German Social Democracy, *Die Neue Zeit*, from 1917–23; a teacher at the SPD party school from 1906, he wrote a number of influential works on the kinship structure of Australian aborigines, the Inca Empire, ancient technology, and the origin of marriage and the family; initially an opponent of Revisionism, in 1914 he supported Germany's entry in World War I and moved to the Right; in his last years argued that socialism could be peacefully introduced through state intervention in the economy.

Dade, Heinrich (1866–1923), German agricultural economist, served as General Secretary of the War Committee of German Agriculture during World War I; wrote a major work on the agricultural policy of the German Empire. He defended German imperialism and colonial expansion.

Dante, Alighieri (1265–1321), Italian poet and one of the greatest figures in world literature; author of the *Divine Comedy*, the first major literary work to appear in the Italian vernacular. He also wrote works on political philosophy. He was one of Marx's favorite writers.

Dareste, Rodolphe-Madeline Cléophas de la Chavanne (1824–1911), jurist and writer on legal history, wrote important study on property relations in Algeria that was referred to by Kovalevsky and Marx.

Darius III (380–330 BC), the last king of the Archaemenid Empire of Persia. Defeated by Alexander the Great at the Battle of Issus and the Battle of Guagamela, he died from wounds inflicted by two of his generals (Bessus and Nabarzanes) as he was fleeing from Alexander's forces.

Davanzati, Bernardo (1529–1606), Italian economist and historian who wrote several books on the history of coinage and the use of money in commercial transactions; his work helped pave the way for the modern banking system; he also translated Tacitus' *Annals* into Italian.

Demosthenes of Peaenia (birth date unknown; died 377 BC), a wealthy sword maker and owner of many slaves who fought for Athens during the Peloponnesian War against Sparta; he was the father of the famous orator of the same name.

Destutt de Tracy, Antoine comte de (1754–1836), French philosopher and economist; an ally of the Marquis de La Fayette during the French Revolution and imprisoned by the Jacobins; member of the sensualist school of philosophy of Condillac and Locke, he is credited with first using the term "ideology." He was a strong supporter of laissez-faire economics and defended the interests of property owners against workers. Thomas Jefferson wrote the Preface to the US edition of his *Principles of Political Economy*.

Dietzgen, Joseph (1828–88), German socialist writer and philosopher; met Marx during the 1848 Revolutions and lived for many years in the US; his *The Nature of Human Brain Work* argued that mental concepts are mere reflections of material and social relations.

Drucki-Lubecki, Franciszek Ksawery (1778–1846), Polish politician, served as Minister of the Treasury in Congress Poland from 1821 to 1830. A supporter of Tsar Alexander I of Russia, he was part of the political faction of "Conciliators," which argued that Poland's short-term economic development could best be assured through union with Russia.

Dubois, Jean-Antoine (1765–1848), French Catholic missionary in India, lived for many years in Mangalore and Mysore; he rejected Western society and dressed and lived like an Indian, and expressed strong appreciation for Hindu culture and religion; his major work is *Hindu Manners, Customs, and Ceremonies*.

Dühring, Eugen Karl (1833–1921), German socialist theorist, proponent of crude positivistic materialism and a critic of Marx and Marxism. Highly influential among many leading socialists of the time (included Eduard Bernstein and August Bebel initially), he was critiqued by Engels in *Herr Dühring's Revolution in Science*, a chapter of which was written by Marx. Argued for a harmony of the interests between capital and labor; became an advocate of German nationalism and anti-Semitism. He was also sharply criticised by Friedrich Nietzsche.

Edward III (1312–77), King of England from 1327 until his death, he initiated the Hundred Years' War with France, initially enjoying considerable success; many of his conquests in France were lost towards the end of his life.

Ehrenreich, Paul M.A. (1855–1914), German ethnologist and anthropologist who visited and researched the indigenous peoples of central and eastern Brazil, including the Botocudo (also known as Aimorés, Aimborés or Krenak people). In 1887–88 he accompanied Karl von den Steinem on the second Xingu expedition. He later made several ethnographic studies on Indian and East Asian societies.

Eichhorn, Karl Friedrich (1781–1854), German jurist, politician, and historian; wrote extensively on German constitutional law. A follower of Friedrich Carl von Savigny.

Elizabeth I of England (1533–1603), Queen of England from 1558 to 1603;

under her reign, England emerged as a major commercial and imperial power.

Engel, Ernst (1821–96), German economist and statistician; formulated Engel's law, which stipulates that as income rises the proportion of total income spent on food declines.

Ernst, Paul (1866–1933), German journalist and playwright; a supporter of the German Social-Democratic Party in the 1890s and contributed to *Die Neue Zeit*; corresponded with Engels on issues of women's emancipation; became a leader of "The Young," an anarchist current that was expelled from the SPD.

Erasmus of Rotterdam (1466–1536), Dutch Renaissance Humanist, most famous as author of *The Praise of Folly*, a satirical attack on the popular customs, morals and traditions of European society. Although friendly to Marin Luther, he remained within the Catholic Church and defended (contrary to most of the Protestants) the doctrine of free will.

Faucher, Julius (1820–78), German economist and politician, defender of an unrestricted free market; emigrated to England in 1850, returned to Germany in 1861, where he became a member of the House of Prussia for the National Liberal Party.

Fawcett, Henry (1833–84), British economist and politician; author of *Manual of Political Economy* (1863) and *The Economic Position of the British Laborer* (1865). A follower of Jeremy Bentham and John Stuart Mill, he was associated with the English Radicals; elected to Parliament as a member of the Liberal Party, he supported workers' rights and women's suffrage.

Ferrand, William (1809–1889), English landowner, conservative politician, and member of the British House of Commons from the 1830s to the 1860s; a protectionist and opponent of extending assistance to the poor through social legislation; he defended an idealized feudalism, defending absolute monarchy and a powerful church.

Fourier, François-Marie-Charles (1772–1837), French utopian socialist and radical defender of democracy, women's emancipation, and gay rights; his writings were a major influence on the young Marx, who held his work in high regard throughout his life. Marx refers to Fourier's work numerous times in the *Grundrisse* and *Capital*.

Frazer, James George (1854–1942), British anthropologist, author of the 12-volume *The Golden Bough*, a study of myths and rituals from around the world. He is considered the founder of religious anthropology.

Frederick, Charles, Grand Duke of Baden (1728–1822), ruler of Baden-Durlach in southwest Germany from 1746 until his death. He was a relatively enlightened social reformer who outlawed serfdom and torture.

Friedrich I, Barbarossa (1122–1190), German Holy Roman Emperor from 1155 until his death. One of the most powerful rulers of the European Middle Ages, he restored imperial authority, imposed imperial rule over much of

Italy, and helped lead the Third Crusade. He also presided over a revival of Roman law.

Friedrich II (1194–1250), Holy Roman Emperor from 1220 until his death. Presided over the Roman Empire at the peak of its power and influence; an avid patron of the arts and sciences and supporter of rationalism; an opponent of the Papacy, he encouraged cooperation and dialogue between Christians and Muslims.

Fumée, Martin (1540–1601), French writer and aristocrat, Lord of Marly-la-Ville, translated work of Lopez de Gomara on the Spanish conquest of the Americas into French; he also wrote under the pen name of Marly de Châtel.

Gambetta, Léon (1838–82), French bourgeois politician, an anti-monarchist, he nevertheless supported the suppresion of the Paris Commune; during the Commune he fled Paris in a hot-air balloon; elected to the Chamber of Deputies in 1879. He generally supported the interests of the lower middle class and petty-bourgeoisie.

Gamito, António Candido Pedroso (1806–66), Portuguese explorer, sought to cross equatorial Africa from coast to coast in 1831, but was stopped at Lake Mwereu, on the border between present-day Zambia and the Democratic Republic of the Congo, by resistance from the Kazembe people; the journal of his expeditions recorded important information about the ethnography of Central Africa.

Gaup, Ernest Theodor (1796–1859), German jurist who specialized in the history of German law; author of the two-volume *German City Rights in the Middle Ages*.

Gelfand, Israel Lazarevich (1867–1924), pen name Alexander Parvus, Russian Social Democrat and Marxist theorist; in the 1890s, became active in the German Social Democratic movement; 1895–96, editor of the *Leipziger Volkszeitung*; 1898–99, chief editor of the *Sächsische Arbeiter-Zeitung* in Dresden; worked closely with Leon Trotsky in 1904–05 in developing the theory of "permanent revolution"; during the Russian Revolution of 1905, member of the St. Petersburg Workers' Council; supported Germany's intervention in World War I; after Bolshevik Revolution of 1917, offered to assist the Bolsheviks, but Lenin turned him down; became a trader and businessman.

Genovesi, Antonio (1712–69), Italian philosopher and political economist, strongly influenced by John Locke's empiricism; wrote one of the first works in Italian on political economy, *Lezioni di Commercio*; although he was close to the mercantilists, he argued that labor is an important source of value.

Gillen, Francis James (1855–1912), Australian anthropologist and ethnologist, explored central Australia and lived among the aborigines; wrote several books on aboriginal society and culture.

Girard, Philippe Henri de (1775–1845), French engineer and inventor who helped found the textile industry in Poland, in the 1820s, in the city of Zyrardow, which is named after him. He also invented the use of tin cans to store and preserve food.

Gladstone, William (1809–1898), major British politician; Chancellor of the Exchequer, 1853, leader of the Liberal Party and Prime Minister of Great Britain in 1868–74, 1880–85, 1886, and 1892–94.

Gneisenau, August Neidhardt von (1760–1831), Prussian general who served as Field Marshal during the Napoleonic Wars. Along with Gerhard von Scharnhorst, he argued for major reforms in the Prussian military in the face of several major defeats; captured Napoleon during the Battle of Waterloo in 1814.

Goethe, Johann Wolfgang von (1749–1832), German poet, prose writer, dramatist, and naturalist; foremost representative of German classical literature, and one of Rosa Luxemburg's favorite writers; author of *Faust*.

Gómara, Francisco López de (1511–66), Spanish historian who wrote an account of Cortés' conquest of Mexico. Although he knew Cortés personally and the book has some important anecdotes, modern historians question many aspects of its claims to accuracy.

Gracchus, Gaius (154 BC–121 BC), younger brother of Tiberius Gracchus, promoted land reform by restricting the size of landed estates in favor of poorer peasants; appealed to the support of plebeians against patrician landed interests; served as Tribune from 121 to 122 BC; alienated many plebeian supporters when he advocated extending citizenship to non-Roman Italians.

Gracchus, Tiberius (163 BC–133 BC), Roman politician, formulated with his brother Gaius the Gracchi reforms, which sought to ameliorate the conditions of the peasants by providing them with lands owned by patricians; elected as Tribune in 133 BC, he promoted a policy of land reform by limiting the amount of land that could be owned by any individual; facing intense opposition by the patricians, he was murdered by them in 133 BC.

Gray, John (1799–1883), economist and neo-Ricardian socialist; a supporter of the labor theory of value, he argued that the unequal distribution between the proceeds of labor and workers' wages should be redressed by eliminating the competitive free market and replacing it with cooperative communities run by the workers.

Gregory VII (1015–85), served as Pope from 1073 until his death. Greatly expanded the power of the papacy through a series of reforms, which included creating a new canon law, imposing his will during the investiture controversy against Henry IV of the Holy Roman Empire, and adopting the election of future popes by a College of Cardinals.

Grosse, Ernst (1862–1927), German sociologist and Sinologist who proposed studying "primitive" peoples based on their artistic and cultural formations.

Guizot, François Pierre Guillaume (1787–1874), French historian and conservative politician, strong supporter of King Louis Philippe from 1830 to 1848 and virulent opponent of social revolution; after being removed from power by the 1848 Revolution, he devoted himself to writing a series of historical works that were severely criticized by Marx and Engels.

Haller, Karl Ludwig von (1768–1854), Swiss jurist and politician, opposed democracy as well as the model of the centralized state that came out of the French Revolution; a fierce reactionary, he opposed all the major revolutionary movements of his time. Hegel strongly criticized his *Restauration der Staatswissenschaften* (Restoration of the Science of the State) in his *Philosophy of Right*.

Handelmann, Heinrich Gottfried (1827–1891), German historian and philologist, wrote histories of Brazil, Haiti, the United States, Denmark, and the Hanseatic League.

Hardenberg, Karl August von (1750–1822), Prussian statesmen who promoted a series of important liberal forms, such as the abolition of serfdom and guild monopoly, in the aftermath of Prussia's defeat by Napoleon in the Battle of Jena; later in life he became a political reactionary. Served as Prussian Foreign Minister from 1805–06 and chief representative of Prussia at the Congress of Vienna in 1814–15.

Häring, Heinrich, Georg Wilhelm (1798–1871), German historical novelist who wrote under the pseudonym of Willibald Alexis; best known for his novel *Der Roland von Berlin*.

Haxthausen, August Frantz Ludwig Maria von (1792–1866), German economist and scientist, defended the interests of large landed-property owners and worked for the King of Prussia in promoting legislation related to land tenure; as part of his studies of the peasantry, traveled to Russia in the 1840s; authored a three-volume study on Russian agrarian formations, which first brought to Western European attention the importance of the Russian village commune; his work proved influential among Russian radicals and conservatives seeking to renovate society on the basis of its traditional social formations.

Henry VII (1275–1313), ruler of the Holy Roman Empire from 1312 until his death. He aimed to restore the power of the Empire by gaining control of Italy, but failed to achieve his aims; Dante was one of his most fervent supporters.

Henry II of Saabrücken (died 1234), Bishop of Worms from 1217 to 1234.

Hermann, Friedrich Benedict Wilhelm (1795–1868), German economist and statistician; one of Germany's earliest political economists, he drew heavily from the work of Smith and Ricardo while giving greater emphasis than they did to such factors as the role of the public sphere and the consumption levels of the laborer.

Heine, Heinrich (1797–1856), one of Germany's greatest poets, essayists and political journalists; close friend and associate of the young Marx.

Helmholtz, Hermann von (1821–94), German physician and scientist who wrote important studies on optics, visual perception, and the physiology of the nervous system; he was the first to discover the speed by which a signal is carried along a nerve fibre.

Herkner, Heinrich (1863–1932), German economist who wrote a series of studies on industrial and financial crises and their impact on economic development; close to Marxism in his early years, he befriended Friedrich Engels and served as a mentor to the Russian Marxist Alexandra Kollontai; became a conservative by 1907, helping to form the German Society for Sociology, along with Max Weber.

Herschel, William (1738–1822), German astronomer, discoverer of the planet Uranus.

Hildebrand, Bruno (1812–78), German economist, statistician, and politician; member of the historical school of economics, sought to analyze economic development on the basis of contingent empirical circumstances and conditions; he was critical of Ricardo and classical political economy for its emphasis on universal economic laws. Like many members of the historical school, he was a conservative socialist of the "socialism of the chair" variety.

Howitt, Alfred William (1830–1908), English and Australian explorer, natural scientist and anthropologist; moved to Australia in 1852 and for many years served as a magistrate of the Omeo goldfields; in the 1860s began to study the Australian aborigines and published several studies about them, especially about the Kurnai peoples; considered a founding figure of Australian anthropology.

Hughes, John (1814/15–89), Welsh engineer and businessmen; originally made his fortune producing iron and armaments, including of the first ironclad ships for the British navy. In 1868, he moved to Russia to help build the naval fortress at Kronstadt; in the 1870s founded a series of metalworks factories and the self-contained city in Ukraine, now known as Donetsk, that became one of the largest industrial centers in Russia; the city was originally named Hughesovka or Yuzovka in his honor.

Hullmann, Karl Dietrich (1765–1846), German historian. His books include studies of the Byzantine Empire, ancient constitutional law, and the commercial history of ancient Greece. His most famous work is a study of the development of cities in the European Middle Ages.

Humboldt, Friedrich Heinrich Alexander Freiherr von (1769–1859), German naturalist and explorer; between 1799 and 1804 traveled extensively in Latin America; the account of his journey and discoveries was a major impetus to the development of the disciplines of geography and global studies; his work focused more on natural conditions and formations than cultural or social issues, but he was a firm opponent of slavery.

Hutten, Ulrich von (1488–1523), German humanist and satirist, colleague of Martin Luther, Zwingli, and Erasmus; author of *Letters of Obscure Men*, which attacked scholasticism and monkish life. As a result of his support for Franz von Sickingen's war against the German princes he was forced into exile in Switzerland.

Ingram, John Kells (1823–1907), Irish economist and sociologist; an opponent of classical political economy in favor of a positivist approach to economics and the social sciences; a follower of August Comte, he was strongly influenced by the German historical school. Best known for his widely read *History of Political Economy* (1888), he may have been the first to use the term *homo oeconomicus* (economic man).

Ianzhul, Ivan Ivanovich (1846–1914), Russian economist and statistician, taught law at Moscow University from 1876. From 1882 to 1887 he was a factory inspector for the Moscow area. A follower of the historical school in political economy, he supported state intervention in the economy and protectionist trade measures.

Ivan the Terrible (1530–84), ruled Russia as Ivan IV from 1533 until his death. Vastly expanded the territory of Russia by conquering the Khanates of Kazan, Astrakhan and Siberia and became crowned as the first Tsar of Russia. Under his rule Russia emerged as a powerful and centralized multiethnic state. His cruel and relentless repression of the Russian nobility as well as all potential political opponents earned him his sobriquet.

Jarcke, Karl Ernst (1801–52), German jurist and writer who forcefully opposed the revolutionary movements of his time in the name of political conservatism. He was close to the reactionary romanticism of figures such as Karl Ludwig von Haller and Adam Müller. A supporter of Metternich's reactionary policies, he accepted his offer to serve in the Austrian government during the 1830s. He idealized the medieval period as being far superior to modern society.

Kankrin, Yegor Frantsevich Kankrin (1774–1845), Russia's finance minister from 1823 to 1844. He stood for protectionism in tariff policy, in part to cover the chronic budget deficit experienced by Russia but also because he wished to counteract the development of capitalist industry in the country.

Kaufman, Konstantin Petrovich von (1818–82), Russian governor-general of Turkestan from 1867 to 1882, author of *Turkestanskii Albom*, an ethnographic study of the people's of Central Asia.

Kautsky, Karl (1854–1938), German Marxist theoretician and the leading figure from the 1890s to World War I of German Social Democracy and the Second International. In 1882 co-founded the journal *Die Neue Zeit* and was its chief editor until 1917. An ally of Rosa Luxemburg in the revisionist debate of

1898, she broke with him in 1910 as he moved closer to reformism with his "strategy of attrition"; 1917 co-founded the USPD; became a fierce critic of the Bolshevik Revolution after 1917; returned to the SPD in 1920 when much of the USPD's membership joined the German Communist Party.

Kindlinger, Nikolaus (1749–1819), German Franciscan who devoted himself to studies of early German history. A follower of Justus Möser, his main work is *Geschichte der deutschen Hörigkeit* (History of German Bondage).

Knies, Karl (1821–98), German economist associated with the older version of the historical school of economics; attacked classical political economy for its claim that society operates according to universal, abstract economic laws.

Kovalevsky, Maksim Maksimovich (1851–1916), Russian historian, sociologist and anthropologist, author of *Communal Ownership of Land—the Causes, Process and Consequences of its Dissolution*, a study of pre-capitalist communal formations in India, the Middle East, North Africa, and Latin America. Marx made detailed notes on this work shortly after its appearance, in 1879. Marx held numerous in-person discussions with Kovalevsky, beginning in the summer of 1875; subsequently, Kovalevsky became a regular visitor to Marx's household. Luxemburg closely studied and commented on Kovalevsky's work, especially in her *Introduction to Political Economy* and *The Accumulation of Capital*.

Lafitau, Joseph François (1681–1746), French philosopher and Jesuit missionary, lived among the Iroquois from 1712–17 and carefully recorded their customs and traditions in *Mœures des Sauvages américains comparées aux mœurs des premiers temps* (Habits of the American Indians Compared with the Morals of the Earliest Times). He is considered an important precursor to the field of ethnology.

Langovoi, Nikolai Petrovich (1860–1920), Russian scientist who specialized in the study of textile production. Much of his work focused on a theory to explain winding on spinning machines and other types of weaving.

Las Casas, Bartolomé de (1474–1566), Spanish historian and social reformer who condemned the genocidal practices of the Spaniards against the indigenous peoples of the Americas; a Dominican friar, he was among the first European settlers in the New World; served as first resident Bishop of Chiapas and "Protector of the Indians"; author of *Short Account of the Destruction of the Indies* and *History of the Indies*. After returning to Spain in the 1540s, argued in a series of debates that Indians were fully human and worthy of decent treatment; he suggested Indian slaves should be replaced with slaves from Africa, but changed his views on this by the end of his life.

Lassalle, Ferdinand (1825–64), writer and political organiser, major figure in formation of German socialist movement. Participant in 1848–49 revolution; 1849–62, maintained connections with Marx, who ultimately broke from him for being "a future workers' dictator"; in 1863, co-founded the Allgemeine

Deutscher Arbeiterverein (General Union of German Workers), which for many years was the largest socialist organization in Germany. Lassalle's followers merged with the "Eisenachers," the purported followers of Marx, in 1875, despite Marx's strong objections, voiced in his *Critique of the Gotha Program*. Lassallean ideas and approaches continued to influence German Social-Democracy for decades afterwards.

Laveleye, Émile Louis Victor de (1822–92), Flemish economist and Christian socialist, took special interest in preserving the culture of minority groups. Wrote an important work on property forms of "primitive" societies.

Lehmann, Carl (1865–1916), German physician and activist in the socialist movement, involved in publishing and distributing radical literature; in 1899 traveled to Russia and co-authored (with Alexander Gelfand, aka Parvus) *Das hungernde Russland: Reiseeindrücke, Beobachtungen und Untersuchungen* (Starving Russia: Travel Impressions, Observations and Analysis), in 1900.

Leo, Heinrich (1799–1878), German historian and politician; a follower of Gustav von Hugo, he studied under Hegel at Berlin University, though he later repudiated his thought. A political reactionary, he was fiercely anti-Semitic. Author of numerous historical works, including *The Constitution of the Development of Lombard Cities*.

Letourneux, Aristide (1820–90), French military office who wrote a three-volume study of the Kabyles of North Africa between 1868 and 1873.

Lexis, Wilhelm Hector Richard Albrecht (1837–1914), German academic economist, wrote one of the first reviews (in 1885) of Volume 2 of Marx's *Capital*. He rejected the labor theory of value and the distinction between value and price. Engels responded to Lexis's critique of Marx in his "Preface" to Volume 3 of *Capital*.

Liebig, Justus von (1803–1873), German chemist, made important discoveries on the effect of nutrients such as nitrogen and carbon dioxide on crops; his work proved of critical importance in the later development of artificial fertilizers; helped elaborate the principles that led to the modern laboratory; his use of the term "metabolism" to explain the biochemical processes of natural systems had important impact on Marx, who discusses his work in *Capital*.

Linnaeus, Carl (1707–78), Swedish botanist, physician, traveler, and zoologist, and founder of modern taxonomy, the system of scientific classification now used in the natural sciences; one of the first European thinkers to classify human beings as primates and rejected arguments that humans are fundamentally distinct from animals; he was the first to describe the human race as *homo sapiens*.

Lippert, Julius (1839–90), Czech politician and historian, author of *Die Geschichte der Familie* (The History of the Family).

List, Friedrich (1789–1846), German economist, forerunner of the historical school of economics that dominated German academic circles for much of the nineteenth century; moved to the US in the 1820s, where under the influence of Alexander Hamilton's writings became a firm advocate of protectionism; served as US counsel to several European countries, including France and Germany; author of *The National System of Political Economy*, which argued for promoting capitalist development through national protection of domestic industries; an advocate of a strong, national state, he denied pursuit of private interest necessarily promotes public good.

Livingston, David (1813–73), Scottish physician, missionary, and explorer; moved to South Africa as a missionary in 1840; traveled extensively in Africa from the 1850s onwards; first European to see Victoria Falls; navigated the Zambezi River and engaged in an ultimately unsuccessful search for the origin of the Nile River. His letters and writings denouncing the slave trade had an important impact on pubic opinion in Britain and elsewhere, though he often relied on slave traders for supplies in his travels; his explorations and missionary work had the result of opening up much of the interior of Africa to the ravages of European colonization and domination.

Loaysa, Juan García de (1478–1546), Spanish Dominican, served as Confessor for Emperor Charles V of Spain; as President of the American Council of the Indies, proposed lenient treatment for the indigenous peoples under Spanish rule; became Archbishop of Seville in 1539 and Grand Inquisitor (of the Spanish Inquisition) in 1546.

Loskiel, Georg Heimrich (1740–1814), missionary and author, published a report of the work of missionaries in New York, Pennsylvania and Ohio in the 1740s.

Lothair I (795–855), Emperor of the Romans, the successor state to Charlemagne's kingdom, from 817 until his death; his kingdom was divided into three parts as a result of conflict with his brothers Charles and Louis; his territory became known as Lothringen, origin of the name of the French province of Lorraine.

Louis XIV (1638–1715), King of France from 1643 until his death. The longest-reigning king in European history, he centralized the administration of the French state and eliminated some aspects of feudalism in the name of consolidating an absolute monarchy. He was a firm upholder of the notion of the divine right of kings.

Louis XV (1710–74), King of France from 1715 until his death. Under his reign the French lost possession of Canada and other territories to Britain in the Seven Years' War; his military exploits greatly weakened the French economy, although he attempted some reforms, such as altering the tax code near the end of his reign.

Louis XVI (1754–93), King of France from 1774 to 1792, attempted to impose some reforms in the early part of his reign, such as abolishing serfdom, but resisted deeper calls for change and was deposed as a result of the French

Revolution of 1789. In 1793 he was tried and executed by the National Convention for his covert support for the foreign invasion of France.

Louis-Philippe (1773–1850), King of France from 1830 to 1848. Proclaimed King after the 1830 Revolution, he was forced from power by the Revolution of 1848 and spent the rest of his life in England. He was the last king of France.

Lucullus, Lucius Licinius (118– 56 BC), Roman politician and general, helped conquer much of Asia Minor for Rome in the Third Mithridatic War; he accumulated a vast amount of private wealth as a result of his conquests; served as consul of Rome in 74 BC.

Luden, Heinrich (1778–1847), German historian and economist who commented on the work of Adam Smith.

Macaulay, Thomas Babington (1800–59), British poet, politician, and historian; lived in India from 1834, where he served on a number of bodies of the British colonial administration. Influenced by utilitarian philosophers such as Jeremy Bentham and James Mill, he argued that educated Indians should learn English instead of their native languages. "Macaulay's Children" refers to those of Indian ancestry who accept the cultural "superiority" of Western culture. Marx was highly critical of him, accusing him of falsifying history.

Mackenzie, Alexander (1764–1820), Scottish explorer who sought to find the Northwest Passage to the Pacific, becoming the first to complete a recorded crossing of North America north of Mexico, in 1793. The Mackenzie River in northern Canada is named after him.

Maine, Henry James Sumner (1822–88), English historian and jurist, author of a number of works on ancient society; his work highlighted the difference between the contractual nature of social relations of modernity versus status-based social relations of antiquity. An advisor to the British government in India, he wrote an influential work on communal village communities in pre-capitalist societies that was read and studied by Marx and Luxemburg.

Malthus, Thomas Robert (1786–1834), English demographer and economist, popularized the theory that population growth increases faster than the rate of economic growth and availability of resources, thereby precluding the possibility of the progressive improvement of society; supported legislation that would prevent the poor and indignant from having children and large families.

Man, Edward Horace (1846–1929), member of the British colonial administration of India, studied the language and culture of the peoples of the Andaman and Nicobar Islands.

Mangoldt, Hans Karl Emil von (1824–1868), German economist who argued that the profits obtained by capitalist entrepreneurs is a reward for risk-taking. His *Grundrisse der Volkswirtschaftslehre* (Outline of Economics) (1863) proved influential in the later development of neo-classical economics.

Marcel, M. G. (1843–1909), French geographer who made a study of the native inhabitants of Tierra del Fuego in the 1890s. He also authored the original text of *Mutineers of the Bounty*, a story of the famous mutiny against Captain Bligh; the story was used by Jules Verne and many others in retelling the incident.

Marwitz, Alexander von der (1795–1814), Prussian nobleman and soldier, took part in the wars against Napoleon on behalf of Prussian and Russian forces; perhaps best known for his brief affair and correspondence with Rahel Varnhagen, an early proponent of women's liberation.

Maurer, Georg Ludwig von (1790–1872), German historian, wrote a series of influential works on the early social and communal institutions among the Germanic peoples; his work was intensely studied by Marx as well as by Luxemburg.

McCulloch, John Ramsey (1789–1864), Scottish economist, leading figure of the Ricardian school of classical political economy; sought to "defend" the labor theory of value by arguing that nature and machinery are also sources of value. His work was strongly criticized by Marx, who considered his contribution a pale reflection of the accomplishments of Smith and Ricardo

McGee, William John (1853–1912), American inventor and ethnologist; from 1893–1903 headed Bureau of American Ethnology; 1895, he explored Isla del Tiburón in the Gulf of Calfornia, home to the Seri Indians; published his study *The Seri Indians* in 1898.

Medici, Ardingo de (birth and death dates unknown), Italian soldier; first member of the famous Medici family of Florence to hold public office. In 1296 he was elected Gonfaloniere, a post designed to protect citizens from abuses of the wealthier and more powerful classes.

Medici, Averardo de (birth date unknown; died 1346), member of the Cafaggiolo branch of the Medici family and father of Giovanni di Medici, who became the first truly powerful member of the Medici's in Florence.

Medici, Catherine de (1519–89), daughter of a leading member of the Medici family; Queen of France from 1547 to 1559, after marrying King Henry II. After Henry II's death, she exerted considerable political influence as the regent for her three sons Francis II, Charles IX, and Henry III, each of whom served as king of France.

Medici, Cosimo (1389–1464), leading figure in the Medici family who helped consolidate control over Florence in the fifteenth century; although he never held public office, he controlled the city through a series of political appointments and his extensive business dealings in banking and commerce. He was a major patron of artists and the arts, playing a critical role in making possible the Italian Renaissance.

Medici, Francesco de (1541–87), Grand Duke of Tuscany from 1574 until his death. He was a patron of the arts as well as of science, taking a special interest in chemistry and alchemy.

Medici, Lorenzo de (1449–92), Italian statesmen of the Medici family and de facto ruler of Florence at the height of the Italian Renaissance; also known as Lorenzo the Magnificent. He was a patron of many artists, poets, and architects; his largess helped make possible the work of Leonardo da Vinci, Botticelli, and Michelangelo.

Medici, Salvestro de (1331–88), member of the Medici family of Florence, held the position of Gongaloniere in 1370 and 1378, after which he ruled as effective dictator of the city. He was forced into exile in 1382.

Melanchthon, Philip (1497–1560), German religious reformer and founding figure of the Protestant Reformation; worked closely with Martin Luther and helped formulate many of the leading tenets of the Lutheran Church.

Mendeleyev, Dmitri Ivanovich (1834–1907), outstanding Russian scientist who first devised the periodic table of the elements and made important discoveries (as well as inventions) associated with modern chemistry. He helped make St. Petersburg into a major center of scientific research. He also helped found the first oil refinery in Russia.

Metternich, Klemens Wenzel von (1773–1859), Austrian politician, fiercely opposed the French Revolution and helped fashion the political restoration of the old regimes that followed the defeat of Napoleon; formed the "Metternich system" of international alliances whose main purpose was to prevent further revolutionary upsurges in Europe; forced from power as a result of the 1848 Revolutions.

Meyer, Conrad Ferdinand (1825–98), Swiss poet and novelist; author of the epic novel *Hutten's Last Days*, which was a favorite of Luxemburg's.

Meyer, Eduard (1855–1930), German historian, wrote extensively on economic and social relations in the ancient world; best known for his book *Geschichte des Altertums* (History of Antiquity).

Mill, James (1773–1836), Scottish historian, economist, and political theorist; one of the founders of classical political economy. Marx subjected his economic writings to careful scrutiny in the 1840s. His historical works include *The History of British India*, which has been widely criticized for helping to originate the theory of "oriental despotism." Mill also wrote extensively on issues of ethics and psychology from a utilitarian perspective.

Mill, John Stuart (1806–73), British philosopher, economist, and political theorist, best known for formulating the modern theory of utilitarianism. A social reformer who served as a member of the British Parliament allied with the British Radicals, he opposed slavery, restrictions on workers' rights, and championed women's emancipation.

Mommsen, Theodor (1871–1903), German historian and politician, author of influential multi-volume study of ancient Rome; served as professor of Roman history at the University of Berlin from 1861 to 1887; he won the Nobel Prize for Literature in 1902 for his *Roman History*; also wrote a systematic treatment of Roman law. Although he was a Liberal, he opposed Bismarck in favoring cooperation with the Social Democrats. Despite his support for German nationalism, he sharply opposed anti-Semitism.

More, Thomas (1478–1535), English philosopher and statesman and important figure in Renaissance humanism; coined the term "utopia." A religious conservative, he defended the traditions of the Catholic Church against the claims of Luther and other Protestants. Opposed to King Henry VIII's break from the Papacy, he was tried and executed on trumped-up charges of treason.

Morgan, Lewis Henry (1818–81), American anthropologist; author of *Ancient Society*, consisting largely of a study of the Iroquois Indians of North America, which argued that the earliest form of human association was the matrilineal clan. Marx made a critical study of Morgan's work in his *Ethnological Notebooks*, accepting some but not all of his findings. Engels utilized his work less critically in his better-known *Origin of the Family, Private Property, and the State*. Morgan also served for several years as a member of the New York State Assembly as a Republican.

Möser, Justus (1720–1794), German jurist, statesman and social theorist, argued in contradistinction to social contract theories that the state is a natural and organic part of historical development; he was a conservative thinker who idealized the pre-capitalist social order.

Mukanda (birth and death dates unknown), also known as Chief Mkanda of the Chewa, an indigenous African people living southwest of Lake Nyasa in modern-day Malawi. Portuguese travelers to this area in the early 1800s referred to him as the most powerful ruler in the area.

Müller, Adam Heinrich (1779–1829), German political economist and writer, a representative of the school of economic romanticism; a political conservative, he opposed the liberal reform movement in Prussia that followed its defeat by French forces in the Battle of Jena. His literary work extolled the virtues of medieval feudalism. A political ally of Metternich, he worked as a political advisor to the Austrian monarchy.

Mun, Thomas (1571–1641), English economist, associated with the mercantilist school; served as director of the East India Company for several years and defended its practices in his book *A Discourse of Trade from England unto the East Indies*.

Mwata Kazembe III Lukwesa Ilunga (1760–1805), ruler of the Luba-Lunda Kingdom in the southeast of modern-day Congo who fiercely resisted efforts by the Portuguese in the late-1700s to secure domination of the area.

Napoleon I (1769–1821), Emperor of France from 1804 to 1815; ruled as Napoleon I. Rising through the ranks of the military during the French Revolution, he seized control of France and initiated a series of wars against reactionary European powers known as the Napoleonic Wars. Initiated a series of legal reforms that laid the foundation of modern-day France, the Napoleonic Code. Died in exile in St. Helena.

Nasse, Erwin von (1829–1890), German economist and politician, wrote on banking and tax systems as well as agrarian history, especially in England.

Nebuchadnezzar (634–562 BC), King of Neo-Babylonian Empire from 605–562 BC. According to the Old Testament, he conquered Jerusalem in 586 BC, destroyed the First Temple and sent the Jews into the "Babylonian Captivity."

Nettelbeck, Joachim Christian (1738–1824), Prussian seaman and slave trader, best known for his autobiography, *Des Seefahrers und aufrechten Bürgers Joachim Nettelbeck wundersame Lebensgeschichte von ihm selbst erzählt*, (The Seafarer and Citizen Joachim Nettlebeck's Miraculous Life Story, Told by Himself). The work served as the basis for a propaganda film used by the Nazis during World War II.

Nicholas I (1796–1855), Emperor of Russia from 1825 until his death. Among Russia's most reactionary rulers, he ruled through brutal autocratic power. Fostered Russian nationalism and brutally repressed the rights of Russia's many national minorities. His crushing of the Hungarian Revolution of 1848 earned him the enmity of democrats and free-thinkers throughout Europe.

Nicholas II (1868–1918), Emperor of Russia from 1894 to 1917; forced to abdicate by the February Revolution. Presided over Russia during its defeat of Japan in the Russo-Japanese War of 1904–05 and the Russian Revolution that followed; led Russia into World War II, in which four million of his countrymen perished. His regime was marked by severe repression and anti-Semitic pogroms as well as political corruption. He was executed by the Bolsheviks during the Civil War.

Owen, Robert (1771–1858), Welsh social reformer, leading figure in utopian socialism; manager of a textile mill, he became a sharp critic of the inhumanity of capitalist industrialization and a leading figure in the cooperative movement. Although initially a follower of English liberals like Jeremy Bentham, he embraced socialism and became a firm critic of the free market; argued for the creation of freely-associated townships based on common ownership, which he applied in creating New Harmony, Indiana; also established an equitable labor exchange, in which distribution of the products of labor was effected by use of labor notes instead of money.

Palmerston, Henry John Temple (1784–1865), British politician; served as Prime Minister from 1855 to 1858 and 1859 to 1865. A conservative Tory who later switched to the Liberal Party, he presided over the Crimean War with Russia, the Second Opium War against China, and the Sepoy Rebellion against British rule in India. He strongly sympathized with the Confederacy during the US Civil War.

Pappemheim, Gottfried Heinrich Graf zu (1594–1632), field marshal of the

Holy Roman Empire during the Thirty Years' War; Friedrich Schiller extolled his military exploits in his famous trilogy *Wallenstein*.

Pasha, Ismail (1830–95), Viceroy of Egypt from 1863, he helped introduce large-scale cotton cultivation to Egypt in response to the US Civil War; in 1866 became Khedive, making Egypt largely independent of Ottoman rule. He initiated a series of social and political reforms aimed at modernizing Egypt but was widely criticized for granting major economic concessions to a number of European powers.

Passarge, Siegfried (1867–1958), German geographer, Professor at the University of Berlin, wrote on Africa and South America.

Paul III (1468–1549), Pope from 1534 until his death. Leading the Catholic Church during the Protestant Reformation, he was a strong promoter of the counter-reformation, supporting the formation of the Society of the Jesuits. He also authored a series of bulls that officially declared for the first time that Native Americans were human beings who were not to be dispossessed of their holdings.

Parvus, Alexander, see **Gelfand, Israel Lazarevich**

Pellegrini, Carlos (1846–1906), President of Argentina from 1890 to 1892. After becoming President following the severe depression of 1890, he insisted on repaying Argentina's debts to its foreign creditors in Europe. He supported a centralized state and opposed the efforts by many of the *caudillos* to affirm regional or local autonomy at the expense of the central government.

Pericles (495–429 BC), Greek statesman and politician, led Athens during the height of its fame and fortune, from 461 to 429 BC. Known as one of the greatest orators of ancient Greece, he is best known for his Funeral Oration, which extolled the virtues of Greek democracy. He also was responsible for sponsoring some of Athens' most important architectural projects, such as the Parthenon. He died of the plague during the Peloponnesian War with Sparta.

Perthes, Johann Georg Justus (1749–1816), German publisher, founded publishing firm that bears his name; began publishing its widely used world atlas in 1785, which has since gone through many additions and change.

Peter the Great (1672–1725), Tsar of Russia from 1682 until his death. Significantly expanded Russia's territory, both to the East, South, and West, and played an instrumental role in the modernization of Russian society.

Petrarch (1304–74), Italian poet and writer, widely considered the father of modern humanism. His sonnets and lyric poetry exerted great influence on such figures as Dante, Boccaccio, and Chaucer. His effort to reinvigorate Christian culture and religion through a return to ancient Greek and Roman sources is widely credited with paving the way for the European Renaissance.

Philip II (1527–98), King of Spain from 1554 until his death, during the height of its power and influence. His extensive military entanglements in Europe helped squander much of the enormous wealth that flowed into Spain through its exploitation of the Americas, leading to a series of economic crises. Under his reign the Dutch initiated their struggle from Spanish rule. The Philippines is named after him.

Philip IV (1605–1665), King of Spain from 1612 until his death. During his reign the Spanish Empire reached its greatest territorial extent; its possessions included Portugal and much of Italy in addition to the bulk of the Americas. The political rigidity and economic difficulties that beset his reign helped lead to the decline of Spanish power.

Philip II Augustus (1165–1223), King of France from 1180 until his death. One of France's most important monarchs, he checked the power of the nobles and extended royal power by conquering most of the English possessions in France. His reign was marked by considerable economic growth and prosperity. A participant in the Third Crusade, he expelled the Jews from France and waged war against dissident Catholics such as the Cathars of southern France.

Pizarro, Francisco (1475–1541), Spanish conquistador who conquered and destroyed the Inca Empire. His destruction of the indigenous culture and population has earned him the enmity of Andean peoples for generations.

Plekhanov, Georgi (1856–1918), Russian revolutionary and Marxist theoretician; originally a Populist, he became an avowed Marxist in the early 1880s and established, in 1883, the Emancipation of Labor Group; author of many books on politics, economics, and philosophy, he coined the term "dialectical materialism"; leader of the Menshevik faction of the RSDLP from 1903; one of the only party leaders not to return to Russia during the 1905 Revolution, he sharply opposed the Bolsheviks on the basis of an economic determinist and unilinear evolutionist understanding of historical development; a strong supporter of World War I, he sharply opposed the Bolshevik seizure of power as well as left-wing Mensheviks such as Martov; left Russia following the October Revolution.

Ploetz, Karl Julius (1819–81), German historian, produced a number of influential handbooks and studies of ancient and modern history; author of *Auszug aus der alten, mittleren und neueren Geschichte*, published in English as *A Handbook of Universal History*.

Pozdneyev, Alexei M. (1851–1920), Russian linguist and geographer, wrote a series of books on the Mongol peoples; helped found the Oriental Institute of Vladivostok University.

Proudhon, Pierre Joseph (1809–1865), French political theorist and economist, the first person to term himself as anarchist. His early work, such as *What is Property?*, influenced a wide number of radical nineteenth century thinkers, including Marx; his effort to utilize neo-Ricardian principles to organize exchange on the basis of commodity production led Marx to sharply criticize his ideas in the *Poverty of Philosophy*. Advocated workers' cooperatives and private property as well as the formation of a national bank to help redistribute wealth from capital to labor; his ideas had enormous impact on the workers' movements in nineteenth century France.

Putzger, Friedrich Wilhelm (1849–1913), German cartographer, author of a widely used Historical Atlas that is often used in schools today.

Quesnay, François (1694–1774), French economist and leading figure of the Physiocratic school; best known for his *Tableau économique*, the first effort to work out a systematic model of social reproduction; he coined the term *laissez-faire*.

Ratzel, Friedrich (1844–1904), German anthropologist and ethnologist, argued that the physical environment was the deciding factor in human culture; most of his work centered on Africa and Asia.

Rau, Karl Heinrich (1792–1870), German political economist who was strongly influenced by the thought of Adam Smith, although he gave prominence to the role of the state in economic development; his work was highly influential among the German historical school of economics.

Rembrandt, Harmenszoon van Rijn (1606–69), Dutch painter; composed his works at the highpoint of Dutch cultural history; renowned as one of the greatest portrait painters.

Reubens, Peter Paul (1577–1640), Flemish painter who worked in the Baroque style; his works emphasize color and movement, with lavish detail.

Reuchlin, Johann (1455–1522), German humanist and scholar; pioneered the recovery and study and Greek and Hebrew texts that were of central importance in the European Renaissance.

Ricardo, David (1772–1823), English political economist; a central figure in classical political economy, he extended its discoveries with his writings on the labor theory of value, the theory of comparative advantage, and the theory of rent. His ideas proved highly influential among free market economists as well as radical critics of capitalism who sought to address the unequal distribution of the proceeds of labor in capitalism.

Rinaldo, Geovanni (1720–95), Italian economist and politician; wrote several influential works on the nature of money and the balance of trade; served as head of the Council of Political Economy in Tuscany during the 1760s.

Rodbertus, Karl Johann (1805–75), German economist who advocated a conservative version of socialism based on state ownership of the economy; on the basis of the labor theory of value, he argued that workers' share in social wealth becomes progressively reduced with the development of capitalism, leading to the over-production of commodities; favored state intervention in the economy to impose an equilibrium of production and consumption.

Roscher, Wilhelm Georg Friedrich (1817–94), German economist and main founder of the historical school of economics in Germany, which emphasized the rise and fall of economic systems based upon cultural, political, and racial factors; he opposed both socialism and laissez-faire capitalism. Marx refers to his work numerous times in *Capital*, describing it (in Volume 1) as "eclectic professorial twaddle." In *Theories of Surplus Value*, Marx referred to Roscher's work as "the graveyard of the science of political economy."

Rudolph I (1218–91), also known as **Rudolph of Habsburg**. Ruler of the Holy Roman Empire from 1273 until his death; played a pivotal role in raising the Habsburg dynasty to one of the most important and powerful ruling groups in Europe.

Rumford, see **Thompson, Benjamin, Count of Rumford.**

Saint-Simon, Claude Henri de Rouroy, comte de (1760–1825), French political theorist and philosopher; advocated a form of statist socialism based on utilizing the power of modern industry; his advocacy of science as the key to progress helped pave the way for positivism. He was not a revolutionary, appealing instead to the agents of existing society to implement such ideals as full employment, social equality, and meritocracy.

Savigny, Friedrich Carl von (1779–1861), German jurist, historian, and leading figure of the historical school of law; wrote extensively on Roman law and property relations.

Savonarola, Girolamo (1452–1498), Italian friar who opposed the Medici family and helped impose a puritanical regime upon Florence for several years that restricted freedom of artistic, cultural, and religious expression; he especially condemned same-sex relations commonplace in Florence at the time. After falling out with the Pope, he was condemned and executed.

Say, Jean-Baptiste (1767–1832), French political economist, defended classical liberal views of free competition, free trade, and lifting governmental restraints on the activities of businesses; formulated Say's Law, which claims that aggregate supply creates its own aggregate demand. His work was highly influential among such figures as James Mill and John Stuart Mill, as well as later neo-liberal economists.

Scaruffi, Gaspero (1519–84), Italian economist best known for his writings on money and gold coinage.

Schäffle, Albert (1831–1903), German sociologist and political economist, supporter of capitalism but argued (especially in the last decades of his life) for collective ownership of property and planned organization of production; also wrote on ways to replace the existing monetary system through the use of labor-based time chits or vouchers; Marx read and criticized his work, in 1881.

Scharnhorst, Gerhard Johann David Waltz von (1755–1813), Prussian officer and military strategist; Chief of the Prussian General Staff during the Napoleonic Wars. In response to Prussian military defeats, argued that only a modern national army based on merit promotion, universal service and modern weaponry could improve Prussia's fortunes. Died in battle.

Scheibler, Karol (1820–81) German industrialist; originally from Belgium, he moved to Russian-occupied Poland in 1848 and helped establish the textile industry in the city of Łódź, building a series of factories and businesses. He became very wealth during the 1860s, when he managed to obtain supplies of cotton for his factories that were unavailable to other industrialists.

Schiller, Christoph Friedrich von (1759–1805), German poet, historian, playwright and philosopher. One of the most outstanding representatives of the German enlightenment, he made important contributions on aesthetics, ethics, and the meaning of human emancipation. His distinction between overcoming the divide between "formal drive" and "sensuous drive" through the realization of the "play drive" anticipates later utopian thinkers and had an especially important impact on the thought of such twentieth century critical theorists as Herbert Marcuse.

Schippel, Max (1859–1928), German Social Democrat and journalist; originally a follower of Rodbertus and Albert Schäffle, he was a long-time leader of the revisionist wing of the SPD. He supported German imperialism and militarism and was a strong supporter of World War I.

Schmoller, Gustav von (1838–1917), leading *Kathedersozialist*, or "Socialist of the Chair." Leading member of the inductive historical school of economics that opposed both classical political economy and marginal utility theory. Advocated social reforms along the lines of a corporativist union of labor and industry. He was an outspoken supporter of German militarism and imperialism; strong supporter of Bismarck's policies.

Schönberg, Gutav von (1839–1908), German economist; specialized in the field of agricultural economics. Worked closely with members of the German historical school.

Schulze-Delitzsch, Hermann (1808–1883), German left of center economist who organized some of the world's first credit unions and worked to create "people's banks" to make capital more readily available to small businessmen and traders. Ferdinand Lassalle sharply critiqued him (in *Herr Bastiat— Schulze von Delitzsch, der ökonomische Julian, oder Kapital und Arbeit*) for promoting policies that were not conducive to the struggles and aims of the working class.

Shulze-Gävernitz, Gerhart von (1864–1943), German economist whose studies on the Russian economy were used by Luxemburg in *The Industrial Development of Poland*. He also authored a book on the work of the English publicist Thomas Carlyle.

Schurtz, Heinrich (1863–1909), German ethnologist and cultural historian who studied African initiation rites. He opposed Bachofen's theory of "mother right" and matrilineal descent by arguing that early societies were characterized by male bonding and male domination.

Serra, Antonio (1580–1650), Italian philosopher and economist, supporter of mercantilism; best known for his work on the nature of coinage and monetary circulation, he was one of the first economists to emphasize the importance of the balance of trade.

Sharapov, Sergei Fedorovich (1855–1911), conservative Russian writer and economist; advocated the eventual union of all Slavs in a single national state under Russian tutelage. He was a political reactionary who attacked the gold standard on the grounds that it was part of an international Jewish conspiracy. Argued against those who held that the infusion of capital from overseas would enable Russia to become industrialized.

Shcherbatov, A.G. (1850–1915), member of the Russian nobility, a conservative who worked closely with the Slavophiles. Traveled to the Middle East in the 1880s, where he obtained horses that he bred on a special farm in the North Caucasus.

Schüller, Richard (1870–1972), Austrian economist associated with the neo-classical Austrian School of economics; student and follower of Carl Menger. Worked as an official in the Ministry of Trade and Foreign Office in the Austro-Hungarian Empire, prior to World War I; his specialty was foreign trade policy. Emigrated to the US in 1940, where he remained until his death.

Sieber, Nikolai Ivanovitch (1844–88), Ukrainian economist and writer, wrote a thesis in 1871 entitled "The Theory of Value and Capital. D. Ricardo in Connection with Later Explanations," one of the first works in Russian to discuss Marx's *Capital*. Taught political economy at the University of Kiev from 1873 to 1875 and later lived in Switzerland and England, where he met with Marx and Engels. He held that communal forms of social interaction are universal features of early human societies. He also argued that capitalism was an inevitable stage of development Russia was compelled to undergo, interpreting Marxism along strictly evolutionary deterministic lines.

Sismondi, Charles Léonard Simonde de (1773–1842), Swiss economist and historian; denied capitalism tended toward conditions of equilibrium and full employment, arguing that a lack of aggregate demand led to persistent economic crises. Although a critic of classical political economy's emphasis on an unrestricted free market, he was not a socialist but rather called upon the existing state to regulate the distribution of social wealth. His work represents a forerunner of the theory of under-consumptionism.

Skoda, Emil von (1839–1900), Czech engineer and industrialist; built a series of armaments plants that was the largest industrial enterprise in Austro-Hungarian Empire and became known as the Skoda works. It played a pivotal role in arms manufacturing during both World War I and World War II.

Smith, Adam (1723–90), Scottish philosopher and economist, leading figure of classical political economy. Formulated the labor theory of value in his major and pathbreaking work, *The Wealth of Nations* (1776). Although often considered a leading proponent of laissez-faire capitalism, he supported government intervention in the economy to mitigate against monopolies and help ameliorate severe poverty and inequality.

Soden, Friedrich Julius Heinrich, Graf von (1754–1832), German jurist and economist who commented critically on the work of Adam Smith.

Solon (638–558 BC), ancient Greek statesman, lawmaker and poet who is credited with laying the foundations of later Athenian democracy; legislated that the poorest class of Athenian citizens, the *Thetes*, be admitted to the Assembly governing Athens and broadened the financial and property qualifications needed to hold office. His abolition of debt obligations for the poorest citizens helped undermine the power of the Athenian aristocracy.

Sombart, Werner (1864–1941), German economist and sociologist, leading figure in the "Young Historical School" of empirical-based social theory. Studied under Gustav von Schmoller and later befriended such figures as Max Weber and Carl Schmidt. An avowed Marxist in his early years, his major works are *Der modern Kapitalismus* (Modern Capitalism) (1902) and *Why there is no Socialism in the United States* (1906), a highly influential work that promoted the myth of American exceptionalism. By the 1930s he moved to the Right and supported a corporativist fusion of state power and economic development.

Somló, Felix (1873–1920), Hungarian sociologist and ethnographer, part of the school of legal positivism; wrote on totemism and the nature of folklore in ancient societies.

Spencer, Walter Baldwin (1860–1929), British-Australian biologist and anthropologist; in 1894 part of the W.S. Horn scientific expedition that explored central and western Australia; on the basis of his experiences of living among the Aborigines, he wrote extensively on their culture and languages.

Spinoza, Benedict de (1632–77), Jewish-Dutch philosopher and leading figure of Western rationalism; sought to extend Descartes's discoveries by fully integrating geometric methods and veridical knowledge into philosophy. Hegel held that "all true philosophy begins with Spinoza"; Marx carefully read both his political and philosophical works.

Starcke, Carl Nicolai (1858–1926), Danish politician and sociologist who opposed Darwin's theories from an anti-evolutionist perspective.

Stein, Heinrich Friedrich Karl Reichsfreiherr vom und zum (1757–1831), Prussian statesman who introduced a series of political, economic, and military reforms following Napoleon's victory over Prussian forces in 1806.

Steinen, Karl von den (1855–1929), German physician, explorer, and ethnologist; made a journey around the world, 1879–81; best known for his several expeditions to the Xingú region of Brazil between 1884 and 1888, which he recorded in a book about native peoples of central Brazil; he also published works on the culture and languages of the native peoples of the Caribbean.

Storch, Heinrich Friedrich von (1766–1835), German-Russian economist; in 1819 wrote an influential work on political economy that presented a modified form of Adam Smith's classical theory of value; developed the theory of "internal goods"—moral and cultural factors that he considered crucial for economic development.

Sutherland-Leverson-Gower, Anne (1829–88), born Anne Hay-Mackenzie, she married the Marquis of Stafford in 1849 and became the Duchess of Sutherland in Scotland; her wealth largely derived from clearing the highlands to make room for sheep farming, causing Marx to write, "The history of the wealth of the Sutherland family is the history of the ruin and of the expropriation of the Scotch-Gaelic population from its native soil."

Stewart, Dugald (1753–1828), philosopher and mathematician of the Scottish Enlightenment; initially studied under Adam Ferguson, who preceded Adam Smith in proclaiming labor as the source of all value. Taught moral philosophy and economics at Edinburgh University and upheld many of the philosophical ideas of Thomas Reid; he was generally supportive of the democratic and revolutionary movements of his time. Marx refers to his work several times in *Capital*.

Sigurd, Syr Halfdansson (birth date unknown; died 1018), King of Ringerike, a territory in southern Norway; emphasized the importance of farming and led a relatively modest life for a nobleman. He became a Christian in 998.

Tacitus, Publius Cornelius (56–117 AD), Roman historian, author of the *Annals* and the *Histories*, which delineate the reigns of the early Roman emperors. One of the greatest of the ancient historians, he made careful use of official sources and documents and avoided mythological presentations of historical events.

Temple, William (1628–99), English politician and diplomat; served as advisor to Charles II of England; Jonathan Swift served as his secretary for a brief period; wrote a series of essays on the nature of government.

Thompson, Benjamin, Count of Rumford (1753–1814), British physician and scientist; born and raised in New England, he opposed the American Revolution and moved to England; much of his scientific work concerned the generation of heat and furnaces. On the basis of his knowledge of caloric theory, he wrote about the minimum amount of food that is necessary to reproduce the labor power of the industrial worker.

Thompson, William (1775–1833), Irish economist, social reformer, and neo-Ricardian socialist; used Smith and Ricardo's labor theory of value to critique capitalist exploitation by attacking the discrepancy between the value of the product and the value of the workers' wages. He advocated a cooperative form of communism based on the independent resources of the working class.

Thornton, William Thomas (1813–80), English neo-Ricardian economist; 1858–80, secretary for public works in the India office; author of *Over-Population and its Remedy* (1846), which advocated a plan for colonizing Irish wastelands by Irish peasants. Worked with John Stuart Mill for many years and played an important role in Mill's recantation of the theory of the wage fund. He was a major critic of the unrestrained free market and defender of the rights of workers; author of *On Labor, its Wrongful Claims and Rightful Dues, its Actual Present and Possible Future* (1869).

Theopompus of Chios (378–320 BC), ancient Greek historian; wrote a history of Philip II of Macedon and is a source for information about Alexander the Great.

Thierry, Augustin (1795–1856), French historian who was a follower of the utopian socialist Saint-Simon. Supporter of the 1830 Revolution in France, he was a moderate liberal in politics. Moved to the Right after the 1848 Revolutions. Many of his historical works (such as *History of the Conquest of England by the Normans*) dealt with the Middle Ages. His most famous book is *History of the Third Estate*.

Thiers, Adolphe (1797–1877), French politician and historian; Served as Prime Minister of France in 1836, 1840, and 1848. An opponent of Napoleon III, he returned to power in the national elections of February 1871 and sued for peace with the Germans. Forced to flee Paris because of the Paris Commune of 1871, he directed the government forces that broke through the city defences, resulting in the slaughter of tens of thousands of communards. Following his brutal repression of the Commune, he became President of France, only to be forced from power in 1873 by opposition from the monarchists.

Thünen, Johann Heinrich von (1783–1850), German economist who developed a theory of ground rent based on spatial economics by emphasizing such factors as transport costs and access to ports in determining the cost of production. In his later work he emphasized the importance of the class struggle between the industrialist and artisan and expressed considerable support for the latter's demands.

Timiziriavez, Dmitri A. (1837–1903), Russian statistician who worked for the Russian Ministry of Finance. He also served as a trade representative to Romania, Serbia, and Turkey; in 1894 he served as a member of the Russian Ministry of Agriculture and State Property.

Timur (1336–1405), Mongol-Turkic conqueror and founder of the Timurid dynasty; also known as Tamerlane; originally from modern Uzbekistan, he conquered an enormous area, including the Middle East, southern Russia, Persia, and northern India; died while en route to conquer China. Though known as one of the most brutal conquerors in history, he was also a patron of the arts and sciences and helped make his capitol Samarkand one of the most splendid cities of the medieval world.

Trirogov, W. G. (birth and death dates unknown), Russian economist, studied communal land formations among the Russian peasantry. Author of *The Village Community and the Poll Tax* (1882).

Thompson, William (1775–1833), Irish economist, philosopher, and social reformer; an early critic of capitalism, he concluded from the labor theory of value that workers are wrongly dispossessed of the product of their labor. A leading radical neo-Ricardian, his work had an important impact on the cooperative movement and was highly praised by Marx. He was a strong supporter of women's rights and criticized other utopian socialists for authoritarian and anti-democratic tendencies.

Townsend, Joseph (1739–1816), English physician and geologist; a political reactionary, he argued in such works as *A Dissertation on the Poor Laws* against providing public assistance for the poor on the grounds that it leads to overpopulation and a redundant labor force.

Trotha, Lothar von (1848–1920), German militarist and imperialist; in 1900, led a brigade that helped suppress the Boxer Rebellion in China; in 1904–05, led a genocidal campaign against the Herero and Nama peoples in Southwest Africa, in which he ordered his troops to slaughter all men, women and children; an extreme German nationalist and racist, he formed the Thule Society after World War I, which had an important impact on forming the ideology of the young Adolph Hitler.

Tugan-Baranovsky, Iikhail (1865–1919), Ukrainian economist and politician, a representative of "legal Marxism"; helped develop the theory of long waves of capitalist development, later taken up by thinkers such as N. Kondratiev; critical of both the labor theory of value and neo-classical marginal utility theory, he moved away from Marxism after the turn of the century towards neo-Kantianism; criticized extensively in Luxemburg's *Accumulation of Capital*. He became a leading opponent of the Bolsheviks after the Russian Revolution of 1917 and was active in the Ukrainian Party of Socialist-Federalists.

Turgot, Anne-Robert-Jacques, Baron de Laune (1717–81), French economist and politician, a leading figure of the Physiocrats; supported free trade and economic liberalism. Served in several posts in the French government in the 1770s, including Controller-General; sought to reduce France's budget deficit while resisting efforts to increase taxes on land. He supported "enlightened" monarchical rule.

Vanderborght, Richard (1861–1926), German jurist and statistician; his published works mainly focused on the economics of transportation; his major work is *The Economic Importance of the Rhine-Maritime*.

Varnhagen, Rahel (née Levin) (1771–1833), German writer and feminist; part of the romantic movement; advocated women's rights and opposed anti-Semitism. An associate of numerous leading intellectuals of the time, such as Friedrich Schlegel and Alexander von Humboldt; author of numerous letters

(6,000 in all) on social, political, and literary issues, most of which were published after her death.

Verri, Pietro (1728–97), Italian philosopher and economist, close to the French Encyclopaedists of the Enlightenment. Promoted anti-feudal reforms from a mercantilist perspective; a supporter of free trade; author of *Meditations on Political Economy* (1771).

Vorländer, Karl (1860–1928), German neo-Kantian philosopher who explored the ramifications of Kant's philosophy for socialist thought; wrote a widely-acclaimed biography of Kant as well as a history of philosophy; author of *Kant, Hegel, and Socialism* (1920).

Wade, John (1788–1875), English journalist; contributed to *The Spectator* and other periodicals. Wrote numerous articles defending the rights of workers and attacking the inequality and corruption of British society. His book *History of the Middle and Working Classes, with a Popular Exposition of the Economical and Political Principles which have influenced the Past and Present Condition of the Industrious Orders* (1833) was cited by Marx in *Capital*.

Wagner, Adolph (1835–1917), German economist and statist socialist. A political conservative, he opposed the aims of the workers' movement in favor of supporting Bismarck and German imperial expansion; in 1878 he joined the anti-Semitic Christian Social Party. Author one of the first critical discussions of Marx's *Capital* in Germany, which Marx responded to at length.

Waller, Horace (1833–96), editor and missionary; traveled to Central Africa in 1861 and spoke out against mistreatment of the Africans by the Europeans. Returning to England in 1864, he became a member of the committee of the Anti-Slavery Society; edited David Livingstone's journals for publication.

Waltershausen, Sartorius von (1809–76), German geologist; made numerous contributions to mineralogy and the study of volcanoes.

Wenckstern, Adolph Wilhelm von (1862–1914), German academic economist, author of several works on Marx and socialist theory; sought to reconcile Marx's ideas with marginal utility theory. Although sympathetic to aspects of Marx's work, he argued that Marx erred in failing to assign a productive role to the capitalist entrepreneur; also argued society could never dispense with private property and exchange.

Weitling, Wilhelm (1808–1871), German and American radical political activist, considered one of the founders of German communism; a self-educated tailor, became active in socialist and communist circles in the 1830s; in 1837 joined the League of the Just, one of the earliest communist organizations in Europe. Marx initially praised his 1842 work *Guarantees of Harmony and Freedom*. Clashed with Marx during and after the 1848 Revolutions over his advocacy of various schemes to immediately seize power through an enlightened minority. After the 1848 Revolutions, moved to New York, where he became active on behalf of the workers' movements.

Westermarck, Edward (1862–1939), Finnish sociologist who studied marriage and argued the nuclear family is necessary for the survival of the species. Engels sharply criticized him in *Origin of the Family, Private Property, and the State.*

Wilda, Wilhelm Eduard (1800–56), German lawyer and legal historian, specialized in the study of criminal law.

Wirth, Max (1822–1900) (1822–1900), German economist and journalist, primarily known for his studies of the labor market. Most important work was *Geschichte der Handelskrisen*, a study of the history of economic crises.

Witte, Sergei (1849–1915), Russian politician, served in numerous government posts under Tsar Alexander III and Nicholas II; as head of Finance Ministry from 1892 to 1903 presided over the industrialization of Russia. He helped negotiate an end to the Russo-Japanese War of 1905 and advocated the introduction of various reforms after the 1905 Revolution, such as the formation of elected parliament and a constitutional monarchy. A liberal by temperament, he criticized Russia's entry into World War I.

Witzleben, Job von (1783–1837), Prussian military leader; fought in the Battle of Jena, after which he argued for major reforms of the Prussian military.

Wolf, Julius (1862–1937), professor of economics at Zurich University, with whom Rosa Luxemburg studied. He was her faculty adviser in the writing of her doctoral dissertation, *The Industrial Development of Poland*. On completion of that work she received her doctoral degree in 1897.

Wolff, Wilhelm (1809–64), German revolutionary and writer. He was imprisoned in the 1830's for his work as a radical student activist, and subsequently became active in the labor and socialist movements. In 1846 he became a close friend of Karl Marx, who dedicated Volume One of *Capital* to his memory. Originally from Silesia, he wrote a series of important articles in the *Neue Rheinische Zeitung* exposing the deprivations imposed upon the German peasantry.

Zaleski, Witold (1836–1908), Polish statistician and demographer, taught political economy in Warsaw (in 1869) and commerce (from 1873–1906) in Kronenberg. In 1882 he helped direct the census of the Kingdom of Poland and tsarist Russia.

Zetkin, Clara Josephine (1857–1933), German Social Democrat and feminist; 1892–1917, chief editor of the Social Democratic women's publication, *Gleicheit*; 1895–1917, member of the Control Commission of the SPD; 1906–17, member of the SPD's Education Committee; in 1907, became secretary of the International Women's Secretariat; in 1910, an initiator of the practice of holding an annual International Women's Day on March 8; leading figure of the anti-war German Left, she contributed to *Die Internationale* and served as a member of the Spartacus Group. She was one of Luxemburg's closest friends and associates, with whom she carried on a lively and active correspondence.

Ziber, Nikolai, see **Sieber, Nikolai.**

Zurita, Alonzo de (1512–85), Spanish lawyer and historian, known for his chronicles of the conquest of Mexico and the Incan Empire by the Spanish; served as Governor of New Granada (modern-day Colombia and Venezuela) from 1550–52.

Index